The European Green Deal and the Eastern Partnership

The Eastern Partnership (EaP) was launched in 2009 to strengthen institutional, economic, and political relations between the European Union (EU) and the six Partnership countries (Armenia, Azerbaijan, Belarus, Georgia, Moldova, and Ukraine). Further, the adoption of the European Green Deal (EGD) for these countries can be seen as a turning point in policymaking, as well as an indication that the Green Deal will become a guide to transforming the economy and making it more sustainable. This book presents an innovative, geopolitical, multidimensional survey of EaP–EU relations and the future of Europe.

It analyzes the situation of the Partnership countries in the context of sustainable development and explores the historical and strategic context of the integration of the Green Deal and its impact on the development of Europe. It examines the necessary conditions for the operation of the EGD in the countries of the EaP and examines the influence of geopolitical conflicts and their impact on the implementation of the EGD in the region. Finally, the book studies the political, economic, and sociodemographic dimensions of geopolitics and their effect on EGD implementation in the Partnership, identifies and evaluates the key challenges, and features a comparative analysis of the European Green Deal and similar environmental initiatives in other parts of the world. Such an approach helps place European efforts in a global context.

This is a valuable reference for students, scholars, and researchers of economics, politics, geography, history, European studies, international relations, and environmental policy. Policymakers at the European, regional, and local government level will benefit from the book's policy recommendations and comprehensive insights.

Zofia Gródek-Szostak is an Assistant Professor in the Department of Economics and Enterprise Organization, Krakow University of Economics, Poland.

Jadwiga Adamczyk is a Full Professor in the Department of Economics and Enterprise Organization, Krakow University of Economics, Poland.

Karolina Kotulewicz-Wisińska is an Assistant Professor in the Department of Political Science, Krakow University of Economics, Poland.

Agata Niemczyk is an Associate Professor in the Department of Tourism, Krakow University of Economics, Poland.

Karolina Wanda Olszowska is an Assistant Professor in the Department of History, Jagiellonian University, Poland.

Anna Szeląg-Sikora is an Associate Professor in the Department of Production Engineering, Logistics and Applied Computer Science, University of Agriculture, Krakow, Poland.

Routledge Advances in Regional Economics, Science and Policy

Regional Cooperation and Resilience in East Asia
Edited by Sebastian Bobowski

The Business of Affordable Housing
Case Studies of the Commercial Supply of Affordable Homes
Alexander Styhre

Spatial Planning and the European Union
Europeanisation from Within
Eva Purkarthofer

Economic Resilience and Pandemic Response
Edited by Agnieszka Rzepka and Artur Paździor

Lagging Regions in the European Union
Structural, Productivity and Efficiency Aspects
Paweł Dobrzański

Urban Scaling
Allometry in Urban Studies and Spatial Science
Edited by Luca S. D'Acci

Technology-Based Regional Economic Development
Institutional Perspectives from the USA and Japan
Akio Nishizawa and David V. Gibson

The European Green Deal and the Eastern Partnership
Towards Resilient, Sustainable and Integrated Economies
Zofia Gródek-Szostak, Karolina Kotulewicz-Wisińska, Jadwiga Adamczyk, Agata Niemczyk, Karolina Wanda Olszowska and Anna Szeląg-Sikora

For more information about this series, please visit: www.routledge.com/series/RAIRESP

The European Green Deal and the Eastern Partnership

Towards Resilient, Sustainable and Integrated Economies

Zofia Gródek-Szostak, Jadwiga Adamczyk, Karolina Kotulewicz-Wisińska, Agata Niemczyk, Karolina Wanda Olszowska and Anna Szeląg-Sikora

Routledge
Taylor & Francis Group
LONDON AND NEW YORK

First published 2025
by Routledge
4 Park Square, Milton Park, Abingdon, Oxon OX14 4RN

and by Routledge
605 Third Avenue, New York, NY 10158

Routledge is an imprint of the Taylor & Francis Group, an informa business

British Library Cataloguing-in-Publication Data
A catalogue record for this book is available from the British Library

ISBN: 978-1-032-78207-2 (hbk)
ISBN: 978-1-032-78209-6 (pbk)
ISBN: 978-1-003-48673-2 (ebk)

DOI: 10.4324/9781003486732

Typeset in Times New Roman
by KnowledgeWorks Global Ltd.

Contents

List of figures

List of tables

Biographies

Zofia Gródek-Szostak is an Assistant Professor in the Department of Economics and Business at the Krakow University of Economics. She is an accredited consultant of the Polish Agency for Enterprise Development (PARP) in the field of proinnovative consulting services of the National Innovation Network (KSI) and general consulting services of the National Service System (KSU). She is the author of papers on public financing of investments and R&D works and on implementing innovative solutions in enterprises. Additionally, she is a member of the Regional Studies Association (RSA) and The Polish Economic Society (PTE).

Karolina Kotulewicz-Wisińska is an Assistant Professor in the Department of Political Studies, Institute of Political Science, Sociology and Philosophy at the Krakow University of Economics. She specializes in the issues of political and economic transformation in the post-Soviet region, both internal and external. In the internal dimension, her area of research interests are political systems, economic systems and the situation of societies in post-Soviet countries. In the external, her area of research interest is foreign policy and external economic policy. Naturally, a particular area of her research interest is political, economic and social cooperation between the European Union and the countries of the EU's Eastern Partnership program.

Jadwiga Adamczyk is a Full Professor of economic sciences since 2009, employed in Institute of Management at Krakow University of Economics. She is a member of the Presidium of the Committee on Economic Sciences of the Polish Academy of Sciences, and a recognized researcher in the scientific community in the field of sustainable development, corporate social responsibility and management. She is the author/coauthor of seven monographs, including the most important: "The concept of sustainable development in enterprise management" (UEK 2001), "Programming sustainable development of enterprises" (PWE 2007), "Corporate social responsibility" (PWE 2009), "Contemporary determinants of efficiency and development of enterprises" (UEK 2020). The number of her citations is more than 1,200 and her h-index is 10. Moreover, her scientific output includes about 200 scientific positions. Teaching activities include lectures and seminars and more than 400 promoted university graduates.

Agata Niemczyk is an Associate Professor in the Department of Tourism at the Krakow University of Economics. She researches, writes, and lectures on consumer behavior, cultural and business tourism, tourism marketing, territorial marketing, silver economy, green entrepreneurship, and sustainable development. She is member of a number of national and international research teams. She is also a member of the Regional Studies Association (RSA) and The Polish Economic Society (PTE). She is the author and coauthor of more than 250 publications.

Karolina Wanda Olszowska is an Associate Professor in the Jagiellonian University. She is a Turkologist, historian, doctor of humanities, and the Head of the "Preludium 16" grant of the National Science Center researching Turkish–American and Turkish–Soviet relations during 1945–1952. She is the author of numerous scientific texts on Turkey, the Turkic states, and the Caucasus, both from a historical and contemporary perspective. She is the winner of scholarships in Turkey, Russia, and Azerbaijan.

Anna Szeląg-Sikora graduated from the Faculty of Production Engineering and Energetics in 2004 and from the Faculty of Agricultural Engineering and Energetics in University of Agriculture in Krakow. In 2007, she received a PhD of agricultural sciences and in 2014 became a Full Professor. She is an Assistant Professor at the Institute of Agricultural Engineering and Computer Science with a specialization in agricultural engineering.

Acknowledgment

The publication presents the result of the Project no. 093/ZIE/2023/DOS financed from the subsidy granted to the Krakow University of Economics.

Co-financed by the Minister of Science under the "Regional Initiative of Excellence" programme. Agreement No. RID/SP/0039/2024/01. Subsidized amount PLN 6,187,000.00. Project period 2024–2027.

Introduction

The Eastern Partnership (EaP) was launched in 2009 to strengthen institutional, economic, and political relations between the European Union (EU) and the six countries of the Partnership (Armenia, Azerbaijan, Belarus, Georgia, Moldova, and Ukraine). On the one hand, this multifaceted and multipurpose initiative seeks to strengthen the political, economic, and social ties between the EU and the countries mentioned above. On the other hand, it aims to strengthen relations between the EaP countries themselves.

The Partnership is not one of the stages of the EU's further enlargement policy. Participation in the initiative does not guarantee future membership, although it does not preclude it. The EU works with partner countries to enhance political ties and economic integration (COM, 2008). It should be noted that this program marked the beginning of the formal delineation of the EU's foreign policy towards the neighboring countries Armenia, Azerbaijan, Georgia, Belarus, Moldova, and Ukraine. In EU foreign policy, these countries constitute a separate group, which is treated as a single region due to similar historical experiences, similar contemporary problems, and economic ties. This approach was adopted to increase the effectiveness of EU foreign policy in the region (Kotulewicz-Wisińska & Gródek-Szostak, 2021).

The intention of the EU, and at the same time the leading objective of the program, is strong, diversified, and mutually beneficial cooperation with all EaP countries, regardless of the degree of their ambitions for EU membership. The Partnership specified the benefits offered to the beneficiaries of the initiative in exchange for undertaking political and economic reforms in accordance with EU standards. It envisages specific forms of political and economic integration: political association, creation of extensive free trade areas, liberalization of the visa regime, harmonization of law, and strengthening cooperation for energy security. The main objectives of the Eastern Partnership were formulated at the first summit in Prague on May 7, 2009 (Council of the European Union, 2009), where the so-called Prague Declaration was accepted. The document contains the following objectives of the program:

- developing economic, political, and social integration, taking into account the principles of international law and fundamental values, including democracy, the rule of law, and respect for human rights and fundamental freedoms, as well as market economy, sustainable development, and fair governance;

DOI: 10.4324/9781003486732-1

- maintaining and stimulating economic reforms and social and regional development between partner countries;
- reducing socioeconomic differences in partner countries;
- deepening bilateral cooperation between the EU and partner countries;
- multilateral cooperation based on the so-called thematic platforms.

The EaP is a program that promotes stability and seeks to build trust between all parties. At the Partnership Summit in Prague, it was emphasized that conflicts hinder cooperation. Therefore, it is very important to resolve disputes peacefully, taking into account the principles and norms of international law, as well as decisions and documents approved within the Partnership. Additionally, the EaP program is also intended to strengthen ties between individual partner countries.

Since 2009, the geopolitical agenda has changed several times, indeed quite drastically recently. The partnership with the six EaP countries initially focused on other priorities other than the environment. It was more important to support democratization processes and strengthen the rule of law, and even resolve visa issues and increase trade and market access. However, as these priorities have been addressed, for example through bilateral Partnership Agreements and Association Agreements, the scope of cooperation has broadened.

Energy and infrastructure often dominated the negotiating process. Most of the EaP countries strived to achieve energy efficiency while trying to loosen ties with the Russian Federation as the main energy supplier. Unlike most of the EaP countries, Azerbaijan is the only country with high oil and gas production, which makes it fully independent of Moscow. Among other priority areas of cooperation, the EU and the EaP identified the need to support the innovation of outdated infrastructure, and, in some cases, the reconstruction of infrastructure damaged during regional conflicts.

Please note that the Partnership Agreements signed with the six EaP countries already included some environmental elements. They generally concerned the protection of biodiversity, agriculture, and forestry, but missed other important issues, such as reducing pollution, waste management, or clean water. There was also extensive consideration of promoting favorable conditions for bilateral trade relations and investment in specific areas, including those indirectly related to environmental protection, such as the export of food products. In addition, energy issues were part of the overall agenda. However, note that climate change has often gone unnoticed.

Over time, it turned out that the Eastern Partnership countries were not as homogeneous as initially thought, and differences in needs and aspirations played an important role. However, cooperation between the EU and the Partnership is developing, and the identified priorities are increasingly dominated by the growing need to address environmental issues, especially by integrating them into various sectors of economic and social life.

In 2017, the Eastern Partnership Summit endorsed 20 goals for 2020. Their results were clearly oriented towards economic development, governance, and social goals, and economic sectors were mentioned explicitly in political statements. Please note that in 2017, the European Green Deal had not yet been released. One of its goals explicitly linked the energy sector with the climate crisis, that is: "Increasing energy efficiency and the use of renewable energy and reducing greenhouse gas emissions."

The awareness of key environmental issues among policy makers has steadily increased over the years. International processes and agreements have consistently developed recommendations and approaches for integrating environmental concerns into national, regional, and local policy processes. The EU has always been at the forefront of these negotiations and has supported their development and implementation. Similarly, EaP countries have endorsed and adopted a number of global policy goals and instruments, such as the Paris Agreement on Climate Change and the 2030 Agenda of the United Nations and its Sustainable Development Goals.

Increasingly, "green" recommendations have appeared in policy statements at the national level in the countries of the Partnership. One example is combating climate change by "greening" energy sectors, including energy efficiency and renewable energy. Another is the development of sustainable transport, green infrastructure, and sustainable cities, and so on. The process was also facilitated for the EaP countries, because they were involved and benefited from participating in various global and regional policy mechanisms aimed at sustainable development, green transition, and investment (e.g., EBRD, Global Environment Fund, Green Climate Fund, UNDP, etc.) (Augustyn et al., 2022).

The Commission published an announcement outlining the European Green Deal that was released in December 2019. It is based on eight elements that clearly highlight the critical relationships and positive and/or negative implications that each sector has for the environment. The European Green Deal elements include:

1 Increasing the EU's Climate Ambition for 2030 and 2050
2 Supplying clean, affordable and safe energy
3 Mobilizing industry for a clean and circular economy
4 Building and renovating in an energy-resource-efficient way
5 Accelerating the shift to sustainable and smart mobility
6 From "Farm to Fork": a fair, healthy, and environmentally friendly food system
7 Preserving and restoring ecosystems and biodiversity
8 A zero-pollution ambition for a toxic-free environment

The adoption of the European Green Deal for the six Partnership countries can be seen as a turning point in policymaking, as well as an indication that the Green Deal will become a guide to transforming the economy and making it more sustainable.

The Green Deal has also become a new approach to the design and implementation of projects and initiatives in cooperation with the Warsaw University of Technology. According to the approach, environmental components should always be integrated, regardless of the target sector and the issues addressed. "Greening a sector" is officially becoming synonymous with reducing its impact on the environment, making it resistant to changes, while contributing to sustainable development and improving people's lives. Importantly, the Green Deal has the ambition to go beyond the borders of the EU and become a driving force supporting neighboring countries in confronting climate change and loss of biodiversity. The Green Deal can also become a framework for mobilizing EU expertise and financial resources to support neighbors and partners on a more sustainable path. The Partnership, which tends to mirror the EU's flagship project of the strategy, has also embraced the European Green Deal. Thanks to this agreement, the green transformation was high on the EU–EaP negotiation agenda. The importance of greening economic sectors is also evident in the post-2020 Eastern Partnership Agenda and in the joint agreement "Recovery, Resilience, and Reform: post-2020 priorities for an Eastern Partnership." It supplemented the document of March 2020 in light of the changed circumstances caused by the pandemic, but did not fundamentally change the priorities.

This publication is an innovative, geopolitical, and multidimensional look at the conditions of EaP countries to implement the assumptions of the European Green Deal and its impact on the development of partnership members, as well as their readiness to implement the Green Deal.

The main objective of the monograph is to diagnose the situation and readiness of the Partnership countries to implement the assumptions of the European Green Deal and to identify the conditions and challenges of its implementation in the context of relations between the EaP Program and the EU. Its implementation will serve specific objectives, such as:

Objective 1: To diagnose the assumptions, conditions, and situation of the Eastern Partnership countries from the point of view of sustainable development.
Objective 2: To present the essence, character, and mindset from the point of view of the European Green Deal.
Objective 3: To identify conditions for the implementation of the European Green Deal in the countries of the Eastern Partnership Program.
Objective 4: To select and evaluate the most important challenges for the implementation of the European Green Deal in light of the EaP–EU relations and the future of Europe.

To implement the adopted assumptions, a critical analysis of the literature on the subject was used as a research method, as well as a descriptive method, various statistical methods, and inference. A synthetic indicator will be used to illustrate the multidimensional socioeconomic potential of the EU member states, which reflect the set of conditions for the implementation of the Green Deal. Based on the above, comparisons will be made and the leader in the area will be revealed, also as an expression of the possible consequences of the implementation for other EaP members.

The following research questions were formulated:

1 What is the impact of the historical, political, geographical, and cultural conditions of the Eastern Partnership countries on the possibility and readiness to participate in the Program?
2 What is the economic, environmental, and social situation of the countries of the Eastern Partnership? (illustrated, e.g., by a map of countries in multidimensional scaling)

3 What conditions affect the implementation of the Green Deal in the Eastern Partnership countries, and to what extent? (based on, e.g., factor analysis)
4 What are the most important challenges for the full implementation and implementation of the Green Deal in the Eastern Partnership countries in the context of European Union relations and the future of Europe? (based on, e.g., importance ranking)

Despite the literature on the subject (Tsebenko et al., 2023), there is no comprehensive monograph illustrating the subject, which, due to dynamic geopolitical changes, also changes constantly. It can be assumed that the role of the EU policy will be strengthened among the Partnership countries, with a clear limitation towards Belarus, which increases the value of the submitted proposal update. It will be useful for policy makers from European, regional, and local governments, but also for education in universities in political science, regional development, or sustainable development.

Russia's war with Ukraine has radically changed global and regional political dynamics. The six countries of the Eastern Partnership are moving along increasingly divergent trajectories. The European Union granted candidate status to Ukraine and Moldova in June 2022, and confirmed that Georgia could become a candidate country after resolving several key issues, including implementing governance reforms, and ending the political conflict between the ruling Kartuli Otsneba (Georgian Dream) party and the opposition. In turn, long-term tensions between Armenia and Azerbaijan have turned into an open conflict several times since 2020, and Belarus suspended its participation in the Eastern Partnership after fraudulent elections.

The Russian war of aggression against Ukraine makes it crucial for the EU to look at how it adapts its neighborhood and enlargement policy to the new reality, taking into account all its neighbors. The situation in the Eastern Partnership countries and their future development path is very important not only for these countries but also for the future of Europe as a whole. The interconnections between the EaP countries under the European Neighborhood Policy and the European Enlargement Policy require setting a new strategic direction and a greater focus on integrated security in its various dimensions.

The EU has financial instruments to support reforms and transformations in its neighboring countries. It remains attractive due to its internal market, the rule of law, the high standard of living, and the freedom to travel. Therefore, connectivity, resilience, and green transition policies are also attractive in the context of economic, ecological, and social changes in these countries.

The structure of the book includes two parts dealing with the issues of the European Green Deal in the countries of the Eastern Partnership. Part I, "Eastern Partnership within the framework of sustainable development in Europe," includes three chapters: "Assumptions and recommendations of the Eastern Partnership," "Characteristics of the Eastern Partnership countries," and "Situation of the Eastern Partnership countries in the context of sustainable development," which diagnose and analyze the potential, condition, and capabilities of the Eastern Partnership countries to implement the assumptions of the European Green Deal.

Part II, "European Green Deal: Essence, character, and mindset," presents the historical context and assumptions of the proposals presented by the European Commission to adapt the EU's climate, energy, transport, and tax policies to reduce net greenhouse gas emissions by at least 55% by 2030 compared to 1990 levels. The considerations are supplemented by a review of national and regional environmental policies aimed at implementing the objectives of the European Green Deal.

Trends, tendencies, dependencies, and research results described in the publication can be an important comparison source for university researchers. It can provide them with a starting point for further in-depth analyses. The publication will probably also be used by academic teachers of economic, political, geographical, and historical studies. The direct addressees of the book will be students of first- and second-degree studies, as well as postgraduate and third-degree studies (doctoral studies). The study will also be a very good source for those who write scientific and review papers on sustainable development. This book will also be useful as a teaching aid for various trainings/courses/workshops in political, geopolitical, and geography studies. Additionally, the study will be addressed to business practitioners (management staff and employees) of various types of institutions responsible for creating tools and instruments to implement the European Green Deal in the Eastern Partnership countries.

References

Augustyn, A.M., Luchetti, D. & Li, J. (2022). *Localising the green agenda in the Eastern Partnership*. Commission for Citizenship, Governance, Institutional and External Affairs, Brussels.

COM (2008). *Eastern Partnership*, 823 final, Brussels, December 3, 2–3.

Council of the European Union (2009). 8435/09, joint declaration of the Prague Eastern Partnership Summit Prague, May 7, 2009.

Kotulewicz-Wisińska, K. & Gródek-Szostak, Z. (2021). *Determinanty i kierunki systemowego wsparcia sektora małej i średniej przedsiębiorczości w państwach Partnerstwa Wschodniego*. Wydawnictwo Adam Marszałek, Toruń.

Tsebenko, O., Ivasechko, O., Turchyn., Y. & Lukach, N. (2023). The European Green Deal: shaping the future of the Eastern Partnership. *IOP Conference Series: Earth and Environmental Science*, 1150, 012005.

Part I

Eastern Partnership within the framework of sustainable development in Europe

1 Assumptions and recommendations of the Eastern Partnership

The Eastern Partnership (EaP) program aims to enhance relations between the European Union (EU) and Eastern European countries (Moldova, Ukraine, Belarus) and the South Caucasus nations (Armenia, Azerbaijan, Georgia). Its goal is to facilitate their gradual integration into EU policies, programs, and the single market. Notably, the initiative does not include prospective EU membership, but rather supports integration processes through both bilateral and multilateral approaches (see Table 1.1). The bilateral dimension of the EaP emphasizes strengthening individual countries' relations with the EU, while the multilateral dimension involves collaborative activities and initiatives among all partners (Czermińska, 2020).

The bilateral format entails negotiations between partner countries and the EU aimed at implementing political and economic integration measures (such as association agreements and free trade agreements), facilitating social mobility (through visa liberalization), and promoting sectoral cooperation (including energy security, agricultural development, environmental issues, and social policies, among others). The objective of the bilateral dimension of the Eastern Partnership is to foster closer relations between the EU and each partner country, thereby establishing a new legal framework for these bilateral relations (Kotulewicz-Wisińska & Gródek-Szostak, 2021).

The multilateral format complements the bilateral approach by offering partner countries opportunities for exchanging experiences in implementing domestic reforms through mechanisms such as meetings of heads of state, foreign ministers, and expert gatherings. Additionally, it aims to foster stability, build regional confidence (addressing long-standing conflicts), and support political and economic transformations in partner countries. It serves as a forum for sharing information and expertise. The multilateral dimension operates through summits involving heads of state and government, meetings of foreign ministers, and expert sessions organized under four thematic platforms.

The Summits of the Heads of State and Government of EU Member States and the Eastern Partnership (EaP) countries constitute the most significant institutions of the EaP. These summits convene once every two years to assess progress made and provide political impetus for the EaP implementation. To date, six summits have been held: May 7, 2009, in Prague; September 29–30, 2011, in Warsaw; November 28–29, 2013, in Vilnius; May 20–21, 2015, in Riga; November 24, 2017, in Brussels; and December 15, 2021, also in Brussels (Consilium Europa, 2022).

DOI: 10.4324/9781003486732-3

Table 1.1 Dimensions of cooperation within the Eastern Partnership.

Bilateral	*Multilateral*	*Nongovernmental*
1 Support for reforms	1 Thematic platforms:	1 EuroNest Parliamentary Assembly
2 Association agreements	1.1 Democracy, good governance, and stability	2 EaP Civil Society Forum
3 Deep and comprehensive free trade zones	1.2 Economic integration and convergence with sectoral policies	3 Congress of Local and Regional Authorities
4 Mobility and security	1.3 Energy security	4 Eastern Partnership Business Forum
5 Energy security	1.4 People-to-people contacts	
6 Promotion of economic and social development	2 Guiding initiatives:	
	2.1 Integrated border management program	
	2.2 Support for the development of small and medium-sized enterprises	
	2.3 Civil protection and disaster prevention initiative	
	2.4 Regional energy markets, energy efficiency and renewable energy sources	
	2.5 Environmental governance	
	2.6 System for combating the effects of natural and man-made disasters	

Source: Szeligowski (2013); Lustigová (2014).

Meetings of foreign ministers from EU member states and partner countries are held annually to review progress and provide political direction for the implementation of the Partnership's objectives. Other ministries engage in sectoral conferences with ministerial participation to initiate cooperation. These meetings are chaired by the EU High Representative for Foreign Policy. During these meetings, the implementation of directives from heads of state and government is evaluated, and other current international policy issues are discussed. To date, 12 such meetings have been held: December 8, 2009; December 13, 2010; July 23, 2012; July 22, 2013; July 22, 2014; April 20, 2015; May 23, 2016; June 19, 2017; October 15, 2018; May 13, 2019; November 15, 2021; and December 12, 2022.

Thematic platforms (COM, 2008) serve as forums for dialogue and cooperation between the EU and partner countries. They have been established around four main areas of cooperation within the Eastern Partnership.

Platform I: Democracy, good governance, and stability

The following areas of cooperation are considered priorities: democracy and human rights issues, justice, internal freedom and security, and stability and security. Key objectives include improving the functioning of the judiciary, reforming public administration, and combating corruption. Among other initiatives, the Integrated Border Management System is being introduced as part of this platform. The implementation of standardized procedures across all partner countries and the expansion of infrastructure are expected to enhance border security while facilitating the movement of travelers and goods. Establishing robust border management systems and adopting EU standards are essential for Eastern Partnership countries to eventually achieve visa-free travel with the European Union. Furthermore, without the adoption of European border management standards, a free trade agreement cannot be realized. Additionally, Platform I encompasses the flagship initiative for developing a system to combat the effects of natural and man-made disasters.

Platform II: Economic integration and convergence with EU policies

Under Platform II, long-term priorities include legislative approximation (covering areas such as trade), the development of financial and macroeconomic cooperation, the stimulation of socioeconomic development, and environmental protection. The work focuses on regulatory harmonization, support for the development of small and medium enterprises (SMEs), and addressing environmental issues. This is facilitated through specially established expert panels on environment and climate change, trade, SMEs, and transport.

Platform III: Energy security

Within this platform, the following areas are considered to be most relevant: support for infrastructure development and supply diversification, regulatory convergence and harmonization of energy policies, and the promotion of energy efficiency and renewable energy sources. This approach is justified because the EaP countries are located along the strategic transit route for energy resources from Russia and Central Asia to Europe. The platform envisions closer energy cooperation between the EU and the EaP countries, which will not only develop a network of connections but also provide mutual support in the event of an energy crisis. The goals include diversifying raw material supplies, promoting the rational consumption of raw materials by increasing energy efficiency, and enhancing the use of renewable energy. One of the platform's tasks is to harmonize regulations on electricity, gas, oil, renewable energy sources, and energy efficiency.

Platform IV: People-to-people contacts

The Platform's work in this area focuses on stimulating scientific exchanges (particularly in higher education), maximizing the implementation of programs aimed at young people, promoting intercultural dialogue, fostering cooperation in the field of culture, and developing the information society. One of the goals of the EaP is to bring the people of the partner countries and the European Union closer together, which is pursued within the framework of this platform. Cultural cooperation, civil society building, and intercultural dialogue contribute to strengthening ties between countries.

Meetings of the thematic platforms are held at least twice a year at the level of high representatives, who present a report on their activities at the annual meeting of ministers. The work of the thematic platforms is supported by 14 expert panels that address specific issues. These panels review and analyze the situation in each partner country concerning the topics covered by the platforms' work and develop recommendations for action and project proposals (Czermińska, 2020).

There is a divergence of tasks between the European Commission, some EU member states, and EaP countries regarding the clarification of the objectives of the various platforms. While the Commission emphasizes the need for EaP partner states to align their laws with the EU acquis, some EU member states and EaP countries view the thematic platforms as a starting point for EU-funded multilateral projects.

Flagship initiatives make the EaP project more concrete and tangible, enhancing its international visibility. These initiatives are implemented as part of the multilateral dimension of the EaP, with the support of the European Commission, in the following areas:

- the Integrated Border Management Flagship Initiative;
- the Support to Small and Medium Enterprises (SMEs) Flagship Initiative;
- the Prevention, Preparedness and Response to natural and man-made Disasters Flagship Initiative, PPRD-East;
- the Environmental Governance Flagship Initiative;
- the Regional Electricity Markets, Energy Efficiency and Renewable Energy Sources Flagship Initiative;
- the Environmental Governance Flagship Initiative.

Within the framework of multilateral cooperation, informal meetings are held at the level of foreign ministers and sector ministries of partner countries, along with European Commissioners. During these meetings, issues concerning multilateral sectoral cooperation and the development of the Eastern Partnership program are discussed.

Cooperation within the so-called nongovernmental dimension includes, among others, the EuroNest Parliamentary Assembly, the EaP Civil Society Forum, and the EaP Business Forum. The Committee of the Regions also aims to implement the Eastern Partnership through organizing the Going East forum and overseeing the EaP Congress of Local and Regional Authorities—a platform for cooperation between EU local authorities and regional and local authorities of partner countries.

The Eastern Partnership is a project that provides a forum for the exchange of information and experience among partner countries. It is a forum that has a so-called Group of Friends (the official name is the Information and Coordination Group). The Group of Friends is a loose, informal group of countries and international financial organizations that do not officially participate in the EaP, but want to support its ad hoc initiatives. This support consists of either financial or technical assistance for the implementation of individual EaP projects. The group also aims to keep each other informed of activities undertaken and to coordinate cooperation in the region. The Friends of the EaP Group, officially inaugurated in Brussels on September 29, 2010, was joined by the US, Russia, Turkey, Norway, Switzerland, Canada, Japan, the European Bank for Reconstruction and Development, and the World Bank (Mizerska-Wrotkowska, 2011).

Based on the progress made in the first ten years of the EaP, five long-term policy goals for the post-2020 period were identified through consultations launched in 2019 (The Eastern Partnership beyond, 2022). These five goals are discussed as follows.

1. Resilient, sustainable and integrated economies

Strengthening the economy is essential to meeting people's expectations, reducing inequality, and making partner countries attractive places for building their futures. Robust interconnections between the EU and the Eastern Partnership, as well as among the partner countries themselves, are crucial drivers of economic development, regional integration, trade, and mobility. The objective is to create decent jobs and economic opportunities that ensure the prosperity of people living in these partner countries. Consequently, the EU and partner countries will collaborate to foster a resilient, sustainable, and integrated economy through:

- increasing trade and furthering the regional and bilateral integration of economies;
- focusing on the full implementation of association agreements with the Deep and Comprehensive Free Trade Areas, along with other trade agreements, to maximize benefits;
- providing stronger incentives for structural reforms, improving access to finance, and supporting SMEs, particularly those led by women and young entrepreneurs, to promote growth and investment;
- strengthening interconnectedness through greater investment in physical and infrastructure connectivity in transportation, energy, and digital technology;
- continuing to invest in people, with a particular emphasis on the youth;
- better linking education, research, and innovation with the needs of the private sector.

2. Accountable institutions, rule of law and security

Good governance and democratic institutions, the rule of law, effective anticorruption policies, the fight against organized crime, respect for human rights, and security—including support for conflict-affected populations—are crucial preconditions for a functioning market economy and sustainable growth (Agenda, 1992). These elements form the backbone of strong and resilient countries and societies.

The EU and partner countries will renew their commitment to the foundations of the partnership, particularly in the areas of accountable institutions, the rule of law, and security, through:

- proposing ways to better measure the impact of judicial reforms;
- considering progress on rule of law reforms when making aid decisions; the EU's incentive-based approach will continue to benefit partner countries more committed to reform;
- reinvigorating EU support to combat economic crime and corruption;
- continuing cooperation with the EU Civil Protection Mechanism to improve prevention, preparedness, and response to natural and man-made disasters;
- increasing support for security dialogue and cooperation.

3. Environmental resilience and climate change resilience

The European Green Deal underscores that environmental and climate challenges require urgent action by the EU and partner countries. In pursuit of climate neutrality, the EU and partner countries share the responsibility of fulfilling nationally determined contributions to the Paris Agreement, a legally binding international treaty on climate change adopted by 196 countries at the UN Climate Change Conference (COP21) in Paris, France, on December 12, 2015, and entering into force on November 4, 2016. This includes modernizing their economies and reducing their carbon footprints.

The EU and partner countries will work together for a resilient and sustainable future in the areas of:

- transforming the region into equitable and prosperous societies with a modern, resource-efficient, clean, closed-loop, and competitive economy, while intensifying environmental and climate action, including the more sustainable use of natural resources;
- creating new green jobs and economic opportunities related to green transformation;
- developing local and renewable energy sources to halt the loss of biodiversity;
- further investing in environmental management and raising awareness, including through cooperation with civil society;
- accelerating the transition to sustainable and smart mobility;
- scaling up efforts in areas critical to human health and well-being.

4. Digital transformation

A modern data-driven economy can only be fully realized if citizens and businesses have access to high-quality, affordable electronic communications infrastructure and services. The Strategy for Shaping Europe's Digital Future calls for a robust digital presence in the EU neighborhood to facilitate economic growth and stimulate sustainable development.

The EU will continue to invest in partner countries' digital transformation and seek to extend the benefits of the Digital Single Market through:

- supporting the deployment of secure gigabit broadband with very high speeds, particularly in remote or less populated areas, and ensuring the availability of affordable services;
- supporting the implementation of roaming agreements between partner countries and, where appropriate, with the EU;
- strengthening e-government in the EaP region to enhance the efficiency, transparency, and accountability of public administration and facilitate reform;
- increasing support for highly innovative digital start-ups and facilitating their cross-border business collaborations;
- continuing to support and assist partner countries in cybersecurity efforts.

5. Just and inclusive society

Transparent, citizen-centered, and accountable public administrations, along with free and fair elections, are essential to democracy. Together with an engaged civil society, free, pluralistic, and independent media, and the protection of citizens' rights, these elements constitute key ingredients for resilient, fair, inclusive, and democratic societies.

The EU and partner countries will work together for resilient, equitable, and inclusive societies:

- ensuring that authorities involve citizens in decision-making to support democratic systems and enable informed choices.
- continuing to support the capacity of civil society organizations, especially local organizations and youth, to engage meaningfully in policy-making, promote reform, and enhance public accountability.
- promoting a well-functioning media environment and support independent journalists to ensure access to reliable and fact-based information.
- fostering social, economic, and political inclusion for all, including women, children, minority groups, and conflict-affected populations.
- ensuring safe and well-managed mobility and people-to-people contact, while providing support to vulnerable migrants and refugees.

The creation of the Eastern Partnership program was influenced by events in the former Soviet Union and the Central and Eastern European region at the turn of the 20th and 21st centuries. Equally significant is the European Union's long-standing role in international relations since its inception, which shapes its foreign policy towards neighboring regions. As a result, the European Union is cultivating a special relationship with its neighboring countries through various initiatives. The Eastern Partnership faces a persistent risk of slipping off the agenda, despite dedicated efforts from certain EU member states, particularly those in the east. It is imperative that the Eastern Partnership adapts and actively responds to new realities, supporting all partner countries in their aspirations. EU–Eastern Partnership relations should prioritize flexibility and differentiation, employing both bilateral and multilateral approaches tailored to the distinct priorities of each partner. This approach aims to enhance the involvement of regional and local authorities in shaping cooperation priorities with territorial impact. The Eastern Partnership region must prioritize the development of better interconnections to prepare for future economic shocks and mitigate external pressures. New regional transportation and energy infrastructure projects will bolster resilience across all six countries. The Green New Deal offers a promising opportunity for the Eastern Partnership, necessitating increased financial commitment from the EU alongside effective implementation of climate diplomacy tools and instruments. Investments in digital tools and engagement via social media platforms tailored to various age groups are essential for fostering civic participation across Eastern Partnership societies. Furthermore, young researchers from both the EU and Eastern Partnership countries should intensify cooperation in research, information technology, and innovation to drive regional development.

Eastern Partnership countries have a modest economic potential compared to the economic potential of the European Union (see Table 1.2 and Figure 1.1).

In 2022, the analyzed countries collectively represented approximately 0.79% of the total world area and about 0.84% of the global population. However, their economic output, measured by the gross product value, amounted to only 0.37% of the world's total, contrasting starkly with the EU's share, which exceeded theirs by more than 44 times. This disparity results from a multitude of factors, including the diversity of economic structures and varying degrees of participation in the international division of labor (see Table 1.3).

The European Union and the Eastern Partnership countries exhibit notable differences in the size of the private sector's contribution to their economies. Excluding the EU, Ukraine boasts the highest share of the private sector, whereas Azerbaijan shows the lowest. Among the other EaP countries, the private sector's share in GDP creation ranges from 21% to 32%. Armenia, Belarus, Moldova, and Ukraine stand out for their significant reliance on agriculture for national income generation. In contrast, the EU and most EaP countries, except Azerbaijan,

Table 1.2 Share of EU and Eastern Partnership countries in the world by area, population, and GDP in 2022 (in %).

Name	*Area*	*Population*	*GDP*
European Union	3.32	5.63	16.55
Armenia	0.02	0.03	0.02
Azerbaijan	0.07	0.13	0.08
Belarus	0.16	0.12	0.07
Georgia	0.05	0.05	0.02
Moldova	0.03	0.03	0.01
Ukraine	0.46	0.48	0.16

Source: Own compilation based on World Bank data (2022).

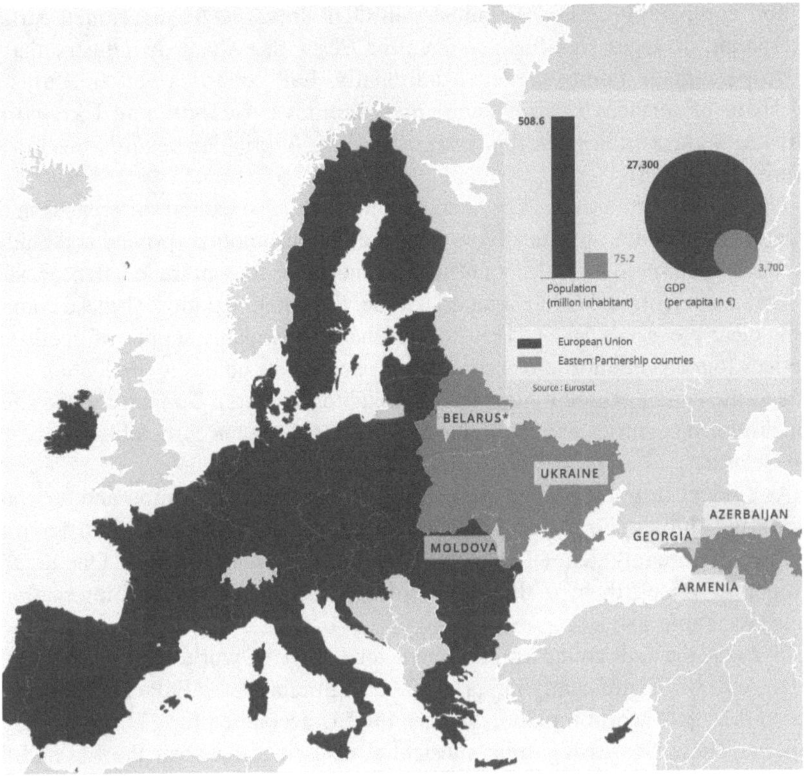

Figure 1.1 Eastern Partnership countries compared to EU countries in 2020.

Source: See https://www.consilium.europa.eu/pl/infographics/towards-stronger-eastern-partnership/ (accessed: 20.02.2024).

Table 1.3 Structure of the EU and Eastern Partnership economies in 2022 (in %).

	*Private sector share in the creation of GDP **	*Structure of GDP creation*			*Demand structure*	
		Farming	*Industry*	*Services*	*Consumption*	*Accumulation*
European Union	56.8	1.73	23.54	64.55	73.65	24.80
Armenia	29.9	10.36	25.56	55.27	83.67	19.40
Azerbaijan	14.9	4.76	55.94	32.20	54.33	12.65
Belarus	24.6	7.71	33.19	48.28	71.15	21.98
Georgia	21.1	6.09	21.54	59.90	89.42	20.71
Moldova	31.8	7.92	20.04	58.03	103.05	26.07
Ukraine	47.0	8.22	19.24	60.77	104.18	12.61

Note: * Data for 2020.

Source: Own compilation based on: World Bank. https://databank.worldbank.org/ (accessed: 07.12.2023); Statistics on small and medium-sized enterprises in EU and the Eastern Partnership countries. The European Commission. https://ec.europa.eu/ and www.eu4business.eu (accessed: 10.03.2021).

exhibit comparable shares of industry in GDP creation. As mentioned earlier, Azerbaijan diverges significantly from the EU with a share of industry that is 32.40 percentage points higher. Additionally, EaP countries vary in terms of the share of services in their economies. Moldova, Georgia, and Ukraine report the highest indices in this category, while Azerbaijan records the lowest Azerbaijan (2018).

The analyzed countries, as indicated by the data, also exhibit differences in the structure of demand, specifically in the share of consumption (private and public) and accumulation in GDP. In countries with negative foreign trade balances, such as Armenia, Georgia, Moldova, and Ukraine, the combined total of these components clearly exceeds 100%. This implies that the available supply of goods and services for consumption and accumulation exceeds the domestic production value (due to the deficit caused by imports outweighing exports). Conversely, the situation differs in countries with a surplus in foreign trade balances, notably Azerbaijan and Belarus.

As evident from the data presented above, the European Union and the Eastern Partnership countries form a group characterized by significant differentiation in their broadly defined economic potential and its utilization. One notable distinction among them is the varying degrees of engagement in international trade (see Table 1.4).

In 2019, the EaP countries accounted for 0.56% of world exports, while the EU's share was significantly larger at 27.66%. Similarly, the EaP countries represented 0.56% of world imports, whereas the EU accounted for 27.78% of global imports. These figures highlight substantial disparities between the EU and the EaP countries, with the EU's export and import shares exceeding those of the EaP by over 49 times and nearly 50 times, respectively. Moreover, the participation of these analyzed countries in international flows of productive capital, accompanied by labor and technical knowledge, is crucial to understanding their economic dynamics.

Table 1.4 Share of EU and EaP countries in international trade in 2022 (in %).

Name	*Share in world exports*	*Share in world imports*
European Union	27.66	27.78
Armenia	0.02	0.03
Azerbaijan	0.17	0.06
Belarus	0.15	0.15
Georgia	0.03	0.05
Moldova	0.02	0.04
Ukraine	0.17	0.23

Source: Own compilation based on data: Trade Statistics for International Business Development. https://www.trademap.org/ (accessed: 07.12.2023) and United Nations Conference on Trade and Development. https://unctadstat.unctad.org/ (accessed: 07.12.2023).

Table 1.5 Share of EU and EaP countries in the world's accumulated stock of productive capital in 2022 (in %).

Name	*Share of cumulative inflows*	*Share of cumulative outflows*
European Union	25.242	31.933
Armenia	0.016	0.001
Azerbaijan	0.067	0.067
Belarus	0.036	0.003
Georgia	0.050	0.008
Moldova	0.011	0.001
Ukraine	0.116	no data

Source: United Nations Conference on Trade and Development. See https://unctadstat.unctad.org/wds/TableViewer/tableView.aspx (accessed: 07.12.2023).

The intensity of international capital flows, including productive capital, varies over time. Nonetheless, the degree of participation in these flows can be assessed by considering the initial shares of the analyzed countries in the accumulated stock of inflows and outflows (Table 1.5).

In 2022, the EaP countries' share in global cumulative inflows of productive capital through foreign direct investment was minimal, standing at only 0.296%. Even smaller was their share in global cumulative outflows of this capital, amounting to just 0.080%. Compared to the broader capital expansion of the European Union, these shares were negligible.

Moreover, among the countries analyzed, the European Union can be regarded as a leader not only in terms of its broadly defined economic potential but also in the degree to which this potential is utilized, including its participation in the international division of labor (see Table 1.6).

Table 1.6 Economic potential of the EaP countries and the degree of its utilization against the EU in 2022 (basic indicators. EU = 100%).

		Armenia	*Azerbaijan*	*Belarus*	*Georgia*	*Moldova*	*Ukraine*	*European Union*
Area		0.68	1.98	4.74	1.59	0.77	13.77	100
Population		0.62	2.27	2.06	0.83	0.58	8.48	100
GDP		0.12	0.47	0.44	0.15	0.09	0.96	100
Participation in the trade of goods	Import	0.11	0.20	0.55	0.19	0.13	0.82	100
	Export	0.08	0.61	0.56	0.11	0.05	0.61	100
Participation in the trade of services	Import	0.10	0.31	0.20	0.12	0.06	1.09	100
	Export	0.15	0.23	0.33	0.21	0.08	0.06	100
Accumulated productive capital stock	Inflow	1.056	−4.734	1.707	2.152	0.626	0.387	100
	Outflow	0.013	0.047	0.049	0.103	0.015	0.009	100

Source: Own calculations based on the World Bank Trade Map and United Nations Conference on Trade and Development (2023).

From the perspective of economic potential and its utilization, the Eastern Partnership countries form a relatively homogeneous group but can be categorized into two distinct groups. Ukraine represents the first group with significant potential surpassing that of Poland, yet not fully leveraging it as effectively as Poland does. The second group comprises countries with comparatively smaller potential and suboptimal utilization. Moldova and Belarus, for instance, pursue policies focused on strictly autonomous economic development. In Armenia, economic growth relies heavily on the construction, agriculture, and mining sectors, with less emphasis on services. This economic structure results in considerable disparities compared to Belarus (Armenian economy, 2018). Conversely, Azerbaijan's economy is impacted by the "Dutch disease," with growth heavily dependent on the oil extraction and distribution sectors, rather than income generation in non-resource sectors (Zulfigarov & Neuenkirch, 2019). Georgia's economic development relies on external financing, excluding debt financing, but struggles to advance the real sector of its economy, with predominant resource allocation in construction and trade sectors (Mekvabishvili & Beridze, 2018).

This described state of affairs is reflected in the rankings of international competitiveness of the analyzed countries, or more accurately, their international competitive capacity. On theoretical grounds, two fundamental and evolving components can be distinguished within a country's national economy's international competitive capacity. First, there is the real component, often referred to as the "real zone,"[1] which encompasses tangible economic activities. Second, there is the institutional or systemic component, which pertains to the regulatory and economic systems governing the functioning of the national economy. These components are interdependent and evolve over time (Misala, 2008, p. 37). The institutional component,[2] or sphere of regulation, of a national economy's international competitive capacity encompasses numerous elements, many of which are challenging to quantify. Under conditions of a more or less market economy, one crucial factor is the degree of privatization, which varies significantly among the countries analyzed (refer to data in Table 1.6). Conversely, indicators such as economic freedom and perceptions of corruption represent an inverse measure of this degree (see Table 1.7).

Among the EaP countries, Georgia stands out for its significant degree of economic freedom, while Belarus, Moldova, and Ukraine continue to exhibit relatively limited economic freedom. Armenia and Azerbaijan fall in between with an average degree of economic freedom. It is noteworthy that in the EaP countries in 2022, compared to 2014, there is a relatively lower corruption perception index. This trend may be attributed to the presence of economic freedom, which typically fosters economic growth and acts as a significant buffer against the spread of corruption. Corruption often proliferates at the interface between the state and private sectors (Misala, 2008).

Currently, there is an ongoing debate regarding the role of government authorities in shaping the international competitive capacity of national economies. There

Table 1.7 Index of economic freedom and corruption in the Eastern Partnership countries in selected years: 2014 and 2022.

	Armenia	*Azerbaijan*	*Belarus*	*Georgia*	*Moldova*	*Ukraine*
Index of economic freedom according to Heritage Foundation[a]						
2014	68.9	61.3	50.1	72.6	57.3	49.3
2022	65.3	61.6	53.0	71.8	61.3	b.d.
Index of corruption[b] according to Transparency International						
2014	37 (94)	29 (126)	31 (119)	52 (51)	35 (103)	26 (142)
2022	46 (63)	23 (157)	39 (91)	56 (41)	39 (91)	33 (116)

[a] The value of the total economic freedom index ranges from 0% to 100%, with the following distinctions depending on its value:
1 – completely free economies, where the IEF ratio is 80–100%;
2 – economies with a significant degree of economic freedom, where the IEF ratio is 70–79.9%;
3 – economies with a medium degree of economic freedom, where the IEF ratio is 60–69.6%;
4 – economies with a fairly limited degree of economic freedom, where the IEF ratio is between 50–59.9%.
5 – repressed economies (with very high state intervention and a very low degree of economic freedom), where the IEF ratio is between 0 and 49.9%.

[b] Since 2012, according to Transparency International's methodology, the Corruption Perception Index (CPI) ranges from 1 to 100. A higher index indicates lower perceived corruption. In parentheses, the rank of the analyzed country is provided for the corresponding years: 2014 out of 153 countries surveyed and 2022 out of 180 countries surveyed.

Source: Źródło: Heritage Foundation. See https://www.heritage.org/index/ (accessed: 28.11.2023); Transparency International. See https://www.transparency.org/ (accessed: 28.11.2023).

is a prevailing notion that enhancing the effectiveness and efficiency of government operations can be achieved through "slimming down" or streamlining government structures. However, it is also recognized that the effective functioning of government can serve as a unique case of a pure public good. This includes ensuring the development of economic infrastructure and human capital resources, which has far-reaching implications (Misala, 2008).

The size of "government" can be measured in various ways, but analyzing the shares of budget revenues and expenditures as a percentage of a country's GDP is typically fundamental. Different approaches to assessing the optimal size of government have generally led researchers to similar conclusions. Optimal government size, in terms of achieving the best economic performance for a society, is typically considered to be around 17% to 21% of the society's income. This translates to government spending comprising approximately 19% of the national income (Kwaśnicki, 2020).

As indicated by the data presented in Table 1.8, all Eastern Partnership countries exhibit budget revenues and expenditures exceeding 20% of their respective GDPs. This signifies a relatively high proportion of "government" involvement in economic activity across these nations. Particularly noteworthy is that, except for Belarus and Georgia, public investment financing remains low in these

Table 1.8 Basic data on public finances in EaP countries during 2014–2021 and in 2022 (shares of GDP in %).

	Budget revenues		*Budgetary expenditure*		*Public finance balance*	
	2014–2021	*2022*	*2014–2021*	*2022*	*2014–2021*	*2022*
Armenia	23.77	25.09	27.57	27.32	−3.80	−2.23
Azerbaijan	29.48	22.93	30.35	23.96	−0.88	−1.03
Belarus*	28.66	26.47*	27.43	26.49*	1.23	−0.03*
Georgia	23.89	26.80	23.61	23.18	0.27	3.62
Moldova	30.45	33.57	32.33	36.83	−1.88	−3.25
Ukraine	27.01	42.32	29.91	58.64	−2.90	−16.32

Note: * In the case of Belarus, there are data for 2021.

Source: Own compilation based on data from the Central Statistical Offices of Armenia, Azerbaijan, Belarus, Georgia, Moldova, and Ukraine

countries. This includes investment in economic infrastructure, which generates "external benefits" for the private sector and reinforces development incentives (Misala, 2008).

Economic challenges and a lack of clear improvement are underscored by the Human Development Index (HDI) (see Table 1.9). Despite Armenia ranking 85th globally in human development in 2021, significant social inequalities persist, and the middle class remains weak (Melkumyan, 2017). This is attributed to an underdeveloped small- and medium-sized enterprise sector and entrenched economic systems within Armenia. Additionally, the country has faced an unstable financial situation since the beginning of its transition, marked by considerable financial and credit risks (Vardomskiy et al., 2016).

In Azerbaijan, a significant issue lies in the inadequate diversification of the national economy, which adversely affects its HDI. As a result, Azerbaijan's ranking in the UNDP's HDI dropped from 78th to 91st place. The country also faces severe inequality, highlighted by a high Gini index of 65% (Gini Index, 2022). Moreover, approximately 2.5 million people are employed in the shadow economy, and the middle class, crucial for societal development, comprises only 4% of the total population (Mashalla, 2020).

However, in terms of the HDI, Georgia improved significantly, ranking 63rd among surveyed countries in 2021. This marks notable progress compared to

Table 1.9 Human Development Index for 2014 and 2021.

	Armenia	*Azerbaijan*	*Belarus*	*Georgia*	*Moldova*	*Ukraine*
2014	0.733 (85)	0.751 (78)	0.798 (50)	0.754 (76)	0.693 (107)	0.747 (81)
2021	0.759 (85)	0.745 (91)	0.808 (60)	0.802 (63)	0.767 (80)	0.773 (77)

Source: Own compilation based on UNDP Human Development Index (2023).

its distant ranking of 76th in 2014. In 2021, life expectancy in Georgia was reported at 76.7 years according to the World Bank. Georgia also boasts high literacy and education rates among its citizens, with 98% of the total population having secondary education as of 2016. Healthcare expenditures in the same year amounted to 8.4% of GDP, with public funds covering only 36.6% of total spending. Most healthcare costs are borne directly by citizens from their own income sources.

In 2021, Moldova was ranked 80th in the HDI, placing it alongside countries such as Turkmenistan (91st), Egypt (97th), Uzbekistan (101st), and Libya (104th) (Human Development Reports, 2022). Over the past 15 years, Moldova has maintained this position in the ranking. These trends are closely tied to demographic shifts in the country, where the population has decreased significantly from 4.3 million people to 2.6 million over the past 30 years (Biroul National de Statistica al Republicii Moldova, 2023).

In the 2021 HDI ranking, Ukraine performed slightly better than Moldova, securing the 77th position. A child born in Ukraine today can achieve only 63% of the productivity of an educated adult. This indicator has seen slight improvement over the past 30 years, driven by a 2.3-year increase in life expectancy and a 2.6-year increase in the duration of education (Sharipov, 2020).

The top-performing country in the discussed ranking is Belarus, which was ranked 60th in 2021. Between 1995 and 2021, Belarus saw a notable increase in its HDI rating from 0.659 to 0.808, marking a 22.61% improvement. Over the same period, life expectancy for Belarusians increased by 3.9 years, while the average length of schooling rose by 3.8 years and the expected length of schooling by 2.5 years (Human Development Index, 2023).

In conclusion, it is evident that all EaP countries lag behind European countries in the indicators discussed. Investing in the education system, healthcare, and social welfare could offer potential solutions to improve these outcomes. When considering economic potential indicators, significant disparities exist between the European Union and the EaP countries. Moreover, there is a noticeable difference in the effectiveness of utilizing this potential between the EU and the EaP countries, with the latter exhibiting lower and varying degrees of effectiveness in comparison to the EU.

The EaP countries within the EU are increasingly setting development goals to leverage their strategic location between the markets of Europe and Asia (Dobbs et al., 2021). However, the relatively poor quality of infrastructure has hindered further trade and local economic development (Kunzel et al., 2019). Enhanced trans-Asian land transit could potentially catalyze greater trade integration for Eastern European countries, the Caucasus, and Central Asia (EECCA). In recent years, China has significantly strengthened its position as a central player in global value chains, with trade between China and Europe now averaging more than USD 1 billion per day. This presents opportunities for EECCA countries in sectors such as industrial and consumer goods, textiles, and machinery and equipment (OECD, 2021). Despite these opportunities, logistics infrastructure

Table 1.10 The World Bank's Logistic Performance Index. Infrastructure indicator (2012–2018). Score from 1 to 5 (best).

Country	*LPI Score*	*Customs Score*	*Infrastructure Score*	*International shipment Score*	*Logistics competence Score*	*Tracking & tracing Score*	*Timeliness Score*
Armenia	2.51	2.39	2.39	2.55	2.45	2.38	2.84
Azerbaijan	2.45	2.53	2.69	2.56	2.14	2.18	2.62
Belarus	2.54	2.29	2.39	2.47	2.53	2.44	3.1
Georgia	2.45	2.38	2.36	2.38	2.27	2.37	2.92
Moldova	2.52	2.31	2.21	2.69	2.36	2.36	3.1
Ukraine	2.83	2.46	2.38	2.77	2.76	3.08	3.45

Source: World Bank (2021b). Logistics Performance Index (database). See https://lpi.worldbank.org/international/aggregated-ranking (accessed: 20.03.2024).

performance in EaP countries, as measured by the World Bank's Logistic Performance Index (LPI) infrastructure index, has not shown a clear upward trend over the past decade (Table 1.10).

Poor-quality infrastructure results in high transportation costs, which in turn hinders competitiveness. With few exceptions, such as Azerbaijan, the economies in the region continue to grapple with challenges stemming from underperforming transport infrastructure and services, as evidenced by various infrastructure indicators (Table 1.11).

In terms of energy, all countries have achieved universal access to electricity. However, energy infrastructure assets, particularly transmission and distribution lines, generally suffer from poor quality due to inadequate investment in the maintenance and replacement of existing facilities over the past decade. This has resulted in high power grid losses and frequent blackouts. Coal remains the primary energy source only in Ukraine, while natural gas and other fossil fuels continue to be key components of energy mixes in EaP countries. Even in countries like Georgia, where hydropower is the largest source of electricity, seasonal fluctuations necessitate supplementing with imported natural gas. Continued investment in fossil fuel power generation poses the risk of locking some EaP countries into unsustainable development paths (OECD, 2021).

Energy consumption, including fuel combustion from transportation, constitutes more than half of all greenhouse gas (GHG) emissions in the EaP countries, ranging from 62% in Belarus and Georgia to 75% in Azerbaijan (World Bank, 2021). This high percentage is partly due to outdated and inefficient infrastructure, as well as insufficiently insulated buildings. There are significant opportunities to improve energy efficiency, which would lead to reductions in greenhouse gas emissions. Ukraine stands out as the largest GHG emitter among the EaP countries in absolute terms, primarily due to its large population. Ukraine's emissions are nearly double those of the other five EaP countries combined. However, Ukraine's emissions have decreased since independence and are now less than half of the pre-independence levels. Per capita, Belarus is the largest emitter, closely followed by Ukraine.

Table 1.11 Selected infrastructure indicators in the EU Eastern Partnership.

	Armenia	*Azerbaijan*	*Belarus*	*Georgia*	*Moldova*	*Ukraine*
		Energy				
Electricity production from coal sources (% of total) 2019	0	0	<0.1	0.1	0	30.8
Electric power transmission and distribution losses (% of output) 2019	11.1	9.8		6.8	18.8	10.3
		Transport				
Quality of roads. 1 (worst)–7 (best). WEF 2019	3.6	5.2		3.8	2.6	3.0
Quality of train services. 1 (worst)–7 (best). WEF 2019	3.1	5.2		3.9	3.0	4.2
Quality of seaport services. 1 (worst)–7 (best). WEF 2019	2.4	5.1		3.8	2.3	3.9
Quality of air transport infrastructure. 1 (worst)–7 (best). WEF 2019	4.6	5.8		4.4	4.4	4.0
		Water and sanitation				
People using safely managed drinking water services (% of the population with access) 2017	86.5	73.6	94.5	80.0	72.9	92.0
People using safely managed sanitation services (% of the population with access) 2017	48.2		80.5	27.2		68.5

Source: World Bank (2021a); World Economic Forum (2019).

The economic development strategies of the Eastern Partnership countries highlight the imperative of addressing infrastructure bottlenecks and enhancing connectivity. Several subregional projects, programs, and strategies are geared towards improving transportation infrastructure to bolster connectivity, enhance service delivery, and bolster competitiveness (see Table 1.12). One prominent initiative is the European Union's Transport Corridor Europe-Caucasus-Asia (TRACECA), which aims to strengthen trade and transport links and foster broader economic relations between the EU and 12 countries, including 5 of the 6 Eastern Partnership countries. These regional programs aim to develop sufficient infrastructure to ensure high levels of transport connectivity and integration across various modes of transport (OECD, 2018).

Recently, some Eastern Partnership economies have emerged as significant recipients of Chinese investment, totaling more than USD 20.6 billion between 2005 and 2020 (American Enterprise Institute, 2021). According to the China Global Investment Tracker, which monitors China's investment projects worldwide, the

Table 1.12 Regional transport corridor initiatives in Eastern Europe, the Caucasus, and Central Asia, including the EaP countries.

Project name	*Amount of investment (in USD billion)*	*Countries or continents covered*
Belt and Road Initiative (BRI)	900–8,000	**Europe**, Asia, Africa
The Central Asia Regional Economic Cooperation (CAREC) Program	31.5	Afghanistan, **Azerbaijan**, People's Republic of China, Georgia, Kazakhstan, the Kyrgyz Republic, Mongolia, Pakistan, Tajikistan, Turkmenistan, Uzbekistan
Transport Corridor Europe Caucasus Asia (TRACECA)	0.16	**Armenia, Azerbaijan**, Bulgaria, **Georgia**, Kazakhstan, Kyrgyzstan, Iran, **Moldova**, Romania, Turkey, **Ukraine**, Uzbekistan, Tajikistan, Turkmenistan, plus EU member states.
Trans-Asian Railway (TAR)	75.6	Afghanistan, **Armenia, Azerbaijan**, Bangladesh, **Belarus**, Bhutan, Brunei, Cambodia, China, India, Indonesia, Iran, Kazakhstan, Laos, Mongolia, Nepal, Pakistan, South Korea, Russia, Sri Lanka, Tajikistan, Thailand, Turkey, Turkmenistan, Uzbekistan, Vietnam.

Source: ITF (2019); OECD (2021).

majority of these investments in the Eastern Partnership region are concentrated in the energy sector, comprising nearly half (48%, or USD 9.9 billion) of all investments. The transportation sector follows as the second largest recipient with 24.5% (USD 5 billion), followed by real estate (8%) and metals (8%). Among the Eastern Partnership countries, Ukraine has received the largest share of Chinese investments amounting to USD 10.5 billion, primarily directed towards energy and transportation sectors. Belarus follows with USD 5.4 billion invested in the energy, transportation, agriculture, and real estate sectors. Azerbaijan received USD 2.2 billion, mainly focused on metals and real estate, while Georgia attracted USD 2.1 billion, primarily in transportation infrastructure.

The OECD (2021) database on major infrastructure investment projects in transport, energy, industry, and water (for detailed methodology and scope, refer to the Reader's Guide) reveals a total value of approximately USD 120 billion for planned and under-construction projects across the six Eastern Partnership countries. Energy projects constitute nearly half of this investment, amounting to 46% or USD 55 billion. Transportation projects follow closely, representing 35% or USD 42 billion of the total. Industrial and mining projects make up the remaining 16%, totaling USD 19 billion.

Within energy projects (OECD, 2015; OECD, 2018; Karatayev et al., 2021; OECD, 2021), electricity generation projects dominate the investment landscape, comprising more than half of the total investment value at 63% or USD 40 billion. This category is followed by investments in oil and gas pipelines, which account for 13% or USD 8.5 billion, and oil and gas production projects at 11% or USD 7.1 billion. In terms of electricity investments, capital-intensive nuclear power projects in Armenia and Belarus collectively represent slightly over half of all electricity-related investments in the Eastern Partnership countries. Hydroelectric projects, particularly in Georgia, make up 29.8% of electricity investments, while other renewable energy sources, primarily wind, account for an additional 15.7%. Many Eastern Partnership countries have prioritized energy security and are diversifying their energy mix away from a heavy dependence on natural gas. Armenia and Belarus have chosen to focus on nuclear energy as part of their energy strategies, while other countries in the region are increasingly turning to renewable energy sources to enhance energy diversity and sustainability.

In conclusion, one of the critical challenges for the future of the Eastern Partnership, alongside integration in trade and economics, investment and financial access, and investment in human capital, is the establishment of stronger interconnections. Sustainable, rules-based, and secure interconnections are indispensable for fostering cooperation between the EU and partner countries alike.

In the realm of transportation, the EU is prioritizing long-term investment strategies, as outlined in the Trans-European Transport Network (TEN-T) Indicative Investment Action Plan. This plan aims to upgrade critical physical infrastructure such as roads, railways, ports, facilities on the inland waterways, airports, and logistics centers. These upgrades are crucial for enhancing interconnections between the EU and partner countries, as well as within the EaP region itself. Support for these initiatives will be facilitated through pooled financial instruments and guarantees under the Neighborhood Investment Platform. Furthermore, the EU intends to enhance the adoption of EU and international transport standards, particularly focusing on road safety, as articulated in the 2018 Declaration on Road Safety adopted by the Eastern Partnership. Efforts are also underway to advance agreements on the Common Aviation Area and improve aviation safety measures. Recognizing the strategic importance of EaP countries in linking Europe and Asia, the EU is committed to promoting and supporting partner countries in implementing strategies that foster continental connectivity.

Furthermore, within the framework of the Eastern Partnership program, EU support for infrastructure development and supply diversification systems is of significant importance. This includes regulatory alignment and harmonization of energy policies, as well as the promotion of energy efficiency and the utilization of renewable energy sources (Schoenefeld, 2021). This strategic approach is justified by the EaP countries' geographical position along crucial transit routes for raw materials from Central Asia to Europe. Under the energy security platform, closer cooperation between the EU and the EaP countries is envisioned. This cooperation aims not only to develop a network of energy connections, but also to enable mutual assistance in case of energy crises in any of the EaP countries. The overarching objectives include diversifying raw material supplies, promoting rational consumption through improved energy efficiency, and increasing the share of renewable energy sources. Harmonizing regulations across the electricity, gas, oil, renewable energy sources, and energy efficiency sectors is a key task in achieving these goals.

Notes

1 Broad own and foreign resources and broad economic infrastructure.
2 The system of functioning of the economy refers to the framework of rules and structures that guide economic activities within a country. It encompasses the existing property relations and value systems, governing the organization, programming, control, and financing of economic life.

References

Agenda (1992). UN conference on environment and development. UNCED.

American Enterprise Institute (2021). China global investment tracker. http://www.aei.org/china-global-investment-tracker/ accessed on 30.12.2023.

Armenian Economy (2018). Armenian economy, in the second half of 2018. https://www.kavkaz-uzel.eu/blogs/83781/posts/35830 accessed on 27.11.2023.

Azerbaijan (2018). Resource model of economic growth. *Analytical Center for the Government of the Russian Federation*, 39, 9.

Biroul National de Statistica al Republicii Moldova (2023).

COM (2008). Eastern Partnership, 823 final, Brussels, December 3, 2–3.

Consilium Europa (2022). https://www.consilium.europa.eu/pl/policies/eastern-partnership/ accessed on 17.11.2023.

Czermińska, M. (2020). Europejskie Partnerstwo Wschodnie – wymiar polityczny. ekonomiczny i bezpieczeństwa zacieśniania stosunków ze wschodnimi sąsiadami Unii Europejskiej. *Krakowskie Studia Międzyanrodowe*, XVII(2), 197.

Dobbs, M., Gravey, V. & Petetin L. (2021) Driving the European green deal in turbulent times. *Politics and Governance*, 9, 316–326.

Gini Index (2022). Word bank estimate. https://data.worldbank.org/indicator/ accessed on 21.11.2023.

Human Development Index (2023). https://hdr.undp.org/data-center/human-development-index#/indicies/HDI accessed on 22.11.2023.

Human Development Reports (2022). http://hdr.undp.org/en/data# accessed on 22.11.2023.

ITF (2019). Enhancing connectivity and freight in Central Asia. International Transport Forum Policy Papers. No. 71. OECD Publishing, Paris.

Karatayev, M., Lisiakiewicz, R., Gródek-Szostak, Z., Kotulewicz-Wisińska, K. & Nizamova, M. (2021). The promotion of renewable energy technologies in the former Soviet bloc: why, how, and with what prospects? *Energy Reports*, 7, 6983–6994. https://doi.org/10.1016/j.egyr.2021.10.068

Kotulewicz-Wisińska, K. & Gródek-Szostak, Z. (2021). *Determinanty i kierunki systemowego wsparcia sektora małej i średniej przedsiębiorczości w państwach Partnerstwa Wschodniego*. Wydawnictwo Adam Marszałek, Toruń.

Kunzel, P., De Imus, P., Gemayel, E.R., Herrala, R., Kireyev, A.P. & Talishli. P. (2019). *Opening up in the Caucasus and Central Asia: policy frameworks to support regional and global integration*. International Monetary Fund, Washington, DC. https://www.imf.org/en/Publications/Departmental-Papers-Policy-Papers/Issues/2018/06/19/Opening-Up-in-the-Caucasus-and-Central-Asia-Policy-Frameworks-to-Support-Regional-and-Global-45910 accessed on 30.12.2023.

Kwaśnicki, W. (2020). Fiskalizm i rozwój gospodarczy. http://www.old.pafere.org/artykuly.n1963.fiskalizm_i_rozwoj_gospodarczy.html accessed on 30.01.2020.

Lustigová, P. (2014). *The place and status of the Eastern Partnership policy in the European external relations law*. [in.] *From Eastern Partnership to the association. A legal and political analysis*. Ed. N. Šišková. Cambridge Scholars Publishing, Newcastle.

Mashalla, T. (2020). Are Azerbaijanis "richer" than they really are? data publikacji 22.01.2020 https://newcaucasus.com/economy/18506-azerbaydzhantsyi-bogache-chem-na-samom-dele.html accessed on 10.11.2023.

Mekvabishvili, E. & Beridze, T. (2018). The "Thorny road" of economic reforms in post-communist Georgia: retrospective and perspective. *Ekonomisti*, 1, 21–29.

Melkumyan, Y. (2017). Armenia's 'middle class': stability characteristics and the challenge of erosion. *Caucasus Analytical Digest*, 95, 2–5. https://nbn-resolving.org/urn:nbn:de:0168-ssoar-88091–8

Misala, J. (2008). *Uwarunkowania rozwoju gospodarczego Polski. wschodnich krajów sąsiedzkich. Estonii. Łotwy i Mołdowy oraz współpracy gospodarczej Polski z tymi krajami w okresie transformacji.* [in.] *Współpraca gospodarcza Polski ze wschodnimi krajami sąsiedzkimi oraz Estonią. Łotwą i Mołdową.* Ed. J. Misala. Politechnika Radomska, Radom.

Mizerska-Wrotkowska, M. (2011). *Geneza i instytucjonalizacja Partnerstwa Wschodniego.* [in.] *Między sąsiedztwem a integracją. Założenia. funkcjonowanie i perspektywy Partnerstwa Wschodniego Unii Europejskiej.* Ed. A. Szeptycki. Dom Wydawniczy ELIPSA, Warszawa.

OECD (2015). *Creating incentives for greener products: a policy manual for Eastern Partnership countries.* OECD Green Growth Studies. OECD Publishing, Paris.

OECD (2018). *Enhancing connectivity through transport infrastructure: the role of official development finance and private investment (The development dimension).* OECD Publishing, Paris. https://dx.doi.org/10.1787/9789264304505-en accessed on 30.12.2023.

OECD (2021). *Sustainable infrastructure for low-carbon development in the EU Eastern Partnership: Hotspot analysis and needs assessment.* [in.] *Green finance and investment.* OECD Publishing, Paris. https://doi.org/10.1787/c1b2b68d-en accessed on 30.12.2023.

Schoenefeld, J.J. (2021). The European Green Deal: what prospects for governing climate change with policy monitoring? *Politics and Governance*, 9, 370–379.

Sharipov, A. (2020). Human Development Index: Ukraine. lower European Union and Central Asia. data publikacji 17.IX. 2020. https://hromadske.ua/ru/posts/indeks-chelovecheskogo-razvitiya-ukraina-nizhe-urovnya-evropy-i-centralnoj-azii accessed on 20.11.2023.

Szeligowski, D. (2013). Partnerstwo Wschodnie. Analiza efektywności na przykładzie Ukrainy. Working Paper Series, WP 10–01, 3–29.

The Eastern Partnership beyond 2022: Reinforcing Resilience – an Eastern Partnership that delivers for all. https://www.consilium.europa.eu/pl/policies/eastern-partnership/eastern-partnership-policy-beyond-2020/ accessed on 16.11.2023.

United Nations Conference on Trade and Development. (2023). https://unctadstat.unctad.org/wds/TableViewer/tableView.aspx accessed on 07.12.2023.

Vardomskiy, L., Pylin, A. & Ilina, M. (2016). Economy of Armenia: the ideas, models and development results. *Scientific paper, Under the common redaction of L. Vardomskiy. Moscow. RAS Institute of Economy*, 39(6). https://inecon.org/docs/Vardomsky_Pylin_Ilyina_paper_2016.pdf accessed on: 20.11.2023

World Bank (2021a). World development indicators (database). https://datacatalog.worldbank.org/dataset/world-development-indicators accessed on 30.12.2023.

World Bank (2021b). Logistics performance index (database). https://lpi.worldbank.org/international/aggregated-ranking accessed on 30.12.2023.

World Economic Forum (2019). The Global Competitiveness Report 2019. World Economic Forum. Geneva. http://www3.weforum.org/docs/WEF_TheGlobalCompetitivenessReport2019.pdf accessed on 30.12.2023.

Zulfigarov, F. & Neuenkirch, M. (2019). Azerbaijan and its oil resources: curse or blessing? *Universitat Trier. Research Papers in Economics*, 11(19), 1–19 https://www.econstor.eu/bitstream/10419/207043/1/1667010700.pdf accessed on 30.12.2023.

2 Characteristics of the Eastern Partnership countries

Economic dimension

Following the collapse of the USSR, the countries involved in the Eastern Partnership (EaP) began the challenging process of systemic political and economic transformation. Armenia, Azerbaijan, Belarus, Georgia, Moldova, and Ukraine faced the primary challenge of overcoming economic stagnation by gradually accelerating economic growth. Since their independence, several factors influencing this goal have been presented in six subchapters, each dedicated to one of these countries.

The research method used in this chapter is the analysis of secondary data on macroeconomic indicators. To evaluate the process of macroeconomic stabilization, the method of analysis of the so-called pentagon of macroeconomic stabilization (PMS) was used (Misala, 2008), which was developed in 1990 at the Institute of Market Conditions and Foreign Trade Prices. This method focuses on observing the development of key indicators such as:

a GDP growth rate, a synthetic measure of economic development and citizens' wealth.
b Registered unemployment rate (U), the ratio of the labor force willing to work to the number of employed.
c Inflation rate (CPI), an indicator of internal balance, measured by the rise in consumer goods.
d Public sector debt rate (G), the ratio of the state budget balance to GDP.
e External debt rate (CA), the ratio of the current account balance to GDP.

The area of the considered pentagon is defined by:

$$\mathbf{PMS} = \left[\left(\Delta GDP * U\right) + \left(U * CPI\right) + \left(CPI * G\right) + \left(G * CA\right) + \left(CA * \Delta GDP\right)\right] * K$$

where PMS is the pentagon of macroeconomic stabilization; and *K* is the ½ sin 72°, a constant coefficient of value 0.475, representing half of the sine of the angle at the central vertex of each of the triangles labeled a, b, c, d, and e. This angle is assumed to be 72°, one-fifth of a full circle.

DOI: 10.4324/9781003486732-4

Achieving an optimal solution (i.e., PMS = 1 = 5 x 0.200) is practically impossible due to various factors. Significant considerations include the fact that, similar to the so-called macroeconomic stabilization index quadrilateral, where the state budget condition is not considered, the goal is to optimize competing (rather than complementary) economic policy objectives to a greater or lesser extent (e.g., accelerating economic growth can reduce unemployment but also creates inflationary pressure and a tendency to increase external debt, and vice versa). However, technical considerations also imply the need for caution when interpreting the calculated real areas of each triangle in the pentagon of macroeconomic stabilization.

Most values (sides) of the pentagon are expressed as percentages, except for the side representing inflation, expressed in thousandths of appropriate values, specifically units. Thus, it is reasonable to use a logarithmic scale for this value and to interpret the results cautiously. The proposed approach and analysis are conventional but noteworthy.

The total area of the pentagon consists of the sum of five triangles:

a Real Sphere Triangle, representing economic growth and unemployment rate ($\Delta \boldsymbol{GDP} * \boldsymbol{U}$).
b Stagflation Triangle, representing unemployment and inflation ($\boldsymbol{U} * \boldsymbol{CPI}$).
c Budget and Inflation Triangle ($\boldsymbol{CPI} * \boldsymbol{G}$).
d Financial Balance Triangle ($\boldsymbol{G} * \boldsymbol{CA}$).
e External Sector Triangle ($\boldsymbol{CA} * \Delta \boldsymbol{GDP}$).

An important feature and advantage of the PMS model is the ability to isolate the area (or indexes) of macroeconomic stabilization dependent mainly on internal factors (areas of triangles a, b, and c, labeled **PMS1 = a + b + c**) and the area (or indexes) of stabilization largely dependent on external factors (area of triangle d, especially e, labeled **PMS2 = d + e**). Analyzing the appropriate indexes and areas allows for forming significant conclusions. Based on the analysis, it is possible to indicate the directions of changes in the broad process of macroeconomic stabilization, specifically progressing stabilization or deepening destabilization. Moreover, analyzing changes in each of the proposed indices and their groups (i.e., synthetic indices PMS1 and PMS2) can assess the achievement of specific stabilization policy goals, highlighting areas of greatest achievement and main threats to stabilization.

The method used in this chapter identifies the most critical internal and external factors affecting the economic development of the EaP countries. Statistical data from the World Bank and Central Statistical Offices of Armenia, Azerbaijan, Belarus, Georgia, Moldova, and Ukraine were used for the analysis. Although the research primarily covers 2014–2022, the specificity of economic changes in these countries since the early 1990s is presented for a better understanding of the problem, significantly impacting their economic development.

Armenia

Armenia's economic development is influenced by various interacting factors. Located in the South Caucasus region, Armenia has the smallest population of the six countries (2.96 million as of 2022) (Data Statistical Committee of the Republic of Armenia, 2024). Its economy is characterized by low income levels, determined by the domestic market capacity and strong dependence on foreign economic ties. Additionally, due to its geographical and geopolitical location, the country incurs high logistical and transportation costs, further reducing the efficiency of the Armenian economy and state budget revenues. Moreover, large defense expenditures and support for Nagorno-Karabakh have hindered economic growth. On the other hand, the extensive Armenian diaspora (estimated at 11 million globally) supports its historical homeland and is a crucial developmental asset. Armenia's economic development is affected by limited domestic demand, usually met through imports; a narrow range of exported goods primarily directed to the EU and Russia; modest internal financial resources (the state cannot borrow extensively in its national currency); limited external borrowing possibilities (low credit rating [Fitch Ratings, 2024]), and transportation blockade risks.

Additionally, regardless of growth dynamics, the country's expenditures always exceed its revenues. This deficit is covered by foreign loans and remittances, including diaspora and international organization aid. Foreign direct investments play a significant role in reducing financial imbalance but do not sufficiently reach sectors of the Armenian economy that could enhance the state's export potential. This imbalance heavily impacts the sociopolitical state of society, posing additional risks for foreign investors and the country's political situation (Vardomsky et al., 2016). Armenia's economic development relies on a small group of oligarchs exploiting the country's geopolitical isolation. In this regard, Armenia resembles Ukraine, where political competition coexists with an oligarchic monopoly in the economy. This dependency in Armenia is a significant obstacle to economic reforms (Stronski, 2017).

From 1992 to 2022, Armenian authorities used various methods to influence economic growth, leveraging global experiences and considering geopolitical and economic conditions. Consequently, the nominal GDP dynamics during this period resemble a zigzag: slow growth during 1992–1999 and 2010–2019 interrupted by periods of rapid economic growth during 2000–2008 and 2020–2022 (Figure 2.1).

The 1990s in Armenia's economic history were marked by a severe economic crisis. During market transformation, Armenia struggled with the disruption of cooperative ties with former Soviet republics. For instance, in the late 1980s, 70% of Armenia's total production was based on imports (raw materials, components), and 60% of the total production was exported (Vardomsky, 2012). The economic problems were exacerbated by the conflict over Nagorno-Karabakh with Azerbaijan, leading to a transportation blockade.

These factors contributed to the country's deindustrialization, resulting in job losses, social inequalities, and a sudden rise in poverty. The decline in industrial employment was accompanied by an increase in low-income sectors (in the 1990s, industrial employment fell by 60%, while agricultural employment increased by 457%). Radical agricultural reforms were implemented during 1991–1993 to address economic issues. As a result, 400.000 hectares of agricultural land were

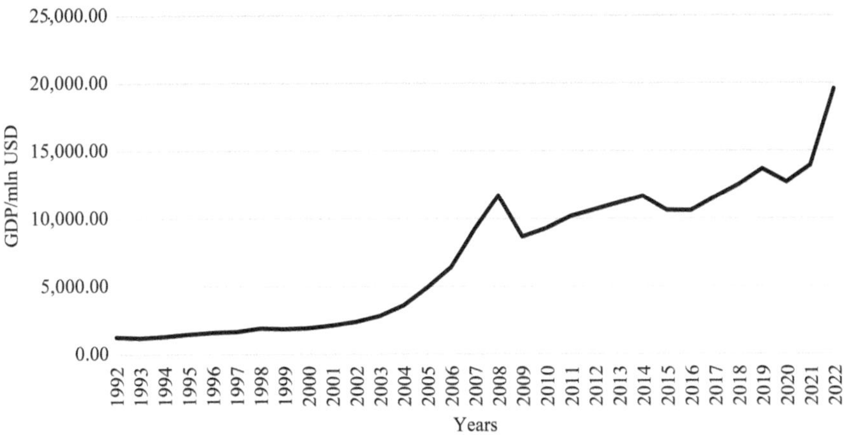

Figure 2.1 Armenia Nominal GDP Dynamics 1992–2022 (million USD).
Source: World Bank (2017, 2021).

privatized, and agriculture became a key economic sector despite a declining GDP share (from 26% in 1998 to 11% in 2022) (Dunamalyan et al., 2023).

In 1999, according to the World Bank, 55% of Armenia's population lived below the national poverty line, with per capita income below subsistence minimum (Sinitsina, 2006). Income declines and high inflation significantly reduced the purchasing power of society. Poor living standards, difficult living conditions, and lack of prospects led to the emigration of about one million people (Ashotova, 2016).

The decline in industrial potential affected the size and structure of foreign trade. In the late 1990s, imports in Armenia exceeded exports by 35 times, mainly due to structural and financial obstacles to increasing export production. The growing trade deficit generated a balance of payments deficit, leading to foreign loans.

At that time, part of Armenia's economic policy involved privatizing state property and liberalizing the economy. State property privatization began in 1994. Economic liberalization increased the private sector's share to 75% and privatization revenues to 66% of GDP (1998). Market reforms included trade liberalization (1992), national currency (dram) convertibility (1997), significant reduction of price regulation for goods and services, and complete abolition of wage regulation. Tax reform (1997) and customs reform (1998) led to Armenia's 2003 WTO membership.

High inflation was also a problem. To reduce it, restrictive monetary policy was implemented, and a stable exchange rate for the national currency was maintained. This policy limited exports and stimulated imports, ultimately leading to foreign currency outflows. These measures, similar to those in other former Soviet countries, resulted in "dollarization" of the economy, development of the "gray economy," and deepening income polarization, negatively impacting Armenia's political situation (Vardomsky, 2012).

During 2000–2008, Armenia doubled its GDP despite deindustrialization. Industrial employment fell by 28.7%, and the industry's GDP share dropped to 15%. The country's industrial structure further simplified, and the industry was no longer the economic growth engine. Economic growth was driven by exports, which increased over 3.5 times. Growth was also stimulated by a threefold increase in remittances from citizens working abroad. Nearly USD 7 billion were transferred to Armenia, with USD 5.3 billion entering the Armenian banking system (Sputnik News, 2017). This strengthened the republic's banking system and increased fixed asset investments by 39% annually. The construction sector rapidly developed, driven by remittances invested in real estate, as well as by the newly launched housing program. Armenia used its deposits of tuff, marble, travertine, and limestone for building materials. The construction sector's GDP share rose from 10.22% in 2000 to 25.31% in 2008, alongside real estate. Improved economic conditions were reflected in per capita income, which increased from USD 442 in 2000 to USD 3,071 in 2008, and poverty levels decreased from 53.5% in 2000 to 26.7% in 2008. Foreign direct investment in Armenia grew symmetrically from USD 513 million to USD 3.643 billion during this period.

Economic growth concentrated mainly in the capital, where most construction projects were implemented, exacerbating regional socioeconomic development disparities and increasing political tensions during the 2008 presidential elections.

In 2008, inflation rose to 8.95% (from −0.79% in 2000), and the Armenian dram strengthened to 306 dram/USD (555 dram/USD in 2000). The dram's appreciation hindered exports and encouraged imports, leading to a sixfold increase in the foreign trade deficit. Economic performance was also affected by internal political contradictions following the March presidential elections and the August Russian–Georgian conflict, disrupting Armenia's trade. Moreover, by the second half of 2008, the global financial crisis began impacting the country's economy.

At the end of the first decade of the 21st century, Armenia's economic situation deteriorated due to declining domestic demand, reduced capital inflows, increased economy crediting costs, poor economic diversification and export (Armbanks, 2010), oligopolies (TERT AM, 2013), and high corruption levels (27 in 2009, Transparency International, 2009). Additionally, the tax and customs system's imperfections and unequal treatment of economic entities exacerbated the situation.

As a result of the global financial crisis's impact on Armenia's economy in 2009, GDP growth slowed, and structural changes occurred. From 2010 to 2015, traditional growth factors such as agriculture (6.08% annual growth), industry (10.02%), and exports (16.37%) contributed to economic growth, alongside sectors like IT (5% of GDP in 2015) and tourism, generating income mainly from increasing foreign tourists (17%) (own calculations based on statistical data of arrivals [Knoema, 2024]).

Armenia's economic openness created new opportunities, but poor risk management exposed the economy to continuous shocks from crises in 2008, 2015, and 2020 (Table 2.1). During these periods, Armenia's economy demonstrated both high vulnerability and relatively quick recovery ability. Although the 2008–2009 economic recession was overcome by 2014 (with 3.4% GDP growth), external market dependence, geopolitical changes, and focus on mineral resources prevented the Armenian economy from exiting a long crisis cycle. In 2021, Armenia showed a clear trend towards breaking free from the "resource curse," as the share

Table 2.1 Armenia. Basic macroeconomic categories development 2014–2022.

	GDP growth rate	*Unemployment rate*	*Inflation rate*	*Budget deficit/ Surplus share in GDP*	*Current account deficit/Surplus share in GDP*
2014	3.6	17.6	2.98	−1.9	−7.8
2015	3.2	18.5	3.73	−4.8	−2.7
2016	0.2	18.0	−1.40	−5.5	−1.0
2017	7.5	17.8	0.97	−4.8	−1.3
2018	5.2	19.0	2.52	−1.6	−7.2
2019	7.6	18.3	1.44	−0.8	−7.1
2020	−7.2	18.2	1.21	−5.1	−4.0
2021	5.8	15.5	7.18	−4.5	−3.5
2022	12.6	13.5	8.64	−2.2	0.8

Source: Own calculations based on data from the World Bank (2017, 2021) and the Statistical Committee of the Republic of Armenia (2024).

of mineral products and base metals decreased to 39.3% of total merchandise exports and 25.1% of total goods and services exports. This share further decreased to 24.3% of total merchandise exports in 2022, mainly due to re-exports, estimated by experts at 15% of total goods and services exports. In 2021, service exports amounted to USD 1.7 billion, with tourism accounting for 46.3%, IT 21.9%, transport services 18.0%, and construction services 5.2%. Notably, Armenian service exports have been steadily growing for over ten years (except for 2020), and Russian immigration in 2022 could drive tourism and IT growth (IT employment increased by 9.100 people, or 39%) (Dunamalyan et al., 2023).

Analyzing Armenia's GDP structure in 2014, 2018, and 2022 (Figure 2.2) reveals the significant role of industry and water supply, whose importance is increasing.

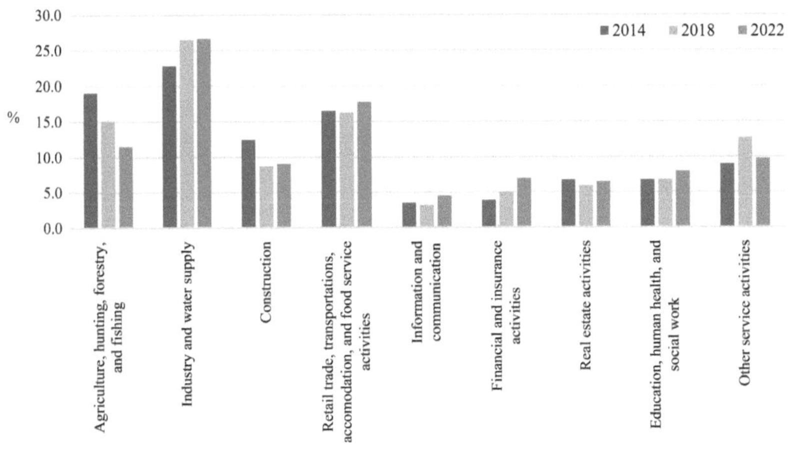

Figure 2.2 Gross domestic product by main economic activities in Armenia in 2014, 2018, and 2022.

Source: Own calculations based on the Statistical Yearbook of Armenia (2016, 2020, 2023).

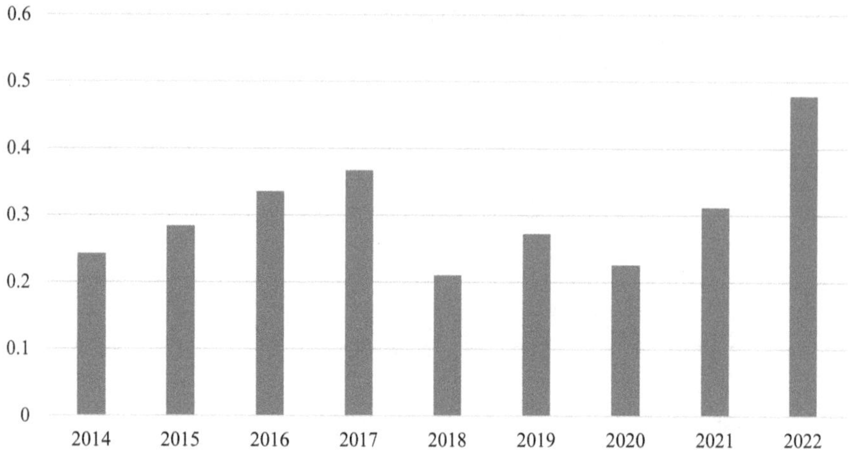

Figure 2.3 Armenia. PMS index development 2014–2022.

Source: Own calculations based on Table 2.1.

It accounts for 25% of GDP. Agriculture's GDP share has been replaced by Retail Trade, Transportation, Accommodation, and Food Service Activities, which now represent nearly 20% of GDP. Construction's share is also noteworthy, accounting for almost 10% of GDP. Other sectors contribute relatively low shares to GDP.

Complementing the above content is the analysis of the synthetic PMS index for this country, reaching a relatively low level, with the highest in 2022 (Figure 2.3, Table 2.2).

During the entire analyzed period, the values of the partial indicators of the PMS fluctuated. Generally speaking, the values of indicators a, b, and c (Table 2.2)

Table 2.2 Armenia. Value and relative importance of macroeconomic stabilization indexes 2014–2022.

Specification	*2014*	*2015*	*2016*	*2017*	*2018*	*2019*	*2020*	*2021*	*2022*
a	0.0250	0.0161	0.0216	0.0276	0.0086	0.0190	0.0104	0.0446	0.0704
b	0.0254	0.0161	0.0302	0.0302	0.0085	0.0201	0.0201	0.0361	0.0480
c	0.1247	0.0931	0.1059	0.1165	0.1247	0.1588	0.1059	0.0837	0.0939
d	0.0318	0.0666	0.0756	0.0749	0.0318	0.0340	0.0454	0.0582	0.1082
e	0.0357	0.0920	0.1026	0.1182	0.0370	0.0406	0.0443	0.0891	0.1580
PMS1	0.1750	0.1253	0.1576	0.1742	0.1417	0.1979	0.1363	0.1643	0.2123
PMS2	0.0675	0.1585	0.1783	0.1931	0.0687	0.0747	0.0897	0.1473	0.2662
PMS	0.2425	0.2838	0.3359	0.3674	0.2105	0.2726	0.2261	0.3117	0.4785
PMS1/PMS, in %	72.17	44.14	46.92	47.43	67.35	72.60	60.31	52.73	44.37
PMS2/PMS, in %	27.83	55.86	53.08	52.57	32.65	27.40	39.69	47.27	55.63
a/PMS1, in %	14.28	12.85	13.68	15.83	6.08	9.58	7.59	27.11	33.17
b/PMS1, in %	14.50	12.84	19.15	17.32	5.97	10.17	14.75	21.98	22.62
c/PMS1, in %	71.22	74.32	67.18	66.85	87.95	80.25	77.66	50.91	44.21
d/PMS2, in %	47.07	41.98	42.42	38.77	46.23	45.57	50.58	39.53	40.63
e/PMS2, in %	52.93	58.02	57.58	61.23	53.77	54.43	49.42	60.47	59.38

Source: Own calculations based on Table 2.1.

increased in 2022 compared to 2014. From 2014 to 2022, due to the current account deficit, the partial indicators reflecting the financial equilibrium triangle and the external sector deteriorated.

In 2014 and during 2018–2021, internal factors had a significant influence on the shaping of the macroeconomic stabilization coefficient, while during 2015–2017 and in 2022, external factors were more influential. For a precise analysis, it is worth examining the correlation coefficients between Armenia's economic growth rate from 2014 to 2022 and the shaping of the unemployment rate, inflation level, state budget condition, and current account balance with foreign countries (Table 2.3).

During 2014–2022, Armenia's economic growth rate was moderately negatively correlated (significant dependence) with the shaping of the unemployment rate (average indicator value: −0.5494). Notably, the negative correlation coefficient between the variables in most of the time intervals covered by the study indicated that GDP increases were high enough to improve the labor market.

Armenia's economic growth rate was moderately correlated (significant dependence) with the inflation rate (average indicator value: 0.5674). Positive correlation occurred in all time intervals except for the 2017–2019 period. GDP increases improved employment indicators but contributed more significantly to changes in the inflation level.

During the analyzed period (2014–2022), a significant positive relationship was observed between the GDP growth rate and public sector debt (state budget deficit) and a weak correlation between the GDP growth rate and foreign debt rate. In the first case, this relationship means that GDP growth contributed to the increase in public sector debt. In the second case, it means that GDP growth was practically unrelated to changes in the foreign debt rate. In the first instance, the increase in internal debt was due to a budgetary imbalance characterized by expenditures exceeding budget revenues. In the case of foreign debt, from 2014 to 2022, changes in the GDP growth rate corresponded periodically to increases or decreases in this

Table 2.3 Armenia. Correlation coefficients between GDP growth rate and changes in other elements of the pentagon.

	GDP growth rate - unemployment rate	*GDP growth rate - inflation rate*	*GDP growth rate - public sector debt*	*GDP growth rate - foreign debt rate*
2014–2016	−0.0438	0.9705	0.7283	−0.7669
2015–2017	−0.3742	0.3684	0.8104	−0.0636
2016–2018	0.0518	0.7540	0.3705	−0.2506
2017–2019	−0.8940	−0.9438	−0.2923	0.4808
2018–2020	0.4679	0.5117	0.9997	−0.984
2019–2021	−0.3713	0.4313	0.6922	−0.4853
2020–2022	−0.9957	0.9875	0.8751	0.8210
2014–2018	0.0515	0.3699	0.2888	−0.1512
2019–2022	−0.6795	0.6766	0.7103	0.3583
2014–2022	−0.5494	0.5674	0.5350	0.1856

Source: Own calculations based on Table 2.1.

debt. For instance, in 2021, Armenia's foreign debt amounted to USD 6.643 billion, increasing by USD 583 million (9.6%). Public finances debt at the end of 2021 amounted to USD 9 billion, or 60.8% of GDP (Statistical Committee of the Republic of Armenia, 2024).

According to the Statistical Committee of Armenia, GDP grew by 12.6% in 2022, the highest figure in the past 15 years. This growth, given in dollars, does not account for inflation. In contrast, real GDP growth, considering inflation, was 4.3%, below the real growth rates in 2017 and 2019, which were 6.53% and 6.16%, respectively. Factors contributing to this growth rate of Armenian GDP in 2022 include (Dunamalyan et al., 2023):

- events in Ukraine, which may have caused an inflow of capital and skilled labor from Russia (about 200,000 Russians emigrated to Armenia), Ukraine, and Belarus (to a lesser extent);
- economic sanctions imposed on Russia increased the share of remittances in GDP and unprecedented growth in Armenian exports (77.7%) as well as re-exports, which are not officially recorded, and imports (63.5%);
- a declining trend in labor migration from Armenia to Russia since 2013;
- an increase in the importance of the light industry in Armenia's economic development, with its share being 9% in 2018; there is potential for growth in the export of light industry products, which is significant for ensuring and increasing employment levels;
- unemployment decreasing to 13.5%.

However, a crucial component of the economy, the people, cannot be overlooked, and the country's population size shows a declining trend. In 2022, Armenia's population was 2.78 million, about 4% less than in 2014. Women dominated the population structure, particularly in 2022. Detailed information is presented in Figure 2.4.

The economy's potential, and the potential of human capital, is shaped by many indicators, including the Human Capital Index (HCI), which calculates the contributions of health and education to worker productivity. Although statistics on this index are incomplete, the published data show that while it was 0.581 in 2018, it was 0.578 in 2022, confirming a moderately (though declining) state of human capital considering the components describing the HCI. In contrast, the Human Development Index (HDI), which includes indicators of average life expectancy, education level, and living standards, does not show progress in this regard. In 2018, Armenia ranked 84th with an index value of 0.771, but in 2022, it achieved one place lower with an index value of 0.759. Thus, the declines mentioned earlier are also observed in this area. Complementing the demographic potential is their financial condition, here seen in simplified terms, as it relates to the Gini index. In Armenia, at the beginning of the analyzed period, it was relatively high; the highest level was reached in 2018, and in subsequent years it began to decrease, highlighting the decreasing inequalities in income distribution among Armenia's population. This results from increasing incomes, primarily due to social benefits

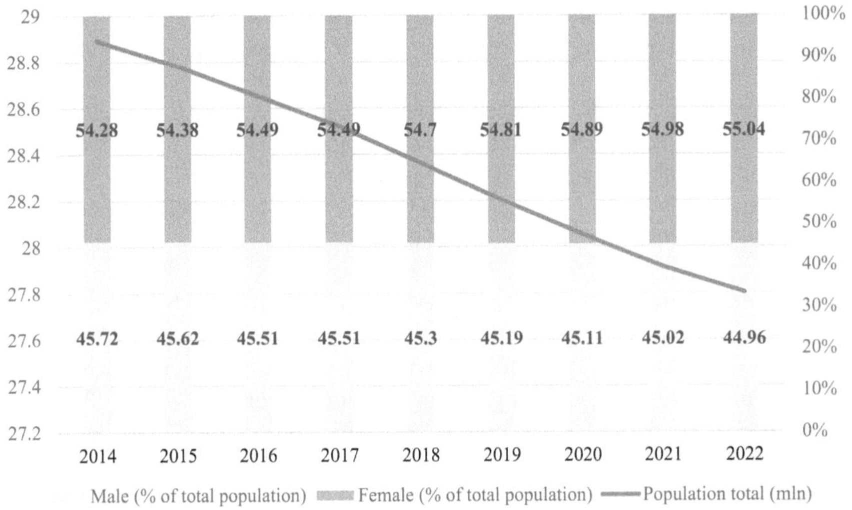

Figure 2.4 Population size and structure by gender in Armenia from 2014 to 2022.

Source: World Bank (2023).

and, above all, financial aid from those who emigrate for economic purposes and transfer money to their relatives in Armenia.

Summarizing the issue of Armenia's economic development conditions, it should be noted that currently, the conflict in Ukraine significantly impacts Armenia's economic outcomes. Additionally, the observed decline in agriculture, healthcare, and social security shows the lack of impact of global events on the structure of the Armenian economy. Similar to the early 2000s, the inflow of money contributes to one or several selected sectors against the backdrop of the decline of others (e.g., agriculture), which may lead to events that occurred in the past. Maintaining all the premises that contributed to GDP growth may cause "Dutch disease" and the emergence of new "bubbles" in the Armenian market. The main premises include the war in Ukraine, Western sanctions on Russia, and the protection of human capital in Armenia. If hostilities cease and many Russian citizens return to Russia, the combination of factors influencing Armenia's economy may change fundamentally (Dunamalyan et al., 2023).

Azerbaijan

Azerbaijan's primary economic sector is the extraction and processing of oil and natural gas. The oil and gas sector generates over 30% of the country's GDP. The exploitation of natural resources in this country is subject to a state monopoly. Oil reserves are estimated at approximately 0.96 billion tons (about 7 million barrels), which constitutes about 1% of the world's oil production. Proven natural gas reserves at the end of 2020 were estimated at 2.8 trillion cubic meters, accounting for about 0.7% of world reserves (WNP, 2020).

At the beginning of the transition in the 1990s, the country faced problems such as the breakdown of economic ties with former republics, a sudden decline in public orders, and structural changes due to modifications in price ratios. Additional economic problems stemmed from political instability and the armed conflict around Nagorno-Karabakh. Therefore, the economic crisis faced by Azerbaijan after the collapse of the former USSR was quite severe (Figure 2.5).

Considering the dynamics of nominal GDP, the economic development of Azerbaijan can be divided into the following stages:

1 **Transformational decline (1992–1995)**: GDP decreased by 58%. During this period, industrial production fell significantly (on average by 24%), agricultural production (on average by 15%), and investments fell by 43%. High inflation was a serious problem (average annual rate of 1,029%). The budget deficit rose to 9.5% of GDP, and the country's foreign exchange reserves were virtually depleted. As a result, incomes fell significantly, unemployment rose, and over 60% of Azerbaijani citizens fell below the poverty line (Rustamov, 2010).
2 **Stabilization and reentry onto the growth path (1996–2000):** The goal of Azerbaijan's authorities was to implement structural reforms, with a priority on financial reform and achieving macroeconomic stabilization. The result of the actions taken was the stabilization of consumer prices and a rise in production. The average annual GDP growth rate was 7.1% (Rustamov, 2010).
3 **Investment surge (2001–2004)**: During these years, investment outlays increased sharply (average annual growth of 51%). The share of foreign direct investments (FDI) in GDP was over 25%. Considering the indicator's value, it should be noted that Azerbaijan became a world leader, because it was more than three times the

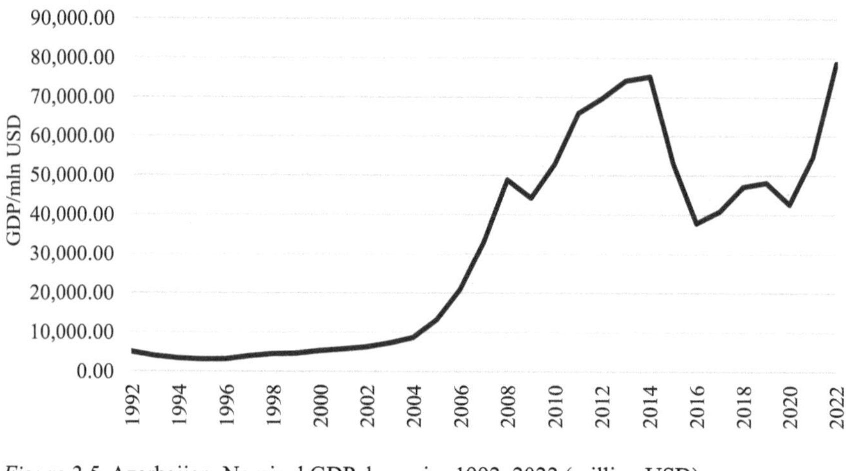

Figure 2.5 Azerbaijan. Nominal GDP dynamics 1992–2022 (million USD).

Source: World Bank (2021).

average for Central and Eastern European countries and Baltic countries, more than five times the value for CIS countries, and more than seven times the average FDI-to-GDP ratio in BRICS countries (Rustamov, 2010).

4 **Economic boom (2005–2008):** Rapid economic growth resulted from large-scale investments in the oil sector in previous years. The challenge was to make the oil boom a driving force for record growth for the entire economy (including the non-oil sector). During 2005–2007, the annual GDP growth rate was 30%. Due to the impact of the global financial crisis, GDP growth during 2008–2009 was 9% annually. Overall, from 2005 to 2009, the country's GDP grew more than 3.3 times, with an average annual growth rate of 25% (author's calculations based on World Bank data).

5 **Stabilization of economic growth (2009–2014):** From 1992 to 2014, Azerbaijan's GDP, expressed in current dollars, grew from USD 1.2 billion to USD 75.3 billion (a record increase for former Soviet republics), and GDP per capita increased from USD 159 in 1992 to USD 8,000 in 2014. During the boom years, Azerbaijan's budget dependency on oil and gas revenues increased sharply. During 2003–2007, the share of transfers from the State Oil Fund (SOF) to the budget averaged about 10% of GDP, while during 2010–2014, it exceeded 50% of GDP, reaching 58.2% in 2014. During 2010–2014, the oil sector shrank by an average of 2.9% annually. GDP outside the oil sector grew by an average of 8.8%, mainly due to the construction industry (average annual growth of 18.2%) and retail trade (average annual growth of 10%). At the same time, 72.6% of investments in construction came from the state budget. Thus, from 2010 to 2014, Azerbaijan's GDP growth was due to the development of the non-oil sector (JSC Kommersant, 2017).

6 **Decrease in economic growth (2015–2016):** The decline in Azerbaijan's GDP growth rate was largely due to the threefold drop in world oil prices. Azerbaijan's authorities took hasty actions to prevent deepening the economic crisis. Among other things, they tried to maintain the depreciating national currency. The Central Bank of Azerbaijan spent half of its foreign exchange reserves for this purpose by mid-2015, and in 2016, after announcing a transition to a floating exchange rate, it allocated an additional 20% of total foreign exchange reserves. This situation accelerated the depreciation of the national currency. It once again showed that Azerbaijan's economy is highly dependent on the extraction and export of natural resources (Mustafajewa, 2017).

7 **Reentry onto the growth path (2017–2019):** Economic growth during this period was due to improved foreign market conditions, resulting in increased Azerbaijani exports and growth in the non-oil sector. Moreover, during 2016–2017, Azerbaijan's economy faced the problem of double-digit inflation. The rapid increase in inflation was due to the revaluation of the manat in the face of the country's economy's high dependence on imports. By the end of 2019, inflation remained at 5%, supported by government policies and the fact that the exchange rate shock ceased to impact price dynamics. The main risk to the country's sustained economic growth remains Azerbaijan's heavy dependence

on resource extraction. The recovery of industrial production was solely due to the development of the extraction industry, and the share of processing fell to 28% of total industrial production (63% in 1997). Unfavorable trends in the credit segment only exacerbate the situation (ACRA, 2018).

8 **Decrease in economic growth (2020–2021):** During this period, the COVID-19 pandemic impacted economic growth by reducing economic activity within the country and disrupting global supply chains. Nonetheless, in 2021, Azerbaijan recorded a 5.6% GDP growth after GDP had decreased by 4.3% in 2020. Significant increases in 2021 were recorded in the non-oil sector (6.7%) compared to its decline in 2020 (2.6%). Exports of oil products from January to October 2021 amounted to USD 2 billion. The basis for Azerbaijan's export growth was actions initiated during 2014–2015, resulting in the opening of Azerbaijani Trade Houses in various countries, creating new agricultural and industrial parks, and taking a number of other actions (Hasanli, 2021).
9 **Reentry onto the growth path in 2022:** In 2022, GDP grew by 4.6% compared to the previous year. In the oil sector, value added decreased by 2.7%, while in the non-oil sector, it increased by 9.1%. In the GDP structure, the share of industry was 51.1%, trade and repair services was 8.2%, transportation and related services was 6%, agriculture was 4.8%, construction was 4.8%, restaurant and hotel services was 1.6%, ICT was 1.4%, and the share of other sectors was 14.7%. The primary economic problem was the rise in inflation, which was about 14% at the end of 2022. The causes of rising prices in Azerbaijan are diverse. First, it is the increase in transportation service costs, especially after 2020. Second, the conflict in Ukraine contributed to the rise in grain market prices, mainly due to the limitation of export capabilities and Azerbaijani grain. Third, the conflict in Ukraine also contributed to the rise in energy raw material prices, which, in turn, indirectly impacted the increase in goods and services prices in Azerbaijan's domestic market. Moreover, in 2022, Azerbaijani citizens working abroad transferred USD 2.779 billion to the country through remittances. This significant increase in remittance volume to the country was associated with about a 5.5-fold increase in funds sent from Russia to Azerbaijan (Mahmudov, 2023). Foreign debt share decreased from 17% to 9.5% of GDP, or to USD 7 billion (TAdviser, 2023). This was possible because Azerbaijan recorded a positive current account balance (over USD 17.7 billion), meaning that exports exceeded imports. This is feasible because the main export commodity is energy raw materials, which account for 90% of the export commodity structure (Report News Agency, 2022).

In this context, it can be stated that the process of stabilizing the Azerbaijani economy during 2014–2022 was uneven. This is evidenced by the analysis of the synthetic PMS index. The index value was relatively low, reaching its highest value in 2022 (Figure 2.6, Table 2.4). The value of the indicator was relatively low, reaching its peak in 2022 (Figure 2.6, Table 2.4).

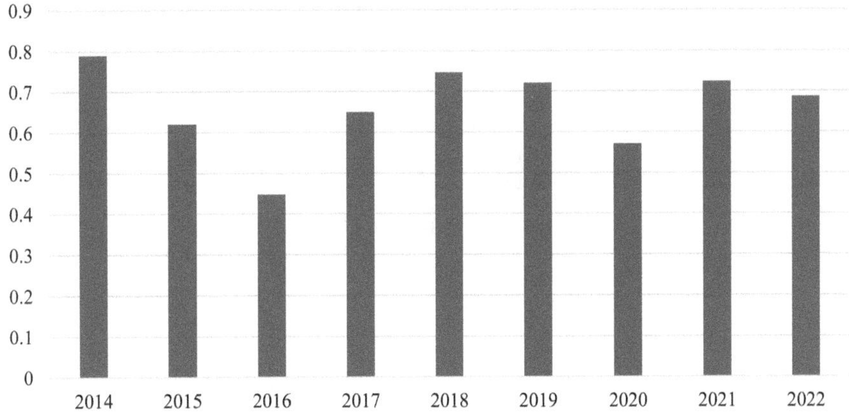

Figure 2.6 Azerbaijan. PMS index development 2014–2022.

Source: Own calculations based on Table 2.4.

From 2014 to 2022, the value of the macroeconomic stabilization indicator PMS for Azerbaijan ranged from 0.4478 to 0.7894.

During the entire analyzed period, the values of the partial indicators of the PMS fluctuated (Table 2.5). Overall, in 2022 compared to 2014, the values of indicators a and e increased, while the values of indicators b, c, and d decreased. From 2014 to 2022, due to difficulties in maintaining a balanced state budget, the values of the partial indicators representing the financial equilibrium triangle worsened.

During 2014–2016 and 2018–2020, internal factors had a significant influence on the shaping of the macroeconomic stabilization coefficient, while in 2017 and during 2021–2022, external factors were more influential. For a precise analysis, it is worth examining the correlation coefficients between Azerbaijan's economic growth rate

Table 2.4 Azerbaijan. Basic macroeconomic categories development 2014–2022.

	GDP growth rate	*Unemployment rate*	*Inflation rate*	*Budget deficit/ Surplus share in GDP*	*Current account deficit/Surplus share in GDP*
2014	2.8	4.91	1.39	0.52	13.57
2015	1.1	4.96	4.01	0.53	−0.42
2016	−3.1	5.00	12.45	0.41	−3.60
2017	0.2	5.00	12.94	1.53	4.12
2018	1.5	4.90	2.26	0.28	12.68
2019	2.5	5.00	2.61	0.25	8.70
2020	−4.3	7.24	2.76	2.39	−0.74
2021	5.6	6.04	6.65	1.10	14.96
2022	4.6	5.65	13.85	1.03	29.82

Source: Own calculations based on data from the World Bank (2021) and the State Statistical Committee of the Republic of Azerbaijan (2022).

Table 2.5 Azerbaijan. Value and relative importance of macroeconomic stabilization indexes 2014–2022.

Specification	*2014*	*2015*	*2016*	*2017*	*2018*	*2019*	*2020*	*2021*	*2022*
a	0.1288	0.1242	0.0948	0.1121	0.1242	0.1207	0.0785	0.1288	0.1293
b	0.1609	0.1286	0.0966	0.0949	0.1448	0.1269	0.1100	0.1012	0.0932
c	0.1694	0.1354	0.1085	0.1132	0.1524	0.1425	0.1603	0.1293	0.1112
d	0.1694	0.1210	0.0847	0.1800	0.1694	0.1694	0.1361	0.1800	0.1800
e	0.1609	0.1109	0.0632	0.1494	0.1552	0.1609	0.0862	0.1839	0.1724
PMS1	0.4591	0.3882	0.2999	0.3201	0.4214	0.3901	0.3487	0.3592	0.3338
PMS2	0.3303	0.2319	0.1479	0.3294	0.3246	0.3304	0.2224	0.3639	0.3524
PMS	0.7894	0.6201	0.4478	0.6495	0.7460	0.7204	0.5711	0.7231	0.6862
PMS1/PMS, in %	58.15	62.61	66.97	49.28	56.49	54.14	61.06	49.67	48.64
PMS2/PMS, in %	41.85	37.39	33.03	50.72	43.51	45.86	38.94	50.33	51.36
a/PMS1, in %	28.04	31.98	31.62	35.01	29.47	30.95	22.50	35.84	38.74
b/PMS1, in %	35.06	33.14	32.21	29.63	34.36	32.53	31.54	28.16	27.93
c/PMS1, in %	36.90	34.88	36.17	35.35	36.17	36.52	45.96	35.99	33.32
d/PMS2, in %	51.28	52.19	57.26	54.64	52.19	51.28	61.22	49.46	51.07
e/PMS2, in %	48.72	47.81	42.74	45.36	47.81	48.72	38.78	50.54	48.93

Source: Own calculations based on Table 2.4.

from 2014 to 2022 and the shaping of the unemployment rate, inflation level, state budget condition, and current account balance with foreign countries (Table 2.6).

During 2014–2022, Azerbaijan's economic growth rate was negatively and clearly correlated with the unemployment rate (average indicator value: −0.2769). Notably, the negative correlation coefficient between the variables in most of the time intervals covered by the study indicated that GDP increases were high enough to improve the labor market.

Conversely, from 2014 to 2022, Azerbaijan's economic growth rate was weakly negatively correlated with the inflation rate (average indicator value: −0.0004). Positive correlation occurred in the time intervals of 2019–2021, 2020–2022, and

Table 2.6 Azerbaijan. Correlation coefficients between GDP growth rate and changes in other elements of the pentagon.

	GDP growth rate - unemployment rate	*GDP growth rate - inflation rate*	*GDP growth rate - public sector debt*	*GDP growth rate - foreign debt rate*
2014–2016	−0.9542	−0.9985	0.9363	0.8318
2015–2017	−0.6658	−0.6285	0.4005	0.6750
2016–2018	−0.7182	−0.6893	0.1506	0.9623
2017–2019	−0.0751	−0.8884	−0.9098	0.5965
2018–2020	−0.9848	−0.6322	−0.9923	0.9092
2019–2021	−0.7014	0.7188	−0.7541	0.9954
2020–2022	−0.9462	0.7066	−0.9906	0.8256
2014–2018	−0.2951	−0.8870	−0.2076	0.8339
2019–2022	0.7105	0.5566	−0.9022	0.7903
2014–2022	−0.2769	−0.0004	−0.3777	0.8007

Source: Own calculations based on Table 2.4.

2019–2022; in all other time intervals, the correlation was negative. GDP increases also contributed to changes in the inflation level.

During the analyzed period (2014–2022), a clear negative relationship was observed between the GDP growth rate and public sector debt (state budget deficit), while a very high correlation was observed between the GDP growth rate and foreign debt rate. In the first case, this relationship means that GDP growth contributed to the decline in public sector debt. In the second case, it means that GDP growth contributed to the increase in foreign debt. In the first instance, the increase in internal debt was due to budgetary imbalance characterized by expenditures exceeding budget revenues. In the case of foreign debt, from 2014 to 2022, changes in GDP growth rate corresponded periodically to increases or decreases in this debt.

An idiosyncrasy of the Azerbaijani economy is its very high dependence on the oil sector, resulting in a growing problem of "Dutch disease" in the post-crisis years, manifested by (EurAsia Daily, 2016):

- a very low and decreasing share of manufactured goods in exports and economic growth primarily driven by sectors such as construction and services;
- a chronically overvalued manat exchange rate against the US dollar;
- increased dependence on food imports to 22% during 2010–2019;
- concentration of FDI in the oil and gas sector and uneven regional economic development (almost two-thirds of GDP is attributed to the Absheron Peninsula).

The high dependence on the oil and gas sector distorts the sectoral structure of the Azerbaijani economy (Table 2.7).

Table 2.7 Azerbaijan. Share of the oil and non-oil sectors in GDP during 2008–2022, in %.

	Oil sector	*Non-oil sector*	*Net taxes on production and imports*
2008	55.44	37.86	6.70
2009	45.13	46.98	7.89
2010	48.06	45.16	6.78
2011	49.60	44.54	5.86
2012	44.73	49.07	6.20
2013	40.87	52.47	6.66
2014	36.27	56.25	7.48
2015	28.27	62.78	8.95
2016	32.36	59.50	8.14
2017	35.65	57.05	7.30
2018	40.24	52.02	7.74
2019	36.84	54.45	8.71
2020	28.13	62.43	9.44
2021	37.02	54.85	8.13
2022	46.64	45.91	7.44

Source: Own study based on data from the Central Statistical Office of Azerbaijan, www.stat.gov.az.

Azerbaijan is a country unfamiliar with depopulation. In 2022, compared to 2014, the population increased by over 6%. During the studied period, the population structure by gender remained unchanged, with a slight predominance of women (Figure 2.7).

As a country of over 10 million people, Azerbaijan had a moderate HDI level. In 2021, it ranked 91st out of 191 countries worldwide, with an HDI value of 0.745. Interestingly, the HCI did not perform as favorably. Statistical data do not provide a complete base in this regard, and the available data indicate a declining level of this index from 0.597 in 2017, 0.629 in 2018, to 0.577 in 2020 (World Bank, 2017, p. 2013).

Summarizing the problem of Azerbaijan's economic development conditions, it is essential to note the clear dominance of the oil sector in generating national income. Actions taken after 2009 to develop the non-oil sector have not resulted in dynamic GDP growth. This situation may indicate improper allocation of resources among national economy sectors and the intensification of the "Dutch disease" problem. Therefore, the country should aim to diversify its economy and primarily develop non-oil sectors.

Belarus

In the early 1990s, the dissolution of the USSR and the severance of cooperative ties led to a significant deterioration of Belarus's economic situation. According to Soviet experts in 1987, due to the hypothetical severance of cooperation with other republics, using its resources, Belarus could ensure only 3.8% of the total final production, while Russia could ensure 64%, Ukraine 14.8%, and Kazakhstan 27.1%

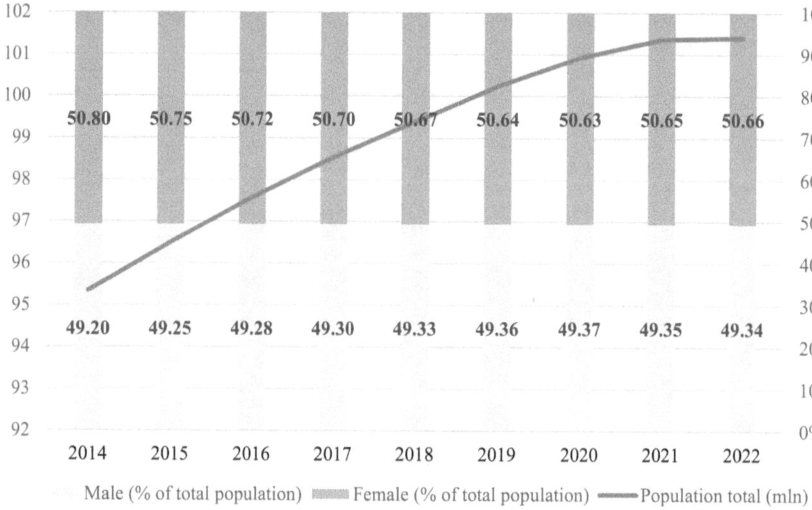

Figure 2.7 Population size and structure by gender in Azerbaijan from 2014 to 2022.
Source: World Bank (2017, p. 2023).

(Vardomsky, 2012). This indicator reveals the function that Belarus served in the Soviet economy, which was essentially that of an "assembly facility."

In Belarus from 1992 to 1996, structural changes were characterized by spontaneity, resulting from halted, reduced, or ceased production due to loss of markets, lack of raw materials, non-competitiveness, and unprofitability of production. Thus, from 1992 to 1995, Belarus's GDP decreased by 22.4% (Figure 2.8), along with industrial production (including construction) by 41.7%, investments in fixed assets by 42.4% (own calculations based on World Bank data), and agricultural production by 27% (data for the years 1990–1996; see Pavlovets & Shiptenko, 2017). At the same time, inflation rose significantly, reaching 2,221% in 1994! Real disposable income decreased by 19% in 1992, fell by another 21% in 1994, and by 13% in 1995 (Shurubovich, 2012).

Following the presidential elections in July 1994, initiatives by A. Lukashenko were aimed at achieving financial stabilization and strengthening the national currency, the Belarusian ruble. Therefore, monetary and financial policies were tightened, efforts were made to reduce the budget deficit, and crediting of the economy on preferential terms was limited. This policy essentially achieved its main goal by significantly reducing inflation. However, containing price growth through monetary supply restrictions contributed to a deepened production decline, reduced investment activity, and lowered living standards (Shurubovich, 2012).

The economic situation in Belarus began to improve only after 1996. This was possible due to (Shurubovich, 2012):

- changes in economic policy, shifting the focus from macroeconomic stabilization (1996–1997) to stimulating economic growth (1998–1999) (Pavlovets & Shiptenko, 2017), using instruments such as state budget subsidies for economically important industrial sectors (Sinyak, 2002),[1] and granting them favorable loans and reliefs;
- development of trade and economic cooperation with CIS countries, mainly with Russia (during 1995–1999, Belarus and Russia signed several integration documents[2]);

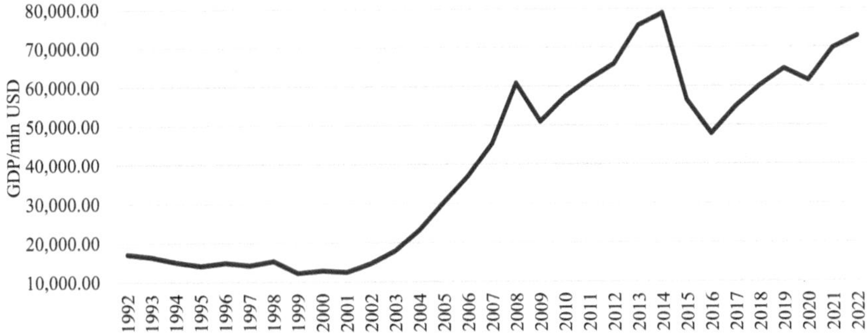

Figure 2.8 Belarus. Nominal GDP dynamics 1992–2022 (million USD).

Source: World Bank (2021).

- active regulatory role of the state by utilizing available production potential (in major economic matters, decisions are made personally by the President of Belarus, who has the necessary powers to do so);
- dominant position of state ownership in the economy (Pavlovets & Shiptenko, 2017)[3] (the Belarusian government controls the achievement of important forecast parameters, which are mandatory for state enterprises);
- the increase in consumer demand due to rising wages and the state's active social policy, which, aiming to improve living standards, became a guarantor of maintaining social stability in the country.

As a result of these factors, the Belarusian economy emerged from transformational recession between 1996 and 2000. In 2000, compared to 1991, the country's GDP was 89.7%, industrial production was 102%, consumption was 113%, real incomes of society were 92%, agricultural production was 75%, and investments in fixed assets were 50% (Vardomsky, 2012).

Conversely, the group of factors that inhibited economic growth in Belarus at that time included (Vardomsky, 2012):

- inflation caused by the increase in money circulation due to concessional loans granted to leading industrial enterprises[4];
- negative trade balance[5];
- low profitability of key economic sectors (Pavlovets & Shiptenko, 2017),[6] leading to rising inter-enterprise debt due to the inability to settle mutual obligations (this problem was typically addressed by additional money issuance, which led to increased inflation).
- change in the country's industrial structure, reducing the share of sectors responsible for producing high value-added goods.[7]

Compared to the 1990s, the socioeconomic situation in Belarus improved in the 2000s, with most economic indicators showing growth. During this time, the so-called "market socialism" Belarusian economic model was fully developed (Pavlovets & Shiptenko, 2017).The socioeconomic development of the country during this period can be divided into several stages:

1 **Period of rapid growth (2001–2008):** These years are considered the most prosperous period of economic development for Belarus, driven by both internal and external factors. The primary generator of growth was the favorable global economy, increased demand in the Russian market, and concessional prices on imported energy resources from Russia. High export revenues enabled the Belarusian government to pursue an active investment policy. However, significant economic problems were not resolved, such as technological restructuring of the outdated industry and its energy intensity, which was twice as high as in highly developed countries. The other challenges include inflation, which rose with the increase in money circulation, the underutilization of opportunities

associated with the inflow of FDI, and the high share of state ownership in GDP (two-thirds of enterprises and 80% of fixed assets). There is also the excessive regulation of economic activity, frequent changes in regulations, and continuous inspections of enterprises (especially private ones) by supervisory authorities (Vardomsky, 2012).

2 **Economic crisis period (late 2008–2009):** The global financial crisis severely impacted Belarus's real economic sector. This occurred due to worsening conditions in global markets and decreased demand for Belarusian goods, especially in the Russian market. Consequently, Belarus abolished import duties on selected raw materials and non-domestically produced metals and components, raised import duty rates on consumer goods, abolished export duties on Belarusian goods, and introduced preferential tariffs on gas, electricity, and heat for energy-intensive industries. In January 2009, the Belarusian Central Bank devalued the national currency by 20% against the US dollar and the euro, and under IMF pressure, the government revised budget expenditures and froze wages in the budget sector (Vardomsky, 2012).

3 **Post-crisis period (2010–2011)**: Due to the anti-crisis measures taken by the Belarusian authorities and the receipt of financial assistance from abroad in 2010, there was a brief improvement in basic macroeconomic indicators. However, this trend could not be maintained, so in the spring of 2011, Belarus's economy faced significant difficulties caused by a severe shortage of foreign currency. The shortage was triggered by the rapidly increasing negative trade balance, the injection of money into the economy and social sphere after 2009, and cyclical problems. This situation led to the suspension of production in industrial plants dependent on imports and a rapid increase in goods prices. The Central Bank of Belarus was forced to perform a sudden 56% devaluation of the Belarusian ruble. This measure nearly halved the negative foreign trade balance. Following Belarus's sale of the second half of "Beltransgaz" shares to Gazprom in November 2011,[8] the country's financial situation improved partially (Vardomsky, 2012: Vlasenko, 2018).

4 **Striving for political-economic stability (2012–2013):** Since 2011, Belarus's restrictive monetary policy, which limited enterprises' access to financial resources for investments, contributed to industrial decline while increasing finished goods inventories. Moreover, measures contributing to the growth of internal and external imbalances were taken in the Belarusian economy. The internal imbalances were exacerbated by wage increases from January to November 2012, which outpaced labor productivity growth by five times. External imbalances were driven by low export competitiveness, chronic negative trade balance, and current account deficits (International Bank for Reconstruction and Development / The World Bank, 2013; Mukha, 2013). The service sector (mainly the IT industry) became a significant factor in economic growth. Consequently, from 2012 to 2014, there was an increase in foreign currency lending to the economy, driven by a significant interest rate difference between ruble and foreign currency loans post-2011. This situation led to a new generation of macroeconomic imbalances (Vlasenko, 2018).

5 **Period of the "Belarusian model" failure (2014–2016)** (Pavlovets & Shiptenko, 2017): The devaluation of the Belarusian ruble against global currencies at the turn of 2014–2015 initiated a two-year economic recession in Belarus. The largest losses were suffered by export-oriented enterprises due to exchange rate differences and debt value loss. By the end of 2015, the number of unprofitable entities increased to 20% of all enterprises, with their net losses amounting to 5% of GDP. The global economic downturn exposed serious problems in Belarus's real sector. The main cause of many large enterprises' unsatisfactory financial condition lies in the internal organization of business processes, associated with errors in strategic planning, faulty coordination, and low management competencies. The recession during 2015–2016 resulted from an overall decline in macroeconomic efficiency (Kotulewicz-Wisińska & Gródek-Szostak, 2021).

6 **Attempt to enter the growth path (2017–2022):** Economic activity increased during 2017–2018. Demand rose due to increased incomes and consumer lending. Labor productivity increased, providing a positive contribution (1.2%) of the qualitative component to real GDP growth. Quantitative indicators also had a positive impact. Overall, the economic growth in 2017 was sufficient to offset the decline in 2016 (Table 2.8). In the real sector of the economy, sales of finished products increased and inventories decrease (Institute of Economics of the National Academy of Sciences of Belarus, 2016a; 2016b). Conversely, the results for 2019 were most influenced by a decline in enterprise investment activity (Institute of Economics of the National Academy of Sciences of Belarus, 2019).

During 2019–2020, the COVID-19 pandemic significantly impacted Belarus's macroeconomic outcomes, leading to a slowdown in economic activity. In 2019, the GDP growth rate was only 1.4% compared to 2018, while 2020 saw a GDP decline of 0.9%. According to Belarusian economists, the main factors influencing GDP growth were reduced oil supplies from Russia due to price disputes and

Table 2.8 Belarus. Basic macroeconomic categories development 2014–2022.

	GDP growth rate	*Unemployment rate*	*Inflation rate*	*Budget deficit/ Surplus share in GDP*	*Current account deficit/Surplus share in GDP*
2014	1.7	5.91	18.12	1.04	−6.63
2015	−3.8	5.88	13.54	1.8	−3.24
2016	−2.5	5.84	11.84	1.3	−3.38
2017	2.5	5.65	6.03	2.8	−1.74
2018	3.1	4.76	4.87	3.8	0.04
2019	1.4	4.16	5.60	3.9	−1.93
2020	−0.9	4.05	5.55	1.35	−0.29
2021	2.4	3.90	9.46	4.76	3.10
2022	−4.7	3.57	15.21	3.72	3.46

Source: Own calculations based on data from the World Bank (2021) and the National Statistical Committee of the Republic of Belarus (2023).

a decline in global market prices for mineral fertilizers. This happened because the largest shares in Belarus's GDP are from the export of mineral fertilizers and the processing of Russian oil (Losyakina & Gospodarik, 2022).

In 2021, the GDP growth rate was 2.4% compared to 2020. This time, the main growth drivers were a strong post-pandemic recovery in the global economy, characterized by increased demand and rising raw material prices. Belarus expanded its export of petrochemical products, machinery, and food both in terms of price and volume. The IT sector continued to develop. Consequently, during January–September 2021, Belarusian exports of goods and services amounted to USD 34.9 billion, and imports to USD 32.2 billion, representing a 32.3% increase in exports and a 29.6% increase in imports compared to the same period in 2020. At the same time, the current account balance for January–September 2021 was a positive USD 1.1 billion (2.1% of GDP), whereas it was a negative USD 416.2 million (0.9% of GDP) in the same period of 2020. Belarus's macroeconomic policy became more flexible and balanced compared to the previous crises (2009, 2011). Russia continued to support Belarus, particularly by helping to refinance debts amounting to USD 1 billion and not halting oil supplies despite US sanctions on the company "Naftan" (Ilex, 2021).

In 2022, Belarus's GDP fell by 4.7% due to a decline in industrial production, trade volumes, and transportation amidst Western sanctions. Redirecting exports to Russia and increasing imports from that country helped mitigate the crisis's impact on some sectors of the Belarusian economy. However, in 2022, the IT sector and the external sector weakened (Ilex, 2022).

Analyzing the structure of Belarus's GDP in 2014, 2018, and 2022 (Figure 2.9), it is evident that industry and water supply play a key role, accounting for nearly

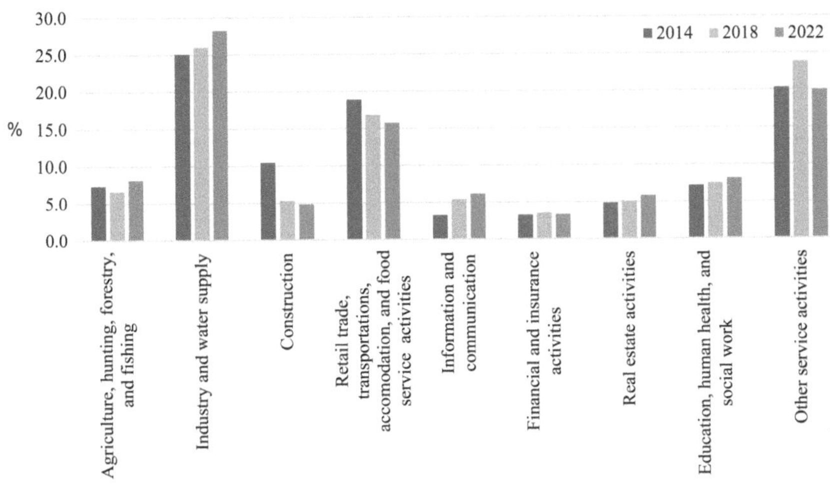

Figure 2.9 Gross domestic product by main economic activities as a % of GDP in Belarus in 2014, 2018, and 2022.

Source: Own elaboration, based on the National Statistical Committee of The Republic of Belarus.

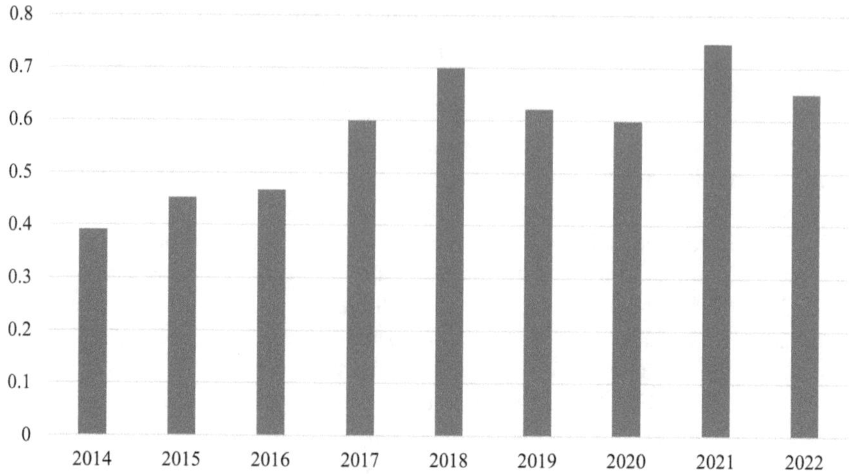

Figure 2.10 Belarus. PMS index development 2014–2022.

Source: Own calculations based on Table 2.8.

one-third of GDP. It should also be noted that the share of agriculture in GDP is small compared to the next dominant sector (i.e., retail trade, transportation, accommodation, and food service activities), although its importance decreased in 2022 compared to 2014. The declined share of construction in Belarus's GDP structure is notable.

The macroeconomic stabilization indicator PMS calculated based on macroeconomic data shows that the process of macroeconomic stabilization in Belarus was uneven (Figure 2.10 and Table 2.9).

Table 2.9 Belarus. Value and relative importance of macroeconomic stabilization indexes 2014–2022.

Specification	*2014*	*2015*	*2016*	*2017*	*2018*	*2019*	*2020*	*2021*	*2022*
a	0.1086	0.0948	0.0991	0.1207	0.1334	0.1242	0.1150	0.1368	0.1040
b	0.0819	0.0932	0.0966	0.1117	0.1234	0.1192	0.1192	0.1140	0.1040
c	0.1047	0.1112	0.1153	0.1412	0.1543	0.1490	0.1333	0.1341	0.1223
d	0.0514	0.0900	0.0900	0.1225	0.1581	0.1293	0.1286	0.2012	0.2012
e	0.0443	0.0632	0.0661	0.1035	0.1310	0.0998	0.1026	0.1609	0.1207
PMS1	0.2952	0.2993	0.3110	0.3736	0.4111	0.3923	0.3675	0.3849	0.3289
PMS2	0.0958	0.1532	0.1561	0.2260	0.2890	0.2291	0.2321	0.3621	0.3219
PMS	0.3910	0.4525	0.4671	0.5996	0.7001	0.6214	0.5987	0.7470	0.6507
PMS1/PMS, in %	75.51	66.14	66.58	62.31	58.72	63.13	61.38	51.53	50.54
PMS2/PMS, in %	24.49	33.86	33.42	37.69	41.28	36.87	38.62	48.47	49.46
a/PMS1, in %	36.80	31.69	31.88	32.31	32.44	31.64	31.28	35.54	31.20
b/PMS1, in %	27.74	31.15	31.06	29.91	30.03	30.28	32.44	29.62	31.61
c/PMS1, in %	35.46	37.16	37.06	37.78	37.53	37.98	36.28	34.84	37.19
d/PMS2, in %	53.70	58.74	57.66	54.22	54.69	56.45	55.61	55.56	62.50
e/PMS2, in %	46.30	41.26	42.34	45.78	45.31	43.55	44.39	44.44	37.50

Source: Own calculations based on Table 2.8.

Table 2.10 Belarus. Correlation coefficients between GDP growth rate and changes in other elements of the pentagon.

	GDP growth rate - unemployment rate	*GDP growth rate - inflation rate*	*GDP growth rate - public sector debt*	*GDP growth rate - foreign debt rate*
2014–2016	0.7305	0.8812	−0.8889	−0.9814
2015–2017	−0.9470	−0.9998	0.8627	0.9637
2016–2018	−0.6535	−0.9983	0.9521	0.9004
2017–2019	0.5454	−0.4793	−0.2479	0.8228
2018–2020	0.8996	−0.7985	0.8788	0.0963
2019–2021	−0.4896	0.7554	0.9971	0.4967
2020–2022	0.6531	−0.6488	0.2271	−0.1595
2014–2018	−0.2229	−0.4226	0.5479	0.2612
2019–2022	0.7092	−0.7098	0.2865	−0.3870
2014–2022	0.0347	−0.5107	0.3230	−0.0895

Source: Own calculations based on Table 2.8.

From 2014 to 2022, internal factors played the most significant role in the macroeconomic stabilization process. However, during 2021–2022, external factors also had a relatively large impact.

There was a weak correlation (practically no relationship) between Belarus's GDP growth rate and the unemployment rate from 2014 to 2022 (average indicator value 0.0347) (Table 2.10).

The negative correlation in four of the studied time intervals indicates that GDP growth/decline could contribute to a decrease/increase in the unemployment rate.

From 2014 to 2022, Belarus's GDP growth rate was moderately negatively correlated (significant dependence) with the inflation rate (average indicator value -0.5107). Positive correlation occurred during 2014–2016 and 2019–2022; in all other time intervals, the correlation was negative. This suggests that changes in the GDP growth rate might have contributed to decreases/increases or increases/decreases in inflation.

During the studied years, a clear positive relationship (low correlation) was observed between the GDP growth/decline rate and public sector debt (state budget deficit) (average indicator value 0.3230). A weak negative correlation (practically no relationship) was observed between the GDP growth/decline rate and the foreign debt rate (average indicator value -0.0895). In the first case, this relationship means that GDP increase/decrease contributed to the increase/decline in public sector debt. In the second case, it means that GDP growth/decrease contributed to the increase in foreign debt.

These described changes are accompanied by demographic changes in the country. Belarus's population is shrinking year by year, with noticeable depopulation. In 2022, compared to 2014, the population decreased by over 2%, with the gender structure remaining unchanged, showing a dominance of women in this respect (Figure 2.11).

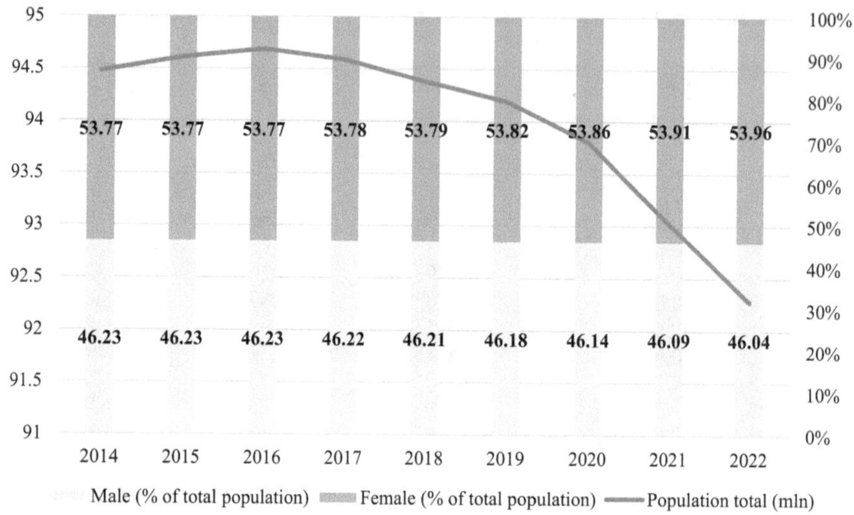

Figure 2.11 Population size and structure by gender in Belarus from 2014 to 2022.
Source: World Bank (2017, p. 2023).

Additionally, there is a reduction in income inequality in society. The Gini index for the described country decreased (Figure 2.12) from 27.2 in 2014 to 24.4 in 2022.

Evaluating the value of society through the lens of the two previously proposed indicators emphasizes high HDI levels. In 2014, it was 0.812, and in 2021, it was 0.808, still above 0.8. The decline in the index placed Belarus in 60th position in the world ranking in 2021, down from 53rd in 2014. The availability of statistical data regarding the HCI allows noting that in 2020, it was at a relatively high level of 0.700.

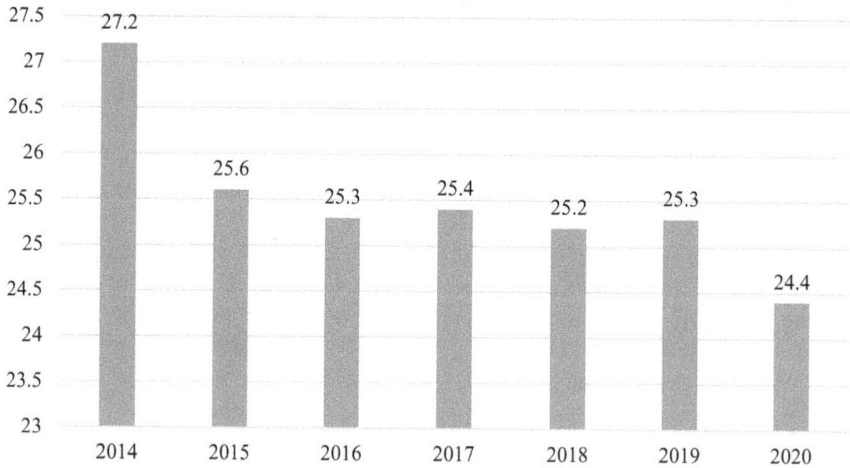

Figure 2.12 The Gini index for Belarus during 2014–2021.
Source: World Bank (2017, 2023).

In summary, it should be noted that the overall conditions for Belarus's economic development are quite varied. Although the economic model of the country initially helped it escape the trap of transformational decline, it now requires reducing the scale of state intervention in the economy and increasing the role of market mechanisms, which respond flexibly to rapidly changing conditions. Currently, the economic situation in Belarus is significantly influenced by the persistent risk of additional sanctions being imposed on the country and the unfavorable economic situation in Russia due to its armed aggression against Ukraine.

Georgia

Following the collapse of the USSR and the restoration of independence, Georgia faced a severe economic crisis, characterized by the largest GDP decline among former Soviet states. From 1991 to 1994, the country's economic development was significantly impacted by the initial economic policies of transformation, political instability, and internal armed conflicts. In 1992, President Z. Gamsakhurdia decided to halt trade with the Russian Federation, negatively affecting industrial and agricultural performance. As a result, industrial production decreased by 43%, and the country's GDP fell by nearly 45%.

The loss of the former Soviet market was the most significant problem for the Georgian economy because the republic lost organized supplies of raw materials and markets for goods and services. The recession in the CIS led to a more than 90% reduction in the export of Georgian agricultural products, and the armed conflict in Abkhazia nearly halted the influx of tourists from Russia. Adaptation to open competition and the disappearance of internal subsidies led to the closure of many enterprises. A significant portion of the skilled workforce was pushed out of industry. Under external pressures, an economy based on going abroad for work emerged in the country (Grigoriev et al., 2008).

Initial reforms (1994–1998)

Reforms implemented between 1994 and 1998, based on the "Washington Consensus" and supported by IMF and World Bank loans, contributed to macroeconomic and financial stabilization. In 1995, inflation was reduced, privatization of small and medium enterprises began, trade with foreign countries was liberalized, market prices for bread were introduced, and laws on commercial banks, land reform, and taxation were adopted. The introduction of the national currency (lari) and the adoption of a balanced budget had a beneficial effect on the economy. In 1995, Georgia saw a 2.6% increase in production, and from 1996 to 1997, the average annual GDP growth rate was 11% (Figure 2.13).

The resumption of economic growth was made possible by leveraging the country's transit potential. Georgia was invited to participate in regional infrastructure projects in a transport-logistic capacity, which encouraged foreign investment. For instance, during 1997–1998, high FDI was related to the construction of the

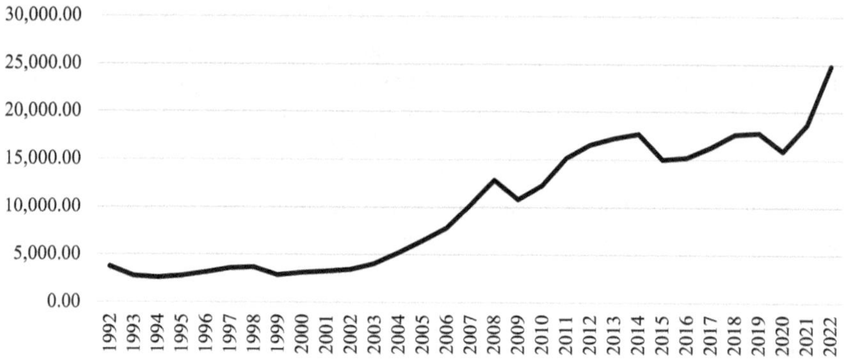

Figure 2.13 Georgia. Nominal GDP dynamics 1992–2022 (million USD).
Source: World Bank (2017, 2023).

Baku–Supsa pipeline and the Supsa terminal (project value USD 370 million), leading to a 66% increase in investment outlays (Vardomsky, 2012).

The Russian financial crisis in 1998 had a profoundly negative impact on Georgia's economy, manifested by a sudden drop in Georgian exports to the Russian market, which was a leading market for Georgian goods (before 1998, Russia accounted for over one-third of Georgian exports). As a result, in 1998, Georgia's economic growth rate suddenly fell to 3.1% and continued to decline for the next two years (Сауран, 2015).

In 2000, Georgia joined the World Trade Organization (WTO), facilitating the development of economic ties abroad, especially imports. Dynamic economic growth in Georgia began in 2001 due to increased domestic demand, export growth, and the development of noncompeting sectors (construction, services, financial intermediation), as well as income from the transit of energy resources. From 2003, additional economic growth was driven by FDI inflows related to the construction of pipeline networks on Georgian territory for transporting energy resources (the Baku–Tbilisi–Ceyhan oil pipeline and the Baku–Tbilisi–Erzurum gas pipeline). Consequently, over 90% of total investments flowed into the transport and construction sectors. Investment levels were very low in other sectors, including industry (Сауран, 2015).

By the late 1990s, Georgia had transitioned from an agrarian-industrial state to a transport-service state, specializing in regional projects of international significance. For example, if in 1996 agriculture and industry accounted for 50.1% of GDP, by 2010 they accounted for only 19.9% (Table 2.11). During this period, the share of trade, transport, and communications increased. In short, Georgia's economy has a structure that hinders achieving balanced development ensuring stable growth (Yeghiazaryan, 2007).

In the case of Georgia, foreign subsidies play an important role in ensuring economic growth and influence the country's economic policy. Already under E. Shevarnadze's rule, the Georgian economy stagnated and was maintained mainly

Table 2.11 The structure of the Georgian economy during 1996–2022.

	Agriculture	*Industry*	*Construction*	*Trade*	*Transport and communications*	*Administration*	*Other sectors*	*GDP*
1996	33.2	16.9	6.1	11.6	5.7	2.9	23.6	100
1998	26.2	13.3	8.5	11.0	11.5	4.1	25.4	100
2000	20.6	12.2	8.8	12.4	14.1	3.6	28.3	100
2002	19.2	12.8	9.9	12.7	14.2	4.2	27.0	100
2004	16.4	12.2	12.1	12.7	13.4	5.8	27.4	100
2006	11.2	12.4	10.6	13.6	11.6	8.5	32.1	100
2008	8.9	11.1	8.5	13.9	10.0	14.9	32.7	100
2010	8.5	11.4	7.9	14.6	10.0	11.3	36.3	100
2012	8.2	12.1	9.7	14.4	9.6	9.7	36.3	100
2014	8.5	9.6	9.6	12.0	6.9	0.9	41.9	100
2016	7.3	7.8	11.5	11.1	6.2	1.0	43.3	100
2018	6.8	8.8	11.1	11.3	6.8	1.3	43.2	100
2019	7.2	10.1	10.6	11.5	6.5	1.5	52.6	100
2020	9.5	10.8	8.7	14.7	6.0	0.8	49.5	100
2021	8.3	11.4	7.3	15.4	6.1	1.0	50.5	100
2022	6.9	9.5	7.9	15.6	6.2	1.2	52.7	100

Source: Own study based on the National Statistics Office of Georgia (2023).

thanks to grants and money transfers from abroad. At the turn of the 21st century, the key economic problem of the country was widespread poverty, ineffective and corrupt state apparatus, unregulated property problems, and many others (Сауран, 2015).

From 2004–2007, Georgia's economy underwent a new phase of development following M. Saakashvili's rise to power in November 2003 after the "Rose Revolution." The new president set the goal that "Georgia should become the world's cheapest and most business-friendly economy." During this period, significant market reforms led to renewed GDP growth.

Over five years, the Georgian government initiated over 70 reforms, including the reform of the executive branch (reducing its size, reforming the Ministry of Internal Affairs, and combating corruption), large-scale privatization, and the liberalization of the national economy. In 2005, tax reform reduced the number of taxes from 21 to 7, and in 2006 to 6, and their rates were lowered. Tax amnesty was granted for income earned before 2004. These changes contributed to a threefold increase in tax revenues (Bendukizhze & Saakashvili, 2007). In 2007, the new Customs Code eliminated all export and import quotas, and the average import duty rate was 1.5%—the lowest global tariff rate at the time. This precedent allowed Georgia to maintain a high trade turnover despite the Russian embargo and the global financial crisis (Avalani, 2011). The largest state enterprises were put up for sale through privatization. The then-Minister of Economy noted in 2005 that Georgia's future was not in making comfortable privatization deals but in developing existing and creating new enterprises. He believed the government should aim to develop small- and medium-sized enterprises, not large industrial plants (Simonyan, 2005). Radical reforms also affected the social sphere. In education, a voucher system was introduced, directing funding to the educational institution chosen by the student's parents (Tytysh & Makarenko, 2015). The entire healthcare sector was privatized, and a health insurance system was introduced (BBC, 2011).

The reforms of 2004–2007 were highly regarded by international organizations. According to EBRD, Georgia was one of the most reformed economies in the CIS after Armenia. In 2010, the structural reform index for Georgia was 3.11 (European Bank for Reconstruction and Development, 2010). The World Bank ranked Georgia three times among the top five countries for the pace and effectiveness of reforms.

During 2004–2007, despite dynamic economic growth, Georgia faced challenges such as

- high inflation, as one of the symptoms of the "Dutch disease." (The supply of foreign currency exceeded the demand for it. On the one hand, this led to the strengthening of Georgian lari, and on the other, to an increase in consumer prices.) (Esebua, 2020);
- unbalanced economic growth, characterized by the high development of financial services, bank lending, real estate, and construction, but a very low development of the real economy sectors (industry and agriculture);
- high current account deficit, indicating unstable economic growth (consumption exceeding production);
- high dependence on external financing sources, mainly FDI and remittances from migrants (Papava, 2010).[9]

During 2008–2009, Georgia's economy underwent significant changes due to internal structural issues and external factors (the war with Russia in August 2008 and the negative impact of the global financial crisis). In 2008, Georgia's economy contracted by 5%, and in 2009, by another 3.7%. FDI decreased, remittances from Georgians working abroad fell, and export values dropped. The banking sector felt the global financial crisis's impact most strongly, experiencing difficulties in securing foreign loans and widespread withdrawal of deposits by the public. However, the country managed to secure additional financial resources abroad. In the fall of 2008, the IMF granted Georgia a loan of USD 1.173 billion with an extended repayment period until July 2011. By the end of 2011, under World Bank decisions, Georgia received USD 4.5 billion (USD 2 billion in grants, USD 2.5 billion in loans). This financial assistance helped halt GDP decline, slightly calmed social unrest, and supported the implementation of an anti-crisis economic policy aimed at infrastructure and social projects (А.Г.Пылин, 2010).

From 2010 to 2019, Georgia experienced positive GDP growth, with the economy growing at an average annual rate of 4.87%. In 2010, GDP growth was driven by increases in manufacturing (20.3%), trade and financial intermediation (over 14%), and the transport, hotel, and restaurant services sector (about 13%), thanks to increased exports and the dynamism of private sector lending. However, agriculture saw a decline of 1.7% (Vardomsky, 2012). In 2011, a new Tax Code came into effect, which contributed to increased central budget revenues. However, Georgia was unable to reduce the current account deficit due to rising prices for energy resources, goods, and services in the domestic market during 2011–2012. During 2012–2013, a decline in domestic demand led to price drops and deflation, caused by the low purchasing power of the population. Therefore, to sustain economic growth, the Georgian Central Bank reduced the base interest rate to a historically low level (3.75 pp) in 2013. Although this policy contributed to slow price growth, global prices for energy resources and the devaluation of national currencies in neighboring countries negatively affected this dynamic. The economic downturn in neighboring countries impacted the decline in Georgian exports, reduced remittances from Georgians working abroad, and decreased tourism revenues (Analytical Center for the Government of the Russian Federation, 2019).

Table 2.12 presents the values of Georgia's key macroeconomic categories from 2014 to 2022. In 2014, according to the newly adopted "Social-economic Development Strategy of Georgia – Georgia 2020," further economic development was partly dependent on the development of the real sector of the economy (Government of Georgia, 2018). As part of this strategy, an agricultural development fund was established, a cooperation law was adopted, a three-tier preferential loan program was launched to increase access to financial services, and some types of agricultural production were subsidized (Beridze & Mekvabishvili, 2018). Financial problems in 2013 (Echo of the Caucasus, 2015; Reuters, 2015), led to a 30% devaluation of the national currency in 2014 (Stronski, 2017). Additionally, the US dollar still played a significant role in Georgia (mainly due to foreign loans); although in 2015, the Georgian government announced a move away from dollarization of the economy. In 2018, the Georgian lari weakened against the dollar (−3.3%), and in 2019, the lari lost nearly 10% of its value (Analytical Center for the Government of the Russian Federation, 2019). By the end of April, the Georgian lari had depreciated to a record low of 3.46 lari/USD. Conversely, in February 2022, the Georgian currency strengthened by 15.5% compared to April 2021 (Georgia Online, 2022).

Table 2.12 Georgia. Basic macroeconomic categories development 2014–2022.

	GDP growth rate	*Unemployment rate*	*Inflation rate*	*Budget deficit/ Surplus share in GDP*	*Current account deficit/Surplus share in GDP*
2014	4.4	17.44	1.75	0.00	−10.12
2015	3.0	16.51	3.11	2.36	−11.82
2016	2.9	16.60	3.90	1.40	−12.49
2017	4.8	13.94	3.62	3.19	−8.06
2018	4.9	12.67	4.46	4.93	−6.78
2019	5.1	11.57	4.85	4.20	−5.92
2020	−6.8	11.73	5.20	−2.01	−12.52
2021	10.5	11.85	9.57	−0.33	−10.43
2022	10.4	11.68	11.90	3.57	−4.52

Source: Own study based on the data of the World Bank (2021b) National Statistics Office of Georgia (Geostat, 2023).

In 2020, Georgia's macroeconomic indicators were negatively affected by the COVID-19 pandemic, leading to a significant economic downturn. However, from 2021 onwards, the Georgian economy began to recover and return to a growth trajectory. From 2021 to 2022, economic experts observed that the growth in economic activity was driven not so much by increased production but rather by favorable international conditions and an unforeseen mass relocation of over 100,000 Russians. This relocation led to an unprecedented increase in remittances from the Russian Federation. According to the National Bank of Georgia, USD 1,256 million was transferred from Russia to Georgia via electronic transfer systems in the first nine months of 2022, accounting for 40.6% of the total remittances received by Georgian commercial banks (Oraghvelidze, 2024).

From 2014 to 2019, the inflation rate in Georgia was relatively stable, fluctuating between 2% and 5%. However, a sharp increase in inflation was observed from 2020 to 2022. In 2020, inflation rose to 5.20%, and by the end of 2022, it reached 11.68%. This dramatic rise can be attributed to the pandemic and post-pandemic crises, which were notably driven by "increased access to financial resources and stimulation of aggregate demand" (PBServices, 2024).

The economic indicators for Georgia are complemented by the synthetic PMS index (Figure 2.14). Notably, the PMS values are low compared to the previously described countries.

During the entire analyzed period, the values of the partial indicators of the PMS fluctuated (Table 2.13). Generally speaking, the values of indicators a, b, c, and d increased in 2022 compared to 2014. During 2014–2016 and 2020–2021, due to the current account deficit, the partial indicators reflecting the financial equilibrium triangle and the external sector deteriorated.

Throughout the analyzed period, the macroeconomic stabilization coefficient was significantly influenced primarily by external factors (i.e. the development status of the real sector, the price level in the internal market, and the situation on

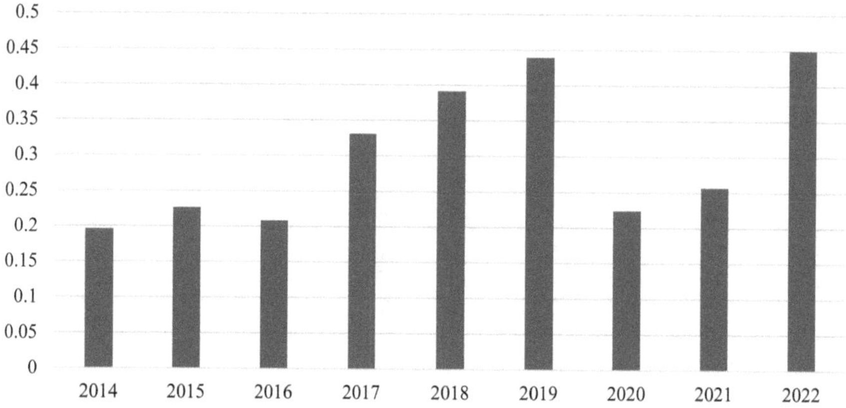

Figure 2.14 Georgia. PMS index development 2014–2022.

Source: Own calculations based on Table 2.12.

Table 2.13 Georgia. Value and relative importance of macroeconomic stabilization indexes 2014–2022.

Specification	*2014*	*2015*	*2016*	*2017*	*2018*	*2019*	*2020*	*2021*	*2022*
a	0.0259	0.0322	0.0322	0.0604	0.0690	0.0802	0.0491	0.0905	0.0905
b	0.0272	0.0338	0.0322	0.0563	0.0617	0.0694	0.0694	0.0604	0.0580
c	0.1429	0.1603	0.1439	0.1608	0.1543	0.1543	0.1056	0.1059	0.1288
d	0	0	0	0.0287	0.0575	0.0718	0	0	0.0862
e	0	0	0	0.0246	0.0493	0.0636	0	0	0.0862
PMS1	0.1959	0.2263	0.2082	0.2774	0.2850	0.3039	0.2242	0.2568	0.2773
PMS2	0	0	0	0.0534	0.1067	0.1355	0	0	0.1724
PMS	0.1959	0.2263	0.2082	0.3308	0.3917	0.4394	0.2242	0.2568	0.4497
PMS1/PMS, in %	100	100	100	83.87	72.75	69.17	100	100	61.66
PMS2/PMS, in %	0	0	0	16.13	27.25	30.38	0	0	38.34
a/PMS1, in %	13.20	14.22	15.56	21.75	24.20	26.38	21.92	35.26	32.65
b/PMS1, in %	13.86	14.95	15.45	20.29	21.66	22.85	30.98	23.51	20.90
c/PMS1, in %	72.94	70.82	69.10	57.96	54.14	50.77	47.10	41.24	46.45
d/PMS2, in %	-	-	-	53.85	53.85	53.03	-	-	50.00
e/PMS2, in %	-	-	-	46.15	46.15	46.97	-	-	50.00

Source: Own calculations based on Table 2.12.

the labor market). As can be seen from the data in Table 2.14, during 2014–2022, the economic growth rate of Georgia was weakly correlated (virtually no relationship) with the unemployment rate (average value of the indicator 0.0438). Notably, the negative correlation coefficient between the variables during 2015–2019 meant that GDP increases were high enough to improve the labor market.

During 2014–2022, Azerbaijan's economic growth weakly correlated (virtually no relation) with the unemployment rate (average indicator value: 0.0438). Notably, the negative correlation coefficient between the variables in most of the time intervals covered by the study indicated that GDP increases were high enough to improve the labor market. Between 2015 and 2019, Georgia's GDP growth was

Table 2.14 Georgia. Correlation coefficients between GDP growth rate and changes in other elements of the pentagon.

	GDP growth rate - unemployment rate	*GDP growth rate - inflation rate*	*GDP growth rate - public sector debt*	*GDP growth rate - foreign debt rate*
2014–2016	0.9891	−0.9517	−0.8888	0.9759
2015–2017	−0.9999	0.1195	0.8685	0.9955
2016–2018	−0.9617	0.2324	0.8911	0.9854
2017–2019	−0.9733	0.9217	0.4133	0.9540
2018–2020	0.3653	−0.8422	0.9939	0.9945
2019–2021	0.2257	0.6940	0.4602	0.5043
2020–2022	0.2362	0.9378	0.7287	0.6984
2014–2018	−0.1040	−0.0534	0.0001	−0.0550
2019–2022	0.0939	0.2215	0.2337	0.0957
2014–2022	0.0438	0.1631	0.1431	0.0573

Source: Own calculations based on Table 2.12.

accompanied by a decline in unemployment. In contrast, in 2020, primarily due to the COVID-19 pandemic, the decline in GDP corresponded with an increase in unemployment. In the following years, 2021–2022, this trend stabilized.

During the analyzed period, Georgia's economic growth rate was weakly positively correlated (practically no relationship) with the inflation rate (average indicator value 0.1631). Notably, negative correlation occurred during 2014–2016 and 2018–2020. Although GDP growth contributed to a decline in inflation, there was an increase in inflation during 2020–2022.

The economic growth rate was also relatively weakly correlated (practically no relationship) with the state of public sector finances. Fluctuations in the state budget surplus corresponded to GDP growth.

Similarly, a relatively weak positive correlation (practically no relationship) was observed between the GDP growth rate and the external debt rate. However, when considering three-year time intervals from 2014 to 2022, high positive correlation was present in all three-year intervals. This means that GDP growth was accompanied by an increase in the country's external debt.

The reforms carried out in Georgia did not reduce unemployment, which remains a primary cause of emigration and the high unemployment rate. According to Geostat, in 2018, 20% of the country's population lived in conditions of absolute poverty. Poverty levels among those under 17 years old (25.5% in this age group) were 6 percentage points higher than among those aged 18–64 years (19.5%). Due to a doubling of social expenditure between 2010 and 2018, the poverty rate decreased by 17.2 percentage points (from 42.7%). According to the World Bank, the Gini index, representing income inequality, remained high in Georgia and was 37.9 in 2018 (Analytical Center for the Government of the Russian Federation, 2019).

The Gini index in Georgia showed variability between 2014 and 2021 (Figure 2.15). Georgia exhibited relatively the highest income distribution inequalities among

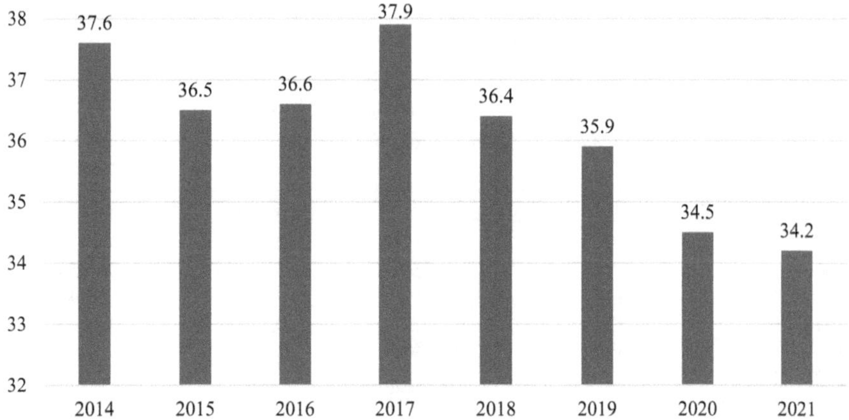

Figure 2.15 Gini index in Georgia during 2014–2021.

Source: World Bank (2021).

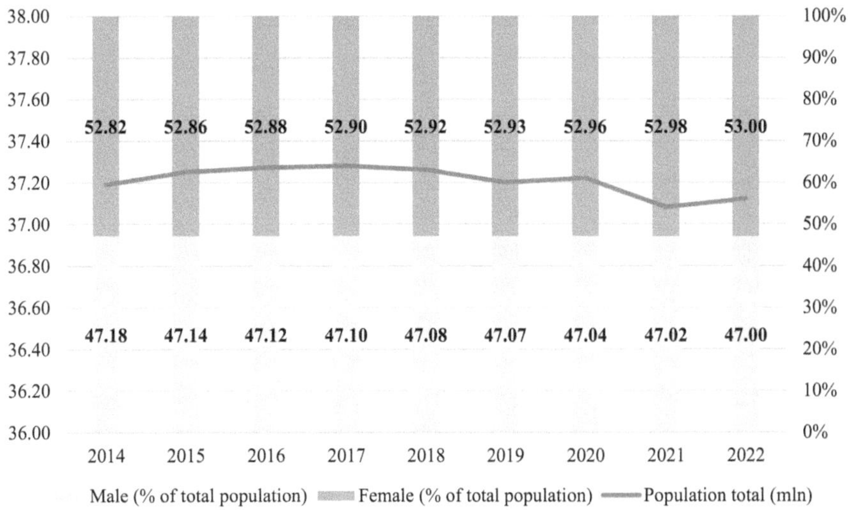

Figure 2.16 Population size and structure by gender in Georgia during 2014–2022.
Source: World Bank (2021).

the analyzed countries. The highest intensity of this phenomenon was recorded in 2017; the lowest in 2021.

Georgia's population numbers 3.7 million people and fluctuated around this level throughout the analyzed period, with a clear dominance of women in its structure (Figure 2.16). Analysis of the HDI indicates that Georgia ranked 63rd in the world in 2021, achieving a high HDI value of 0.82. Complementing this picture is the HCI. In this area, Georgia lost its 2017 position in 2020, reaching a level of 0.56 versus 0.61.

In summary, Georgia's development occurred under challenging circumstances. Since the beginning of economic transformation, over one million citizens have emigrated. The main reason for this ongoing issue is the persistently high double-digit unemployment rate. This remains one of the most significant problems facing the Georgian economy. Moreover, Georgia's economy is highly dependent on external financing. Despite these challenges, Georgia stands out among former Soviet Union countries in terms of the scope of economic reforms, which also impacts the country's social dimension.

Moldova

The economic transformation in the Republic of Moldova was accompanied by a severe economic crisis. Contributing factors included the breakdown of economic ties with the former Soviet economic complex[10] (Poisic, 2008), a "shock" price model influenced by Russia's "shock therapy,"[11] and the Transnistrian conflict that disrupted internal socioeconomic connections in the republic. These factors led to a

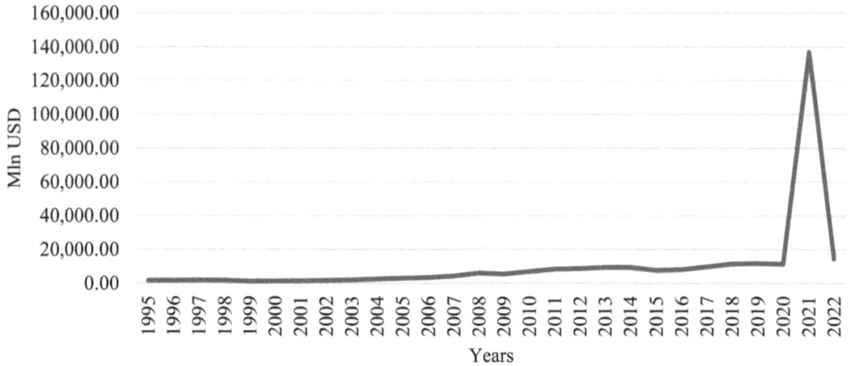

Figure 2.17 Moldova. Nominal GDP dynamics 1995–2022 (million USD).

Source: World Bank (2021).

sharp decline in GDP (Figure 2.17), industrial production, and investments in fixed assets, very high inflation, a significant budget deficit, and a decline in the standard of living (Kotulewicz, 2000).

By the mid-1990s, the initial phase of the transition to a market economy had concluded in Moldova, based on the "Program for Transition to a Regulated Market Economy for 1992–1995,"[12] adopted on November 21, 1990, and later recommendations from the International Monetary Fund.[13] This phase saw the liberalization of prices and trade and achieved relative economic stabilization, although at a level incomparably lower than in 1989.

The transformation in Moldova had both political and economic dimensions. Democratic institutions were being established, the Constitution was adopted (July 1994), police and defense forces were formed, and the foundations of a market economy were created. The introduction of the national currency (the Moldovan leu) in 1993 contributed to shaping financial and credit policies, implementing tax reforms, and establishing a banking system comprising the Central Bank and 22 commercial banks (Batranciuc, 2011). Moldova joined the Council of Europe and became a member of the UN and other international organizations.

Privatization was a key economic reform in Moldova in the 1990s. Mass voucher privatization was carried out based on two programs from 1993 to 1994 and 1995 to 1996. A third program for monetary privatization from 1997 to 1998 was extended several times due to slow progress (Percisncaia & Dodon, 2001). By the end of 2000, around 500 enterprises had been privatized. Overall, 60% of industrial plants and over 80% of small enterprises changed ownership through privatization programs (Vardomsky, 2012).

Agricultural Reforms and Challenges Under the "Pământ" (Land) program were implemented until the end of 2005, state farms were dismantled, and agricultural land was distributed among private farmers. Despite other programs ("Moldovan Countryside" in 2005; "Strategy for Agro-industrial Sector Development for 2006–2015" in 2006), the difficult situation in agricultural production could not be reversed. The agricultural sector requires thorough modernization and a transition to intensive development.

The 1990s reforms in Moldova did not yield the expected results. With the breakdown of economic ties with former Soviet republics and the lack of its own energy raw material base, the economic transformation was accompanied by deep deindustrialization. In 1999, the industry's share in GDP was 17.5% (33.3% in 1991), and agriculture's share was 24.5% (42.7% in 1991). During this period, the share of services increased from 24% to 57.9% (Kotulewicz, 2002). Consequently, by 2000, the country's GDP was 51% of its 1991 value.[14] All other macroeconomic indicators also tended to decline except for consumer prices, which increased by 3,234 times (Vardomsky, 2012).

Until 1998, Moldova's main trading partners were CIS countries, particularly Russia and Ukraine. Limited export potential meant that food, wine, tobacco, and agricultural raw materials dominated the export structure (75.8% of total exports in 1997). In contrast, mineral raw materials, especially energy resources, dominated Moldovan imports (37% of total imports in 1997).

The ongoing deindustrialization contributed to increased poverty and mass emigration of citizens in search of work abroad. This situation was exacerbated by unfair income distribution, with a 1:15 income disparity between the rich and the poor. Real income fell by 70% (Fokina, 2017). Additionally, by the end of 1999, due to the impact of the Russian financial crisis, Moldova was on the brink of insolvency. The collapse of trade with Russia led to the diversification of Moldova's foreign trade directions.[15]

Moldova only began to gradually rebuild its economy after 2000, and economic revival occurred later than in other CIS countries (Severin, 2000). The transition to a phase of economic growth was accompanied by:

- improvement in foreign trade, mostly due to economic growth in Russia;
- increased domestic demand for goods and services was fueled growth in wages and remittances from Moldovans working abroad;
- a significant reduction in inflation due to restricted monetary growth, with inflation decreasing from 43.7% in 1999 to 4.4% in 2003. Although inflation rose to 12.5% in 2004, it was brought down to 10% in 2005 and slightly increased to 12.8% in 2008 (Moldova, 2006);
- a halted decline in industrial production;
- increased privatization of the state sector characterized by financial inflows to the state budget (Percisncaia & Dodon, 2001).

From 2001 to 2005, economic revitalization encompassed virtually all sectors of the economy, including industry, construction, transport, communications, and trade (Moldova, 2006). Moldova's GDP grew by 6.6% in 2003, 7.4% in 2004, and 7.5% in 2005. Overall, between 2003 and 2006, Moldova's GDP increased by 44%.[16] This growth was driven primarily by rising domestic demand, which was largely fueled by remittances from Moldovan citizens working abroad (Amambayeva, 2004). However, this created a vicious cycle where the country increased imports to meet domestic demand, leading to a growing trade deficit and negatively impacting the financial situation, including increased debt.

In 2006, the GDP growth slowed, and other economic indicators deteriorated due to Russia's import ban on Moldovan wine. This led to a 50% reduction in Moldovan wine production and declines in related industries such as glass, paper, and cardboard manufacturing. As a result, Moldova's industrial production abruptly fell by 6.9%. This crisis, caused by an external factor, highlighted the state of Moldova's economy and the country's dangerous dependence on the wine industry and certain agricultural sectors. Diversification and modernization of the economy were essential but faced significant obstacles, including a severe shortage of domestic financial resources and foreign investment.

Moldova's investment domain was characterized by high levels of risk, which discouraged substantial foreign investment in the real sector. This risk was associated with underdeveloped infrastructure, administrative barriers, corruption, a high share of the shadow economy, a lack of qualified personnel, political instability, and other factors.

To improve the situation, Moldova adopted the "Strategy for Attracting Foreign Investment and Supporting Exports for 2006–2015." This strategy emphasized using FDI to transition from economic stagnation to a "smart" economy based on innovation and modern technologies (Fokina, 2017). Reforms carried out between 2001 and 2007 led to enhanced cooperation with the EU under the Action Plan for 2005–2007. The regime of autonomous trade preferences granted by the EU changed the geographical structure of Moldova's foreign trade, increasing the share of the EU and reducing the share of CIS countries (Kotulewicz-Wisińska, 2017).

In 2008, Moldova's GDP grew by 7.2%. Key achievements included macroeconomic stabilization, which involved reducing inflation to 7.3%, increasing production in industry, agriculture, and services, and boosting domestic demand. The Moldovan government introduced a zero tax rate on reinvested income, implemented a tax amnesty, and legalized capital, which supported the country's budget through VAT revenues. This year also saw high levels of export and import turnover. A significant achievement was the inflow of USD 707 million in FDI, with cumulative FDI amounting to USD 1.7385 billion (Vardomsky, 2012).

In 2009, Moldova's economy was severely impacted by the global financial crisis, leading to a 6.0% decline in GDP. Industrial production fell by 22.2%, agricultural production by 9.6%, exports by 18.4%, and imports by 33.1%. However, the trade deficit decreased by 40.1%, (National Bureau of Statistics of the Republic of Moldova, 2009), contributing to a reduction in the current account deficit from 16.1% of GDP in 2008 to 8.1% in 2009 (Calac, 2010). FDI also decreased significantly, and the decline in remittances from Moldovan citizens working abroad negatively affected 40% of households and reduced domestic demand (National Bureau of Statistics of the Republic of Moldova, 2009).

In 2009, Moldova experienced record-low inflation—zero inflation—but the budget deficit increased to 6.9% of GDP. To address this deficit, Moldova secured foreign loans, including USD 142 million from the IMF, USD 24 million from the US "Millennium Challenge" program, EUR 3.5 million from the Council of Europe, and EUR 400,000 from the UNDP (Vardomsky, 2012). Despite these measures, the main macroeconomic indicators were highly unstable. In 2009, the Moldovan government's policies led to a 17% devaluation of the national currency. These actions significantly impacted the social sphere, with the official unemployment rate increasing from 3.9% in 2008 to 5.7% in 2009. Approximately 10% of Moldovan citizens were forced to leave the country in search of livelihood. The internal political crisis, starting after the parliamentary elections in April 2009 and ending with the election of the president in March 2012, exacerbated the economic crisis. Additionally, foreign loans, particularly those from the IMF, added to Moldova's economic burden, and the government abandoned social promises aimed at improving citizens' living standards. The economic situation was further worsened by insufficient diversification in the production sector and the lack of structural reforms, affecting the course of macroeconomic stabilization in subsequent years.

From 2010 to 2022, Moldova's economy exhibited relatively positive growth, with an average GDP growth rate of 3.35%. Notably, there were clear declines in GDP growth in 2015 (due to the banking fraud scandal) and 2020 (due to the COVID-19 pandemic). Data on GDP (Table 2.15) show that in 2022, GDP increased nominally by one-third compared to 2014, and in real terms, it grew by 16%.

However, the recorded level of economic growth remains so modest that it does not allow for greater convergence with the countries of Central and Eastern Europe and does not allow for a significant increase in the standard of living of the population. There are many reasons for this, ranging from extreme climatic phenomena or the increasing migration of the labor force to trade discrepancies with some external partners (the situation of Moldovan exports to the Russian Federation after the signing of the Association Agreement with the EU). Added to this are the shocks

Table 2.15 GDP in current prices, per capita, purchasing power parity (PPP), growth dynamics in Moldova from 2014 to 2022.

Specification	*GDP (current USD) in millions*	*GDP growth (annual %)**	*GDP per capita, PPP (constant 2017 international, USD) in the thousands*
2014	11609.5	3.60	11.1
2015	10553.3	3.20	11.5
2016	10546.1	0.20	11.6
2017	11527.4	7.50	12.5
2018	12457.9	5.20	13.2
2019	13619.2	7.60	14.3
2020	12641.6	−7.20	13.4
2021	13878.9	5.80	14.2
2022	19513.4	12.60	16.1

Note: *Annual percentage growth rate of GDP at market prices based on constant local currency.

Source: World Bank (2021).

caused by events such as the "billion-dollar theft"[17] or numerous political crises that have weakened the quality of governance of state institutions and undermined the state's ability to intervene and provide support in times of crisis, such as the COVID-19 pandemic example.

Even if, for a longer time span, there is evidence of growth in the national economy, the quality of this growth is fragile, and long-term sustainability is highly questionable. The consumption-based growth model reveals its limitations in conditions where migration trends change from periodic migration for labor purposes to final migration determined by economic factors. These weaknesses were very noticeable during the COVID-19 pandemic, when the state entered the crisis with low levels of competitiveness and economic freedom, but also in the context of deepening systemic weaknesses caused by corruption, low competition, and difficulties in accessing financing (Expert-Group, 2020). As a result, state support has been modest, amounting to just 0.4% of GDP, while funds of up to 5% of GDP have been allocated globally. As a result, the COVID-19 pandemic had a significant impact on the size of GDP, resulting in a recession that saw GDP in 2020 fall by 8.32% by 2019.

GDP per capita by purchasing power parity showed a similar trend, except for the COVID 2020–2021 year. Practically, despite the increase in GDP, the size of GDP per capita by purchasing power parity compared to countries among Europe remains quite modest. If in the period 2014–2022, the value of the indicator increased by almost one-third, this growth did not contribute to Moldova's advancement in this ranking.

Over the past decade, the structure of Moldova's national economy has not changed significantly. The economic growth model is still based on consumption and money transfers from citizens working abroad, and this factor stimulates the development of the trade sector. Such a model also contributes to the development of the construction sector, which appears to still have the resources to sustain this trend. In contrast, the traditional sectors of the national economy—agriculture and industry—are characterized by moderate development, despite the impact on them of shocks not necessarily dependent on the intentions of policymakers, namely the impact of climatic conditions on agricultural performance or the impact of external factors on selected industries.

Since 2014, the economic structure of the Republic of Moldova has not seen significant changes (Figure 2.18). Trade remains the sector with the largest share in GDP creation, and the strengthening of its position is mainly due to the unchanging annual volume of remittances from Moldovan citizens who work abroad (EU4Environment, 2021). In second place is manufacturing, which in recent years has overtaken the agricultural sector in terms of its share of GDP, mainly due to increased foreign investment and increased export opportunities. In contrast, agriculture is an industry heavily dependent on climatic conditions, yielding modest results especially in drought years. In practice, despite efforts to modernize the agricultural sector, systemic problems remain unresolved and some even get worse. Thus, the situation regarding the development of the irrigation system and related to increasing access to water sources remains a serious problem in the context of

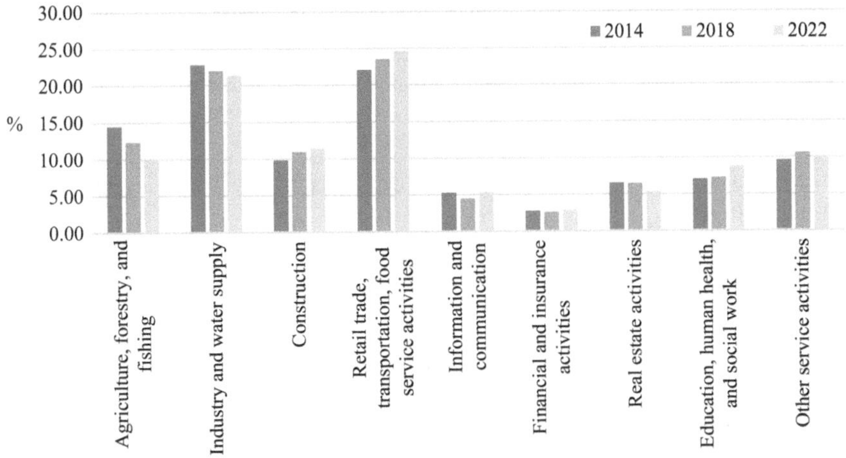

Figure 2.18 Gross domestic product by main economic activities in Moldova in 2014, 2018, and 2022.

Source: World Bank (2021), National Bureau of Statistics of the Republic of Moldova (2014, 2018, 2022).

the increasingly frequent occurrence of drought. In addition to this, it should be noted that some types of agricultural products have been dependent on selected markets (such as apples and other fruits), and exports have often been the result of political decisions. Problems also exist in the case of animal products, the export of which faces difficulties (EU4Environment, 2021).

Against the backdrop of problems in several sectors of the economy, industries such as construction, transportation, and services (especially the IT sector) are strengthening their position. The construction sector has seen growth thanks to sustained demand for housing, especially in Chisinau. Demand is being driven both by remittances and by easier access to housing loans following the implementation of the state's "Prima Casă" program and the reform of the financial system.

In 2014, the Population and Housing Census contributed to a clear picture of the labor market situation, including unemployment. Even if its level has remained quite low in recent years, below 5%, it does not reflect the real situation of job seekers. There are still many people who avoid registering with the National Employment Agency due to temporary emigration abroad and getting caught up in the wave of seasonal migration.

The unemployment rate had been on a downward trend since 2014. By 2018, there was an improvement in the employment rate, mainly due to a decrease in the unemployment rate and a reduction in informal employment. This situation was also influenced by the fiscal reform carried out in the same year. As a result of the reform, which resulted in fiscal loosening (the establishment of a unified personal income tax of 12%), both the number of informal workers and the number of

Table 2.16 Moldova. Key macroeconomic categories for Moldova's economy during 2014–2022.

	GDP growth rate	*Unemployment rate*	*Inflation rate*	*Budget deficit/ Surplus share in GDP*	*Current account deficit/Surplus share in GDP*
2014	4.99	3.9	5.1	−1.74	−6.05
2015	−0.34	3.7	9.7	−2.21	−5.93
2016	4.65	4.2	6.4	−1.85	−3.61
2017	4.18	4.1	6.6	−0.64	5.83
2018	4.08	3.0	3.1	−0.84	−10.77
2019	3.55	5.1	4.8	−1.48	−9.42
2020	−8.28	3.8	3.8	−3.49	−7.69
2021	13.93	3.2	5.1	−1.22	−12.41
2022	−5.02	3.1	28.7	−3.20	−17.11

Source: Own calculations based on data from the World Bank (2021) and the National Bureau of Statistics of the Republic of Moldova (2009, 2014, 2018, 2022).

unemployed decreased by tens of thousands of people. As a result, the unemployment rate reached its lowest level ever—about 3% (Table 2.16).

Notably, Moldova has a fairly high level of informal employment, which is more than 22% of the total workforce (National Bureau of Statistics of the Republic of Moldova, 2020). Construction and agriculture are sectors in which, for years, more than half of the employed are people without formal employment contracts. The number of these citizens is augmented by those who are unemployed but not seeking work or who do not meet the conditions for being considered unemployed. This is particularly true of those who are temporarily working abroad, for whom periods of residence at home are interspersed with periods of work abroad.

The data presented in Table 2.16 show that the process of stabilizing the Moldovan economy from 2014 to 2022 was chaotic. From 2014 to 2016, an improvement in the synthetic PMS indicator was observed (Figure 2.19). During this time, the indicator's value increased from 0.4831 to 0.5274. In contrast, the indicator's value

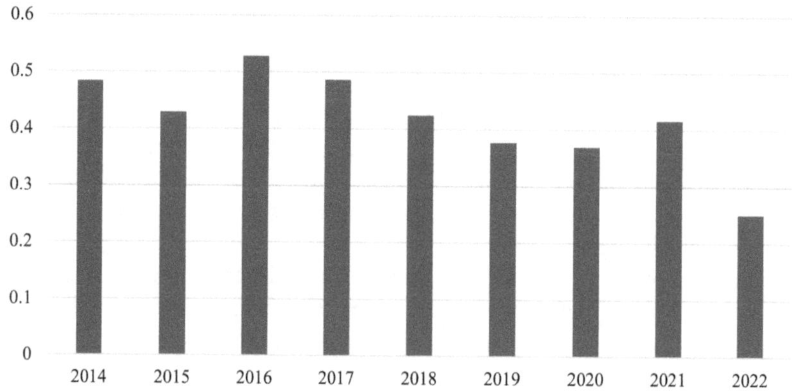

Figure 2.19 Moldova. PMS index development 2014–2022.

Source: Own calculations based on Table 2.16.

Table 2.17 Moldova. Value and relative importance of macroeconomic stabilization indexes 2014–2022.

Specification	*2014*	*2015*	*2016*	*2017*	*2018*	*2019*	*2020*	*2021*	*2022*
a	0.1466	0.1222	0.1380	0.1380	0.1466	0.1251	0.0831	0.1711	0.0977
b	0.1312	0.1140	0.1192	0.1156	0.1438	0.1158	0.1367	0.1312	0.0877
c	0.1137	0.0918	0.1098	0.1141	0.1336	0.1137	0.1016	0.1137	0.0651
d	0.0424	0.0492	0.0741	0.0567	0	0.0106	0.0272	0	0
e	0.0493	0.0513	0.0862	0.0616	0	0.0119	0.0210	0	0
PMS1	0.3915	0.3280	0.3670	0.3677	0.4241	0.3545	0.3214	0.4160	0.2506
PMS2	0.0916	0.1005	0.1604	0.1183	0	0.0225	0.0482	0	0
PMS	0.4831	0.4285	0.5274	0.4860	0.4241	0.3770	0.3696	0.4160	0.2506
PMS1/PMS, in %	81.03	76.54	69.59	75.65	100	94.03	86.96	100	100
PMS2/PMS, in %	18.97	23.46	30.41	24.35	0	5.97	13.04	0	0
a/PMS1, in %	37.45	37.25	37.60	37.52	34.57	35.27	25.85	41.12	39.01
b/PMS1, in %	33.51	34.77	32.48	31.45	33.92	32.65	42.54	31.54	34.99
c/PMS1, in %	29.05	27.98	29.92	31.03	31.51	32.08	31.61	27.34	26.00
d/PMS2, in %	46.23	48.92	46.23	47.95	-	47.07	56.53	-	-
e/PMS2, in %	53.77	51.08	53.77	52.05	-	52.93	43.47	-	-

Source: Own calculations based on Table 2.16.

decreased annually from 2017 to 2020 and in 2022, with the exception of 2022, when the PMS indicator value was 0.4160.

The unsystematic nature of the Moldovan economy's stabilization process from 2014 to 2022 is also confirmed by the partial indicators of the synthetic five-sided macroeconomic stabilization indicator (Table 2.17).

The changes in the value of the PMS indicator in Moldova and its low level were due to the influence of many factors. While the level of this indicator (growth/stabilization) from 2014 to 2022 was primarily the result of internal factors, significant influence from external factors was evident in the periods 2014–2017 and 2020–2021.

For a more detailed analysis of selected macroeconomic indicators, it is worth examining the correlation coefficients between the economic growth rate of Moldova from 2014 to 2022 and the corresponding trends in the unemployment rate, inflation level, state budget condition, and current account balance abroad (Table 2.18). These

Table 2.18 Moldova. Correlation coefficient between GDP growth rate and changes in other elements of the pentagon.

	GDP growth rate - unemployment rate	*GDP growth rate - inflation rate*	*GDP growth rate - public sector debt*	*GDP growth rate - foreign debt rate*
2014–2016	0.7381	−0.9857	0.9924	0.3691
2015–2017	0.9705	−0.9939	0.7158	0.6921
2016–2018	0.6373	0.7308	0.4222	0.9797
2017–2019	−0.6070	0.3499	0.9906	0.7296
2018–2020	0.0871	0.0630	0.9831	−0.9199
2019–2021	−0.2699	0.9576	0.9294	−0.9813
2020–2022	−0.5040	−0.3323	0.9998	−0.1379
2014–2018	0.9811	0.8826	−0.8680	−0.5610
2019–2022	0.6719	0.5627	−0.3627	−0.6710
2014–2022	0.8389	0.4720	−0.5671	−0.6135

Source: Own calculations based on Table 2.16.

correlations indicate that from 2014 to 2022, the greatest impact on the economic growth rate was exerted by unemployment, the level of foreign debt, and the public sector deficit. Inflation had the least influence on GDP growth.

During the period 2014–2022, economic growth was strongly correlated with the unemployment rate (the correlation coefficient was 0.8389). It is noteworthy that the correlation coefficient between the analyzed variables was negative from 2017 to 2022, suggesting that GDP increases were significant enough to contribute to substantial improvements in the labor market.

The economic growth rate in Moldova during this period was relatively moderately positively correlated with the inflation rate. While high economic growth improved employment indicators, it also contributed to rising inflation. An observed moderate negative correlation between the economic growth rate and public sector debt (state budget deficit) was noted during the analyzed period. In Moldova, expenditures have exceeded revenues (mainly from taxes) for years.

Conversely, Moldova's economic growth rate was relatively highly negatively correlated with the foreign debt ratio. The deficit in the current account balance stemmed from a negative trade balance, increased consumer spending (especially in 2021 and 2022, primarily due to high energy prices), and rising foreign debt.

The primary resource of any economy is its people. Analyzing Moldova's demographic profile from 2014 to 2022, a clear depopulation trend emerges (Figure 2.20).

For years, Moldova has experienced a persistent negative natural population growth, which, coupled with increasing emigration (mainly for employment purposes), supports the claim that Moldova is facing rapid depopulation, especially in

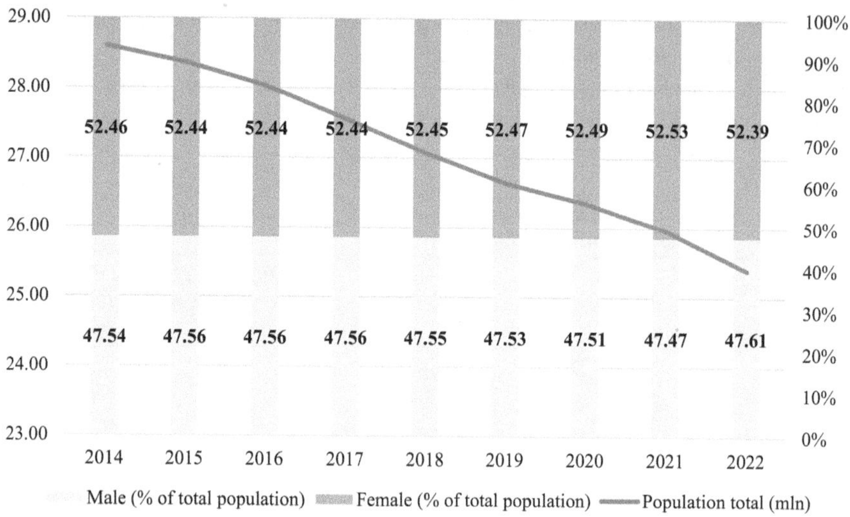

Figure 2.20 Population size and structure by gender in Moldova from 2014 to 2022.

Source: World Bank (2021), National Bureau of Statistics of the Republic of Moldova (2009, 2014, 2018, 2022).

rural areas. During 2014–2021, the number of residents permanently living in the country decreased by 356,000, resulting in a total population of 2.5 million as of January 1, 2022 (Figure 2.20).

This declining population trend has been consistent throughout the analyzed period. Despite this decline, the gender ratio remains stable, with a clear predominance of women. As a result, figures such as a population of 3.5 million include those temporarily absent and residing abroad. Simultaneously, government decisions increasingly rely on other data, particularly the number of residents with permanent residence, which stood at 2.5 million in 2022 (Figure 2.20).

Observing the HDI, it should be noted that according to 2022 data, Moldova ranked 86th among 191 countries surveyed. The HDI value of 0.763 places Moldova in the group of countries with relatively high social development. Over the past 30 years, Moldova's HDI increased by 10.9% (from 0.690 to 0.763). However, existing inequalities in Moldova have led to losses in social development. Moldova's HDI reduction due to inequality stands at 8.5 percent. Moldova recorded a 0.156 Gender Inequality Index value in 2022, ranking 41st out of 166 countries. In 2022, Moldovan women had an HDI value of 0.776 compared to 0.751 for men, resulting in a Gender Development Index value of 1.033, one of the highest in the Europe and Central Asia region (UNDP, 2024a).

Analyzing the country's demographic profile, it is important to address socioeconomic inequalities. In the Republic of Moldova, the Gini coefficient, which measures the level of socioeconomic inequality, shows a decreasing trend due to rising incomes. In Moldova from 2014 to 2022, the Gini coefficient decreased from 26.8 to 25.7. A significant factor contributing to this situation was the increase in external migration of low-income individuals. Labor migration results in a significant volume of annual remittances directed to the national economy. As a result, the share of remittances received by households in the lowest 20% income bracket doubled from 2014 to 2021, reaching 18% of total disposable income, comparable to households with the highest incomes. Consequently, the number of households with adverse socioeconomic status decreased, especially among those whose members work in the agricultural sector, where wages are among the lowest. However, such conclusions should be approached with caution, considering certain shortcomings in Moldova's statistics. There is a noted underrepresentation of high-income households in the country's statistics. Furthermore, it is becoming increasingly common to underestimate declared incomes in household surveys compared to consumption expenditures. This causes the national statistical data to be underestimated, providing an incomplete picture of the phenomenon (EU4Environment, 2021).

In summary, a stabilized economy is characterized by stable fundamental macroeconomic parameters, a balanced state budget, and a balanced payment balance, particularly the current account balance. Such a state remains an unattainable goal for the Moldovan economy. This situation arises because the Moldovan economy remains highly sensitive to both external factors and long-standing unresolved internal issues. As is known, external factors, especially in the short term, constitute a set of independent factors, in this case, from the Moldovan economy. The current model of economic development in Moldova relies on the government's response to emerging imbalances and socioeconomic challenges, compounded by the unresolved issue of purposeful strategic national economic development.

Ukraine

In the former USSR, Ukraine, which served as a major industrial hub and agricultural granary, produced 20% of the total industrial and agricultural output (Vardomsky, 2012).

Ukraine's industry is characterized by a high degree of diversification. In the eastern part of the country, economic development is primarily driven by metallurgy, which includes all stages of technological processes, from ore mining and enrichment to producing finished goods such as pig iron, non-ferrous metals, and their alloys. The iron ore deposits located in Kryvyi Rih (Dnipropetrovsk region) are among the richest in the world (Ukraine ranks fourth in terms of iron ore reserves, after Russia, Brazil, and Australia, and sixth in terms of extraction). Additionally, the close proximity of rich coal deposits as a major energy source and a well-developed machinery, aerospace, space, and defense industry further support this region's economy (Kotulewicz, 2015).

In central Ukraine, with Kyiv as the capital, key industries include machinery manufacturing, metal, food, pharmaceutical, chemical, petrochemical, energy, and building materials production. Leading sectors in machinery manufacturing encompass the aerospace and space industry, electronics, and the production of devices and tools. In this region, highly developed agriculture provides the raw material base for the country's agri-food industry (Kotulewicz, 2015).

In western Ukraine, the economy is dominated by the food, fuel, refinery, chemical, forestry, oil and gas extraction, machinery, energy, light, and metal-processing industries, and agriculture. Food products account for 65% of consumer goods production. Industry contributes 23% to the regional gross product, while agriculture accounts for 12% (Kotulewicz, 2015).

The most challenging period for Ukraine's economy was the 1990s, during which the economy shrank drastically. The country's elites at the time rejected the idea of "shock therapy" as a means to establish economic foundations. In 1992, it was decided to introduce a temporary currency, the Ukrainian karbovanets, during the transition period, which led to hyperinflation in the early 1990s.

Among CIS countries, Ukraine experienced a significant GDP decline, which contracted by 61% from 1990 to 1999 (Figure 2.21). The primary driver of this change was the suppression of economic activity, mainly due to external factors, which were further exacerbated by internal factors. Together, these factors caused a decline in the value of both capital assets and human capital.

Most economic sectors recorded a steep decline, but domestic and foreign trade and investment were the most affected. Industrial and agricultural production plummeted drastically due to the sudden severance of trade and industrial ties with former USSR republics and economic issues in CIS countries. Consequently, in 1992 compared to 1991, the overall value of Ukrainian exports decreased fivefold,

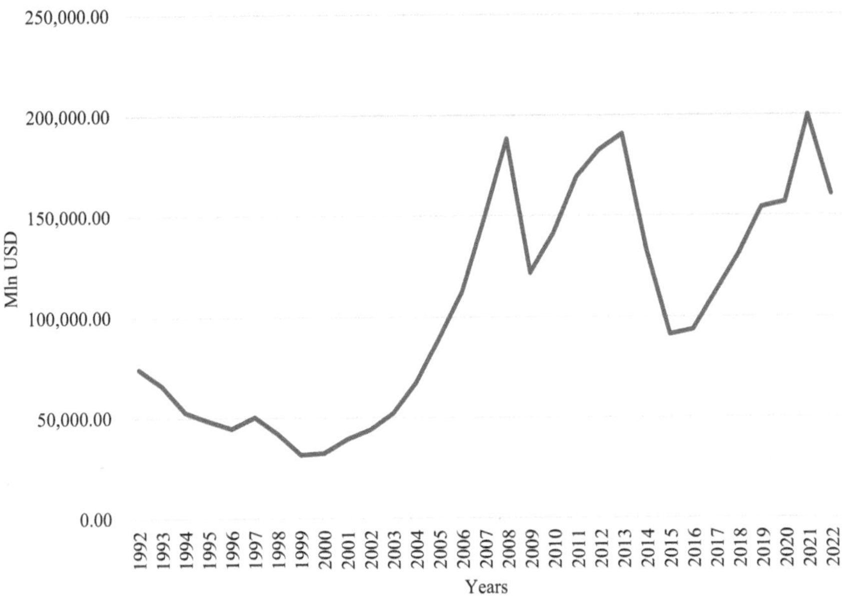

Figure 2.21 Ukraine. Nominal GDP dynamics 1992–2022 (million USD).

Source: World Bank (2021).

while exports to CIS countries dropped eightfold. In contrast, trade with the rest of the world at the beginning of the 1990s experienced a smaller decline of 30–40%. In subsequent years, Ukraine actively engaged in trade, with its trade volume in 2000 being twice as high as in 1991.

The aforementioned problems led to a reduction in the number of employed persons by 6.5 million from 1990 to 1999, with the largest employment declines in industry and construction. As a result, real incomes fell by 72%, making poverty Ukraine's main problem. In 2000, the relative poverty rate was 26.4% with a monthly income of 156 hryvnias, and the poverty rate was 13.9% with a monthly income of 125 hryvnias. Furthermore, in 2000, the average monthly expenses of over 80% of the population were below the subsistence minimum (270 hryvnias) (Osipova, 2005). In the 1990s, widespread poverty not only significantly reduced domestic demand but also caused a decline in birth rates, an increase in mortality rates, and the emigration of 2.5 million citizens. During this period, the population decreased from 51.1 million to 45.6 million.

The recession spiral from 1990 to 1999 led to significant changes in the economic structure. During this period, the share of industry in GDP decreased from 41.9% to 33.2%, agriculture and forestry from 22.3% to 14.1%, and construction from 8.1% to 4.9%. Conversely, the share of services increased from 27.75% to 47.8%.

This situation was exacerbated by a very sharp and long-term decline in investment activity. By the end of the 1990s, investments in fixed assets did not exceed a quarter of the level of the already poor 1991. The investment crisis was a response to the sharp decline in aggregate demand from the state, economic entities, and households. At the time, the modest value of FDI could not remedy the situation.

The prolonged decline was caused by delayed and inconsistent economic reforms, the granting of privileges to enterprises linked to the government, and large state budget obligations during Leonid Kravchuk's term. Between 1991 and 1994, Ukraine experienced the highest inflation among CIS countries because the government addressed state social payment issues by printing additional money. The economic recession was further deepened by (Burakovsky & Novitsky, 2003):

- the strong inertia of state administrative institutions, which hindered the development of the monetary system;
- a significant discrepancy between government policies and the limited capacity of emerging market entities to adapt to rapidly changing economic conditions;
- the mentality of the managerial corps and a lack of financial resources for technological adaptation of production to changing conditions;
- the spread of corruption and the formation of the so-called elite in power (Dergachev, 2000).

Under these conditions, Ukraine's most stable economic sector turned out to be the transit of energy resources. Due to geopolitical changes, Ukraine became one of the leading transit countries globally. Revenues from energy resource transit and re-export played a crucial role in stabilizing the country's financial situation and shaping the Ukrainian capitalist class.

The economic situation in Ukraine slightly improved during Leonid Kuchma's administration as state expenditures were significantly reduced. Between 1994 and 1999, the budget deficit decreased from 8.9% of GDP to 1.5% of GDP. Furthermore, in 1994, price controls on most goods were abolished, foreign trade was liberalized, a unified exchange rate was introduced, and voucher privatization began. In 1996, the national currency, the hryvnia, was introduced and became convertible in 1997. Financial stabilization enabled Ukraine to obtain large loans from the IMF and EBRD, increasing its debt from 2.0% of GDP in 1995 to 27.6% of GDP in 1998.

From 2000 to 2008, the Ukrainian economy developed dynamically, with an average annual GDP growth rate of 6.92%. During this period, industrial production grew by an average of 22.74% annually, and investments in fixed assets by 30.45%. Economic growth was driven by favorable conditions in global commodity and financial markets, particularly in Russia and the EU, favorable gas prices from Russia until 2006, over a 4.5-fold increase in Ukrainian exports, and a nine-fold increase in retail trade. This situation resulted in an increase in disposable incomes from USD 635 in 2000 to USD 3,923 in 2008. However, the poverty rate in Ukraine remained almost unchanged at 27%, prompting about 20–25% of the labor force to seek employment outside Ukraine (CES, 2023). The outflow of the labor force led to a more than 16-fold increase in remittance inflows from abroad.

Between 2000 and 2008, the share of remittances in Ukraine's GDP increased from 1.29% to 3.61%. Although the share of the "shadow economy" in the Ukrainian economy decreased, it remained relatively high at 36.65% of GDP in 2008 (The Global Economy, 2015).

At the end of May 2008, Ukraine joined the WTO. However, in the fall of that year, the situation in global capital markets deteriorated suddenly, as evidenced by a decline in demand for export goods. In 2009, Ukraine entered a crisis with serious financial and economic imbalances due to weak political institutions and the lack of budgetary and structural reforms. Consequently, in 2009, GDP growth was −14.76% compared to 2008. Industrial production decreased by 13.85%, the share of main trading partners in foreign trade (mainly, the EU, CIS, and Turkey) declined, investments in capital assets fell by 60%, disposable income per capita dropped by USD 1,346, the public finance deficit increased by 14.16 percentage points relative to GDP, and foreign debt rose by 29.32%.

During 2010–2011, Ukraine experienced economic recovery. The driving force was export growth, which contributed to increased industrial production in sectors such as chemical, metallurgical, and machinery manufacturing. Ukraine also saw an increase in FDI, primarily related to the purchase of existing assets by foreign investors rather than the creation of new economic entities (Vardomsky, 2012).

However, the years 2012–2015 marked another economic downturn in Ukraine. The main factors were the stagnation in the real economy,[18] a decline in domestic demand,[19] rising foreign debt,[20], a sudden decrease in foreign exchange reserves,[21] increased demand for external loans, low diversification of energy raw material import directions, and a decline in FDI.[22] The difficult economic situation was further exacerbated by the geopolitical conflict with the Russian Federation. It is worth noting that due to Russian aggression in 2014, Ukraine recorded a negative real GDP growth of -6.6%.

However, from 2016 to 2019, Ukraine's economy began to grow again (Table 2.19). This growth was largely driven by increased industrial production, mainly in the

Table 2.19 Ukraine. Basic macroeconomic categories development 2014–2022.

	GDP growth rate	*Unemployment rate*	*Inflation rate*	*Budget deficit/ Surplus share in GDP*	*Current account deficit/Surplus share in GDP*
2014	−6.6	9.27	12.07	−4.54	−3.44
2015	−9.8	9.14	48.70	−1.55	5.53
2016	2.2	9.35	13.91	−2.30	−2.00
2017	2.5	9.50	14.44	−1.41	−3.10
2018	3.4	8.80	10.95	−1.90	−4.91
2019	3.2	8.19	7.88	−1.96	−2.68
2020	−3.8	9.48	2.73	−5.18	3.36
2021	3.5	9.82	9.36	−3.36	−1.94
2022	−29.1	25.8	10.18	−16.17	4.97

Source: Own study based on the data of the World Bank (2021) and the State Statistics Service of Ukraine (2024).

manufacturing sector, and agricultural production (except in 2017). An important reason for the growth in these two sectors was the rise in prices for key export commodities—grain and metals (Ivanov, 2019). Ukraine managed to reduce the budget deficit to 2% of GDP, inflation decreased, the Ukrainian hryvnia strengthened against the US dollar, and the average monthly wage in the national economy more than doubled. A positive influence also came from generational change in politics. Over 80% of the deputies elected in the summer 2019 parliamentary elections were new (Aslund, 2019).

In 2020, Ukraine's real GDP declined by 3.8%. The main factors behind this drop were the restrictions imposed worldwide due to the COVID-19 pandemic and a significant 24.4% decrease in investment. The fall in investment resulted not only from uncertainties related to infections but also from "unresolved renewable energy issues." Amid the crisis, the government had to cut funding and guaranteed tariffs for renewable energy producers, causing an additional downturn in this industry. Residents' incomes were eroded by nearly 10% inflation, primarily driven by a 7.2% increase in processed food prices. According to the national economic audit, due to untapped potential over the past decade, Ukraine lost a trillion dollars. Ukrainians suffered this loss due to constant shifts in policy direction, incomplete reforms, lack of a long-term economic strategy, corruption, and ineffective governance (Szymański, 2020).

In 2021, thanks to coordinated efforts by the authorities and international partner support, Ukraine achieved the highest GDP in its history (over USD 195 billion). However, this growth was destroyed by Russia's invasion of Ukraine in February 2022. The outbreak of the armed conflict caused Ukraine's GDP to decline by over 29% in 2022.

Nevertheless, high unemployment remained a problem. Since 2014, the unemployment rate had been rising. In 2019, the unemployment rate was 8.19%, and it reached nearly 10% in 2021. The increase in the unemployment rate in 2021 was higher than in neighboring Central and Eastern European countries, including EU countries. Unlike in EU countries, a large number of unofficially unemployed individuals are not registered with employment offices and thus are not included in overall statistics, leading to measurement inaccuracies. The average unemployment rate in Ukraine exceeded the European average by almost 37.9%. Due to the Russian invasion in February 2022, nearly 41% of Ukrainians stopped working, and nearly every second Ukrainian lost their job. Among those still employed, 24% worked part time or remotely. In a country where one-third of businesses do not operate and 45% operate below capacity, finding a job is a significant challenge (Petryshyn, 2022).

By the end of 2014, consumer prices had risen by 24.9% due to the devaluation of the hryvnia, increases in administratively regulated prices, and rapid inflationary expectations.

That year also saw increased fees for transportation, medicines, and food (primarily vegetables, fruits, and to a lesser extent, meat and dairy products). The National Bank of Ukraine's balanced monetary policy led to a decrease in inflation at the end of 2015, with the annual inflation rate reaching 9.14%. The annual inflation rate in 2016 was 9.35%, and in 2017, it reached 9.50%. According to the National Bank of Ukraine, this increase was due to rising prices for vegetables and fruits, dairy and meat products, higher fuel prices, and increased excise taxes and alcohol prices. In 2018, inflation dropped to 8.80% due to a slowdown in consumer price growth and favorable conditions in the currency market. In 2019, it was 8.19%, and in 2020, it rose to 9.48%. While pandemic inflationary pressures intensified at the end of 2021, in 2022, the Russian aggression drove inflation higher. With the invasion came increases in fuel, gas, and food prices (Petryshyn, 2022).

In recent years (comparing 2021 to 2009), total state and state-guaranteed debt increased by 8.4 times, foreign debt by 7.3 times, and domestic debt by 10.6 times. In 2014, total state and state-guaranteed debt, expressed in hryvnias (UAH), rose significantly by UAH 516.5 billion, or 53%. The primary reason for this increase was expenditures related to the war in eastern Ukraine. To make ends meet, Ukraine had to take out a substantial loan in 2020. It is noteworthy that there are fewer willing to lend to Ukraine. During 2020, Ukraine's state and state-guaranteed debt increased by UAH 553.6 billion, or 27.7%. This increase in state debt and guarantee obligations was mainly due to the need to finance the state budget deficit and allocate funds to combat COVID-19. Part of this increase is related to the devaluation of the national currency (from 24.12 UAH per USD at the beginning of 2020 to 28.17 UAH per USD at the end of the year, a 16.8% increase).

The structure of Ukraine's public debt is characterized by a very large share of the government sector (about 88.42%), a systematic increase in the share of foreign debt (by place of issuance), and a very high (nearly 50%) share of debt in the form of securities. Expenditures on debt servicing now constitute the largest part of Ukraine's budget expenses. Loans taken out long ago have stopped driving the economy and now serve only to refinance existing obligations. In 2022 (during the war), Ukraine's debts increased by almost USD 3.5 billion. Ukraine spends huge amounts on the war. According to the Ministry of Finance, the state spends about USD 10 billion (UAH 300 billion) per month on the war. The main source of military and other expenditures is the state budget (Petryshyn, 2022).

Therefore, it is worth analyzing the GDP structure in Ukraine in 2014, 2018, and 2022. As presented in the data shown in Figure 2.22, the key economic sectors generating the largest percentage of GDP are Retail Trade, Transportation, Accommodation and Food Service Activities, and Industry and Water Supply, although their share in GDP systematically declined over the studied period. Nonetheless, the sector of Other Economic Activities deserves particular attention, as its share in GDP consistently grew and, notably, in 2022 exceeded that of 2014 by 14 percentage points.

Analyzing the PMS index level, it is evident that from 2014 to 2022, Ukraine's macroeconomic stabilization process was uneven and maintained at a relatively low

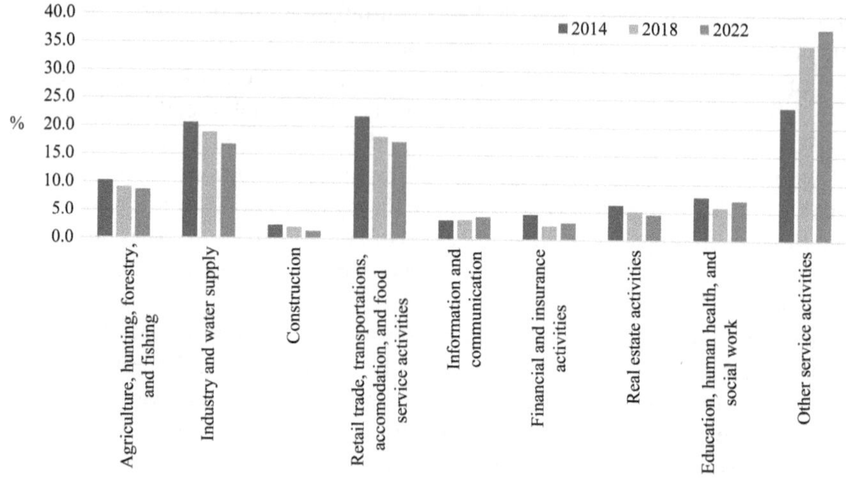

Figure 2.22 Gross domestic product by main economic activities as a % of GDP in Ukraine in 2014, 2018, and 2022.

Source: Own calculations based on National Accounts of Ukraine for 2022, State Statistics Service of Ukraine, Kyiv, 2024.

level (Figure 2.23). Nevertheless, from 2014 to 2020, the macroeconomic stabilization index in Ukraine increased from 0.3183 to 0.4840. However, in 2022, due to Russia's armed invasion of Ukraine, the macroeconomic situation of the Ukrainian economy experienced significant destabilization, as previously discussed.

From 2014 to 2019, there was a significant improvement in the value of the real sector triangle, which illustrates the relationship between GDP growth and unemployment (Table 2.20). Between 2014 and 2020, the stagflation and budget triangles also improved. However, in 2021, the value of this index decreased due to instability related to the increasing threat of Russian aggression. From 2014 to 2020, the value

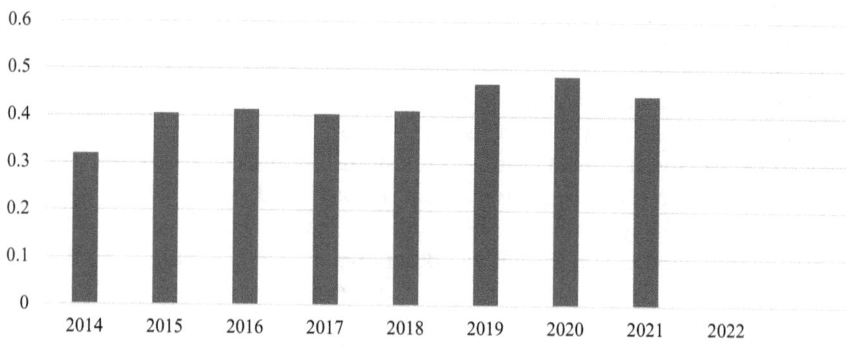

Figure 2.23 Ukraine. PMS index development 2014–2022.

Source: Own calculations based on Table 2.17.

Table 2.20 Ukraine. Value and relative importance of macroeconomic stabilization indexes 2014–2022.

Specification	*2014*	*2015*	*2016*	*2017*	*2018*	*2019*	*2020*	*2021*	*2022*
a	0.0601	0.0506	0.0885	0.0885	0.1000	0.1000	0.0698	0.0917	0
b	0.0708	0.0483	0.0684	0.0684	0.0788	0.0844	0.0930	0.0755	0
c	0.0746	0.0647	0.0851	0.0916	0.1036	0.0890	0.0890	0.0866	0
d	0.0582	0.1482	0.0787	0.0741	0.0635	0.0847	0.1059	0.0817	0
e	0.0546	0.0920	0.0920	0.0805	0.0714	0.0952	0.1265	0.1072	0
PMS1	0.2055	0.1636	0.2420	0.2485	0.2756	0.2880	0.2516	0.2538	0
PMS2	0.1128	0.2402	0.1706	0.1546	0.1350	0.1800	0.2323	0.1888	0
PMS	0.3183	0.4038	0.4126	0.4031	0.4106	0.4679	0.4840	0.4426	0
PMS1/PMS, in %	64.55	40.52	58.64	61.65	67.13	61.54	51.99	57.34	-
PMS2/PMS, in %	35.45	59.48	41.36	38.35	32.87	38.46	48.01	42.66	-
a/PMS1, in %	29.23	30.92	36.58	35.62	36.29	34.73	27.64	36.13	-
b/PMS1, in %	34.48	29.53	28.26	27.52	28.59	29.30	36.98	29.73	-
c/PMS1, in %	51.61	61.71	46.10	47.95	47.07	47.07	45.57	43.25	-
d/PMS2, in %	48.39	38.29	53.90	52.05	52.93	52.93	54.43	56.75	-
e/PMS2, in %									

Source: Own calculations based on Table 2.19.

of the indicator d, which provides information about Ukraine's financial situation, improved, resulting from the reduction of the budget deficit.

From 2014 to 2022, the increase in the value of the PMS in Ukraine primarily resulted from the intensive impact of internal factors. The exception was 2015, when external factors had a greater influence, and their impact did not significantly diminish in subsequent years.

In examining the correlation coefficients between Ukraine's economic growth rate and the trends in unemployment, inflation, the state budget, and the current account balance (Table 2.21), it should be noted that during the period 2014–2022, Ukraine's economic growth rate was relatively moderately (significantly correlated)

Table 2.21 Ukraine. Correlation coefficients between GDP growth rate and changes in other elements of the pentagon.

	GDP growth rate - unemployment rate	*GDP growth rate - inflation rate*	*GDP growth rate - public sector debt*	*GDP growth rate - foreign debt rate*
2014–2016	0.9211	−0.6738	0.0197	−0.5922
2015–2017	0.9186	−0.9994	−0.3480	−0.9954
2016–2018	−0.9015	−0.9276	0.1832	−0.9901
2017–2019	−0.7667	−0.7650	−0.9515	−0.5301
2018–2020	−0.8695	0.9382	0.9999	−0.9715
2019–2021	−0.2843	0.9843	0.8848	−0.9889
2020–2022	−0.9729	−0.8249	0.9965	−0.8210
2014–2018	0.0597	−0.3112	0.1865	0.0545
2019–2022	−0.7963	−0.7546	0.9526	−0.4769
2014–2022	−0.5512	−0.4419	0.8956	−0.2833

Source: Own calculations based on Table 2.19.

negatively correlated with the unemployment rate (average coefficient −0.5512). Notably, between 2014 and 2018, there was a relatively low correlation between GDP size and the unemployment rate. However, during the period 2020–2022, this correlation was nearly perfect. This means that an increase/decrease in GDP could cause a decrease/increase in unemployment.

Ukraine's economic growth rate from 2014 to 2022 was relatively moderately (significantly correlated) negatively correlated with the inflation rate. A stronger correlation was observed from 2019 to 2021.

During the period 2014–2022, the GDP growth rate and the budget deficit were relatively highly positively correlated (average coefficient 0.8956). However, during the period 2018–2020, the correlation (average coefficient 0.9999) indicated a nearly perfect relationship between economic growth and the budget deficit. However, during the period 2018–2020, the correlation (average coefficient 0.9999) indicated a nearly perfect relationship between economic growth and the budget deficit. This implies that economic growth contributed to an increase in the budget deficit.

Conversely, from 2014 to 2022, the GDP growth rate and the current account balance were relatively weakly negatively correlated (average coefficient −0.2833). This suggests that economic growth had a positive impact on reducing Ukraine's foreign debt.

One of the pillars of this potential is the people, the citizens of Ukraine. The data analysis presented in Figure 2.24 indicates that the population of Ukraine has been systematically, although slowly, decreasing. This situation accelerated dramatically in 2022 with the outbreak of war in Ukraine. A significant portion of the population, including men, sought new places to live. As a result, the population of Ukraine in 2022 is characterized by a clear predominance of women.

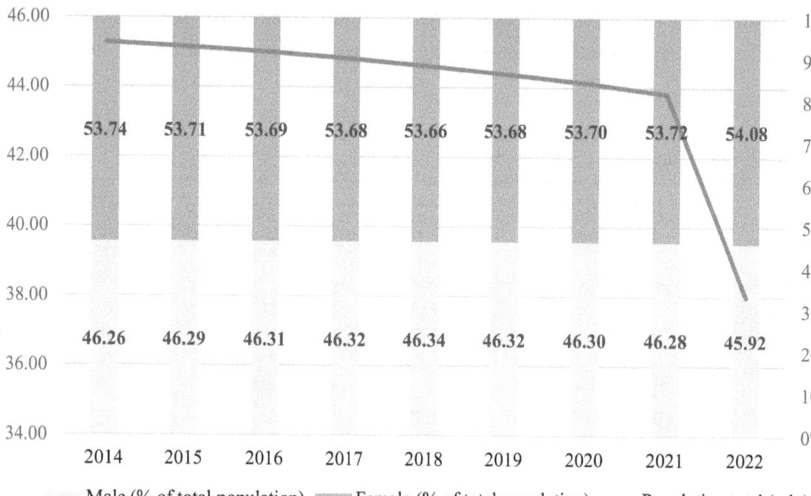

Figure 2.24 Population size and structure by gender in Ukraine from 2014 to 2022.

Source: World Bank (2021).

In turn, the HCI for this country remained stable from 2017 to 2020, ranging from 0.63 to 0.64. Conversely, the level of social development indicates a relatively high status, as evidenced by the HDI, which reached 0.77 in 2014, 0.78 in 2018, and 0.77 in 2021, placing Ukraine in the 77th position among 191 countries worldwide. It is also worth noting the scale of income inequality in the country. In Ukraine, unlike the previously mentioned countries, inequalities increased until 2019, but slightly decreased in the last studied year (Figure 2.25). This is due not only to social benefits but also to remittances from those working abroad. Statistics are available up to 2021. World Statistics does not provide more recent data. The war in Ukraine affects the lack of data.

The presented content allows for outlining the socioeconomic profile of the EaP member countries. The economy is a living organism that undergoes continuous changes under the influence of its environment. In current times, these changes are challenging and unpredictable. The concept of resilience (Zimmerman, 2013) can assist in adapting to unfavorable conditions.

In summary, it should be noted that since gaining independence, the Ukrainian economy still requires substantial investment for industrial modernization. Modernizing production will not only reduce the energy intensity of the national economy but also increase productivity, thereby boosting the supply and competitiveness of Ukrainian export goods. This direction of change, in the near future, will allow for the diversification of Ukrainian exports and policies, leading to the country's development. The armed aggression by Russia against Ukraine means that, on one hand, the Ukrainian economy will need enormous financial resources for postwar reconstruction; on the other hand, it continually delays the moment when Ukraine can fully exploit its economic potential.

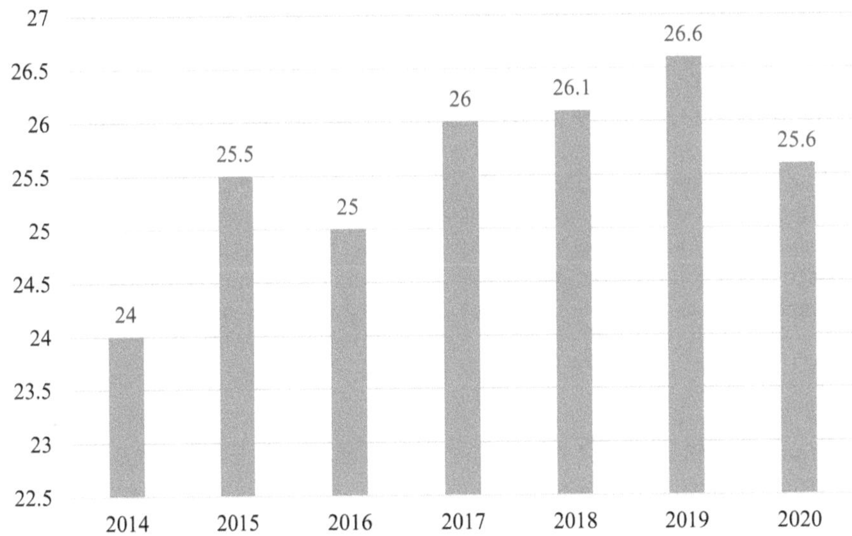

Figure 2.25 Gini index in Ukraine in 2014–2021.

Source: World Bank (2021). In 2021 and 2022, some data is unavailable.

Economic challenges

The Partnership countries are obliged to step up action in areas that are essential to the health and well-being of citizens, make economies more resource-efficient, develop new green jobs and other economic opportunities related to the green transition, develop local and renewable energy sources, and manage natural resources to maximize sustainability.

One of the challenges facing the Partnership countries is to intensify efforts for more sustainable urban development and further improve the provision of ecosystem services, such as access to water and sanitation, waste management, green spaces, and urban mobility.

Reducing production waste is a key starting point for increasing competitiveness at a relatively low cost. It is necessary to continue work on promoting sustainable product policy, eco-innovation, extended producer warranty, and other ways to prevent and reduce the amount of waste and its management, green public procurement, and better information for consumers.

Measuring progress towards green growth generates economic opportunities for the Partnership countries. The applied indexes measure green economy innovation, public and private environmental spending, energy subsidies, and organic farming. Therefore, the analysis covers the economic opportunities associated with green growth, assessing the effectiveness of policies in areas with a focus on technology and innovation, environmental goods and services, investment and financing, pricing, taxes, and transfers.

Changes in the EU's relations with the Partnership countries—caused by Russia's aggression in Ukraine—are associated with a modification of the EaP program. The task of the EU is to gradually include candidate countries in EU policies and support interested partners in the area of security. An important task facing the EU is the effective implementation of economic aid and support for the development of civil society in the EaP countries.

In view of the above, the EU faces the task of extending its neighborhood policy with a security-related component—combined with resilience, support for the rule of law, and norms of social standards. In addition, investment in the infrastructure and integration of the energy markets of the EU's eastern neighbors strengthens energy security and connectivity on both sides and limits Russian influence in these countries. Therefore, diversification policy for the Partnership countries will play an important role in the future by renewable energy, which requires comprehensive investments and can be implemented as part of the EU Green Deal.

Armenia

Like other former Soviet Union countries, Armenia achieved universal access to electricity. Although increased investments in the energy sector are crucial for Armenia's further development, the affordability of energy for households remains a central policy issue. Households spend an average of 12.4% of their budgets on energy and 6% on electricity alone. Up to 11.2% of households are classified as "electricity poor," and 52.5% as "energy poor" (Gabrielian, 2018; Andrusevych et al.,

2021). As increased investments put pressure on raising electricity rates, regulators face the challenge of addressing energy poverty among low-income households (World Bank, 2017). Following the collapse of the Soviet Union and the energy crisis of the early 1990s, Armenia experienced a complete breakdown of its heating system. Minimal adoption of "autonomous heating," where small gas boilers heat a building or group of buildings, led Armenians to use inefficient, individual gas boilers (OECD, 2018). Armenia eliminated most subsidies related to the energy system inherited from the Soviet era, yet subsidies remain as targeted support for low-income households and lost budget revenues due to tax exemptions for diesel and natural gas (exempt from excise duty).

Modern Armenia's power infrastructure performs worse compared to neighboring countries. Armenia's electricity transmission and distribution systems lead to losses of 11.1% of transmitted electricity, whereas loss rates are lower in Azerbaijan (9.8%) and Georgia (6.8%) (World Economic Forum, 2019). Armenia's power sector also suffers from reliability issues—34% of entities experience power outages, more than in Azerbaijan (16%) but less than in Georgia (54%) (World Bank, n.d.). The age and lack of maintenance are major factors contributing to the poor performance of Armenia's power infrastructure. Electrical substations are on average around 35 years old, and most have not undergone major upgrades or overhauls since construction (World Bank, 2017). Unlike Georgia, Moldova, and Ukraine, Armenia is not a contracting party of the EU Energy Community but has been an observer since 2011 (Energy Community, 2019).

Armenia is a net energy importer. In 2018, Armenia's domestic energy production covered just over a quarter (0.82 Mtoe) of the total primary energy supply, with the shortfall made up by imports (2.27 Mtoe). However, Armenia is a net exporter of electricity, exporting to Iran (140 kgoe) (IEA, 2019a; 2019b). Armenia does not have confirmed oil resources and has very limited local natural gas resources, which remain untapped. As a result, Armenia is fully dependent on imported natural gas, its main energy source, and oil (IEA, 2018). The vast majority of Armenia's gas imports come from Russia (2 billion cubic meters annually, about 80%), with a smaller share from Iran (500 million cubic meters annually, about 20%). Although Armenia and Iran have expressed interest in increasing cross-border gas trade, Armenia faces the challenge of balancing energy security concerns from diversifying gas supplies with the risk of violating US-imposed sanctions on Iran (Harutyunyan, 2019).

Energy security is one of Armenia's main goals in the energy sector. The primary challenge is its reliance on old power plants whose operational life has reached or exceeded its limit. This applies especially the Metsamor nuclear power plant, the only nuclear plant not only in Armenia but in the entire South Caucasus. Metsamor was supposed to be shut down in 2016, but its lifespan was extended to 2026 due to insufficient replacement capacity (OECD, 2018). Armenia must increase investments in energy infrastructure not only due to growing energy demand but also due to the urgent need to replace outdated generation capacity. One way that Armenia seeks to improve energy security is through the development of renewable energy. Armenia aims to source 21% of its energy from renewables by 2020 and 26% by 2025. These renewable energy goals included specific targets: 377 MW of installed hydroelectric capacity by 2020, 397 MW by 2025; 50 MW of wind and geothermal by 2020, 100 MW by 2025; and 40 MW of solar PV by 2020, 80 MW by 2025 (IEA, 2016). Armenia introduced tax incentives for households generating electricity from small photovoltaic (PV) and wind installations for their own use and distribution through the national grid (Bertelsmann Stiftung, 2020).

Armenia's strategic program for 2014–2025 highlights several large-scale projects to achieve the country's energy security and diversification goals. Armenia plans to improve its grid connections with the Georgian and Iranian power systems through the construction of new transmission lines and substations, as well as the modernization of existing infrastructure. Armenia aims to allocate 0.3% of its annual budget to improving energy efficiency and the national transmission and distribution system. Regarding generation, Armenia's strategic program emphasizes the rehabilitation of the Vorotan hydropower plant and preliminary work on utilizing the country's geothermal potential (Government of Armenia, 2014).

The mining sector also plays a significant role in environmental degradation, especially in the Eastern Europe, Caucasus, and Central Asia (EECCA) region, as highlighted in the latest OECD analysis (OECD, 2019). In Armenia, the enforcement of national legislation and international standards in the mining sector is weak, and proposed expansions of existing mines and the establishment of new ones have prompted a strong response from civil society calling for better environmental management (Bertelsmann Stiftung, 2020).

Armenia has been a party to the UNECE Convention on Environmental Impact Assessment in a Transboundary Context since 1997 and the related Protocol on Strategic Environmental Assessment since 2011. Armenia's 2014 law "On environmental impact assessment and expertise" covers both EIA and SEA requirements, but the SEA provisions in particular are not fully aligned with the Protocol. The EU-funded program EaP GREEN and its successor program, EU4Environment, implemented jointly by the OECD, UNECE, UNEP, UNIDO, and the World Bank, have been helping Armenia improve its environmental assessment processes.

Armenia has adopted a number of environmental protection regulations impacting the climate; however, many of the existing regulations and policies in the country do not focus on climate change. In response to this issue, the government has decided to develop national action plans for all climate-sensitive sectors, and recent strategies (e.g., the National Disaster Risk Management Strategy of 2017) have begun to incorporate climate change concerns (Table 2.22). Armenia is also in the process of updating its NDC with support from the EU-funded EU4Climate program (EU4Climate, 2020).

Armenia is committed to the green transformation of its economy. Based on national policies and commitments arising from international treaties, investments and reforms supporting Armenia's transition to a green economy focus on the following key areas (Table 2.23).

Table 2.22 Armenia. Main strategic documents in force.

	Status	*Time horizon*	*Sectoral coverage*	*Main objectives*
First Nationally Determined Contribution (NDC)	Submitted in 2017	2015–2030	Economy-wide	• Conditional target: Limit total aggregate emissions between 2015 and 2050 to 633 million tCO_2e • Main sectors targeted for emission reduction: energy, transport, urban development, industrial processes, waste management, land use, and forestry • Main adaptation tool: "ecosystem approach" to climate change adaptation
Strategic Program of Prospective Development (2014–2025)	Adopted in 2014	2014–2025	Economy-wide	• Focus on job creation, development of human capital, improvement of the social protection system, and modernization of public administration and governance
Program of the Government of the Republic of Armenia 2017–2022	Adopted in 2017	2017–2022	Economy-wide	• Adopt new Law on Energy by 2020 • Develop long-term development program for power system

Source: OECD (2021)

The green transformation aims to combat climate change while addressing broader challenges related to sustainable development, in line with the 2030 Agenda and the Sustainable Development Goals (SDGs). To achieve these goals, the Armenian government has initiated the development of over 30 sectoral strategies, as well as a comprehensive transformation strategy for Armenia for

Table 2.23 Armenia. Key domains of the greening transformation.

I. Resource efficiency and clean production	IV. Energy saving and improvement of energy efficiency	VII. Transition to smart and green multimodal transportation
II. Sustainable planning, management, use and reuse of drinking and irrigation water resources	V. Development of power sector and green transition to low carbon energy	VIII. Sustainable, energy efficient urban development
III. Development of sustainable and efficient agriculture and forestry	VI. Waste management (solid waste and wastewater)	IX. Service sector, smart solution, big data, data storage

Source: Central Bank of Armenia (2023).

Table 2.24 Armenia. National strategies.

01	**First INDC and Paris Agreement**: According to the first INDC submitted in 2015 to the UNFCC, followed by ratification of Paris Agreement in 2017, Armenia is committed to pursuing economy-wide climate mitigation measures.	04	**Armenia-EU Comprehensive and Enhanced Partnership Agreement (CEPA)** comprises of several processes and reforms covering 2030 Agenda, through its framework of SDG-aligned targets and indicators.
02	**Updated NDC (2021–2030)** aims to double renewables in energy generation. Five key components are geared towards transition: sustainable energy production, industrial processes, agriculture, waste, and forestry	05	**The 2021–2026 Government Program** emphasizes the Sustainable Development and Green Economy focusing on decarbonization of economy and gradual phase-out from fossil fuels.
03	**Armenia's Transformation Strategy 2020–2050** targets ambitious SDGs based on three interrelated elements of sustainable development: economic growth, social cohesion, and protection of the environment	06	**Importance of energy efficiency and sustainable energy development** is emphasized through a number of national strategies—ESRE, NEEAPs, and Energy Sector Development Strategy up to 2040.

Source: Central Bank of Armenia (2023).

2020–2050. All these initiatives are essential steps addressing the 5Ps of sustainable development: People, Planet, Prosperity, Peace, and Partnership. Several national documents form the foundation for Armenia's sustainable development trajectory (Table 2.24).

The government's program for 2021–2026 prioritizes environmental protection. This will focus on enhancing the country's resilience to climate change through adaptive and mitigative policies. Priorities include the efficient use of water resources, such as the management of Lake Sevan; improvement of waste management; sustainable forest management and specially protected natural areas; biodiversity and biological safety; ensuring the gradual reduction and limitation of the use of single-use polyethylene products; reviewing the threshold for the taxation of metallic minerals; harmonizing environmental protection regulations with the guidelines outlined in the Armenia–EU Comprehensive Extended Partnership Agreement; and ongoing cooperation with international organizations operating in this field. Within the infrastructure development priorities, two sectors have a particular impact on the environment:

1 Water management: The goal is to improve water supply (including for drinking and irrigation) and drainage management through reforms which include:

- reconstruction of the emergency sections of "Arpa-Sevan" tunnel;
- building reservoirs;

Renewable Energy	Electric Vehicles (EVs)	Energy Efficiency (EE) in Buildings
• The 2021 Energy Strategy aims for 1,000 MW of solar PV capacity by 2030. • Supportive policy stances including auctions, a feed-in tariff policy covering project investment horizons, net metering, import tax incentives, and VAT incentives to encourage renewable energy uptake.	• VAT exemptions on import of EVs (extended until end of 2023). • Government of Armenia (GoA) plans to scale up charging infrastructure and additional free parking facilities for electric vehicles.	• Mandatory EE requirements for newly constructed residential multiapartment buildings. • Mandatory energy audits for buildings constructed with state funds. • Definition of labeling requirements for energy-saving devices and equipment. • The EU's EE Directive (EED) and the Energy Performance of Buildings Directive (EPBD) are transposed in Armenian national regulatory framework as part of EU-Armenia CEPA implementation.

Figure 2.26 Low carbon development highlights in Armenia.

Source: Own study based on Central Bank of Armenia (2023).

- promoting the use of water-saving irrigation systems;
- implementing 10 priority anti-flood programs;
- carrying out the restoration of water supply and drainage systems in 11 cities and 41 rural settlements, and rehabilitating of distribution networks.

2 Energy independence and security (Figure 2.26). The overall goal is to ensure a reliable and high-quality supply of electricity and gas to consumers, including from renewables. Policy measures include:

- a gradual liberalization of the electricity market;
- modernization of the second power unit of the Armenian NPP by 2026 (and for another 10 years through additional investment) and construction of a new nuclear power unit;
- increasing the share of solar energy production to 15% by 2030;
- promotion of energy efficiency measures under the requirements of the Armenia–EU Comprehensive Extended Partnership Agreement;
- implementation of knowledge-based and smart energy sector programs (Table 2.20) (Central Bank of Armenia, 2023).

In conclusion, decarbonizing the energy sector means reducing its carbon dioxide emission intensity (i.e., decreasing emissions per unit of generated electricity). The power sector is often considered the "easiest" to decarbonize compared to highly dispersed sectors like transport, due to the large number of available solutions and the relative ease of transitioning to a relatively limited number of solutions. Armenia has made the decarbonization of the energy sector a key factor in its low-emission development strategy (Table 2.25).

Table 2.25 SWOT analysis of Armenia.

Strengths	**Weaknesses**
• Increase in investments in the energy sector. • Availability of targeted subsidies for low-income households. • Elimination of most subsidies related to the Soviet-era energy system. • Introduction of tax incentives for households generating electricity from small photovoltaic and wind installations for their own use and distribution through the national grid. • Development of national action plans for all climate-sensitive sectors, with recent strategies (e.g., the National Disaster Risk Management Strategy of 2017) beginning to incorporate climate change concerns.	• Up to 11.2% of households are classified as "electricity poor," and 52.5% as "energy poor." • Lost budget revenues due to tax exemptions for diesel and natural gas (exempt from excise duty). • Reliability issues—34% of entities experience power outages, more than in Azerbaijan (16%) and less than in Georgia (54%). • Lack of confirmed oil resources and very limited local natural gas resources, which remain untapped. • Dependence on old power plants whose operational life has reached or exceeded its limit.
Opportunities	**Threats**
• The challenge of balancing energy security concerns from diversifying gas supplies with the risk of violating US sanctions on Iran. • Increasing investments in energy infrastructure due to growing energy demand and the urgent need to replace outdated generation capacity. • Development of renewable energy. Armenia aims to source 26% of its energy from renewables by 2025. • Improving the connection of the energy grid with the Georgian and Iranian power systems through the construction of new transmission lines and substations, as well as the modernization of existing infrastructure. • Utilizing the country's geothermal potential. • The EU-funded program EaP GREEN and its successor program, EU4Environment, implemented jointly by the OECD, UNECE, UNEP, UNIDO, and the World Bank, have been helping Armenia improve its environmental assessment processes.	• Electricity transmission and distribution systems lead to losses of 11.1% of transmitted electricity, whereas loss rates are lower in Azerbaijan (9.8%) and Georgia (6.8%). • Armenia is not a contracting party of the EU Energy Community but has been an observer since 2011. • Complete dependence on imported natural gas, the main energy source, and oil. • The majority of Armenia's gas imports come from Russia (2 billion cubic meters annually, about 80%), with a smaller share from Iran (500 million cubic meters annually, about 20%).

Source: Own study.

Azerbaijan

Given its relatively small size, Azerbaijan's total emissions account for just 0.1% of the total global greenhouse gas (GHG) emissions. In the 1990s, following the dissolution of the Soviet Union, Azerbaijan's GHG emissions and GDP both halved. GHG emissions dropped from 78 $MtCO_2e$ in 1990 to 38 $MtCO_2e$ in 1997, coinciding with a decline in GDP (World Bank, 2021). Over the past twenty years, Azerbaijan's emissions have slowly increased but have not exceeded the 1990 level since 2012. On the other hand, Azerbaijan's economy has grown rapidly since the late 1990s; by 2017, it was 2.5 times larger than before independence. As a result, the GHG intensity of Azerbaijan's economy has more than halved, from 3.5 $kgCO_2e$ per dollar (in constant 2010 dollars) in 1990 to 1 $kgCO_2e$ per dollar GDP in 2012 (OECD, 2021). Energy (including fuel combustion in transport) is responsible for the majority of GHG emissions in Azerbaijan—accounting for 75.3% in 2012. Although this is a significant share, it is lower than in 1990 when energy accounted for 87.2% of total emissions.[23] Azerbaijan's energy-related emissions were 38.5% lower than in 1990, while emissions from all other sources have gradually increased since independence. Agriculture accounted for 13.6% of emissions in 2012, industrial processes 5.8%, and waste 4.8% (Ministry of Ecology and Natural Resources Republic of Azerbaijan, 2015).

Azerbaijan's energy sector benefits from better quality infrastructure compared to other strategic sectors; however, the country's electricity transmission and distribution systems perform worse than those of its neighbors. While Georgia's power grids result in losses of 7.3% of electricity production, Azerbaijan's transmission and distribution networks experience a loss rate of 9.7% (IEA, 2019b). Like other former Soviet Union countries, Azerbaijan has achieved universal access to electricity.

Azerbaijan's economy is driven by the oil and gas sector, which accounts for about 90% of the country's exports and 30% to 50% of its GDP, depending on oil prices. Revenue from oil exports, and increasingly from gas, has brought substantial wealth to Azerbaijan and improved the standard of living (IMF, 2021). The dynamics of the domestic oil and gas sector significantly influence economic growth, both through industrial activity and consumer spending related to employment and wages.

Although the hydrocarbon-based growth model has brought significant benefits, Azerbaijan now recognizes both the limitations and opportunities of transitioning to clean energy. Azerbaijan's economy remains heavily dependent on fossil fuels. Oil and natural gas still account for over 90% of exports and one-third of GDP (Figure 2.27). Although the sharp rise in energy prices caused by Russia's invasion of Ukraine brings short- and medium-term gains and accelerated growth, exposure to global energy price declines remains a fundamental characteristic of Azerbaijan's economy.

The non-oil private sector is constrained by several factors, including access to skilled labor and financing, as well as market competition bottlenecks, with

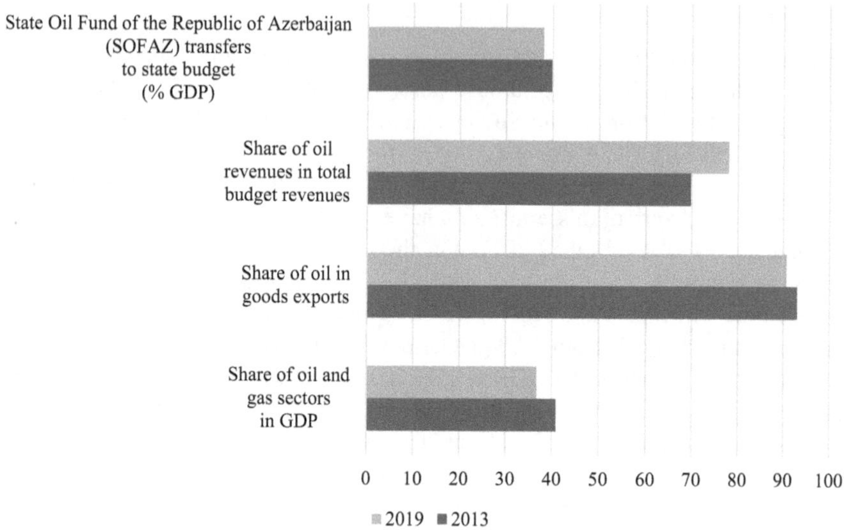

Figure 2.27 Azerbaijan. Oil and gas contribution to key aggregates.

Source: World Bank Group (2023).

state-owned enterprises maintaining a significant presence in the economy (World Bank Group, 2023). Policy declarations, such as the "National Priorities for Socio-Economic Development" (UNESCO, 2022 and the "Republic of Azerbaijan Socio-Economic Strategy for 2022–2026" (SEDS, 2022), acknowledge the limitations of hydrocarbon-driven growth.

The SEDS for 2022–2026 recognizes the country's limited progress in finding other sources of comparative advantage and sets forth an ambitious economic diversification program focused on digital technologies, human capital, and new areas of industrial export. It also commits Azerbaijan to significant investments in transitioning to clean energy, including renewable energy, electric mobility, and energy efficiency, along with enabling reforms such as cost-reflective energy pricing. By 2060, a global net-zero economy would reduce Azerbaijan's exports by nearly 3.4% of GDP compared to the business-as-usual (BAU) scenario, even if Azerbaijan meets its climate targets for 2030 and 2050. Additionally, global decarbonization policies may indirectly increase the costs of diversification and development of non-hydrocarbon sectors. From 2016–2021, Azerbaijan ranked 115th out of 133 countries in terms of economic complexity. Current policies will not enable Azerbaijan to achieve its nationally determined contributions (NDC) goals, but they can be met with relatively moderate additional efforts. Azerbaijan is not currently on track to meet its NDC+ goals, which aim to reduce GHG emissions by 35% by 2030 and 40% by 2050 (relative to 1990 levels). In the BAU scenario, energy and industrial process–related emissions would only be 28% lower than 1990 levels by 2030 and only 30% lower by 2050. To achieve NDC+ goals, renewable energy would need to account for about 20% of energy production by 2030 and 40% by 2050 (compared to 7% in 2022). Moreover, policies supporting improved energy efficiency across all end-use sectors should be adopted to achieve a 5% reduction in final energy demand by 2030 and 15% by 2050 compared to the BAU scenario. More than half of the additional GHG emission reductions required in the net-zero scenario compared to the BAU scenario must come from improved energy efficiency. Reducing fugitive emissions from fossil fuel extraction and transport also poses a challenge in achieving the 2030 NDC target at a relatively low cost.

Further investments in clean energy post-2030 to fully decarbonize the energy sector by 2050 would need to be combined with ongoing aggressive reductions in fugitive emissions, large-scale electrification of end-use sectors, significant efficiency gains, and the introduction of zero-emission energy carriers in sectors that cannot be electrified. Azerbaijan would need to install approximately 30 GW of wind and PV power plants by 2060, in addition to storage capacity and carbon capture and storage (CCS) systems in biomass power plants. In the transport sector, emissions would be reduced primarily through the adoption of clean fuel vehicles (mainly electric, but also biofuels and green hydrogen), improved energy efficiency, and a shift to lower-carbon transportation modes (especially rail). By 2060, total final energy demand would need to be nearly half of the BAU scenario's demand for that year, with electricity accounting for about 60% of this demand.

Early decarbonization could bring net economic benefits, even if global fossil fuel prices remain higher for longer. In the national net-zero scenario, the natural gas available for export would increase by 35% by 2060, as a smaller share of gas production is consumed domestically, while in the BAU scenario, it would remain essentially unchanged. If international fossil fuel prices stay higher than assumed in the net-zero scenario (as is currently the case due to Russia's invasion of Ukraine), a faster pace of domestic decarbonization would free up resources for export earlier. This would lead to 5–10% additional natural gas available for export annually in the medium term (2030–2050) compared to the baseline net-zero scenario, helping Azerbaijan capture gains from higher global prices. This increased natural gas export would help meet the currently growing demand for natural gas as a transitional fuel (especially in Europe), but its role would remain temporary, because global decarbonization is ultimately expected to reduce demand for all fossil fuels (Table 2.26).

According to World Bank Group estimates (2023), the average incremental investments will amount to approximately USD 1.35 billion annually (or about 4% of GDP), with nearly 60% expected to come from the public sector. While several measures for both decarbonization and resilience need to be supported by public funds (starting with strengthening the energy system to enable the penetration of renewable energy sources [RES] or consolidating and maintaining existing

Table 2.26 Economic costs, investment, and benefits of Azerbaijan's decarbonization and resilience 2060 pathway.

Compared to BAU, until 2060	*Net increase in CAPEX9 (A) (USD billions, discount)*	*Net increase in OPEX (B) (USD billions, discounted)*	*Net economic costs (A + B) (USD, billions/% of GDP, discounted)*	*Annual net investment (USD, billions/% of GDP, discounted)*	*Estimated split of the net increase in investment, public/private (% / %)*	*Welfare Gains (% change compared to cumulative discounted GDP)*	*Estimated co-benefits (compared to cumulative discounted GDP), %*
Decarbonization							
Electricity	[7.6]	[6.2]	[13.8]/[1.0]	0.17/0.5	17/83		
Transport	11.2	−6.7	4.4/0.3	0.34/1.0	51/49		
Residential	2.9	9.1	12.0/0.9	0.07/0.2	20/80		
Industry and Other	4.8	3.5	8.3/0.6	0.14/0.4	0/100		
Decarbonization total	**18.9**	**5.8**	**24.7/1.9**	**0.72/2.1**	**30/70**	**−0.17**	**[1.4]**
Resilience							
Water Efficiency	14.8	2.8	17.6/1.2	0.60/1.9	95/5	[>1]	
Climate Smart Agriculture	1.1	0.7	1.8/0.1	0.03/0.1	40/60		
Resilience total	**15.9**	**3.5**	**19.4/1.3**	**0.63/2.0**	**92/8**	**[>1]**	
TOTAL	**34.8**	**9.3**	**44.1/3.2**	**1.35/4.1**	**59/41**	**[0.83]**	**[>1.4]**

Source: World Bank Group (2023).

infrastructure), a larger portion (investments in renewable energy and the adoption of climate-friendly agriculture) can and should be financed through commercial and private sector funds (Table 2.27).

In summary, Azerbaijan has been effective in attracting private investments in the energy sector, but most of these have focused on oil and gas extraction for export markets (where the majority of FDI lies), while domestic energy sectors have seen marginal private sector involvement.

Table 2.27 SWOT analysis of Azerbaijan.

Strengths	**Weaknesses**
• Azerbaijan's economy is driven by the oil and gas sector, which accounts for about 90% of the country's exports and 30% to 50% of its GDP. • The dynamics of the domestic oil and gas sector significantly influence economic growth, both through industrial activity and consumer spending related to employment and wages.	• Azerbaijan's economy remains heavily dependent on fossil fuels. • Azerbaijan's exposure to global energy price declines remains a fundamental characteristic of its economy. • The non-oil private sector is constrained by several factors, including access to skilled labor and financing. • The country has made limited progress in finding other sources of comparative advantage.
Opportunities	**Threats**
• Policy declarations, such as the "National Priorities for Socio-Economic Development" (Azerbaijan 2030) and the "Republic of Azerbaijan Socio Economic Strategy for 2022–2026" (SEDS, 2022), acknowledge the limitations of hydrocarbon-driven growth. • An ambitious economic diversification program focuses on digital technologies, human capital, and new areas of industrial export. • A need for significant investments in transitioning to clean energy, including renewable energy, electric mobility, and energy efficiency, along with enabling reforms such as cost-reflective energy pricing. • Further investments in clean energy post-2030 aim for the full decarbonization of the energy sector by 2050. • This involves continuous aggressive reduction of fugitive emissions, large-scale electrification of end-use sectors, substantial efficiency gains, and the introduction of zero-emission energy carriers in sectors that cannot be electrified.	• Azerbaijan is not currently on track to achieve its NDC+ goals, which aim to reduce GHG emissions by 35% by 2030 and 40% by 2050 (relative to 1990 levels). • Several measures for both decarbonization and resilience need to be supported by public funds, starting with strengthening the energy system to enable the penetration of renewable energy sources (RES) and consolidating and maintaining existing infrastructure.

Source: Own study.

Belarus

Belarus is one of the least energy self-sufficient countries in the world. Domestic production covers only about 15% of Belarus's energy demand, with the shortfall made up by imports, primarily from a single supplier, Russia (IEA, 2020). In 2018, Belarus imported 20 billion cubic meters (15 Mtoe) of natural gas for domestic use, which is the main fuel for generating electricity and heat, while producing only 128 kgoe domestically. The supply of Belarusian oil fuels the country's large refining industry.

During Russia's war with Ukraine, the Lukashenko regime has supported Russia. Sanctions imposed by the West in this context affect many sectors of the Belarusian economy, such as petrochemicals (Żochowski, 2021). The deteriorating economic situation from the regime's perspective has forced the abandonment or postponement of "secondary" goals such as decarbonization, waste management, and water pollution control (Heinrich-Böll-Stiftung, 2023). The Belarusian regime assesses the impact of Western sanctions on achieving global SDGs as follows:

- the sanctions imposed on Belarus (and Russia) have harmed the achievement of SDGs in other parts of the world, especially regarding goals 1 (hunger), 7 (affordable and clean energy), and 13 (climate);
- despite the sanctions, Belarus claims to be successfully progressing towards all SDGs, having already achieved 80% of them (UNCTAD conference, 2021);
- while sanctions threaten the achievement of SDGs, they also create new opportunities by strongly motivating the utilization of existing reserves and the combination of all available resources to ensure sustainable development (Brantsevich, 2022).

Following the Kremlin's policy of isolating from the West, Belarusian authorities currently model their sustainable development agenda primarily on the green agenda controlled by the Russia-led Eurasian Economic Union (EAEU), whose actions are often declarative, derivative, or in the early stages of development. In October 2022, the Eurasian Integration Research Center published the results of the first stage of developing the concept of implementing green principles in the EAEU. This work is conducted under the Green Eurasia project, whose scientific and methodological aspects are officially controlled by the Research Council on Global Environmental Issues of the Russian Academy of Sciences to "facilitate the creation of a unified environmental and climate policy in the Eurasian countries, including the EAEU member states" (Yurgens & Romov, 2023). Decarbonization itself is seen as a challenge largely created by developed countries as a tool of unfair competition, as they transitioned to a new technological order. Another report published by the Center in May 2023 expressed this more explicitly: "Currently and in the future, the technological and social goals of the Green Transformation should be implemented according to the principles of sustainable development, with only nominal linkage to carbon emission reductions" (Yurgens & Romov, 2023). Belarus's agenda in the aforementioned areas is limited to private and local

Table 2.28 SWOT analysis of Belarus.

Strengths	Weaknesses
• Diverse industries that leverage the country's human capital. • Social and political awakening of Belarusian citizens. • The Belarusian opposition has gained international support and financial backing. • Russian gas pipelines transporting natural gas to Poland, Germany, and from Vilnius to Kaliningrad pass through Belarusian territory. • Russian oil pipelines transporting oil to Poland, Germany, the Czech Republic, Slovakia, and Hungary pass through Belarusian territory. • A transit country with roads connecting Russia–Ukraine and Central Europe (EU countries).	• One of the least energy self-sufficient countries in the world. • Domestic production covers only about 15% of energy demand, with the shortfall made up by imports, primarily from Russia. • High energy intensity of the economy. • High degree of technological obsolescence in industry. • Sustainable development policy currently limited to local and regional projects. • High level of state intervention in the economy. • Economic dependence on Russia, especially following the outbreak of full-scale war in Ukraine. • "Brain drain" of well-educated citizens leaving the country.

Opportunities	Threats
• The economic and social crisis in Belarus may help the opposition take power. • Support from the EU and USA for democratic changes in Belarus. • Rapid and flexible adaptation to changing economic and political conditions.	• Sanctions imposed by the West affect many sectors of the Belarusian economy, such as petrochemicals. • Policy of isolating from the West. • Growing demographic crisis caused by significant labor emigration.

Source: Own study.

initiatives (e.g., regional sustainable development forums) that are tailored to meet SDG requirements but, upon closer inspection, are not genuinely linked to them (Table 2.28).

The Belarusian finance market has only made the first steps in the implementation of the green agenda. In mid-2019, BIK Ratings started introducing the practice of ESG-rating of local businesses. The Council of Ministers adopted a resolution titled "On Adopting Criteria of Green and Adaptation Projects and Requirements for Green and Adaptation Projects Verification System." The Belarusian green taxonomy has yet to be published, but its name suggests it is conceptually similar to the Russian one (Yurgens & Romov, 2023).

In summary, based on publicly available materials, it should be noted that sustainable development policy in Belarus is currently limited to local and regional projects. Amid anti-Western rhetoric, ordinary state regulations and economic stimulation are only superficially placed in the context of SDGs. The tendency to turn to the Eurasian "ecosystem" as an alternative to Western norms is also visible in the areas of energy, climate, and ecology.

Georgia

In July 2023, the Georgian government presented a long-term low-emission development strategy to 2050 (LT-LEDS). LT-LEDS was officially adopted in April 2023 with support from the European Union and UNDP under the EU4Climate program (ICI, 2023). The LT-LEDS project lays the foundation for a carbon-neutral future for Georgia and will play a crucial role in updating the national climate action plan, setting a clear course for sustainable, low-emission growth.

Georgia adopted its first National Climate Strategy (NCS) for 2030 and Action Plan (CSAP) for 2021–2023 (CSAP, 2021) in 2021. The CSAP is a mechanism for planning and implementing coordinated efforts to achieve the goals outlined in the NDC. The strategy includes GHG reduction targets while considering future priority areas. As an integral part of the strategy, the CAP (Climate Action Plan) includes specific actions to achieve these goals. The CAP in its current form is a detailed three-year (2021–2023) implementation plan. Within the LT-LEDS project, advisory support has been provided over the past six years in the following areas (ICI, 2023):

- Developing the updated NDC and CSAP.
- Developing the Monitoring and Reporting Scheme.
- Elaborating long-term decarbonization pathways for the transport sector.
- Preparing policy and feasibility studies for the agricultural sector.
- Elaborating a roadmap for the Climate Change Law and conducting educational activities to raise awareness about climate change.

The Georgian LT-LEDS places special emphasis on technological transformation and the modernization of economic sectors, particularly energy-efficient technologies and renewable energy sources, as the foundation for low-emission development. Innovative technologies, including climate technologies, are key to economic development and decarbonization by 2050. Georgia plans to combine low-emission development with economic growth by introducing innovative approaches and technologies that reduce GHG emissions (Table 2.29).

Georgia aims to become "green" by 2050 through a transition to energy-efficient technologies and renewable energy sources. Technological transformation and modernization are key to economic development and decarbonization by increasing efficiency, minimizing losses, and utilizing low-emission technologies. Georgia plans to integrate low-emission development with economic growth by introducing innovations that simultaneously reduce GHG emissions. Georgia has made significant progress in improving energy security and transitioning to a cleaner and more sustainable energy system (BDD, 2021).

The long-term vision for Georgia's energy sector involves "decarbonizing" the sector by maximizing the use of renewable energy sources and improving energy efficiency across all sectors of the national economy. Achieving carbon neutrality by mid-century will be the ultimate goal of Georgia's long-term low-emission development strategy.

Table 2.29 Share of sectoral GHG emissions in national GHG emissions. WaM optimistic and WaM pessimistic scenarios.

Sector	*WaM Optimistic scenario*				*WaM Pessimistic scenario*			
Energy	68%	64%	59%	46%	67%	66%	61%	50%
Industrial Processes and Product Use (LPPU)	12%	15%	18%	25%	12%	15%	17%	21%
Agriculture	12%	14%	16%	19%	13%	13%	15%	18%
Waste	8%	6%	7%	10%	6%	7%	7%	6%
Total excluding Land Use, Land Use Change and Forestry (LULUCF)	100%	100%	100%	100%	100%	100%	100%	100%
LULUCF	−33%	−44%	−61%	−101%	−31%	−44%	−63%	−105%
Total including LULUCF	70%	57%	40%	-1%	69%	56%	37%	−5^

Source: Ministry of Environmental Protection and Agriculture of Georgia (2015; 2023).

The LT-LEDS highlights the critical importance of introducing innovative policies and new technologies that require external (international) technical, technological, and financial assistance to achieve the ultimate goal of carbon neutrality by mid-century. Moreover, climate mitigation policies should be implemented in line with principles of social justice and a just transition. Measures implemented under climate mitigation policies create opportunities for new, decent jobs, contributing to regional and national economic development alongside GHG emission reductions. Therefore, low-emission development becomes a tool not only for reducing GHG emissions but also for achieving social welfare goals.

In the context of decarbonization challenges, it is important to note that the transport sector is one of the largest sources of GHG emissions in Georgia. In 2015, the transport sector was responsible for emitting 4.2 $MtCO_2e$, accounting for about 24% of total national emissions (Day et al., 2021). Decarbonization scenarios indicate that in the baseline scenario, GHG emissions from this sector are expected to increase by 71% to 7.1 $MtCO_2e$ by 2030:

- Freight transport is expected to be the subsector with the largest growth in the baseline scenario, with GHG emissions more than doubling due to the anticipated large increase in commercial activity.
- The forecast for GHG emissions in freight transport largely depends on the extent to which freight activity can be shifted from road trucks to rail and the pace at which the rail network can be electrified.
- GHG emissions from passenger transport are expected to increase by 49% from 2015 to 2030, roughly in line with the expected increase in demand for passenger activity over the same period, as improvements in vehicle emission intensity are offset by an increase in the share of passenger activity in private light-duty vehicles.

In the CSAP scenario, where Georgia fully implements the mitigation actions included in the climate strategy and action plan, GHG emissions from this sector are expected to increase by 34% to 5.6 $MtCO_2e$ by 2030:

- While emissions from freight transport in the CSAP scenario follow the same upward trend as in the baseline, the trend for passenger transport emissions is reversed, leading to a 7% decrease in absolute emissions from 2015 to 2030.
- The modal share of commercial vehicles is expected to decrease significantly by 14.8% from 2015 to 2030, while the share of buses nearly doubles. The modal share of rail and marshrutkas also increases by 2.5% and 4.3%, respectively.

Emissions for the transport sector in "best-in-class" and "Paris Agreement-compliant" scenarios peak in the short term and decline to zero by mid-century. From a financial and practical standpoint, the vision for climate finance as part of the LT-LEDS Climate Finance Strategy (CFS) considers the factors necessary to secure public, private, and international funds for the successful implementation of LT-LEDS (BDD, 2021) (Table 2.30).

Table 2.30 SWOT analysis of Georgia.

Strengths	**Weaknesses**
• Development of a long-term low-emission development strategy to 2050 (LT-LEDS). • Adoption of the National Climate Strategy (NCS) for 2030 and the Action Plan (CSAP) for 2021–2023. • Association agreement with the EU signed in 2016. • EU candidate status since December 2023. • An important transport corridor for energy resources to the European Union. • A crucial transport corridor connecting former Soviet Republics with the EU. • A significant transport route connecting the Persian Gulf countries with the Black Sea.	• The transport sector is one of the largest sources of GHG emissions in Georgia. • Georgia has high capital costs, which pose a significant barrier to attracting funds and the development process. • The Georgian energy grid is connected to the Russian energy network. • Relatively low pipeline capacity running through Georgia.
Opportunities	**Threats**
• Increased demand for Azerbaijani energy in the EU could contribute to increasing pipeline capacity. • Important transport corridors passing through Georgia that bypass Russia and lead to Europe may gain significance, be expanded, and become routes for goods from China to the EU.	• Construction of alternative transport corridors through Armenia and Iran may reduce the importance of the route through Georgia. • A pipeline built on the Black Sea floor near the Russian-occupied Crimea peninsula poses a security threat. • Introduction of the "Foreign Influence Transparency Act."

Source: Own study.

In summary, the climate finance system involves mobilizing local, national, and international financial resources to support climate change mitigation, adaptation, and low-emission development. It is crucial to develop financing policies and procedures that align with Georgia's LT-LEDS and meet investment requirements to achieve its main goals. This is significant because, like other developing countries, Georgia faces high capital costs, which pose a substantial barrier to attracting funds and to the entire development process.

Moldova

Moldova has shown significant progress in its commitment to adaptive initiatives, as evidenced by the development and adoption of several strategic and cross-sectoral documents outlining the country's vision for mitigating both current and anticipated climate risks to the economy and population. These documents include the climate adaptation strategy and its implementation action plan (developed in 2014), as well as various national strategic documents covering different socioeconomic domains and sectoral development documents for national priority sectors such as agriculture, water resources, public health, forestry, energy, and transport. To strengthen these commitments, Moldova incorporated an adaptation component into its updated Nationally Determined Contributions (NDC) or NDC2, submitted to the United Nations Framework Convention on Climate Change (UNFCCC) in 2020. This adaptation component includes cross-sectoral and sectoral adaptation actions and measures consistent with the National Development Strategy: Moldova 2030 and the overarching adaptation goal of the Paris Agreement. It recognizes the necessity to improve the policy environment for adaptation and strengthen government regulatory and institutional capacities.

In August 2023, the National Climate Change Adaptation Program to 2030 was adopted, along with an Action Plan aimed at accelerating the implementation of adaptation commitments. Additionally, efforts are underway to develop the second version of the National Adaptation Plan, which would include a specialized focus on the agriculture sector (IMF, 2023).

The draft Integrated National Energy and Climate Plan (NECP) 2025–2030, serving as a roadmap for achieving the country's decarbonization goals, was presented for consultation from February 5 to 19, 2024. The document was developed by the Ministry of Energy with support from the European Union through the "Coping with the Impact of the Energy Crisis in the Republic of Moldova" program, implemented by UNDP Moldova. The NECP outlines goals for renewable energy, energy efficiency, and GHG emissions. The plan is a legal commitment of the Republic of Moldova and concerns only the territories controlled by constitutional authorities (UNDP, 2024b).

The structure of the national energy policy plan is based on five dimensions of the energy union and describes public policies and investments aimed at achieving the goals set out in each dimension (Figure 2.28).

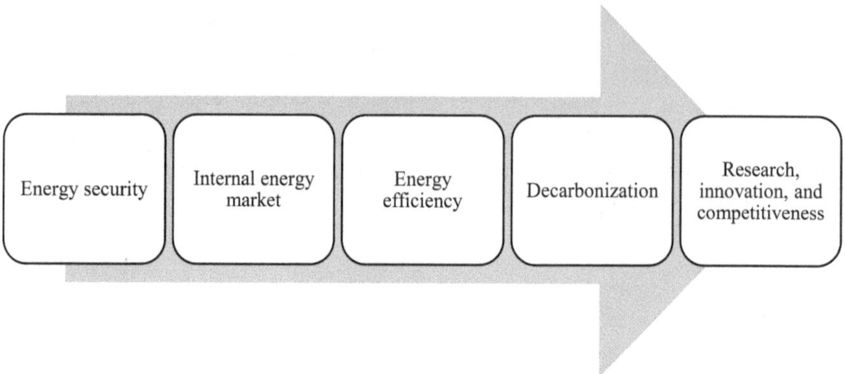

Figure 2.28 Moldova. Structure of the national energy policy plan.

Source: Own study.

In the dimension of decarbonization, the document prioritizes replacing firewood with renewable energy sources and energy-efficient technologies, reaching a capacity limit of 600 MW of wind power and 200 MW of photovoltaics. It also aims to reduce GHG emissions from 8.75 $MtCO_2$ to 7.45 $MtCO_2$ excluding sequestration.

The European Union and UNDP have supported the government of the Republic of Moldova in developing its first-ever Low Emissions Development Programme (LEDP). The program, which came into effect on January 1, 2024, systematizes policies and sectoral action plans aimed at achieving the GHG emission reduction targets outlined in the updated Nationally Determined Contribution (NDC) submitted in March 2020 to the UNFCCC.

According to the program, by 2030, GHG emissions are to be reduced relative to 1990 levels (UNDP, 2023a) :

- in the energy sector by 81%, ;
- in the transport sector by 52%,
- in the buildings sector by 74%, ;
- in the industrial sector by 27%, ;
- in the agricultural sector by 44%, and ;
- in the waste sector by 14%.

Mitigating climate change requires joint global efforts, and the Republic of Moldova, despite accounting for less than 1% of global GHG emissions, is an active participant in efforts to limit global warming (Table 2.31).

In summary, considering international efforts to reduce CO_2 emissions and combat climate change, extensive investments create significant opportunities for decarbonizing Moldova's transport sector. Moldova's commitment in this area

Table 2.31 SWOT analysis of Moldova.

Strengths	**Weaknesses**
• The development and adoption of several strategic and cross-sectoral documents outlining the country's vision for mitigating both current and anticipated climate risks to the economy and population. • Replacement of firewood with renewable energy sources and energy-efficient technologies. • Association and Free Trade Agreements with the EU (2014, extended to Transnistria in 2016). • EU candidate status since 2022. • International financial support.	• Energy dependence on Russia. • The poorest country in Europe. • Separatist movement in Transnistria. • Corruption, oligarchic system, and weak civil society.
Opportunities	**Threats**
• Diversification of energy supply through Romania and the transport corridor through the Black Sea. • Achieving energy independence from Russia. • Moldova's accession to the European Union. • Moldova's accession to NATO. • Overcoming separatist tendencies in Transnistria and Gagauzia and fully integrating them into Moldova.	• Further deepening of energy dependence on the Russian Federation. • Intensification of separatist movements in Transnistria and eventual secession from Moldova. • Financially unsustainable replacement of Russian energy supplies with Romanian resources in the long run. • Increased social dissatisfaction due to rising energy prices, which may support pro-Russian sentiments in society. • Intensification of separatist tendencies in the Autonomous Territorial Unit of Gagauzia.

Source: Own study.

contributes to environmental protection and climate change mitigation. Strengthening the knowledge base and promoting joint platforms dedicated to climate-friendly mobility and decarbonization plays a decisive role.

Ukraine

Before the war with Russia, Ukraine had the most energy- and resource-intensive economy in Europe, particularly due to the large share of high-energy-consuming industries such as metallurgy. Currently, as a result of the ongoing war, many industrial plants located in eastern and southeastern Ukraine have been destroyed. The reconstruction of the industrial sector presents an opportunity to eliminate past dependencies on fossil fuels and dirty technologies and replace oligarchic control of the industry with a multi-stakeholder ownership structure. By rebuilding the sector in line with sustainable development and climate neutrality principles, Ukraine could become a major supplier of green goods and raw materials, such as green steel, to the EU and the rest of the world, thereby facilitating global decarbonization. This process would be challenging due to the significant need for investment and the supply of costly, best available technologies. However, it would form the basis for Ukraine's economic revival, especially in the areas most affected by the war (GLOBSEC, 2023).

In July 2022, an international conference on Ukraine's postwar reconstruction (URC2022) was held in Lugano, Switzerland, where its plan was presented and the so-called Lugano Declaration was signed. This document sets the framework for the political process that will guide Ukraine's reconstruction after the end of the Russian aggression. The reconstruction plan includes, in particular, a transition towards sustainable development, emission reductions, and a shift to renewable energy sources.

In June 2023, Ukraine presented its energy strategy to 2050 at the Ukraine Recovery Conference in London. This strategy envisions the decarbonization of Ukraine's energy sector by 2050. Considering the country's ambitions to join the EU, pathways to net-zero GHG emissions in Ukraine by 2050 were analyzed. Ukraine is committed to achieving rapid, deep, and sustained reductions in GHG emissions while ensuring affordable, reliable, and secure energy for all Ukrainians, and developing long-term, low-emission development strategies in line with the EU goal of net-zero emissions by 2050 (Ministry of Energy of Ukraine, 2023).

With 68% of Ukraine's coal capacity damaged or destroyed (UNDP, 2023b), the Ukrainian government is considering phasing out coal from the energy sector by 2035. Ukraine also plans to significantly increase electricity production using wind, solar, nuclear, and biofuel technologies (Ministry of Energy, 2023), and to improve system balancing with robust energy storage capabilities. The country's goal is to become a leading European green energy hub focused on carbon-neutral electricity production. Currently, Ukraine is actively engaged in developing its commercial potential and striving for smooth integration with EU energy markets. Additionally, it aspires to play a key role in the emerging EU hydrogen economy. Similarly, the country is considering developing certified gas storage facilities to enhance energy security and flexibility in Ukraine and Europe. Furthermore, engagement in global energy equipment production chains is expected to foster economic growth and technological advancement in the country.

Before the war, Ukraine had a mixed situation in the energy sector, with pro-European legislative changes and positive developments in increasing energy efficiency and renewable energy occurring alongside rising coal consumption. The war reversed some of the positive energy trends, because many renewable energy facilities were destroyed or ceased operation, while power outages caused by shelling of energy infrastructure forced businesses and civilians to use fossil fuel generators. However, after the war, Ukraine is expected to continue decarbonizing the sector, accelerating economic growth and ensuring long-term economic

Table 2.32 SWOT analysis of Ukraine.

Strengths	Weaknesses
• Developed Energy Strategy aiming for the decarbonization of Ukraine's energy sector by 2050. • Engagement in developing its commercial potential and striving for smooth integration with EU energy markets. • Engagement in global energy equipment production chains fostering economic growth and technological advancement. • Obtaining EU candidate status in June 2022. • Initiation of EU accession negotiations in December 2023. • International support and financial backing for pro-European reforms. • Important transport routes passing through Ukrainian territory.	• The most energy- and resource-intensive economy in Europe. • Ruin of many industrial plants in eastern and southeastern Ukraine due to the ongoing war. • Ongoing armed conflict on parts of Ukrainian territory. • Loss of Crimea and Donbas. • Corruption, nepotism, and oligarchic rule. • Devastation caused by prolonged conflict. • Significant demographic losses. • Unstable political situation.
Opportunities	**Threats**
• Rebuilding the industrial sector offers an opportunity to eliminate past dependencies on fossil fuels and dirty technologies, replacing oligarchic control with a multi-stakeholder ownership structure. • Ongoing threat of another outbreak of war, even after signing a peace treaty. • Secession of Crimea and Donbas from Ukraine. • Loss of access to most Black Sea ports. • Continuous threat of war may prevent NATO accession.	• Even after signing a peace treaty, Ukraine may be threatened by another outbreak of war. • Secession of Crimea and Donbas from Ukraine. • Loss of access to most Black Sea ports. • The continuous threat of war may prevent Ukraine from joining NATO.

Source: Own study.

resilience, given the significant potential for developing wind, solar, and biomass energy (Table 2.32).

In summary, Ukraine can rapidly accelerate the development of renewable energy sources by ensuring the further adoption of legal and regulatory frameworks in line with the EU Green Deal, including the introduction of market-based energy prices for all consumers. The development of electricity storage and balancing rapid energy production with the potential use of natural gas, biomethane, and hydrogen is also necessary. In conclusion, under favorable investment conditions and stakeholder engagement in reforms, Ukraine can meet its own energy needs and supply low-emission and renewable energy to the EU.

Notes

1 This group includes industries such as machinery, metal processing, chemical and petrochemical, energy, light industry, food, building materials, forestry, and wood processing. These industries, except for the last four, were integrated into the economy of the former USSR and depended on the import of raw materials and resources. The utilization rate of the aforementioned production capacities in 2000 was 61%.
2 These include the Agreement on the Customs Union of January 6, 1995; the Agreement on the Establishment of the Association of Russia and Belarus of April 2, 1996; the Agreement on the Union of Belarus and Russia of April 2, 1997; and the Agreement on the Establishment of the Union State of December 8, 1999.
3 In 1997, 65.1% of all employees in the economy were employed in state-owned enterprises, and these entities accounted for 61% of total industrial production.
4 According to World Bank data, inflation in Belarus increased from 52.7% in 1996 to 293.7% in 1999.
5 UNCTAD data shows that the negative foreign trade balance rose to USD 1.32 billion in 2000. This was caused by the Russian economic crisis, which made the export of Belarusian goods to Russia unprofitable and increased the costs of importing raw materials and semi-products from Russia due to the depreciation of the Russian ruble.
6 In 1997, the profitability in the industry was 13.2%, in 1998 it was 14.5%, and in 1999 it was 17.1%.
7 The share of the machinery and metal processing industry decreased from 34.2% in 1991 to 20.5% in 2000, and the number of people employed in research units dropped threefold (from 59,300 to 22,300).
8 Gazprom and Beltransgaz signed the contracts for gas supply to and transit across Belarus from 2012 through 2014. Gazprom and the State Property Committee of the Republic of Belarus also entered into the purchase and sale agreement for the remaining 50% stake in Beltransgaz.
9 Approximately 20% of Georgian citizens live outside the country, and the amount of money transfers through the banking system exceeds USD 1 billion.
10 In 1990, 29% of the total Moldovan industry, in which 36% of the republic's total workforce was occupied, with a share of 48% of the total value of the republic's industrial and manufacturing assets, was strongly linked to the country's industry. Notably, at that time two-fifths of the economic potential of the MSR and one-seventh of the population was located on the territory of the now unrecognized Transnistrian Moldovan Republic.
11 Until 1993, the Soviet ruble was the legal currency in Moldova.
12 The program did not take into account the country's capacity to leverage its economic potential, which was significantly weaker than the then average for the countries of the former USSR.
13 Following the recommendations of the MFR, between 1993 and 1999, the Moldovan government pursued a restrictive monetary policy aimed at healing the financial system by reducing budget and household spending.
14 Own calculations based on World Bank data.
15 In 2001, Moldova became a member of the World Trade Organization (WTO).
16 Own calculations based on World Bank data.
17 Between January 2012 and November 2014, three Moldovan banks, Banca de Economii, Banca Socială and Unibank, were involved in a money laundering scheme. The banks issued loans to front companies, after which part of the money was returned to Moldova to secure new loans while the other part of the money was stolen. Most of the money was laundered with the involvement of two Latvian banks – the so-called Core Laundering Mechanism.
18 Over this four-year period, industrial production contracted year by year. According to Ukrstat data, the decline was 4.3% in 2013 compared to 2012, 10.1% in 2014 compared to 2013, and 12.3% in 2015 compared to 2014.

19 According to Ukrstat, the largest drop in domestic demand occurred in 2015 compared to 2014, amounting to 19.8%.
20 According to the Central Bank of Ukraine, foreign debt increased by 12.6% between 2012 and 2014. The currency structure of debt in 2015 was as follows: 78.2% in US dollars, 11.4% in euros, and 1.9% in Russian rubles.
21 According to the Central Bank of Ukraine, gold reserves in 2015 were 49.3% lower than in 2012, and foreign exchange reserves were 54.2% lower.
22 According to the Central Bank of Ukraine, FDI in 2013 was 53.6% of the value in 2012. During 2014–2015, it was only 5.4% of the value in 2012.
23 For more details, see Chapter 3.

References

ACRA (2018). Oil dependence recovers along with Azerbaijan economy coming out of stagnation. https://www.acra-ratings.ru/research/838/?lang=en accessed on 12.04.2024.
Amambayeva, E. (2004). Two missions - one problem. *Ekonomicheskoe Obozrenie*, 38(582) of October 22. http://logos-pres.md/arhiv-nomerov/
Analytical Center for the Government of the Russian Federation (2019). Georgia: features of economic growth. *Bulletin on Current Trends in the World Economy*, 46, 15–18.
Andrusevych, A., Andrusevych, N. & Mishchuk, Z. (2021). Greening the Eastern Partnership: regional dimension of the future perspectives. Discussion Paper, FES EU Office and the FES Regional Office Dialogue Eastern Europe.
Armbanks (2010). Armenian government draws lessons from crisis situation – PM. http://www.armbanks.am/2010/05/22/11508/ accessed on 27.3.2024.
Ashotova, A.L. (2016). *Economic consequences of the international migration of skilled labor (on the example of the Republic of Armenia).* Dissertation, Russian-Armenian University, Yerevan, 70–71.
Aslund, A. (2019) Ukraine's affairs are much better than they seem. https://nv.ua/opinion/ekonomika-ukrainy-chego-ozhidat-ot-zelenskogo-poslednie-novosti50063099.html accessed on 27.03.2024.
Пылин А.Г. (2010). Экономическое развитие Грузии в условиях «двойного внешнего шока». Мир перемен, 2010, № 2. imepi-eurasia.ru/mir.php#pylin210
Avalani, M. (2011). Modernization of customs control in Georgia: changes, results, prospects. *Caucasus and Globalization*, 5(3–4), 73–84.
Batranciuc, D.D. (2011). Historical and economic peculiarities of the development of the banking system of the Republic of Moldova. *Voprosy ekonomiki i parvo*, 5, 177.
BBC (2011). Georgia is privatizing hospitals and clinics. https://www.bbc.com/russian/international/2011/07/110704 accessed on 19.04.2024.
BDD (2021). Basin data and directions. Ministry of Finance of Georgia, Tbilisi.
Bendukizhze, K. & Saakashvili, M. (2007). Great renaissance: Georgia. https://old.inliberty.ru/library/667-Velikoe-vozrozhdenie-Gruziya accessed on 19.04.2024.
Beridze, T. & Mekvabishvili, E. (2018). "Thorny path" of economic reforms in post-communist Georgia: retrospective and perstektive. *Ekonomist*, 1, 26.
Bertelsmann Stiftung (2020). BTI 2020 country report Armenia. Bertelsmann Stiftung. https://www.ecoi.net/en/file/local/2029509/country_report_2020_ARM.pdf accessed on 12.02.2024.
Brantsevich, T. (2022). Despite sanctions, Belarus confidently continues to move towards achieving the Sustainable Development Goals. https://www.sb.by/articles/tseli-i-prepyatstviya.html accessed on 12.02.2024.
Burakovsky, I.V. & Novitsky, V.E. (2003). *Economic transformations in Ukraine. Political and economic transformations in Russia and Ukraine.* Three Squares, Moscow.
Calac, D. (2010). Balance of payments and investment hunger. *Logos Press Economic Review*, 14, 8.

Сауран (2015). Georgia: economic development of the country in the 1990s. http://cc-sauran.kz/rubriki/economika/113-gruziya-ekonomicheskoe-razvitie-v-1990.html accessed on 19.04.2024.
Central Bank of Armenia (2023). National sustainable finance roadmap of Armenia. https://www.cba.am/EN/pmessagesannouncements/National_Sustainable_Finance_Roadmap_06.10.2023.pdf accessed on 13.02.2024.
CES (2023). Ukrainian refugees: how many are there, their intentions & return prospects. Second wave. https://ces.org.ua/en/refugees-from-ukraine-final-report/ accessed on: 25.03.2023
CSAP (2021). Climate change strategy and action plan. https://policy.asiapacificenergy.org/node/4445 accessed on 13.02.2024.
Data Statistical Committee of the Republic of Armenia (2024). https://statbank.armstat.am/ accessed on 27.3.2024.
Day, T., Gonzales-Zuñiga, S. & Lui, S. (2021). Decarbonisation scenarios for the transport sector in Georgia. New Climate Institute. https://newclimate.org/resources/publications accessed on 26.02.2024.
Dergachev, V.A. (2000). East European Geopolitical Knot: Ukraine between East and West. Problems of Post-Soviet Countries, Vyp. 1, IMEPI RAS, Moscow, p. 19.
Dunamalyan, N.A., Davtyan, V.S. & Tavadyan, A.A. (2023). Economic development as a method of foreign policy risk compensation: the case of Armenia. *Journal of International Analytics*, 14(1), 92–110. (in Russ.) https://doi.org/10.46272/2587-8476-2023-14-1-92-110
Echo of the Caucasus (2015). Georgia: economic results of the year. https://www.ekhokavkaza.com/a/26772772.html accessed on 10.09.2023.
Energy Community (2019). Implementation report. https://www.energy-community.org/implementation/IR2019.html accessed on 28.01.2024.
Esebua, N. (2020). Economic crisis in Georgia: the banking system is going into the stone age. http://www.banki.ru/news/bankpress/?id=1180446 accessed on 20.09.2020.
EU4Climate (2020). Armenia country profile. https://eu4climate.eu/wp-content/uploads/countries/EU4Climate-ARMENIA.pdf accessed on 13.02. 2024.
EU4Environment (2021). Spre o Transformare Verde a Republicii Moldova, Analiza situației din 2021 (Towards green transformation of the Republic of Moldova: State of Play in 2021). https://www.eu4environment.org/app/uploads/2022/03/Report-Green-Growth-Indicators-Republic-Moldova-2021-ROM.pdf
EurAsia Daily (2016). Baku syndrome: a large-scale crisis in the Caspian sea is inevitable? https://eadaily.com/ru/news/2016/01/29/bakinskiy-sindrom-masshtabnyy-krizis-na-kaspii-neminuem accessed on 2.09.2023.
European Bank for Reconstruction and Development (2010). Transition report 2010. Recovery and reform. London, 116–117.
Expert-Group (2020). *Raportul de Stare Țării*, https://www.expert-grup.org/ro/biblioteca/raportul-de-stare-a-tarii accessed on: 30.11.2023
Fitch Ratings (2024). Armenia. https://www.fitchratings.com/research/sovereigns/armenia-08-02-2024 accessed on 27.03.2024.
Fokina, L. (2017). 25 years of Independence of the Republic of Moldova: main results. https://www.imemo.ru/files/File/magazines/rossia_i_novay/2017_02/25Let_nezavisimosty_Fokina.pdf accessed on 5.10.2020.
Gabrielian, S. (2018). Investment firm sues Armenia over railway deal. Radio liberty. https://www.azatutyun.am/a/29472531.html accessed on 28.01.2024.
Georgia Online (2022). Georgian currency strengthened by more than 15% against the dollar. https://www.apsny.ge/2022/eco/1644348074.php accessed on 16.05.2024.
GLOBSEC (2023). The green recovery of Ukraine: a challenging but nonnegotiable way to succeed in the world of tomorrow. https://www.globsec.org/ accessed on 27.02.2024.
Government of Armenia (2014). Republic of Armenia 2014-2025 Strategic Program of Prospective Development. https://www.gov.am/en/prsp/ accessed on: 01.12.2023

Government of Georgia (2018). Social-economic development strategy of Georgia "GEORGIA 2020." https://www.adb.org/sites/default/files/linked-documents/cps-geo-2014-2018-sd-01.pdf accessed on 10.05.2024.

Grigoriev, L., Kondratiev, S., Salikhov, M. (2008). Difficult way out of the transformation crisis (the case of Georgia). *Economic Issues*, 10, 83–86.

Harutyunyan S. (2019). Iran looks to boost gas supplies to Armenia. Radio Liberty. https://www.azatutyun.am/a/30045968.html accessed on 28.01.2024.

Hasanli, A. (2021). Economic outcomes of 2021: Azerbaijan takes new heights. https://report.az/en/business/economic-results-of-2021-azerbaijan-takes-new-heights/ accessed on 11.04.2024.

Heinrich-Böll-Stiftung (2023). Izolacja i represje na Białorusi: konsekwencje dla polityki środowiskowej. https://pl.boell.org/pl/2023/01/19/izolacja-i-represje-na-bialorusi-konsekwencje-dla-polityki-srodowiskowej accessed on 22.01.2024.

ICI (2023). Georgia's path to a carbon-neutral future https://www.international-climate-initiative.com/en/iki-media/news/georgias-path-to-a-carbon-neutral-future/accessed on: 01.12.2023

IEA (2016). Scaling up renewable energy program for Armenia (SREP Armenia). https://www.iea.org/policies/5674-scaling-up-renewable-energy-program-for-armenia-srep-armenia?country=Armenia&qs=armenia accessed on 12.2.2024.

IEA (2018). IAEA country nuclear power profiles: Armenia, 2018 Edition. International Atomic Energy Agency, Vienna. https://www-pub.iaea.org/MTCD/Publications/PDF/cnpp2018/countryprofiles/Armenia/Armenia.html

IEA (2019a). *World Energy Balances 2019*. International Energy Agency, Paris. https://doi.org/10.1787/3a876031-en accessed on 13.02.2024.

IEA (2019b). *World Energy Statistics 2019*. International Energy Agency, Paris. https://doi.org/10.1787/2e828dea-en accessed on 14.02.2024.

IEA (2020). Belarus energy profile. https://www.iea.org/reports/belarus-energy-profile#key-energy-data accessed on 23.02.2024.

Ilex (2021). There was no collapse. How the Belarusian economy fared in 2021. https://ilex.by/kollapsa-ne-sluchilos-kak-ekonomika-belarusi-prozhila-2021 god/ accessed on 19.04.2024.

Ilex (2022). How the Belarusian economy shrank by 4.7% in 2022 and what will happen next. https://ilex.by/kak-belorusskaya-ekonomika-szhalas-na-4-7-v-2022-godu-i-chto-budet-dalshe/ accessed on 19.04.2024.

IMF (2021). Republic of Azerbaijan. IMF Country Report No. 21/278 https://www.elibrary.imf.org/view/journals/002/2021/278/article-A001-en.xml accessed on: 01.12.2023

Institute of Economics of the National Academy of Sciences of Belarus (2016a). Analytical note "Results of socio-economic development of the Republic of Belarus in 2016." http://economics.basnet.by/index/20 accessed on 27.03.2024.

Institute of Economics of the National Academy of Sciences of Belarus (2016b). Socio-economic development of the Republic of Belarus in 2011-2015 and measures to ensure sustainable balanced development of the economy in the future. Minsk, pp. 6–7.

Institute of Economics of the National Academy of Sciences of Belarus (2019). On the results of socio-economic development of the Republic of Belarus in 2018. http://economics.basnet.by/files/2018_Itogi.pdf accessed on 19.04.2024.

International Bank for Reconstruction and Development / The World Bank (2013). DOING BUSINESS2013 Smarter Regulations for Small and Medium-Size Enterprises. https://www.doingbusiness.org/content/dam/doingBusiness/media/Annual-Reports/English/DB13-full-report.pdf accessed on: 30.11.2023

Ivanov G. (2019) , Ukraine: economy in datails, Kommersant Dengi, nr 7 from 13.03.2019. https://www.kommersant.ru/doc/3898920.

JSC Kommersant (2017). Rich oil past. https://www.kommersant.ru/doc/3229878 accessed on 12.04.2024.

Knoema (2024). Number of arrivals. https://knoema.ru/atlas/Armenia/ accessed on 4.04.2024.

Kotulewicz, K. (2000). Economic reforms in Moldova in the 1990s. *Zeszyty Naukowe Akademii Ekonomicznej w Krakowie*, 555, 97–108.

Kotulewicz, K. (2002). *Uwarunkowania i przebieg transformacji systemowej w Republice Mołdawii*. Krakow University of Economics, Dostępne w Archiwum UEK - nr 356/544.

Kotulewicz, K. (2015). *Geostrategiczny wybór Rosji u zarania trzeciego tysiąclecia. Tom II. Unia Europejska jako partner strategiczny Federacji Rosyjskiej na początku XXI wieku. Cześć II. Aspekt gospodarczy*. Wydawnictwo Uniwersytetu Jagiellońskiego, Kraków, 63–64.

Kotulewicz-Wisińska, K. (2017). Moldova and Ukraine between the Russian Federation and the European Union. The economic aspect. *Nowa Polityka Wschodnia*, 2(13), 61–70.

Kotulewicz-Wisińska, K. & Gródek-Szostak, Z. (2021). *Determinanty i kierunki systemowego wsparcia sektora małej i średniej przedsiębiorczości w państwach Partnerstwa Wschodniego*. Wydawnictwo Adam Marszałek, Toruń.

Losyakina, Y.V. & Gospodarik, C.G. (2022). Analysis and forecasting of the economic growth of the Republic of Belarus after Covid-19. https://elib.bsu.by/bitstream/123456789/285730/1/79-85.pdf accessed on 14.04.2024.

Mahmudov, K. (2023). Economy of Azerbaijan in 2022. The most used and remembered word is inflation. https://turan.az/en/macroeconomy/economy-of-azerbaijan-in-2022-the-most-used-and-remembered-word-is-inflation-773957 accessed on 11.04.2024.

Ministry of Ecology and Natural Resources Republic of Azerbaijan (2015). Third National Communication to the United Nations Framework Convention on Climate Change. Republic of Azerbaijan. https://unfccc.int/sites/default/files/resource/azenc3.pdf.

Ministry of Energy (2023). With support of Ministry of Energy and German Federal Ministry of Education and Research, educational initiative to implement EU Green Deal launched in Ukraine. https://www.kmu.gov.ua/en/news/za-pidtrymky-minenerho-ta-federalnoho-ministerstva-osvity-ta-naukovykh-doslidzhen-nimechchyny-v-ukraini-startuie-osvitnia-initsiatyva-z-vprovadzhennia-zelenoho-kursu-eu-greendeal accessed on 30.11.2023

Ministry of Energy of Ukraine (2023). Report for COP28. Clean energy roadmap: from reconstruction to decarbonization in Ukraine. https://www.pnnl.gov/sites/default/files/media/file/Ukraine%20NZW%20COP28%20report%202023.pdf

Ministry of Environmental Protection and Agriculture of Georgia (2023). Georgia`s long-term low emission development strategy. Tbilisi, p. 10.

Misala, J.(2008). *Współpraca gospodarcza Polski ze wschodnimi krajami sąsiedzkimi oraz Estonią, Łotwą i Mołdawią. Dotychczasowy rozwój i perspektywy*. Radom, 276–277.

Moldova (2006). A guide for entrepreneurs. UNIDO, Warsaw, 30.

Mukha, A. (2013). Review of the Belarusian economy in 2012. Forecast for 2013 (I). https://nmnby.eu/news/analytics/5090.html accessed on 18.04.2024.

Mustafajewa, K. (2017). Has the Azerbaijani economy found the bottom? https://www.bbc.com/russian/features-38899321 accessed on 11.04.2024.

National Bureau of Statistics of the Republic of Moldova (2009). Socio-Economic Development of the Republic of Moldova. Chisinau.

National Bureau of Statistics of the Republic of Moldova (2014). https://statistica.gov.md/en/gross-domestic-product-in-the-republic-of-moldova-in-2014-9497_2546.html accessed on: 01.12.2023

National Bureau of Statistics of the Republic of Moldova (2018). https://statistica.gov.md/en/gross-domestic-product-in-the-republic-of-moldova-in-2018-9497_1439.html accessed on: 01.12.2023

National Bureau of Statistics of the Republic of Moldova (2020). https://statistica.gov.md/en/statistic_domains accessed: 01.12.2023

National Bureau of Statistics of the Republic of Moldova (2022). https://statistica.gov.md/en/statistic_indicator_details/12 accessed on: 01.12.2023

National Statistical Committee of the Republic of Belarus (2023). https://www.belstat.gov.by/en/ofitsialnaya-statistika/real-sector-of-the-economy/ accessed on: 30.11.2023.

National Statistics Office of Georgia (2023). https://www.geostat.ge/en accessed on: 30.11.2023.

OECD (2018). *Inventory of energy subsidies in the EU's Eastern Partnership countries (Green finance and investment).* OECD Publishing, Paris. https://dx.doi.org/10.1787/9789264284319-en

OECD (2019). Mining and green growth in the EECCA region pre-publication version. https://www.oecd.org/en/publications/mining-and-green-growth-in-the-eecca-region_1926a45a-en.html accessed on 28.02.2024.

OECD (2021). *Sustainable infrastructure for low-carbon development in the EU Eastern Partnership: Hotspot analysis and needs assessment.* [in.] *Green finance and investment.* OECD Publishing, Paris. https://doi.org/10.1787/c1b2b68d-en accessed on 13.02.2024.

Oraghvelidze, I. (2024). Georgia-2023. Economy: the year of Europe with a Russian accent. https://www.ekhokavkaza.com/a/32760930.html accessed on 16.05.2024.

Osipova, I.I. (2005). State program for overcoming poverty in Ukraine. The main results of monitoring: methods, criteria, results, problems and prospects. http://www.insee.fr/en/insee-statistique-publique/colloques/pauvrete/pdf/poverty_UA_Osypova_RU.pdf

Papava, V. (2010). Socio-economic development of Georgia: a view of the medium-term perspective. https://www.researchgate.net/publication/316431030 accessed on 19.04.2024.

Pavlovets, Y., & Shiptenko, C. (2017). Economics of Belarus. Historical essays of the XX-XXI centuries. Book World, Moscow.

PBServices (2024). Georgia in 2023: a report on the country's economy. https://pbservices.ge/ru/blog/gruziya-otchet-ob-ekonomike-strany/#section_7 accessed on 16.05.2024.

Percisncaia, N.P. & Dodon, S.V. (2001). Privatization and its impact on the state budget (experience of the Republic of Moldova). https://cyberleninka.ru/article/n/privatizatsiya-i-eyo-vliyanie-na-gosudarstvennyy-byudzhet-opyt-respubliki-moldova/viewer accessed on 5.10.2020.

Petryshyn, H. (2022). The economic situation in Ukraine before the outbreak of the Russo-Ukrainian war, pp. 58–69, https://cejsh.icm.edu.pl/cejsh/element/bwmeta1.element.ojs-doi-10_34765_sp_0322_a04/c/ articles-2195816.pdf accessed on 17.05.2024.

Poisic, M. (2008). Industry of Moldova: yesterday, today, tomorrow. Information-analytical portal "AVA". Chisinau. https://ava.md/2008/07/30/promyshlennost-moldovy-vchera-segodnya/ accessed on 15.09.2023.

Report News Agency (2022). Azerbaijan's economy in 2022: challenges, achievements and expectations. https://report.az/en/finance/azerbaijan-s-economy-in-2022-challenges-achievements-and-expectations/ accessed on 11.04.2024.

Reuters (2015). Georgia's GDP growth slowed to 0.5% in Jan 15/14. https://www.reuters.com/article/georgia-gdp-idRUL5N0W14CB20150227 accessed on 10.09.2023.

Rustamov, E.S. (2010). Macroeconomic policy and institutional development in oil-exporting countries (on the example of Azerbaijan), Abstract of a dissertation for the degree of Doctor of Economics, Russian Academy of Sciences Institute of Economics, Moscow 2010, p. 27. https://www.econ.msu.ru/cmt2/lib/a/1711/file/Rustamov.pdf accessed on 11.04.2024.

SEDS (2022). Government of Azerbaijan 2022a 'Republic of Azerbaijan Socio-Economic Strategy for 2022-2026,' approved on July 21, 2022. https://static.president.az/upload/Files/2022/07/22/5478ed13955fb35f0715325d7f76a8ea_3699216.pdf

Severin, I. (2000). Moldova - the only country in the CIS with negative economic growth. "Ekonomicheskoe obozrenie", No. 35 (387) of September 22.

Shurubovich, A. (2012). Socio-economic development of Belarus: stages, trends, problems. https://www.imemo.ru/files/File/magazines/rossia_i_novay/2012_02/ASUR_social.pdf accessed on 20.03.2024.

Simonyan, Y. (2005). The future of the Georgian economy is not in endless privatizations. *Nezavisimaya Gazeta*, July 5. http://www.ng.ru/ideas/2005-07-05/11future.html accessed on 19.04.2024.

Sinitsina, I. (2006). Poverty and ways to overcome it in the CIS countries, p. 146, http://www.research.by/webroot/delivery/files/ecowest/2006n1r05.pdf accessed on 27.03.2024.

Sinyak, N.G. (2002). State and trends in the development of enterprise property in the Republic of Belarus. http://www.nestor.minsk.by/sn/2002/36/sn23622.html, accessed on 2.08.2020.

Sputnik News (2017). The ups and downs of the Armenian economy over the past 17 years. https://am.sputniknews.ru/20170709/vzlety-i-padeniya-ehkonomiki-armenii-za-poslednie-17-let-7887171.html accessed on 27.03.2024.

State Statistical Committee of the Republic of Azerbaijan (2022). https://www.stat.gov.az/menu/13/?lang=en accessed on: 30.11.2023

State Statistics Service of Ukraine, Kyiv (2024). https://stat.gov.ua/en accessed: 01.012.2023

Statistical Committee of the Republic of Armenia. (2024). https://armstat.am/en/ accessed on 4.4.2024.

Statistical Yearbook of Armenia (2016). https://armstat.am/en/?nid=586&year=2016 accessed on: 30.11.2023

Statistical Yearbook of Armenia (2020). https://armstat.am/en/?nid=586&year=2020

Statistical Yearbook of Armenia (2023). https://armstat.am/en/?nid=586&year=2023 accessed on: 30.11.2023

Stronski, P. (2017). *Armenia at twenty-five: a rough ride*. Carnegie Endowment for International Peace, Washington, DC.

Szymański, D. (2020). *Państwo „niewykorzystanych szans". Nasz sąsiad znów ma poważne problemy.* https://businessinsider.com.pl/finanse/makroekonomia/ukraina-audyt-gospodarczy-raport-pkb-za-2020-r-i-ruchy-wojsk-rosji/bdrtgh0 accessed on 17.05.2024.

TAdviser (2023). Economy of Azerbaijan. https://www.tadviser.ru/index.php/Статья:Экономика_Азербайжана accessed on 11.04.2024.

TERT AM (2013). Yes, there is an oligopoly in Armenia - final press conference of Tigran Sargsyan (live broadcast). https://www.tert.am/ru/news/2013/12/27/tigransargsyan-oligopolia/1498299 accessed on 27.03.2024.

The Global Economy (2015). Ukraine: shadow economy, percent of GDP. https://www.theglobaleconomy.com/Ukraine/shadow_economy/ accessed on 25.03.2023.

Transparency International (2009). Corruption perception index. https://www.transparency.org/reaserch/cpi/cpi_2009/0 accessed on 25.03.2024.

Tytysh, G. & Makarenko, O. (2015). Former Minister of Education of Georgia: the main customer of education reform is society. https://life.pravda.com.ua/society/2015/01/11/187439/ accessed on 19.04.2024.

UNCTAD conference (2021). Fifteenth session of the United Nations Conference on Trade and Development (UNCTAD 15). 03–07 October 2021. Bridgetown, Barbados and Geneva, Switzerland https://unctad.org/meeting/fifteenth-session-united-nations-conference-trade-and-development-unctad-15 accessed on: 01.12.2023

UNDP (2023a). The low emissions development programme was approved, bringing Moldova one step closer towards a carbon-free economy. https://www.undp.org/moldova/press-releases/low-emissions-development-programme-was-approved-bringing-moldova-one-step-closer-towards-carbon-free-economy accessed on 27.02.2024.

UNDP (2023b). Towards a green transition of the energy sector of Ukraine. https://www.undp.org/sites/g/files/zskgke326/files/2023-06/undp-ua-energy-damageassessment.pdf accessed on 27.02.2024.

UNDP (2024a). Human Development Report 2023–2024. https://moldova.un.org/en/265691-human-development-report-2023-2024 accessed on 17.04.2024.

UNDP (2024b). The Integrated National Energy and Climate Plan – a roadmap for green economy and energy – was publicly consulted. https://www.undp.org/moldova accessed on 27.02.2024.

UNESCO (2022). Azerbaijan 2030: national priorities for socio-economic development. https://www.unesco.org/creativity/en/policy-monitoring-platform/azerbaijan-2030-national-priorities-socio-economic-development accessed: 01.12.2023

Vardomsky, L.B. (2012). (ed.). *Social and Economic Development of PostSoviet Countries: Summary of 20 Years*. Moscow: IE RAN. Original in Russian (Вардомский Л. Б. Социально-экономическое развитие постсоветских стран: Итоги двадцатилетия. М.: ИЭ РАН).

Vardomsky, L.B., Pylin, A.G. & Ilyina, M.Y. (2016). *Economy of Armenia: ideas, models and development results*. Russian Academy of Science, Institute of Economics, https://inecon.org/docs/Vardomsky_Pylin_Ilyina_paper_2016.pdf accessed on: 20.11.2023
Vlasenko, M. (2018). Economic development in Belarus: quality of growth and efficiency of distribution of basic resources. http://www.research.by/webroot/delivery/files/wp2018r01.pdf. accessed on 18.04.2024.
WNP (2020). *Azerbejdżan ma coraz więcej gazu*, https://www.wnp.pl/gazownictwo/azerbejdzan-ma-coraz-wiecej-gazu,401456.html,accessed accessed on 5.04.2024.
World Bank (n.d.), Enterprise surveys: infrastructure. https://www.enterprisesurveys.org/en/data/exploretopics/infrastructure accessed on 28.01.2024.
World Bank (2017). Future Armenia: systematic country diagnostic. https://elibrary.worldbank.org/doi/abs/10.1596/29791 accessed on 8.01.2024.
World Bank (2021a). World development indicators (database). https://datacatalog.worldbank.org/dataset/world-development-indicators accessed on 14.01.2024.
World Bank (2021b) National Statistics Office of Georgia (Geostat, 2023)
World Bank Group (2023). Azerbaijan. Country climate and development report (English). Washington, DC. http://documents.worldbank.org/curated/en/099112723161524095/P17904806938f5083093a707fa0352e87a5 accessed on 16.02.2024.
World Economic Forum (2019). https://www3.weforum.org/docs/WEF_TheGlobalCompetitivenessReport2019.pdf accessed on: 01.12.2023
Yeghiazaryan, A. (2007). Georgia: structural problems of the economy and Turkish economic expansion (1994–2007). REGNUM, Yerevan – Moscow,7, 17–30.
Yurgens, I.Y., & Romov, R.B. (2023). Enabling green integration and building a common sustainable development space in the EAEU. MGIMO, Moskov.
Zimmerman, M.A. (2013). Resiliency theory: a strengths-based approach to research and practice for adolescent health. *Health Education & Behavior*, 40(4), 381–383.
Żochowski, P. (2021). Bolesne sankcje sektorowe UE wobec Białorusi. Ośrodek Studiów Wschodnich. https://www.osw.waw.pl/pl/publikacje/analizy/2021-06-25/bolesne-sankcje-sektorowe-ue-wobec-bialorusi accessed on 27.03.2024.

3 Situation of the Eastern Partnership countries in the context of sustainable development

Resource and environmental productivity of economy

This section analyzes the issue of productivity in the use of natural and environmental resources in the Eastern Partnership (EaP) countries. In this context, nine indicators of environmental resource productivity were examined: the size of greenhouse gas (GHG) emissions, CO_2 productivity, final energy consumption, energy intensity, the share of renewable energy in final energy consumption, the volume of waste generation and recycling, and the volume of fertilizer use and water consumption. These indicators provide information on the efficiency of energy and natural resource use in economic activities, encompassing both production and consumption. The results illustrate the key challenges associated with the transition to a low-carbon and resource-efficient economy.

1. **Greenhouse gas emissions.** Rising greenhouse gas emissions have serious environmental consequences and increase vulnerability to climate change. The increase in greenhouse gas emissions results in higher temperatures, degradation of climatic conditions, and an increased frequency and intensity of extreme weather events. Of particular interest is carbon dioxide (CO_2), which constitutes the largest portion of greenhouse gases. Converting all other greenhouse gases—methane (CH_4), nitrous oxide (N_2O), hydrofluorocarbons (HFCs), perfluorocarbons (PFCs), and sulfur hexafluoride (SF_6)—into carbon dioxide equivalents (CO_2e) allows for their comparison and the determination of their individual and total contributions to global warming. Emission intensity is the average emissions of a given pollutant from a specific source relative to the intensity of a particular activity. This metric is also used to compare the environmental impact of different fuels or activities. Terms such as "emission factor" and "carbon intensity" are often used interchangeably (World Bank, 2023b). Statistics on greenhouse gas emissions, sourced from www.climatewatchdata.org, cover the period 2014–2020.
2. **Productivity (emission efficiency) of CO_2.** Productivity of greenhouse gas emissions is an indicator that reflects the correlation between emissions and the dynamics of economic development. This indicator shows the amount of economic output, expressed as gross domestic product (GDP) in USD, relative to a

DOI: 10.4324/9781003486732-5

certain amount of greenhouse gas production. For example, an increase in productivity means that the production of a unit of GDP corresponds to a reduction in greenhouse gas emissions. Conversely, a decrease in productivity indicates that the production of a unit of GDP corresponds to an increase in greenhouse gas emissions. Productivity is calculated as the ratio of GDP in constant 2015 prices to greenhouse gas emissions. Data for GDP in constant prices are sourced from the World Bank website and cover the period 2014–2020.

3. **Final energy consumption.** The development of the green economy is significantly influenced by how energy is used. Reducing the consumption of fossil fuels in primary energy production leads to lower CO_2 emissions and helps maintain a clean environment. Energy productivity is an indicator that reflects the relationship between energy consumption and economic development. This indicator shows the amount of economic output, expressed as GDP, relative to a certain amount of energy consumption. For example, an increase in energy productivity means that producing a unit of GDP corresponds to a reduction in energy consumption. The productivity index is calculated as the quotient of GDP at purchasing power parity (PPP) in constant 2017 prices and the amount of primary energy production. The data are sourced from the websites of the Central Statistical Offices of the Eastern Partnership Program countries and cover the period 2014–2022, except for Belarus and Ukraine, for which data are available from 2014 to 2020.
4. **Energy intensity.** Energy intensity measures the amount of energy consumed per unit of GDP. The energy intensity index is calculated as the ratio of total energy consumption, expressed in grams of oil equivalent, to GDP at constant 2017 prices. A reduction in energy intensity indicates that less energy is needed to produce the same amount of GDP and is associated with an increase in energy efficiency. Additionally, a reduction in energy intensity implies that economic growth has been accompanied by more efficient use of energy resources. The data are sourced from the websites of the Central Statistical Offices of the Eastern Partnership Program countries and cover the period 2014–2022, except for Belarus and Ukraine, for which data are available from 2014 to 2020.
5. **Share of renewable energy in final energy consumption**. Renewable energy sources provide an alternative to fossil fuels and contribute to reducing greenhouse gas emissions. They diversify energy supplies and reduce dependence on volatile oil and gas markets. The data are sourced from the websites of the Central Statistical Offices of the Eastern Partnership Program countries and cover the following years: Armenia (2014–2021), Azerbaijan, Georgia, and Moldova (2014–2022), Belarus (2014–2019), and Ukraine (2014–2020).
6. **Waste production.** Waste refers to products or substances that, once consumed, are no longer suitable for use in human activities such as production or consumption. Waste is a significant source of environmental pollution. The data are sourced from the websites of the Central Statistical Offices of the Eastern Partnership Program countries and cover the period 2014–2022, with exceptions for Georgia (2015–2022, municipal waste only) and Ukraine (2014–2020).

7. **Waste recycling.** Waste utilization refers to the reintroduction of waste into the economic cycle as secondary raw materials or processed for use as intermediate or finished energy products. Waste utilization plays a crucial role in maintaining a healthy environment. By reintroducing waste into the economic cycle, the consumption of natural resources is reduced, thereby lessening the environmental impact. The data are sourced from the websites of the Central Statistical Offices of the Eastern Partnership Program countries and cover the period 2014–2022, with exceptions for Georgia (no data on waste recycling) and Ukraine (data available 2014–2020).
8. **Use of fertilizers.** The sustainability of agricultural systems is a crucial element of green growth. One aspect of progress toward green growth can be evaluated by analyzing the intensity of mineral fertilizer use, as intensive use of nitrates or phosphates can cause environmental pollution. In international practice, fertilizer balances are conducted to estimate the pollution potential of mineral fertilizers. The data are sourced from the websites of the Central Statistical Offices of the Eastern Partnership Program countries and cover the period 2014–2022, with exceptions for Armenia, where data are available only for 2014–2017.
9. **Use of water.** The rational use of water resources is fundamental to ensuring sustainable socioeconomic development. Water is essential not only for stimulating agricultural sector development but also for maintaining public health at a satisfactory level. Efficient use of scarce water resources is a key indicator of progress towards achieving green economic growth. To assess the relationship between water consumption and economic dynamics, water productivity is calculated. This indicator shows the value of national output, expressed as GDP in USD, derived from a given amount of water used. For example, an increase in water productivity signifies that the production of one dollar of GDP was achieved with a reduced amount of water consumption. The data are sourced from the websites of the Central Statistical Offices of the EaP countries and cover the period 2014–2022.

Resource and environmental productivity of economy in terms of individual Eastern Partnership countries

Armenia

Greenhouse gas emissions

Armenia, despite contributing minimally to anthropogenic greenhouse gas emissions, actively pursues measures to address climate change. The Republic of Armenia ratified the United Nations Framework Convention on Climate Change in May 1993. In December 2002, Armenia further ratified the Kyoto Protocol, and in February 2017, it signed the Doha Amendment to the Kyoto Protocol and the Paris Agreement. In May 2019, Armenia ratified the Kigali Amendment to the Montreal Protocol, demonstrating its commitment to phasing out hydrofluorocarbons

(HFCs). These actions underscore Armenia's engagement in a multilateral process aimed at combating climate change (Republic of Armenia, 2021a).

The Republic of Armenia submitted its intended Nationally Determined Contribution (INDC) to the UNFCCC Secretariat in September 2015. The INDC encompassed a preparatory period from 2015 to 2019, followed by a subsequent phase starting in 2020 with a long-term perspective up to 2050 (Republic of Armenia, 2021a). On April 22, 2021, the Armenian government approved Armenia's Nationally Determined Contribution for the ten-year implementation period (2021–2030), establishing an unconditional mitigation target of reducing emissions by 40% from 1990 levels by 2030. Additionally, in 2018, Armenia became a member of the NDC Partnership to facilitate the implementation of its nationally determined contributions (Republic of Armenia, 2021b).

Armenia, a landlocked country with fragile mountain ecosystems, is already experiencing the adverse impacts of climate change and grappling with water scarcity issues. Consequently, the policies and adaptation measures currently being implemented hold significant importance for Armenia's pursuit of its socioeconomic development objectives. In this context, Armenia's Nationally Determined Contribution (NDC) adheres to the principles of a green economy and aligns with the Sustainable Development Goals (SDGs), which are integral to Armenia's socioeconomic development agenda.

The Republic of Armenia promotes policies aimed at increasing the share of renewable energy in the power generation sector, expanding demand-side solar power generation, enhancing energy conservation across all sectors of the economy, including the deployment of high-efficiency equipment in industry and construction, promoting environmentally friendly vehicles, and improving road infrastructure within the transport sector (Republic of Armenia, 2021b).

According to the Strategic Program for the Development of the Energy Sector of the Republic of Armenia, the government aims to increase the total share of solar power generation to at least 15%, equivalent to 1.8 billion kWh, by 2030. In pursuit of this goal, significant legislative and regulatory reforms have been implemented in recent years to promote and expand renewable energy sources, specifically focusing on scaling up electricity generation through photovoltaic (solar PV) power plants. These efforts are intended to bolster Armenia's energy security and competitiveness while aligning with environmental standards and commitments (Republic of Armenia, 2021b).

Evolution of the greenhouse gas emission rate

In the Republic of Armenia, greenhouse gas emissions, with carbon dioxide (CO_2) comprising three-fifths of these emissions, showed an upward trend after 2013. By 2020, compared to 2014 levels, greenhouse gas emissions, including CO_2, had increased by 14.12% and 23.15%, respectively.

The Republic of Armenia bears a minimal historical responsibility for GHG emissions. In 2020, Armenia emitted approximately 10.42 $MtCO_2$-equivalent (excluding the Land Use, Land-Use Change, and Forestry sector) and 10.46 $MtCO_2$-equivalent (including the LUCF sector), accounting for less than 0.02% of total global emissions (Climate Watch Data, 2024). Armenia's per capita net and total GHG emissions were notably lower than the global averages: net emissions were 3.52 tCO_2 equivalent per capita, and total emissions were 3.53 tCO_2 equivalent per capita in Armenia, compared to 5.94 tCO_2 equivalent per capita and 6.12 tCO_2 equivalent per capita globally (Climate Watch Data, 2024).

From 1990 to 2020, Armenia saw a significant decrease in total direct GHG emissions (excluding LUCF), with emissions in CO_2 equivalent declining by approximately 57.27%. Specifically, emissions decreased from 24.39 $MtCO_2$ equivalent in 1990 to 10.42 $MtCO_2$ equivalent in 2020. Similarly, net greenhouse gas emissions (including LUCF) decreased by about 57.34% over the same period, from 24.52 $MtCO_2$-equivalent in 1990 to 10.46 $MtCO_2$-equivalent in 2020 (Climate Watch Data, 2024).

From 2014 to 2020, greenhouse gas emissions in Armenia exhibited an upward trend, as illustrated in Figure 3.1. During this period, annual emissions averaged approximately 9.53 $MtCO_2$ equivalent. Annual changes fluctuated around this average, ranging from 9.13 to 10.42 $MtCO_2$ equivalent. Carbon dioxide (CO_2) emissions constituted the majority, accounting for 59.77% of total greenhouse gas emissions.

Specifically, CO_2 emissions from 2014 to 2020 followed a steady trajectory, hovering around an annual average of approximately 5.70 $MtCO_2$ equivalent. Annual variations in CO_2 emissions ranged between 5.48 and 6.75 $MtCO_2$ equivalent.

Between 2014 and 2020, the composition of greenhouse gas emissions by sector remained relatively stable (Figure 3.2). The proportion of emissions attributed to the energy sector saw a slight rise from 68.13% to 70.61%, while emissions from

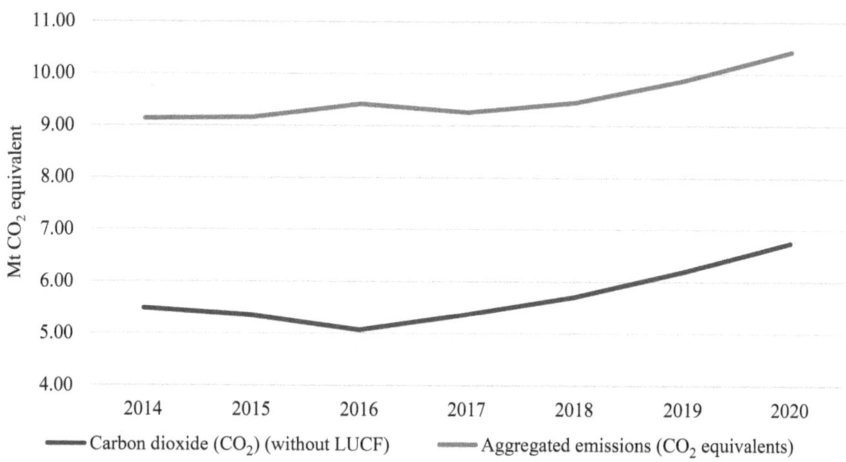

Figure 3.1 Armenia. Greenhouse gas emissions, including CO_2 between 2014 and 2020, in $MtCO_2$ equivalent.

Source: Climate Watch Data (2024).

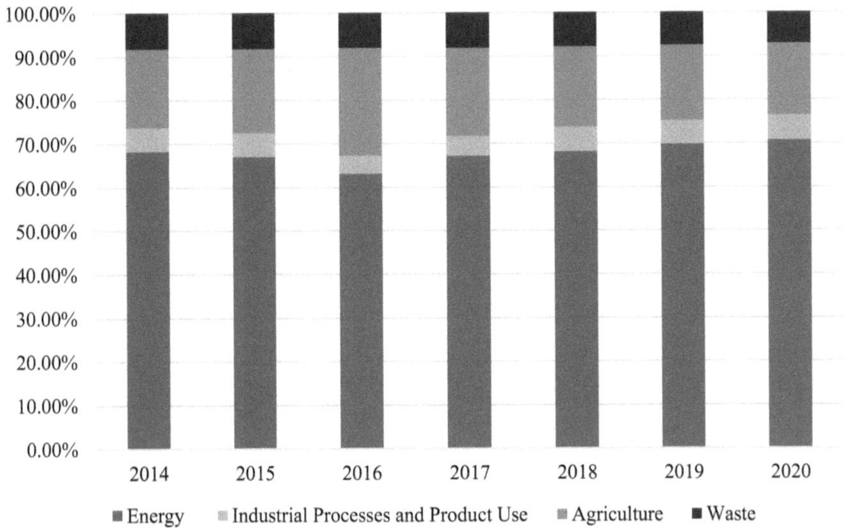

Figure 3.2 Armenia. Structure of greenhouse gas emissions by sector from 2014 to 2020, in %.

Source: Climate Watch Data (2024).

industrial processes and product use increased marginally from 5.48% to 5.67%. Conversely, the share of emissions from the agriculture and waste sectors experienced declines, decreasing from 18.18% to 16.62% and from 8.21% to 7.11%, respectively.

Productivity index (emission efficiency) of CO_2

In the Republic of Armenia, greenhouse gas emissions, including CO_2, increased after 2013 alongside economic growth. Between 2014 and 2020, Armenia experienced overall economic expansion, despite a 7.20% GDP decline in 2020 compared to 2019. Nevertheless, GDP grew by 16.77% from 2014 to 2020. Concurrently, there was an observed increase in CO_2 emission productivity under these conditions, as depicted in Figure 3.3. From 2014 to 2017, CO_2 productivity rose from 1.87 USD/kg to 2.12 USD/kg, but decreased thereafter, reaching 1.77 USD/kg in 2020. In contrast, greenhouse gas productivity increased from 1.12 to 1.30 USD/kg CO_2 equivalent between 2014 and 2019, then declined to 1.15 USD/kg CO_2 equivalent in 2020. In 2020, despite the GDP decrease relative to 2019, greenhouse gas emissions, including CO_2, increased by 5.54% and 8.91%, respectively. These findings indicate that while Armenia strives to decouple economic growth from CO_2 emissions, achieving this goal remains contingent upon GDP dynamics.

The CO_2 productivity indicator is calculated as the quotient of GDP at purchasing power parity in constant 2017 prices and the volume of CO_2 emissions in kilograms. From 2014 to 2020, the average value of this indicator was 5.48 GDP/kg.

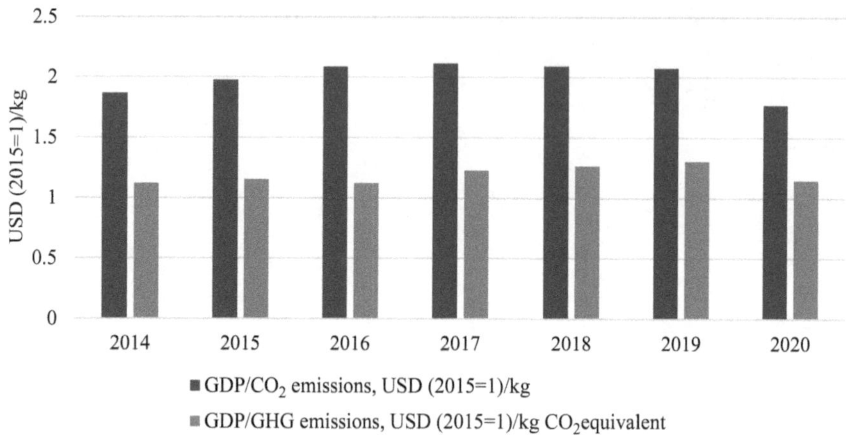

Figure 3.3 Armenia. Productivity of greenhouse gases and CO_2 from 2014 to 2020.
Source: Climate Watch Data (2024).

Notably, between 2014 and 2017, the indicator increased from 5.86 GDP/kg to 6.64 GDP/kg. However, from 2018 to 2020, there was a decline in the indicator from 6.57 GDP/kg to 5.55 GDP/kg. Overall, across the entire period, there was a decrease in the indicator from 5.86 GDP/kg to 5.55 GDP/kg, reflecting a decline of 5.18%.

Final energy consumption

Since 2015, the Republic of Armenia has consistently published an official energy balance, providing detailed information on energy consumption and methodology. Therefore, the analysis for Armenia spans from 2015 to 2022. During this period, Armenia's primary energy supply and final energy consumption have shown an upward trend. Importantly, the growth in energy supply outpaced GDP growth over the study period, leading to an increase in energy productivity.

Between 2015 and 2021, Armenia's primary energy supply rose from 3.3 to 4 million tons of oil equivalent. This increase in energy supply corresponded with a rise in energy consumption, as depicted in Figure 3.4. Comparing 2022 to 2015, total energy consumption escalated from 2.2 to 2.9 million tons of oil equivalent, marking a 33.39% increase. During the period 2015–2022, the agricultural sector exhibited the most rapid growth in energy consumption, soaring from 39.3 to 103.4 thousand tons of oil equivalent, more than tripling in volume. Other sectors also saw notable increases in energy consumption. Specifically, the residential sector experienced the largest rise, climbing from 693 to 996 thousand tons of oil equivalent over the same period. Energy consumption in the transportation sector increased by 36.61%, from 649 to 887 thousand tons of oil equivalent. In the industrial sector, energy consumption grew by 35.61%. Additionally, non-energy sectors saw a 38.13% increase, reaching 71 thousand tons of

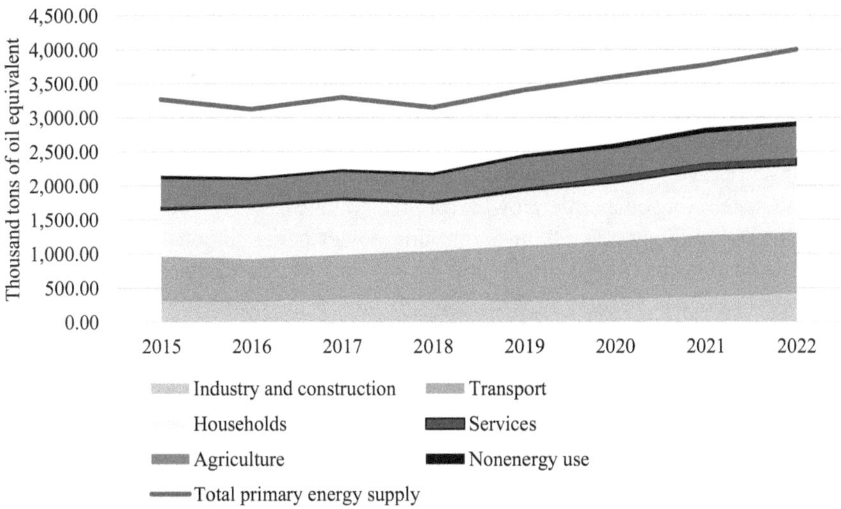

Figure 3.4 Armenia. Primary energy supply and final energy consumption by sector during 2015–2022, in thousand tons of oil equivalent.

Source: Statistical Committee Republic of Armenia (2023).

oil equivalent from 51 thousand tons. In contrast, energy consumption in the service sector rose by 13.59%.

Between 2015 and 2022, there were slight changes in the structure of total energy consumption, as illustrated in Figure 3.5. The share of the agricultural sector in total energy consumption decreased from 18.97% to 16.15%, while the residential sector's share increased from 32.25% to 34.72%. The share of the industrial and construction sector remained stable at 14.61%. In contrast, the transportation

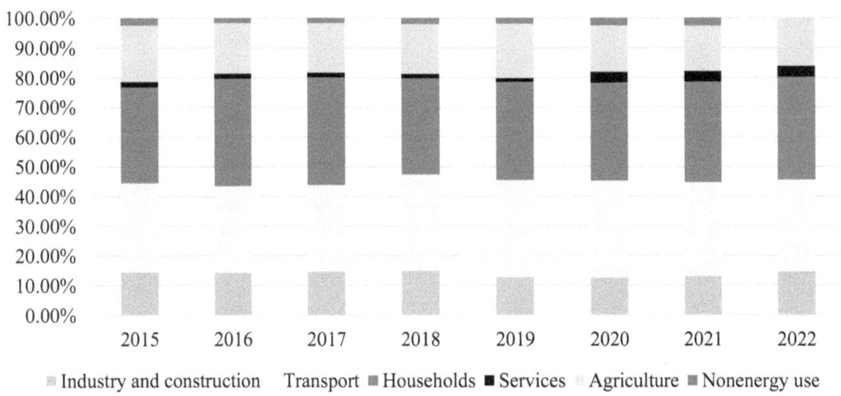

Figure 3.5 Armenia. Structure of total energy use from 2015 to 2022, in %.

Source: own compilation based on data from Statistical Committee Republic of Armenia (2023).

sector accounted for 30.95% of total energy consumption throughout the period. Additionally, there was an increasing trend in the share of total energy consumption attributed to the services sector and non-energy industries.

In 2022, compared to 2015, Armenia's primary energy supply increased by 22.52%, while GDP at purchasing power parity in constant 2017 prices grew by 34.80%. This suggests that the increase in energy productivity may have contributed to decoupling economic growth from the volume of energy consumption. Calculating the quotient of GDP at purchasing power parity in constant 2017 prices and the volume of energy production reveals that the energy productivity index rose by 10.02% from 2015 to 2022. Specifically, it increased from USD 10.14 to USD 11.15 per gram of oil equivalent.

Energy intensity

The Republic of Armenia experienced an increase in energy productivity and a slight reduction in energy intensity after 2014. However, not all sectors of the economy saw a decline in energy intensity. Between 2015 and 2022, growth in GDP was outpaced by an increase in final energy consumption, leading to an overall rise in energy productivity and a modest decrease in energy intensity across the economy (Figure 3.6). For instance, in 2015, it took 203.7 grams of oil equivalent to produce one US dollar's worth of final energy consumption. By 2021, this ratio had increased to 225.06 grams of oil equivalent per USD, marking a 10.49% rise. The agricultural sector, however, saw an increase in energy intensity despite an 11.36% growth in gross value added from 2015 to 2022. Energy consumption in agriculture rose by 13.59% on average during this period. In 2015, energy intensity in agriculture stood at 38.64 grams of oil

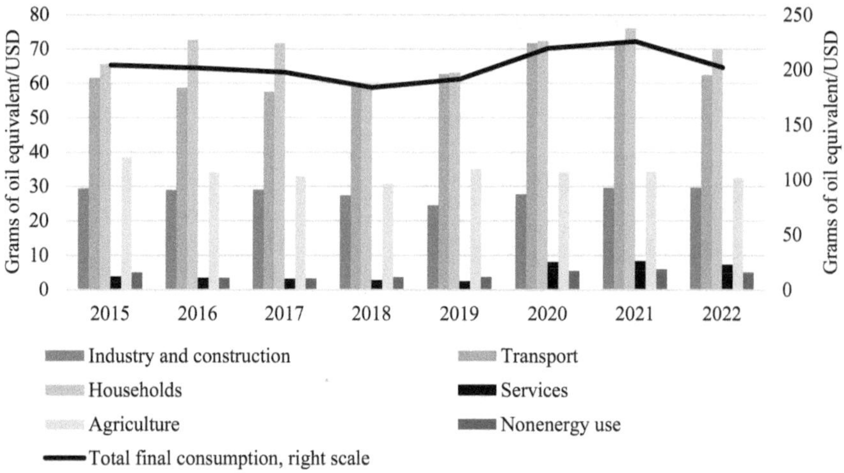

Figure 3.6 Armenia. Energy intensity from 2015 to 2022, in grams of oil equivalent/USD.

Source: Own compilation based on data from Statistical Committee Republic of Armenia (2023).

equivalent per USD, decreasing to 32.56 grams in 2022, representing a 15.74% reduction. Contrarily, the industrial sector did not witness a decrease in energy intensity, maintaining a level of 29.43 grams of oil equivalent per USD. Meanwhile, energy intensity in services surged by 119.78% from 3.72 to 8.18 grams of oil equivalent per USD from 2015 to 2021.

Share of renewable energy in total energy consumption

In the Republic of Armenia, the supply of renewable energy increased from 2015 to 2021, despite a decrease observed in 2020. Consequently, the share of renewable energy in both primary energy supply and final energy consumption also rose. In 2021, hydropower dominated Armenia's renewable energy supply at 65.89%, followed by wood combustion at 15.94%, with solar energy ranking third at 14.20%. This highlights the early stages of development in Armenia's modern renewable energy generation sector. Programme of the Government of the Republic of Armenia 2021-2026, https;//www.gov/am/en/gov-program/

In Armenia, between 2015 and 2021, the supply of renewable energy increased from 287 to 353 thousand tons of oil equivalent, marking a growth of 23.17%. However, there was a decrease in 2020, with renewable energy supply dropping to 255 thousand tons of oil equivalent, reflecting an 11.15% decline compared to 2015. Despite this fluctuation, it is noteworthy that from 2014 to 2021, there was an increase in the share of renewable energy in primary energy production, while the share of renewable energy in total energy consumption decreased (Figure 3.7). Specifically, in 2015, renewable energy accounted for 13.35% of primary energy supply, which decreased slightly to 12.43% by 2021.

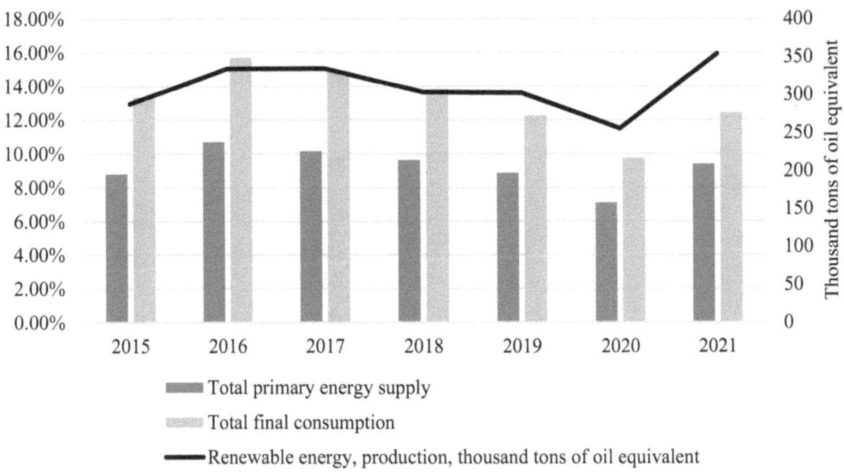

Figure 3.7 Armenia. Renewable energy supply (thousand tons of oil equivalent) and the share of renewable energy in primary energy production and total energy consumption from 2015 to 2021, in %.

Source: own compilation based on data from Statistical Committee Republic of Armenia (2023).

Waste generation

In Armenia, two noticeable trends have emerged. First, manufacturing waste has shown a tendency to increase, particularly noticeable after 2015. Second, there has been a concurrent increase in the amount of waste generated by the public.

Since 2015, there has been a clear trend of increasing production waste, as depicted in Figure 3.8. In 2015, almost 48 million tons of waste were generated, and by 2021, this volume had increased by 88.68% to 88.74 million tons. Meanwhile, the volume of waste collected from the population has shown fluctuations. Over the period 2014–2022, there was a 2.89% increase in 2022 compared to 2014. The peak volume of waste collected from the population occurred in 2020, totaling 573,000 tons, marking the highest volume recorded throughout the study period.

From 2014 to 2021, there was a notable increase of 69.30% in the amount of production waste generated. During the same period, VAT—an indicator reflecting the production process, expressed in current prices—also increased by 69.84%. This suggests a close correlation between the production process and waste generation, as shown in Figure 3.44. In contrast, the dynamics of municipal waste, specifically waste collected from the population and household consumption, exhibited different trends between 2014 and 2022 (Figure 3.9). While municipal waste production surpassed household consumption dynamics during 2015–2017 and 2020–2021, the reverse occurred during 2018–2020 and 2021–2022. Over the entire period 2014–2022, household waste increased by 2.89%, whereas household consumption grew by an average of 30.94% annually. This indicates that the current consumption habits of the population are less likely to accelerate waste generation.

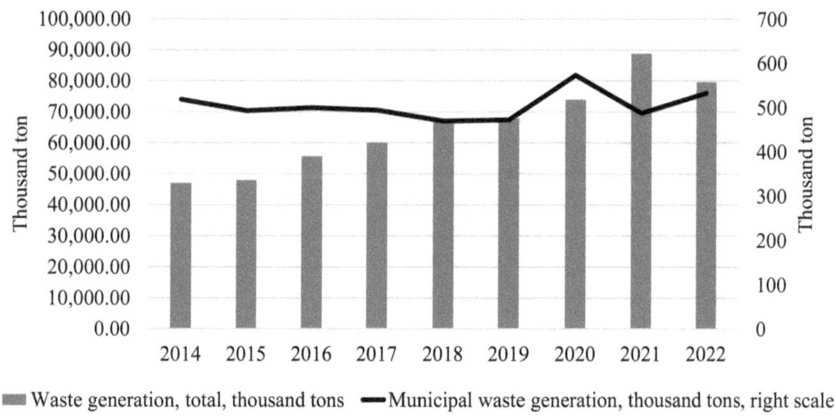

Figure 3.8 Armenia. Production of production waste and municipal waste from 2014 to 2022, in thousands of tons.

Source: Own compilation based on data from World Bank (World Bank Open Data, 2023) and Statistical Committee Republic of Armenia (2023).

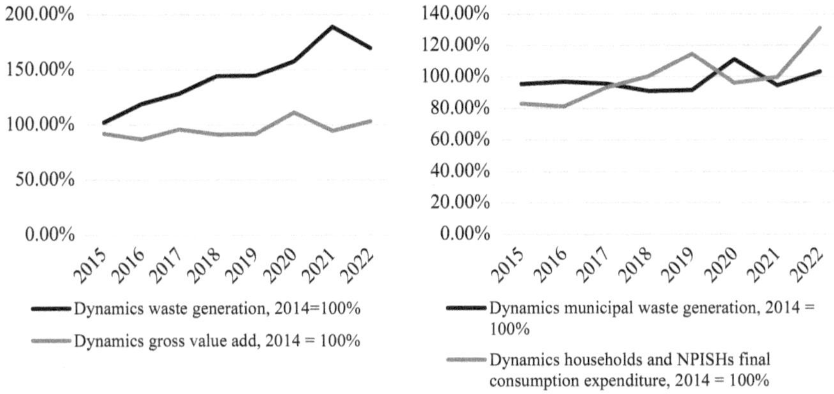

Figure 3.9 Armenia. Dynamics of production waste, municipal waste, VAT, and household consumption from 2015 to 2022, in %.

Source: Own compilation based on data from World Bank (World Bank Open Data, 2023) and Statistical Committee Republic of Armenia (2023).

Waste recycling—evolution of the indicator

In the Republic of Armenia, data is collected on "used waste," which includes both waste disposed of and waste used for energy production.

In 2018, the highest amount of waste disposed of reached 1,603.6 thousand tons, marking the peak between 2014 and 2022 (Figure 3.10). Over this period, the volume of disposed waste fluctuated from a minimum of 9.1 thousand tons to the maximum of 1,603.6 thousand tons. Additionally, in 2018, the ratio of disposed waste to produced waste peaked at 2.37%. Throughout 2014–2022, this ratio varied

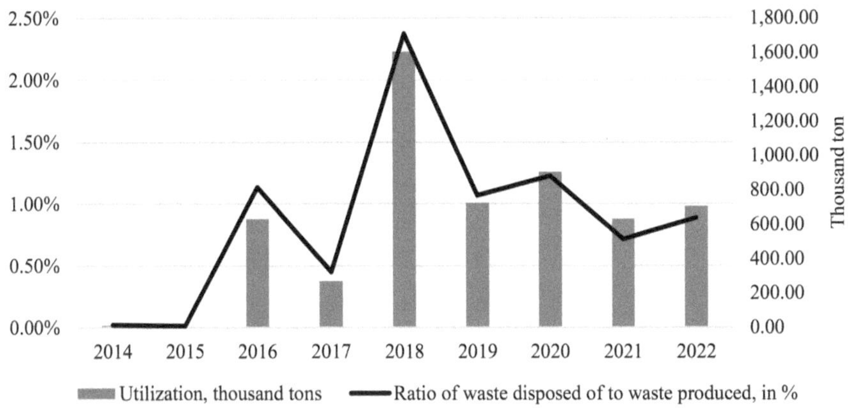

Figure 3.10 Armenia. Waste disposed (thousands of tons) and the ratio of waste disposed to waste produced from 2014 to 2022, in %.

Source: Own compilation based on data from World Bank (World Bank Open Data, 2023) and Statistical Committee Republic of Armenia (2023).

between 0.01% and 2.37%, highlighting fluctuations in waste disposal relative to waste production.

Use of fertilizers

In the Republic of Armenia, fertilizer balances are not prepared, but there is available information that allows for the analysis of mineral fertilizer consumption intensity, with data only accessible for the years 2014–2017. Armenian agricultural production predominantly relies on the use of organic fertilizers.

In general, there has been an increase in the use of mineral fertilizers and a decrease in the use of organic fertilizers in Armenia after 2013 (Figure 3.11). The introduction of mineral fertilizers into agricultural land increased from 54.41 thousand tons in 2014 to more than 93.02 thousand tons in 2017. Conversely, the consumption of organic fertilizers decreased over the same period. In 2014, 3154.7 thousand tons of organic fertilizers were used, compared to more than 3075.2 thousand tons in 2017.

The increase in fertilizer use was also accompanied by a rise in the amount of mineral fertilizer applied per hectare of soil. Between 2014 and 2017, the application rate for chemical fertilizers increased from 190.89 to 341.5 kg/ha (Figure 3.12). In contrast, the application rate for organic fertilizers remained stable at 11.08 kg/ha during this period. Specifically, in 2017, there was a 2.52% decrease in the use of organic fertilizers and a 70.97% increase in the use of mineral fertilizers compared to 2014.

Most mineral fertilizers used are nitrates, followed by phosphates, with potassium fertilizers having the smallest share. Between 2014 and 2017, all types

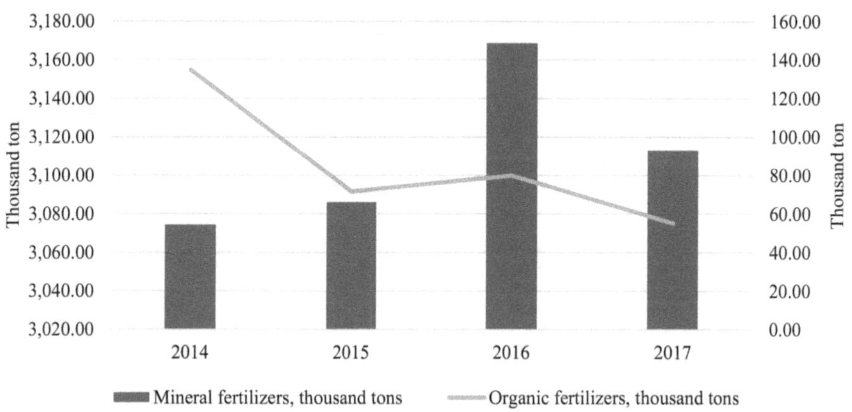

Figure 3.11 Armenia. Consumption of chemical and natural fertilizers on farms and peasant farms (farmers) during 2014–2017, in thousands of tons.

Source: Own compilation based on data from World Bank (World Bank Open Data, 2023) and Statistical Committee Republic of Armenia (2023).

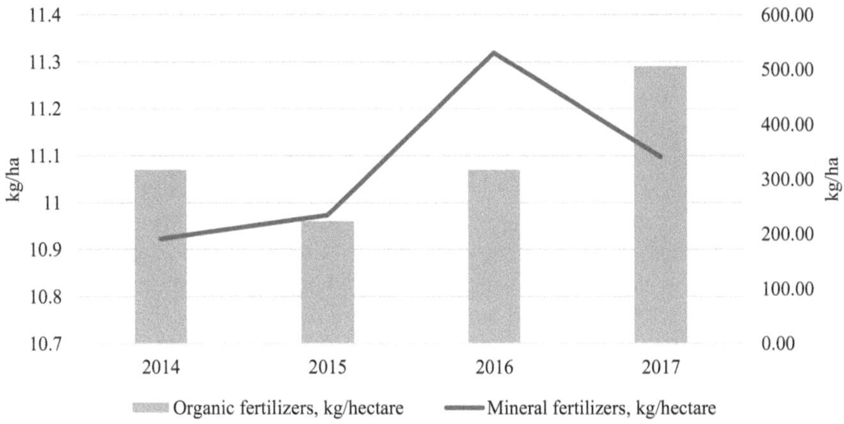

Figure 3.12 Armenia. Consumption of chemical and natural fertilizers on farms and peasant farms (farmers) during 2014–2017, in kg/ha.

Source: Own compilation based on data from World Bank (World Bank Open Data, 2023) and Statistical Committee Republic of Armenia (2023).

of fertilizers were consumed to varying degrees (Figure 3.13). The consumption of nitrates increased by 85.27%, from 48.64 to 90.11 thousand tons. Conversely, phosphate fertilizer consumption decreased significantly by 99.17%, from 2.78 thousand tons to 23 tons during the same period. Potassium fertilizer consumption also saw a decline of 87.65%, from 1.7 thousand tons to 210 tons.

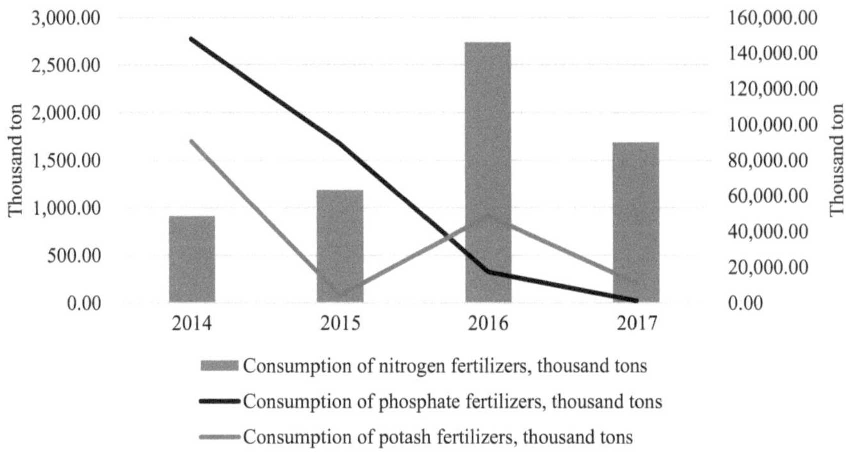

Figure 3.13 Armenia. Types of mineral fertilizers used on farms and peasant farms (farmers) during 2014–2017, in tons.

Source: Own compilation based on data from World Bank (World Bank Open Data, 2023) and Statistical Committee Republic of Armenia (2023).

Water consumption

From 2014 to 2022, water consumption in Armenia showed a steady increase. In 2014, the total water consumption was 2,112.8 million m³, and by 2022, it had risen to 2,422.3 million m³. Most sectors experienced consistent water consumption patterns over this period (Figure 3.14). On average, 167.74 million m³ of water were consumed annually for production purposes, constituting 7.53% of the total water consumption. The agricultural sector stands out as the largest consumer of water in Armenia (Global Water Partnership (GWP), n.d.). Over the period 2014–2022, agriculture averaged an annual water consumption of 1,932.76 million m³, which accounts for 86.71% of the total water consumed in the country. Domestic water consumption during this period was 129.5 million m³ annually, representing 5.81% of the national water consumption.

If water consumption exhibited stable evolution from 2014 to 2022, GDP expressed in USD at constant 2017 prices saw a notable increase of 39.11% over the same period. This increase contributed to improved water productivity, marking a decoupling of economic growth from water consumption. Water productivity is calculated as the ratio of GDP in constant 2017 prices at purchasing power parity to the volume of water consumption. Comparing 2022 to 2014, water productivity rose from 15.19 to 18.43 USD/m³, reflecting a notable increase of 21.34%.

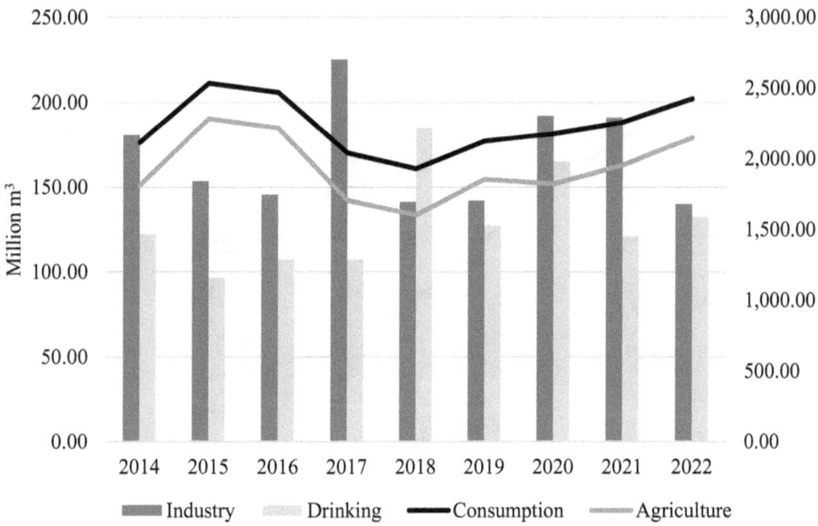

Figure 3.14 Armenia. Water consumption by economic sector during 2014–2022, in million m³.

Source: Own compilation based on data from World Bank (World Bank Open Data, 2023) and Statistical Committee Republic of Armenia (2023).

Azerbaijan

Greenhouse gas emissions

On January 10, 1995, Azerbaijan ratified the United Nations Framework Convention on Climate Change (UNFCCC). Subsequently, on April 30, 1997, the State Commission on Climate Change (the Commission) was established by decree of the President of the Republic of Azerbaijan. This commission was tasked with overseeing the fulfillment of the commitments made by the Republic of Azerbaijan under the UNFCCC (Ministry of Ecology and Natural Resources Republic of Azerbaijan, 2021, p. 33).

On March 11, 2020, the President of the Republic of Azerbaijan issued a decree approving the new composition of the Commission. The Commission is chaired by the Deputy Prime Minister of Azerbaijan, with the Minister of Ecology and Natural Resources of the republic serving as the deputy chairman. The members of the Commission include the Minister of Finance, Minister of Economy, Minister of Agriculture, Minister of Health, Deputy Minister of Foreign Affairs, Deputy Minister of Transport, Communications and Advanced Technologies, President of the National Academy of Sciences of Azerbaijan, President of the State Oil Company of Azerbaijan (SOCAR), Chairman of the Open Joint Stock Company (OJSC) "Azerenergy," and Chairman of the Azerbaijan OJSC for Land Reclamation and Water Management (Ministry of Ecology and Natural Resources Republic of Azerbaijan, 2021, p. 33).

A working group composed of specialists from the relevant state bodies was established by taking into account the importance of the active role of the relevant state bodies in this process, the strengthening of interagency relations, and the significance of the recently approved State Commission in ensuring the implementation of the commitments of the Republic of Azerbaijan under the UN Framework Convention on Climate Change. The Action Plan of the Working Group is approved (Ministry of Ecology and Natural Resources Republic of Azerbaijan, 2021, p. 33).

The Action Plan consists of two courses of action: (1) Developing Inventory and Monitoring, Reporting, and Verification (MRV) systems, and (2) evaluation of GHG emission reduction measures by sectors (Ministry of Ecology and Natural Resources Republic of Azerbaijan, 2021, p. 33).

The Ministry of Ecology and Natural Resources is the National Designated Authority responsible for implementing the commitments arising from the UN Framework Convention on Climate Change. The Ministry has appointed a national coordinator for the Convention. At the same time, a working group is established to increase the efficiency and diversify activities in this area (Ministry of Ecology and Natural Resources Republic of Azerbaijan, 2021, p. 33). The Climate Change Center was established under the National Hydrometeorological Department that is attached to the Ministry of Ecology and Natural Resources. The main purpose of the Center is to coordinate the country's climate change activities and establish a relevant database (Ministry of Ecology and Natural Resources Republic of Azerbaijan, 2021, p. 33).

The Republic of Azerbaijan is actively participating not only in the implementation of the United Nations Framework Convention on Climate Change, as well as the Kyoto Protocol and the Paris Agreement (Republic of Azerbaijan, 2023, p. 4).

According to Article 4 of the Paris Agreement, Azerbaijan has committed to reducing its greenhouse gas emissions by 35% by 2030. This pledge reflects a significant ambition considering the country's domestic circumstances, particularly its economic diversification plans for the coming decade (Republic of Azerbaijan, 2023, p. 4).

Since Azerbaijan is actively engaged in international cooperation under Article 6 of the Paris Agreement, the current version of its nationally determined contributions (NDCs) encompasses the elements outlined in Table 3.1.

Evolution of the greenhouse gas emission rate

In Azerbaijan, greenhouse gas emissions, including CO_2, have shown a relatively steady trend since 2013. Specifically, in 2020 compared to 2019, greenhouse gas emissions, including CO_2, increased by 5.91% and 6.39%, respectively.

Table 3.1 Azerbaijan's nationally determined contributions to 2050 (updated in 2023).

The Republic of Azerbaijan aims to achieve a 40% reduction in greenhouse gas emissions by 2050 compared to 1990 levels, contingent upon international support in the form of financing, technology transfer, and capacity building, to ensure sustainable socioeconomic development.	
In accordance with the instructions contained in Decision 4/CMA.	
Quantitative data as of the reference date (including base year, if applicable):	
Reference (base) year	1990
Quantitative data as of the reference date	In the 4th National Communication of Azerbaijan, the total volume of greenhouse gas emissions for the reporting year (taking into account the absorption volume in the land use, land-use change and forestry (LULUCF) sector) is assumed to be 79 Mt CO_2 equivalent*
Objective regarding numerical reference	Reduction of greenhouse gas emissions by up to 40% compared to 1990 level, taking into account the maximum absorption capacity of forests and other ecosystems.
Conditions for changing reference indicators	Total greenhouse gas emissions into the atmosphere can be updated and recalculated through methodological improvements. Updates will be included in the next Biennial Update Report or Biennial Transparency Report and National Communication.
Deadlines and/or terms for execution:	
The deadlines and/or terms for execution, as well as the start and end date, in accordance with any relevant decision made at the Conference of the Parties of the Paris Agreement	From 1 January 2023 to 31 December 2050.

(Continued)

Table 3.1 (Continued)

Consideration of paragraphs 31 (c) and (d) of decision 1/CP.21 by the country	In its 4th National Communication, Azerbaijan recorded updated information on sources included in the greenhouse gas inventory. Information on greenhouse gas emissions into the atmosphere from sources that have not been accounted for due to lack of data will be included in the reports after restructuring of the Monitoring, Reporting and Verification (MRV) system in accordance with the requirements of the improved transparency format specified in Article 13 of the Paris Agreement. If air emissions from these sources are significant, i.e., if they are considered a key emission sector, Azerbaijan will provide relevant clarifying information on these emissions in the next reports to the UNFCCC Secretariat.
Scale and scope:	
General description of the target	Target covering all sectors
The Nationally Determined Contributions includes sectors, gases, benchmarks and areas including, where applicable, sectors under Guidelines of the Intergovernmental Panel on Climate Change.	The target includes: 1 Energy, industrial processes and product use, agriculture, land use, land use change and forestry, waste sector 2 Greenhouse gases: carbon dioxide (CO_2), methane (CH_4), nitrogen oxide (N2O), hydrofluorocarbons (HFCs), perfluorocarbons (PFCs).

Source: Republic of Azerbaijan (2023, pp. 4–6 [w]) https://www.climatewatchdata.org/countries/AZE?end_year=2020&start_year=1990, accessed: 5.02.2024. [w] = [in].

* It should be noted that during the GHG inventory for 1990 (base year), there was some missing data to calculate emissions/absorbances for all categories mentioned in the relevant methodological guidelines prepared by the IPCC in 2006. In this regard, when inventories are conducted in subsequent years based on more complete data for the base year, the GHG emission figure for that year may be subject to change in the assessment. Moreover, due to the lack of data for the occupied territories of Azerbaijan for about 30 years, it is foreseen to recalculate emissions/absorbances for this period.

The Republic of Azerbaijan's historical responsibility for greenhouse gas emissions is small. In 2020, Azerbaijan emitted about 55.35 $MtCO_2$-equivalent (excluding LULUCF) and 53.45 $MtCO_2$-equivalent (with LULUCF), less than 0.21% of total global emissions (Climate Watch Data, 2024). In Azerbaijan, total and net per capita GHG emissions were lower than the global average (Azerbaijan: net emissions were 5.30 tCO_2 equivalent per capita, total emissions were 5.48 tCO_2 equivalent per capita; World: net emissions were 5.94 tCO_2 equivalent per capita, total emissions were 6.12 tCO_2 equivalent per capita) (Climate Watch Data, 2024). Between 1990 and 2020, the dynamics of Azerbaijan's total direct GHG emissions (excluding LUCF), expressed in CO_2 equivalent, showed a downward trend, decreasing by about 26.67%: from 75.48 $MtCO_2$ equivalent in 1990 to 55.35 $MtCO_2$ equivalent in 2020. Net greenhouse gas emissions (from LUCF) decreased

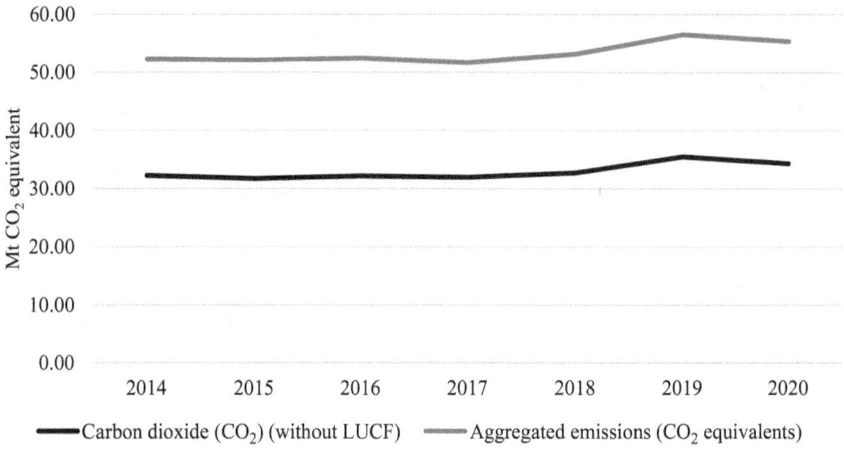

Figure 3.15 Azerbaijan. Greenhouse gas emissions, including CO_2 from 2014 to 2020, in $MtCO_2$ equivalent.

Source: Climate Watch Data (2024).

by about 27.66% over the same period: from 73.89 $MtCO_2$-equivalent in 1990 to 53.45 $MtCO_2$-equivalent in 2020 (Climate Watch Data, 2024).

From 2014 to 2020, greenhouse gas emissions in Azerbaijan followed an increasing trend, as depicted in Figure 3.15. During this period, annual emissions averaged around 53.39 $MtCO_2$ equivalent, with minor fluctuations ranging between 51.76 and 56.54 $MtCO_2$ equivalent. Carbon dioxide (CO_2) emissions constituted approximately 60.09% of the total greenhouse gas emissions. Specifically, CO_2 emissions exhibited a stable pattern, hovering around an annual average of approximately 32.97 $MtCO_2$ equivalent, with annual variations between 31.77 and 35.52 $MtCO_2$ equivalent.

Between 2014 and 2020, the composition of greenhouse gas emissions by sector in Azerbaijan showed relatively stable patterns, as illustrated in Figure 3.16. The energy sector remained the largest contributor, although its share decreased slightly from 77.01% to 75.24%. In contrast, emissions from industrial processes and product use increased marginally from 2.53% to 2.76%. The agriculture sector saw a slight rise in its contribution to emissions, from 13.36% to 14.22%, while the waste sector also experienced a slight increase, from 7.10% to 7.77%.

Productivity (emission efficiency) of CO_2

In Azerbaijan, the period after 2013 witnessed relatively stable greenhouse gas emissions, including CO_2, alongside fluctuating GDP dynamics. Specifically, while Azerbaijan's economy showed growth between 2014–2015 and 2017–2019, it experienced contractions in 2015 and 2020. GDP increased by 2.12% in 2019 compared to 2014 but declined by 2.27% in 2020 compared to 2019. Despite these variations in GDP, greenhouse gas emissions remained relatively constant during

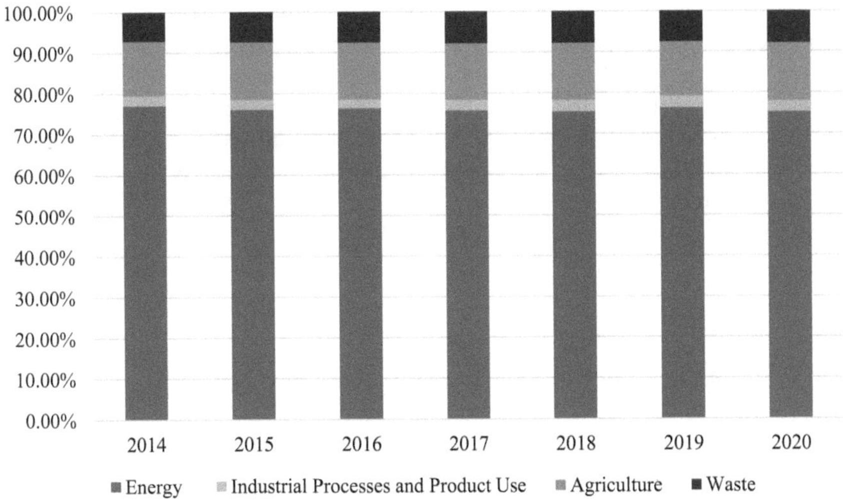

Figure 3.16 Azerbaijan. Structure of greenhouse gas emissions by sector from 2014 to 2020, in %.

Source: Climate Watch Data (2024).

this period. Under these circumstances of stable emissions and uneven economic growth, there was a decrease in CO_2 productivity as depicted in Figure 3.17. Specifically, CO_2 productivity declined from 1.63 USD/kg to 1.50 USD/kg CO_2 equivalent between 2014 and 2020. In contrast, greenhouse gas productivity increased from 0.99 USD/kg to 1.08 USD/kg over the same period. These results

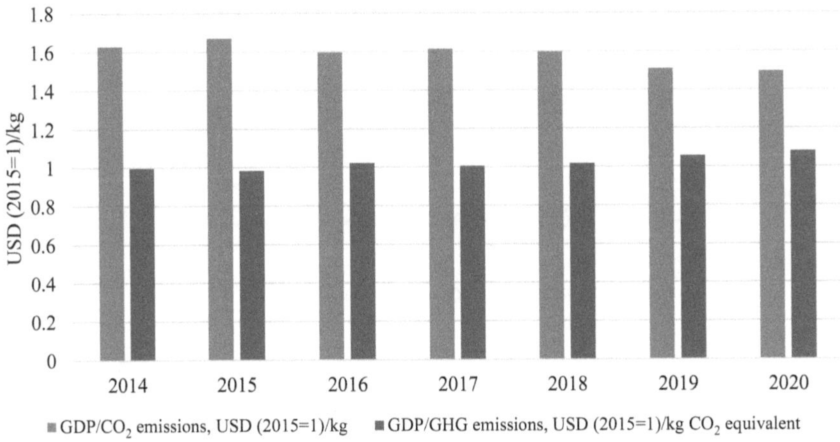

Figure 3.17 Azerbaijan. Productivity of greenhouse gases and CO_2 from 2014 to 2020.

Source: Climate Watch Data (2024).

indicate that while Azerbaijan aims to decouple economic growth from CO_2 emissions, achieving this goal remains contingent upon the dynamics of GDP.

The indicator of CO_2 productivity is derived from the quotient of GDP at purchasing power parity expressed in constant 2017 prices and the volume of CO_2 emissions in kilograms. Over the period 2014–2020, the average value of this indicator was 4.29 GDP/kg. It's important to note that this value fluctuated marginally during these years. However, across the entire period analyzed, the indicator decreased from 4.40 to 4.04, marking an 8.15% decline.

Final energy consumption

In Azerbaijan, primary energy supply and final energy consumption grew from 2014 to 2022. Between 2014 and 2022, energy supply growth was three times higher than GDP growth.

Overall, between 2014 and 2022, the supply of primary energy in Azerbaijan increased from 15.10 to 18.66 million tons of oil equivalent. This growth in energy supply corresponded with an increase in energy consumption across various sectors (Figure 3.18). Specifically, in 2022 compared to 2014, total energy consumption rose from 8.24 to 11.02 million tons of oil equivalent, representing a notable increase of 33.70%.

Between 2014 and 2022, energy consumption in Azerbaijan experienced significant growth across various sectors. The services sector notably saw the fastest increase, rising from 665,000 to 1,064,000 tons of oil equivalent, marking an increase of more than 60%. Similarly, other sectors also showed substantial

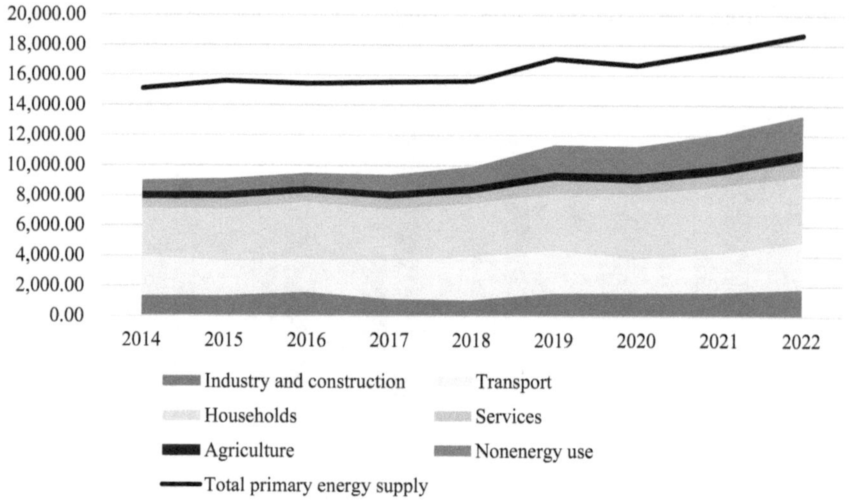

Figure 3.18 Azerbaijan. Primary energy supply and final energy consumption by sector from 2014 to 2022, in thousand tons of oil equivalent.

Source: The State Statistical Committee of the Republic of Azerbaijan (2023).

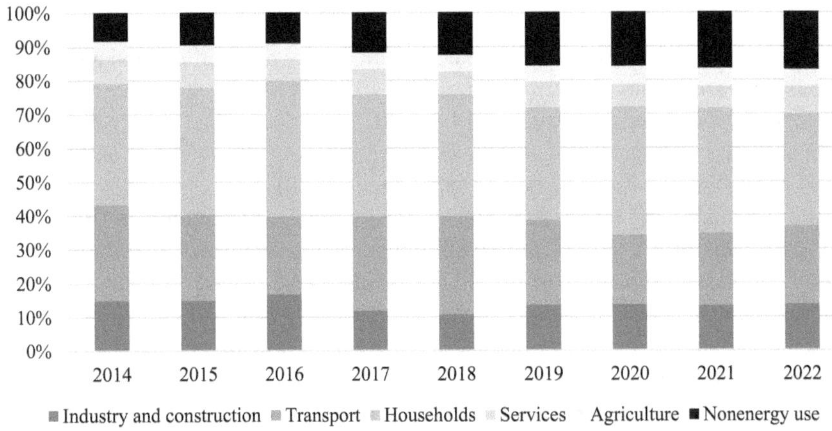

Figure 3.19 Azerbaijan. Structure of total energy use from 2014 to 2022, in %.

Source: Own compilation based on data from The State Statistical Committee of the Republic of Azerbaijan (2023).

growth in energy consumption during this period. The agricultural sector witnessed a notable increase from 461.8 to 649.5 thousand tons of oil equivalent, reflecting growth in energy demand for agricultural activities. In the residential sector, energy consumption rose by 37.91%, reaching 4.45 million tons of oil equivalent by 2022. In the industrial sector, energy consumption increased by 35.61%, climbing from 1.329 to 1.793 million tons of oil equivalent. The transport sector also saw growth, with energy consumption expanding by 19.67%, from 2.56 to 3.06 million tons of oil equivalent. Azerbaijan's non-energy sector experienced the most dramatic increase in energy consumption, surging by 203.34% from 751.2 to 2.279 thousand tons of oil equivalent, highlighting substantial energy demand growth in this area.

Between 2014 and 2022, Azerbaijan's overall energy consumption structure exhibited minimal changes (Figure 3.19). The agricultural sector's share in total energy consumption remained consistent, averaging 5.66%. Meanwhile, the transportation sector saw a slight decrease in its share from 31.05% to 27.80%. In contrast, the residential sector's share increased from 39.15% to 42.01%. The industrial and construction sectors maintained their share at 15.52% throughout the period under review. Notably, there was a significant increase in the share of total energy consumption by non-energy industries, rising from 9.11% to 20.68%.

In 2022, compared to 2014, primary energy supply in Azerbaijan increased by 23.66%, while GDP at purchasing power parity in constant 2017 prices grew by 7.98%. This indicates that despite the increase in energy supply, economic growth did not sufficiently decouple from energy consumption volume. Calculating the quotient of GDP at purchasing power parity and the volume of energy production over the period 2015–2022 shows a decline in energy productivity by 12.68%, dropping from USD 9.40 to USD 8.21 per gram.

Energy intensity

In Azerbaijan, there was a noticeable decline in energy productivity and a simultaneous increase in energy intensity after 2013. This trend was pervasive across all sectors of the economy. Between 2014 and 2022, the rise in final energy consumption outpaced GDP growth, resulting in decreased energy productivity and heightened energy intensity across the economy (Figure 3.20).

For instance, the energy intensity of final energy consumption in 2014 was 156.98 grams of oil equivalent per US dollar, which increased to 194.37 grams of oil equivalent per US dollar by 2022, marking a 23.82% rise. Notably, the residential sector exhibited the highest energy intensity in terms of energy consumption throughout this period, averaging 72.32 grams of oil equivalent per US dollar. Among all sectors, services experienced the most significant increase in energy intensity. Despite a marginal 0.21% rise in gross value added from 2014 to 2022, energy consumption surged by an average of 60.06%. In the services sector, energy intensity soared from 12.67 grams of oil equivalent per US dollar in 2014 to 18.77 grams of oil equivalent per US dollar in 2022, marking a substantial 48.23% increase. Contrarily, the industrial sector did not see a reduction in energy intensity; it escalated from 25.32 grams of oil equivalent per US dollar in 2014 to 31.63 grams of oil equivalent per US dollar in 2022. This represents a 24.92% increase in energy intensity over the eight-year period. Similarly, other economic sectors such as agriculture, transportation, residential, and non-energy industries also witnessed an upward trajectory in energy intensity during the review period.

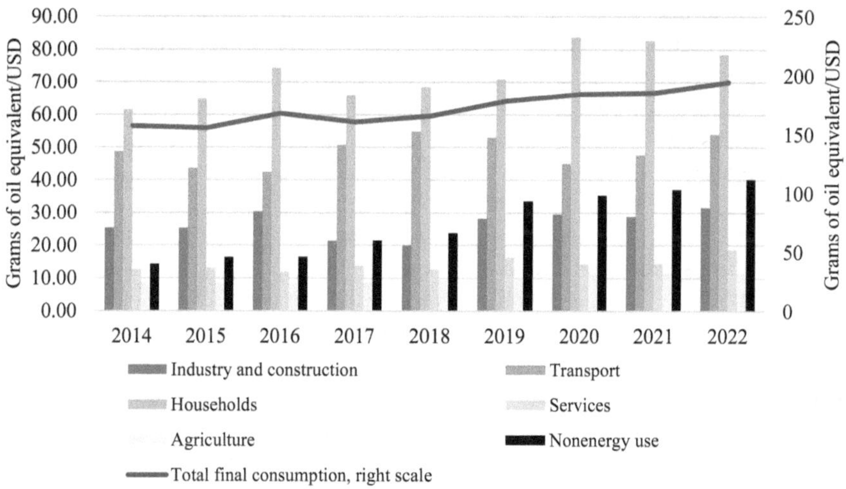

Figure 3.20 Azerbaijan. Energy intensity from 2014 to 2022, in grams of oil equivalent/USD.

Source: Own compilation based on data from The State Statistical Committee of the Republic of Azerbaijan (2023).

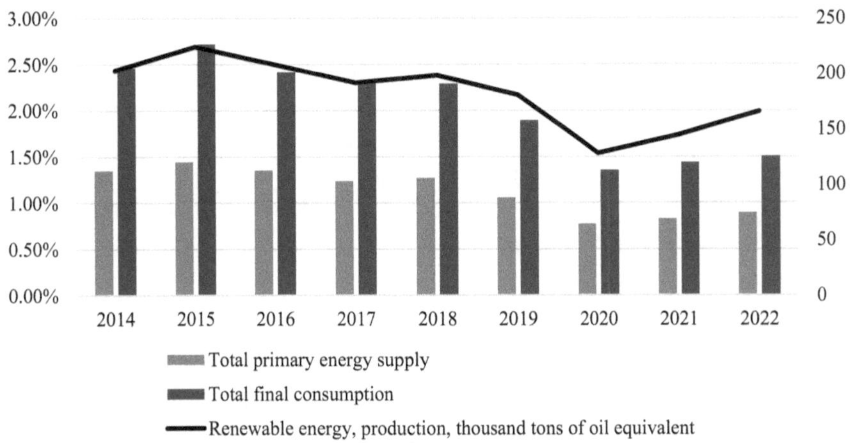

Figure 3.21 Azerbaijan. Renewable energy supply (thousand tons of oil equivalent) and share of renewable energy in primary energy production and total energy consumption from 2014 to 2022, in %.

Source: Own compilation based on data from The State Statistical Committee of the Republic of Azerbaijan (2023).

Share of renewable energy in total energy consumption

In Azerbaijan, the supply of renewable energy exhibited fluctuations between 2014 and 2022, contributing to a decrease in its share within both primary energy supply and final energy consumption. As of 2022, the composition of renewable energy sources in Azerbaijan's energy mix was dominated by hydropower, which accounted for 82.85% of renewable energy supply. Following hydropower, wood combustion made up 9.66%, while wind energy and solar energy held smaller shares of 4.35% and 3.14%, respectively. This distribution underscores the early stage of development of modern renewable energy generation sectors in Azerbaijan.

In Azerbaijan, between 2014 and 2022, the supply of renewable energy fell from 202.7 to 165.6 thousand tons of oil equivalent, a decrease of 18.30%. As a result, there were declines in the share of renewable energy in primary energy production and in total energy consumption between 2014 and 2022 (Figure 3.21).

Waste generation

In Azerbaijan, two trends are noticeable. Production waste tended to increase, especially after 2016. At the same time, the amount of waste generated by the public increased.

Since 2016, there has been a clear trend of increasing production waste (Figure 3.22). Almost 1.03 million tons of waste were generated in 2014. By 2022, the volume of waste generated increased by 28.68% to 1.33 million tons. The volume of waste collected from the population was also characterized by growth. During the 2014–2022 period, the volume of waste increased by 96.20% in 2022

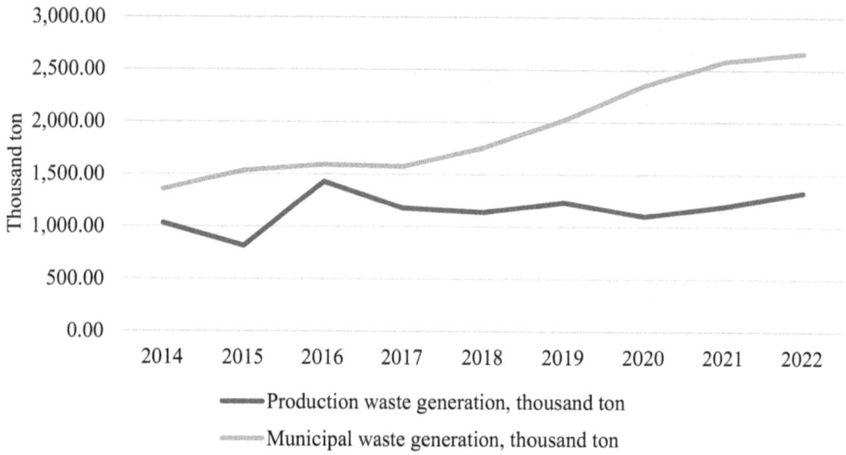

Figure 3.22 Azerbaijan. Generation of production waste and municipal waste from 2014 to 2022, in thousands of tons.

Source: Own compilation based on data from The State Statistical Committee of the Republic of Azerbaijan (2023).

compared to 2014. In 2020, Azerbaijan collected 2.66 million tons of waste from the population, and this was the largest volume of waste in the entire study period.

From 2014 to 2021, the amount of production waste generated was increased by 28.68%. In the same period, VAT—an indicator showing the production process, expressed in current prices—increased by 4.75%. In this context, the separation of the production process from waste generation is not confirmed (Figure 3.22). There was a similar trend for municipal waste. From 2014 to 2022, waste collected from the population and household consumption were characterized by a clear growth rate. As a result, compared to household consumption, the amount of waste collected from the population grew faster (Figure 3.23). In this interval, the dynamics of municipal waste production exceeded the dynamics of household consumption. Between 2014 and 2022, the amount of waste from households increased by 96.20%, while household consumption declined by 20.12% on average per year. Thus, the current consumption pattern of the population is conducive to accelerated waste generation.

Waste recycling—evolution of the indicator

In Azerbaijan, data is collected on "used waste," which includes both waste disposed of and waste used for energy production.

The most waste was disposed of in 2018—848.3 thousand tons of waste. During 2014–2022, the amount of disposed waste ranged from 497.3 to 848.3 thousand tons (Figure 3.24). At the same time, in 2018, the ratio of disposed waste to produced waste reached the highest value of 29.29%. In 2014–2022, the ratio ranged between 20.12% and 41.37%.

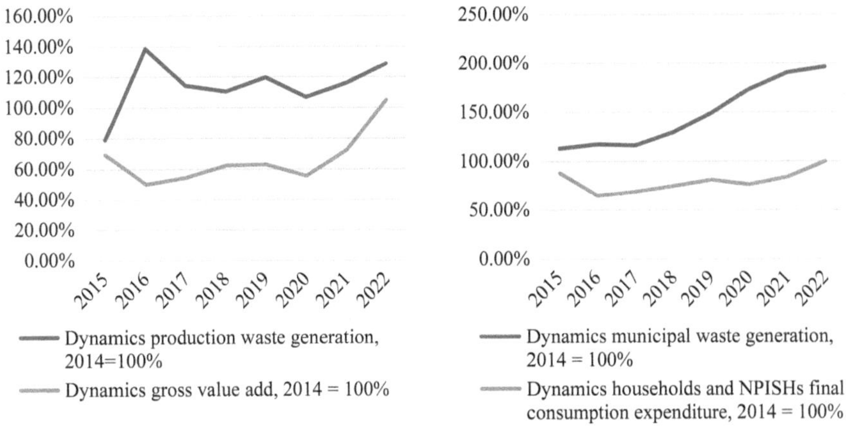

Figure 3.23 Azerbaijan. Dynamics of production waste, municipal waste, VAT, and household consumption from 2015 to 2022, in %.

Source: Own compilation based on data from The State Statistical Committee of the Republic of Azerbaijan (2023).

Use of fertilizers

Fertilizer balances are maintained in Azerbaijan, revealing an upward trend in the consumption of mineral fertilizers alongside stable usage of organic fertilizers. Notably, organic fertilizer consumption predominates (Figure 3.25). Mineral fertilizer application increased significantly from 107.6 thousand tons in 2014 to over

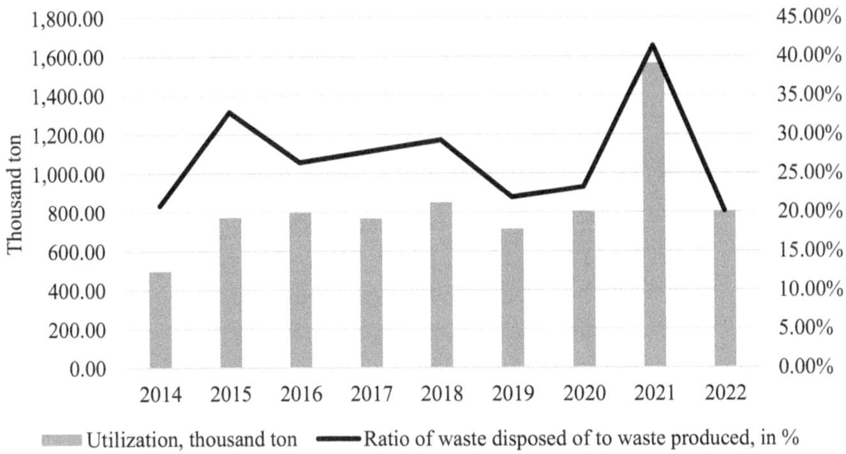

Figure 3.24 Azerbaijan. Waste disposed (thousands of tons) and the ratio of waste disposed to waste produced from 2014 to 2022, in %.

Source: Own compilation based on data from The State Statistical Committee of the Republic of Azerbaijan (2023).

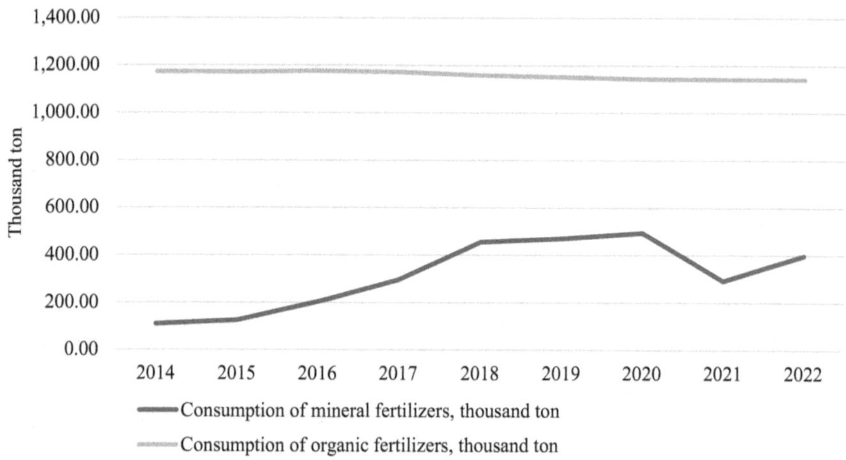

Figure 3.25 Azerbaijan. Consumption of chemical and natural fertilizers on farms and peasant farms (farmers) during 2014–2017, in thousands of tons.

Source: Own compilation based on data from The State Statistical Committee of the Republic of Azerbaijan (2023).

396.7 thousand tons in 2022. Conversely, there was a slight decline in the use of organic fertilizers. Specifically, while 1172 thousand tons of organic fertilizers were applied in 2014, this figure decreased marginally to just over 1141 thousand tons by 2022 for agricultural purposes.

The rise in fertilizer consumption coincided with an increase in the quantity of mineral fertilizers applied per hectare of land. From 2014 to 2022, the application rate rose from 59.8 to 208.8 kg/ha for chemical fertilizers. In contrast, the rate for organic fertilizers remained steady at 610 kg/ha (Figure 3.26). By 2022, compared to 2014, there was a 2.65% decrease in the use of organic fertilizers, while the use of mineral fertilizers surged by 268.38%.

Most mineral fertilizers are nitrates. In second place are phosphates, and the smallest share is potassium fertilizers. During 2014–2017, all types of fertilizers were consumed to varying degrees (Figure 3.27). The amount of nitrates consumed increased by 85.27%, or from 48.64 to 90.11 thousand tons.

During the same period, the amount of phosphate fell by 99.17%, or from 2.78 thousand tons to 23 tons. Potassium fertilizer consumption also declined by 87.65%, or from 1.7 thousand tons to 210 tons.

Use of water

From 2014 to 2022, water consumption in Azerbaijan exhibited consistent growth. Starting at 8,115 million m^3 in 2014, it increased to 10,528 million m^3 by 2022. Across most sectors, water consumption showed a steady upward trend

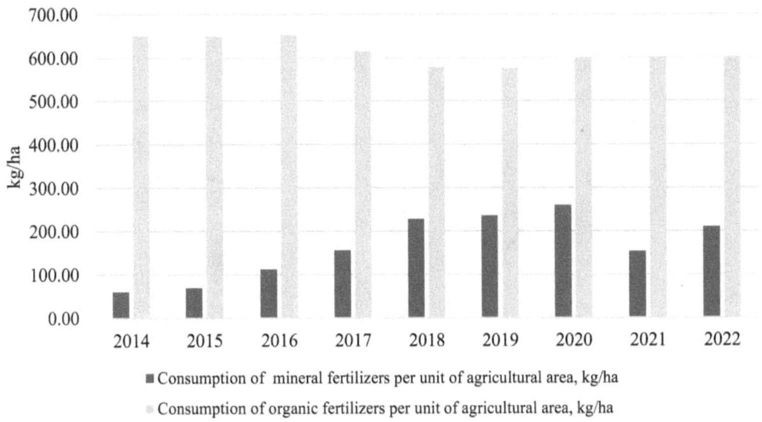

Figure 3.26 Azerbaijan. Consumption of chemical and natural fertilizers on farms and peasant farms (farmers) during 2014–2017, in kg/ha.

Source: Own compilation based on data from The State Statistical Committee of the Republic of Azerbaijan (2023).

(Figure 3.28). On average, 2,206.89 million m^3 of water were used annually for production purposes during this period, constituting 23.62% of total water consumption. In Azerbaijan, the agricultural sector emerged as the largest consumer of water. From 2014 to 2022, agriculture averaged an annual water consumption of 6,757.78 million m^3, accounting for 72.33% of total water consumption. Domestic water consumption over the same period amounted to 313.56 million m^3, representing 3.36% of the national economy's total water consumption.

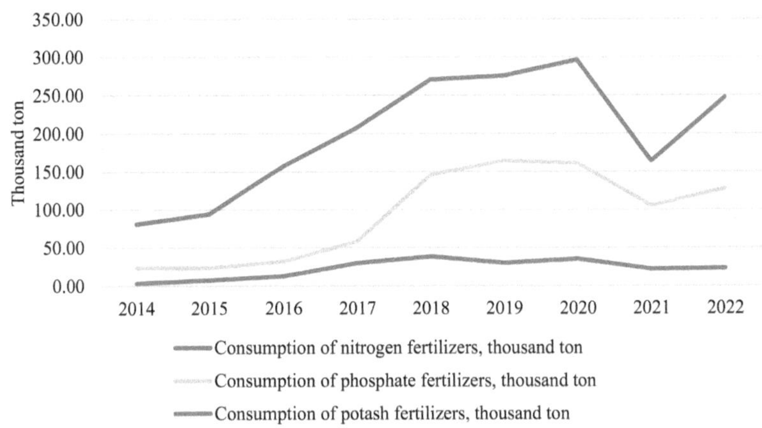

Figure 3.27 Azerbaijan. Types of mineral fertilizers used on farms and peasant farms (farmers) during 2014–2022, in thousands of tons.

Source: Own compilation based on data from The State Statistical Committee of the Republic of Azerbaijan (2023).

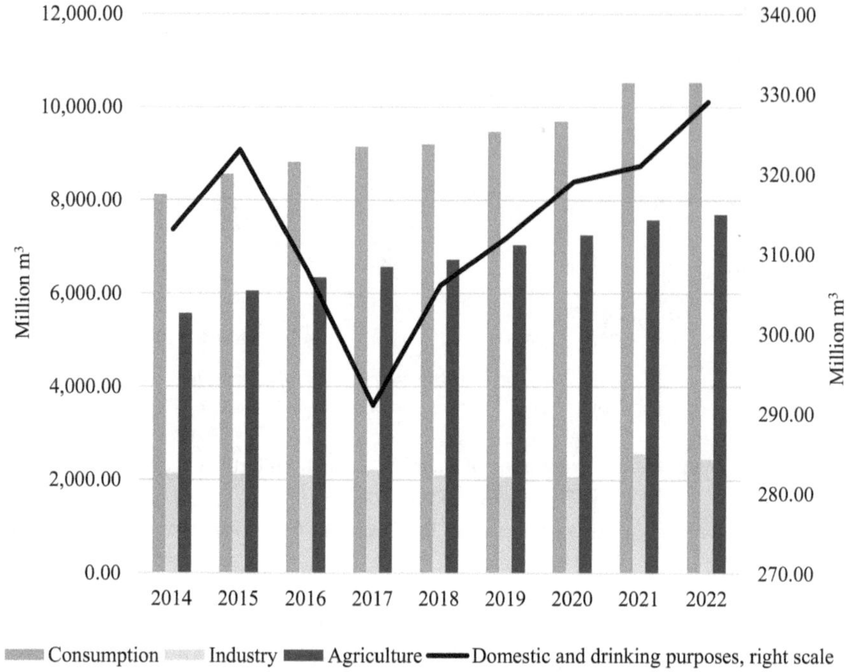

Figure 3.28 Azerbaijan. Water consumption by economic sector during 2014–2022, in million m^3.

Source: Own compilation based on data from The State Statistical Committee of the Republic of Azerbaijan (2023).

If water consumption in Azerbaijan increased by 29.74% between 2014 and 2022, concurrently GDP expressed in USD at 2017 constant prices rose by 39.11%. Despite this economic growth, water productivity declined, indicating a failure to achieve decoupling of economic growth from water consumption. Expressed as the ratio of GDP at 2017 constant prices at purchasing power parity to the volume of water consumption, productivity decreased from 17.47 USD/m^3 in 2014 to 14.54 USD/m^3 in 2022, marking a decline of 16.77%.

Belarus

Greenhouse gas emissions

The Republic of Belarus places great importance on addressing climate change, as demonstrated by its participation in all major international agreements in this field. Belarus signed the United Nations Framework Convention on Climate Change (UNFCCC) on June 11, 1992, ratified it on May 11, 2000, and became a full party to the UNFCCC on August 9, 2000 (UNFCCC, 2006a). Subsequently, on August 26, 2005, Belarus signed a document to accede to the Kyoto Protocol, becoming a full party on November 24, 2005. Decision 32/CMP.1 submitted Belarus' request to be included in Annex B of the Protocol to the parties of the Kyoto Protocol, outlining its commitment to reduce greenhouse gas emissions to 95% of the 1990 levels. Inclusion in Annex B is crucial for Belarus, as it determines the country's eligibility to participate in the Kyoto Protocol's economic mechanisms and to acquire financial resources under the flexibility mechanisms (UNFCCC, 2006a).

Since joining the Kyoto Protocol, Belarus has been actively working to create the conditions necessary for fulfilling its commitments. The country is establishing the legislative, institutional, and technical foundations for its full and effective participation in the Kyoto Protocol's flexibility mechanisms, and the National Action Plan on Climate Change has been approved (UNFCCC, 2006a).

Additionally, according to the document "Nationally Determined Contribution of the Republic of Belarus" (INDC), which was prepared in accordance with paragraphs 13 and 14 of Decision 1/CP.20 of the Conference of the Parties to the UNFCCC in preparation for the 21st Conference of the Parties, Belarus has committed to reducing greenhouse gas emissions by at least 28% by 2030 compared to the 1990 base year (Ministry of Natural Resources and Environment of the Republic of Belarus, 2018), excluding the Land Use, Land-Use Change and Forestry sector (hereinafter referred to as "LULUCF") and without any additional conditions. The commitment did not imply using international carbon market mechanisms or mobilizing foreign financial resources for the implementation of the best available technologies (UNEP, 2021).

In light of the establishment of an Inter-Ministerial Working Group on Climate Change by decree of the Minister of Natural Resources and Environmental Protection of the Republic of Belarus on May 20, 2015, Belarus is further strengthening its commitment to climate action. This group includes representatives from various ministries and government bodies, such as the Ministry of Natural Resources, the Ministry of Foreign Affairs, the Ministry of Energy, the Ministry of Economy, the Ministry of Finance, the Ministry of Forestry, and the Ministry of Agriculture and Food, as well as experts (Ministry of Natural Resources and Environment of the Republic of Belarus, 2018).

In October 2021, in alignment with Article 4 of the Paris Agreement, the Republic of Belarus pledged to make a more ambitious contribution to the global response to climate change by setting both unconditional and conditional economy-wide GHG reduction targets. Considering the country's economic situation and capabilities, the new unconditional target is to reduce GHG emissions by at least 35% by 2030 from 1990 levels, including the land use, land-use change, and forestry (LULUCF) sector. Additionally, the new conditional target aims to reduce GHG emissions by at least 40% by 2030 from 1990 levels, also including the LULUCF sector, contingent upon the use of international financing mechanisms to implement the best available technologies for ensuring these reductions (UNEP, 2021).

Evolution of the greenhouse gas emission rate

In the Republic of Belarus, after 2013, emissions of greenhouse gases, including CO_2 (carbon dioxide accounts for 3/5 of greenhouse gases), had a downward trend. In 2020 compared to 2019, emissions of greenhouse gases, including CO_2 respectively decreased by 5.14% and 7.79%.

The Republic of Belarus' historical responsibility for greenhouse gas emissions is small. In 2020. The Republic of Belarus emitted about 87.87 $MtCO_2$-equivalent (without the LUCF sector) and 86.30 $MtCO_2$-equivalent (with the LUCF sector), which is less than 0.18% of total global emissions (Climate Watch Data, 2024). In Belarus, total and net per capita GHG emissions were significantly higher than the global average (Belarus: net emissions were 9.20tCO_2 equivalent per capita, total emissions were 9.37tCO_2 equivalent per capita; World: net emissions were 5.94tCO_2 equivalent per capita, total emissions were 6.12tCO_2 equivalent per capita) (Climate Watch Data, 2024). Between 1990 and 2021, the dynamics of total direct GHG emissions (excluding LUCF), expressed in CO_2 equivalent, in Belarus showed a downward trend, decreasing by about 38.13%: from 142.02 $MtCO_2$ equivalent in 1990 to 87.87 $MtCO_2$ equivalent in 2020. Net greenhouse gas emissions (from the LUCF) decreased by about 33.06% over the same period: from 128.92 $MtCO_2$-equivalent in 1990 to 86.30 $MtCO_2$-equivalent in 2020 (Climate Watch Data, 2024).

From 2014 to 2020, greenhouse gas emissions showed a steady growth rate (Figure 3.29). During this period, annual emissions averaged 89.60 $MtCO_2$ equivalent. Annual changes oscillated slightly around this value and ranged between 87.32 and 92.63 $MtCO_2$ equivalent. Carbon dioxide emissions account for 63.40% of all greenhouse gas emissions. From 2014 to 2020, CO_2 emissions evolved steadily and oscillated slightly around an annual average value of

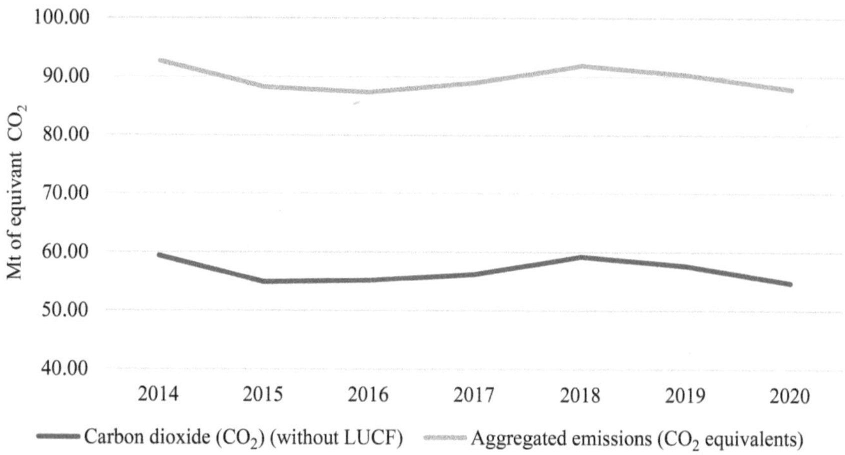

Figure 3.29 Belarus. Greenhouse gas emissions, including CO_2, in $MtCO_2$ equivalent.
Source: Climate Watch Data (2024).

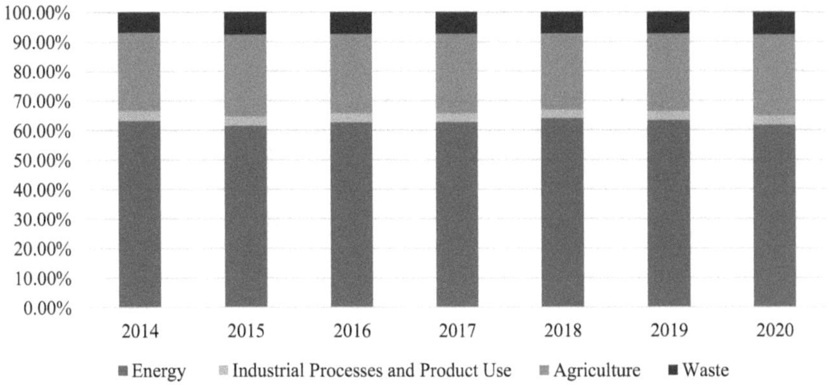

Figure 3.30 Belarus. Structure of greenhouse gas emissions by sector, in %.

Source: Climate Watch Data (2024).

about 56.79 $MtCO_2$ equivalent. Annual fluctuations oscillated between 54.80 and 59.43 $MtCO_2$ equivilent.

Between 2014 and 2020, the structure of greenhouse gas emissions by sector did not change significantly (Figure 3.30). The share of emissions generated by the energy sector decreased slightly from 63.26% to 61.76%, and emissions determined by industrial processes and product use decreased from 3.42% to 3.21%. The share of emissions from the agriculture and waste sectors was characterized by an increase from 26.49% to 27.48% and from 6.82% to 7.55%, respectively.

Productivity (emission efficiency) of CO_2

In Belarus after 2013, the decline in greenhouse gas emissions, including CO_2, was accompanied by fluctuations in GDP dynamics. In 2014 and during 2017–2019, the Belarusian economy experienced growth dynamics. During 2015–2016 and in 2020, there was a decline in GDP. In 2020, compared to 2014, GDP was 0.10% lower at USD 58.6 billion. Under the conditions of decreasing CO_2 emissions and fluctuating GDP, a slight decrease in CO_2 productivity was observed (Figure 3.31). The level of CO_2 productivity during 2014–2020 decreased slightly from 1.01 USD/kg to 0.93 USD/kg. In contrast, greenhouse gas productivity from 2014 to 2020 increased slightly from 0.63 to 0.67 USD/$kgCO_2$ equivalent. The results obtained show that Belarus is making efforts to decouple economic growth from CO_2 emissions.

The value of the indicator—CO_2 productivity—can be calculated using the quotient of the size of GDP at purchasing power parity expressed in constant 2017 prices and the volume of CO_2 emissions expressed in kilograms. Thus, during 2014–2020, the average value of the indicator was equal to 3.12 GDP/kg. It should be noted that the value of the indicator remained at a relatively constant level during these years. Accordingly, Belarus saw a slight increase from 3.04 GDP/kg to 3.29 GDP/kg over the entire period under review, an increase of 8.34%.

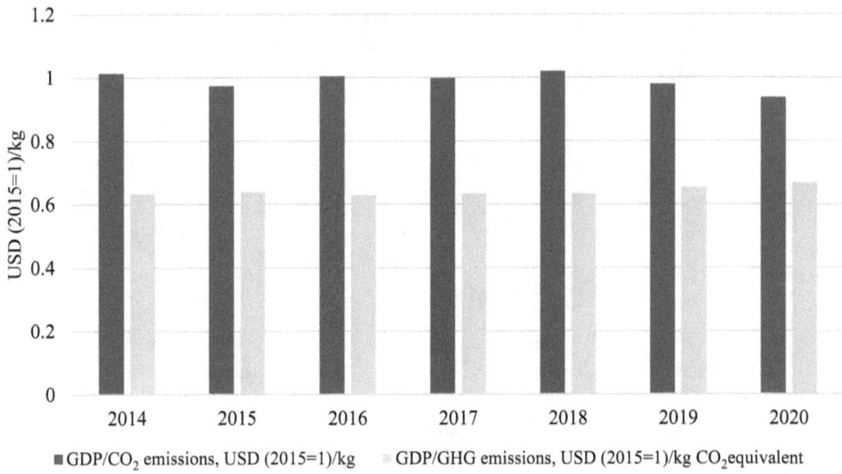

Figure 3.31 Belarus. Greenhouse gas and CO_2 productivity.

Source: Climate Watch Data (2024).

Final energy consumption

In Belarus, energy balance data is available for the period 2014–2020. During this timeframe, both primary energy supply and final energy consumption declined. Notably, the decline in energy supply was more significant than the decline in GDP over the same period.

Overall, between 2014 and 2020, the supply of primary energy in Belarus decreased from 27.6 to 25.9 million tons of oil equivalent (Toe). This reduction in energy supply also resulted in a decrease in energy consumption. As shown in Figure 3.32, total energy consumption decreased from 18.8 million Toe in 2014 to 17.8 million Toe in 2020, representing a decrease of 5.63%.

Consumption levels in the residential and agricultural sectors remained essentially unchanged between 2014 and 2020. On the other hand, sectors such as transportation, services and industry saw a decline in energy consumption. Thus, in the industrial sector, the decrease was 9.18% (i.e. consumption fell from 6.7 million Toe in 2014 to 6 million Toe in 2020). In the transportation sector, energy consumption decreased by 8.50%, or from 4.1 to 3.8 million Toe. Also, the services sector saw an 8.07% decrease in energy consumption, from 1.9 to 1.8 million Toe.

Between 2014 and 2020, the structure of total energy consumption in Belarus changed slightly (Figure 3.33). The industrial sector remained the largest consumer, accounting for 34.28% of total energy consumption in 2020. The residential sector followed, with its share increasing by 1.79 percentage points to 28.30% over this period. The transportation sector ranked third, with a share of 21.41% in 2020. The service sector's share remained stable, averaging 9.88% of total energy consumption. In contrast, the agricultural sector accounted for an average of 6.17% of total energy consumption.

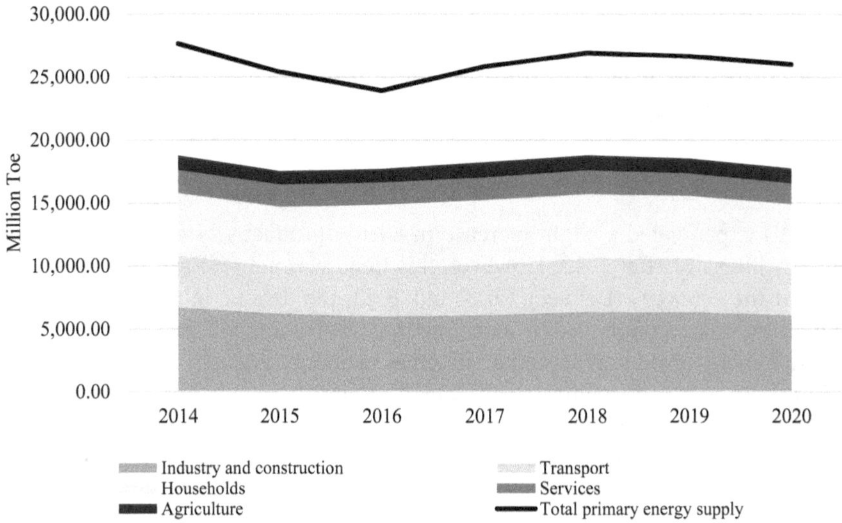

Figure 3.32 Belarus. Primary energy supply and final energy consumption by sector, in thousand tons of oil equivalent.

Source: National Statistical Committee of the Republic of Belarus (2022).

In 2020, compared to 2014, the supply of primary energy in Belarus decreased by 6.15%, while the volume of GDP at purchasing power parity (PPP) in constant 2017 prices remained virtually unchanged. This outcome suggests that changes in energy productivity have not contributed significantly to decoupling economic

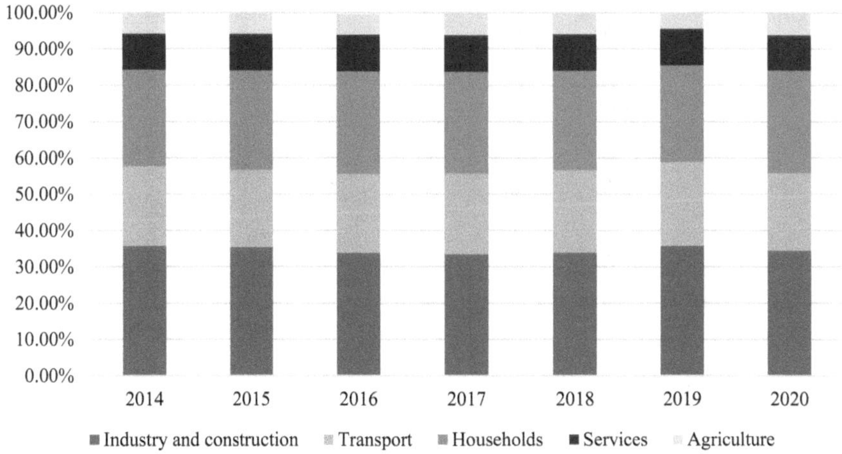

Figure 3.33 Belarus. Structure of total energy use, in %.

Source: Own compilation based on data from National Statistical Committee of the Republic of Belarus (2022).

growth from energy consumption. However, if we calculate the ratio of GDP at PPP in constant 2017 prices to the volume of energy production, the resulting energy productivity index indicates a slight increase of 6.45%, rising from 6.54 to 6.96 USD per gigajoule (GO) between 2014 and 2020.

Energy intensity

Belarus experienced a slight increase in energy productivity and a decrease in energy intensity after 2013. However, this trend was not uniform across all sectors of the economy. Between 2014 and 2022, the decline in final energy consumption was accompanied by a decline in GDP, leading to a modest increase in overall energy productivity and a reduction in energy intensity (Figure 3.34). In 2014, final energy consumption amounted to 319.40 grams of oil equivalent per US dollar, whereas in 2020, this ratio decreased to 301.72 grams of oil equivalent per USD, reflecting a decrease of only 5.54%. The industrial sector, being the most energy-intensive, saw its energy intensity index drop from 113.76 grams of oil equivalent per USD in 2014 to 103.42 grams of oil equivalent per USD in 2020, marking a decrease of 9.09%.

Contrarily, the agricultural sector saw the largest increase in energy intensity. From 2014 to 2020, gross value added in this sector fell by 24.54%, while energy

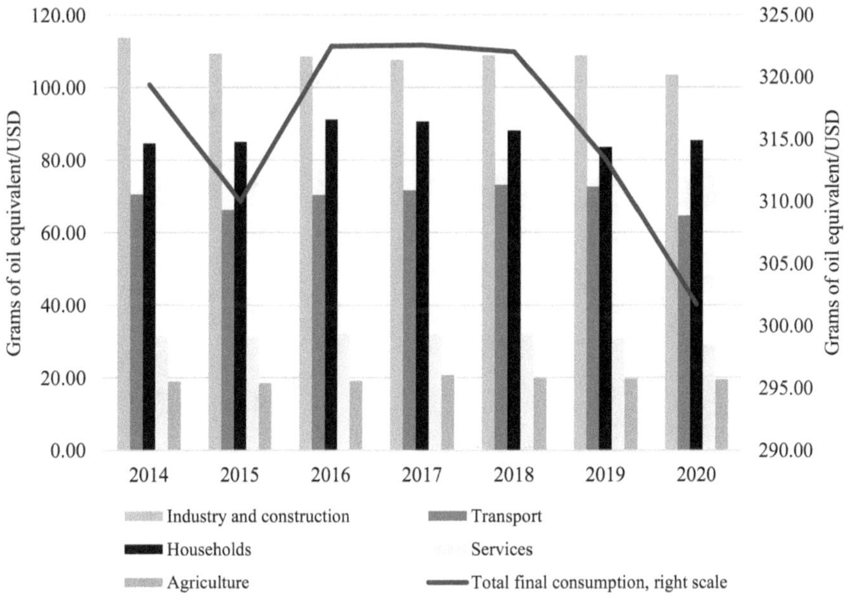

Figure 3.34 Belarus. Energy intensity, in grams of oil equivalent/USD.

Source: Own compilation based on data from National Statistical Committee of the Republic of Belarus (2022).

consumption rose by an average of 1.97%. Consequently, the energy intensity in agriculture increased from 18.99 grams of oil equivalent per USD in 2014 to 19.39 grams of oil equivalent per USD in 2020, an increase of 2.08%. Similarly, the housing sector did not see a reduction in energy intensity, which rose from 84.66 grams of oil equivalent per USD to 85.38 grams of oil equivalent per USD. In contrast, the transportation sector achieved a reduction in energy intensity, decreasing from 70.52 grams of oil equivalent per USD to 64.59 grams of oil equivalent per USD, a decrease of 8.41%.

Share of renewable energy in total energy consumption

In Belarus, the growth of renewable energy was notable between 2014 and 2019, leading to an increasing share of renewable sources in both primary energy supply and final energy consumption. By 2019, wood energy dominated the renewable energy supply with a share of 7.00%, followed by hydropower at 0.116%, and biogas production at 0.10%. Wind energy and solar energy accounted for 0.06% each, highlighting the early stage of development in modern renewable energy generation sectors. Despite these advancements, the overall supply of renewable energy in Belarus increased from 1.44 million tons of oil equivalent in 2014 to 1.89 million tons in 2020, representing a decrease of 31.47%. However, the share of renewable energy in primary energy production rose from 5.2% in 2014 to 7.3% by 2019 (Figure 3.35).

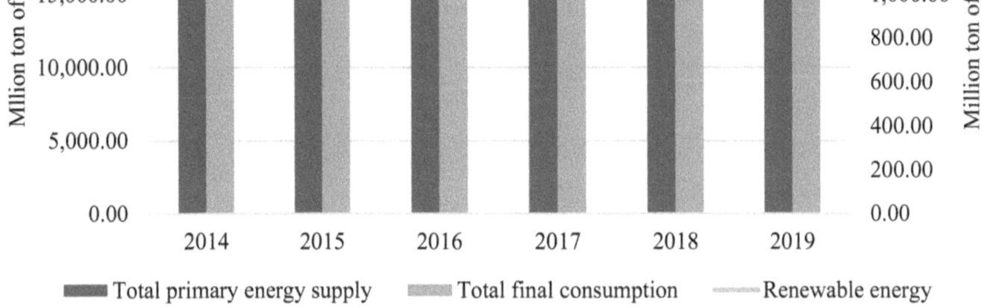

Figure 3.35 Belarus. Renewable energy supply (thousand tons of oil equivalent) and share of renewable energy in primary energy production and total energy consumption, in %.

Source: Own compilation based on data from National Statistical Committee of the Republic of Belarus (2022).

Waste generation

In Belarus between 2014 and 2022, two notable trends emerged regarding waste generation. First, production waste showed an increasing trend, particularly noticeable after 2016, although there was a decrease in 2022 (Figure 3.36). Second, simultaneously, there was a steady increase in waste generated by the public. Specifically, the amount of production waste increased from nearly 52.53 million tons in 2014 to approximately 62.25 million tons in 2021, marking an 18.51% rise. However, in 2022, there was a significant 23.69% decrease in production waste. Conversely, waste collected from the population showed a consistent upward trajectory. Over the period of 2014 to 2022, the volume of waste collected increased by 7.32%, with approximately 4 million tons of waste collected in 2022 alone.

From 2014 to 2021, the amount of production waste generated was increased by 18.51%. In the same period VAT—an indicator showing the production process, expressed in current prices—decreased by 12.38%. In this context, the separation of the production process from waste generation is not confirmed (Figure 3.37). There was a similar trend for municipal waste. From 2014 to 2022, waste collected from the population and household consumption had different dynamics. As a result, compared to household consumption, the amount of waste collected from the population grew faster. In this interval, the dynamics of municipal waste production exceeded the dynamics of household consumption. Between 2014 and 2022, the amount of waste from households increased by 7.32%, while household consumption decreased by 22.11% on average per year. Thus, the current pattern of population consumption does not reduce the volume of municipal waste.

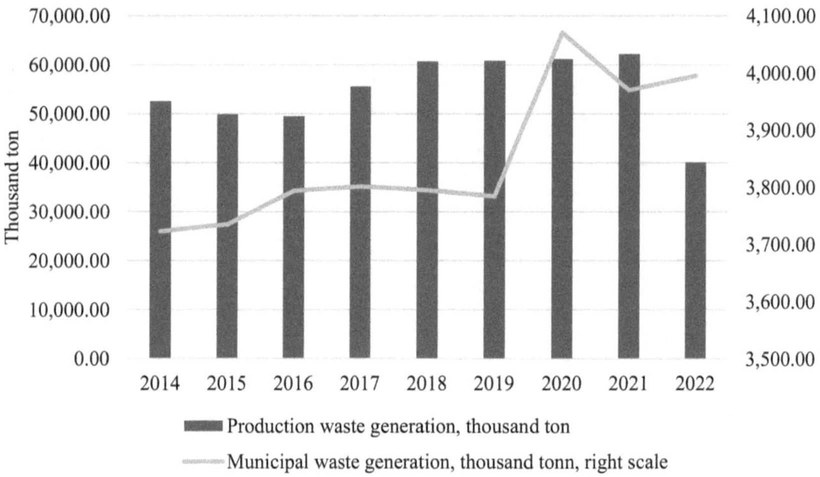

Figure 3.36 Belarus. Production of production waste and municipal waste from 2014 to 2022, in thousands of tons.

Source: Own compilation based on data from National Statistical Committee of the Republic of Belarus (2022).

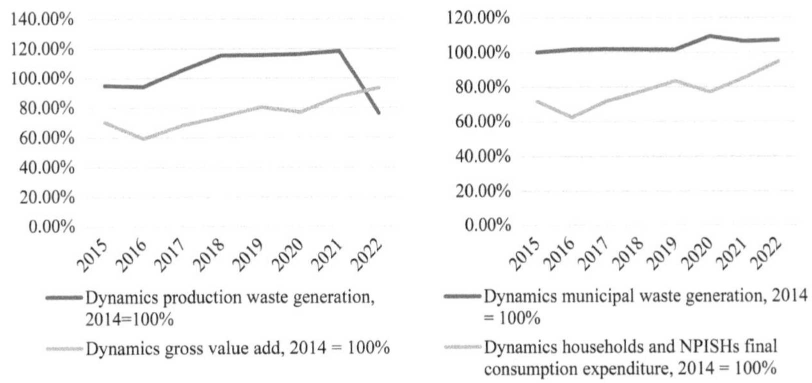

Figure 3.37 Belarus. Dynamics of production waste, municipal waste, VAT, and household consumption from 2015 to 2022, in %.

Source: Own compilation based on data from National Statistical Committee of the Republic of Belarus (2022).

Waste recycling—Evolution of the indicator

Belarus disposed of the most waste in 2022—20.05 million tons of waste. From 2014 to 2022, the amount of waste disposed ranged from 12.75 to 22.65 million tons (Figure 3.38). At the same time, in 2022, the ratio of disposed waste to produced waste reached its highest value, at 45.47%. From 2014 to 2022, the ratio oscillated between 23.78 and 45.47%.

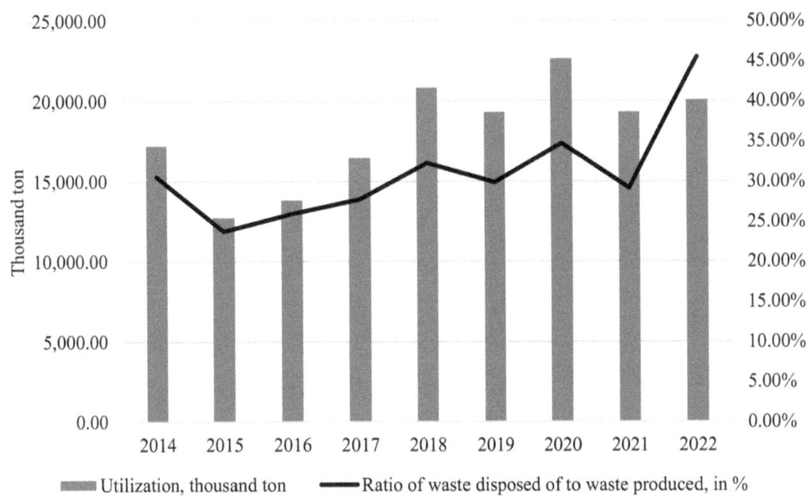

Figure 3.38 Belarus. Waste disposed (thousands of tons) and the ratio of waste disposed to waste produced between 2014 and 2022, in %.

Source: Own compilation based on data from National Statistical Committee of the Republic of Belarus (2022).

Fertilizer use

In Belarus, the fertilizer balance sheet reveals a declining trend in both mineral and organic fertilizer consumption, with organic fertilizers predominating (Figure 3.39). Specifically, the consumption of mineral fertilizers decreased from 1.22 million tons in 2014 to slightly over 1.10 million tons in 2022. Conversely, there was a slight decrease in the consumption of organic fertilizers. In 2014, approximately 52.32 million tons of organic fertilizers were used, compared to more than 50.84 million tons in 2022 for agricultural land fertilization.

Between 2014 and 2022 in Belarus, there was a noticeable decline in fertilizer use per hectare of soil, accompanied by specific changes in application rates. The application rate for mineral fertilizers decreased from 162 kg/ha in 2014 to 153 kg/ha by 2022. Conversely, the application rate for organic fertilizers remained stable at 6.8 tons/ha (Figure 3.40). Comparing 2022 to 2014, there was a reduction in the use of organic fertilizers by 10.10% and a slight decrease in the use of mineral fertilizers by 2.83%. These trends indicate a strategic shift towards more sustainable agricultural practices and possibly improved efficiency in fertilizer application over the analyzed period.

Most mineral fertilizers are potassium fertilizers. Nitrates are second, and phosphates account for the smallest share. During 2014–2017, all types of fertilizers were consumed to varying degrees (Figure 3.41). The amount of nitrates consumed increased by 1.45%, or from 456.1 to 462.7 thousand tons. During the same period, the amount of phosphate fell by 35.55%, or from 153.3 thousand tons to 98.8 tons. Potassium fertilizer consumption also fell by 12.36%, or from 609.3 thousand tons to 534 tons.

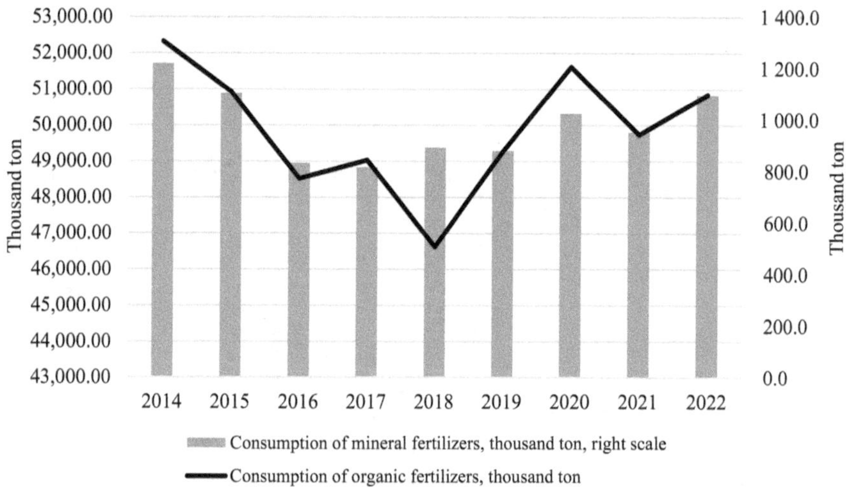

Figure 3.39 Belarus. Consumption of chemical and natural fertilizers on farms and peasant farms (farmers) during 2014–2017, in thousands of tons.

Source: Own compilation based on data from National Statistical Committee of the Republic of Belarus (2022).

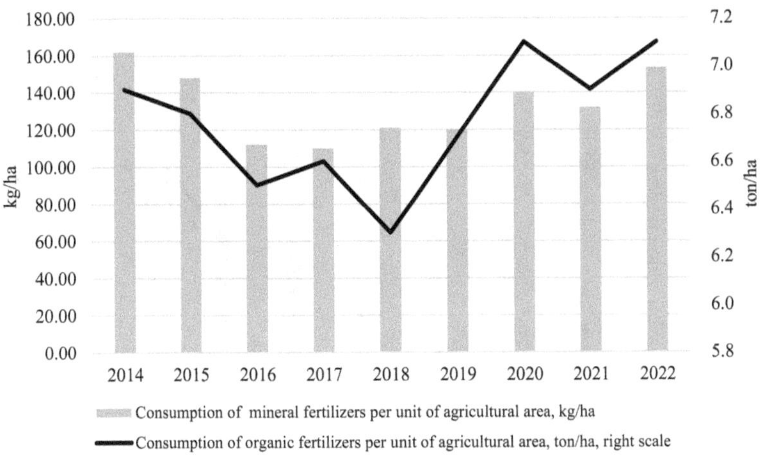

Figure 3.40 Belarus. Consumption of chemical and natural fertilizers on farms and peasant farms (farmers) during 2014–2017, in kg/ha.

Source: Own compilation based on data from National Statistical Committee of the Republic of Belarus (2022).

Water consumption

Between 2014 and 2022, Belarus experienced a decline in water consumption, with total usage decreasing from 1,370.8 million m^3 in 2014 to 1,270.5 million m^3 in 2022. This decline in water consumption varied across different sectors (Figure 3.42). The industrial sector was the largest consumer of water in Belarus, averaging 503.97 million m^3 annually for production needs during this period,

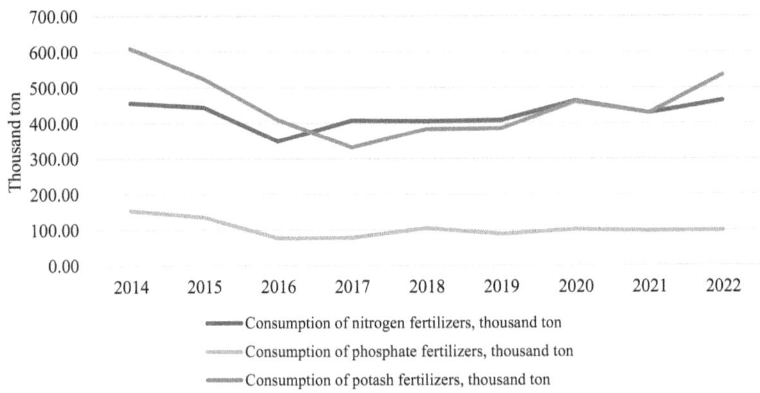

Figure 3.41 Belarus. Types of mineral fertilizers used on farms and peasant farms (farmers) during 2014–2022, in thousands of tons.

Source: Own compilation based on data from National Statistical Committee of the Republic of Belarus (2022).

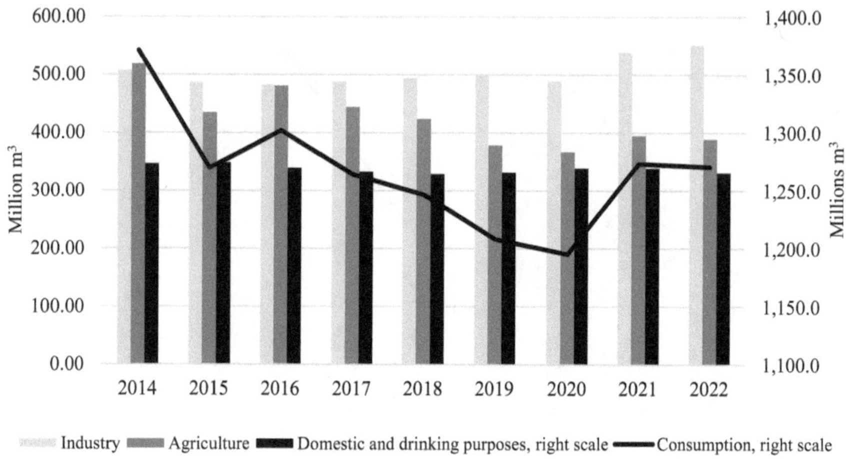

Figure 3.42 Belarus. Water consumption by economic sector during 2014–2022, in million m³.

Source: Own compilation based on data from National Statistical Committee of the Republic of Belarus (2022).

which accounted for 39.79% of total water consumption. The agricultural sector followed closely, using an average of 425.45 million m³ of water annually, representing 33.59% of total water consumption in the country. Household water consumption over the same period averaged 337.31 million m³ annually, making up 26.63% of total water consumption in the national economy.

If water consumption fell by 7.32% between 2014 and 2022, then GDP expressed in USD at 2017 constant prices increased by 15.87%. As a result, water productivity increased and a decoupling of economic growth from water consumption was achieved. If one expresses productivity as the ratio of GDP at 2017 constant prices at purchasing power parity to the volume of water consumption, then in 2022 compared to 2014, the level of productivity increased to 163.80 from 131.01 USD/m³, an increase of 25.02%.

Georgia

Greenhouse gas emissions

Georgia became a party to the United Nations Framework Convention on Climate Change in 1994. The Kyoto Protocol to the Convention was ratified by the Georgian Parliament on May 28, 1999. Subsequently, on February 21, 2017, the Government of Georgia approved the Paris Agreement. Furthermore, on January 17, 2020, Georgia joined the Amendment to the Doha Amendment to the Kyoto Protocol, which is an integral part of the United Nations Framework Convention on Climate Change (Ministry of Environmental Protection and Agriculture of Georgia, 2015; 2021).

In 2016, the EU–Georgia Association Agreement entered into force, highlighting the importance of cooperation in various aspects of climate change. These include mitigation and adaptation to climate change, emissions trading, integration of climate considerations into sectoral policies, and the development of clean technologies. The agreement specifically emphasizes the necessity of collaboration in preparing technology transfer activities based on Georgia's Low Carbon Development Strategy, Nationally Appropriate Mitigation Actions (NAMA), and Technology Needs Assessment (TNA) (Ministry of Environmental Protection and Agriculture of Georgia, 2019b).

On June 7, 2017, Georgia ratified the Paris Agreement and began preparing the Nationally Determined Contribution (NDC) document. At the same time, the Ministry of Environmental Protection and Agriculture of Georgia began to develop the "Climate Action Plan for 2021–2030" (Ministry of Environmental Protection and Agriculture of Georgia, 2019b).

In 2021, Georgia submitted an updated Nationally Determined Contribution (NDC) and developed its 2030 Climate Change Strategy along with the 2021–2023 Climate Change Action Plan (CSAP). This comprehensive framework includes detailed indicators and metrics specifically tailored for seven key economic sectors (Ministry of Environmental Protection and Agriculture of Georgia, 2023b).

Georgia, as a Contracting Party to the Energy Community Treaty, is actively aligning and implementing EU legislation (Acquis Communautaire) in accordance with the Energy Community Treaty and Georgia's Protocol of Accession to the Energy Community Treaty. Following consultations involving the Energy Community, the European Commission, and the Government of Georgia, a new greenhouse gas reduction target was established for Georgia to achieve by 2030. This target aims to reduce greenhouse gas emissions by 47% compared to 1990 levels, including the land use, land use change, and forestry sector (LULUCF). On December 15, 2022, the Energy Community Council of Ministers endorsed this target through an Executive Order. Georgia plans to incorporate this updated commitment into its revised Nationally Determined Contribution (NDC) in 2025.

Evolution of the greenhouse gas emission rate

In Georgia, greenhouse gas emissions, primarily comprising CO_2 (carbon dioxide constituting more than half of total emissions), have shown relatively stable trends since 2013. By 2020, compared to 2014 levels, greenhouse gas emissions increased by 5.14%. Specifically, CO_2 emissions rose by 18.50% during the same period.

Georgia's historical responsibility for greenhouse gas emissions is small. In 2020, Georgia emitted about 17.67 $MtCO_2$ equivalent (without the LUCF sector) and 17.69$MtCO_2$ equivalent (with the LUCF sector), accounting for less than 0.04% of total global emissions (Climate Watch Data, 2024). In Georgia, total and net per capita GHG emissions were below the global average (Georgia: net emissions were 4.75 $MTCO_2$ equivalent per capita, total emissions were 4.75 $MTCO_2$ equivalent per capita; World: net emissions were 5.94 $MTCO_2$ equivalent per capita, total emissions were 6.12 $MTCO_2$ equivalent per capita) (Climate Watch

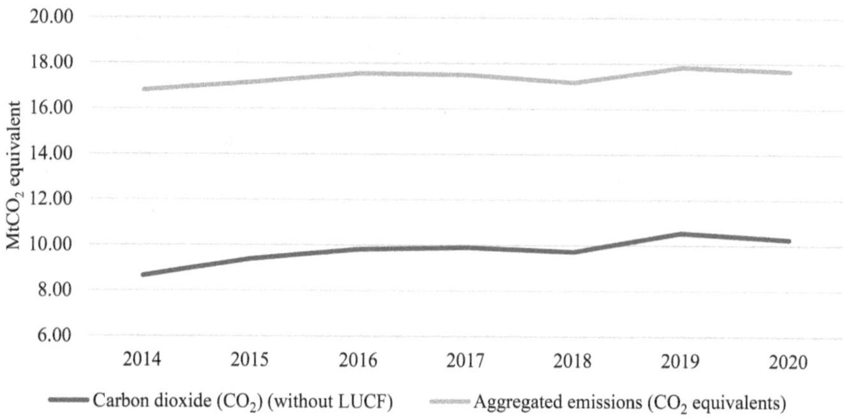

Figure 3.43 Georgia. Greenhouse gas emissions, including CO_2, in $MtCO_2$ equivalent.
Source: Climate Watch Data (2024).

Data, 2024). Between 1990 and 2021, the dynamics of total direct GHG emissions (excluding LUCF), expressed in CO_2 equivalent, in Georgia showed a downward trend, decreasing by about 64.46%: from 49.72 $MtCO_2$ equivalent in 1990 to 17.67 $MtCO_2$ equivalent in 2020. Net greenhouse gas emissions (from LUCF) decreased by about 43.54% over the same period: from 31.33 $MtCO_2$ equivalent in 1990 to 17.69 $MtCO_2$ equivalent in 2020 (Climate Watch Data, 2024).

From 2014 to 2020, greenhouse gas emissions in Georgia exhibited stable dynamics, as illustrated in Figure 3.43. Over this period, annual emissions averaged approximately 17.38 million metric tons of CO_2 equivalent ($MtCO_2$ equivalent). Annual variations fluctuated slightly around this average, ranging between 16.81 and 17.84 $MtCO_2$ equivalent. Carbon dioxide (CO_2) emissions constituted the majority, accounting for 56.09% of total greenhouse gas emissions. Specifically, CO_2 emissions followed a steady trend during the same period, oscillating around an annual average of approximately 9.76 $MtCO_2$ equivalent. Annual fluctuations in CO_2 emissions ranged between 8.65 and 10.55 $MtCO_2$ equivalent.

Between 2014 and 2020, the structure of greenhouse gas emissions by sector did not change significantly (Figure 3.44). The share of emissions generated by the energy sector increased from 55.77% to 58.54%, and the share of emissions determined by industrial processes and product use increased from 10.18% to 11.60%. The share of emissions from the agriculture and waste sectors was characterized by a decrease from 14.88% to 11.76% and from 19.17% to 18.10%, respectively.

Productivity (emission efficiency) of CO_2

In Georgia, since 2013, there has been a slight increase in greenhouse gas emissions, including CO_2 emissions, alongside positive GDP growth. For instance, in 2020 compared to 2014, GDP grew by 14.07%. This period of increased CO_2 emissions and GDP growth also saw a rise in CO_2 productivity, as depicted in

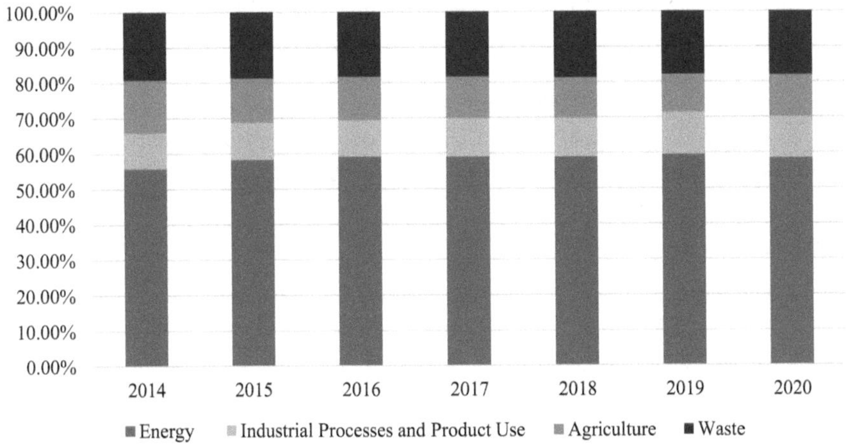

Figure 3.44 Georgia. Structure of greenhouse gas emissions by sector, in %.

Source: Climate Watch Data (2024).

Figure 3.45. Specifically, CO_2 productivity increased slightly from 0.60 USD/kg in 2014 to 0.62 USD/kg in 2020. Conversely, the productivity of greenhouse gases, measured as US dollars per kg of CO_2 equivalent, decreased from USD 1.16 to USD 1.07 over the same period. These findings indicate that while Georgia is making efforts to decouple economic growth from CO_2 emissions, there remains a dependency on GDP for achieving this goal.

The value of the indicator—CO_2 productivity—can be calculated using the quotient of the size of GDP at purchasing power parity expressed in constant 2017 prices and the volume of CO_2 emissions expressed in kilograms. Thus, during 2014–2020, the average value of the indicator was equal to 5.16 GDP/kg. It should

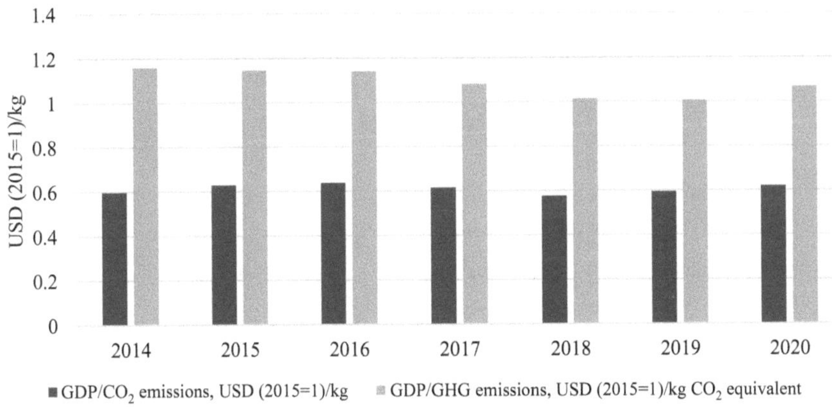

Figure 3.45 Georgia. Greenhouse gas and CO_2 productivity

Source: World Bank (World Bank Open Data, 2023); Climate Watch Data (2024).

be noted that during 2014–2017, there was a decrease in the value in question from 5.27 GDP/kg to 5.11 GDP/kg. In contrast, in 2018 there was an increase in the value of the indicator to 5.46 GDP/kg. In subsequent years, there was again a decrease in the value of the indicator to 5.07 GDP/kg. Accordingly, Georgia saw a decrease from 5.27 GDP/kg to 5.07 GDP/kg over the entire period under review, a decrease of 3.74%.

Final energy consumption

In Georgia, primary energy supply and final energy consumption grew from 2014 to 2022. From 2014 to 2022, GDP growth exceeded energy supply growth by 11.13 percentage points.

Overall, between 2014 and 2022, primary energy supply in Georgia increased from 4.5 million Toe to 5.7 million Toe. This rise in energy supply corresponded with an increase in energy consumption, as illustrated in Figure 3.46. Consequently, in 2022 compared to 2014, total energy consumption rose from 4 million Toe to 5.2 million Toe, marking an increase of 29.03%.

Between 2014 and 2022, Georgia experienced notable increases in energy consumption across various sectors. The industry and construction sector saw the fastest growth, with energy consumption rising from 613,000 Toe to 891,000 Toe, an increase of more than 45%. Similarly, the agricultural sector exhibited substantial growth, doubling its energy consumption from 12.1 thousand Toe in 2014 to 29.6 thousand Toe in 2022. In the residential sector, energy consumption increased

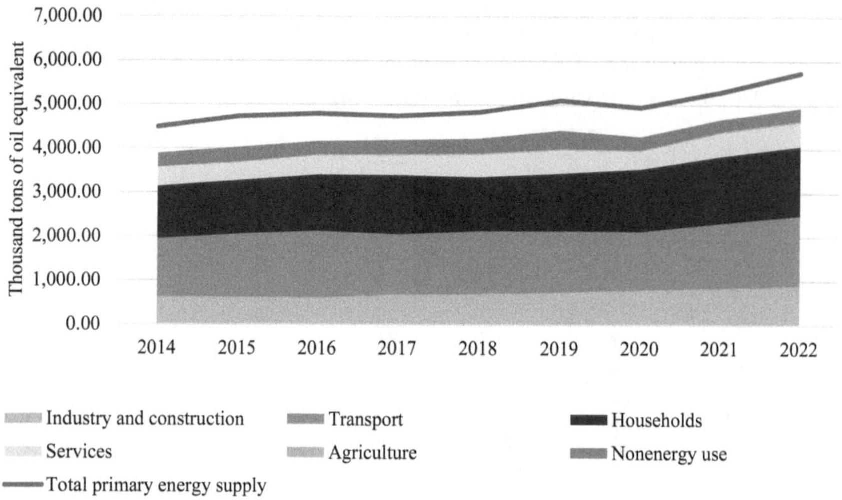

Figure 3.46 Georgia. Primary energy supply and final energy consumption by sector, in thousand tons of oil equivalent

Source: Energy Balance of Georgia 2015 (p. 14–17), 2016 (p. 14–17), 2017 (p. 14–17), 2018 (p. 14–17), 2019 (p. 14–17), 2020 (p. 14–17), 2021 (p. 14–17), 2022 (p. 14–17), 2023 (pages 14–17).

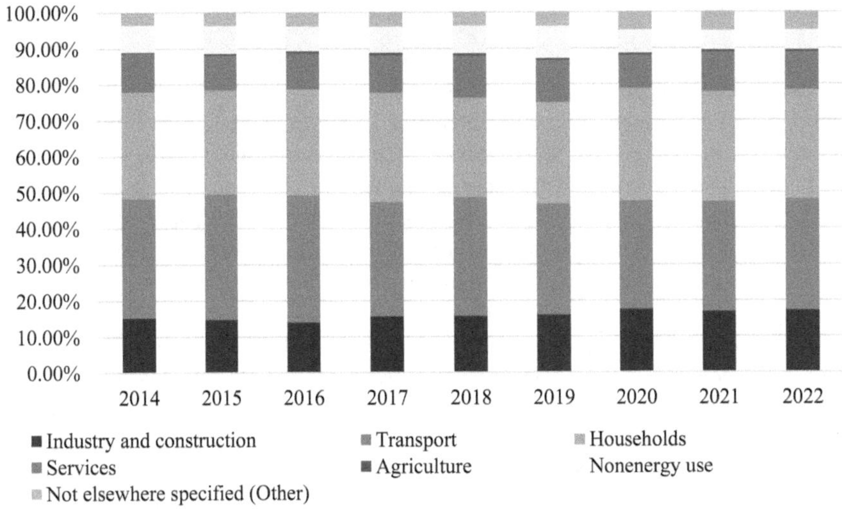

Figure 3.47 Georgia. Structure of total energy use, in %

Source: Own compilation based on data from National Statistics Office of Georgia.

by 32.30%, reaching 1.6 million Toe by 2022. Energy use in the transportation sector also grew significantly, rising by 19.95% from 1.3 million Toe to 1.6 million Toe over the same period. Conversely, Georgia's non-energy sector experienced a decrease in energy consumption, declining by 5.32% from 306 thousand Toe in 2014 to 290 thousand Toe in 2022.

Between 2014 and 2022, the structure of total energy consumption in Georgia remained relatively stable, as depicted in Figure 3.47. The agricultural sector's share of total energy consumption remained unchanged at an average of 0.57%. In contrast, the transportation sector's share of total energy consumption decreased from 33.01% to 30.69%, while the residential sector's share increased slightly from 29.60% to 30.35%. The industrial and construction sector saw a modest increase in its share of total energy consumption, rising from 15.23% to 17.17%. Conversely, non-energy industries experienced a decrease in their share of total energy consumption, declining from 7.62% to 5.59% over the period reviewed.

In 2022, compared to 2014, Georgia experienced a 27.98% increase in primary energy supply, while GDP at purchasing power parity in constant 2017 prices rose by 39.11%. This suggests a potential decoupling of economic growth from energy consumption volume, possibly influenced by increased energy productivity. Calculating the quotient of GDP at purchasing power parity in constant 2017 prices and the volume of energy production reveals that the energy productivity index from 2014 to 2022 improved by 8.70%. Specifically, this index increased from USD 10.18 to USD 11.06 per gram (g) of energy, highlighting enhanced efficiency in energy use relative to economic output over the period analyzed.

Energy intensity

Between 2014 and 2022, Georgia observed a slight increase in energy productivity and a decrease in energy intensity, although not all sectors of the economy experienced reductions in energy intensity. The overall trend was influenced by an increase in final energy consumption alongside economic growth, as illustrated in Figure 3.48. Specifically, the energy intensity of the economy improved from 277.16 grams of oil equivalent per US dollar in 2014 to 257.09 grams of oil equivalent/USD in 2022, marking a decrease of 7.24%. In the transportation sector, which is the most energy-intensive by volume of energy consumption, energy intensity decreased significantly from 91.50 grams of oil equivalent/USD in 2014 to 78.90 grams of oil equivalent/USD in 2022, a decrease of 13.78%. Conversely, the agricultural sector experienced the largest increase in energy intensity. Despite a 1.59% decrease in gross value added from 2014 to 2022, energy consumption in this sector surged by 144.63%. Consequently, energy intensity in agriculture increased from 0.83 grams of oil equivalent/USD in 2014 to 1.47 grams of oil equivalent/USD in 2022, reflecting a rise of 75.85%. In the industrial sector, energy intensity also increased slightly from 42.21 grams of oil equivalent/USD in 2014 to 44.13 grams of oil equivalent/USD in 2022. Conversely, the residential sector saw a decrease in energy intensity from 82.05 grams of oil equivalent/USD to 78.04 grams of oil equivalent/USD, representing a reduction of 4.89%.

Share of renewable energy in total energy consumption

In Georgia, the supply of renewable energy declined from 2014 to 2022. As a result, the share of renewable energy in primary energy supply and in final energy

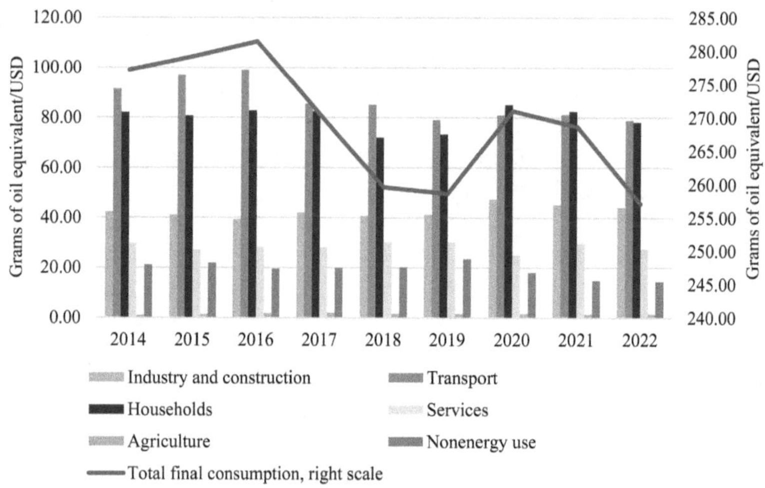

Figure 3.48 Georgia. Energy intensity, in grams of oil equivalent/USD

Source: Own compilation based on data from Energy Balance of Georgia 2015 (p. 14–17), 2016 (p. 14–17), 2017 (p. 14–17), 2018 (p. 14–17), 2019 (p. 14–17), 2020 (p. 14–17), 2021 (p. 14–17), 2022 (p. 14–17), 2023 (pages 14–17).

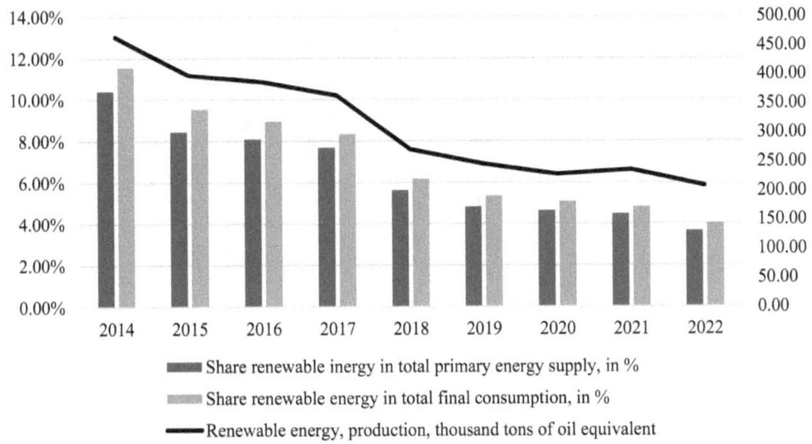

Figure 3.49 Georgia. Renewable energy supply (thousand tons of oil equivalent) and share of renewable energy in primary energy production and total energy consumption, in %.

Source: Own compilation based on data from National Statistics Office of Georgia (2023b).

consumption was declining. In Georgia in 2022, renewable energy supply was dominated by energy derived from wood combustion (99%) and trace amounts of biomass and biogas (0.20%). This fact indicates the embryonic stage of development of the modern renewable energy generation sector.

In Georgia, between 2014 and 2022, the supply of renewable energy decreased significantly from 465 thousand Toe to 208 thousand Toe, marking a decline of 55.25%. Consequently, there was a reduction in the share of renewable energy both in primary energy production and in total energy consumption over the same period, as depicted in Figure 3.49.

Waste generation

Georgia does not keep statistics on production waste. Therefore, the issue of municipal waste for 2015–2022 will be discussed. The amount of waste generated by the public in Georgia has increased over the time period under review (Figure 3.50). Almost 774.7 million tons of waste were generated in 2015. By 2022, the amount of waste generated increased by 34.90% and amounted to 1045.1 million tons of waste.

Waste recycling—evolution of the indicator

Western societies have developed robust systems for waste segregation, collection, and recycling, whereas Georgia, as a transitional state, is in the initial stages of establishing a modern waste management framework and confronting the challenge of eliminating illegal landfills and dumping sites. The country operates through

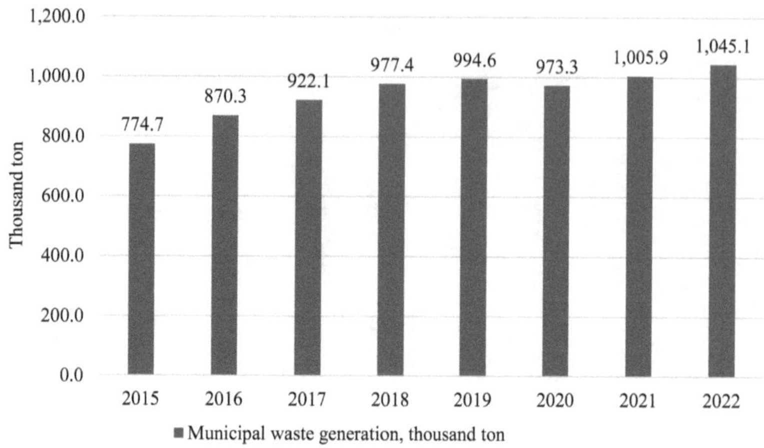

Figure 3.50 Georgia. Municipal waste production from 2015 to 2022, in thousands of tons.
Source: Own compilation based on data from National Statistics Office of Georgia (2023b).

its Solid Waste Management Company, tasked with critical functions such as rehabilitating old landfills, establishing transfer stations, constructing new regional landfills, and progressively implementing a modern waste management system. Currently, the company manages 53 municipal waste sites and landfills, and since 2013, it has been constructing new regional landfills in compliance with EU standards, assisting municipalities in adopting advanced waste management and separate collection protocols (The Solid Waste Management Company of Georgia, n.d.).

Furthermore, Georgia is actively engaging with international organizations and donors to introduce modern waste management models. Through collaboration with the European Union, the United Nations Development Program (UNDP), and the Government of Sweden, the country has developed the necessary legal framework for implementing the Extended Producer Responsibility (EPR) system. This initiative led to the adoption of technical regulations effective from September 1, 2020, governing the management of four waste types under the EPR: waste electrical and electronic equipment (WEEE), waste oils, tires, and batteries and accumulators. Future plans include extending EPR regulations to cover used packaging materials and end-of-life vehicles. The EPR system promotes the separate collection and recycling of waste, aiming to minimize landfill use, conserve resources, and reduce environmental risks, aligning with broader goals of environmental and public health protection. Originating in Sweden in 1990, EPR has been successfully implemented across Europe and globally (EU4Georgia, n.d.)

Use of fertilizers

In Georgia, a fertilizer balance sheet reveals that the consumption trends of mineral and organic fertilizers have remained relatively stable. Notably, organic fertilizer consumption has shown dominance (Figure 3.51). Specifically, while

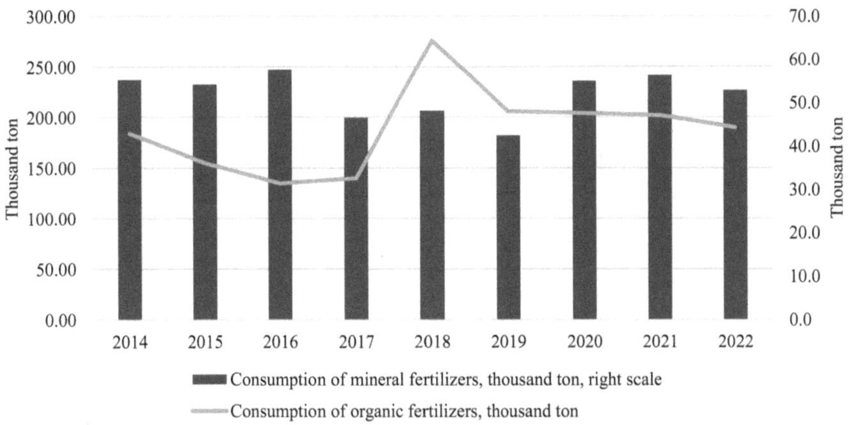

Figure 3.51 Georgia. Consumption of chemical and natural fertilizers on farms and peasant farms (farmers) from 2014 to 2022, in thousands of tons.

Source: Own compilation based on data from National Statistics Office of Georgia (2023b).

55.3 million tons of mineral fertilizers were applied to the land in 2014, this figure decreased slightly to nearly 53 million tons by 2022. Conversely, there has been a slight increase in the consumption of organic fertilizers over the same period. In 2014, approximately 184 million tons of organic fertilizers were used, and this increased to around 190 million tons by 2022 for agricultural purposes.

Water consumption

In Georgia, between 2014 and 2022, there was a notable decline in water consumption. Specifically, water usage decreased from 1,583 million m^3 in 2014 to 1,197 million m^3 in 2022. The evolution of water consumption varied across different sectors (Figure 3.52). Over this period, an annual average of 340 million m^3 of water was utilized for production purposes, constituting 26.45% of the total water consumption. The agricultural sector accounted for the highest water consumption, using an average of 640 million m^3 annually, which equates to 49.83% of the total water consumed. Domestic water consumption during this period totaled 304.96 million m^3, representing 23.72% of the total water consumption in the national economy.

If water consumption fell by 24.40% between 2014 and 2022, then GDP expressed in USD at 2017 constant prices increased by 39.11%. As a result, water productivity increased and decoupling of economic growth from water consumption was achieved. If one expresses productivity as the ratio of GDP in 2017 constant prices at purchasing power parity to the volume of water consumption, then in 2022 compared to 2014, the productivity level increased to 52.98 from 28.79 USD/m^3, an increase of 25.02%.

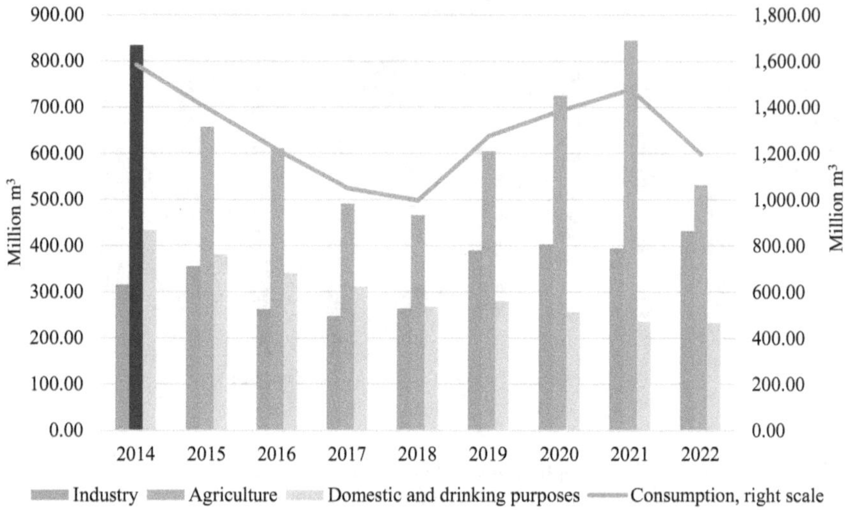

Figure 3.52 Georgia. Water consumption by economic sector during 2014–2022, in million m^3.

Source: Own compilation based on data from National Statistics Office of Georgia (Natural Resources of Georgia and Environmental Protection, 2022, p. 43; Natural Resources of Georgia and Environmental Protection, 2014, p. 40).

Moldova[1]

Greenhouse gas emissions

The Republic of Moldova is committed to several international agreements aimed at mitigating greenhouse gas emissions. Moldova signed the United Nations Framework Convention on Climate Change (UNFCCC) on June 12, 1992, and subsequently ratified it through parliamentary approval on March 16, 1995. The UNFCCC aims to stabilize greenhouse gas concentrations in the atmosphere at a level that prevents dangerous anthropogenic interference with the climate system (UN Environment, 2021).

In accordance with these provisions, Moldova has committed itself to various agreements that guide its future actions. The Republic is a signatory to the Protocol established during COP 3 in Kyoto in 1997. This Protocol mandates that industrialized countries and those listed in Annex I of the Convention must collectively reduce their direct greenhouse gas emissions by at least 5% from 1990 levels over the period spanning 2008 to 2012. Moldova ratified the Kyoto Protocol on March 13, 2003. As a non-Annex I Party during the Kyoto Protocol's initial commitment period, Moldova was not bound by specific obligations to reduce greenhouse gas emissions.

Moldova has been a party to the Copenhagen Accord since January 2010. As part of Annex II, which outlines mitigation actions for developing countries, Moldova committed to "reducing its total national greenhouse gas emissions to at least

25% below 1990 levels by 2020. This pledge involves implementing economic mechanisms aimed at global climate change mitigation, in alignment with the principles and provisions of the Convention."

The Doha Amendment to the Kyoto Protocol was approved at COP 18 in Doha in 2012. The amendment includes new obligations for Annex I countries under the Kyoto Protocol for the second commitment period (Jan. 1, 2013–Dec. 31, 2020); a revised list of greenhouse gases to be reported by Annex I countries in the second commitment period; and a series of amendments to several Kyoto Protocol articles that specifically regulate certain issues related to the first commitment period, which were to be amended to remain valid for the second commitment period as well. According to the Doha Amendment to the Kyoto Protocol, industrially developed countries are to reduce greenhouse gas emissions by at least 18% in the second commitment period compared to the base year (1990). As of June 15, 2022, 148 countries have ratified the Doha Amendment to the Kyoto Protocol, the vast majority of which are non-Annex I countries of the UNFCCC and the Kyoto Protocol. The Doha Amendment entered into force on December 31, 2020 (UNFCCC, 2023).

At COP 19 in Warsaw in 2013, parties agreed to transfer their intended Nationally Determined Contributions (INDCs) (Decision 1/CP.19), for inclusion in the new 2015 Climate Agreement, which was considered and adopted by COP 21 in 2015 in Paris. This climate agreement established a new commitment period (Jan. 1, 2021—Dec. 31, 2030) for reducing greenhouse gas emissions. The COP 19 also approved the "General Guidelines for National Measurement, Reporting and Verification of Nationally Supported Appropriate Mitigation Actions by Parties - Developing Countries (Decision 21/CP.19)." The document laid a solid foundation for a new Climate Agreement in 2015.

The Republic of Moldova actively participated in the negotiations leading to the adoption of the Paris Agreement at COP 21 in 2015. This landmark agreement, which entered into force on November 4, 2016, aims to strengthen the global response to climate change by keeping global temperature rise well below 2°C above preindustrial levels and pursuing efforts to limit it to 1.5°C. The agreement also aims to enhance countries' ability to adapt to the adverse impacts of climate change and to foster climate resilience and low greenhouse gas emissions development. Moldova signed the Paris Agreement on December 21, 2016, in New York, demonstrating its commitment to global climate action. The agreement was subsequently ratified by the Parliament of the Republic of Moldova through Law No. 78 of May 4, 2017, which was published in the Official Gazette No. 1, 162–170 on May 26, 2017.

On September 25, 2015, the Republic of Moldova officially announced its Intended Nationally Determined Contribution and related information to ensure clarity, transparency, and understanding with regard to the provisions of Decisions 1/CP.19 and 1/CP.20. Accordingly, the Republic of Moldova has committed to achieve an unconditional target of 64–67% reduction in greenhouse gas emissions by 2030 compared to the level recorded in the reference year (1990), and to make every effort to reduce greenhouse gas emissions by 67% compared to 1990.

The reduction commitment could be conditionally increased to about 78%, according to the global agreement, which regulates important issues such as the provision of low-cost financial resources, technology transfer, and technical cooperation, access to all of this to a degree that meets the challenges of global climate change. Greenhouse gas emission reduction targets have been set in the emission budget covering the period from January 1, 2021, to December 31, 2030. The set greenhouse gas emission reduction targets, specified in the Intended Nationally Determined Contribution of the Republic of Moldova, were then officially approved at the national level by Government Decision No. 1470 dated December 30, 2016, on the approval of the Low Carbon Development Strategy of the Republic of Moldova until 2030 and the Action Plan for its implementation.

On April 3, 2020, the Republic of Moldova submitted to the UNFCCC Secretariat an updated nationally determined contribution (NDC Registry, 2023). According to this, the Republic of Moldova has committed to achieving more ambitious GHG reduction targets by 2030. Thus, the unconditional target is to increase GHG reductions from 64–67% to 70% from the level recorded in the base year (1990), and the conditional target is to increase from 78% to about 88% from the level recorded in 1990, respectively. The new targets for reducing greenhouse gas emissions were introduced as part of the Low Carbon Development Program to 2030 and the Action Plan for its implementation. These documents were approved in September 2023 and came into effect on January 1, 2024 (UNDP, 2023).

Evolution of the greenhouse gas emissions indicator

In the Republic of Moldova, after 2013, emissions of greenhouse gases, including CO_2 (carbon dioxide accounts for two-thirds of greenhouse gases), have undergone a relatively stable evolution. In 2020 compared to 2019, greenhouse gas emissions, including CO_2, increased by 5.34% and 11.66%, respectively.

The Republic of Moldova's historical responsibility for greenhouse gas emissions is small. In 2020. The Republic of Moldova emitted about 12.99 $MtCO_2$ equivalent (excluding the LUCF sector) and 13.17 $MtCO_2$ equivalent (with the LUCF sector), which is less than 0.01% of total global emissions (Climate Watch Data, 2024). In Moldova, total and net per capita GHG emissions were significantly lower than the global average (Moldova: net emissions were 4.96 tCO_2 equivalent per capita, total emissions were 5.03 tCO_2 equivalent per capita; World: net emissions were 5.94 tCO2 equivalent per capita, total emissions were 6.12 tCO_2 equivalent per capita) (Climate Watch Data, 2024). Between 1990 and 2021, the dynamics of total direct GHG emissions (excluding LUCF), expressed in CO_2 equivalent, showed a downward trend in the Republic of Moldova, decreasing by about 65.94%: from 38.14 $MtCO_2$ equivalent in 1990 to 12.99 $MtCO_2$ equivalent in 2020. Net greenhouse gas emissions (from LUCF) decreased by about 65.26% over the same period: from 37.91 $MtCO_2$ equivalent in 1990 to 13.17 $MtCO_2$ equivalent in 2020 (Climate Watch Data, 2024).

From 2014 to 2020, greenhouse gas emissions were characterized by constant dynamics (Figure 3.53). During this period, annual emissions amounted to about

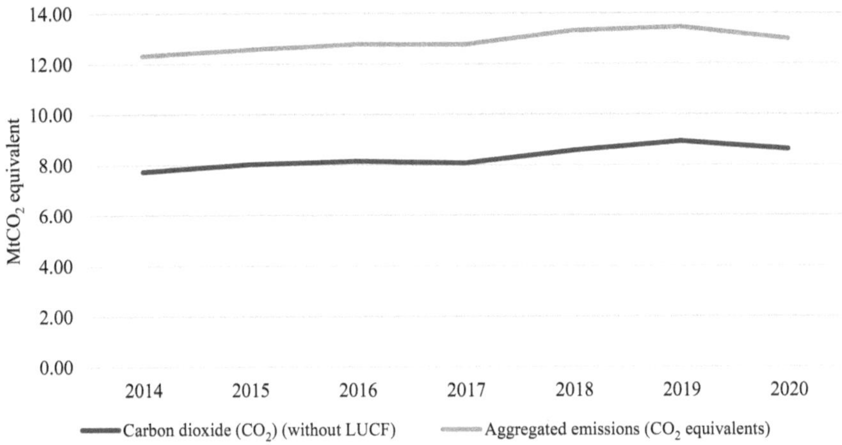

Figure 3.53 Moldova. Greenhouse gas emissions, including CO_2, in $MtCO_2$ equivalent.
Source: Climate Watch Data (2024).

12.88 $MtCO_2$ equivalent. Annual changes ranged slightly around this value and ranged between 12.33 and 13.45 $MtCO_2$ equivalent. Carbon dioxide emissions account for two-thirds of all greenhouse gas emissions. From 2014 to 2020, CO_2 emissions evolved steadily and oscillated slightly around an annual average value of about 8.29 $MtCO_2$ equivalent. Annual fluctuations oscillated between 7.71 and 8.92 $MtCO_2$ equivalent.

Between 2014 and 2020, the structure of greenhouse gas emissions by sector did not change significantly (Figure 3.54). The share of emissions generated by the energy sector increased slightly from 68.57% to 69.90%, and emissions determined by industrial processes and product use increased from 5.75% to 7.31%. The share of emissions from the agriculture and waste sectors remained relatively constant at around 13.41% and 11.21%, respectively.

Productivity (emission efficiency) of CO_2.

In the Republic of Moldova, following 2013, greenhouse gas emissions, including CO_2, exhibited a relatively stable trend alongside GDP growth. Over the period spanning 2014 to 2020, Moldova's economy generally showed upward momentum, despite a downturn in GDP during 2014–2015. By 2020, GDP measured in USD at current prices had risen by 22.68% compared to 2014. Concurrently, under conditions of sustained CO_2 emissions and expanding GDP, there was an observed increase in greenhouse gas productivity, rising from 0.63 USD/kg to 0.65 USD/kg from 2014 to 2020 (Figure 3.55). In contrast, CO_2 productivity experienced a slight decline, decreasing from 1.01 USD/kg to 0.98 USD/kg CO_2 equivalent over the same period. These findings suggest Moldova's ongoing efforts to decouple economic growth from CO_2 emissions.

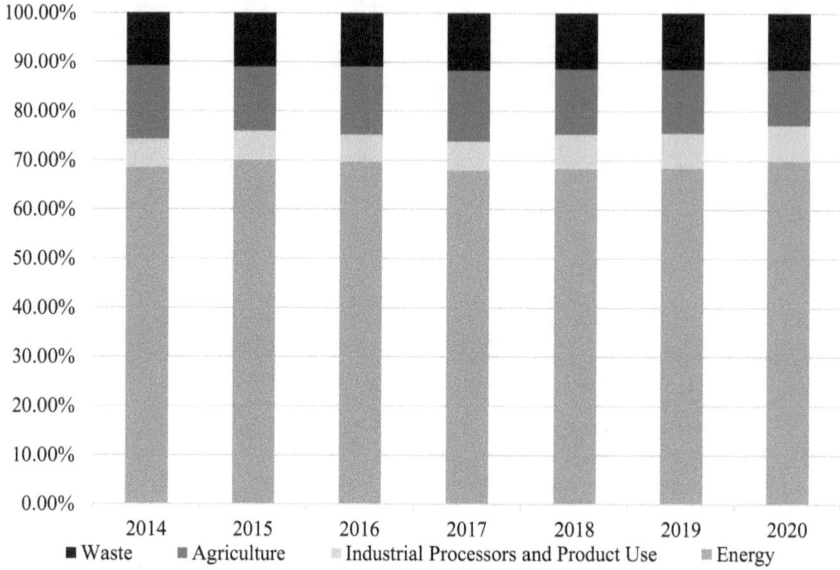

Figure 3.54 Moldova. Structure of greenhouse gas emissions by sector, in %.
Source: Climate Watch Data (2024).

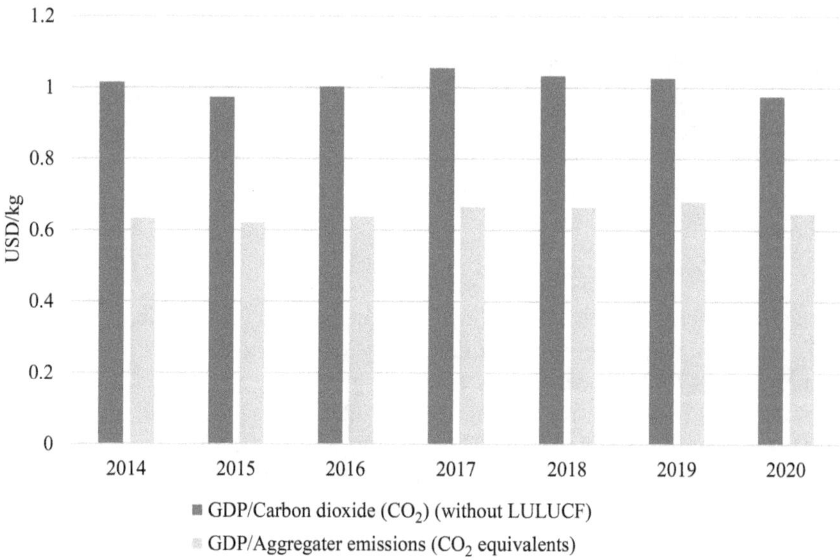

Figure 3.55 Moldova. Production of greenhouse gases and CO_2 in the Republic of Moldova.
Source: Own compilation based on data from Climate Watch Data (2024); World Bank (2022).

The value of the indicator—CO_2 productivity—can be calculated using the quotient of the size of GDP at purchasing power parity expressed in constant 2017 prices and the volume of CO_2 emissions expressed in kilograms. Thus, during 2014–2020, the average value of the indicator was equal to 3.76 PPC (production possibilities curve)/kg. It should be noted that during 2014–2017 there was an increase in the value in question from 3.77 PPC/kg to 3.92 PPC/kg. On the other hand, a decrease in the value of the indicator from 3.84 PPC/kg to 3.62 PPC/kg was recorded between 2018 and 2020. Accordingly, Moldova saw a decrease from 3.77 PPC/kg to 3.63 PPC/kg over the entire period under review, a decrease of 3.83%.

Final energy consumption

In the Republic of Moldova, primary energy supply and final energy consumption increased after 2013. The growth of energy supply was lower than the growth of GDP. As a result, there was an increase in energy productivity.

Overall, from 2013 onwards, primary energy supply in the referenced region exhibited growth until 2021, with a subsequent decline noted in 2022. Between 2014 and 2021, primary energy supply increased from 2.7 to 3.2 million tons of oil equivalent, marking an 18.81% rise. However, in 2022, there was a 6.16% decrease in primary energy supply compared to the previous year. This increase in energy supply correspondingly drove an uptick in energy consumption (Figure 3.56). Specifically, comparing 2021 to 2014, total energy consumption rose from 2.4 to 2.9 million tons of oil equivalent, reflecting a 21.38% increase. Conversely, in

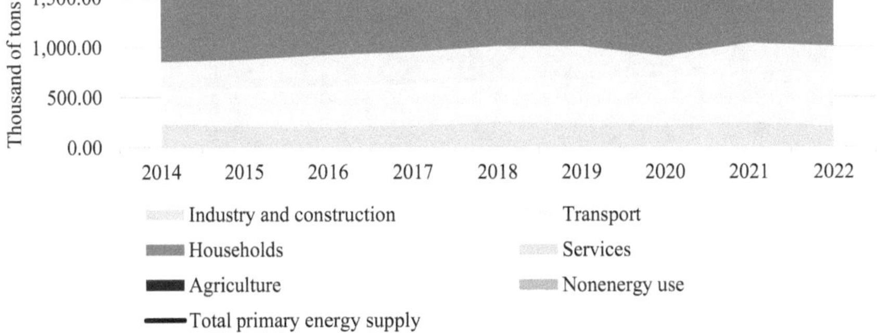

Figure 3.56 Moldova. Primary energy supply and final energy consumption by sector, in thousands of tons of oil equivalent.

Source: Biroul Național de Statistică al Republicii Moldova (2023).

2022 compared to 2021, there was a decrease in total energy consumption volume by 11.35%.

Between 2014 and 2022, the transportation sector experienced the fastest growth in energy consumption, increasing from 618 to 793 thousand Toe, representing a 28.32% rise. Other sectors also saw fluctuations in energy consumption over this period, with increases observed from 2014 to 2021 and decreases noted in 2022. Specifically, from 2014 to 2021, the residential sector recorded the largest increase in energy consumption, rising from 1.2 to 1.4 million Toe. The agricultural sector saw a substantial 51.56% increase, from 64 to 161 thousand Toe, while the non-energy sector's consumption rose by 36.54%, from 52 to 71 thousand Toe. Energy consumption in the trade and public services sector increased by 18.37%, and the industrial and construction sectors grew by 4.26% during this period. However, in 2022, all sectors except transportation experienced a decrease in energy consumption, largely attributed to increases in natural gas and electricity prices.

Between 2014 and 2022, the structure of total energy consumption changed slightly (Figure 3.57). The share of the residential sector in total energy consumption decreased from 49.61 to 42.82%, while the share of transportation increased from 25.65 to 30.59%. In contrast, the industrial and construction sector's share of total energy consumption also decreased from 9.76 to 8.33%. In contrast, the trade and public services sector accounted for 10.17 to 10.19% of total energy consumption during the period under review. level of energy consumption. The upward

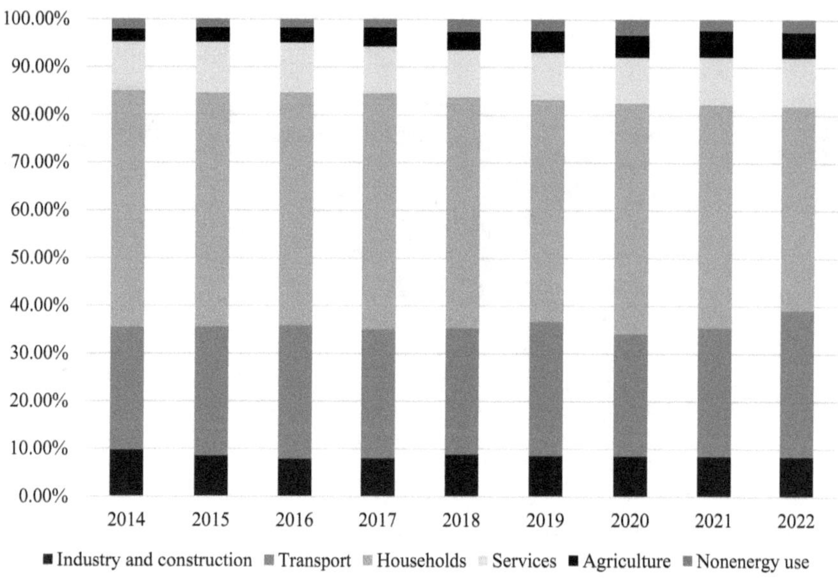

Figure 3.57 Moldova. Structure of total energy use, in %.

Source: Own compilation based on data from Biroul Național de Statistică al Republicii Moldova (2023).

trend was characterized by the size of the share of total energy consumption in agriculture and non-energy industries.

In 2022, compared to 2014, primary energy supply in Moldova increased by 11.50%, while GDP expressed in USD at constant 2017 prices increased by 16.23%. This outcome suggests that the increase in energy productivity may have contributed to decoupling economic growth from energy consumption. Calculating the quotient of economic output, expressed in GDP at purchasing power parity in constant 2017 prices, and energy production indicates that the energy productivity index increased by 4.24% from 2014 to 2022, rising from 10.85 to 11.31 USD/g.

Energy intensity

The Republic of Moldova saw an increase in productivity and a decrease in energy intensity after 2013. However, not all sectors of the economy saw a decrease in energy intensity. Between 2014 and 2022, the increase in final energy consumption was overtaken by GDP growth. These changes conditioned an increase in energy productivity and a decrease in energy intensity across the economy (Figure 3.58). Thus, if in the case of final energy consumption in 2014. 307.85 grams of oil equivalent cost one US dollar, in 2022 the ratio was 284.99 grams of oil equivalent/USD, a decrease of 7.42%. An industry with a significant reduction in energy intensity is industry and construction. In this sector, gross value added in 2022 compared to 2014 increased by 97%, while energy consumption on average increased by only 0.62%. As a result, the energy intensity of industry and construction fell by

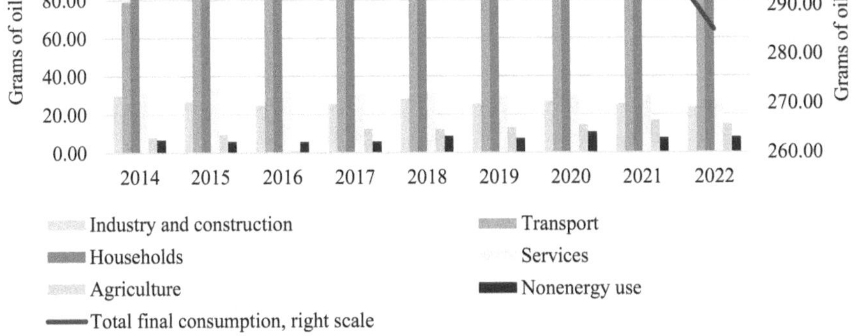

Figure 3.58 Moldova. Energy intensity, in grams of oil equivalent/USD.

Source: Own compilation based on data from Biroul Național de Statistică al Republicii Moldova (2023).

20.92%, from 30.03 to 23.75 grams of oil equivalent/USD. At the same time, there was an increase in energy intensity in agriculture. Gross value added in agriculture increased by 22.47% and energy consumption by 115.63%. As a result, in the agricultural sector, energy intensity increased by 85.52%, from 8.18 to 15.17 grams of oil equivalent/USD.

Share of renewable energy in total energy consumption

In the Republic of Moldova, the supply of renewable energy increased between 2014 and 2021, despite a decline in 2019. Consequently, the share of renewable energy in both primary energy supply and final energy consumption also grew. However, renewable energy supply in Moldova is predominantly composed of biofuels and waste, highlighting the nascent stage of development in modern renewable energy generation sectors.

Overall, Moldova's renewable energy supply was increasing after 2013, although there was a decline in 2019. and in 2022 there was a recorded decline. Between 2014 and 2021, the supply of renewable energy increased from 641 to 742 thousand tons of oil equivalent, an increase of 15.76%. However, in 2019 and in 2022, the supply of renewable energy decreased to 660 and 499 thousand tons of oil equivalent, respectively. Following these changes, the supply of renewable energy in 2019 increased by 1.87% compared to 2014, in 2022 it decreased by 22.15% compared to 2014. Despite these fluctuations, it should be noted that between 2014 and 2022 there were increases in the share of renewable energy in primary energy production and in total energy consumption (Figure 3.59). While

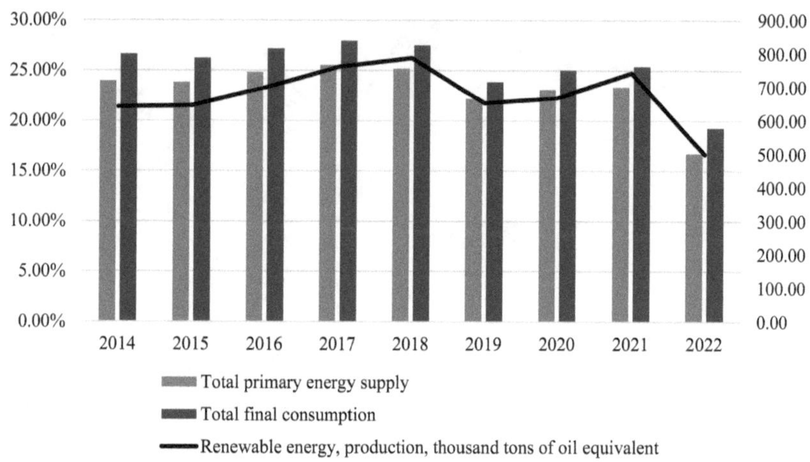

Figure 3.59 Moldova. Renewable energy supply (thousand tons of oil equivalent) and share of renewable energy in primary energy production and total energy consumption, in %.

Source: Own compilation based on data from Biroul Național de Statistică al Republicii Moldova (2023).

in 2014 renewable energy accounted for 23.97% of primary energy supply, in 2022 this share was only 16.71%. During the same period, the share of renewable energy in final energy consumption fell from 26.61 to 19.25%.

However, in the Republic of Moldova, unlike other European countries, the share of biofuels and waste in primary renewable energy supply is extremely high. Biofuels and waste account for 98–99% of primary renewable energy supply. In contrast, more than 80% of biofuels and waste is firewood. This fact indicates that renewable energy in the Republic of Moldova is mainly obtained by cutting down trees, and modern renewable energy generation processes are at an early stage of development.

Waste generation

In the Republic of Moldova, two trends are noticeable. Production waste has rather decreased, especially after 2015. At the same time, the amount of waste generated by the public is increasing.

Since 2015, there has been a noticeable trend towards reducing production waste (Figure 3.60). For instance, production waste generation decreased significantly from almost 4 million tons in 2015 to approximately 1.2 million tons by 2019. Concurrently, there was an increase in waste collected from households, particularly after 2018. Between 2014 and 2016, the volume of household waste remained relatively stable around 2 million m^3, but from 2017 to 2021, there was a more pronounced growth in the volume of household waste. As a result, by 2021, the volume of waste collected from the population had reached nearly 2.2 million m^3.

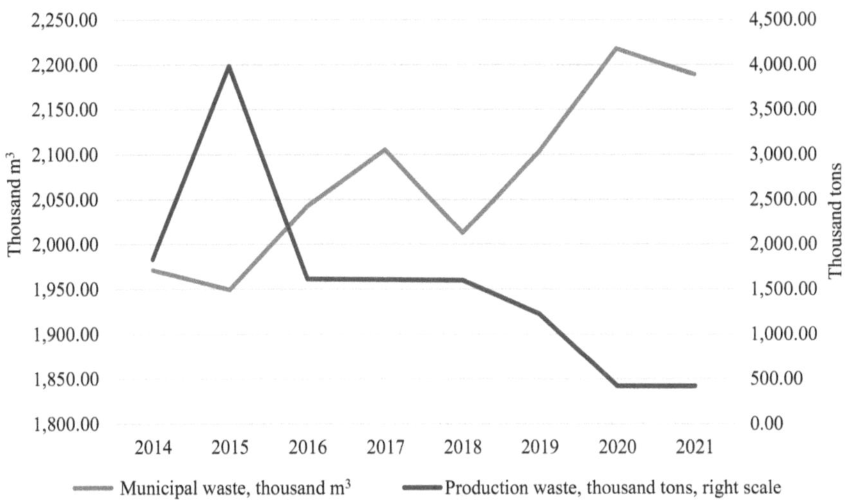

Figure 3.60 Moldova. Generation of production waste and municipal waste.

Source: Own compilation based on data from Biroul Național de Statistică al Republicii Moldova (2023).

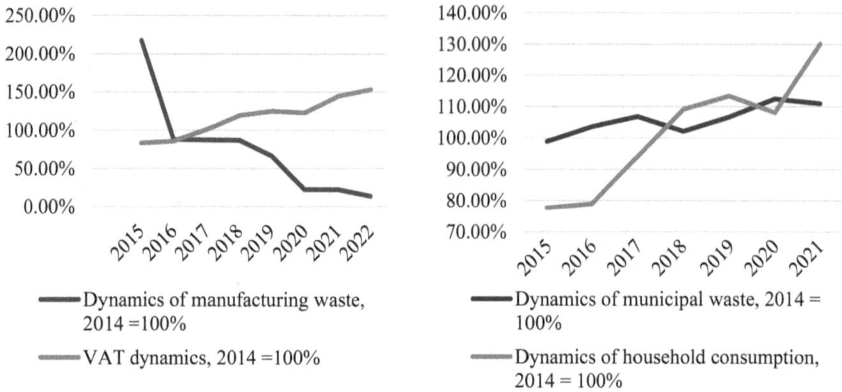

Figure 3.61 Moldova. Dynamics of production waste, municipal waste, VAT, and household consumption, in %.

Source: Own compilation based on data from Biroul Național de Statistică al Republicii Moldova (2023) and World Bank (World Bank Open Data, 2023).

From 2014 to 2021, the amount of production waste generated was reduced by 85.53%. In the same period VAT—an indicator showing the production process, expressed in current prices—increased by 53.24%. In this context, the separation of the production process from waste generation is confirmed. However, the situation is different for municipal waste. Waste collected from the population and household consumption had similar dynamics during 2014–2017. As a result, the amount of waste collected from the population grew faster compared to household consumption (Figure 3.61). In 2018, household consumption exceeded municipal waste production, then during 2019–2020, municipal waste production again exceeded household consumption. In 2021, on the other hand, it was observed that it was household consumption that exceeded municipal waste production. Between 2014 and 2021, the amount of household waste increased by 11.05%, while household consumption increased by an average of 5.22% per year. Thus, the current consumption pattern of the population continues to promote accelerated waste generation.

Waste recycling—evolution of the indicator

In the Republic of Moldova, data is collected on "used waste," which includes both recycled waste and waste used for energy production.

The most waste was disposed of in 2018—709 thousand tons of waste. Between 2014 and 2022, the amount of disposed waste ranged from 172 to 709 thousand tons (Figure 3.62). At the same time, in 2020, the ratio of disposed waste to produced waste reached the highest value of 73.98%. During 2014–2022, the ratio ranged between 15.09% and 64.91%.

The "On the Approval of the National Waste Management Program for the years 2022–2027 and the Action Plan for its implementation for the period 2023–2027, 2023"

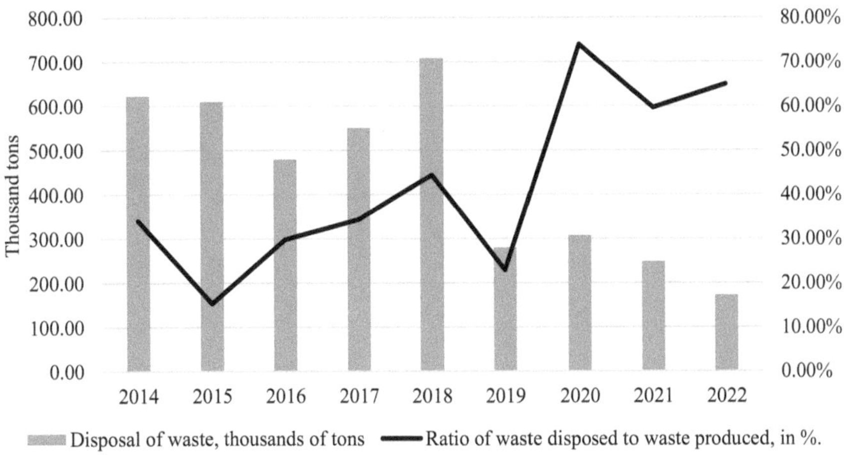

Figure 3.62 Moldova. Waste disposed (thousands of tons) and ratio of waste disposed to waste produced, in %.

Source: Own compilation based on data from Biroul Național de Statistică al Republicii Moldova (2023).

(Republic of Moldova, 2023) provides information on the level of recycling of certain categories of municipal waste. However, this information is not official data and is only an estimate by the program's authors. Thus, it was estimated that in 2021 the recycling rate for plastic waste was 3.0%, and the recycling rate for paper waste was 22.0%. A higher recycling rate applies to glass waste and increased from 35.12% in 2018 to 41.5% in 2019. In 2021, the rate value was only 33.0%.

Use of fertilizers

In the Republic of Moldova, formal fertilizer balance sheets are not regularly compiled. However, available data allows for the analysis of mineral fertilizer consumption trends. There has been a notable rise in the use of mineral fertilizers in Moldova. Despite this increase, it has not corresponded to a significant rise in crop production.

In general, there has been an increase in the consumption of both mineral and organic fertilizers after 2013 (Figure 3.63). While 72.4 thousand tons of mineral fertilizers were applied to agricultural land in 2014, this increased to over 67.9 thousand tons by 2022. Regarding natural fertilizers, their usage has shown a more fluctuating pattern, despite an overall upward trend. Specifically, while 28.1 thousand tons of natural fertilizers were utilized in 2014, this amount grew to more than 82.6 thousand tons by 2022 for agricultural purposes.

The increase in fertilizer use was also accompanied by an increase in the amount of fertilizer applied per hectare of soil. Between 2014 and 2021, the rate increased from 83.6 to 96.9 kg/ha for chemical fertilizers and from 18.7 to 83.3 kg/ha for organic

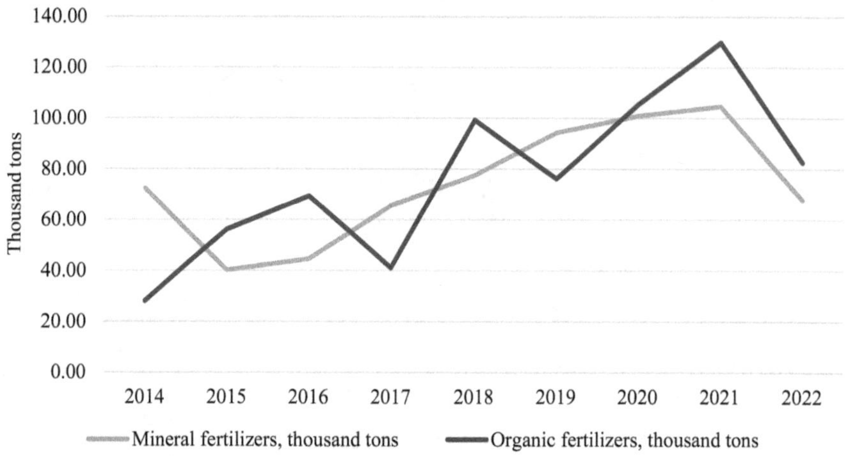

Figure 3.63 Moldova. Consumption of chemical and natural fertilizers on farms and peasant holdings (farmers), in thousands of tons.

Source: own compilation based on data from Biroul Național de Statistică al Republicii Moldova (2023).

fertilizers (Figure 3.64). In 2022, there was a decrease in the use of mineral fertilizers and organic fertilizers by 38.18% and 37.21%, respectively, compared to 2021.

Most mineral fertilizers used in Moldova are nitrates, followed by phosphates, with potassium fertilizers constituting the smallest share. Between 2014 and 2021, there was a notable increase in the consumption of all types of fertilizers

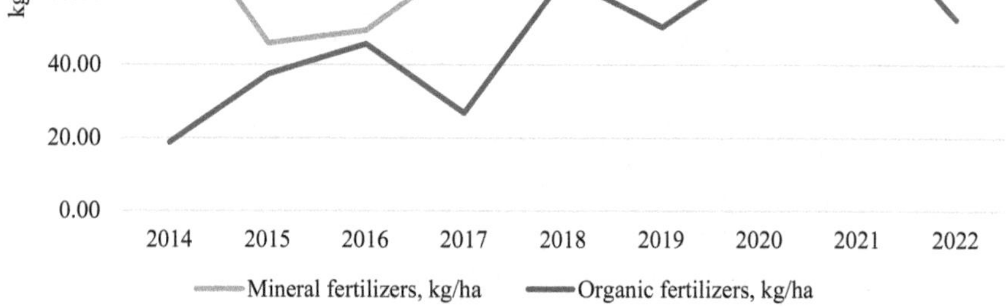

Figure 3.64 Moldova. Consumption of chemical and natural fertilizers on farms and peasant farms (farmers), in kg/ha.

Source: Own compilation based on data from Biroul Național de Statistică al Republicii Moldova (2023).

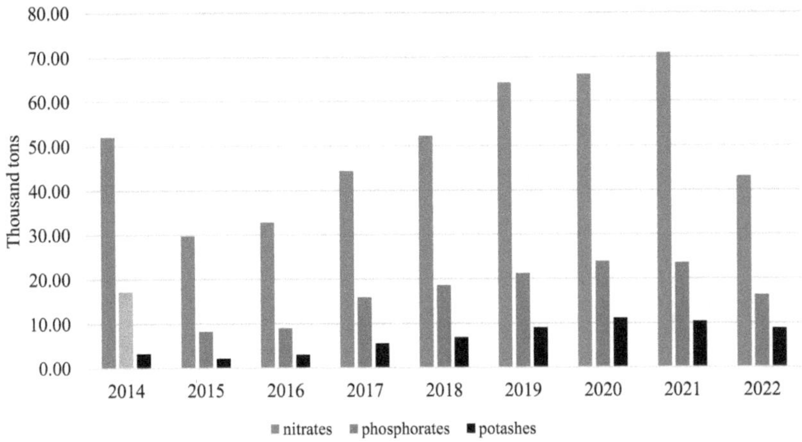

Figure 3.65 Moldova. Types of mineral fertilizers used on farms and peasant farms (farmers), in thousands of tons.

Source: Own compilation based on data from Biroul Naţional de Statistică al Republicii Moldova (2023).

(Figure 3.65). Specifically, the use of nitrates surged by nearly 1.5 times, rising from 52 to 71 thousand tons. Concurrently, phosphate consumption increased from 17.2 to 23.5 thousand tons during the same period. Potassium fertilizer usage also saw a significant uptick, more than tripling from 3.2 to 10.3 thousand tons. However, in 2022, the consumption of all three types of fertilizers decreased.

Water consumption

In the Republic of Moldova, water consumption remained stable after 2010, while GDP grew. Consequently, there was an increase in water productivity. However, this advance did not allow the Republic of Moldova to improve its position compared to other countries in Europe.

From 2014 to 2022, water consumption in Moldova remained relatively stable. In 2014, the country used 785 million m^3 of water, and by 2020, this figure had barely changed, totaling 787 million m^3. Water consumption across most sectors showed a consistent pattern of evolution (Figure 3.66). Annually, approximately 581 million m^3 of water were utilized for production needs, constituting roughly three-quarters of the total water consumed. Agriculture accounted for 38–40 million m^3 annually, primarily for irrigation purposes. Domestic water consumption during this period amounted to 112 million m^3.

If water consumption showed a stable evolution from 2014 to 2022, then GDP expressed in USD at 2017 constant prices increased by 16.23%. As a result, water productivity increased and a decoupling of economic growth from water consumption was achieved. If one expresses productivity as a ratio of GDP in 2017 constant

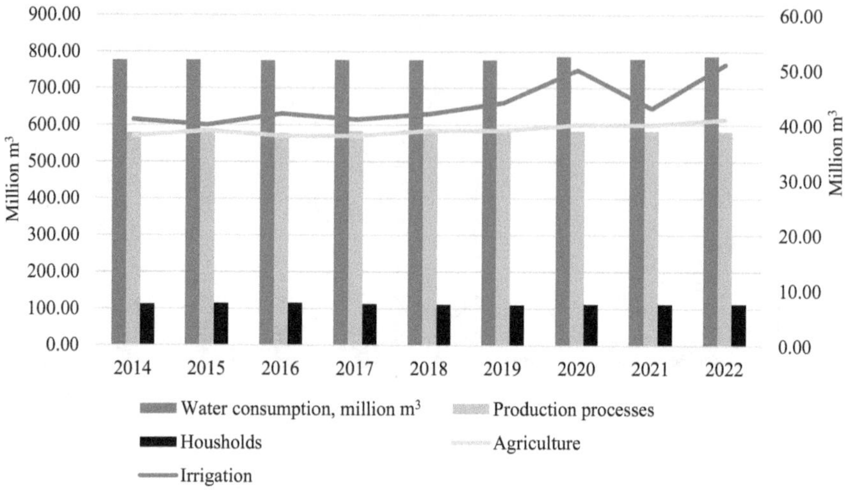

Figure 3.66 Moldova. Water consumption by economic sector, in million m^3.

Source: Own compilation based on data from Biroul Național de Statistică al Republicii Moldova (2023).

prices at purchasing power parity, then in 2022 compared to 2014, the productivity level increased from 37.42 to 42.88 USD/m^3, an increase of 14.60%.

Ukraine

Greenhouse gas emissions

Ukraine signed the UNFCCC in June 1992 and subsequently joined Annex I of the UNFCCC in August 1997 (UNFCCC, 1998). In the spring of 2004, Ukraine ratified the Kyoto Protocol, thus assuming commitments aimed at mitigating the adverse impacts of global climate change (UNFCCC, 2006b). Ukraine has pledged to achieve a 65% reduction in greenhouse gas emissions by 2030 compared to 1990 levels. This reduction is intended to be achieved without compromising food production in Ukraine, ensuring that the Ukrainian economy develops sustainably (UNFCCC, 2016).

Evolution of the greenhouse gas emission rate

In Ukraine, after 2013, greenhouse gas emissions, including CO_2 (carbon dioxide accounts for two-thirds of greenhouse gases), followed a further downward trend. In 2020 compared to 2019, greenhouse gas emissions, including CO_2, decreased by 23.96% and 30.31%, respectively.

Ukraine's historical responsibility for greenhouse gas emissions is relatively minor. In 2020, Ukraine emitted approximately 227.34 $MtCO_2$ equivalent (excluding the LUCF sector) and 224.44 $MtCO_2$ equivalent (including the LUCF sector),

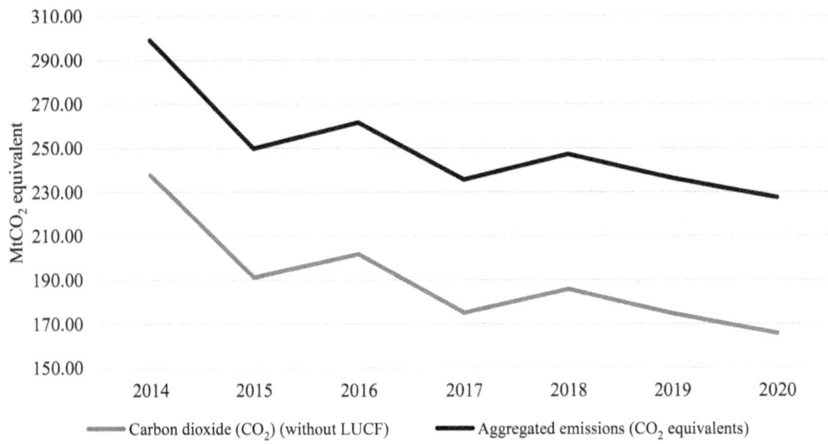

Figure 3.67 Ukraine. Greenhouse gas emissions, including CO_2, in $MtCO_2$ equivalent.
Source: Climate Watch Data (2024).

which collectively accounts for less than 0.47% of global emissions (Climate Watch Data, 2024). Ukraine's total and net per capita greenhouse gas (GHG) emissions were lower than the global averages: net emissions were 5.15 tCO_2 equivalent per capita for Ukraine compared to the global average of 5.94 tCO_2 equivalent per capita, and total emissions were 5.09 tCO_2 equivalent per capita for Ukraine compared to the global average of 6.12 tCO_2 equivalent per capita (Climate Watch Data, 2024). From 1990 to 2020, Ukraine experienced a significant decline in total direct GHG emissions (excluding LUCF), which decreased by approximately 72.47% from 825.87 $MtCO_2$ equivalent in 1990 to 227.34 $MtCO_2$ equivalent in 2020. Similarly, net greenhouse gas emissions (including LUCF) decreased by about 71.47% over the same period, from 786.55 $MtCO_2$ equivalent in 1990 to 224.44 $MtCO_2$ equivalent in 2020 (Climate Watch Data, 2024).

From 2014 to 2020, greenhouse gas emissions were characterized by constant dynamics (Figure 3.67). During this period, annual emissions amounted to about 250.87 $MtCO_2$ equivalent. Annual changes oscillated slightly around this value and ranged between 298.99 and 227.34 $MtCO_2$ equivalent. Carbon dioxide emissions account for 75.21% of all greenhouse gas emissions. From 2014 to 2020, CO_2 emissions steadily evolved and oscillated slightly around an annual average value of about 190.18 $MtCO_2$ equivalent. Annual fluctuations oscillated between 237.73 and 165.66 $MtCO_2$ equivalent.

Between 2014 and 2020, the distribution of greenhouse gas emissions across sectors in Ukraine remained relatively stable (Figure 3.68). The proportion of emissions attributed to the energy sector decreased from 81.83% to 75.02%. Conversely, emissions from industrial processes and product use increased from 2.79% to 4.28%. Similarly, the share of emissions originating from the agriculture sector rose from 10.77% to 14.22%, while emissions from the waste sector increased from 4.61% to 6.47%.

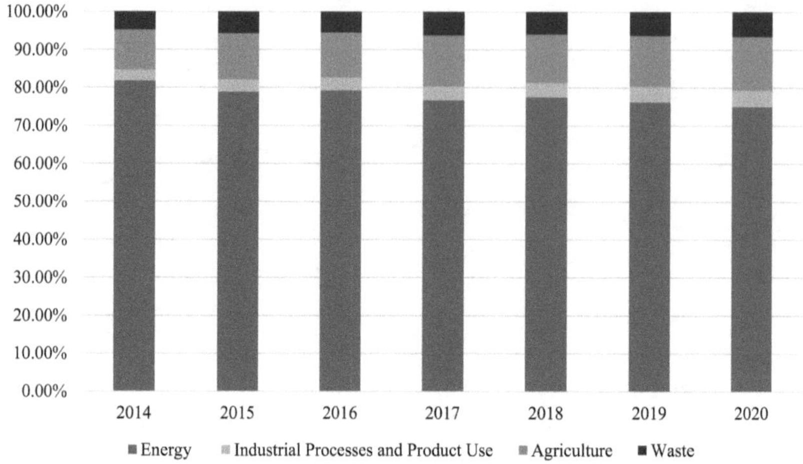

Figure 3.68 Ukraine. Structure of greenhouse gas emissions by sector, in %.

Source: Climate Watch Data (2024).

Productivity (emission efficiency) of CO_2

In Ukraine, following 2013, the trend of declining greenhouse gas emissions, including CO_2, did not consistently coincide with uniform GDP growth. While the Ukrainian economy showed growth dynamics between 2014 and 2019, there were declines in GDP in 2015 and 2020. Specifically, GDP decreased by 2.75% in 2020 compared to 2014. Amidst these fluctuations in GDP and decreasing CO_2 emissions, there was a notable decrease in greenhouse gas (GHG) productivity from 2.96 to 2.32 USD/kg CO_2 equivalent from 2014 to 2020 (Figure 3.69). Conversely, CO_2 productivity increased during this period, rising from 0.42 USD/kg to 0.59 USD/kg. These findings indicate that while Ukraine is endeavoring to decouple economic growth from CO_2 emissions, the linkage between emissions and GDP remains evident.

The value of the indicator—CO2 productivity—can be calculated using the quotient of the size of GDP at purchasing power parity expressed in constant 2017 prices and the volume of CO_2 emissions expressed in kilograms. Thus, during 2014–2020, the average value of the indicator was equal to 2.73 GDP/kg. It should be noted that during 2014–2017, there was an increase in the value in question from 2.24 GDP/kg to 2.88 GDP/kg. On the other hand, in 2018 the value of the indicator fell to 2.81 GDP/kg, and in the period 2021–2020 it increased again to 3.13 GDP/kg. Therefore, in Ukraine, over the entire period under review, there was an increase from 2.73 GDP/kg to 3.13 GDP/kg, an increase of 39.56%.

Final energy consumption

In the case of Ukraine, data on the energy balance is available for the period 2014–2020. Therefore, the analysis covers the range from 2014 to 2020. In Ukraine, primary energy supply and final energy consumption have been declining over the

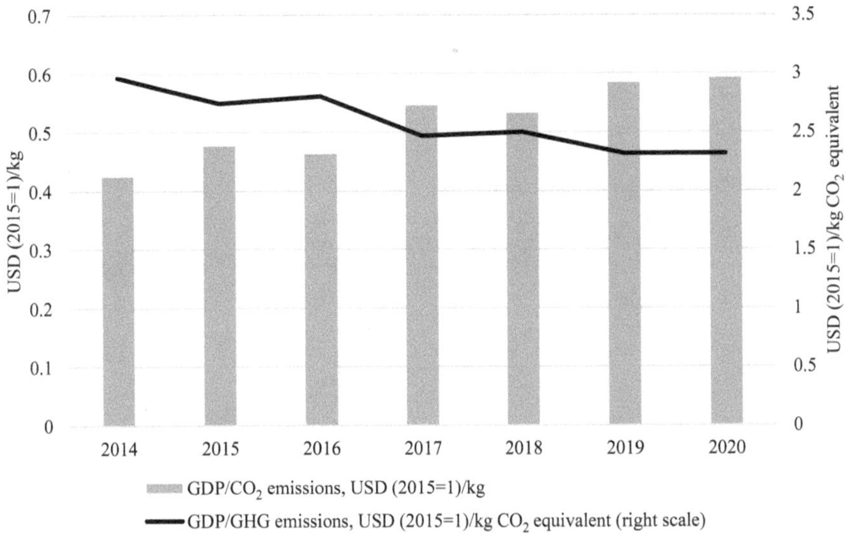

Figure 3.69 Ukraine. Greenhouse gas and CO_2 productivity.

Source: World Bank (World Bank Open Data, 2023); Climate Watch Data (2024).

period studied. Between 2014 and 2020, the decrease in energy supply was greater than the decrease in GDP by 15.53 percentage points. Overall, primary energy supply decreased from 105.68 to 86.36 million tons of oil equivalent between 2014 and 2020. The decline in energy supply also led to a decline in energy consumption (Figure 3.70). Thus, in 2020 compared to 2014, total energy consumption decreased from 61.46 to 47.44 million tons of oil equivalent, a decrease of 22.27%.

Between 2014 and 2020, energy consumption in Ukraine exhibited diverse trends across different sectors. The services sector notably increased its energy consumption from 4.66 to 4.86 million Toe, marking a growth of over 4%. Conversely, other sectors experienced reductions in energy consumption during the same period. Specifically, the residential sector saw the most substantial decline, decreasing from 20.38 to 13.60 million Toe, representing a significant 33.28% decrease. The industrial and transportation sectors both experienced reductions in energy consumption by approximately 22.43% and 22.42%, respectively. Similarly, the agricultural sector reduced its energy consumption from 2 to 1.66 million Toe, a decline of 17.52%. In contrast, energy consumption in the non-energy sector increased by 5.11%, rising from 3.5 to 3.68 million Toe.

Between 2014 and 2020, the structure of total energy consumption in Ukraine exhibited minor changes, as depicted in Figure 3.71. The industrial sector consistently maintained a stable share, accounting for an average of 31.84% of total energy consumption throughout this period. In the transportation sector, there was an initial increase in its share from 16.80% in 2014 to 20.19% by 2019, followed by a decrease to 16.77% in 2020. Conversely, the residential sector saw its share decrease from 33.17% to 28.47% over the same period. The agricultural sector

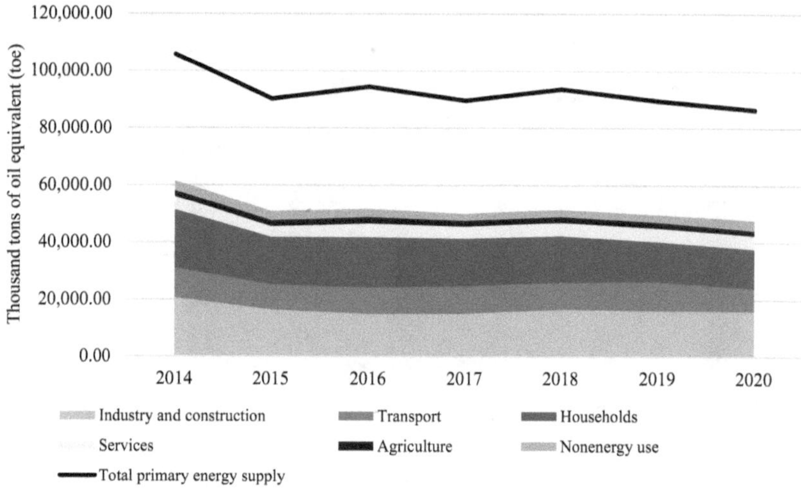

Figure 3.70 Ukraine. Primary energy supply and final energy consumption by sector, in thousand tons of oil equivalent.

Source: State Statistics Service of Ukraine (State Statistics Service of Ukraine (https://ukrstat.gov.ua/), 2021).

maintained the lowest share of energy consumption, averaging 3.70% throughout the period under review. Notably, non-energy industries experienced a notable increase in their share of total energy consumption, rising from 5.69% to 7.70%.

In 2020, compared to 2014, primary energy supply in Ukraine decreased by 18.28%, while GDP at purchasing power parity in constant 2017 prices decreased by 2.75%. This suggests that the decline in energy productivity has contributed to

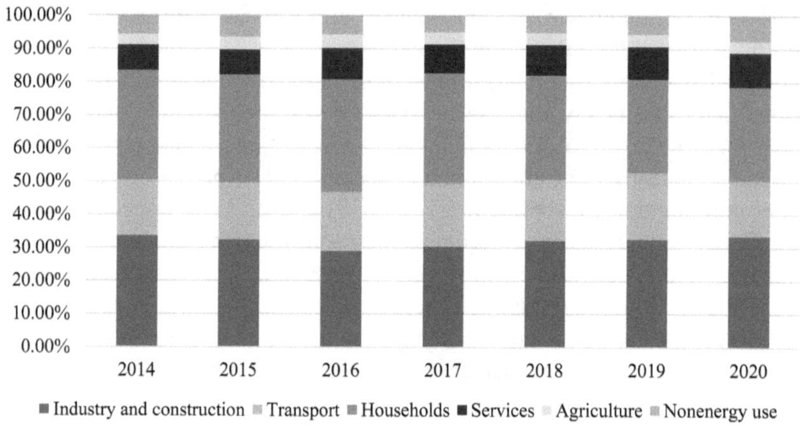

Figure 3.71 Ukraine. Structure of total energy use, in %.

Source: Own compilation based on data from State Statistics Service of Ukraine (State Statistics Service of Ukraine (https://ukrstat.gov.ua/), 2021).

the decoupling of economic growth from the volume of energy consumption. Calculating the ratio of GDP at purchasing power parity in constant 2017 prices to the volume of energy production reveals that energy productivity between 2014 and 2020 increased by 19.01%, from 5.04 to 6.00 USD/g.

Energy intensity

In Ukraine, after 2013, there was a slight increase in energy productivity and a significant decrease in energy intensity. However, not all sectors of the economy experienced a reduction in energy intensity. Between 2014 and 2020, despite an increase in final energy consumption, there was a decrease in GDP. These changes led to an overall increase in energy productivity and a decrease in energy intensity across the economy (Figure 3.72). For instance, in 2014, 609.17 grams of oil equivalent cost one US dollar in terms of final energy consumption. By 2020, this ratio decreased to 486.89 grams of oil equivalent per USD, marking a decrease of 20.07%. The industrial sector, which accounts for the highest volume of energy consumption, also saw a decrease in energy intensity. In 2014, its energy intensity ratio was 203.88 grams of oil equivalent per USD, which decreased to 162.62 grams of oil equivalent per USD by 2020, a decline of 20.24%. Similarly, the transport sector experienced a 20.22% decrease in energy intensity over the same period. The housing sector in Ukraine

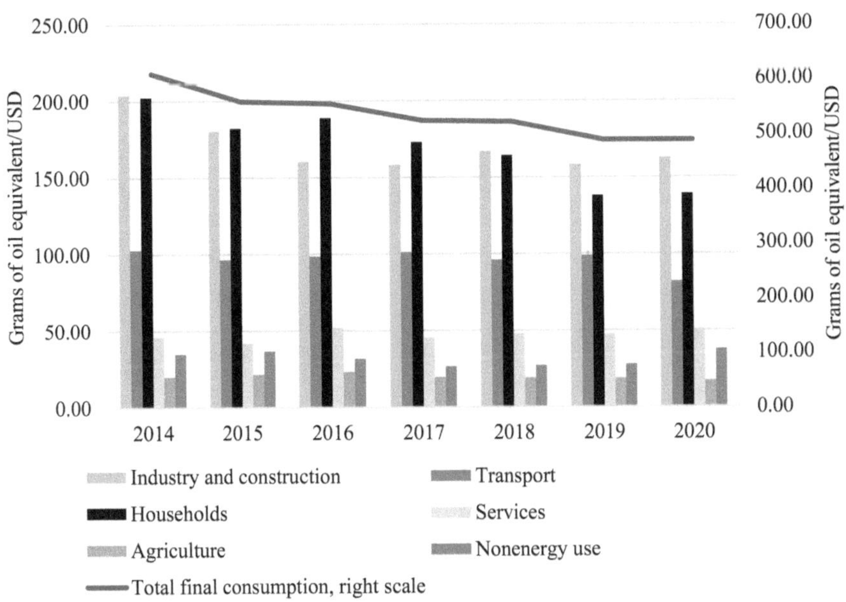

Figure 3.72 Ukraine. Energy intensity, in grams of oil equivalent/USD.

Source: Own compilation based on data from State Statistics Service of Ukraine (State Statistics Service of Ukraine (https://ukrstat.gov.ua/), 2021).

observed the largest decrease in energy intensity, dropping from 202.04 grams of oil equivalent per USD in 2014 to 138.62 grams of oil equivalent per USD in 2020, representing a decrease of 31.39%. Conversely, the agricultural sector recorded the smallest decrease in energy intensity, with a reduction of 15.19% between 2014 and 2020.

Share of renewable energy in total energy consumption

In Ukraine, between 2014 and 2020, there was an increase in the supply of renewable energy. Consequently, the share of renewable energy in both primary energy supply and final energy consumption also grew. However, Ukraine's renewable energy supply is predominantly sourced from biofuels and waste. This highlights the early stage of development of the modern renewable energy generation sector in the country.

Between 2014 and 2020, the supply of renewable energy in Ukraine more than doubled, increasing from 2.8 to 5.7 million tons of oil equivalent, marking a growth of 103.32%. Consequently, there were notable increases in the share of renewable energy within both primary energy production and total energy consumption (Figure 3.73). Specifically, in 2014, renewable energy accounted for 2.65% of primary energy supply, which rose to 6.58% by 2020. Similarly, the share of renewable energy in final energy consumption increased from 4.55% in 2014 to 11.90% by 2020.

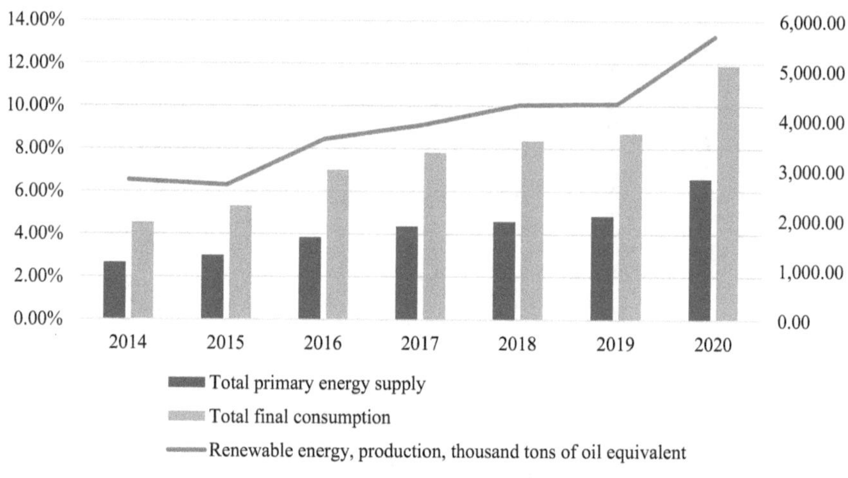

Figure 3.73 Ukraine. Renewable energy supply (thousand tons of oil equivalent) and share of renewable energy in primary energy production and total energy consumption, in %.

Source: Own compilation based on data from State Statistics Service of Ukraine (State Statistics Service of Ukraine (https://ukrstat.gov.ua/), 2021).

Waste generation

Two trends are evident in Ukraine. Both production waste and household waste show a declining trend (Figure 3.74). In 2014, approximately 355 million tons of waste were generated, increasing by nearly a third to 463 million tons by 2020. Similarly, the volume of waste collected from households fluctuated around 11.5 million m³ during 2015–2016 but began to increase from 2017 to 2020. Consequently, by 2020, the volume of waste collected from the population reached nearly 12.6 million m³.

Between 2014 and 2020, the amount of production waste generated increased by 30.25%. During the same period, VAT—an indicator reflecting the production process in current prices—increased by 15.65%. This suggests that the separation of the production process from waste generation is not confirmed (Figure 3.75). However, the situation differs for municipal waste. Waste collected from the population and household consumption exhibited distinct dynamics from 2015 to 2018. Consequently, the amount of waste collected from the population grew faster compared to household consumption (Figure 3.75). Nevertheless, in 2019, household consumption exceeded municipal waste production. This trend continued in 2020 as well. In 2020, compared to 2014, the amount of household waste increased by 17.56%, while household consumption rose by 20.34%. If this trend continues, Ukraine will succeed in reducing municipal waste creation.

Waste recycling. Evolution of the indicator

In Ukraine, data is collected on "used waste," encompassing both recycled waste and waste utilized for energy production. The peak disposal of waste occurred

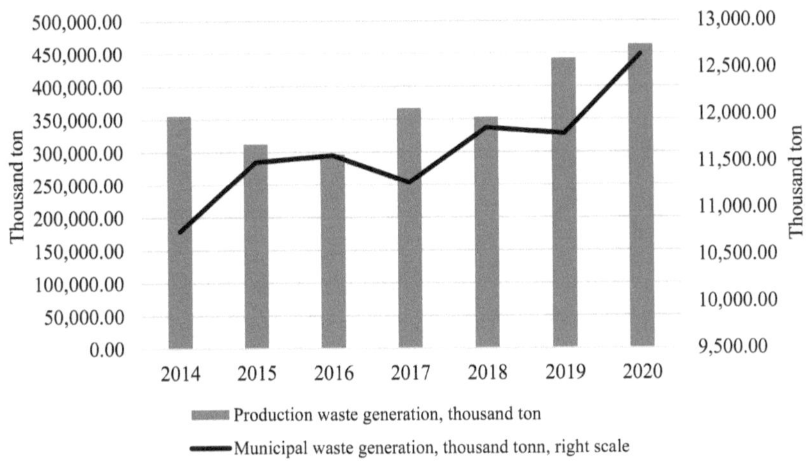

Figure 3.74 Ukraine. Generation of production waste and municipal waste.

Source: Own compilation based on data from State Statistics Service of Ukraine (State Statistics Service of Ukraine (https://ukrstat.gov.ua/), 2021).

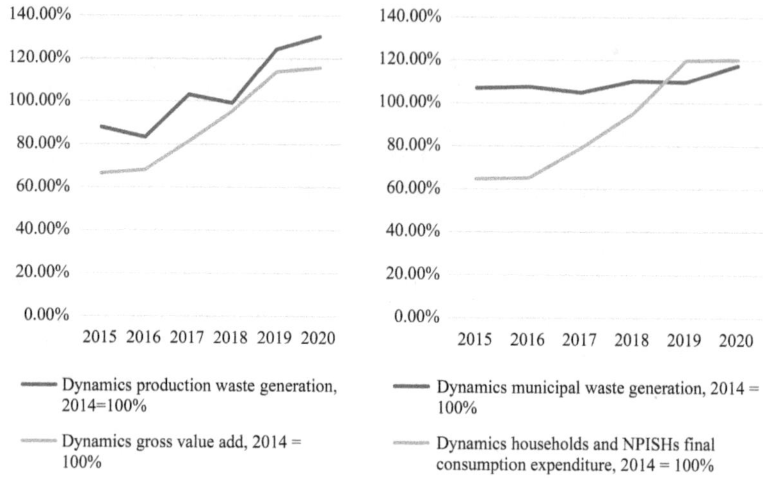

Figure 3.75 Ukraine. Dynamics of production waste, municipal waste, VAT, and household consumption, in %.

Source: Own compilation based on data from State Statistics Service of Ukraine (State Statistics Service of Ukraine (https://ukrstat.gov.ua/), 2021).

in 2014, totaling 109 million tons. Between 2014 and 2022, the disposed waste fluctuated between 85 and 109 million tons (Figure 3.76). Concurrently, the ratio of disposed waste to produced waste peaked at 30.78% in 2014. Over the period 2014–2022, this ratio varied between 30.78% and 21.74%. These findings indicate a reduction in the volume of recycled waste.

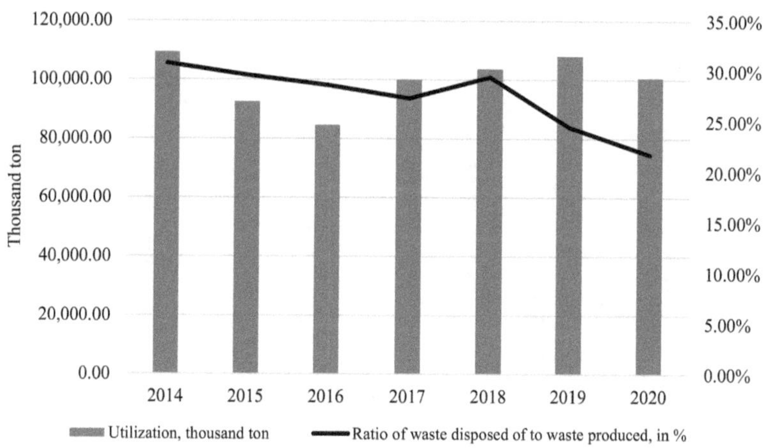

Figure 3.76 Ukraine. Waste disposed (thousands of tons) and ratio of waste disposed to waste produced, in %.

Source: Own compilation based on data from State Statistics Service of Ukraine (State Statistics Service of Ukraine (https://ukrstat.gov.ua/), 2021).

Use of fertilizers

A fertilizer balance sheet is compiled in Ukraine, providing the basis for analyzing the intensity of mineral fertilizer consumption. Ukraine has experienced accelerated growth in mineral fertilizer usage over the review period. However, this increase has not been paralleled by a significant rise in crop production, which remains largely contingent on weather conditions. Generally, there has been an uptick in the utilization of both mineral and organic fertilizers since 2013 (Figure 3.77). Whereas 1.5 million tons of mineral fertilizers were applied in 2014, over 2.9 million tons were utilized by 2021. The onset of Russia's full-scale invasion of Ukrainian territory in 2022 led to a reduction in agricultural land area and subsequently, fertilizer consumption. Natural fertilizer use exhibited a more fluctuating trend, with a subdued upward trajectory. For instance, whereas 9.9 million tons of natural fertilizers were used in 2014, nearly 12 million tons were applied in 2021 to fertilize agricultural lands. In 2022, there was a decrease in organic fertilizer consumption due to Russia's military actions and reduced sowing areas.

The increase in fertilizer use was also accompanied by an increase in the amount of fertilizer applied per hectare of soil. Between 2014 and 2021, the rate increased from 72.2 to 139.6 kg/ha for chemical fertilizers and from 485.2 to 536.1 kg/ha for organic fertilizers (Figure 3.78). In 2022, there was a decrease in the use of mineral fertilizers and organic fertilizers by 27.65% and 7.69%, respectively, compared to 2021.

Most mineral fertilizers predominantly consist of nitrates, followed by phosphates, with potassium fertilizers constituting the smallest portion. Consumption

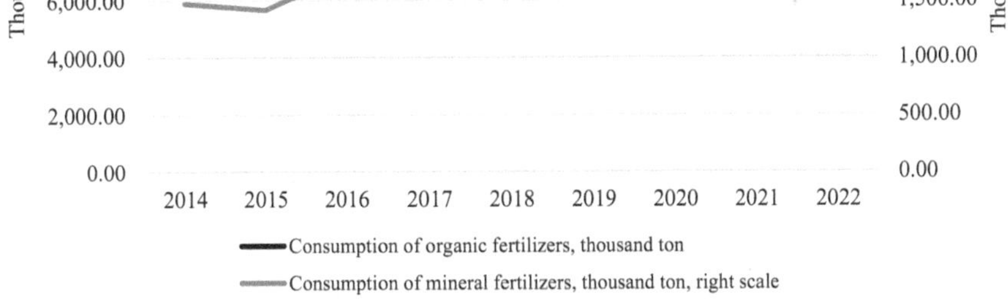

Figure 3.77 Ukraine. Consumption of chemical and natural fertilizers on farms and peasant holdings (farmers), in thousands of tons.

Source: Own compilation based on data from State Statistics Service of Ukraine (State Statistics Service of Ukraine (https://ukrstat.gov.ua/), 2021).

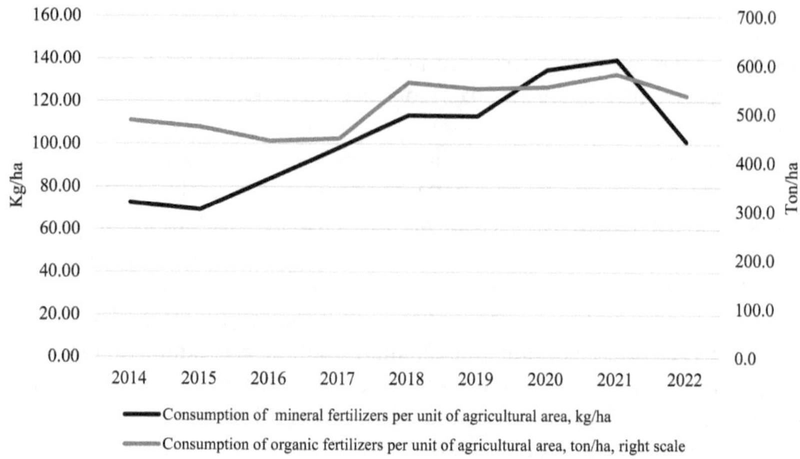

Figure 3.78 Ukraine. Consumption of chemical and natural fertilizers on farms and peasant farms (farmers), in kg/ha.

Source: Own compilation based on data from State Statistics Service of Ukraine (State Statistics Service of Ukraine (https://ukrstat.gov.ua/), 2021).

of all fertilizer types markedly increased between 2014 and 2021 (Figure 3.79). The usage of nitrates nearly doubled, rising from 1 to 1.97 million tons. Similarly, phosphate consumption more than doubled, from 241 to 501 million tons, during the same period. Potassium fertilizer consumption also almost doubled, increasing from 209 to 404,000 tons. However, in 2022, the use of all three types of fertilizers declined.

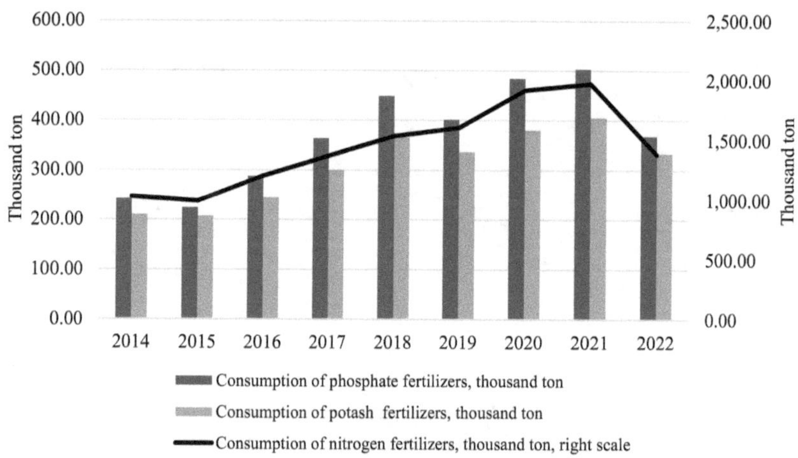

Figure 3.79 Ukraine. Types of mineral fertilizers used on farms and peasant farms (farmers), in thousands of tons.

Source: Own compilation based on data from State Statistics Service of Ukraine (State Statistics Service of Ukraine (https://ukrstat.gov.ua/), 2021).

Water consumption

In Ukraine, water consumption remained stable between 2015 and 2020. The volume of water consumed was 7,125 million m^3 in 2015 and 7,238 million m^3 in 2020, showing no significant decrease. However, notable variations occurred in other years: in 2014, the consumption was 8,710 million m^3, while in 2021 and 2022, it decreased to 6,143 and 3,401 million m^3, respectively. A similar trend was observed across most sectors of Ukraine's national economy (Figure 3.80). From 2014 to 2022, an average of 4,771 million m^3 of water was annually used for production needs, comprising about three-fifths of total water consumption. Agricultural purposes accounted for an annual average of 1,339 million m^3 of water, nearly one-third of the total. Domestic water consumption averaged 1,305 million m^3 annually during the period in question.

If water consumption showed a declining trend from 2014 to 2022, GDP expressed in USD at 2017 constant prices also remained at a similar level except for 2022, in which, due to the war, the value of the indicator compared to 2014 decreased by 28.67%. Despite this, there was an increase in water productivity in Ukraine and a decoupling of economic growth from water consumption was achieved. If one expresses productivity as a ratio of GDP in constant 2017 prices at purchasing power parity, then in 2022, compared to 2014, the productivity level rose to 111.70 USD/m^3 from 61.15 USD/m^3, an increase of 82.67%.

Summary

In conclusion, it is notable that all countries are implementing measures to reduce CO_2 emissions. The effectiveness of these efforts is reflected in the CO_2 productivity index. Countries like Armenia, Azerbaijan, Georgia, and Ukraine exhibit a strong

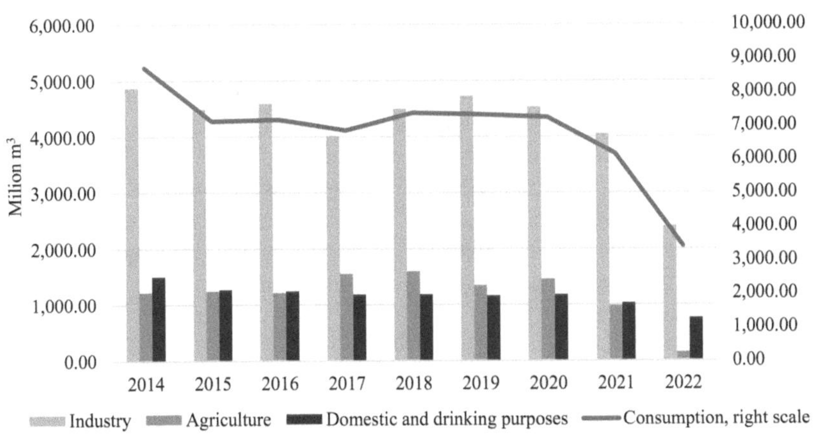

Figure 3.80 Ukraine. Water consumption by economic sector, in million m^3.

Source: Own compilation based on data from State Statistics Service of Ukraine (State Statistics Service of Ukraine (https://ukrstat.gov.ua/), 2021).

dependency of CO_2 productivity on GDP. Conversely, while Belarus and Moldova are striving to decouple economic growth from CO_2 emissions, their impact on the CO_2 productivity index remains minimal. Among the Eastern Partnership countries, varying outcomes were observed regarding final energy consumption. Specifically, Armenia, Georgia, Moldova, and Ukraine experienced an increase in energy productivity between 2014 and 2022, potentially contributing to decoupling economic growth from energy consumption. In contrast, changes in energy productivity in Azerbaijan and Belarus did not lead to such decoupling, influenced by the energy intensity of their economies. Ukraine notably demonstrated a clear reduction in energy intensity alongside an increase in economic productivity. Conversely, Armenia, Belarus, Georgia, and Moldova saw slight decreases in energy intensity despite increases in economic productivity. Azerbaijan, where energy intensity rose across all sectors of the national economy and final energy consumption outpaced GDP growth, represents a contrasting case. Across all six countries, the renewable energy sector remains in an early developmental stage, primarily reliant on wood combustion with minimal utilization of biomass and biogas.

Concurrently, waste production has generally increased, with Armenia, Azerbaijan, Belarus, Georgia, and Ukraine failing to confirm decoupling the production process from waste generation. Moldova stands out as the exception where successful decoupling was achieved during the study period. Regarding waste recycling, all countries except Georgia are actively engaged in this practice. Moldova showed a significant increase in waste recycling, whereas Ukraine witnessed a decline in materials processed through recycling initiatives. Moreover, mineral fertilizer usage has increased in all countries without corresponding gains in agricultural production, increasingly subject to climatic influences. Finally, Armenia, Belarus, Georgia, Moldova, and Ukraine have shown signs of decoupling economic growth from water consumption, whereas Azerbaijan has not observed such decoupling.

Natural resource base in European Partnership countries

This section examines whether and how the Eastern Partnership economies are sustaining their natural asset base. Six indicators are utilized to assess water resources, forests and land, organic farming, biodiversity, and protected areas. This framework allows for evaluating whether the natural asset base is preserved within sustainable limits concerning quantity, quality, and value. Progress is gauged through monitoring natural resources and other environmental assets, along with the flows of environmental services including renewable and nonrenewable resources, biodiversity, and ecosystems.

1. **Water resources.** Surface water resources and groundwater resources that are or can be used in the national economy. *Water intake* from natural water bodies involves extracting water from surface and groundwater sources for various uses. This includes well water obtained during natural resource extraction. *Water loss* during transportation refers to the loss of water from the point of extraction to its destination due to factors such as evaporation, filtration, leakage, and other

forms of dissipation. *Renewable internal freshwater resources per capita* refer to a country's internal renewable resources (internal river flows and groundwater from precipitation) relative to population. The indicator is calculated based on World Bank demographic estimates. The *level of water scarcity* represents the share of freshwater withdrawals by all major sectors in the total available renewable freshwater resources. The main sectors defined in the ISIC standards include: agriculture, forestry and fishing; manufacturing; energy production and supply; and services. The indicator is also called intake intensity.

2. **Forest resources.** The *total area of the forest fund* includes the portion of a country's territory occupied by forests, as well as the area devoted to forest management. Forestation rate means the area with planted or naturally growing trees of at least 5 meters in height in relation to the total area of the country. This indicator does not include trees in agricultural production systems (e.g., fruit orchards) and trees in parks and urban gardens.
3. **Soil resources.** The use of the land fund shows the structure of the land fund as of January 1, 2014–2022, by land category.
4. **Organic farming.** The area of land under organic farming means the area of land cultivated with organic agri-food production in accordance with the legislation of the countries under study. The number of farmers covered by organic farming includes those engaged in organic agri-food production in accordance with the principles of organic production as defined in the laws of the Eastern Partnership countries on organic agri-food production and national and international standards in this regard, certified in an established manner.
5. **Biodiversity.** Protected plant and animal species are a number of fauna and flora species threatened with extinction and protected by law, included in the Red Books[2] of the EaP countries.
6. **Natural protected areas.** The *area of natural protected areas* is the portions of land, water surface and air space on which there are natural complexes and objects of special natural, scientific, cultural, aesthetic, recreational and leisure value, which are completely removed or partially removed from economic use and for which a special system of protection has been established. The *share of protected natural areas* shows the area of natural areas protected by the state in relation to the total area of the country. The data is calculated by the authors and presented as a total for each of the EaP countries.

Armenia

Water resources

Proper management of water resources plays a key role in Armenia's socioeconomic development. The Republic has water resources at a moderately sufficient level. Armenia's water resources come mainly from rivers and groundwater. About 9,500 rivers flow through the country, of which 400 rivers are rivers with a length of more than 10 km and tributaries (Excerpt N54, 2017). There are several major rivers in the republic, including the Araks, Hrazdan, and Vorotan rivers, which are important sources of water used for irrigation electricity production and water supply for cities. All of Armenia's rivers are tributaries of the Araks and Kura rivers. Most of these rivers are small and are fed by fresh water from melting snow and groundwater (German–Azerbaijan Chamber of Commerce, 2023). The average annual total river runoff is 6,250 million m^3, of which 3,029 million m^3 comes from springs and groundwater. About 950 million m^3 of water comes from the Araks and Ahuryan border rivers. There are 14 major river basins in the country (Water Resources Management in Armenia, 2024).

Armenia boasts approximately 100 freshwater lakes and ponds. Lake Sevan, the country's largest freshwater reservoir, serves as a vital multipurpose water source for irrigation and power generation. As of 2022, its surface area measures 1,278.42 km^2, with a water level recorded at 1,900.57 meters (Statistical Committee Republic of Armenia, 2023). Plans are underway to raise Lake Sevan's water level by 6.5 meters over the next 30 years, thereby enhancing its water reserves. This initiative is expected to play a crucial role as a strategically significant natural resource for Armenia's energy and other economic sectors (Excerpt N54, 2017). Armenia has constructed 74 water reservoirs with a total usable capacity of 988 million m^3. An additional 31 water reservoirs are currently under construction, which upon completion will provide Armenia with an additional 832 million m^3 of water reserves (Water Resources Management in Armenia, 2024).

Water intake indicator

Although Armenia is not a water-scarce country, it faces a serious water shortage problem (Figure 3.81) due to the high demand for public water supply and high water consumption in agriculture (German–Azerbaijan Chamber of Commerce, 2023)

In 2022, the volume of water withdrawn was substantial, amounting to 68% of total renewable water resources, approximately 3,071.1 million m^3 annually (Figure 3.81). From 2014 to 2022, water losses across sectors of the national economy showed a decreasing trend, with a 13.10% reduction in losses by 2022 compared to 2014 levels. During this period, an increase in water withdrawal was noted, largely driven by heightened consumption in the agricultural sector, where irrigation, processing industries, and households play pivotal roles. Conversely, water consumption for production needs in the mining sector has decreased.

Forest resources

Armenia is characterized by a relatively small forest cover, comprising 11.54% of its total land area, equivalent to 334 thousand hectares, of which 328.26 thousand hectares are forested areas (Figure 3.82). This total includes approximately 50 thousand hectares of artificially planted forests. The predominant tree species in Armenia's forests are beech, oak, hornbeam, and pine. Additionally, the country is home to numerous rare species that grow in limited regions and represent some of the oldest flora species. These include taxa such as common ivy, wild jasmine, oriental plane tree, Caucasian elm, clematis, among others (WWF, 2024).

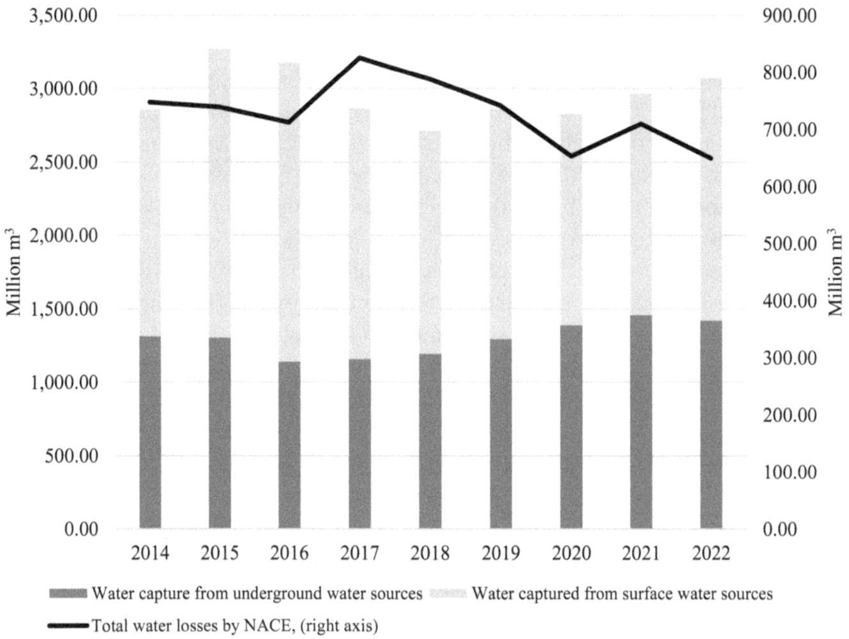

Figure 3.81 Armenia. Water capture during 2014–2022.

Source: Statistical Committee Republic of Armenia (2023).

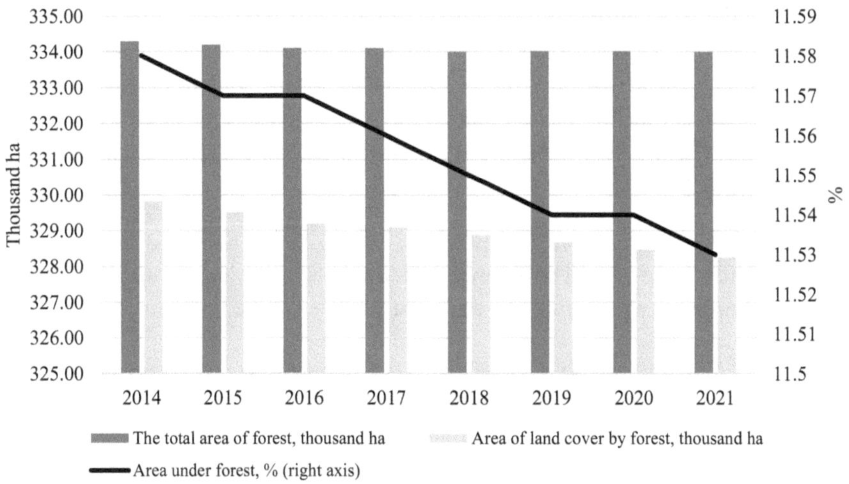

Figure 3.82 Armenia. Forest resource indicators from 2014 to 2022.

Source: Statistical Committee Republic of Armenia (2023).

Armenia's forest cover is unevenly distributed, primarily located in the central mountainous regions at elevations ranging from 500 to 2,100 meters in the north and up to 2,500 meters in the south. Approximately 64% of Armenia's forests are concentrated in the Lori and Tavush regions, with another significant forested area found in Syunik in the south. In the mountainous zones, there are small patches of natural forests totaling 17,000 hectares. On average, Armenia has 0.1 hectares of forest per capita, which is below the global average range of 0.5 to 0.8 hectares per capita (World Bank, 2023a).

In Armenia, forests are characterized by a high degree of degradation. Estimates from the feasibility study for a national forest inventory (NFI) in 2005 (which was not undertaken) suggest that 70% of Armenia's forests are degraded or overmature (World Bank, 2023a). This results from cutting old high-quality mixed oak and beech forests mainly through sanitary cuts and the lack of application of silvicultural measures. Mature forests became young low-quality coppice hornbeam forests because of high-grade cuttings, including unregulated timber exports. In the few planted conifer forests in the basin of Lake Sevan, approximately one quarter of the forest stands around the lake have been clear-cut, leading to accelerated erosion. According to FAO-FRA (2020), out of the official forest area of 28,470 hectares, 310,000 hectares are naturally regenerating forests. For 1990, the same statistic was 321,000 hectares, suggesting a loss in natural forest cover of 11,000 hectares over 30 years. Contrary to the official forest cover level of 11%, many national forestry experts and civil society organizations assert that the real forest cover of Armenia is 7–8% (World Bank, 2023a).

Armenia's natural forests are mainly deciduous (97%). There are four types of forests in the country:

- More than 40% of the forests are predominantly beech (*Fagus orientalis*). These forests are found on sloping hillsides at an altitude of 800–2,000 meters. In these forests, there are such tree species as Caucasian lime (*Tilia cordata*), Litinov birch (Betula litwinow), and spindle tree (*Euonymus europaeus*).
- Oak forests cover about one-third of the forested areas and grow at elevations between 600 and 2,000 meters above sea level. These forests also include other broadleaf species such as ash, hornbeam, Georgian maple, cork elm, and field maple.
- Forests rich in hornbeams occupy about 14% and may be mixed with oak and wild fruit tree species. These forests are found at elevations of 800–1,800 meters. Hornbeam also occurs as a secondary species in the few remaining natural pine forests.
- The fourth forest type is the pistachio/wild fruit tree forest (sea buckthorn, pistachio, almond, and wild cherry). It is found in the north of the country at altitudes of 900–1,200 meters and in the south at altitudes of 1,800–2,000 meters (World Bank, 2023a).

The main forest species (beech, oak, and hornbeam) cover 81.3% of Armenia's total forest area and account for 93.96% of the total timber resources.27 Other tree species-Caucasian pine, birch, elm, maple, ash, pear, apple, yew, hazel, plane, walnut, and others—are mainly represented together with the forest-forming species and occupy 18.7% of the forest area.

Deforestation and forest degradation are the major environmental problems in the country. According to FAO-FRA (2020), during 1990–2020, Armenia lost 6,260 hectares of forests. Moreover, 11,000 hectares of naturally regenerated primary forests were degraded into secondary forests during the same period. The average growing stock over bark in the Armenian forests decreased from 19.43 m^3/ha in 1990 to 11.63 m^3/ha in 2015 (FAO-FRA 2020) and the declining trend most likely continued after that period. A 1993 inventory estimate indicated the total standing wood volume to be 42 million m^3 (about 127 m^3 per ha) with an annual average growth of 0.45 million m^3 (less than 1.5 m^3/ha and year). The figures for both wood stock and annual growth seem to be extremely low. Either they are not accurate estimates or the existing natural forests overall are heavily degraded in terms of wood stock. An Organization for Security and Co-operation in Europe (OSCE) study in 2006 estimated the standing timber stock to be even lower, 28 million m 3,56 which corresponds to 85 m^3/ha. These findings suggest that some degree of forest degradation most likely has occurred in much larger areas beyond the 11,000 hectares reported above (World Bank, 2023a).

Degradation levels are set to increase. Continuous land degradation and increasing drought are expected to lead to changes in Armenia's forest cover. Armenia's Fourth National Communication to the United Nations Framework Convention on Climate Change (UNFCCC) (NC4) (MoE, 2020) forecasts a potential loss of forest and woodlands of 14,000–17,500 hectares (around 3–4%) by 2030 as a result of changes to ecosystems and growing conditions as well as an increased frequency of forest fire, pest and disease outbreaks, and invasive species. In the forest areas of the country, overuse of forest resources, exacerbated by the effects of climate change, has resulted in erosion, landslides, and disturbance to the hydrological cycle (World Bank, 2023a).

Soil resources

In general, Armenia has 14 types, 27 subtypes, and a lot of families, varieties, and species of soils. The total number of soils is 228. In addition to the area of soil types listed in Table 3.2, nearly 358,000 hectares of the country are covered by the rock outcrops, sands, infrastructure, and residential zones.

Armenia has experienced minimal changes in the extent of its soil resources over the past decade. Factors such as urbanization, population density, and infrastructure expansion have had little impact on the structure of the land base. Consequently, Armenia remains primarily an agricultural nation. However, extensive portions of agricultural land are fragmented and susceptible to erosion, thereby constraining agricultural productivity.

Armenia's land resources are predominantly agricultural, comprising approximately 67% of the total land area, totaling 2.04 million hectares. Agricultural land use has remained stable over the years, with arable land accounting

Table 3.2 Natural soil zones and soil types in Armenia.

Natural soil zone	*Soil types*	*RSG (respective soil group)*	*Territory*		*Altitudes*
Thousand hectares			%		
Semidesert	1 Semidesert brown	Calcisols	152.0	5.8	850–1,250
	2 Irrigated	Antrosols	53.0	2.0	
	meadow-brown	Solonetz-	2.0	0.1	
	3 Paleohydromorphic	Solonchaks	29.0	1.1	
	4 Saline-alkaline	Solonetz-			
	hydromorphic	Solonchaks			
Dry-prairie	Mountainous chestnut	Kastanozems	242	9.2	1,250–1,900
Prairie	1 Mountainous	Chernozems	718.0	27.4	1,300–2,450
	blacksoils	Chernozems	13.0	0.5	
	2 Meadow blacksoils	Antrosols	48.0	1.8	
	3 Bottomland	Regosols and	18.0	0.7	
	– terraced	rocк			
	4 Soils of Lake	outcrops			
	Sevan				
Forest	1 Mountainous-	Acrisols	133.0	5.2	500–2,400
	brown forest	Acrisols	15.0	0.6	
	2 Mountainous sod –	Acrisols	564.0	21.6	
	carbonate forest +				
	3 Mountainous cinnamonic forest				
Mountainous - meadow	1 Mountainous -	Umbrisols	346	13.2	2,200–4,095
	meadow	Phaeozems	283	10.8	
	2 Mountainous - meadow prairie				
Total area			2616.0	100.0	

Source: Ghazaryan (2013).

for more than 70% and perennial plantations making up just over 10% of the total agricultural land (Figure 3.83). In recent years, Armenia has experienced a slight decrease of 7,000 hectares in uncultivated land. As of 2022, approximately 20 thousand hectares of land remain uncultivated, representing 1% of the total agricultural land area. However, soil quality is under pressure from erosion, insufficient grazing, and inadequate soil conservation practices (Statistical Committee Republic of Armenia, 2023). Roughly 40% of Armenia's agricultural land is affected by erosion, significantly reducing its productivity compared to noneroded land, which yields 3–4 times more (Convention on Biological Diversity, 2024).

The other types of land included in the land fund remain on the register in the same areas, namely: forest and conservation fund land, 11.22%; township land, 5.12%; and water fund land, 0.87%. The exception to this rule is the land in the reserve fund, which currently amounts to 0.62 thousand hectares, and over 2012–2022, their areas have not changed.

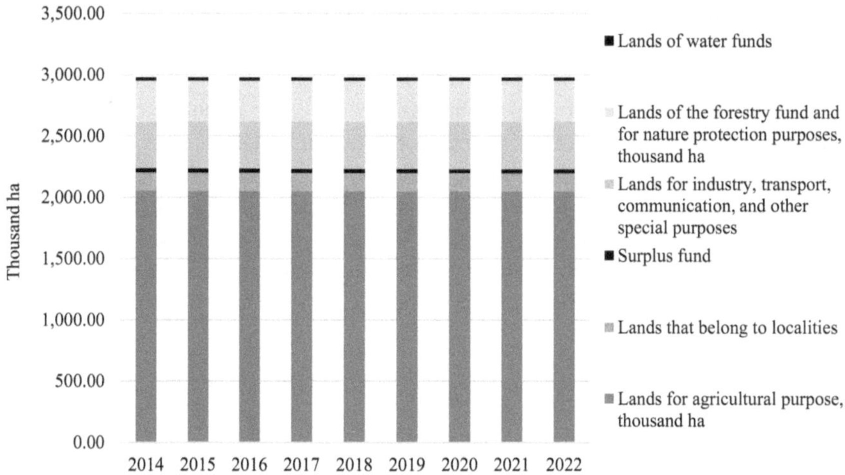

Figure 3.83 Armenia. Land resources by land category during 2014–2022, in thousand hectares.

Source: Statistical Committee Republic of Armenia (2023).

Organic farming

The Republic of Armenia adopted a law on organic agriculture in 2008. This came into force in 2009. This makes Armenia one of the first former Soviet countries to have its own organic law. The Law of the Republic of Armenia of 8 April 2008 No. 23-N on Organic Agriculture is based on the principles of the Codex Alimentarius (EcoConnect, 2021).

Thus, already in the early 1990s, about 80% of the agricultural land was privatized. About 350 thousand privately run family farms were established. The average farm size is 0.5 to 1 hectare. In 2019, the eco-certified cultivated area of the Republic of Armenia was 594 ha. This is 0.04% of the total cultivated area. The area used for ecological wild collection is considerably larger. It amounts to 8,570 ha. The certified organic area in the Republic of Armenia has shrunk by 21% in the past 10 years. In 2019, 2,358 hives were certified organic in the Republic of Armenia (Willer et al., 2021).

The decline of the organically certified area can probably be explained by the end of the projects to promote organic farming. Because the farmers cannot generate any additional yield through their organic certification and do not receive any financial support, neither from the Republic of Armenia nor from aid organizations, they drop out of the process (EcoConnect, 2021).

The organic certified farms in the Republic of Armenia are exclusively producers of plant products. There is no certified organic animal production so far. As in conventional agriculture, the production of fruits plays an essential role in organic farming. In Armenia, apricots are the most important fruit grown after wine. According to FAO statistics, 10,363 hectares of apricots were grown conventionally and organically in total in 2019. This is only 4,000 hectares less than wine. Pomegranates, apples, pears, and plums are also grown. Furthermore, raspberries and blackberries are grown in Armenia (EcoConnect, 2021).

Another important ecological production sector in the Republic of Armenia is wild collection. In the regions of Armenia where cultivation is not possible, plants are collected wild to make teas and medicinal products. As described above, Armenia has a rich flora. The plant parts taken from the ecologically certified wild collection areas include nettles, thyme, mint, lime blossom, sea buckthorn, liquorice, oregano, rose hips, raspberries, blackberries cornelian cherry, and sea buckthorn. Wild collection is an important source of income for the rural population in remote areas (EcoConnect, 2021).

Biodiversity

The Republic of Armenia is considered a small landlocked country located in the Caucasus region of Eurasia. The diversity of Armenia's landscape and the peculiarities of its terrain are critical factors in the formation and evolution of the country's flora and fauna. Biodiversity in Armenia includes more than 200 species of edible plants, 40 species of edible fungi, more than 1,000 forage plants, 350 species of honey plants, 350 ether plants, 120 dye plants, 100 vitamin-producing plants, and 60 gum plants; about 10% of Armenia's flora is believed to have medicinal properties. About 3% of the flora (123 species) are local endemics of Armenia (Convention on Biological Diversity, 2024).

A comprehensive survey of Armenia's flora and fauna was conducted between 2007 and 2010. In 2010, the Government of the Republic of Armenia approved an update of the Red Book and gave it legal status. The new edition includes 452 plant species (12.5% of the flora) and 308 animal species (2% of the fauna), as well as 40 species of fungi and 155 species of invertebrates. The assessment was based on the criteria of the IUCN Red List of Threatened Species and aerial data on these species, mapped using GIS. The most endangered mammals include Leopard (*Panthera pardus,* "Critically Endangered"), Armenian mouflon (*Ovis orientalis,* "Endangered"), Bezoar goat (*Capra aegagrus,* "Vulnerable"), Transcaucasian bear (*Ursus arctos,* "Vulnerable"), European marbled polecat (*Vormela peregusna*, "sensitive"), European otter (*Lutra,* "Endangered"), and Pallas' cat (*Otocolobus manul,* "Regionally Extinct") (Convention on Biological Diversity, 2024).

The link between biological resources and Armenia's socioeconomic landscape is unmistakable. Biological resources play a pivotal role in Armenia's economy, notably by providing raw materials for agriculture, food production, and various industries, as well as fostering recreational opportunities. Among Armenia's natural ecosystems, forests are arguably the most crucial economically. Local communities predominantly utilize open forests for timber and seasonal grazing. Additionally, these forests are rich in herbs and edible plants, which residents gather for personal consumption and for sale in local markets (Convention on Biological Diversity, 2024). Biodiversity loss has accelerated significantly over the past century due to industrial development, agriculture, urbanization, energy demands, and intensive exploitation of forests, grasslands, and other ecosystems. The primary threats to biodiversity stem directly or indirectly from human activities, including habitat alteration, overexploitation, pollution from sewage and mineral fertilizers, overgrazing, plowing, illegal logging, tourism development, introduction of invasive species, climate change, and inadequate irrigation practices leading to salinization and soil erosion. Anthropogenic impacts are particularly pronounced in forested areas, semi-desert, and steppe ecosystems, as well as in the aquatic environment of Lake Sevan (Convention on Biological Diversity, 2024).

Natural protected areas

Specially protected areas serve to effectively protect biodiversity in Armenia. Their total area is 383,100 hectares, which is 12.1% of the country's total area (or 7% of the total area if the area of Lake Sevan is not included) (Figure 3.84).

Only 54% of Armenia's specially protected areas consist of forest ecosystems, yet these areas safeguard 70% of the country's flora and fauna. Armenia's network of protected areas encompasses four national parks (Sevan, Dilijan, Lake Arpi, Arevik), three state reserves (Khosrov, Shikahogh, Erebuni), and 232 natural monuments within 27 state reserves. Efforts to expand the network are ongoing, with plans to establish two additional protected areas in southern Armenia (Gnishik and Khustup), as well as the conversion of the Shikahogh State Reserve into the Shikahogh Biosphere Reserve in the Syunik region, supported by financing from the KfW Development Bank (Entwicklungsbank) (Convention on Biological Diversity, 2024).

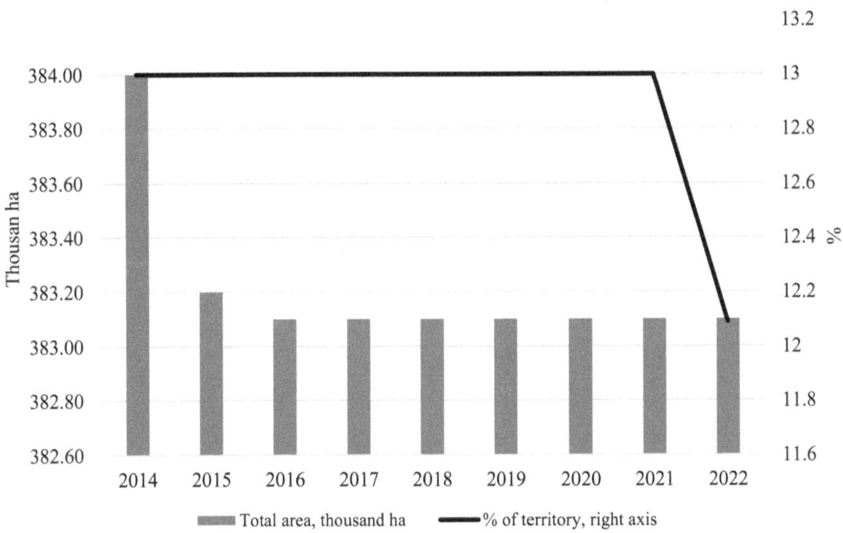

Figure 3.84 Armenia. Area of natural protected areas.

Source: Statistical Committee Republic of Armenia (2023).

As can be seen from the data presented in the chart, the area of protected areas in Armenia decreased by 900 hectares between 2014 and 2022. This decrease is mainly conditioned by the decrease in the area of forest cover.

Azerbaijan

Water resources

In Azerbaijan, the main facilities of the hydrographic network—rivers, lakes, and reservoirs —are unevenly distributed in different parts of the country. Azerbaijan's water resources are limited compared to other countries in the South Caucasus and account for only 15% of the region's water resources. The sources of the country's surface water resources are rivers, lakes, reservoirs, and glaciers. Surface water resources are mainly concentrated within rivers and 67–70% of river water resources come from the territory of neighboring countries (Ministry of Ecology and Natural Resources Republic of Azerbaijan, 2021).

Rivers

The republic of Azerbaijan features a river network comprising more than 8,350 rivers, with two exceeding 500 km in length, while the majority are shorter than 10 km (Table 3.3). Among these, the Kura River and its tributaries constitute Azerbaijan's primary river system, flowing directly into the Caspian Sea. The Kura River, crucial as Azerbaijan's main water source, traverses Turkey, Georgia, and Azerbaijan. Its total catchment area spans 188,000 km^2, with Azerbaijan's portion accounting for 258,000 km^2, or 31%. The Kura River passes through various cities including Mingachevir, Yevlakh, Shirvan, and numerous other regions within the

Table 3.3 Azerbaijan: River resources as at 2021.

Rivers	*Shore that the river flows in to*	*Length (km)*	*Water catchment area (km^2)*		*Altitude (m)*
			Source	*Mouth*	
Kura River	Caspian Sea	1515	188,000	2,740	-27
Araz	Kura River (right)	1072	10,2000	2,990	-11
Ganikh	Mingachevir Water Reservoir	414	16,920	2,560	75
Gabirri	Mingachevir Water Reservoir	389	4,840	2,560	51
Khami	Kura River (right)	220	8,340	2,422	255
Aghstafachay	Kura River (right)	133	2,586	3,000	210
Kurekchay	Kura River (right)	186	2,080	3,100	18
Arpachay	Araz (left)	126	2,630	2,985	780
Hakarichay	Araz (left)	113	5,540	3,080	268
Samur	Caspian Sea	216	4,430	3,600	-27
Pirsaat	Caspian Sea	119	2,280	2,400	-11
Bolgarchay	Mahmudchala lake	163	2,170	1,710	-17

Source: Republic of Azerbaijan (2021, p. 20).

Table 3.4 Azerbaijan: Water resources of lakes as of the end of 2021.

Lakes	*Location*	*Water catchment area (km²)*	*Volume (million m³)*
Sarısu	Kura-Araz lowland	65.7	59.1
Aghzibirchala	Shabran	13.8	10.0
Goygol	Kurekchay basin	0.79	24.0
Hajigabul	Kura-Araz lowland	8.4	12.1
Boyuk-Shor	Absheron peninsula	16.2	27.5
Aghgol	Kura-Araz lowland	56.2	44.7
Jandargol	The border of Georgia	10.6	51.0

Source: Republic of Azerbaijan (2021).

country. Azerbaijan's major transboundary rivers encompass 21 watercourses, including the Kura, Araz, Ganikh, Gabirri, Samur, Astara, and several smaller rivers that feed into the Kura and Araz basin (Ministry of Ecology and Natural Resources Republic of Azerbaijan, 2021).

The Araz River, Azerbaijan's second-largest river and a right tributary of the Kura River, flows through Turkey, serving as the border between Turkey and Armenia, Turkey and Azerbaijan, and Iran and Azerbaijan. Its total catchment area covers 102,000 km^2, with Azerbaijan's portion amounting to 18%, or 18,740 km^2 (Ministry of Ecology and Natural Resources Republic of Azerbaijan, 2021).

Lakes

There are about 450 lakes in Azerbaijan with a total area of 395 km^2, 10 of which are larger than 10 km^2 (Table 3.4). The largest lake of the Republic is Sarysu Lake located in the Kura-Araz plain (water area 65.7 km^2, volume 59.1 million m^3). Tufangol (surface area 0.01 km^2, volume 0.11 million m^3) is the highest mountain lake located in the Demiraparanchay basin and at an altitude of 3,277 m. One of the most picturesque lakes of the Republic is the famous Goy-Gol Lake. The lake was formed in the middle reaches of the Aghsuchay after a strong earthquake in 1139.

Azerbaijan has built 140 water reservoirs and artificial water bodies, covering a total area of 982.84 km^2 and holding a total volume of 21,464 million m^3. More than 60 of these reservoirs have a capacity exceeding 1 million m^3. These reservoirs, constructed both within and outside riverbeds (Table 3.5), are primarily used for irrigation. Reservoirs and hydropower plants built on the Kura, Araz, and Tartar rivers—such as Shamkir, Mingachevir, Yenikand, Varvara, Araz, and Sarsang—serve multiple purposes, including power generation, irrigation, and water supply. Mingachevir Reservoir, the largest in the Republic, was put into operation in 1953.

Groundwater

Usable groundwater in the Republic of Azerbaijan is limited and unevenly distributed. However, the territory is rich in highly mineralized raw thermal and

Table 3.5 Azerbaijan: Water resources of water reservoirs as of the end of 2021.

Water reservoir	*Water catchment area (km²)*	*Volume (million m³)*
Mingachevir	605	15,730
Shamkir	116	2,677
Yenikand	22.61	158.5
Varvara	22.5	60
Araz	145	1,254
Sarsang	13.85	565
Jeyranbatan	13.89	186
Khanbulanchay	2.46	52
Sirab	1.54	12.7
Aghstafachay	6.38	120
Khachinchay	1.76	23

Source: Republic of Azerbaijan (2021,, p. 21).

hydromineral waters, which are of significant energy and industrial importance and are found in the deep layers of Earth's crust. Additionally, Azerbaijan has 16 sources of medicinal drinking water and 14 sources of mineral waters with medical significance. The country also has deposits of iodine-bromine waters, which have proven industrial resources and have been exploited for many years, playing an important role in the national economy (Ministry of Ecology and Natural Resources Republic of Azerbaijan, 2021).

Water intake ratio

In Azerbaijan, internal water resources amount to 35 billion m^3/year, which is about 3,529 m^3 per capita (data for 2017) (Azerbaijan Water, 2024). Since the Soviet era, water has been polluted as a result of agricultural activities and the chemical industry. Moreover, mining activities have led to heavy metal contamination, and untreated domestic wastewater causes organic pollution. Wastewater treatment plants are in short supply, and those that exist often do not function properly. Climate change could further threaten the water quality of Azerbaijan's two rivers (Kerres, 2010).

Groundwater resources in Azerbaijan are renowned for their mineral drinking water quality and are used for medicinal purposes. The Nakhichevan Autonomous Republic is particularly rich in mineral groundwater. Water losses in irrigation systems, estimated at 50%, lead to waterlogging and salinization. Moreover, only 6,000 km^2 of irrigated land, which are the most naturally saline areas, have drainage. Increased water levels in the Caspian Sea have also contributed to the salinization of coastal lands. Salinity is particularly prevalent in the Kura-Araks plain (UNECE, 2004).

Nearly 30% of the Caspian Sea's coastal area is vulnerable to contamination, and more than half of the rivers longer than 100 km are considered polluted. All lakes in the low-lying parts of the country are exposed to changes in their thermal, biological, and chemical regimes. The lakes of the Absheron Peninsula and the

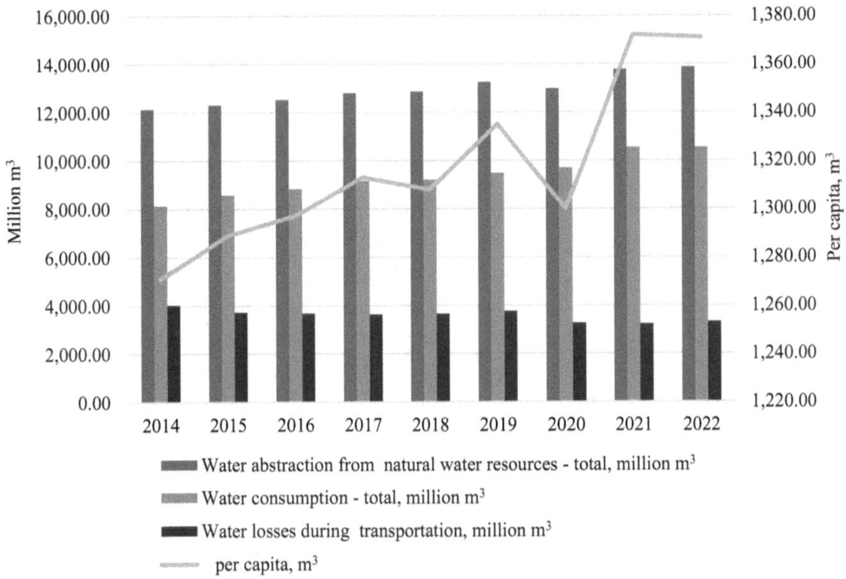

Figure 3.85 Azerbaijan. Water intake 2014–2022.

Source: The State Statistical Committee of the Republic of Azerbaijan (2023).

Kura-Araks Plain, covering a total area of more than 200 km^2, are in critical condition. The main sources of pollution of water resources are industry, agriculture, the municipal sector, energy, heating, and recreation (UNEP/GRID-Arendal, 2005). The irrational use of water resources and the pollution of water bodies can be attributed to the poor equipment of cities, regional centers, and other settlements with sewage systems and wastewater treatment plants, as well as the aging of existing technical facilities (Figure 3.85).

The amount of water withdrawn is quite high, accounting for about 40% of renewable water resources or an annual volume of about 13,841 million m^3 (Figure 3.85). One reason for the high values of water abstraction is consumption and relatively high losses during transportation. From 2014 to 2022, transport water losses showed a relatively stable evolution, fluctuating between 3.2 and 4.0 billion m^3. During this period, there was an increase in the amount of water withdrawn by the agricultural sector and industry, with increases of 38.05% and 14.23%, respectively. In the household sector, water consumption increased by only 5.11%, despite population growth in the Republic.

Forest resources

Azerbaijan's forests are mainly deciduous, with less than 3% of them evergreen. Deciduous forests, including dry and moist subtropical forests, are found on mountain slopes, along river corridors, and on plains (Azerbaijan FAA 119, 2020). Azerbaijan's mountain forests are mainly oriental beech (*Fagus orientalis*), oak (mainly

Quercus iberica) or hornbeam (*Carpinus caucasica*). In some areas, oak and hornbeam grow together in mixed oak-hornbeam forest. In foothill forests in the lower mountain range up to 1,000 meters above sea level, oaks and hornbeams also dominate. At higher altitudes, the trees are replaced by rhododendron (*Rhododendron caucasicum*) shrubs in the western, wetter part of the Greater Caucasus, and pine (*Pinus silvestris*) or juniper (*Juniperus*).

The southeastern tip of Azerbaijan, bordering the Caspian Sea and Iran, is a unique mixed landscape encompassing the Talyish Mountains, which rise to more than 2,000 meters, the adjacent lowlands and wetlands of Lankaran, and humid subtropical zones in the lower part up to 500 meters above sea level, a climate unusual for Azerbaijan, with a dry season in July and August and abundant rainfall the rest of the year. The relict subtropical forests of this zone include species that originated in the Tertiary, including many endemic tree and shrub species, other higher plants, and insects. Forests include ironwood (*Parrotia persica*), chestnut oak (*Quercus castaneifolia*), Caucasian elm (*Zelkova carpinifolia*), Caucasian persimmon (*Diospyros lotus*), Lankaran acacia (*Albiccia julibrissina*), and many endemic plant species. Much of the plain has been adapted for cultivation, including grapes, citrus, and other tropical fruits, as well as cattle grazing.

The dry subtropical forest is found mainly along parallel mountain ranges of the Greater Caucasus at elevations up to 600 meters, including areas around the Mingachevir Reservoir in western Azerbaijan, near the border with Georgia. Some patches of this forest also occur in the foothill zone of the Lesser Caucasus. It consists primarily of various species of juniper (*Juniperus*), wild pistachio (*Pistacia mutica*), Caucasian oak (*Quercus iberica*), wild fig tree (*Ficus carica*), Caucasian blackberry (*Celtis caucasica*), wild almond (*Amygdalus fenzlianum*), Caucasian pear (*Pyrus caucasicum*), and other trees that are distant relatives of cultivated species and can thrive in dry climates.

Along the riverbanks are several areas of remnant riparian forests, known as "tugay," that have not been logged or flooded due to anthropogenic water regimes. These forests are characterized by distinctive white and black poplar (*Populus alba*, *Populus nigra*), oak (*Quercus longipes*, now *Q. iberica*), wing nut (*Pterocarya fraxinifolia*), and other trees. Tugay forests account for just over 1% of Azerbaijan's total forest cover.

In 2021, Azerbaijan's forest fund covered 1,143.3 thousand hectares, which is about 14% of the country's total area. Of this, approximately 1,040.7 thousand hectares are forested (Figure 3.86). The majority of Azerbaijan's forests (85%) are located on high mountain slopes, providing soil protection, water retention, climate purification, and other benefits. The remaining 15% are plain forests. In mountainous regions, forests cover 20–60% of the total area, while in lowland areas, the coverage ranges from 0.5–2.0%. On average, each person in the republic has access to 0.14 hectares of forest area and 17 m^3 of firewood. In Azerbaijan, 88% of the forests are deciduous, 8.9% are mixed forests, and 0.06% are coniferous forests. These forests span different age classes, with an average age of 86 years in mountainous zones and 40–60 years in the plains. The country's average annual

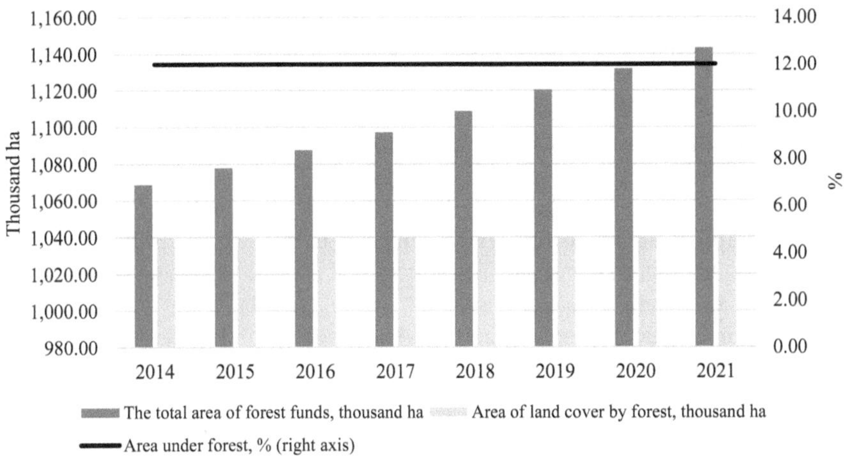

Figure 3.86 Azerbaijan. Forest resource indicators from 2014 to 2022.

Source: The State Statistical Committee of the Republic of Azerbaijan (2023).

growth of firewood is 1.5 million m^3, with an average stock of 172 m^3 of firewood per hectare (eco.gov.az/az).

Between 2014 and 2022, Azerbaijan saw an increase in the areas included in the forest fund, while the forest-covered area remained constant at 1,040.7 thousand hectares. However, from 2015 to 2022, the volume of timber resources in Azerbaijan decreased by a third. In 2015, the country had 151.9 million m^3 of timber, but by 2022, this volume had reduced to only 103.7 million m^3.

Soil resources

Vertical soil zonality predominates in the territory of the republic. There are 25 types and 60 subtypes of soils in the country (Ministry of Ecology and Natural Resources Republic of Azerbaijan, 2021).

Chestnut soils (gray-brown) are widespread in the Republic at altitudes of 400–800 m. The amount of humus in these soils is 2.5–3.5%. In the Greater and Lesser Caucasus Mountains, Ganja-Gazakh, and Mil-Karabakh plains, in the low mountainous areas of Ajinohur and Jeyranchol, these lands rise up to 600 m, and in Nakhchivan to more than 1,000 m.

Mountain-forest soils occur in the mountains at an altitude of 700–2,000 m. Brown mountain-forest soils are widespread in the lower zones and relatively arid areas. The amount of humus in these soils with sparse forests and shrubs is 5–7%. Brown mountain-forest soils occur in the upper parts. Due to heavy rainfall, brown mountain-forest soils are widespread in the Lankaran region. Nakhchivan does not have this type of soil due to the arid climate.

Mountain-black soils occur in the south-east of the Greater Caucasus, and in the north of the Karabakh and Murovdagh ranges. Humus in these soils is 6–6.5%.

Yellow and red soils are found in the lower parts of the Talysh Mountains and Lankaran lowland. These soils with a humus content of 8–12% are rich in iron oxide.

The Alazan-Ayrichay valley, Samur-Davachi lowland, and Shollar plain are covered with meadow-forest soils. Alluvial-meadow soils occur in the northern foothills of the Talysh Mountains, on the shores of the Gizilaghaj Bay, along the Kura River and the Main Shirvan Collector. The plots of land intended for agricultural purposes under the territorial planning of land use are considered agricultural lands. Agricultural land includes agricultural areas, lands under forest strips, on-farm roads, communications, swamps, ponds, and buildings and structures required for conducting agricultural activities. Agricultural areas (arable lands) include lands sown with grains, perennial crops, derelict lands, meadows, pastures, and grazing fields.

The total land fund in the country is more than 8.641 million hectares. Of this, 4.78 million hectares or 55% are agricultural lands, including 1.45 million hectares of irrigated land. About 2.06 million hectares of agricultural land are arable lands and 3.88 million hectares of the country's lands are nonagricultural (Figure 3.87). Azerbaijan is one of the countries having limited land resources. The agricultural land per capita in the country is equal to 0.47 hectares, including 0.2 hectares of crop field. The per capita area of pastures and hayfields is limited. Except for foothills and the south-eastern part of the country, for most, agricultural

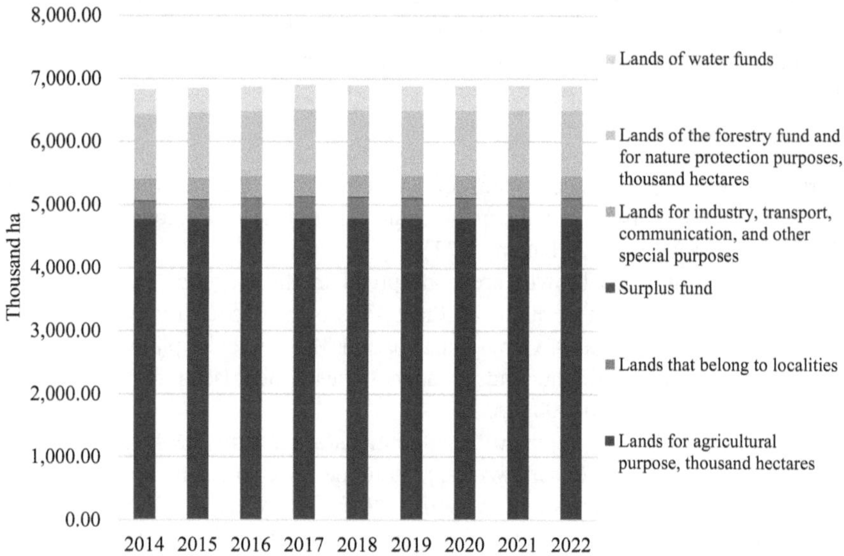

Figure 3.87 Azerbaijan. Land fund by land category during 2014–2022, in thousand hectares.

Source: The State Statistical Committee of the Republic of Azerbaijan (2023).

land's irrigation water is a very important means of agricultural production. This is due to the specifics of arid and semi-arid climates.

The other types of land included in the land fund remain on the register in the same areas, namely: forest and conservation fund land, 15.11%; village land, 4.54%; water fund land, 5.73%, and industrial and infrastructure land, 4.98%.

Organic farming

In Azerbaijan, about 4.8 million hectares are used by the agricultural sector, of which 43% is arable land, 50.6% is grassland and pasture, and 5.7% is perennial crops. In Azerbaijan, such an organization as in Georgia ELKANA does not yet exist. The Ganja Agribusiness Association (GABA)—inspired by the soil scientist Professor Amin Babayev—plays an essential role in the development of organic agriculture. This association is the initiator and leading force of the Azerbaijan Federation of Organic Agriculture Movements (AzFOAM) and has been a member of the International Federation of Organic Agriculture Movements (IFOAM) since 2002 (EcoConnect, 2022).

In 2005, GABA started preparing a legal framework for organic agriculture in Azerbaijan. In 2008, the Law of the Republic of Azerbaijan on Ecologically Clean Agriculture was adopted. Since 2008, "ecologically clean" has been used as a synonym for organic or biological (cf. Republic of Azerbaijan, 2008; EcoConnect 2022). Despite the existing law and its regulations, there is a gap in the practical implementation (e.g., in the registration or supervision of inspection and certification bodies). Therefore, all control and certification functions are carried out by foreign control bodies (Certification bodies) (EcoConnect, 2022).

GABA had launched an initiative to establish a national control body, Azekosert. This was established with financial and technical support from the Strengthening Organic Agriculture in the South Caucasus project and registered by the Ministry of Justice on the December 5, 2005. Azekosert Ltd is the only private organic certification body in Azerbaijan dealing with inspection and certification of organic food and agricultural production (EcoConnect, 2022).

The organic products are mainly certified according to EU legislation by foreign companies and thus enter the European market. There are also products destined for the USA and certified according to the National Organic Program (NOP) (EcoConnect, 2022).

According to IFOAM and FIBL statistical data, there were a total of 40,779 hectares certified as organic in Azerbaijan in 2020. Of these, 38,080 hectares were agricultural land (including conversion land); 2,126 hectares were a wild collection of fruits, nuts, berries, and aromatic medicinal plants; and 573 hectares were of aquaculture (cf. FiBl & IFOAM-Organics International, 2021; EcoConnect, 2022).

Azerbaijan's global share of organically farmed agricultural land is 0.05%; its share of organically farmed agricultural land in Asia is 0.216% (Table 3.6). Azerbaijan is one of the ten countries in Asia with the highest share of organic agriculture in the total agricultural area (EcoConnect, 2022).

Table 3.6 Main crops produced in Azerbaijan and certified as organic (including those in conversion), in 2014.

Culture	*Organic area (ha)*	*Organic share (%)*	*Fully converted area (ha)*	*In conversion (ha)*
Cereals	1,598	0.2	0	1,598
Oilseeds	126	0.7	50	76
Protein crops (dried legumes)	6	0,005	2	4
Citrus fruits	21	0.9	2	19
Grapes	41	0.3	1	40
Olives	13	0.7	5	8
Fruits	754	1.5	112	642
Subtropical Fruits	495	4.8	180	315
Vegetables	213	0.2	55	158

Source: EcoConnect (2022, p. 14).

In 2020, there were 466 producers and processors. No importers or exporters are reported. In 2020, domestic sales of organic products amounted to about EUR 3 million, which corresponds to about EUR 0.3 per person (cf. Willer & Lernoud, 2016). Because there is no reliable data collection system in Azerbaijan, these figures can provide some guidance, but need to be updated and based on trustworthy data sources (EcoConnect, 2022).

Biodiversity

Flora. The country's flora includes 5,000 plant species in 176 families and 1,142 genera. In terms of the total number of species, the flora of Azerbaijan is much richer than in the other republics of the South Caucasus. Plant species found in the country account for 66% of the total number of plant species growing in the Caucasus. The Republic of Azerbaijan is rich in relict species rooting back to the tertiary period. There are over 240 endemic plant species in the country (Fourth National Communication to the United Nations Framework Convention on Climate Change. Republic of Azerbaijan, Baku, 2021, p. 22). Broad-leaved forests are spread at an altitude of 600–1800 m above sea level in the mountainous areas of the Greater and Lesser Caucasus. Coniferous forests occur locally in the Eldar plain (*Eldar pine*), in the mountainous regions of the Greater and Lesser Caucasus, and around Goygol (Fourth National Communication to the United Nations Framework Convention on Climate Change. Republic of Azerbaijan, Baku, 2021, p. 22).

Fauna. The fauna of Azerbaijan includes 100 species of mammals, 360 species of birds, 61 species of reptiles, 10 species of amphibians, 100 species of fish, and more than 15,000 insects. (Fourth National Communication to the United Nations Framework Convention on Climate Change. Republic of Azerbaijan, Baku, 2021, p. 22).

Invertebrates. About 25,000 species of invertebrates were found in Azerbaijan, 90% of them belong to the type of arthropods (Fourth National Communication to the United Nations Framework Convention on Climate Change. Republic of Azerbaijan, Baku, 2021, p. 22)..

Cyclostomes The fauna of Azerbaijan includes one species of round-mouthed fish—the Caspian lamprey (*Caspimyzon wagneri*). It is included in the first edition of the Red Book of the Republic of Azerbaijan as a rare species (Fourth National Communication to the United Nations Framework Convention on Climate Change. Republic of Azerbaijan, Baku, 2021, p. 22)...

Fish. Ninety-five species of Azerbaijan's ichthyofauna are considered indigenous, and the rest are introduced species. Out of the bony fish (*Osteichthyes*), 101 species of fish pertaining to a total of 13 groups were recorded in the Azerbaijani section of the Caspian Sea (10 groups) and inland waters.

Amphibia. Amphibians in different landscapes vary according to species composition and distribution. Due to the warm climate and rich food, the species composition is relatively rich in the plains, semi-deserts, and foothills. (Fourth National Communication to the United Nations Framework Convention on Climate Change. Republic of Azerbaijan, Baku, 2021, p. 22)..

Reptiles. The modern vertebrate fauna of Azerbaijan includes 54 species of reptiles. Most species of reptiles live in semi-deserts (Fourth National Communication to the United Nations Framework Convention on Climate Change. Republic of Azerbaijan, Baku, 2021, p. 22)...

Birds. Ornithofauna in Azerbaijan is very rich with 394 bird species from 60 families were recorded in this area. Of these, 40% are nonmigrating and found in Azerbaijan all year round, 27% are wintering, and more than 10% are recorded during migration. One of the largest migration routes in Eurasia passes through Azerbaijan. Every year, about 1.5 million waterfowl alone pass through the territory of Azerbaijan, using it as a stop for rest and feeding (Fourth National Communication to the United Nations Framework Convention on Climate Change. Republic of Azerbaijan, Baku, 2021, pp. 22–23).

Mammals. Finally, 107 species of mammals are registered in Azerbaijan. The most common mammal species in Azerbaijan are water rat (*Arvicola terrestris*), brown rat (*Rattus norvegicus*), wolf (*Canis lupus*), jackal (*C. aureus*), fox (*Vulpes vulpes*), weasel (*Mustela nivalis*), badger (*Meles*), and wild boar (*Sus scrofa*) (Fourth National Communication to the United Nations Framework Convention on Climate Change. Republic of Azerbaijan, Baku, 2021, p. 23).

Under the current legislation, rare and endangered species of animals and plants in their natural habitat within the country are under special protection and are included in the Red Book of the Republic of Azerbaijan. As an official document, the Red Book of the Republic of Azerbaijan contains information on the status, distribution, and protection of animal and plant species (subspecies, populations) throughout the territory of the Republic of Azerbaijan, including the part of the Caspian Sea belonging to the Republic of Azerbaijan (Fourth National Communication to the United Nations Framework Convention on Climate Change. Republic of Azerbaijan, Baku, 2021, p. 23).

The protection of flora and fauna in the country is enshrined both in the country's legislation and in the first edition of the Red Book of plants and animals of the Azerbaijan SSR, published in 1989. In this list of species requiring protection, 140 species of flora and 108 species of fauna of Azerbaijan are included by scholars. (Fourth National Communication to the United Nations Framework Convention on Climate Change. Republic of Azerbaijan, Baku, 2021, p. 23)

In the latest (2013) edition of the Red Book of the Republic of Azerbaijan approved in 2000, the protection status of 300 species of plants (266 higher and 20 lower) and fungi (146 higher and 20 lower) and 223 species of animals (1 Oligochaeta species, 1 Crustacea species, 1 Mollusca species, 71 Insecta species, 6 Amphibia species, 14 Reptilia species, 9 Pisces species, 72 Aves species, and 42 Mammalia species) were reassessed by experts in cooperation with the representatives of various organizations of the country. (Fourth National Communication to the United Nations Framework Convention on Climate Change. Republic of Azerbaijan, Baku, 2021, p. 23)

Natural protected areas

Between 2014 and 2022, the share of protected areas consistently remained at 10.31% of the total size of Azerbaijan's territory, or 8,928.6 km^2 (eco.gov.az/az/).

Specially protected natural areas and monuments represent Azerbaijan's national wealth, acknowledged for their ecological, scientific, cultural, and aesthetic significance. The status of these areas is delineated by the Law on Environmental Protection and the Law on Specially Protected Natural Areas and Monuments. In Azerbaijan, these specially protected natural areas are classified based on their conservation goals and specific utilization purposes:

- State nature reserves, including biosphere reserves
- National and nature parks
- Ecological parks
- Nature monuments
- State sanctuaries
- Zoological parks
- Botanical and dendrological parks
- Spas and resorts

National parks. Azerbaijan has embarked on a new trajectory with the establishment of its first national park, Shirvan National Park, in 2003, marking a significant step forward for the country and its citizens. Since then, four additional national parks have been established, with ongoing efforts in this direction. Currently, the total area of specially protected areas in Azerbaijan, including national parks, amounts to 594,939.1 hectares, constituting 7% of the country's total area. Specifically, the established national parks cover a total area of 117,700 hectares and encompass six sites: Shirvan, Ordubad, Ag-Gol, Hirkan, ltiagaj, and Absheron. Future plans include the establishment of Shag Dag National Park to safeguard the Greater Caucasus mountain ecosystem, Samur-Yalama National Park along the

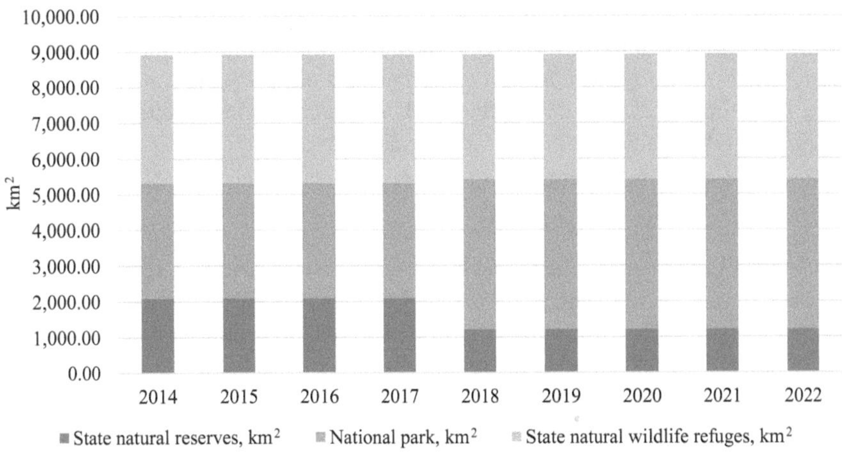

Figure 3.88 Azerbaijan. Surface area of protected areas during 2014–2022, in km².

Source: The State Statistical Committee of the Republic of Azerbaijan (2023).

Caspian Sea in the north, and Goygol National Park, which will further expand the protected area to 11% of Azerbaijan's territory.

Reserves. The first nature reserve areas protecting Azerbaijan's remarkable nature were established in the 1930s in Goygol, Zagatala and Gizilaghaj. The adoption of the Law on Nature Protection of Azerbaijan in 1969 contributed to the increase in the number of reserves. Shortly after that date, six other specially protected areas were established, namely the state nature reserves of Shirvan, Basitchay, Garayazi, Aggol, Ismayilli, Ilisu and Altiaghaj. By 2003, the total area of specially protected areas was 478,000 hectares, accounting for 5% of the country's area. In 2003 and 2004, the area of protected nature areas increased by almost 117 thousand hectares. Currently, there are 13 state nature reserves and 19 state nature reserves, which cover the most important ecosystems (Figure 3.88).

Between 2014 and 2022, significant changes occurred in the area of various types of protected areas in Azerbaijan. During this period, the area occupied by reserves decreased by 42.26%, currently totaling 1207.2 km². Similarly, areas dedicated to wildlife protection saw a decrease of 2.88%. In contrast, the area designated for national parks increased by 30.74%, reaching 4213.7 km² by 2022.

Belarus

Water resources

In Belarus, water resources play a crucial role, both environmentally and economically. The Republic's renewable water resources consist of river runoff and groundwater, primarily derived from precipitation within its borders (internal runoff) and inflows from neighboring countries. Medium and large rivers are the primary source of surface water, with their annual flow volume typically ranging from

57.900 million m³ during average water abundance years to 92.400 million m³ in water-abundant years. Conversely, in water-scarce years (constituting 5% of supply), river flows decrease to 37,200 million m³ annually. Notably, 55% of Belarus's total annual river flow belongs to the Black Sea basin, while the remaining 45% is attributed to the Baltic Sea basin (Minpriroda, 2024c).

Rivers

Seven major rivers, each longer than 500 km, traverse Belarusian territory: Western Dvina, Neman, Neris, Dnieper, Sozh, and Pripyat. Six of these rivers are transboundary, with only the Berezina River being entirely within Belarusian borders (Table 3.7). In total, Belarus boasts 20,800 rivers of varying sizes, collectively measuring 90.6 thousand km in length (Minpriroda, 2024c).

Most of the river flow, amounting to 34,000 million m³ annually (59%), originates within Belarusian territory (local runoff). The remaining 41%, equivalent to 23,900 million m³ per year, comes from neighboring countries such as Russia and Ukraine. The majority of local river flow (73%) is generated in the drainage basins of the Western Dvina, Nemunas, and Dnieper rivers. Transit runoff, which contributes significantly, arrives primarily via the Dnieper (32%), Pripyat (31%), and Western Dvina (28%). The distribution of local runoff exhibits marked seasonal variability. During the spring months, approximately 42–47% of the annual flow occurs along rivers in the western and central parts of Belarus (including the Nemunas, Neris, and Berezina basins), with the remainder distributed throughout the rest of the year, accounting for 52–62% (Minpriroda, 2024c).

The unevenness of the annual flow is mitigated to a certain extent through the construction of reservoirs. Belarus has developed 153 reservoirs with a combined volume of 3,100 million m³, out of which approximately 1,240 million m³ are usable. This constitutes slightly over 13% of the total flow generated within the

Table 3.7 Belarus: River water resources as of the end of 2022.

Rivers	*Length (km)*		*Catchment area (km²)*	
	Total	*In Belarus*	*Total*	*In Belarus*
Dnepr	2,145	689	50,4000	67,460
Western Dvina	1,020	345	87,900	33,150
Neman	914	431	98,200	34,610
Western Bug	831	169	73,470	9,990
Pripyat	761	495	121,000	50,900
Goryn	659	83	27,700	1,200
Sozh	648	493	42,140	21,700
Berezina	613	613	24,500	24,500
Vilia	510	267	25,100	10,920
Pticchi	421	421	9,470	9,470
Shara	325	325	6,990	6,990

Source: National Statistical Committee of the Republic of Belarus (2022).

country. Reservoir types in Belarus are predominantly canal (river) reservoirs, accounting for 35%, while lake-type reservoirs make up 13% of the total (Minpriroda, 2024c).

There are approximately 10,800 lakes in Belarus, with the majority (75%) classified as small lakes measuring up to 0.1 km^2 in area. Lakes larger than 1.0 km^2 are notable, collectively holding between 6,000 to 7,000 million m^3 of water. The largest of these lakes are situated within the Western Dvina basin, accounting for 72% of the total water supply, followed by lakes in the Nemunas basin at 20%. Lakes in the Pripyat and Dnieper river basins also contribute significantly to Belarus's water resources (Minpriroda, 2024c).

Water intake ratio

In terms of per capita water resources, Belarus enjoys a relatively favorable situation, surpassing European countries and significantly outpacing some neighboring nations. The rate of water supply from total water resources averages 6.2 thousand m^3 per person in Belarus. For comparison, in Europe, this rate averages 4.6 thousand m^3 per person, while in Poland and Ukraine it is 1.7 thousand m^3 per person, and in Russia it is 30 thousand m^3 per person (Eco Future Project, 2024).

In Belarus, the ecological status of surface water bodies is assessed based on surface water monitoring conducted under the State Environmental Monitoring System. This monitoring covers 160 sites with 297 observation points located at medium-sized and large water bodies. Between 2015 and 2020, Belarus observed an improving trend in the ecological status of surface waters, with 72.4% of them achieving a good or higher classification. Only 1.2% of surface waters were significantly impacted by anthropogenic stresses during this period (National Legal Internet Portal of the Republic of Belarus, 2022).

Currently, Belarus recognizes and approves a balanced groundwater resource of 6.35 million m^3 per day across 609 deposits within its territory. Among these, water from 605 groundwater deposits is suitable for domestic and drinking purposes, while the remaining four deposits are suitable for technical purposes. Additionally, the investigated and approved underground mineral water resources amount to approximately 62.13 thousand m^3 per day (National Legal Internet Portal of the Republic of Belarus, 2022).

The amount of water withdrawn is quite small, accounting for 2.22% of total renewable water resources or an annual volume of about 1,450 million m^3 (Figure 3.89).

From 2014 to 2022, transport water losses were characterized by a downward trend, and in 2022, transport water losses accounted for 50% of the value of transport losses compared to 2014. A reduction in the amount of water withdrawn was observed in the time frame, and the main factor determining this evolution is a reduction in water consumption by the agricultural sector, processing industry, and by households. On the other hand, there is an increase in water consumption for the production needs of companies in the electric power sector.

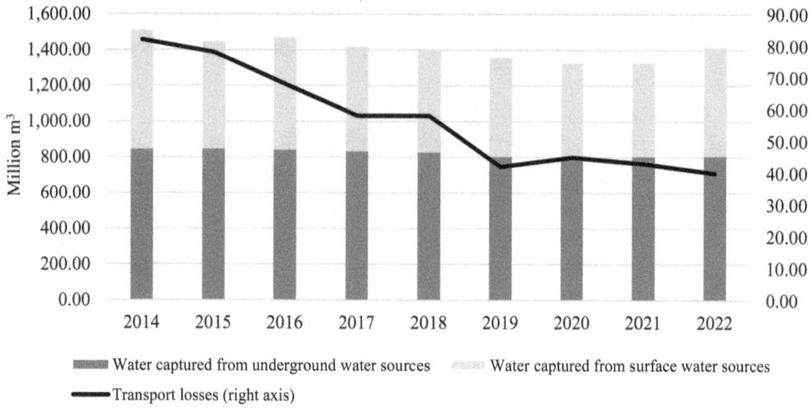

Figure 3.89 Belarus. Water capture during 2014–2022, in million m^3.

Source: National Statistical Committee of the Republic of Belarus (2022).

Forest resources

The forest fund of Belarus totals more than 9.7 million hectares and the forest cover of the territory is 40.1% (Figure 3.90). The standing timber stock is estimated at 1.7 billion m^3. The annual increase is 31.9 million m^3 of wood. Each resident of the republic accounts for 1 hectare of forested land and more than 180 m^3 of wood reserve, which is two times higher than the average European level. The annual gain in "timber" considerably exceeds its annual cutting, keeping the balance between economic and ecological components in favor of ecology. The forests of Belarus are the exclusive property of the state (SB News, 2014).

In recent decades, Belarus has experienced a significant increase in the proportion of mature forests, driven by both natural processes and the forestry policies implemented by the Ministry of Forestry aimed at rationalizing forest management. Since 1994, the share of mature forests has risen by 4.7%, reaching 14.7% in 2019. This increase has led to a corresponding rise in timber production. For instance, in 2016, Belarusian forest organizations harvested approximately 20 million m^3 of timber, a figure that exceeded 25 million m^3 by 2020. Nearly half of this timber volume was obtained through mechanical felling methods, with all harvested wood utilized by Belarusian wood processing industries (President of the Republic of Belarus, 2024).

Forests cover one-third of the territory of Belarus. Forests in the territory of Belarus are state-owned and mostly belong to the Committee of Forestry (about 7 million hectares, or 76.1% of the total forest fund area). The rest of the forest owners are represented by the Security Committee, collective farms and associations, the research institutes, and government (Atroshchanka & Minkevich, 2004).

All forests in Belarus are divided into four categories: environmental protection, recreational and health, protective, and operational. The area of operational forests today is approximately 5.4 million hectares, protective forests is 2.3 million

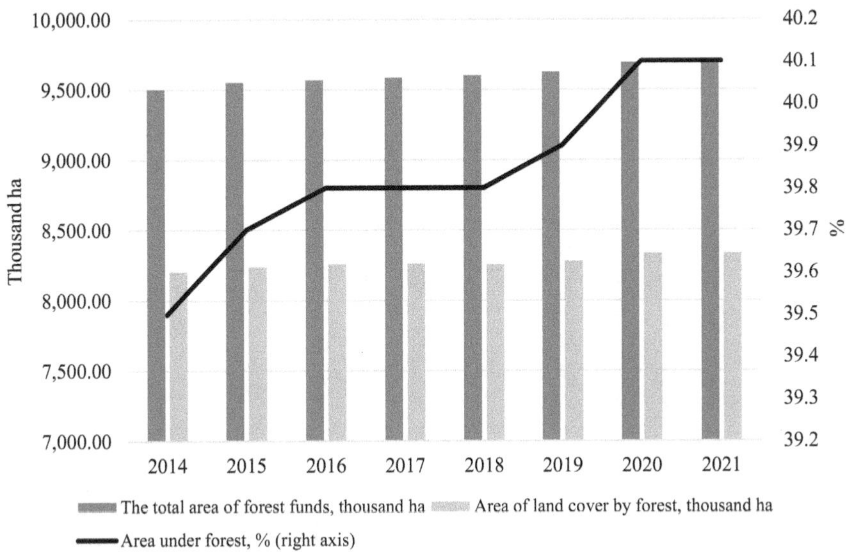

Figure 3.90 Belarus. Forest resource indicators from 2014 to 2022.

Source: National Statistical Committee of the Republic of Belarus (2022).

hectares, environmental forests is 1.6 million hectares, and recreational and recreational forests is 0.36 million hectares. However, economic activity is carried out mainly in production forests (BELTA, 2024).

In 2022, Belarus's total timber resources amounted to 1.9 billion m^3, reflecting an 11.17% increase since 2014. Timber resources per hectare of forest land rose by 73 m^3, reaching 221 m^3, while mature and overgrown plantings increased by 59 m^3, attaining 272 m^3/ha. The average age of plantings also grew from 44 to 56 years. During the 2014–2022 period, there was an increase in timber harvested for sale. In 2022, 25.7 million m^3 were cut for this purpose, a 31.46% rise compared to 2014. The area of forest subjected to logging in 2022 was 511 thousand hectares, compared to 523 thousand hectares in 2014. The felling carried out during this period was associated with maintenance, cleaning, and sanitation work.

Soil resources

Land is a cornerstone of Belarusian national wealth and a vital natural resource serving diverse functions. It functions as an integral part of the natural environment, a fundamental element for economic activities, a pivotal resource in agriculture and forestry, and a significant object within property relations. According to the State Land Cadastre of the Republic of Belarus, the total land area as of January 1, 2022, stood at 207. 8 thousand hectares. This places Belarus 14th in Europe by land area. The structure of the land fund categorized by land type is illustrated in Figure 3.91.

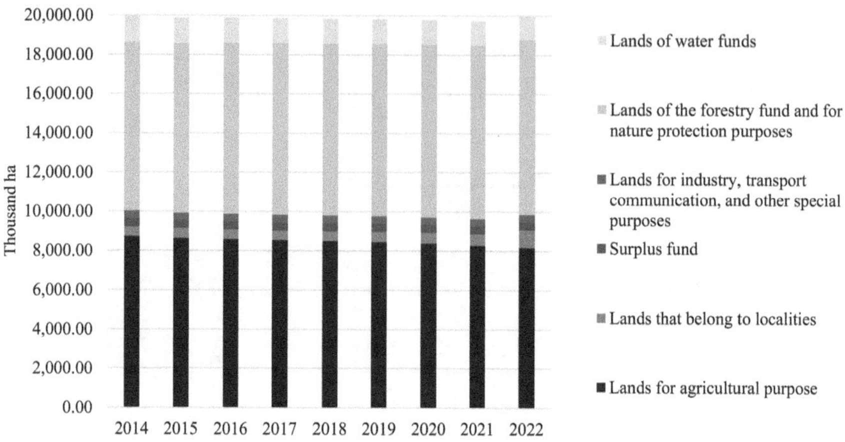

Figure 3.91 Belarus. Land fund by land category during 2014–2022, in thousand hectares.
Source: National Statistical Committee of the Republic of Belarus (2022).

There were no significant changes in the structure of the land fund in Belarus between 2014 and 2022. The largest share of this structure, as in previous years, is agricultural land (68.45%) and forest land (17.7%). The share of land occupied by buildings was 6.20% of the total land structure. It should be noted that there was an increase of 47.62% in this category of land during the period under review. Land belonging to the water land fund accounted for 4% and other land amounted to 3.60%.

The soil cover of Belarus is quite complex in terms of composition, as well as basic properties, with a total of 11 soil types identified. Under the influence of many soil-forming processes, the following types of soils were formed:

- turf and podosols (45.1%),
- bogs (14.4%),
- swamp-pebble soils (9.0%),
- turf-carbonate soils (0.2%), and
- floodplain soils (8.4%) (Tsapko, 2018).

In Belarus, arable land holds particular significance as the most intensively utilized part of the soil resources. Arable land covers 28% of the total agricultural land in the country. Between 2014 and 2022, the area of agricultural land decreased by 214 thousand hectares. The primary causes of land degradation include water erosion, wind erosion, radioactive and chemical pollution, mineralization of drained peat soils, reduced fertility of agricultural land, transformations due to mining and construction activities, floods, waterlogging, burning of drained peatlands, and irrational land use practices. Moreover, Belarus has 300 deposits of construction materials that are mined using open-pit methods, alongside mining activities for potash salt and table salt. Industrial peat mining has led to significant destruction of large areas. Disturbed lands, mostly concentrated in the Minsk and Gomel regions (including the city of Gomel), refer to areas where the soil cover has been partially or completely disturbed due to mining activities. Additionally, soil contamination with chemicals exceeding its natural decomposition capacity further contributes to soil fertility reduction (Tsapko, 2018).

Organic farming

On November 18, 2019, the law "On the production on the circulation of organic products" came into force in Belarus. Two bodies are accredited for the certification of organic products and their production processes in Belarus: the product certification body Republican Unitary Enterprise "Scientific and Practical Center of the National Academy of Sciences of Belarus on Food" and the product and service certification body Republican Unitary Enterprise "Belarusian State Institute of Metrology" (In Belarus.... 2020). Currently, about 1,500 hectares of land are used for organic farming in Belarus, and 30 entrepreneurs are engaged in production (Kostyushin, 2019).

Belarus possesses significant potential for developing organic agriculture, owing to its favorable climatic conditions, abundant soil resources, low levels of environmental pollution, well-developed transport infrastructure, and robust research and scientific capabilities. According to data from FiBL, Belarus ranked among the top ten countries in Europe in terms of the growth dynamics of organic farming acreage in 2018. However, the share of land dedicated to organic farming as a proportion of the total agricultural land area is currently only 0.02%, significantly below the global average of 1.5%. Nevertheless, Belarus holds promising prospects for expanding its organic farming sector. Land monitoring data indicates that there are 410 thousand hectares of uncultivated land and 15.2 thousand hectares of fallow land, accounting for 5% and 0.2% of agricultural land, respectively. These areas theoretically offer potential for organic agricultural production (National Agency of Investments and Privatization, 2020).

According to the National Strategy for Sustainable Socio-Economic Development of the Republic of Belarus for the period up to 2030, the aim is to increase the share of areas devoted to organic agriculture to 3–4% of the total agricultural land area by 2030. This ambitious target underscores the anticipated rapid growth of organic farming within the country. By integrating uncultivated and fallow lands into agricultural use, Belarus anticipates achieving a 5.2% share of organic agricultural land in the total agricultural area within a relatively short timeframe. Belarus specializes in the organic cultivation of wheat, rapeseed, barley, buckwheat, and oats, highlighting its focus on key staple crops within the organic sector (National Agency of Investments and Privatization, 2020).

Biodiversity

Natural complexes and ecological systems cover 57% of the territory of the Republic of Belarus. These ecosystems encompass diverse habitats including forests

(41.5%), thickets (3.2%), meadows (3.8%), swamps (4.1%), and water bodies (2.2%). Among these ecological systems, several are crucial for biodiversity conservation. They include deciduous forests, coniferous forests, and black alder forests, which support a variety of flora and fauna. Additionally, wet or periodically flooded meadows, swamps, lakes, and the ecological systems found in valleys and riverbeds play significant roles in maintaining biodiversity and ecological balance within Belarus (Minpriroda, 2024b).

About 14,000 species are known in the flora, which include about 4,100 species of higher plants (1,400 species are native), 442 species of bryophytes, 669 species of lichens, and more than 9,000 species of lower plants (algae and fungi). Over the past century, about 50 native species of wild plants have disappeared from the territory of Belarus (Minpriroda, 2024b).

The mammalian fauna is represented by 76 species belonging to 6 orders - insectivores (11 species), bats (19), carnivores (13), lagomorphs (2), rodents (25), even-toed ungulates (6 species). 332 species of birds were registered, of which at least 230 species nest in Belarus (Minpriroda, 2024b).

Over the past 30 years, the number of species of flora and fauna added to the Red Book of Belarus that are considered rare or endangered has increased (Figure 3.92).

According to the Central Statistical Office of Belarus, between 1990 and 2022, the number of rare or endangered animals increased from 85 to 203 species, and the number of flora species increased from 65 to 303.

Natural protected areas

Specially protected natural areas play a major role in the preservation of biological and landscape diversity in Belarus. According to the Law of the Republic of

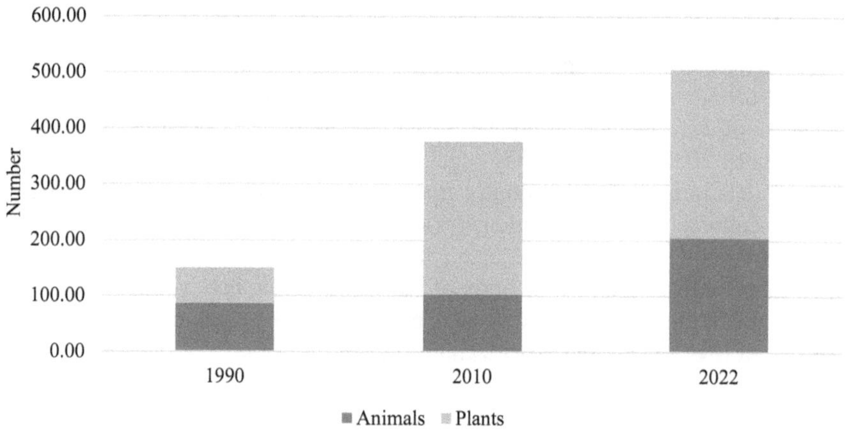

Figure 3.92 Belarus. Protected species of plants and animals (included in the Red Book).
Source: National Statistical Committee of the Republic of Belarus (2022).

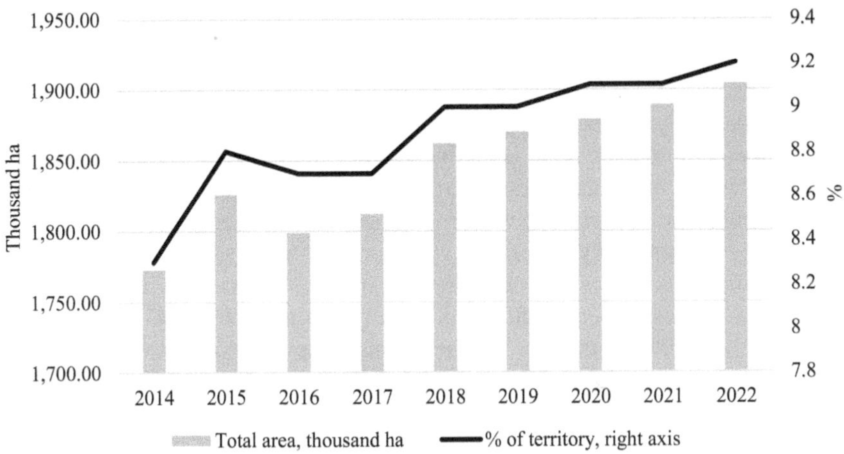

Figure 3.93 Belarus. Surface area of protected areas during 2014–2022.

Source: National Statistical Committee of the Republic of Belarus (2022).

Belarus "On Specially Protected Natural Areas" (dated October 20, 1994), these are areas located on the territory of the Republic of Belarus with unique, standard, or other valuable natural complexes and objects that are of special ecological, scientific, and (or) aesthetic significance, due to the fact that a special regime of protection and use is applied to them (Minpriroda, 2024a).

Currently, Belarus has several types of protected areas based on their functions and nature conservation systems. These territories are categorized as follows: reserves, national parks, temporary reserves, and nature monuments (Figure 3.93). As of now, Belarus has one reserve, which is the Berezinsky Biosphere Reserve, and four national parks: Belovezhskaya Pushcha, Pripyat, Lake Braslav, and Lake Narochansky. Additionally, there are temporary reserves and nature monuments of both national and regional importance. The number and area of these temporary reserves and nature monuments fluctuate from year to year.

Between 2014 and 2022, the area of protected areas increased by 1.773 million hectares to 1.904 million hectares, an increase of 7.39%. In 2022, the share of protected areas in the total size of the national territory was 9.2%. According to current legislation, within the territories of national parks and reserves in Belarus, the dual objectives of preserving biological and landscape diversity are balanced with restrictions on economic activities and the promotion of ecotourism. Several specially protected natural areas in Belarus hold international conservation status: eight republican reserves ("Olmansky marshes," "Middle Pripyat," "Prostyr," "Kotra," "Osvevsky," "Yelnya," "Sporovsky," and "Zvanets") are designated as wetlands of international importance. Additionally, 6 protected areas are recognized as key botanical areas, and 14 are listed for their significance in the conservation of European wild birds (Minpriroda, 2024a).

Georgia

Water resources

Georgia stands out as one of Europe's most water-rich nations, boasting ample renewable water resources comprising rivers, lakes, reservoirs, glaciers, and groundwater. However, these resources are unevenly distributed across the country, with concentrations primarily in the western regions, while eastern regions of Georgia often faces water scarcity issues. The rivers in eastern regions of Georgia are part of the unified Mtkvari river system, draining into the Caspian Sea, whereas rivers in western regions of Georgia flow individually into the Black Sea. In western regions of Georgia, the total river flow, including transit flow, amounts to 49.8 km^3, whereas in eastern regions of Georgia, it totals 16.5 km^3 (National Statistics Office of Georgia, 2023a).

Rivers

Georgia has 25,075 rivers with a total length of 54,768 km, 99.4% of which are small rivers with a total length of less than 25 km. The Black Sea basin includes more than 17,000 rivers (with a total length of 32,574 km). Internal renewable surface water resources in the Black Sea basin are estimated at 49.8 km^3/year. In the western part of the country, the main rivers running from north to south include the Inguri (length on Georgian territory, 213 km), Rioni (327 km), and Khorokhi (26 km).

In contrast, internal renewable surface water resources in the Caspian Sea basin are estimated at 16.5 km^3/year. In the eastern part of the republic, the main rivers include Terek and Andijskoye, which rise in the north of the country and flow northeast into the Russian Federation before flowing into the Caspian Sea, and Alazani, Lori, and Kura, which begin in Georgia and then flow through the territory of neighboring Azerbaijan and flow into Lake Adzhinour before flowing southeast into Azerbaijan and then flowing into the Caspian Sea.

There are two tributaries of the Kura River on Turkish territory: the Mtkvari, for which the estimated flow from Turkey is 0.91 km^3/year, and the Potskhovi, for which the estimated flow from Turkey is 0.25 km^3/year. The inflow of the Debet River, a southern tributary of the Kura River, is estimated at 0.89km3/year from Armenia. In turn, renewable groundwater resources according to Georgian estimates amount to 17.23 km^3/year, of which 16 km^3/year is drained by the surface water network (overlap). Therefore, the volume of internal renewable water resources in Georgia totals 58.13 km^3/year. The total actual renewable water resources in Georgia are 63.33 km^3/year (Water Action Hub, 2024).

Georgia's largest river is the Rioni, with an annual outflow of 12.6 km^3 In western Georgia, there are large rivers such as the Inguri (5.9 km^3), Chorohi (8.9 km^3), Kodori (4.1 km^3), Supsa (1.4 km^3), Bzib (3.0 km^3), and others. In eastern Georgia, there are rivers such as the Kura (7.2 km^3), Alazani (3.1 km^3), Aragvi (1.4 km^3), Big Liahvi (1.4 km^3), Khrami (1.0 km^3), Lori (0.8 km^3), and others (Global Water Partnership, 2024).

Lakes

Georgia is home to approximately 860 lakes, covering a combined area of 170 km^2, which constitutes 0.24% of the country's total area. These lakes are characterized by their diverse origins, including tectonic, glacial (the most abundant), lacustrine, coastal, karst, sufozie, landslide, and anthropogenic lakes. Most of Georgia's lakes are freshwater, with minimal salt content. Lake Paravani is the largest in terms of area, Lake Tabatskuri leads in volume, and Lake Ritsa is renowned as the deepest lake in the South Caucasus region (National Statistics Office of Georgia, 2023a).

Water reservoirs

There are 44 water reservoirs on the territory of Georgia, with a total area of 163 km^3 and a total volume of 3.315 million m^3. Of these reservoirs, 36 are located in the east of the country and 8 are located in the west of the country.

Water in Georgia is primarily utilized for irrigation and hydroelectric power generation, with water supply being the least significant use. The largest hydroelectric dam in the country is situated on the Inguri River, boasting a reservoir capacity of 1.092 km^3. Additionally, Georgia has constructed 31 dams specifically for irrigation purposes, with a cumulative capacity of 782 million m^3. Among these, the largest irrigation reservoirs include the Sioni Reservoir on the Lori River with a capacity of 325 million m^3, the Tbilisi Reservoir on the Kura River holding 308 million m^3, and the Dalimta Reservoir on the Lori River with a capacity of 180 million m^3.

In addition, on the main ridge of the Caucasus mountains there are 734 glaciers with a total area of 513 km^2.

Among the factors affecting the river ecosystem, the issue of water consumption is of great importance, because the use of water for economic activities, especially irrigation, results in lower water levels (i.e., a reduction in water resources) (National Statistics Office of Georgia, 2023a).

Groundwater

Groundwaters—fresh, mineral, and thermal—hold significant importance among Georgia's mineral resources, playing a crucial role in the country's national economy. Freshwater availability per capita in Georgia is 2.5 times higher than the global average. Groundwater serves multiple purposes including drinking, medicinal uses, and as a source of thermal energy. Georgia possesses substantial reserves of fresh groundwater totaling 21.7 km^3, which corresponds to 23% of the national precipitation. The distribution of groundwater resources varies across the country, increasing from east to west. Moreover, Georgia boasts abundant thermal waters that have potential applications in agriculture and energy sectors. Groundwater resources in Georgia are categorized based on their salinity and temperature characteristics:

- fresh drinking water (salinity not more than 1.0 g/l);
- thermal water - therapeutic (20-350C), heat-and-power (40-1080C); and
- mineral water (general salinity above 1.0 g/l (Natural Resources of Georgia and Environmental Protection, 2023).

Mineral waters in Georgia exhibit remarkable diversity in their chemical compositions. Some mineral waters naturally flow to the surface, characterized by compositions such as carbon dioxide, calcium bicarbonate, sodium calcium bicarbonate, calcium bicarbonate-chloride, and calcium sulfate-chloride. The majority of mineral waters are extracted through boreholes and have compositions that include sodium chloride, sodium calcium sulfate-chloride, and sodium hydrocarbonate-chloride, among others (National Statistics Office of Georgia, 2023).

Water intake ratio

Georgia possesses a total freshwater resource of 100 km^3. However, the country faces significant challenges related to water use, primarily stemming from surface water pollution and inefficient water management practices. Water pollution in Georgia is largely attributed to human activities, with municipal waste from cities introducing organic substances, nitrogen, and phosphorus compounds into water bodies. Among the most polluted rivers are the Kura, Vere, Alazani, Algeti, Saramula (in the Caspian Sea basin), and Rioni (in the Black Sea basin). Despite having centralized sanitation systems in 45 cities, including 33 treatment plants established between 1972 and 1986, many of these facilities are either nonfunctional or operate inadequately. Additionally, local rivers in Georgia are contaminated with industrial waste, including heavy metals like zinc, copper, manganese, and arsenic ions, which result from industrial production activities. Although Georgia's volume of water abstraction in relation to renewable water resources remains relatively small, there has been an observed increase in water consumption between 2014 and 2022, as indicated by Figure 3.94.

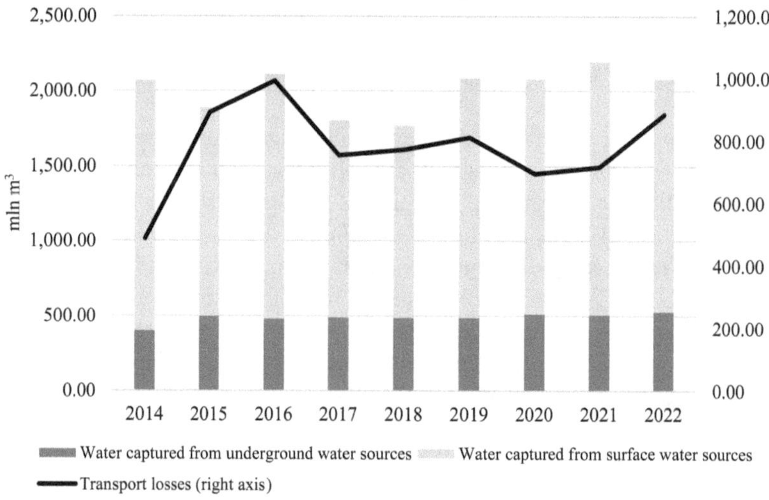

Figure 3.94 Georgia. Water intake during 2014–2022.

Source: National Statistics Office of Georgia (2023).

Between 2014 and 2022, water withdrawal in Georgia has been influenced by several notable trends. Notably, there has been a substantial increase in water losses during transportation, which rose by over 81% during this period. Concurrently, while water abstraction from surface water resources has seen a slight decrease, there has been a significant uptick in water withdrawal from groundwater sources, increasing by nearly 32%. Throughout the study period, there has been a decline in water withdrawal primarily for household purposes. In contrast, there has been an increase in water withdrawal to meet industrial and production needs.

Forest resources

Georgia is a mountainous country, so almost all of the forests (97.7%) are located on the slopes of the mountains. In western Georgia, forests start from sea level and cover lowlands and foothills slopes up to 500 m above sea level. In lowland wetlands, we find willow, poplar in places, Imeretian oak, ash, and beech. Places on the hills and foothills are covered with Kolchida forests (National Statistics Office of Georgia, 2022).

Georgia is rich in forests. The forestation level of Georgia's territory during 2014–2022 was 40.62%. The area of land belonging to the Georgian Forest Fund in 2022 was 3,100,500 hectares (which is 44.5% of the total area of the country), of which about 2,807,800 hectares are forested 98.5% of the forests are of natural origin (Figure 3.95). The remaining 1.5% are man-planted forests; they are found in almost every region and mainly grow pine trees. More than 60% of the forests are located above 1,000 meters above sea level, more than 49% on slopes with an incline of 26% and steeper, and 39% on northern slopes. According to the Ministry

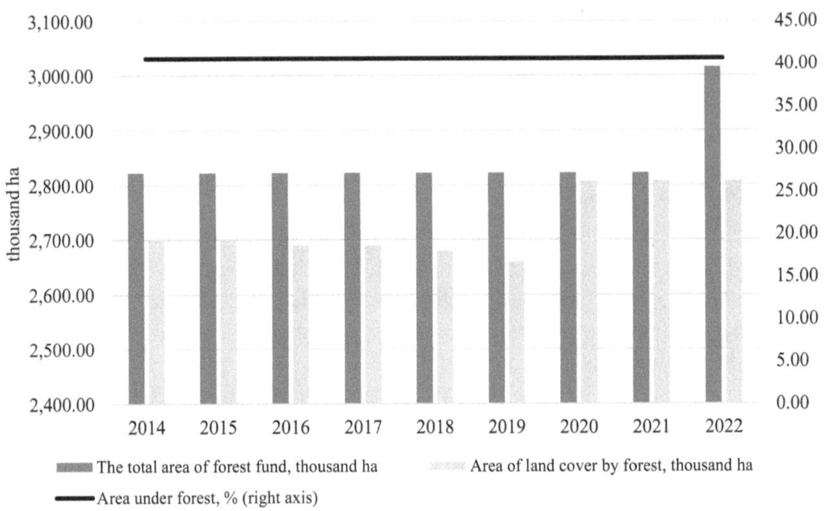

Figure 3.95 Georgia. Forest resources during 2014–2022.

Source: National Statistics Office of Georgia (2023).

of Environmental Protection and Agricultural of Georgia, 24.5% (759 thousand hectares) of Georgia's total forest cover is located in temporarily occupied areas: 547.6 thousand hectares in Abkhazia and 211.6 thousand hectares in South Ossetia (Ministry of Environmental Protection and Agriculture of Georgia, 2023a).

The forest areas of the Greater and Lesser Caucasus hold global significance because they represent the last intact forests within the temperate climate zone. These forests in Georgia serve a dual role: supporting biodiversity and playing a crucial role in various sectors of the national economy.

The average stock of timber mass in Georgia's forests is 231.8 m^3/ha. This includes the volume of single-growth tall trees and coppice (217.6 m^3/ha), standing deadwood (7 m^3/ha), and broken trees (7.2 m^3/ha). Georgia's total timber resources are 528.2 million m^3. The average annual increment is 6 m^3/ha, and the total annual increment is 13.7 million m^3 (Ministry of Environmental Protection and Agriculture of Georgia, 2023a).

According to the National Statistics Office of Georgia, between 2015 and 2022, the volume of cut timber decreased from 712,300 m^3 to 534,000 m^3. The felling of trees carried out was related to maintenance, cleaning, and sanitation work.

Soil resources

Land is one of the main national wealths that needs special care and protection; almost half of natural wealth of Georgia counts on soil. Georgia is a highland country. Lowland zone covers only 46% of the country territory. Georgia is characterized by a great variety of soil types on its small territory, which includes nearly all soils of the world. The spectrum of soil types in Georgia reaches from bog soils in the lowlands of the humid subtropics of West Georgia to meadow-grey-cinnamonic and salty soils in the dry subtropics of East Georgia. Foothill, mountain forest, and mountain-meadow regions show very different soil types. A great variety of rocks, a specific relief with contrasting climatic conditions, and great differences in biodiversity and other soil-forming factors determine the enormous variety of soils in Georgia and its specific geographical distribution (Urushadze et al., 2015).

Due to the diversity of natural conditions, we can find almost all types of soil in Georgia. There are three soil provinces: West, East, and South. By the conditions and processes of soil formation, in each of them, different zones and subzones are distinguished and within the latter—regions and subregions. There are 48 soil regions and 169 subregions in Georgia.

Soil vegetation in Georgia is very diverse: Polydominant Colchis forest on red and yellow soils; alder forest in Kolkheti peat swamp; broadleaf and coniferous forest; highland meadows on the same ridge; eternal snow and glaciers on the main watershed ridge of the Caucasus; forest steppe and steppe landscapes in Eastern Georgia, and mountain steppes with black soil (chernozems) in the highlands of Southern Georgia (National Statistics Office of Georgia, 2022).

The land resources are characterized by a high level of agricultural utilization and a high natural fertility of arable lands. Territorial distribution of lands in Georgia, similarly to other components, is subject to the rule on vertical zoning:

- I zone (up to 250 m above sea level)—mainly characterized by subtropical cultures of Western Georgia.
- II zone (250–500 m)—area of horticulture, viticulture, market-gardening, and intensive field activities (mainly maize).
- III zone (500–1,000 m)—dominates cereals, arable lands, and animal husbandry.
- IV zone (1,000–1,500 m)—grasslands; field activities are weakly developed.
- V zone (1,500–2,000 m)—mainly grasslands.
- VI zone (above 2,000 m)—agriculture does not exist.

The territory of Georgia can be divided into three parts according to utilization types:

1 Agricultural land – 15.8%;
2 Natural – farming area (forest, shrubbery, hay pastures) – 70.6%; and
3 Land not used in agriculture – 13.6%.

Agricultural land is subject to permanent changes in structure and quality, determined by cultivating new areas, intensive melioration activities, and others. Moreover, erosion processes, land salinity, or bogging or flooding and other unfavorable conditions cause a decrease in the size of agricultural land and a worsening of its quality (Figure 3.96). Thus, land resources are under permanent quantitative and qualitative changes (National Statistical Office of Georgia, 2022).

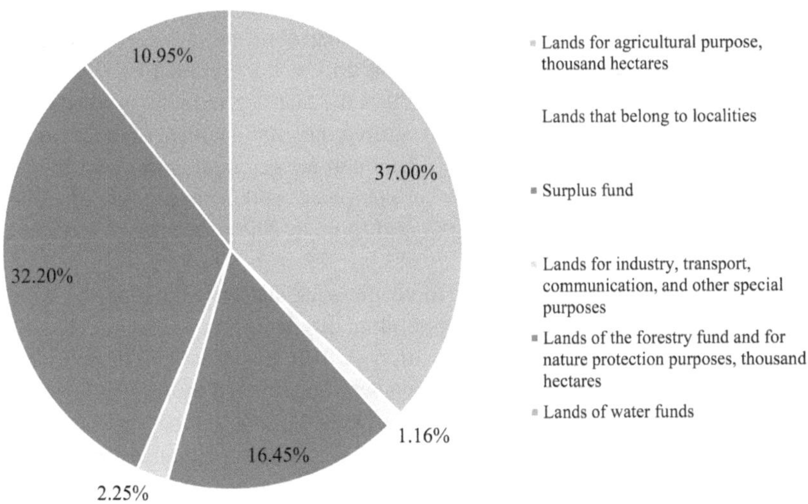

Figure 3.96 Georgia. Land fund by land category in 2004, in %.

Source: National Statistics Office of Georgia (2022).

Georgia's land fund is dominated by agricultural land. The share of these soils is about 37% of the total land fund, or 2.8 million hectares. In addition, agricultural land use has remained virtually the same for years—over 76% is arable land and just over 2.6% is perennial plantations (i.e., vineyards and orchards) (Figure 3.96). The other types of land included in the land fund remain on the register in the same areas, namely, forest and conservation fund land, 32.20%; township land, 1.16%; water fund land, 2.6%; land in the reserve fund, which now accounts for 16.45% of the land fund area; and land used by road and industrial infrastructure, 2.25% (National Statistics Office of Georgia, 2022).

Organic farming

In Georgia, 43.3% (30,300 km^2) of the country's land area is used for agriculture. Annual crops grow on 209.9 thousand hectares (Geostat, 2020) and perennial crops are grown on 109.6 thousand hectares of land (Agricultural Census of Georgia 2014). A group of growers joined together in 1994 to form the Association for Organic Agriculture, ELKANA. ELKANA's proactive work has led to two important results:

- the adoption of the Georgian law on organic agricultural production; and
- the establishment of CAUCASCERT Ltd, the first commercial certification body in Georgia as an independent company (Heinz Gengenbach, 2021).

In 1996, ELKANA became a member of the International Federation of Organic Agricultural Movements (IFOAM). In compliance with IFOAM standards and European Union regulations, the Association has developed and officially registered a bio-production standard, which has been subsequently updated several times. However, since 2009, based on the process of harmonization of Georgian legislation with the EU regulations, the organization has been guided by the standard defined by the EU regulations. The placing of the member farmers' products on the market with a respective status ("bio") required the establishment of a relevant legislative base and certification system. Thanks to active cooperation with the Ministry of Agriculture of Georgia and other competent authorities, a Law of Georgia on Biological Agro-production entered into force in 2006 (Jorjadze & Urushadze, 2015).

In 2011, in parallel with entry into force of the legislation to the office of the then Prime Minister, all the laws related to food quality had to be incorporated exactly in the regulatory framework of food safety, which was practically implemented later. The regulatory framework was considered completed by August 2014 upon enactment of the regulation on labeling, notwithstanding the fact that no relevant technical regulations/standards were developed. Georgia recognizes international organic agro-production standards (Jorjadze & Urushadze, 2015).

As regards to the certification system, ELKANA initiated a project "The Development of Organic Agriculture and Certification System in the South Caucasus," which in 2002 was funded by the Swiss Agency for Development and Cooperation

(SDC) and the Swiss organization HEKS-EPER with the technical support of GIZ—the organization acting on behalf of German Federal Ministry for Economic Cooperation and Development (BMZ). Within the framework of this project, a bio-certification system was established in all the three South Caucasian states, whereas the certification agencies of Armenia (Ecoglobe Ltd, www.ecoglobe.am) and Georgia (Caucascert Ltd, www.caucascert.ge) in 2008 were granted a certificate of accreditation by the Office of the German Accreditation System (DAP) and since the end of 2011 have been on the list of certification bodies approved by the EU regulation under the common name GREEN CAUCASUS and biological certificates awarded by them are recognized on the EU markets (Jorjadze & Urushadze, 2015).

According to 2014 statistics, 0.32% (1,292 ha) of agricultural land area in Georgia is certified as "bio" (area under apples, pomegranate, persimmon, grapes, cereals, legumes, essential oil plants, etc.) (Jorjadze & Urushadze, 2015).

As the umbrella association of Georgian organic farmers, it comprises about 649 individual members and 68 organizations with more than 2,500 farmers, including 519 individual memberships, at the beginning of 2021 (Heinz Gengenbach, 2021). According to the Caucascert inspection body (April 9, 2021), as of 2020, a total of 2,158 hectares of agricultural land has been certified, of which 484 hectares are in conversion. The number of certified clients is 72 (Heinz Gengenbach, 2021).

Biodiversity

FLORA –PLANTS

Due to the diversity of natural, geographic, and climatic conditions, the flora of Georgia is very rich and diverse. The varied relief of Georgia's territory and the complex configuration of mountain rings have resulted in the geographic and ecological isolation of the country's ecosystems and have contributed to a high level of local endemism.

Georgia is home to up to 5,000 species of wild and rare plants and up to 8,300 spore-bearing plants (about 75 species of plants, 600 species of mosses, 600 species of lichens, 5,000 species of fungi, 2,000 species of algae, and others).

Some species that became extinct in the rest of western Eurasia millions of years ago have survived in Georgian territory. Particularly in Kolkhetia, you can still find species such as Caucasian birch, Pontic oak, Kolkhetian ivy, cranberry, cherry laurel, and others. These species represent unique remnants of ancient flora that have persisted in Georgia's diverse and ecologically rich landscapes.

The substantial difference in the climate of East and West Georgia provides the distinction of their vegetation that is reflected in the structure of the vertical belt. In West Georgia, there is no semi-arid and arid belt without forest. The flat areas, slopes, and foothills are covered with forests from the sea shore. Compared with East Georgia, the landscapes of subnival vegetation are less expressed here. Accordingly, in West Georgia, there are only five main belts: forest (1,900 m above sea level); subalpine (1,900–2,500 m); alpine (2,500–3,000 m); subnival (3,000–3,600 m), and nival (3,100 m and above).

In East Georgia, there are six main belts: semi deserts, dry fields and low-density forests (arid light woodlands) (150–600 m); forest (600–1,900 m); subalpine (1,900–2,500 m); alpine (2,500–3,000 m); subnival (3,000–3,500 m), and nival (3,500 m and above). Vegetation of mountain fields prevails in the mountainous forest and subalpine belts of South Georgia, where the vegetation of the mountain fields are mainly presented (National Statistics Office of Georgia, 2023a).

FAUNA

There is a rich and diverse fauna in Georgia, mainly represented by the elements of the subdistrict of the Mediterranean Sea of Pale arctic district, but in the north part of the country, the representatives of European and Siberian subdistricts are also frequently met, while in the southeast district, species of Central Asian subdistrict fauna or others similar to them can be found.

There are around 100 mammal species, more than 330 bird species, about 48 reptile species, 11 amphibian species, and 160 fish species known in Georgia. Thousands of invertebrate species are met, but an exact number has not been determined yet. Animals are distributed by zones, but the species with a great ecologic valence inhabit in several zones (National Statistics Office of Georgia, 2023a).

During the past few decades, the biodiversity of Georgia has significantly reduced. This is related to anthropogenic and natural factors such as loss of habitants, fragmentation and degradation, illegal hunting and fishing, introduction of new species, and nonsustainable use of natural resources (Figure 3.97). At present, the Red List of Georgia contains 139 animal species and 56 wooded plant species; 43 of the animal species and 20 of the plant species are categorized as endangered

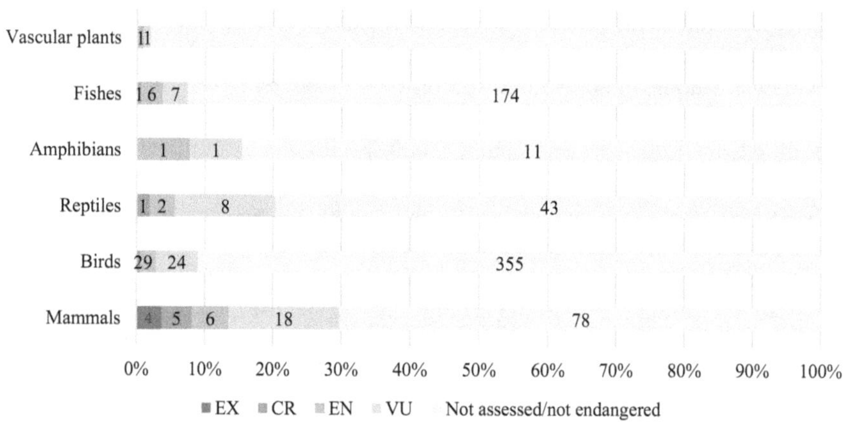

Figure 3.97 The status of animal and plant species in Georgia.

Source: Ministry of Environmental and Natural Resources Protection in Georgia (2015).

(EN) or critically endangered (CR); 44 vertebrate species prevailing in Georgia are also considered globally threatened and included in the IUCN Red List, as vulnerable (VU) or endangered taxa.

Thirty-three species of mammals are on the Red List. Among them, four species are extinct on national level, five species are critically endangered (Lynx, leopard, Striped Hyena, Red Deer, Wild goat), and six species are endangered species (Brown Bear, Common Bottlenose Dolphin, West Caucasian ibex, Chamois). There are 53 species of birds on the Red List. Among them, Saker Falcon and Lesser Kestrel are critically endangered. White Pelican, Lesser White-fronted Goose, Velvet Scoter, White-tailed Eagle, White-headed Duck, Cinereous Vulture, Red-footed Falcon, and Barn Owl are endangered species. The Red List includes 11 species of reptiles, 2 species of amphibians, and 12 species of fish. All species of sturgeon are included among the fishes (Red List, 2003).

Natural protected areas

There are various types of natural-territorial complexes (landscapes) in Georgia, including semi-deserts (East Georgia), Kolkheti humid subtropics (West Georgia), and nival-glacial landscapes. In Georgia, which is a mostly mountainous country, a variation of natural components by altitude and, accordingly, altitudinal zonation with the full spectrum of landscape zones are well represented. Herewith, various types of natural territorial complexes, typical for flat lowlands and small mountain areas of humid, moderately humid, and dry subtropics, are developed in the valleys and lowlands between the mountains. More than 100 types (type, subtype, form) of landscape are spread on the territory of Georgia (National Statistics Office of Georgia, 2023a).

The first national park in Georgia, Saguramo National Park, was established in 1973, on the basis of which Tbilisi National Park was created in 1979 (and then later abolished). National parks are generally created in order to protect relatively large, natural ecosystems of exceptional beauty that are of national and international importance and to conserve the existing biodiversity. In addition, national parks play an important role in the development of eco-tourism, particularly in the promotion of the natural and cultural heritage of Georgia at the international level (Agency of Protected Areas, 2024).

In 1995, the first national park that complies with international standards was established and it was named Borjomi-Kharagauli National Park. Kolkheti National Park was established in 1998, Tusheti and Vashlovani in 2003, and Mtirala in 2006. During past few years, Javakheti and Machakhela National Parks were established, whereas Algeti, Saguramo, and Kazbegi Strict Nature Reserves were awarded the status of national parks. In the coming years, it is planned to expand Kazbegi and Algei National Parks, as well as to create the National Park of Glaciers on the Central Caucasus Mountain Range and Pshav-Khevsureti Protected Areas in the Mtskheta Mtianeti Region (Agency of Protected Areas, 2024).

In 2022, there were 14 nature reserves with an area of 129 thousand hectares, 14 national parks with an area of 497 thousand hectares, 26 managed reserves with

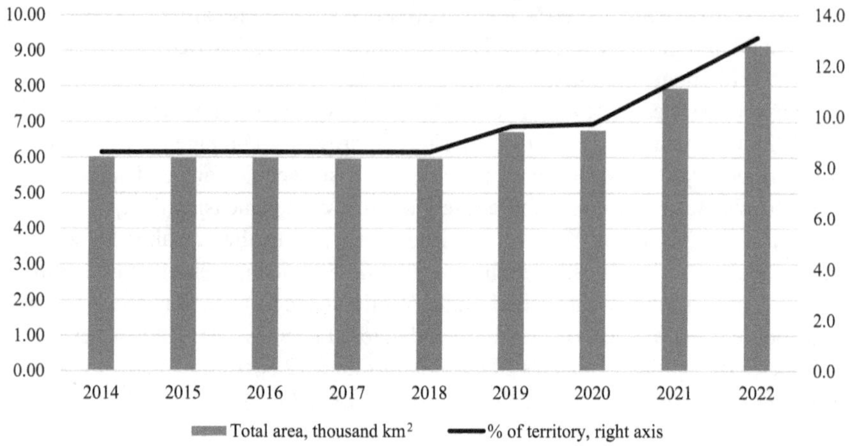

Figure 3.98 Georgia. Surface of protected areas during 2014–2022.

Source: National Statistics Office of Georgia (2023).

an area of 106 thousand hectares, 40 natural monuments with an area of 2.7 thousand hectares, as well as areas of protected landscapes with an area of 165 thousand hectares and one protected area of universal use with an area of 13 thousand hectares (National Statistics Office of Georgia, 2023a). In Georgia, between 2014 and 2022, the area of protected areas increased from 6.01 thousand km^2 to 9.13 thousand km^2 (Figure 3.98). Accordingly, in 2022, 13.1% of the country's territory consisted of protected areas.

Moldova

Water resources

The Republic of Moldova faces challenges due to limited water resources compared to many European countries, heavily relying on the Prut and Dniester rivers, most of whose water originates outside its borders. Despite a significant agricultural sector, characterized by numerous small-scale farmers, Moldova experiences increasing water demand exacerbated by frequent droughts. Irrigation practices often employ inefficient systems with considerable water losses. As a result, Moldova contends with high per capita water abstraction rates, substantial water stress levels, significant transportation losses, and uncertain prospects for reducing these challenges.

Rivers

In the Republic of Moldova, there are 3,621 permanent or temporary rivers, streams, and creeks with a length of more than 16,000 km, 90% of which are less than 10 km long, and only 9 of them exceed 100 km in length.

Table 3.8 Moldova: Water resources as at the end of 2022.

Name	*Rivers*			
	Length (km)		*Catchment area (km²)*	
	Total	*In Moldova*	*Total*	*In Moldova*
Dniestr	1,352	657	72,100	19,070
Prut	976	695	27,500	7,990
Răut	286	286	7,760	7,760
Bâk	155	155	2,150	2,150
Botna	152	152	1,540	1,540
	Lakes			
	Location (district)		**Surface (km²)**	
Beleu	Cahul		9.50	
Manta	Cahul		21.0	
Sălaşu	Anenii Noi		3.72	
Dracele	Cahul		2.65	
Rotunda	Cahul		2.08	
Nistrul Vechi	Căuşeni		1.86	
Roşu	Căuşeni		1.60	
	Artificial lakes			
	Location (district)		**Surface (km²)**	
Dubăsari	Dubăsari		67.5	
Costeşti-Stânca	Râşcani		59	
Cuciurgan	Slobozia		27.3	
Taraclia	Taraclia		15.1	
Ghidighici	Străşeni		6.8	
Ialoveni	Ialoveni		4.4	

Source: Biroul Naţional de Statistică al Republicii Moldova (2023).

All rivers belong to the Black Sea basin and can be grouped as follows: rivers of the Dniester basin, rivers of the Prut basin, and southern rivers flowing into the mouth of the Danube or the Black Sea. Small rivers predominate. The largest include the Dniester (1,352 km, including 657 km on the territory of the country with an annual flow of about 10 km^3), Prut (976 km, including 695 km on the territory of the country, with an annual flow of about 10 km^3), Răut (286 km), Cogalnic (243 km, including 125 km on the territory of the country), Bîc (155 km), and Botna (152 km) (Table 3.8). The density of the hydrographic network averages 0.48 km/km^2 for the country and varies from 0.84 km/km^2 in the north of the country to 0.12 km/km^2 on the left side of the Dniester River (UN Environment, 2023).

The primary sources of water for rivers in the area are snow and rain, with a smaller contribution from groundwater. Precipitation predominantly occurs as transient rainfall, with only about 10% falling as snow. Spring sees elevated water levels as a result of snowmelt, accounting for 40–50% of the annual river flow. During the summer, heavy rainfall can lead to substantial increases in river levels, particularly in smaller rivers, occasionally resulting in severe and catastrophic flooding events (UN Environment, 2021).

Lakes

On the territory of the country, there are 4,475 water reservoirs with an area of about 40.2 thousand hectares, of which only about 60 are natural lakes. The largest of them are lakes located in the Prut riverine meadows (Beleu, 6.26 km^2; Dracele, 2.65 km^2; Rotunda, 2.08 km^2) and in the Dniester riverine meadows (Salas, 3.72 km^2; Ros, 1.16 km^2; Nistrul Vechi, 1.86 km^2) (Table 3.8). However, there are more than 4,250 accumulation lakes for various purposes (irrigation, fishing, recreation, industrial and domestic needs, flood control). Large lakes, among others for powering hydropower plants, were created on the Prut River in cooperation with Romania (Costesti-Stanca, 59 km^2), on the Dniester River (Dubasari, 67.5 km^2; Cuciurgan, 27.3 km^2), and on the Bic River (Ghidighici, 6.8 km^2) (Third Biennial, 2021).

Underground waters

Groundwater plays a special role in the land water balance of the Republic of Moldova. These waters are actively integrated into the hydrological cycle as a component of groundwater flow. The distribution of groundwater resources across the country is uneven, with most of them concentrated in the meadows of the Dniester and Prut rivers. In areas far away from these rivers, the supply of water to underground aquifers decreases. Thus, the groundwater resources of the Republic of Moldova include 17 complexes and aquifers of different ages, which are unevenly distributed throughout the country. The most important of these are six aquifers: the Quaternary groundwater (22 million m^3), Middle Sarmatian (110 million m^3), Lower Sarmatian + Badian (770 million m^3), Cretaceous (110 million m^3), and Upper Sarmatian and Pontic (44 million m^3). In most aquifers, about 50% of the water is potable, with the exception of phreatic water, which is about 20–30%. Deep water resources total 1100 million m^3, and those considered potable account for about 255,000 m^3/day (Tăriță et al., 2013).

About 40% of the rural population in Moldova relies on water supplied from underground layers under hydrostatic pressure. Approximately 4,956 wells are monitored for water usage, with 2,612 wells operational as of 2019. Among these, 1,672 wells are used for drinking water, 657 for technical purposes, 46 for agricultural needs, 220 for industrial use, and 17 for spa purposes. Water supply is also sourced from the first level of water, which is nonpressurized. This includes around 178.7 thousand wells, consisting of 144.9 thousand farm wells and 3094 spring wells, of which 2.060 thousand are developed wells. This source provides about 1.8 million m^3 per day from proven reserves. However, it's important to note that only 50% of the total groundwater used in Moldova is suitable for drinking purposes without prior treatment due to varying degrees of contamination and quality issues.

Water intake ratio

Moldova's internal water resources (rivers and groundwater resources) amount to only 1.6 billion m^3, which is about 550 m^3 per capita (including the population of Transnistria), far below the amount recorded in other European countries. In

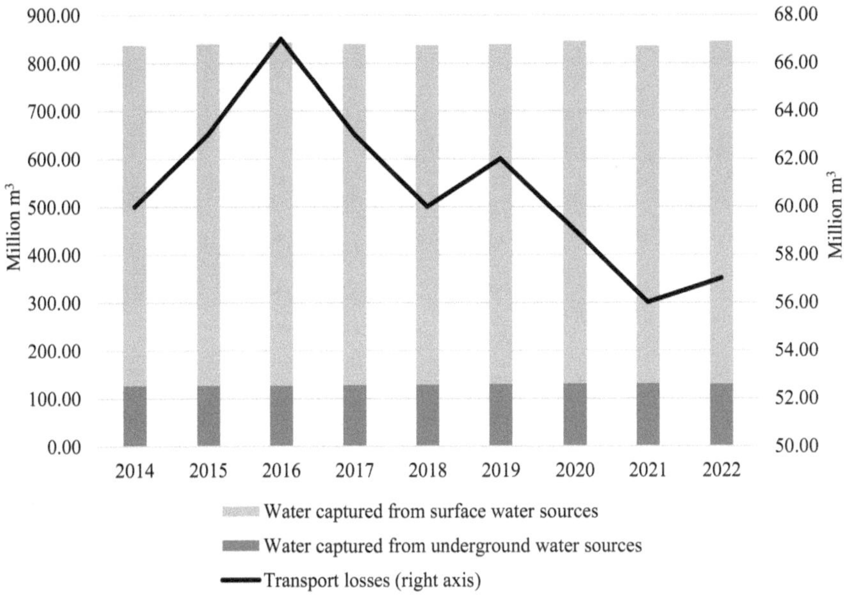

Figure 3.99 Moldova. Water capture during 2014–2022, in million m³.

Source: Own compilation based on data from Biroul Național de Statistică al Republicii Moldova (2023).

general, Moldova's water resources can be considered of poor quality due to the continued neglect of environmental aspects over many years. The data show that the water quality of the Prut and Dniester rivers falls into Class III (moderately polluted), and inland rivers into Classes IV–V (polluted and heavily polluted) (EU4Environment, 2022). Despite the limited water resources, the amount of water abstracted is quite large, accounting for about half of the renewable water resources or an annual volume of about 845 million m³ (Figure 3.99).

From 2014 to 2022, water losses during transportation in Moldova remained relatively stable, fluctuating between 56 and 60 million m³ annually. Over the long term, there has been a reduction in the total amount of water withdrawn. This trend is primarily influenced by the decline in population, leading to a corresponding decrease in household consumption. Conversely, the decline in water consumption for production needs has not been as pronounced, although there has been a slight reduction in recent years.

Forest resources

Despite a slight increase in the forest cover of the national territory, the Republic of Moldova is still a country with limited forest resources (Figure 3.100). This is under conditions in which Moldova is facing serious environmental problems, with climate extremes becoming more frequent in recent years. At the same time, no one

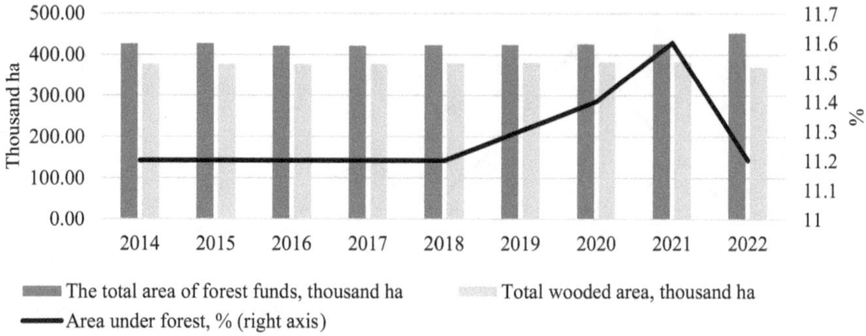

Figure 3.100 Moldova. Forest resource indicators from 2014 to 2022.

Source: own compilation based on data from Biroul Național de Statistică al Republicii Moldova (2023).

doubts that the reduction of forest area is one of the causes of these phenomena, so public policy actions in this regard are absolutely necessary.

The Republic of Moldova remains a low forest-cover country, with the area of land covered by forests increasing slightly in recent years. Most of the forest fund is owned by the state through the "Moldsilva" Agency (85.4%), local public administration authorities (12.8%), and other institutions. During 2014–2021, the area of the forest fund increased from 426 to about 451.7 thousand hectares, mainly due to areas covered by deciduous forests. As a result of these changes, the country's forest cover has increased from 11.1% to 11.6%, with fluctuations depending on the area: in the north, 8.7%; in the center, 15.1%; and in the south, 8.5%.

The slow pace of forest cover growth has garnered increasing attention from policymakers, and the frequency of recent extreme weather events has heightened public awareness that urgent action is necessary. At the Presidential level, a Task Force was established in 2021 to spearhead the development of a National Afforestation Program. This initiative aims to plant a minimum of 100,000 hectares of forests over the next decade, with the ambitious target of achieving 15% forest cover of the country's land area (Presidency of the Republic of Moldova, 2021).

As for wood pulp resources, there has been a slowdown in recent years. Between 2014 and 2021, timber mass resources increased from 49 to 50.1 million m^3, and in 2022, they were only 43.4 million m^3. It should be noted that this was due to the fact that the area of forests where logging was carried out in connection with maintenance, cleaning, and sanitation work was larger than the area of forests subjected to regeneration work (tree planting). Thus, between 2014 and 2022, the area where logging was carried out in connection with maintenance and cleanup work fell from 4,252 to 3,928 hectares, while regeneration covered areas that did not increase continuously, but ranged from 4,992 to 5,304 hectares (Biroul Național de Statistică al Republicii Moldova, 2023).

Soil resources

Moldova has experienced minimal changes in the size of its soil resources over the past decade, as indicated by Figure 3.101. Urbanization, population density, and infrastructure expansion have not significantly altered the structure of the land fund. Consequently, Moldova remains primarily an agricultural nation, with soil standing as its principal natural resource. However, substantial portions of agricultural land are fragmented, and erosion impacts some areas, thereby constraining agricultural productivity.

Moldova's land fund is predominantly composed of agricultural land, accounting for approximately 62% of the total land area, which translates to about 2.5 million hectares. Agricultural land use has remained stable over the years, with arable land comprising more than 70% and perennial plantations (mainly vineyards and orchards) making up slightly over 10%. In recent years, Moldova has observed a decrease in uncultivated land, with about 24 thousand hectares recorded in 2021, constituting 1.1% of total agricultural land. Despite these trends, the quality of Moldova's soil is under pressure from factors such as erosion, lack of proper grazing management, and inadequate soil conservation measures. According to the Land Registry, eroded soils cover approximately 877,600 hectares, including 114,000 hectares classified as highly eroded (Anuarul IPM, 2021). The area affected by erosion has expanded by 283,400 hectares over the past four decades, averaging an increase of about 7,000 hectares annually.

The distribution of land types within Moldova's land fund has remained largely unchanged over recent years. Specifically, forest and conservation fund land occupies 13.4%, village land 9.3%, and water fund land 2.6% of the total land area.

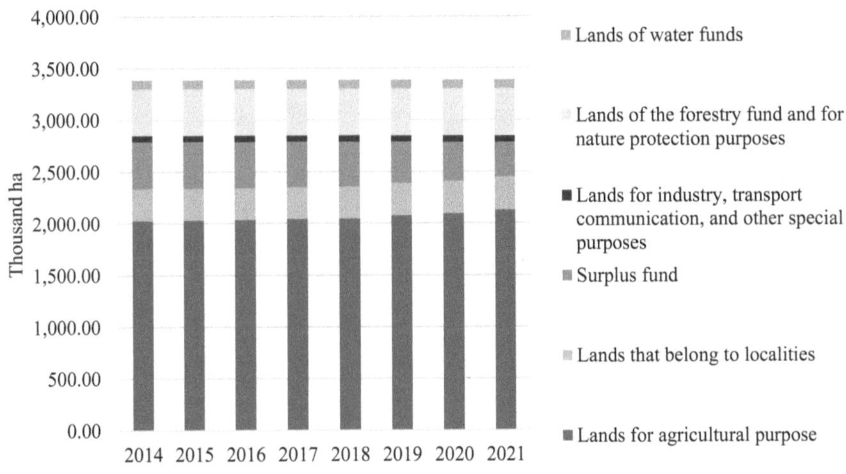

Figure 3.101 Moldova. Land fund by land category during 2014–2021, in thousand hectares.

Source: Own compilation based on data from Biroul Național de Statistică al Republicii Moldova (2023).

However, there has been a notable decrease in land within the reserve fund, which now constitutes 11.2% of the land fund area, marking a reduction of just over 90,000 hectares between 2011 and 2021 (Biroul Național de Statistică al Republicii Moldova, 2023). This decline primarily resulted from the exclusion of land previously occupied by structures and annexes from former agricultural units, subsequently reclassified for agricultural use.

Organic farming

Organic farming in Moldova is not yet considered a distinct sector within agriculture, because both the land area dedicated to it and the number of participants remain relatively small. This situation stems from various factors affecting both consumer demand and producer supply. Despite governmental efforts to promote organic farming through policy initiatives, the support provided remains limited, particularly in financial terms. Agriculture remains a pivotal sector of Moldova's economy, despite its declining contribution to GDP. In 2022, agriculture accounted for approximately 8.29% of GDP, marking a significant decrease from two-thirds of its 2000 levels. Given agriculture's vulnerability to climate impacts, the government has prioritized sustainable agricultural development, including through initiatives like sectoral greening (Republic of Moldova, 2014).

Organic farming in Moldova is defined as the production of agri-food products obtained without certain synthetic chemicals, promoting environmentally friendly production technologies with minimal biodiversity impact. Despite advancements in legislation covering certification, inspection, labeling, and export, the expansion of organic farming capacity remains limited. Both the number of participating farmers and the area under organic cultivation show uncertain trends with unclear prospects (Figure 3.102). According to the "Atlas of Organic Agriculture for 2020," Moldova had 139 certified organic agriculture producers cultivating approximately 28.6 thousand hectares, constituting 1.4% of the country's agricultural land. However, it's essential to acknowledge statistical limitations, because official figures may not encompass producers employing organic practices without certification, including those certified by foreign entities.

Biodiversity

Biodiversity is a natural resource that forms the basis for the proper functioning of ecosystems. The state of biodiversity can be described by the increasing number of endangered plant and animal species. The latest edition of the Red Book presented in 2015 listed two times more plant and animal species compared to the 2001 edition. Under these conditions, the Republic of Moldova needs clear policies and measures to protect rare and vulnerable species by restoring natural habitats.

The flora of the Republic of Moldova comprises approximately 5,500 plant species, with 208 listed in the latest edition of the Red Book. The fauna includes around 17,000 animal species, with 219 categorized as endangered and listed in the Red Book. Typically, the Red Book is updated every decade after reassessing

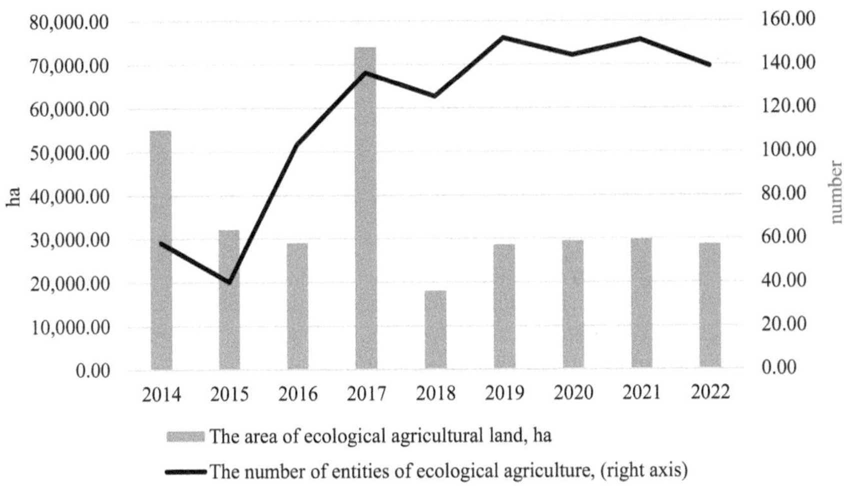

Figure 3.102 Moldova. Organic farming during 2014–2022.

Source: Ministerul Agriculturii și Industriei Alimentare. https://www.madrm.gov.md/ accessed: 30.01.2024

species conservation status and geographic distribution. The latest edition from 2015 nearly doubled the number of protected species, indicating a decline in hunting resources (Figure 3.103). Amphibians and reptiles face a critical situation, with 64% of species threatened, while mammals and birds face risks of 40% and 22%, respectively. Urgent and effective measures are essential to prevent potential extinctions in these categories. Fish populations also show concern, with approximately 27% of species endangered. The Dniester and Prut rivers harbor significant aquatic biodiversity, yet poaching and uncontrolled fishing contribute to depletion

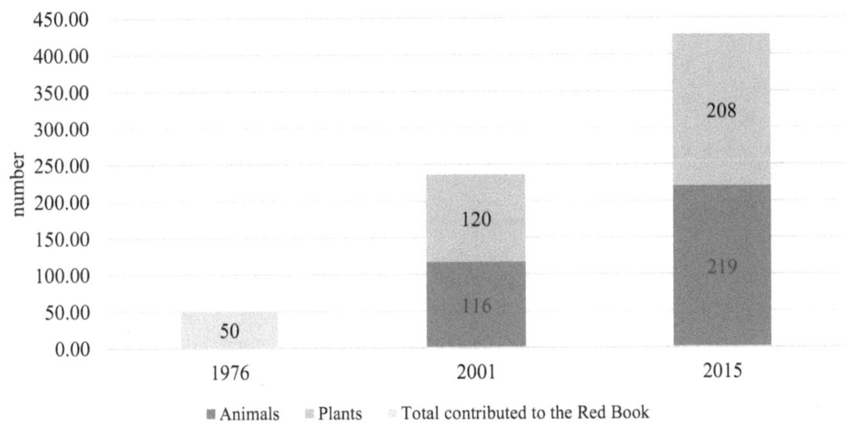

Figure 3.103 Moldova. Protected species of plants and animals (included in the Red Book).

Source: EU4Environment (2021b, p. 54); (2022).

of fish stocks, hindering commercial fishing for years. Oversight of fishing activities by state institutions and control mechanisms remains inadequate for sport, recreational, and commercial fishing purposes (EU4Environment, 2021b, 2021c; Biroul Național de Statistică al Republicii Moldova, 2023).

Natural protected areas

The Republic of Moldova registers small areas of protected areas in relation to the national territory, even if periodically some areas are given this status. Moreover, the goal of preserving nature and related cultural values in these areas is difficult to achieve in conditions where the state is unable to ensure full compliance with the legal framework and limit harmful human interference.

The International Union for Conservation of Nature (IUCN) recognizes protected areas as "clearly delineated geographic spaces, recognized, designated and administered by legislation or other effective means, to achieve long-term conservation of nature, as well as environmental services and associated cultural values." (INCN, Effective protected areas, https://iucn.org/our-work/topic/effective-protected-areas). According to national legislation (Legea No. 1538/1998), the protected areas fund consists of several categories of natural sites and complexes of undisputed primary value for the preservation of biodiversity and natural habitats, the study of natural processes, the restoration of ecological balance, and the environmental education of the population (Republic of Moldova, 1998).

The area of natural areas under state protection in Moldova encompasses approximately 195,000 hectares, accounting for 5.7% of the country's total area and comprising 312 sites. This reflects a consistent expansion over time, marked by legislative designations of protected areas. Significant increases occurred notably in 2007 and 2013 (Figure 3.104), resulting in nearly a threefold expansion

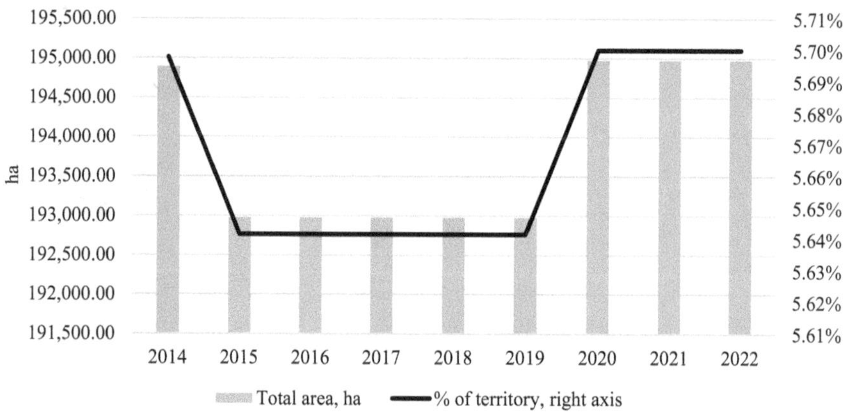

Figure 3.104 Moldova. Surface of protected areas during 2014–2022.

Source: Own compilation based on data from Biroul Național de Statistică al Republicii Moldova (2023).

compared to 15 years ago. Key among these are five renowned scientific reserves: Codru, Iagorlîc, Prutul de Jos, Plaiul Fagului, and Padurea Domnească. These reserves aim to safeguard natural ecosystems, including tree species, shrubs, other plant species, and the entire faunal complex.

Ukraine

Water resources

Water resources in Ukraine play a pivotal role in the country's economic development and the daily lives of its population. However, the supply of water resources in Ukraine is inadequate and primarily depends on river flow, groundwater, and seawater. The potential river flow resources are estimated at 209.8 km^3, with 52.4 km^3 occurring within Ukraine's territory and 157.4 km^3 contributed by tributaries. Groundwater resources amount to 7 km^3, while seawater contributes approximately 1 km^3 to the economy. Per capita water availability in Ukraine averages 1,045 m^3, with the highest levels observed in the western and northern regions of the country (CBITA, 2011).

The distribution of water resources across Ukrainian territory is uneven and does not align with the locations of water-intensive economic sectors. Areas with the smallest amount of water resources coincide with regions that are home to significant water consumers, such as the Donbass, the Kryvyi Rig region, the Autonomous Republic of Crimea, and the southern regions of the country.

In Ukraine, the main consumers of water include industries such as electric power, metallurgy, and the chemical industry, as well as agriculture and municipal services. To address disparities in surface water availability across different regions, Ukraine has constructed 1,100 water reservoirs with a combined capacity of 55 km^3, with the largest reservoirs situated on the Dnieper River. Additionally, there are approximately 29,000 ponds, seven major canals, and ten waterworks in the country. On average, Ukraine's annual total natural water resources amount to 94 km^3, with 56.2 km^3 available for consumption. The majority of these renewable water resources derive from river flows, totaling 85.1 km^3 (excluding the Danube). Of this amount, 60% originates within Ukraine's borders (local flow), while 40% comes from upstream areas (transit flow).

Ukraine's major rivers include:

- Dnieper (total length 2,201 km, 981 km within Ukrainian borders, average annual flow 53.3 km^3).
- Dniester (total length 1,362 km, within Ukrainian borders 705 km, average annual flow 8.7 km^3).
- Southern Bug (total length 806 km, average annual flow 3.4 km^3).
- Siversky Donets (total length 1,053 km, within Ukrainian borders 672 km, average annual flow 5 km^3).

The Danube also flows through the territory of Ukraine at a distance of 174 km, the average annual flow of 123 km^3 is a transit flow.

In total, there are more than 70,000 rivers on Ukrainian territory, but only 117 of them are more than 100 km long. In summer, rivers become shallow, with many of them drying up. In order to retain water formed from melted snow and to regulate the flow, reservoirs have been created on most rivers (a total of 1,057, they can hold 55 km^3 of water). To supply water to lowland areas, canals were built: North Crimean with a length of 400.4 km; Dnipro-Donbas, 550 km; and Siversky Donets-Donbas, 131.6 km. In the south of Ukraine, large irrigation systems have been established (Kakhovskaya, Inguletskaya, and others). In areas with excessive moisture or slow runoff, drainage systems are in operation (Verkhne-Pripyatskaya, Latoritskaya, and others).

The country has more than 20,000 lakes, 43 of which have an area of more than 10 km^2. Large lakes are located in the Danube floodplain and on the Black Sea coast (Yalpug, Sasik, and others). The largest lake in Polesia is Svitaz. Synewyr ejst is the largest lake in the Carpathian Mountains. The total area of the swamps is 12,000 km^2. They are located mainly in Polesia. Estimated underground water resources are 27.4 km^3, of which 8.9 km^3 is not associated with surface flow.

Based on the results of the 1975–1980 regional assessment, it was estimated that Ukraine's groundwater resources amount to 61,6892,000 m^3/day, including with mineralization up to 1,500 mg/dm^3–57,499,900 m^3/day. The projected groundwater resources are distributed unevenly across regions due to differences in geological, structural, and physical–geographical conditions of different regions of Ukraine. Most of the projected resources are concentrated in the northern and western regions of Ukraine; the resources of the southern region are limited. Most projected groundwater resources are concentrated in the Chernihiv region (8,326,700 m^3/day) and the least in Kirovograd (404,600 m^3/day), Chernivtsi (405,300 m^3/day), and Nikolaev (441,600 m^3/day) (Tomiltseva et al., 2017).

Water intake ratio

In general, Ukraine's water resources are considered inadequate. In dry years, water shortages are even experienced in large river basins. The use of water resources is categorized into two main types: water consumption, which involves the removal of water from the source for subsequent use in technological processes such as industry, agriculture (with irrigation), and municipal services; and water use that is realized directly in the water source without the direct consumption of the resource, including hydropower, water transport, fishing, and tourism. Industry consumes the most freshwater, accounting for 48% of total water consumption. Agriculture uses about 40%, while public utilities in cities and other populated areas use approximately 12%. From 2014 to 2022, Ukraine experienced a decrease in water abstraction from both surface and underground sources (Figure 3.105).

Thus, in 2022 compared to 2014, water withdrawal from surface sources decreased by 59.25%, and water withdrawal from groundwater sources decreased by 47.64%. The share of groundwater in total water consumption in 2022 was 16.18%.

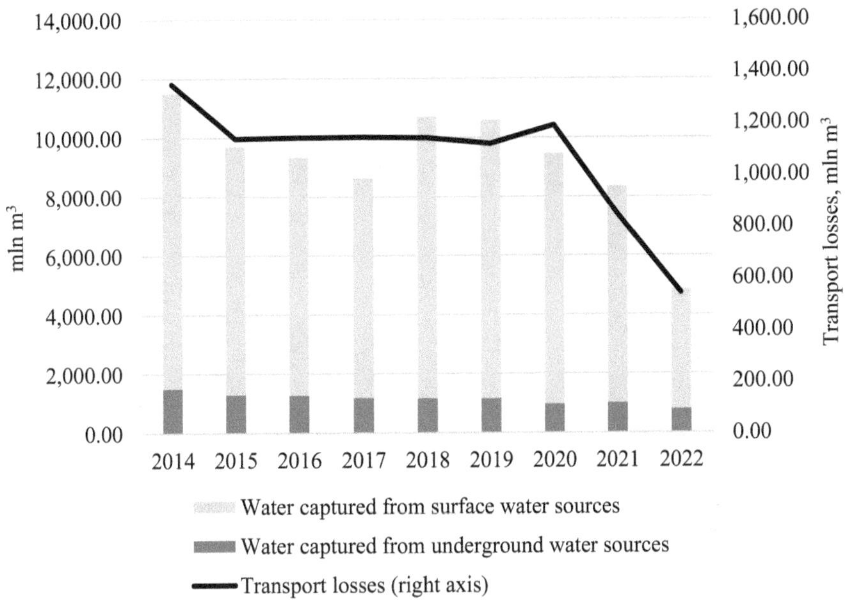

Figure 3.105 Ukraine. Water capture during 2014–2022, in million m^3.

Source: State Statistics Service of Ukraine.

There was also a downward trend in water transportation losses. Between 2014 and 2022, the level of water transportation losses decreased by 59.93%. Overall, there was a decrease in the amount of water withdrawn during this period, primarily driven by reduced water consumption in the agricultural sector, where irrigation is significant, as well as in the processing industry and households.

Among the major problems concerning the rational formation, use, and protection of Ukraine's water resources are several critical issues: pollution of water bodies by harmful emissions and inadequately treated industrial and municipal wastewater; intensive aging of the main fixed assets used for water supply and conservation; low efficiency of water treatment plants; insufficient self-healing and self-purification capacity of water systems; and an unsustainable water management system characterized by extensive use of water resources in production and high water intensity.

Forest resources

The total area of forest plots in Ukraine is 10.4 million hectares (Figure 3.106). Forests of Ukraine according to their purpose and distribution within a country perform mainly ecological (water protection, protective, sanitary and hygienic, etc.) functions and have limited commercial significance (State Forest Resources Agency of Ukraine, 2024).

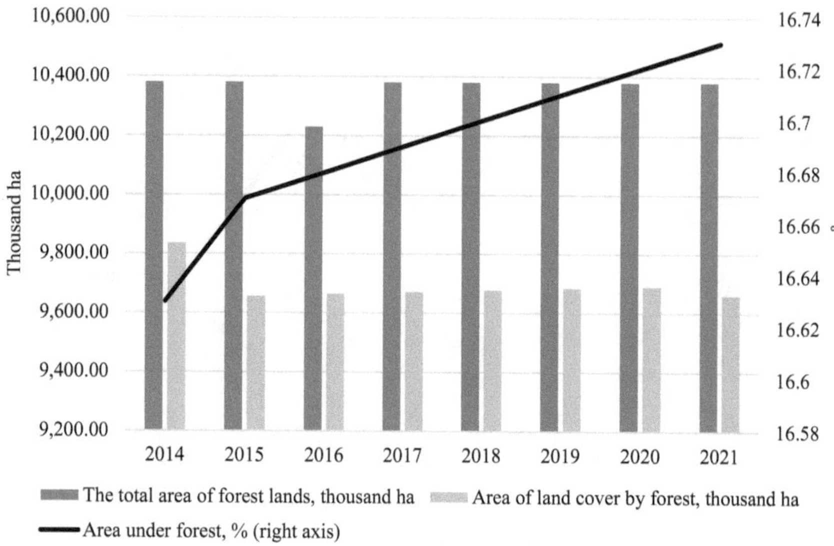

Figure 3.106 Ukraine. Forest ratios 2014–2021.

Source: State Statistics Service of Ukraine.

During the past 50 years, the forest ratio increased 1.5 times and growing stock 2.5 times. Growing stock is estimated to be within 2.1 billion m³. The total average change of growing stock reached 35 million m³. The average annual change of growing stock is 3.9 m³/ha in State Forest Resources Agency of Ukraine forests, varying from 5.0 m³ in Carpathians up to 2.5 m³ in the Steppe region. A gradual increase of growing stock has been carried out, which confirms the significant economic and environmental potential of forests in Ukraine (State Forest Resources Agency of Ukraine, 2024).

The largest share in age structure is middle-aged stands at 45%. The share of mature and over mature stands is only 17%. The average age of forests is around 60 years. A gradual aging of forests is taking place, leading to the deterioration of sanitary conditions (State Forest Resources Agency of Ukraine, 2024).

Ukrainian forests compose of over 30 tree species. The prevailing species are pine (*Pinus silvestris*), oak (*Quercus robur*), beech (*Fagus silvatica*), spruce (*Picea abies*), birch (*Betula pendula*), alder (*Alnus glutinosa*), ash (*Fraxinus excelsior*), hornbeam (*Carpinus betulus*), fir (*Abies alba*) (State Forest Resources Agency of Ukraine, 2024).

According to the Land and Forest Codes of Ukraine, forests may be in state, communal, or private ownership. The majority of forests are state-owned. During the division of land between state and communal ownership to communal property about 1.3 million hectares (12.5%) of forest land was transferred, which are in constant use of enterprises subordinated to local governments. The share of private forest ownership is less than 0.1% of the total area of forest land. About 0.8 million hectares of state-owned forest lands is not given for use and assigned to reserve lands (State Forest Resources Agency of Ukraine, 2024).

Soil resources

The vast majority of land in Ukraine is fertile and very fertile. Approximately 50% of the territory is covered by chernozem, with a humus content[3] of up to 9% and layer thickness varying from 40 cm to 1 m, considered among the most fertile in the world, and 14% are chestnut soils, with a 3–4% humus content and a layer thickness of about 0.5 m. These two types of highly fertile land cover approximately 370 thousand km^2, or 64% of the country's area. Due to the well-developed network of large rivers in their valleys, fluvial muds have developed (about 4.5% of the area), also usually characterized by high fertility. Less fertile are the flat soils occupying about 19% of the state's area, with a humus content of 1–2.5%. The podzolic soils (about 6% of the area), formed mainly on sands, are among the poor soils. Other soil types are found on about 7% of the country's area (Matuszak, 2021).

In various regions of Ukraine, there is a significant variation in the types of soils present. In the northern part of the country, within the mixed forest zone, less fertile feldspathic and podzolic soils dominate. Moving into the forest-steppe belt, black soils are predominantly found. The steppe zone can be further categorized: in the northeast, chernozem soils prevail, while along the coasts of the Black and Azov seas in the south, chernozem soils are also prominent. In the southwest region, particularly in the Carpathian Mountains, podzolic soils and lower-quality brown soils can be observed (Matuszak, 2021, pp. 13–14).

Among the challenges facing Ukrainian agriculture is the gradual degradation of soils. According to the State Land Protection Agency, between 1990 and 2015, the average percentage of humus, a crucial factor for soil fertility, decreased from 3.36% (data for 1986–1990) to 3.16% (data for 2006–2010) (Baliuk et al., 2021). The degradation process has been most pronounced in steppe areas, where humus levels declined from 3.72% to 3.45%. Climate change contributes to this phenomenon, but it is exacerbated by agricultural practices, particularly the dominance of monocultures that include soil-sterilizing oilseed crops (Matuszak, 2021).

Over the past decade, Ukraine has not seen significant changes in the size of its soil resources (Figure 3.107).

Factors such as urbanization, population density, and infrastructure development have not been able to change the land fund structure. As a result, Ukraine remains a predominantly agricultural country, and the country's main natural resource is soil.

In Ukraine, agricultural land dominates the land fund, comprising approximately 68.45% of the total land area, which amounts to 41.3 million hectares. However, the quality of these soils is declining due to erosion, lack of grazing, and insufficient implementation of soil conservation measures. The total area of eroded soil has increased to 13.4 million hectares, with arable land accounting for 10.6 million hectares (32% of the total arable land). Annually, up to 500 million tons of topsoil are washed away from arable land, leading to the loss of 24 million tons of humus.

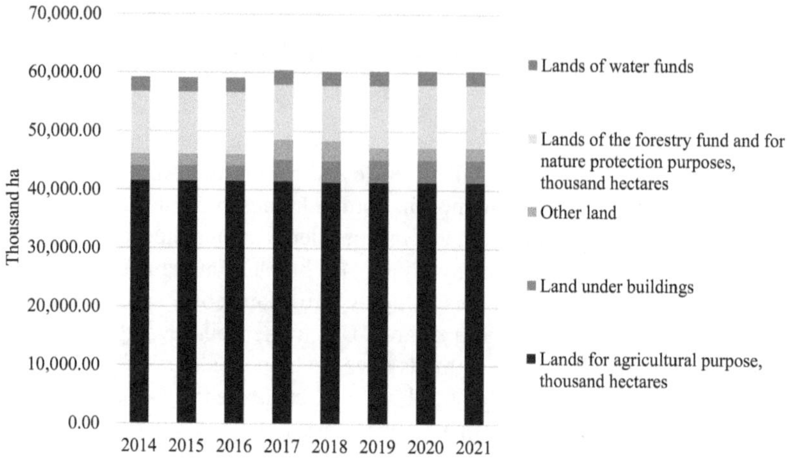

Figure 3.107 Ukraine. Land fund by land category during 2014–2021, in thousand hectares.
Source: State Statistics Service of Ukraine.

Experts estimate that agricultural losses due to soil erosion exceed 9–12 million tons of grain annually. Eroded land includes 4.5 million hectares with moderately and severely eroded soils, among which 68,000 hectares have completely lost the humus horizon. Moreover, more than 50% of Ukraine's arable land is at risk of wind erosion, particularly affecting 12.4 million hectares in the steppe zone (Baliuk et al., 2021).

The other types of land included in the land fund remain on the register in the same areas, namely: forest and conservation fund land, 17.7%; land under buildings, 6.2%; and water fund land, 4.0%.

Organic farming

Ukraine, having significant potential for organic production, export, and consumption in the domestic market, has achieved some results in developing its own organic production. For example, the area of certified agricultural land in Ukraine involved in the cultivation of various organic products is already over 400 thousand hectares (Figure 3.108), and the country was ranked 20th among the world leaders in organic movement in 2017. The share of certified organic land in Ukraine's total agricultural area is about 1%. At the same time, Ukraine occupies the first place in the Eastern European region in the certified area of organic arable land, specializing mainly in the production of cereals, legumes, and oilseeds (Organic in Ukraine, 2021).

Official IFOAM statistics confirm that in 2002, there were 31 organic farms registered in Ukraine. In 2021, there were already 528 organic operators, and the total area of agricultural land on which organic production is carried out was 422 299 hectares. Although in recent years there has been a certain decline in the number of operators and areas under organic production. In the very first year of the Russian invasion, the area under organic farming significantly decreased to 263 619 hectares, as did the number of operators (462). The same can be said about the domestic market for the consumption of organic products, which has significantly "shrunk" to the level of 2017.

This information from the site: the Federation of Organic Movement of Ukraine, https://organic.com.ua/organic-v-ukraini/

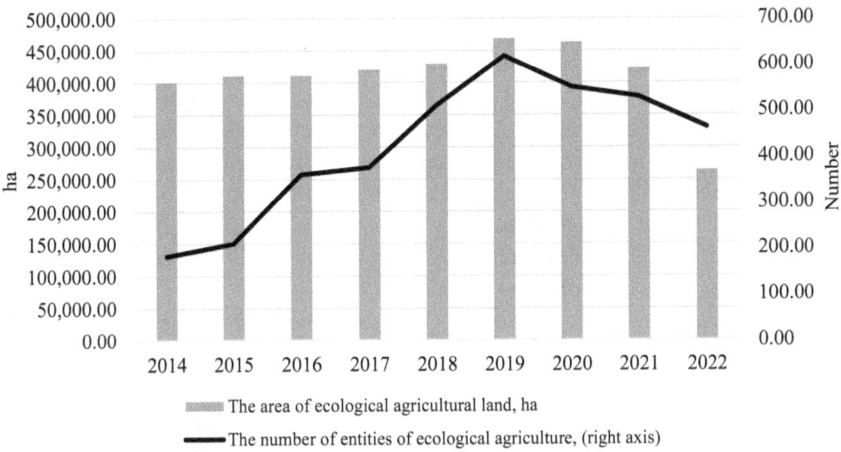

Figure 3.108 Ukraine. Organic farming 2011–2017.

Source: According to IFOAM and the Federation of Organic Movement of Ukraine (2023).

The majority of Ukrainian organic farms are located in the Odessa, Kherson, Kiev, Poltava, Vinnytsia, Zakarpattia, Lviv, Ternopil, and Zhytomyr regions. Ukrainian certified organic farms vary in size from a few hectares, as in most European countries, to several thousand hectares of arable land (Organic in Ukraine, 2021).

Studies of the Federation of Organic Movement of Ukraine show that the modern domestic consumer market for organic products in Ukraine began to develop in the early 2000s, making EUR 100 thousand in 2004; EUR 200 thousand in 2005; EUR 400 thousand in 2006; EUR 500 thousand in 2007; EUR 600 thousand in 2008; EUR 1.2 million in 2009; and EUR 2.4 million in 2010. In 2011, this figure increased to EUR 5.1 million, up to EUR 7.9 million in 2012, up to EUR 12.2 million in 2013, up to EUR 14.5 million in 2014, up to EUR 17.5 million in 2015, up to EUR 21.2 million in 2016, up to EUR 29.4 million in 2017, up to EUR 33.0 million in 2018, up to EUR 36.0 million in 2019, up to EUR 38.0 million in 2020, up to EUR 39.0 million in 2021, and up to EUR 29.0 million in 2022, his information from the site: the Federation of Organic Movement of Ukraine, https://organic.com.ua/organic-v-ukraini/ (Organic in Ukraine, 2021).

One of the complex issues of organic market development is the lack of regulation of the legal framework, which complicates the work of domestic organic producers. It should be noted that the Law of Ukraine "On Production and Turnover of Organic Agricultural Products and Raw Materials" adopted in 2013 is now inactive (this Law was only effective in Ukraine until August 2, 2019). After all, the provisions of the law are imperfect and do not comply with EU legislation in the field of organic production, circulation, and labeling of organic products. This has a negative impact on the functioning of the domestic organic market, the image of the country in the world market "organic"; it creates trade barriers for exporting producers; and the consumer is not protected from falsification of "organic", and the producer from unfair competition (Organic in Ukraine, 2021).

Biodiversity

Occupying less than 6% of Europe's land area, Ukraine possesses a remarkable 35% of Europe's biodiversity. This is attributed to its favorable geographic location, encompassing diverse migration routes and natural zones. Ukraine's rich biodiversity comprises over 70,000 species, including numerous rare, relict, and endemic species. Many of these species require special protection, as evidenced by their inclusion in the Red Book of Ukraine. The latest edition (2009) of the Red Book lists 826 species of flora and 542 species of fauna under special conservation status. (Convention on Biological Diversity, 2020).

Ukraine occupies about 11% of the Carpathian mountain range, which encompasses significant environmental, aesthetic, scientific, educational, recreational, and health resources. Over the past two centuries, forest cover in the plains and foothills of the Carpathian Mountains has decreased. However, more recently, an annual average increase of vegetation of 4 m^3/ha has occurred (fluctuating from 5 m^3/ha in the Carpathians to 2.5 m^3/ha in the steppe zone). There has also been an increase in the area and number of territories and objects protected under the Nature Reserve Fund (Ukraine's protected areas network). Natural and semi-natural vegetation cover about 29% of Ukraine's territory, which is represented mostly by forests (17.7% of the territory), meadows, mires, steppes, and saline habitats. Some of the species found in the country are endemics and relicts. Almost one-quarter of Ukraine's floral species is concentrated in forests (Convention on Biological Diversity, 2020).

The country boasts about 63,000 rivers totaling 206,000 km in length, with the area of coastal protection lines along rivers totaling 1.3 million ha. The area of Ukraine's wetlands comprises around 4.5 million ha. Biological resources of the Black Sea and Azov Sea are depreciating in condition, in general, although in the past few years there has been a trend towards improving their condition. As a result of the calamitous condition of red algae (*Phyllophora* sp.), its exploitation was recently prohibited. In addition, the territories in which the main reserves of red algae are concentrated have been declared botanical *zakazniks* (game reserves) known as "Phyllophora's Field of Zernova" (2008) and "Small Phyllophora's Field of Zernova" (2012). The harvesting of club-rush (a plant of the genus *Scirpus*) has become an important economic activity in some areas during the winter. Annually, thousands of people are engaged in club-rush harvesting and processing in the wetlands of the Danube Delta (Convention on Biological Diversity, 2020).

At the beginning of the second decade of the 21st century, there were positive developments regarding contaminated land, especially those affected by radioactive contamination, and the condition of open land with limited or no vegetation. Data from 2012 indicates that since 2000, the area dedicated to grassland and pasture has increased by 97,200 hectares (Convention on Biological Diversity, 2020).

After two years of war in Ukraine, experts from the Ministry of Environmental Protection and Natural Resources have observed severe environmental damage and the destruction of unique ecosystems. The conflict has devastated relict steppe fragments, particularly in the Donetsk Highlands, wetlands near the mouth of the

Dnieper River, and sections of the Black Sea and Azov Sea coasts. Ministry data reveals that military actions have impacted 60 species of animals and 750 species of plants and fungi. Over 300 million m² of Ukrainian land have been destroyed, with lasting implications for both wildlife and human populations long after the cessation of hostilities (IFAW, 2023; Ber, 2023).

Natural protection areas

The total protected area of Ukrainian territory in 2022 was 6.9% (4,173.01 thousand hectares) (Figure 3.109). Today, protected areas in Ukraine are divided into 11 categories of territories and objects of national or local importance. The first category consists of nature preserves that have been given a supplemental title, that of a "biosphere reserve," under the United Nations' Man and the Biosphere program. According to the State Cadastre of the Nature Reserve Fund, at the beginning of 2021, there were 8,633 territories and objects in the Nature Reserve Fund. The Nature Reserves Fund included five biosphere reserves (the Askaniia-Nova Biosphere Reserve, the Black Sea Biosphere Reserve, the Danube Biosphere Reserve, the Carpathian Biosphere Reserve, and the Uzhanskyi National Nature Park), 19 nature reserves, 53 national nature parks, 85 regional landscape parks, 3,398 nature reserves, 3,580 nature monuments, 802 protected areas, 28 botanical gardens, 13 zoological gardens, 62 arboreta, and 588 garden-park art parks (Open Data Portal, 2023).

No war has taken into account the needs of nature conservation. Meanwhile, war in every armed conflict brings millions of silent casualties. The Russian invasion of Ukraine is no exception. It is along the state border and the coast of the Azov-Czar Sea that the most valuable, unique protected areas are located. The problem is not only about the 100-year-old Askania-Nova or the Black Sea Biosphere Reserve,

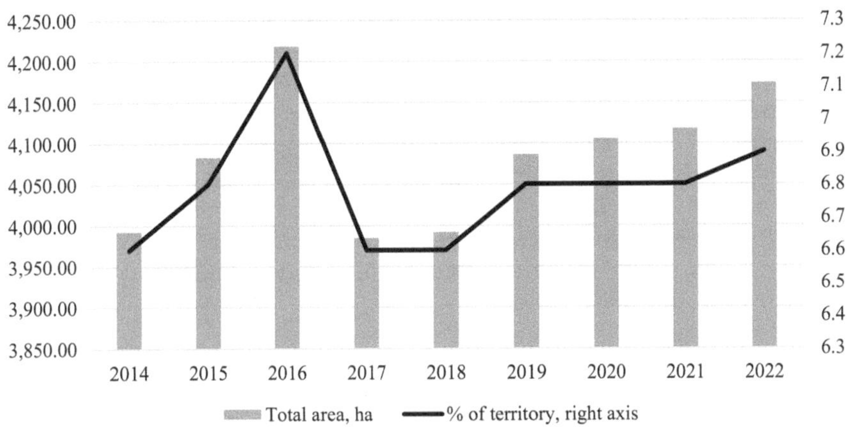

Figure 3.109 Ukraine. Nature protection areas 2014–2022.

Source: State Statistics Service of Ukraine.

which are UNESCO conservation sites, but also about dozens of other unique reserves and national parks.

According to calculations by the Ukrainian Nature Protection Group (UNCG, 2022), the total area of forests in the war zone under the temporary control of Russian invaders or inaccessible to Ukraine is more than 3 million hectares. This represents about 22% of Ukraine's total forest areas.

The conflict zone encompasses 1,654,.736 hectares of pristine steppe currently under occupation forces, constituting approximately 59% of Ukraine's total steppe area, along with 4.514 hectares of shrub vegetation, representing over 10% of such areas in Ukraine. The highest level of protected nature reserves (including national parks, nature reserves, and biosphere reserves) covers a total area of 1,236,366 hectares. Forty-four percent of these reserves are situated within the war zone, under temporary control by Russian invaders, or are currently inaccessible to Ukraine.

Summary

In conclusion, it is evident that the Eastern Partnership countries exhibit varying levels of water resources. Georgia stands out as one of the most water-rich countries in Europe, boasting abundant total renewable water resources. Moldova, including Transnistria, faces the most challenging situation with approximately 550 m^3 per capita, significantly lower compared to other European nations. Meanwhile, other countries in the region generally have adequate water resources, yet they grapple with declining water quality due to agricultural and industrial activities. Moreover, issues such as irrational water use and substantial losses during transportation persist. With progressive climate change, the looming threat of water scarcity is expected to worsen across most EaP countries.

An important natural resource across EaP countries is their forest resources, which vary significantly among the nations. Belarus and Georgia stand out with the highest levels of forestation across their national territories. In contrast, the remaining countries exhibit lower levels of forest cover, influenced by significant environmental challenges and a rising frequency of extreme weather events.

Forests primarily serve ecological functions such as water protection, biodiversity preservation, and environmental sanitation across the EaP countries. However, rapid industrialization, agricultural expansion, urban growth, energy demands, and intensive land use practices have collectively contributed to biodiversity loss in these nations over the past century. Consequently, there is an urgent need for comprehensive policies and measures aimed at protecting rare and vulnerable species through habitat restoration initiatives.

The area of protected areas for EaP countries ranges from 5.7% (Moldova) to 12.1% (Armenia). The size of these areas is variable, because periodically some areas are given protected area status. Moreover, these countries should take care to preserve nature and related cultural values.

The EaP countries are notable for their extensive agricultural areas, which constitute a crucial economic asset. However, the quality of agricultural soils and the extent of agricultural land vary significantly among these nations. An increasingly critical issue that demands attention is land degradation, exacerbated by climate change, leading to continuous fluctuations in both the quantity and quality of soil resources across these countries. One partial solution to this pressing problem is the promotion of organic agriculture, yet its share in overall agricultural production in the region remains relatively modest.

Environmental dimension of quality of life in Eastern Partnership countries

In this area, analyses were undertaken to demonstrate whether greening generates benefits for people. Four indicators were analyzed as follows:

1. **Air pollution.** *Atmospheric emissions of pollutants* means the introduction of pollutants into the atmospheric air from stationary and mobile emission sources (vehicular transportation). All pollutants emitted into the atmospheric air after passing through the dust and gas equipment at organized and unorganized sources of pollution are taken into account. Atmospheric emissions of pollutants (nitrogen oxides and sulfur oxides) on a per capita basis were calculated by relating the volume of emissions of certain pollutants to the average resident population of the territory on a permanent basis.
2. **Exposure of the population to fine particles ($PM_{2.5}$).** Data of fine particles are presented, which consist of various organic and inorganic substances, such as sulfates, nitrates, sodium chloride, soot, mineral dust, and water.
3. **Access to safe drinking water.** A public water supply system comprises a comprehensive network of technological installations, functional facilities, and specialized equipment designed to deliver public water supply services. Key components of the system include intakes, treatment plants, pumping stations equipped with or without hydrophones, storage reservoirs, public water transport networks, and public water supply networks. The percentage of the population with access to safely managed water supply services indicates the extent to which services provide access to improved sources of drinking water. Improved sources encompass various types such as indoor or outdoor water bodies, public taps, protected wells and springs, bottled water, delivered water, and rainwater.
4. **Access to sanitary facilities.** A *public sewerage* system is a set of technological installations and functional and specialized equipment, through which the public sewerage service is provided. The public sewerage system consists, in particular, of the following elements: public sewerage networks, pumping stations, treatment stations, and pre-emission sewers. The *share of the population with access to at least basic sanitation* includes both those using basic sanitation and those using safely managed sanitation. Safely managed sanitation services are those that provide the population with access to both the public sewage system and individually improved sanitation facilities, such as septic tanks, latrines (without access to sewers), and toilets connected to a sewer.

Using these measurements, the chapter considers the impact of environmental conditions and environmental risks on people's quality of life and well-being. In addition, an attempt was made to show the extent to which an increase in income is accompanied (or not) by an increase in overall well-being.

Armenia

Air pollution

Until 1992, the main sources of air pollution in the Republic of Armenia were the energy sector, nonferrous metallurgy, industrial building materials, and chemical industry enterprises, but due to the severe economic crisis, many of these industries were forced to cease operations. The main sources of air pollution in Yerevan are road transportation, urban development, mines, and businesses. In Yerevan, 29 mining licenses have been issued and 405 companies have been allowed to release pollutants into the atmosphere from actual sources. The share of motor vehicles in the mass emission of harmful substances into the atmosphere in the Republic of Armenia is about 65% (IQAir, 2024).

Historically, records began in 2019, when the annual average value was 25.5 μg/m^3 (Table 3.9).

Table 3.9 Armenia: Emissions of pollutants into the atmospheric air by pollutants and years

	2014	*2015*	*2016*	*2017*	*2018*	*2019*	*2020*	*2021*	*2022*
Sulphur dioxide (SO_2). total. 1,000 t/year	32.07	34.14	38.76	38.5	28.61	0.91	0.86	0.76	1.06
Nitrogen oxides (NOX). total. 1,000 t/year	17.17	16.07	16.29	17.4	17.3	19.72	22.99	23.51	22.78
NMVOC. total. 1,000 t/year	23.57	23.15	24.61	25.48	24.73	30.23	36.63	37.74	37.23
Carbon monoxide (CO). total. 1,000 t/year	106.14	104.89	107.86	110.3	112.4	133.04	154.88	159.44	157.63
Hydrocarbons (CH). total. 1,000 t/year	111.2	109	108.35	116.48	102.4	106.86	96.5	98.38	109.42
Ammonia (NH_3) from stationary sources*. 1,000 t/year	0.66	0.68	0.17	0.1	0	0	0.3	..	0.03

(*Continued*)

Table 3.9 (Continued)

	2014	*2015*	*2016*	*2017*	*2018*	*2019*	*2020*	*2021*	*2022*
Dust from stationary sources. 1,000 t/year	4.17	5.04	4.2	5.4	5.9	5.97	6.98	8.49	8.83
Lead. total. t/year	5.9	3.16	1.77	3.71	1.6	0.9	1.11	1.15	1.14
Mercury from stationary sources. t/year	0	0	0	0	0	0	..	..	..
Nickel from stationary sources. t/year	0	0	0	0	0	0	..	..	..
Arsenic from stationary sources. t/year	4.06	6.37	0.5	2.34	0.5	0	..	..	..

Source: Statistical Committee Republic of Armenia, https://statbank.armstat.am/pxweb/en/ArmStatBank/?rxid=9c2c8a86-9f1e-4d5c-8de8-68d419ad463b.

* In 2013, the quantity of Ammonia (NH_3) into the atmospheric air from stationary sources of emission for agriculture is subject to adjustment.

In 2020, there was a slight improvement in air quality, with particulate matter ($PM_{2.5}$) levels recorded at 24.9 μg/m³. This improvement coincided with the onset of the COVID-19 pandemic, during which many vehicles were not in regular use as part of efforts to contain the virus. Additionally, numerous factories and nonessential production units were temporarily closed, leading to reduced emissions into the atmosphere. As a result of these measures, air quality data in most cities showed significant improvements, reflecting cleaner air conditions during that period (Figures 3.110–3.113).

In 2021, the improvement of the inventory was done, and the waste sector has been included and the emissions for previous years (2016–2020) has been recalculated. According to the emissions data for 2021, the waste sector is the main source of pollution with NMVOC (about 75%), then the energy sector within 17% of total emissions. The emissions of NMVOC shows an increasing trend due to the waste sector. Stationary combustion in manufacturing industries and construction accounted for nearly 87% of SOx emissions in 2021. A significant decrease after 2018 (by 98% 2019–2021) was caused by copper production. The energy sector is a main source of CO emissions. In 2021, the shares of emissions from transport and residential combustion sources were 87% and 9.7%, respectively. CO emissions were increased by 39% in 2021 compared to 2016. The increase of CO emissions was mainly a result of the increase in emissions from the transport sector, by 23% during 2016–2021. CO emissions from transport have a variable trend: they increase from 2014 to 2020 and decrease in 2021 (IIR, 2023).

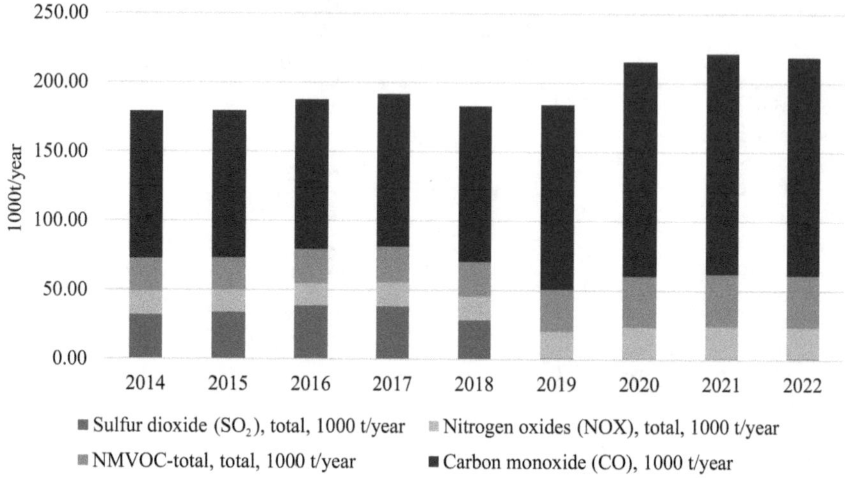

Figure 3.110 Armenia. Emissions of pollutants into the atmospheric air by pollutants and years.

Source: Statistical Committee Republic of Armenia, https://statbank.armstat.am/pxweb/en/ArmStatBank/?rxid=9c2c8a86-9f1e-4d5c-8de8-68d419ad463b.

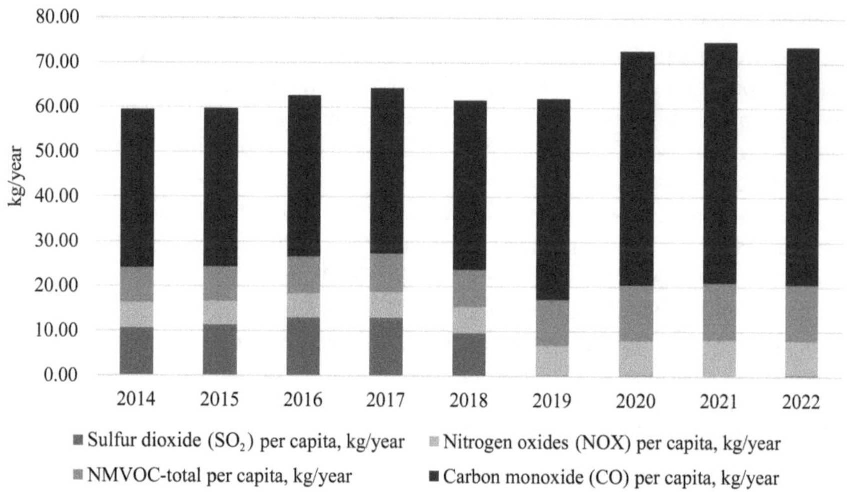

Figure 3.111 Armenia. Emissions of pollutants into the atmospheric air by per capita, kg/year.

Source: www.scws.am/en.

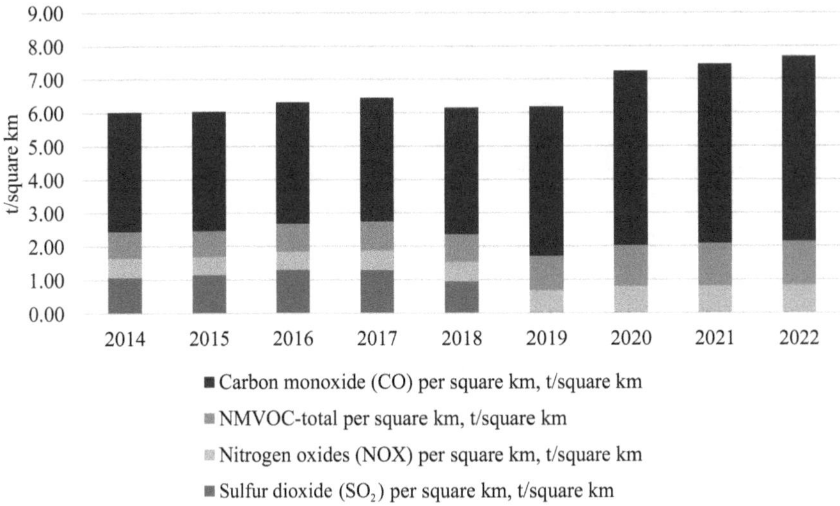

Figure 3.112 Armenia. Emissions of pollutants into the atmospheric air by per km^2, t/km^2.

Source: www.scws.am/en.

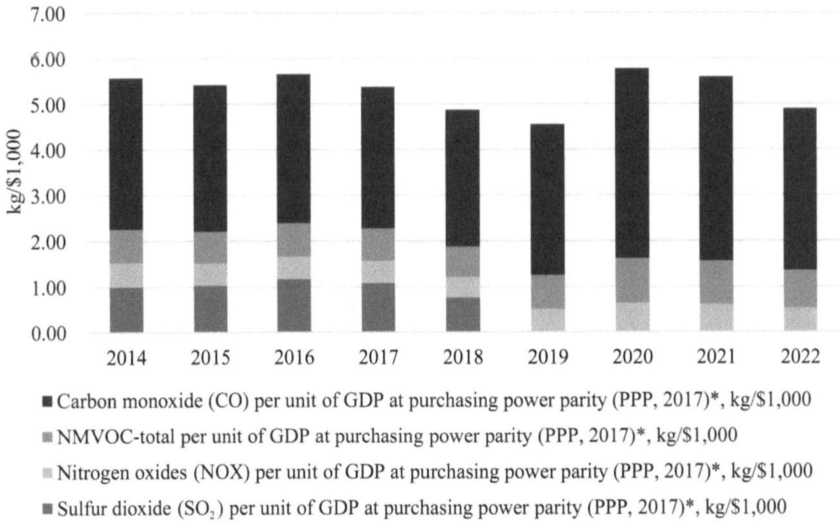

Figure 3.113 Armenia. Emissions of pollutants into the atmospheric air per unit of GDP at purchasing power parity (PPP. 2017), kg/USD 1,000.

Source: Statistical Committee Republic of Armenia, https://statbank.armstat.am/pxweb/en/ArmStatBank/?rxid=9c2c8a86-9f1e-4d5c-8de8-68d419ad463b.

Policymakers in Yerevan are focusing on addressing air pollution primarily through improvements in transportation infrastructure and management, as well as modernizing the vehicle fleet. Despite recent extensive development in Yerevan's road network and planned expansions, the city still lacks dedicated lanes for public transportation and other alternative modes like bicycling, necessitating a strategic approach to utilize roads more efficiently. Efforts to reduce the average age of vehicles are underway, beginning with the replacement of older public transportation vehicles with cleaner alternatives, including electric vehicles. The introduction of electric vehicles into the city's fleet is a key initiative in this regard. Additionally, policymakers have implemented voluntary agreements for industrial energy audits, offering incentives such as small subsidies to encourage companies to enhance their energy efficiency measures (IQAir, 2024).

Exposure of the population to fine particles ($PM_{2.5}$)

Air pollution levels in Yerevan exceed those in Moscow and Istanbul (Table 3.10; Figure 3.114). According to the *New York Times* (Popovich et al., 2019), pollution in Yerevan on the worst day in 2019 in terms of air quality reached 153 µg/m^3. In Giumri, Armenia's second city, the figure was 104 µg/m^3; in Vanadzor, 103µg/m^3; and Stepanakert, 75 µg/m^3. For regional comparison purposes, a $PM_{2.5}$ level of 75 µg/m^3 was recorded in Tbilisi. Although there is no data for Baku, a level of 84 µg/m^3 was registered in the nearby city of Shirvan.

On the international front, looking at major urban centers, $PM_{2.5}$ levels reached 41 µg/m^3 in Moscow, 91 µg/m^3 in Istanbul, 38 µg/m^3 in New York, 75 µg/m^3 in Paris, and 88 µg/m^3 in Berlin.

According to Martirosyana and Khachatrian (2020), motor vehicles are responsible for 68.3% of harmful substance emissions into the atmosphere in Armenia. Lori province stands out as the most polluted among all provinces in Armenia, primarily due to nonvehicular sources. Compared to Vayots Dzor, the province with the cleanest air in Armenia, Lori is significantly worse off, being 138 times more polluted. Furthermore, Lori is three times more polluted than the capital city of Yerevan. As of 2018, Armenia's per capita emissions were reported to be 38.4 kg.

Access to safe sources of drinking water

Despite the natural resources indicated in the natural resource base area, Armenia has faced serious challenges in providing clean and safe water to its citizens over the past two decades. In many parts of the country, water was available for only two to three hours a day, and pressure was low. Often, tap water was unsuitable for drinking and cooking.

The country's problems were familiar to many of its neighbors. When Armenia gained independence from the Soviet Union in 1991, it faced the mammoth task of transforming state-owned utility systems into modern, efficient agencies.

Table 3.10 Armenia: Ambient air quality in urban areas by cities in emissions and years.

		2014	2015	2016	2017	2018	2019	2020	2021	2022
Yerevan	Station 1. Dust. Annual average concentration. mg/m³	90	74	108	148	126	120	124	106	109
	Station 1. Sulfur dioxide. Annual average concentration. mg/m³	17	27	28	25	31	11	99	10	13
	Station 1. Nitrogen dioxide. Annual average concentration. mg/m³	11	14	19	19	20	14	27	19	23
	Station 1. Ground-level ozone. Annual average concentration. mg/m³	12	9	7	6	9	8	6	4	5
	Station 2. Dust. Annual average concentration. mg/m³	88	72	109	115	123	163	89	106	108
	Station 2. Sulfur dioxide. Annual average concentration. mg/m³	20	27	26	38	31	23	11	17	24
	Station 2. Nitrogen dioxide. Annual average concentration. mg/m³	15	13	18	21	19	14	22	16	19
	Station 2. Ground-level ozone. Annual average concentration. mg/m³	17	6	18	7	7	8	4	5	5
	Station 3. Dust. Annual average concentration. mg/m³	65	53	74	95	76	97	114	148	130
	Station 3. Sulfur dioxide. Annual average concentration. mg/m³	18	29	30	28	28	14	10	19	22
	Station 3. Nitrogen dioxide. Annual average concentration. mg/m³	18	15	22	21	12	14	42	34	36
	Station 3. Ground-level ozone. Annual average concentration. mg/m³	8	6	22	7	7	6	5	5	7
Vanadzor	Station 1. Dust. Annual average concentration. mg/m³	114	49	102	153	270	162	235	153	166
	Station 1. Sulfur dioxide. Annual average concentration. mg/m³	14	11	13	13	15	8	79	5	3
	Station 1. Nitrogen dioxide. Annual average concentration. mg/m³	18	14	13	11	12	8	7	4	6
	Station 1. Ground-level ozone. Annual average concentration. mg/m³	-	-	-	-	-	-	-	-	-
	Station 2. Dust. Annual average concentration. mg/m³	116	61	86	177	276	171	225	209	173
	Station 2. Sulphur dioxide. Annual average concentration. mg/m³	12	9	9	13	13	9	79	10	4
	Station 2. Nitrogen dioxide. Annual average concentration. mg/m³	18	13	12	11	10	9	6	6	6
	Station 2. Ground-level ozone. Annual average concentration. mg/m³	-	-	-	-	-	-	-	-	-
	Station 3. Dust. Annual average concentration. mg/m³	130	54	101	141	181	139	192	131	122
	Station 3. Sulfur dioxide. Annual average concentration. mg/m³	12	11	9	11	16	10	80	7	4
	Station 3. Nitrogen dioxide. Annual average concentration. mg/m³	14	11	9	9	8	7	5	4	5
	Station 3. Ground-level ozone. Annual average concentration. mg/m³	-	-	-	-	-	-	-	-	-
Alaverdi	Station 1. Dust. Annual average concentration. mg/m³	200	76	122	226	169	92	175	113	123
	Station 1. Sulfur dioxide. Annual average concentration. mg/m³	15	14	26	22	8	10	11	9	9

(*Continued*)

Table 3.10 (Continued)

	2014	2015	2016	2017	2018	2019	2020	2021	2022
Station 1. Nitrogen dioxide. Annual average concentration. mg/m^3	17	13	10	16	7	7	5	4	6
Station 1. Ground-level ozone. Annual average concentration. mg/m^3	-	-	-	-	-	-	-	-	-
Station 2. Dust. Annual average concentration. mg/m^3	249	63	109	304	369	212	380	242	123
Station 2. Sulfur dioxide. Annual average concentration. mg/m^3	13	15	17	14	16	12	13	11	5
Station 2. Nitrogen dioxide. Annual average concentration. mg/m^3	9	8	8	10	7	8	3	4	4
Station 2. Ground-level ozone. Annual average concentration. mg/m^3	-	-	-	-	-	-	-	-	-
Station 3. Dust. Annual average concentration. mg/m^3	-	-	-	-	-	-	15	135	112
Station 3. Sulfur dioxide. Annual average concentration. mg/m^3	20	26	22	32	34	15	12	13	9
Station 3. Nitrogen dioxide. Annual average concentration. mg/m^3	9	9	8	7	6	6	5	4	5
Station 3. Ground-level ozone. Annual average concentration. mg/m^3	-	-	-	-	-	-	-	-	-

Source: Statistical Committee of the Republic of Armenia, https://statbank.armstat.am/pxweb/en/ArmStatBank/ArmStatBank__8%20Environment__(A)%20Emissions%20of%20pollutants%20into%20the%20atmospheric%20air/EE-a2.px/?rxid=9c2c8a86-9f1e-4d5c-8de8-68d419ad463b.

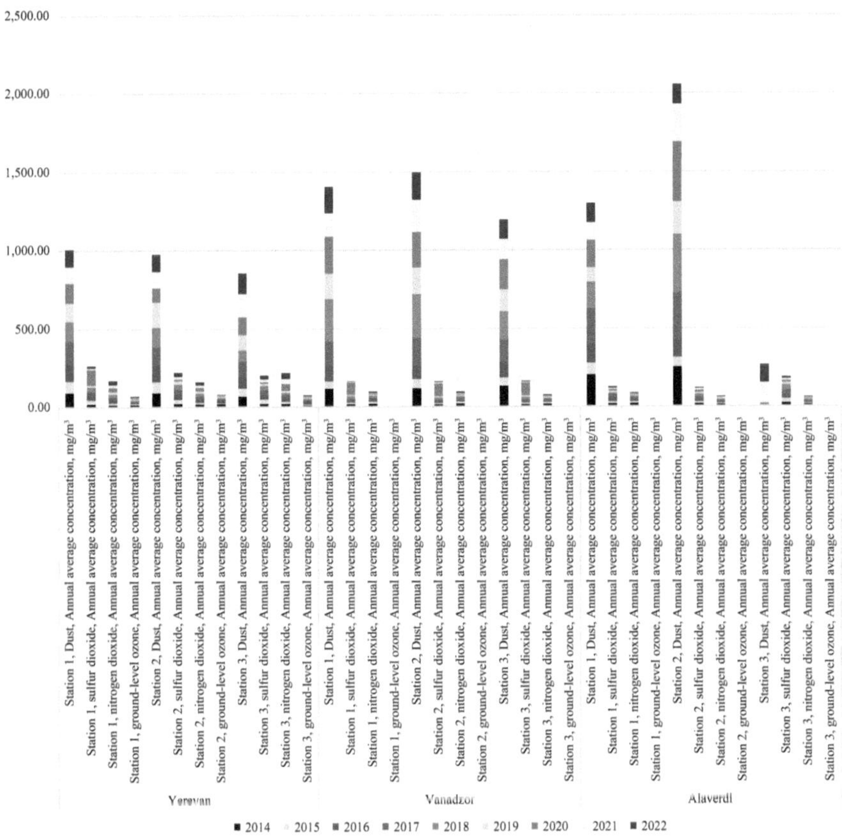

Figure 3.114 Armenia. Emissions of pollutants into the atmospheric air by per unit of GDP at purchasing power parity (PPP. 2017)*. kg/USD 1,000. **GDP is on the basis of purchasing power parity (PPP) in constant 2017 international dollars (http://data.worldbank.org/indicator/NY.GDP.MKTP.PP.KD).

Source: https://statbank.armstat.am/pxweb/en/ArmStatBank/ArmStatBank__8%20Environment__(A)%20Emissions%20of%20pollutants%20into%20the%20atmospheric%20air/EE-a1.px/table/tableViewLayout2/?rxid=9c2c8a86-9f1e-4d5c-8de8-68d419ad463b.

This included the national water and sewerage company and local water agencies throughout the country.

In the 1990s, approximately 60–80% of the water flowing through the system was lost due to leaks or other issues. This figure was more than four times higher than the norm observed in most Western European cities at that time.

Residents of the capital Yerevan and approximately 95% of the urban population in the rest of the country were connected to a centralized Soviet-era water supply system. However, this old system later deteriorated due to neglect and inadequate maintenance (see Figure 3.115). In the years following independence, only

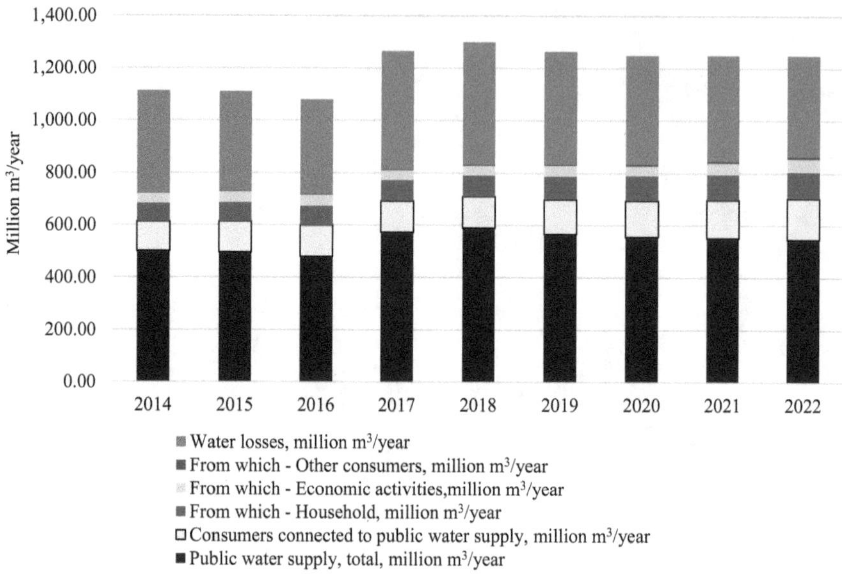

Figure 3.115 Armenia. Public water supply by purpose and years.

Source: www.scws.am/en.

about 15% of the population had continuous access to water (Asian Development Bank, 2014).

Government reforms implemented in the early 2000s enabled the country's main water agency, the Armenia Water and Sewerage Company, to collaborate with private companies aimed at enhancing efficiency and improving service quality (Figure 3.116).

Financial support in 2007, along with technical expertise, was provided through a water supply and sanitation sector project backed by a USD 36 million loan from the Asian Development Bank (ADB). In April 2012, the ADB approved an additional loan of USD 40 million. This funding was earmarked for the construction of 600 km of new pipeline networks to connect an additional 110,000 households, as well as for the rehabilitation of pumping stations and wastewater treatment plants (Asian Development Bank, 2014).

Although Armenia boasts relatively abundant water resources and is classified as a "moderately secure" country with freshwater resources, equal access to drinking water and sanitation remains a problem for many rural communities in Armenia. It is worth noting that as of January 1, 2017, water supply and sanitation services (wastewater treatment) are managed by CJSC "Veolia Djur." About 579 of the 1,002 rural settlements do not have centralized water supply and sanitation services, which is not covered by water supply companies. Local village authorities are responsible for the water supply of these settlements. The issue of ensuring equal access to drinking water and sanitation services was the main topic of

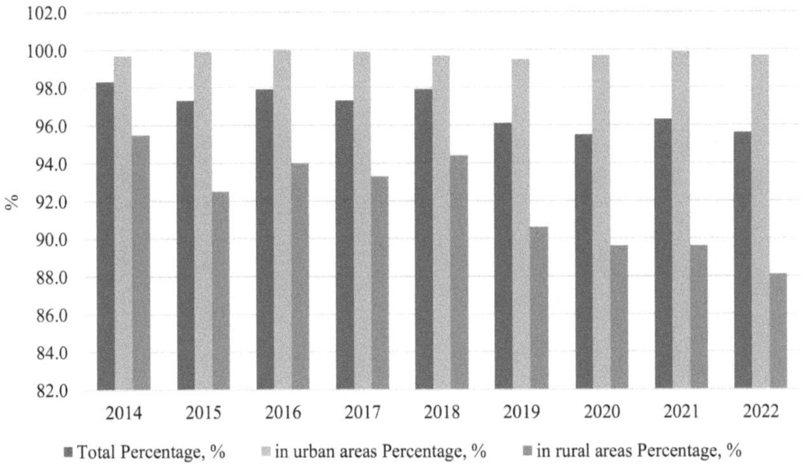

Figure 3.116 Armenia. Population connected to public water supply by indicators and years.

Source: www.statbank.armstat.am.

discussion at the meeting titled. "Implementation of the UNECE/WHO Protocol on Water and Health in Armenia, Georgia and Moldova." The event was held on October 25, 2023 (Armenian National Platform, 2023).

Population connected to the sewage system

Data from the United Nations Children's Emergency Fund (UNICEF, 2022) shows that nearly 4,400 students (1%) and nearly 630 teachers (1.6%) in 70 schools (5%) do not have access to water (both potable/drinking and handwashing) in the 2021–2022 academic year. In addition, nearly 3,600 students (0.9%) and 517 teachers (1.3%) in more than 60 schools do not have access to sanitation and water.

According to the Statistical Committee of Armenia (2022), in the 2021–2022 academic year, 135 of Armenia's 1,354 public schools, with more than 12,500 students and about 1,580 teachers, lacked sanitation.

Due to the scarcity of wastewater treatment plants in Armenia, most wastewater is not treated. As a result, domestic wastewater seeps into nearby streams and surface water resources, polluting them (Figure 3.117).

As of 2021, according to the Water Committee of the Ministry of Territorial Management and Infrastructure (Ministry for the Environment, 2021), only around 8% of the total volume of municipal wastewater is mechanically cleaned, and only approximately 0.13% of the total volume of wastewater has undergone biological treatment (Figure 3.118).

A study conducted by the European Bank for Reconstruction and Development (EVN Report, 2023) between October 2018 and August 2019 found that poor water quality in the lower areas of the Ahuryan River in the Shirak region is attributed to the discharge of domestic wastewater from nearby municipalities.

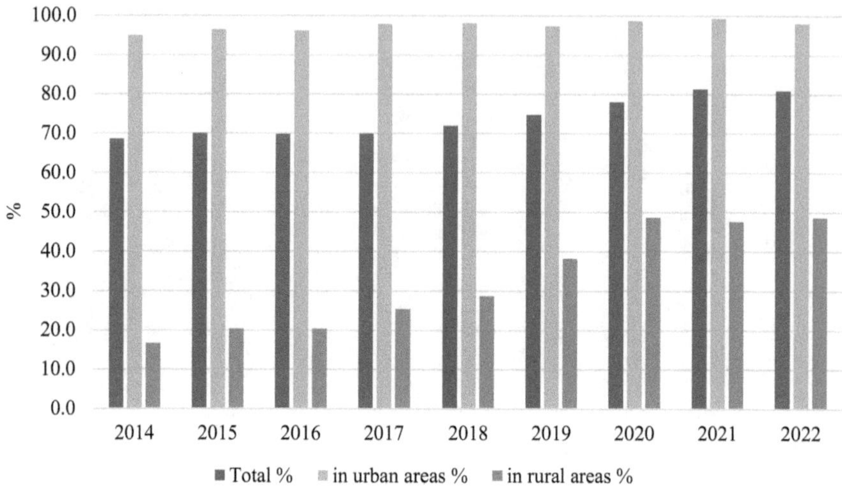

Figure 3.117 Armenia. Population connected to wastewater treatment by indicators and years.

Source: www.statbank.armstat.am.

Notes: Percentage of residents connected to a wastewater collecting system in the total number of households. Only mechanical (primary) treatment is available.

Figure 3.118 Armenia. Wastewater treatment facilities by indicators and years (million m^3/year).

Source: www. statbank.armstat.am.

Azerbaijan

Air pollution

The main sources of air pollution in Azerbaijan are industrial facilities and motor vehicles. According to Mammadova (2015), vehicles alone account for up to 80% of gaseous substances responsible for air pollution. Azerbaijan has over 86,000 motor vehicles, including 70,000 trucks and 20,000 buses. A significant proportion (90%) of these vehicles have been in use for more than five years, contributing to increased air pollution levels. Approximately 500,000 tons of emissions are released into the air annually from motor transport (Yolchiyeva et al., 2020). Technical issues affect about 60% of cars and 25% of trucks, with many vehicles failing to meet environmental standards (Mammadova & Rostamnia, 2022).

Incomplete combustion of fuel is another significant contributor to pollution, with 85% of fuel emissions released into the air as particulate matter. These emissions not only impact air quality but also contribute to increased morbidity and reduce resilience to the effects of climate change. (Table 3.11).

Because economic growth in Azerbaijan was primarily driven by the expansion of the oil and gas industry and transportation infrastructure in Baku and Sumgayit, environmental concerns often took a backseat. The sharp decline in oil prices in 2020 has sparked discussions about the sustainability of an economic model heavily reliant on extraction and heavy industry. Industrialization has already had detrimental effects on Azerbaijan, leading to decreased agricultural productivity (Table 3.12) and the discharge of a significant portion of waste from oil extraction and refining directly into the Caspian Sea (UNSDCF, 2020).

Azerbaijan, with a population of 10.1 million, produces approximately 5.5 tons of CO_2 per person annually (refer to Table 3.12 and Table 3.13). This places Azerbaijan 76th out of 191 countries in terms of per capita emissions (Boyle, 2024).

Table 3.11 Azerbaijan: Total emissions from stationary sources by ingredients, in thousand tons.

	2014	*2015*	*2016*	*2017*	*2018*	*2019*	*2020*	*2021*	*2022*
Total. thousand tons	189.3	178.0	187.6	184.1	170.9	177.0	146.7	156.7	158.4
of which:									
Sulfur dioxide	1.6	1.5	8.5	4.9	0.7	0.7	1.1	2.2	1.0
Nitrogen oxides	19.5	17.6	18.2	22.1	20.8	22.2	21.0	21.4	22.1
Carbon monoxide	32.2	31.9	24.3	25.5	15.2	16.2	17.3	19.5	26.3
NMVOC	9.6	12.9	9.4	10.2	10.6	12.5	10.4	11.5	12.1
Ammonia	0.1	0.02	0.02	0.1	0.2	0.03	0.01	0.01	0.04
Hydrocarbons	116.4	116.9	119.9	113.9	115.1	116.8	92.0	97.0	92.1

Source: www.stat.gov.az.

Table 3.12 Azerbaijan: Emissions of the main pollutants per capita, total. kg/capita.

	2014	*2015*	*2016*	*2017*	*2018*	*2019*	*2020*	*2021*	*2022*
Emissions of the main pollutants per capita, total. kg/capita of which:	19.9	18.4	19.2	18.7	17.2	17.7	14.5	15.5	15.7
Sulfur dioxide	0.2	0.2	0.9	0.5	0.1	0.1	0.1	0.2	0.1
Nitrogen oxides	2.0	1.8	1.9	2.2	2.1	2.2	2.1	2.4	2.2
Carbon monoxide	3.4	3.3	2.5	2.6	1.5	1.6	1.7	1.9	2.6
NMVOC	1.0	1.3	1.0	1.0	1.1	1.2	1.0	1.1	1.2
Ammonia	0.01	0.002	0.002	0.01	0.02	0.003	0.001	0.001	0.004
Hydrocarbons	12.2	12.1	12.3	11.6	11.6	11.7	9.1	9.6	9.1

Source: www.stat.gov.az.

As much as 62% of Azerbaijan's emissions are attributed to carbon dioxide (CO_2), while methane (CH_4) contributes 28.4% and nitrous oxide (N_2O) accounts for 8.7% of total greenhouse gas emissions. Among the sectors contributing to energy-related emissions, the electricity/heat industry stands out, generating 13.7 million tons of greenhouse gases, which represents 24.7% of Azerbaijan's total emissions. Following closely are fugitive emissions and construction, which emit 8.48 million tons and 7.95 million tons of greenhouse gases, respectively (Boyle, 2024).

In 2020, Azerbaijan experienced a significant economic downturn, with its GDP declining by 11.4% compared to the previous year, shrinking from USD 48.2 billion to

Table 3.13 Azerbaijan: Emissions of the main pollutants per area, total. kg/km².

	2014	*2015*	*2016*	*2017*	*2018*	*2019*	*2020*	*2021*	*2022*
Emissions of the main pollutants per area, total. kg/km² of which:	2185.9	2055.4	2166.3	2125.9	1973.4	2043.9	1694.0	1809.5	1829.1
Sulfur dioxide	18.5	17.3	98.2	56.6	8.1	8.1	12.7	25.4	11.5
Nitrogen oxides	225.2	203.2	210.2	255.2	240.2	256.4	242.5	247.1	255.2
Carbon monoxide	371.8	368.4	280.6	294.5	175.5	187.1	199.8	225.2	303.7
NMVOC	110.9	149.0	108.5	117.8	122.4	144.3	120.1	132.8	139.7
Ammonia	1.2	0.2	0.2	1.2	2.3	0.3	0.1	0.1	0.5
Hydrocarbons	1344.1	1349.9	1384.5	1315.2	1329.1	1348.7	1063.5	1120.1	1063.5

Source: www.stat.gov.az.

Table 3.14 Azerbaijan: Emissions of the main pollutants per unit of GDP*, total. kg/USD 1,000.

	2014	*2015*	*2016*	*2017*	*2018*	*2019*	*2020*	*2021*	*2022*
Emissions of the main pollutants per unit of GDP*, total. kg/USD 1,000	1.3	1.2	1.4	1.3	1.2	1.2	1.1	1.1	1.0
of which:									
Sulfur dioxide	0.01	0.01	0.06	0.04	0.005	0.005	0.010	0.02	0.01
Nitrogen oxides	0.1	0.1	0.1	0.2	0.1	0.2	0.2	0.1	0.10
Carbon monoxide	0.2	0.2	0.2	0.2	0.1	0.1	0.1	0.1	0.20
NMVOC	0.1	0.1	0.1	0.1	0.1	0.1	0.1	0.1	0.10
Ammonia	0.001	0.0001	0.0001	0.001	0.001	0.0002	0.0001	0.0001	0.0003
Hydrocarbons	0.8	0.8	0.9	0.8	0.8	0.8	0.7	0.7	0.6

Source: www.stat.gov.az.

* By purchasing power parity prices of 2017.

USD 42.7 billion. Despite this economic contraction, carbon dioxide (CO_2) emissions decreased by 2.1% during the same period. Over the decade from 2010 to 2020, Azerbaijan's GDP declined by 19.3%, while emissions increased by 24.9% (Table 3.14).

For comparison, the compound annual growth rate (CAGR) of GDP in Azerbaijan over the past ten years was -2.1%, and the CAGR of greenhouse gas emissions was 2.2% (Boyle, 2024).

In 2022, the volume of air pollutant emissions from stationary sources and motor vehicles (Figure 3.119) compared to 2021 increased by 50.4 thousand tons and generally made 930.6 thousand tons, of which 83% or 772.2 thousand tons were per the share of harmful emissions from motor vehicles. The volume of emissions of harmful substances from motor vehicles increased by 6.7% and the volume of emissions from stationary sources by 1.1%. The volume of emissions of harmful substances from stationary sources in Baku, the industrial center, decreased by 3.9 thousand tons, in Mingechevir by 1.9 thousand tons, while in Sumgayit, it increased by 1.7 thousand tons.

As a result of preventive measures, 2022, 67% of harmful substances generated from stationary sources were captured and disposed by cleaning devices. During the year for a decreasing quantity of emissions of harmful substances into the atmosphere, 108.7 thousand tons of emissions of harmful substances into the air basin were prevented due to the improvement of technological processes in industrial enterprises and the increasing efficiency of existing cleaning devices. Of the total

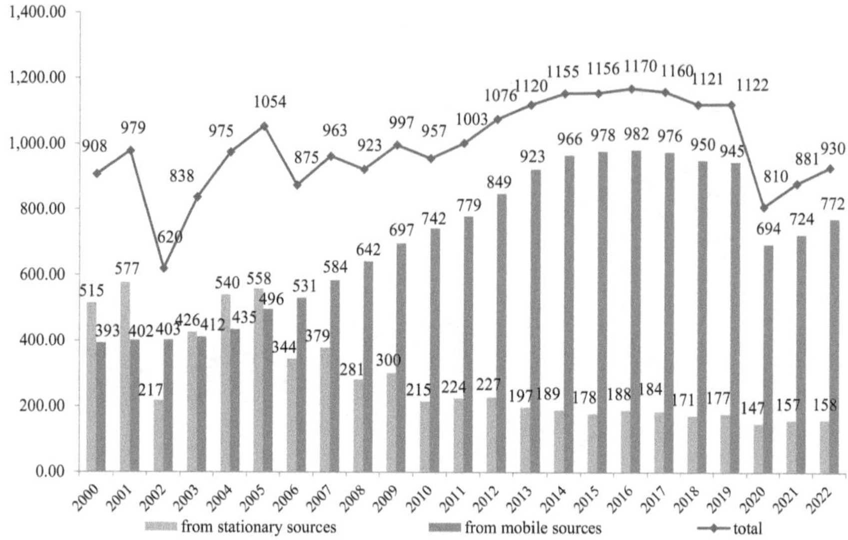

Figure 3.119 Azerbaijan. Compositions of air pollutant emissions from motor vehicles, in thousand tons.

Source: www.stat.gov.az.

harmful emissions released into the atmosphere, 59.5% were carbon oxides, 25.0% were carbohydrates, 12.0% were nitrogen oxide, 0.1% were sulfur anhydrite, and the rest were other pollutants (The State Statistical Committee of the Republic Azerbaijan, 2023).

Exposure of the population to fine particles ($PM_{2.5}$)

Currently, welfare costs associated with air pollution (Table 3.15) by fine particles ($PM_{2.5}$) represent about 5% of the GDP equivalent in Azerbaijan, compared to 3.8% on average in the EU. The mean population exposure to $PM_{2.5}$ is two times higher than the WHO guideline: 21 vs. 10 $\mu g/m^3$ (EU4Environment, 2021a).

The performance of reducing $PM_{2.5}$ and methane emissions, which cause risks to the population's health, will need to be significantly improved for Azerbaijan to ensure social inclusion while pursuing green growth (GGGI Technical Report, 2023).

Access to safe sources of drinking water

Azerbaijan is experiencing water stress conditions with an annual water (Table 3.16) exploitation index of greater than 40%. The annual average of the dependency ratio of Azerbaijan to external inflow is also estimated to be relatively

Table 3.15 Azerbaijan: Ambient air quality*.

	2014	*2015*	*2016*	*2017*	*2018*	*2019*	*2020*	*2021*	*2022*
Average annual concentration of NO_2 by towns. mkg/m^3									
Baku	60	60	50	60	70	70	56	48	44
Ganja	30	30	30	30	30	30	...	41	40
Sumgayit	80	90	90	90	80	70	...	45	45
Average annual concentration of SO_2 by towns. mkg/m^3									
Baku	11	14	19	26	32	33	28	23	32
Ganja	38	38	37	38	37	37	...	35	35
Sumgayit	25	27	26	27	28	26	...	25	26
Average annual concentration of CO by towns. mkg/m^3									
Baku	3,000	2,300	2,200	2,000	2,200	2,300	...	1,531	1,735
Ganja	X	x	x	x	x	x	x	1,074	1,562
Sumgayit	X	x	x	x	x	x	x	1,136	1,326
Average annual concentration of PM_{10} disperse dust from automatic station. mkg/m^3									
Baku	X	x	x	44	44	49	49	41	44
Average annual concentration of $PM_{2.5}$ disperse dust from automatic station. mkg/m^3									
Baku	X	x	x	x	x	x	x	27	28
Ganja	X	x	x	x	x	x	x	28	26
Sumgayit	X	x	x	x	x	x	x	22	21

Source: www.stat.gov.az.

* According to the data of the Ministry of Ecology and Natural Resources.

high (63%). On average, every year, around 10,000 million m^3 of water is used to meet the water demand of different economic sectors, of which 3% is used for households from the water supply system (ENI SEIS II East, 2019a).

Agriculture is the most water-demanding sector (Table 3.17; Table 3.18), accounting for 90% of total water withdrawals annually. Water abstraction increased by 10.3% between 2000 and 2017, while renewable freshwater resources declined by 20% during the same period (ENI SEIS II East, 2019a).

According to the Aqueduct Projected Water Stress Country Rankings, Azerbaijan is among the countries with an "exceptionally high" water stress ranking in the 2020, 2030, and 2040 projections (World Resources Institute, 2015).

Table 3.16 Azerbaijan: Freshwater abstracted (million m^3).

	2014	*2015*	*2016*	*2017*	*2018*	*2019*	*2020*	*2021*	*2022*
Freshwater abstracted including:	11,592	11,689	11,878	12,120	12,167	12,590	12,203	12,968	13,028
Fresh surface water	9,773	9,673	9,803	10,054	10,072	10,224	9,808	10,633	10,672
Fresh groundwater	1,819	2,016	2,075	2,066	2,095	2,366	2,395	2,335	2,356

Source: www.stat.gov.az.

Table 3.17 Azerbaijan: Distribution of freshwater abstracted from natural sources by activity types (million m³).

	2014	*2015*	*2016*	*2017*	*2018*	*2019*	*2020*	*2021*	*2022*
water supply industry	461	426	392	371	401	398	420	395	394
Agriculture. forestry and fishing	10,418	10,654	10,820	11,161	11,237	11,614	11,207	11,962	11,980
Manufacturing	10	10	16	10	8	11	13	3	5
Electricity industry	662	571	626	553	499	556	553	595	641
Other economic activities	41	28	24	25	22	11	10	13	8
Losses during transport	4,008	3,718	3,680	3,627	3,643	3,755	3,267	3,216	3,313
Total freshwater use	7,584	7,971	8,198	8,493	8,524	8,835	8,936	9,752	9,715

Source: www.stat.gov.az.

Population connected to the sewage system

In Baku, the capital's wastewater treatment sector serves 72% of the population (UNECE, 2019). However, only 50% of the wastewater processed by the system is adequately treated. Of the treated water, 90% undergoes only mechanical treatment, while a mere 10% receives secondary biological treatment (UNECE, 2019). In 2017, 32.7% of Azerbaijan's population was connected to wastewater collection systems (STAT, 2019), with most of this coverage achieved in urban areas (UNECE, 2019). Consequently, further improvements are needed to enhance wastewater treatment and extend coverage (Table 3.19; Table 3.20).

According to Ahmadov (2020), wastewater treatment plants are available in only 16 cities and regions, and most of these plants are not fully efficient. In many

Table 3.18 Azerbaijan: Including by activity types (million m³).

	2014	*2015*	*2016*	*2017*	*2018*	*2019*	*2020*	*2021*	*2022*
Households	244	239	264	259	272	277	287	279	285
Agriculture. forestry and fishing	5,928	6,438	6,336	6,561	6,712	7,018	7,235	7,586	7,701
Manufacturing	42	36	47	26	36	39	40	39	34
Electricity industry	1,284	1,153	1,465	1,574	1,437	1,437	1,341	1,811	1,648
Other economic activities	86	105	86	73	67	64	33	37	47

Source: www.stat.gov.az.

Table 3.19 Azerbaijan: Discharge of sewage waters (million m³).

	2014	*2015*	*2016*	*2017*	*2018*	*2019*	*2020*	*2021*	*2022*
Discharge of sewage waters	5,347	5,573	5,669	5,449	5,143	4,863	4,759	5,237	5,082
of which:									
Untreated waste water	257	298	312	319	266	212	221	225	203
Incomplete treated water	8	7	7	6	6	6	3	4	4

Source: www.stat.gov.az.

cases, the quality of water supplied to the population does not meet the required standards. Although the Azerbaijani government has adopted a program to build water supply and wastewater treatment systems in more than 60 cities, local authorities still need to collaborate with donors to address these problems effectively (Ahmadov, 2020).

Table 3.20 Azerbaijan: Main indicators characterizing protection of water resources and their rational use* (million m³).

	2014	*2015*	*2016*	*2017*	*2018*	*2019*	*2020*	*2021*	*2022*
Water abstraction from natural water resources – total	12,123	12,285	12,504	12,781	12,847	13,227	12,961	13,743	13,841
Per capita. m³	1,271	1,289	1,297	1,313	1,308	1,335	1,300	1,372	1,371
Water consumption – total	8,115	8,567	8,824	9,154	9,205	9,472	9,693	10,526	10,528
of which:									
domestic and drinking purposes	313	323	308	291	306	312	319	321	329
Industrial needs	2,144	2,117	2,108	2,224	2,111	2,070	2,073	2,566	2,449
of which drinking water	49	46	43	31	44	42	45	52	90
Irrigation and agriculture supply	55,72	6,057	6,342	6,570	6,722	7,038	7,252	7,575	7,692
Volume of recycled and consequently used water	2,469	2,441	2,346	2,398	2,345	2,358	2,243	2,795	2,653
in percent to total water consumption for industrial needs	54	54	53	52	53	53	52	52	52
Water losses during transportation	4,008	3,718	3,680	3,627	3,642	3,755	3,268	3,217	3,314
Discharge of sewage waters	5,358	5,575	5,673	5,453	5,147	4,863	4,759	5,237	5,083
of which untreated waste water	265	305	319	326	272	218	225	229	208

Source: www.stat.gov.az.

* On the basis of the data of the Joint Open Company of Irrigation and Water Industry

Belarus

Air pollution

By 2020, agriculture, forestry, and fishing accounted for the largest share of emissions (34.2%), followed by manufacturing (33.8%) and electricity generation (21.4%). Petroleum refining represented the largest share within the manufacturing industry (43.1%). Although emissions from stationary sources constitute about one-third of total emissions (Table 3.21), their adverse effects are significant due to the potential release of hazardous compounds and those with long-term impacts (Dziarzhynskaya et al., 2022).

In 2020, mobile sources accounted for 61.5% of gross emissions from all sources in the Republic of Belarus (National Statistical Committee of the Republic of Belarus, 2022). Most of these emissions originate from the city of Minsk and the Minsk and Grodno regions (Medvedev, 2021). The emissions from mobile sources consistently include carbon monoxide, hydrocarbons, nitrogen oxides, particulate matter, and sulfur oxides. The distribution and dispersion of these emissions are influenced by the area's natural, climatic, and meteorological characteristics. However, predicting the real impact of mobile source emissions on public health is challenging due to the variable number of emission sources and the duration of their operation.

Exposure of the population to fine particles ($PM_{2.5}$)

Belarus has an air quality value of 15.5 $PM_{2.5}$, placing it 92nd out of 124 on the global list of countries with the worst air quality.

The most polluted atmosphere in Belarus is over Minsk. According to the analysis, the average concentration of NO_2 in Belarus is relatively low, 0.24×10^{-4} mol/m^2. In general, the lowest concentrations of NO_2 are located in the north of Belarus. Several hotspots are significantly higher, including in the capital's urban area, Minsk, where NO_2 values exceed 0.50×10^{-4} mol/m^2, more than double the average for the country (Abrahamyan et al., 2023).

Table 3.21 Belarus: Emission of harmful pollutants into the air from stationary sources in CIS 1) (thousand tons).

	Air pollutant emissions – total	*including:*				
		Particulates	*Gaseous and liquid matters*	*of which:*		
				sulfuric anhydride (SO_2)	*nitrogen oxides (NO_2)*	*carbon oxide (CO)*
2020	451	24	427	56	45	83
2021	465	26	439	45	47	81

Source: www.stat.gov.az.

Access to safe drinking water sources

Belarus has a high level of per capita water availability compared to the global average and less intensive industrial activity compared to the EU. Its biggest challenge is to improve the efficient use of water by end users, especially households and water-intensive industries such as food processing (Deraviaha & Dubianok, 2020). Agriculture accounts for a smaller share of water use in Belarus (36%) than the global average (69%), but a larger share than the European average (25%). While industry uses a larger share of water in Belarus (25%) than the global average (19%), it uses less than half as much as in Europe (54%). Households use the most water in Belarus (39%), a much higher share of water consumption than the European and global averages (21% and 12%, respectively). Compared to the country's vast renewable freshwater resources and other European countries, annual water consumption rates in Belarus are low. Freshwater abstraction accounts for only 4.8% of total available freshwater resources, well below the 25% threshold that defines the initial water deficit. In 2016, water abstraction amounted to 1.4 billion m^3, with 365 million m^3 coming from surface sources and 819 million m^3 from underground sources (Minpriroda, 2018).

Population connected to the sewage system

The United Nations' report on water shows that 95% of the population in Belarus has access to a safe drinking water source, 86% of the country has a safe sewage treatment plant, and 81% of the country has access to safe sanitation services (United Nations, 2022). While these numbers may seem relatively high, they are critically low compared to Western European countries such as Poland, where 100% of the population has access to drinking water and 93% of the country has access to sanitation services. In June of 2020 (World Bank Blogs, 2020), following the completion of the subsidized "Clean Water Program," the number of people that benefited from quality access and treatment of water rose from 324,000 in 2019 to a staggering 611,766 people at the time of the project's completion. Not only did more people benefit from increased water quality and treatment, 47,520 individuals gained access to much-improved sanitation services through 32 newly constructed utility centers and 154 km of piping that was replaced.

Georgia

Air pollution

According to the World Health Organization (WHO) database, in just 2019, 5,220 people were estimated to have died due to air pollution in Georgia. In other words, according to such estimates, there are 130.6 ambient air pollution-related fatalities per 100,000 Georgians annually—a significantly higher number than most Western European countries, and even higher than Armenia and Azerbaijan in the region (ISET Policy Brief Series, 2023). Pollutants can be emitted by both natural and

Table 3.22 Georgia: Main pollutants (1,000 t/year).

	2014	*2015*	*2016*	*2017*	*2018*	*2019*	*2020*	*2021*
Sulphur dioxide (SO_2) Of which:								
from stationary sources	4.9	4.7	5.2	5.8	5.4	5.0	4.5	5.5
from mobile sources	0.3	0.3	0.3	0.1	0.1	0.1	0.1	0.1
Nitrogen oxides (NO_X). Of which:								
from stationary sources	18.5	19.1	18.0	17.9	17.5	18.1	18.7	18.5
from mobile sources	21.4	23.9	26.1	24.1	22.4	20.5	19.3	20.5
Non-methane volatile organic compounds (NMVOC). Of which:								
from stationary sources	34.1	31.7	32.0	31.3	29.6	29.2	28.5	29.5
from mobile sources	9.2	9.9	11.3	10.8	10.5	10.4	10.1	10.8
Ammonia (NH_3), total. Of which:								
from stationary sources	33.5	37.0	35.6	33.6	32.4	31.9	33.5	33.1
from mobile sources	0.4	0.5	0.7	0.6	0.6	0.6	0.6	0.7
Carbon monoxide (CO). Of which:								
from stationary sources	84.7	73.2	71.7	68.6	53.1	49.6	46.2	49.1
from mobile sources	52.7	57.3	68.3	64.0	60.7	60.4	57.5	62.2

Source: www.geostat.ge/en.

anthropogenic sources. Some of the main categories included in the latter are industry, transportation, energy production, waste, and agriculture (Table 3.22).

In 2020, nitrogen dioxide concentrations exceeding the norm were registered at 12 of 25 indicative monitoring points in Tbilisi. In 8 of these cases, the concentration exceeded the norm by 50% or more. Relatively better results were obtained in 2021, when nitrogen dioxide concentrations exceeded the norm at 9 points out of 25.

According to a 2019 report from the Office of the Public Defender, in 2016 alone, the government had spent GEL 120,050,566 (USD 59,139,562) to cover medical costs of treating diseases related to air pollutants (NO_2, SO_2, CO, O_3, PM_{10}, and $PM_{2.5}$). A World Bank report from 2020 further estimates that the medical burden stemming from ambient and indoor air pollution equals USD 560 million, comprising 3% of Georgia's GDP in 2018 (Maghedani, 2022).

Exposure of the population to fine particles ($PM_{2.5}$)

Considering that the typical Georgian citizen was exposed to 15 μg/m³ of $PM_{2.5}$ in 2015 (measured in mean annual concentration), Georgian air quality is still poor (Table 3.23). With exposure at even 10 μg/m³ of $PM_{2.}$5, the WHO has established, with a 95% confidence rate, the connection between these levels and mortality caused by heart and lung diseases. At the lowest level recorded in 2009 (11 μg/m³ of $PM_{2.5}$), Georgia still exceeded the WHO air quality guideline (Maghedani, 2022).

In addition to industry, transportation—cars, in particular—is a major contributor to air pollution in Belarus. Cars account for 43% of nitrogen oxide emissions.

Table 3.23 Georgia: Amount of suspended particles (1,000 t/year).

	2014	*2015*	*2016*	*2017*	*2018*	*2019*	*2020*	*2021*
Total suspended particulates (TSP). total	25.7	25.8	25.5	25.4	21.6	21.8	20.7	20.4
Of which:								
from stationary sources	24.7	24.7	24.3	24.5	20.8	21.0	19.9	19.6
from mobile sources	1.0	1.1	1.2	0.9	0.8	0.8	0.8	0.8
Patriculate matters (PM_{10}). total	18.7	17.2	17.0	16.3	13.4	12.8	12.0	12.1
Of which:								
from stationary sources	17.8	16.2	15.9	15.2	12.4	11.8	11.0	11.6
from mobile sources	0.9	1.0	1.1	1.0	1.0	1.0	1.0	0.5
Patriculate matters ($PM_{2.5}$). total	16.3	14.4	14.2	13.8	11.0	10.2	9.6	9.6
Of which:								
from stationary sources	15.6	13.6	13.3	12.6	9.8	9.1	8.5	8.9
from mobile sources	0.7	0.8	0.9	1.2	1.2	1.1	1.1	0.7

Source: www.geostat.ge/en.

Underdeveloped public transportation contributes to increased emissions from the transportation sector, with both intercity and intracity routes remaining problematic. As a result, even those who would use public transportation whenever possible are compelled to buy private cars. Due to economic difficulties, most people cannot afford a new vehicle—83% of registered cars (1.47 million) are 10 years old or older, and 23% are more than 30 years old (Maghedani, 2022).

Access to safe drinking water sources

Georgia has been improving its water supply network during recent years. About 40.5% of the total population was not connected to the water supply in 2015, but this had decreased by 6.3% in 2018. Although Georgia is a non-water-stressed country, about 34.2% of the population in Georgia were not connected to the public water supply in 2018 and had to manage their water demand by self-supply (Table 3.24). In addition, the water supply network is in poor condition, causing the network to lose 66.4% of the total water losses in the network (ENI SEIS II East, 2019b).

The discrepancy between the totals and the sum in some cases can be explained by using rounded data.

In Georgian households even a connection to the water supply system does not guarantee continued access to drinking water. According to the United Water Supply Company of Georgia (UWSCG), several households connected to the water supply system do not yet have constantly available drinking water with the exceptions of Tbilisi, and the Racha-Lechkhumi and Kvemo-Svaneti regions (ISET, 2021).

Population connected to the sewage system

More than one-third of wastewater discharged into water bodies in Georgia is inadequately treated. Therefore, water quality depends largely on the type of wastewater discharged and how well it is treated. Surface water abstraction for agriculture

Table 3.24 Georgia: Household water use per capita.

	Unit	*2015*	*2016*	*2017*	*2018*	*2019*	*2020*	*2021*	*2022*
Households supplied by water supply industry									
Water supplied to households by water supply industry*	million m³	207.6	213.7	223.4	221.9	223.4	229.2	210.1	208.0
Population connected to water supply industry	million	2.22	2.33	2.44	2.45	2.52	2.57	2.63	2.67
Water use per capita (water supply industry)*	m³	93.5	91.8	91.4	90.6	88.8	89.2	79.9	77.8
Households supplied by self-supply**									
Population not connected to water supply industry (self-supply)	million	1.51	1.40	1.29	1.27	1.20	1.16	1.06	1.06
Estimated water use by households supplied by self-supply per capita***	m³	93.5	91.8	91.4	90.6	88.8	89.2	79.9	77.8
Water use in the country (self supply)	million m³	141.2	128.4	117.5	115.5	106.5	103.5	84.5	82.8
Total household water use (water supply industry and self-supply)									
Total water use by households*	million m³	348.8	342.1	340.9	337.4	329.9	332.6	294.6	290.8
Total population	million	3.73	3.73	3.73	3.72	3.72	3.73	3.69	3.74
Total household water use (water supply industry and self-supply) per capita*	m³	93.5	91.8	91.4	90.6	88.8	89.2	79.9	77.8

Source: www. geostat.ge/en.

* Does not include volume of water used by enterprise employees for personal needs outside the households.

** Includes households supplied by municipalities as well.

*** Estimated based on an average per capita water use by households supplied by the water supply industry.

has more than doubled since 2003. Higher concentrations of agriculture-related pollutants have been recorded near agricultural areas as a result of leaching (European Environment Agency, 2020)

The share of Georgians connected to public water and sewage systems has been steadily increasing. However, as of 2019, one-third of the population still had no

Table 3.25 Georgia: Population connected to wastewater treatment.

	Unit	*2015*	*2016*	*2017*	*2018*	*2019*	*2020*	*2021*	*2022*
Total population of Georgia	million	3.73	3.73	3.73	3.72	3.72	3.73	3.69	3.74
Population connected to water supply industry	million	2.22	2.33	2.44	2.45	2.52	2.57	2.63	2.67
Percentage of population connected to water supply industry	%	59.5	62.5	65.5	65.8	67.7	68.9	71.3	71.5
Population connected to a wastewater collecting system									
Population connected	Million	1.65	1.72	1.78	1.81	1.83	1.87	1.90	1.96
Percentage of total population connected	%	44.2	46.0	47.9	48.6	49.4	50.1	51.5	52.4
Population connected to a wastewater collecting system without subsequent treatment									
Population connected to wastewater collecting system without subsequent treatment	Million	0.45	0.47	0.45	0.47	0.48	0.51	0.54	0.47
Percentage of population connected to wastewater collecting system without subsequent treatment	%	12.1	12.6	12.1	12.6	12.9	13.6	14.5	12.6
Population connected to water supply industry without connection to a wastewater collecting system									
Population connected to water supply industry without connection to a wastewater collecting system	Million	0.57	0.61	0.66	0.64	0.68	0.70	0.73	0.71
Percentage of population connected to water supply industry without connection to a wastewater collecting system	%	25.7	26.3	27.0	26.1	27.1	27.3	27.8	26.7

Source: www. geostat.ge/en.

access to public water supply and about half had no access to sewage disposal systems (Table 3.25).

Moldova

Air pollution

From 2009 to 2019, air pollution remained a top 10 risk factor in Moldova, with lower respiratory infections the fifth-highest cause of deaths and disability combined. Moldova is the sixth most affected EBRD investee economy by ambient air pollution in terms of disability-adjusted life years of the population, meaning ambient air pollution is a serious public health issue on a per capita basis

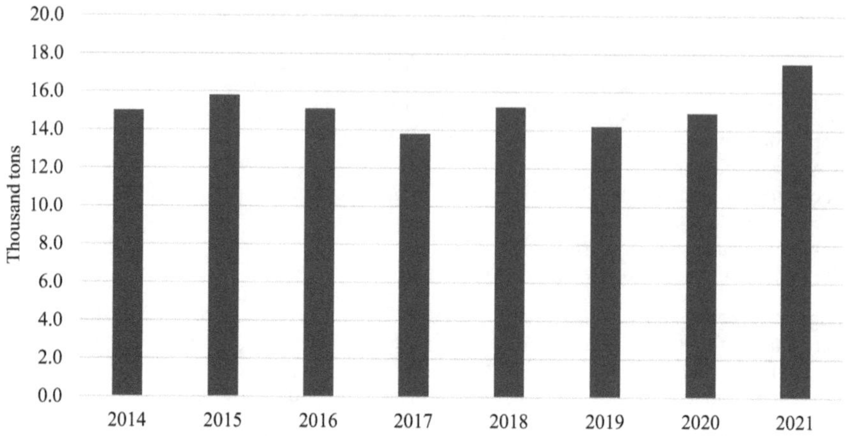

Figure 3.120 Moldova. Emission of pollutants, total (thousand tons).

Source: www.statbank.statistica.md.

(Figure 3.120). Since 2010, Moldova has seen a rise in air-pollutant emissions due to a rapid increase in emissions from road transport, a trend that amplifies environmental and human health risks (European Bank, 2022).

Information is presented without the data on districts from the left side of the river Nistru and municipality Bender.

Exposure of the population to fine particles ($PM_{2.5}$)

One of the direct effects of environmental pollution is the deterioration of human health and damage to ecosystems. The country occupies an average position in relation to other European countries in terms of exposure to $PM_{2.5}$ (Figure 3.121). Moldovans' exposure to $PM_{2.5}$ is decreasing. Between 2010 and 2019, exposure dropped from 18.5 to 14.0 $\mu g/m^3$. In the Republic of Moldova, the changes are in line with the general trend of decreasing population exposure to fine particulate matter in the EU. In addition, in 2019, exposure in the Republic of Moldova was 14 $\mu g/m^3$, which is close to the EU value of 13.5 $\mu g/m^3$ (https://www.expert-grup.org/).

Information is presented without the data on districts from the left side of the river Nistru and municipality Bender.

Access to safe drinking water sources

Between 2011 and 2019, the public water supply network in Moldova expanded rapidly, significantly increasing people's access to safely managed drinking water. However, the expansion of the public water supply networks far outpaced the increase in the length of sewerage networks. This disparity puts additional pressure on water resources, as increased water consumption reduces the amount of

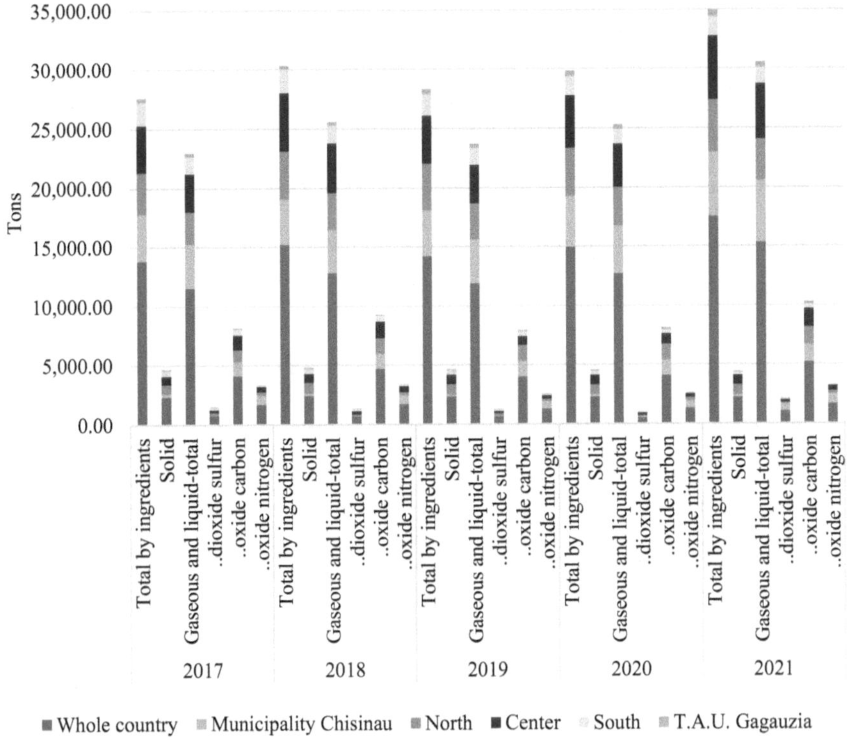

Figure 3.121 Moldova. Emission of pollutants in atmospheric air by stationary sources of economic agents by districts/regions- and ingredients.

Source: www.statbank.statistica.md.

high-quality water returning to the natural water cycle (Table 3.26). Moldova is highly dependent on water sources outside its borders, with a water dependency rate of 86.6% (European Bank, 2022).

Since 2012, there has been a noticeable improvement in the percentage of the population connected to the water supply system. In 2017, 53.5% of the total population was connected to the water supply system, compared to 42% in 2012, with the majority living in urban areas. Currently, almost 93% of the urban population and only 27% of the rural population have access to improved water supply systems. Groundwater serves as the main source of drinking water in rural areas, placing significant pressure on groundwater aquifers. Due to the increase in the population connected to the water supply system, water consumption from the public water supply system also rose by 15% between 2012 and 2017. This increase should be considered as an increase in measured water consumption by 15% in the water supply system (ENI SEIS II East, 2019c).

Table 3.26 Moldova: The main indicators of water use by Needs and Years (million m³).

	2014	*2015*	*2016*	*2017*	*2018*	*2019*	*2020*	*2021*	*2022*
Water abstraction from natural water basins – total	837	840	843	840	837	839	846	836	845
.. water abstraction from underground sources	127	128	126	127	128	129	130	130	129
Water use (without repeated and circulating water) – total	777	777	776	777	777	777	787	780	788
..for production needs	579	579	578	583	582	582	583	583	582
..for agricultural needs	38	39	38	38	39	39	40	40	41
..for irrigation	41	40	40	40	40	41	50	43	51
..for domestic needs	113	114	115	113	111	110	112	112	113
Losses during transportation	60	63	67	63	60	62	59	56	57
Quantity of repeated and circulating water	315	307	295	286	270	256	267	278	239
Wastewater disposal in surface water basins	664	666	666	667	677	678	673	677	675

Source: www.statbank.statistica.md.

Population connected to the sewage system

People's access to waste management systems and water services is increasing but remains insufficient (Table 3.27). The expansion of public water supply networks has improved access to safely managed water services. Between 2014 and 2020, the percentage of the population using safely managed water services increased

Table 3.27 Moldova: Discharge of sewage, mine, and phreatic drainage waters in natural water basins by Indicators and Years (million m³).

	2014	*2015*	*2016*	*2017*	*2018*	*2019*	*2020*	*2021*	*2022*
Discharge waters - total	664	666	666	667	677	678	673	677	675
Conventionally pure waters (without purification)	545	546	544	544	545	546	545	546	545
Polluted waters	10	8	28	8	9	8	8	8	8
..without purification	1	1	2	1	2	2	2	2	2
..insufficiently purified	9	7	26	7	7	6	6	6	6
Normatively treated waters	109	112	94	115	123	124	120	123	121

Source: https://statbank.statistica.md/PxWeb/pxweb/ro/.

from 72.2% to 74.1%. However, despite this progress, Moldova lags far behind other European countries in providing access to safe water sources. In 2020, 97.8% of the European Union population used safely managed water services, which is 23.7% higher than the corresponding percentage in Moldova (https://www.expert-grup.org).

Although Moldova's water quality remains relatively stable, inadequate wastewater management practices, including the lack of tertiary and secondary treatment in many areas, exacerbate the situation (Biotica, 2021). The country's water management system often struggles to fully address the challenges posed by industrial and domestic discharges (Biotica, 2021), leading to significant pollution in most of Moldova's internal rivers. This pollution can pose threats to public health if not properly treated (Ormax, 2021). Additionally, surface water sources such as artificial and natural lakes and ponds tend to be highly saline and mineralized (Ormax, 2021).

Ukraine

Air pollution

The air quality in Ukraine is the poorest in Europe, according to the World Health Organization (WHO, 2024), which identifies Ukraine as having the highest health impacts from air pollution on the continent. This situation is primarily attributed to Ukraine's heavy reliance on fossil fuels, which account for 70% of its primary energy consumption. The combustion of these fuels releases substantial amounts of pollutants into the atmosphere, making them the primary contributors to air pollution in the country. Coal-fired power plants, in particular, are significant sources, with a large fleet of 20 plants continuously emitting sulfur dioxide, particulate matter, and nitrous oxides into the air (Table 3.28).

Table 3.28 Ukraine: Emissions of pollutants and greenhouse gases into atmosphere. Air emissions per area.

Pollutant Type	*2018*	*2019*	*2020*	*2021*
Particulate matters – total	0.6	0.6	0.5	0.5
Particulate matters more 2.5 m/km and less 10 m/km	0.1	0.1	0.1	0.1
Particulate matters 2.5 m/km and less	0.04	0.04	0.04	0.04
Nitrogen dioxide	0.7	0.6	0.6	0.6
Ammonia	0.03	0.03	0.03	0
Sulfur dioxide	1.2	1.2	1	1
Carbon monoxide	3.4	3.3	3	3.1
Non-methane volatile organic compounds	0.4	0.3	0.3	0.3

Source: https://stat.gov.ua.

The impact of the war on air quality in Ukraine is complex, dynamic, and includes both an increase and decrease in air pollution. The main increase in air pollution is due to the following causes (Hryhorczuk et al., 2024):

- Bombings: The concentration of fine particulate matter has increased dramatically due to bombing and the resulting structural fires; in Kiev, for example, the concentration of fine particulate matter on March 19, 2022—less than a month after the start of the Russian invasion—was 27.8 times higher than recommended by the World Health Organization.
- Destruction of fuel depots: During the first 13 months of the war, 36 fuel depots, including 17 oil depots, were destroyed, producing pollution from the burning of 108,000 tons of oil, petroleum products, and gasoline.
- Attacks on industrial facilities: These attacks, such as on fertilizer and nitric acid plants, have resulted in the release of toxic substances, including nitric acid and ammonia.
- Movement of military equipment: The large-scale movement of military equipment, including tanks, artillery, armored vehicles, and trucks, generates large amounts of dust and fossil fuel emissions. These greenhouse gas emissions further contribute to global warming.
- Destruction of buildings: The destruction of residential and other buildings resulted in exposure to toxic residues from explosions, as well as hazardous dust and toxic substances such as alkali dust, cement particles, glass, asbestos, lead, and other heavy metals, and organic substances, including polycyclic aromatic hydrocarbons.
- Fires: Fires occurred frequently and spread widely as a result of military operations and insufficient numbers of firefighters. There were 25 times more forest fires in 2022 than in 2021. More than 183,000 hectares of Ukrainian forests and plantations were burned by fires. Smoke from the fires contains fine and coarse particulates, carbon monoxide, methane, nitrogen oxides, volatile organic compounds, and many other toxic substances.

War has increased Ukraine's vulnerability to climate change and complicated its efforts to reduce greenhouse gas emissions.

Exposure of the population to fine particles ($PM_{2.5}$)

Ukraine ranks among the most affected countries by air pollution in Europe. According to recent data, the average annual exposure to fine particulate matter with a diameter of less than 2.5 micrometers ($PM_{2.5}$) was 20.3 μg/m^3, placing Ukraine 9th in Europe in this regard. Based on the Global Burden of Disease (GBD) database, air pollution was responsible for approximately 42,900 premature deaths in Ukraine in 2019, which accounts for about 10% of all morbidity and mortality in the country (UNDP, 2022). The average annual $PM_{2.5}$ concentration in Ukraine was 20.31 μg/m^3 in 2017. Over the past three decades, this indicator peaked at 28.31 μg/m^3 in 1990 and reached a minimum of 20.31 μg/m^3 in 2017 (Index Mundi, 2018).

In Ukraine's major cities, where air quality is clearly below optimal, improving air quality to a level considered "good" could prevent up to a third of all strokes and cases of chronic obstructive pulmonary disease.

Access to safe drinking water sources

Military activities have led to chemical contamination of freshwater resources in Ukraine through direct and indirect means. Direct contamination occurs through the storage and decomposition of munitions, as well as the release and leaching of explosive residues into water sources. Indirect contamination results from damage to industrial facilities during military actions (Shumilova et al., 2023). Groundwater, which supplies 25% of Ukraine's drinking water needs, is particularly vulnerable to contamination from leaching explosive residues such as perchlorate and nitrate into the soil (Hryhorchuk et al., 2024). During times of conflict, water infrastructure in Ukraine also suffers damage both directly and indirectly due to military attacks. Despite international conventions prohibiting attacks on essential infrastructure like dams, such attacks continue, leading to disproportionate damage to civilian infrastructure. This damage disrupts access to drinking water, sanitation services, and leads to surface and groundwater pollution (Hryhorczuk et al., 2024).

Before the war, Ukraine had a highly developed water sector, which has since been devastated by Russia's invasion. As of July 2023. Ukraine's Ministry of Environmental Protection and Natural Resources documented the destruction of 724 hydraulic facilities, 71 water pumping stations, 64 sewage pumping stations, and 23 water treatment plants (World Bank, 2023b). As a result of the war, 20.7 billion m^3 of wastewater were discharged into surface waters. As of April 2022, about 6 million people in Ukraine—about 15% of the population—had limited or no access to safe water (Shumilova, 2023). After the destruction of the Novaya Kachovka dam in June 2023, about 1.25 million people and more than 300,000 children in Dnipro, Zaporizhzhya, Mykolaiv, and Kherson regions had no stable and safe drinking water supply (Reliefweb, 2023).

Access to sanitary facilities

Before the invasion, Ukraine faced significant disparities in access to centralized water supply and sewage collection and treatment services. Approximately 10 million people lacked access to safely managed water services, and 20 million people lacked access to centralized sewage services. Rural areas experienced lower access rates compared to urban areas, exacerbating inequalities (WAREG, 2023). The total physical damage to the Water Supply and Sewerage (WSS) sector is estimated at a substantial USD 2.2 billion, with approximately USD 0.9 billion incurred between June 2022 and February 2023 alone (WAREG, 2023). The regions most affected by the conflict include Kharkiv, Luhansk, Chernigov, Kyiv, and Donetsk. Critical infrastructure such as wastewater treatment plants, water and sewage networks, and drinking water treatment plants bore the brunt of the damage. Additionally, numerous water and wastewater pumping stations, vital for the operation of WSS systems, suffered extensive damage.

Losses in the water sector are estimated to be around USD 7.5 billion, primarily attributable to several factors exacerbated by the ongoing conflict. These include reduced water consumption due to population displacement and temporary shutdowns or reduced operations in industrial sectors. Furthermore, the collection of water service fees has significantly declined, especially in regions directly affected by the war. Additional economic losses stem from increased energy costs, heightened fuel consumption, rising prices of materials and equipment, tariff deficits, water losses, and expenditures related to chemical reagents, demolition, and debris management.

Summary

The establishment of data management platforms across the six countries has significantly enhanced transparency regarding water information, utilizing official national data sets. Despite these advancements, the EaP countries still face challenges due to inadequate quantity and quality of data, which hampers the preparation of comprehensive water balances. Water resources are crucial for the development of these countries, but they are under escalating pressure exacerbated by climate change. Industries, energy sectors, agriculture, households, and other stakeholders all depend on freshwater resources. Effective water management is therefore essential not only for ensuring economic resilience but also for enhancing human well-being and fostering sustainable livelihoods.

The Association Agreements with Georgia, the Republic of Moldova, and Ukraine, as well as the Comprehensive and Enhanced Partnership Agreement with Armenia, include ambitious, time-bound commitments to reform water policy and implement EU water-related directives.

All countries in the region are modernizing air quality monitoring by gradually establishing automated air quality monitoring networks. The transfer of experience at the regional level and the harmonization of efforts in line with EU standards can significantly improve the access of policymakers and citizens to up-to-date air quality data and its analysis relevant to policy.

Decarbonization in Eastern Partnership countries

This area attempts to examine how progress towards green growth generates economic opportunities for EaP countries. In approaching the identification of challenges in the area of decarbonization in the EaP, here is an inventory of key indicators.

1 **Green economy/environmental innovation.** *The share of environmental technologies in total technologies developed* shows the number of environmental and green economy innovations in relation to the total number of innovations developed. According to the OECD, innovation goes beyond the research and development (R&D) system and is based on companies that implement production processes. They bring goods or services to market, apply new organizational methods or significantly improved marketing concepts. The source of the data is the OECD statistical database.
2 **Public expenditure on environmental protection**. *Government spending on environmental protection* shows the amount of money spent on this purpose and the programs carried out in connection with it. *Government expenditures on environmental protection* are financial resources representing transactions related to the prevention. reduction and elimination of pollution and any other degradation of the environment made by the governments of the Eastern Partnership program countries.

3 **Energy subsidies**. Energy subsidies are direct or indirect financial contributions provided by the state to recipients of energy obtained from fossil sources. These include tax credits/exemptions. excise and other tax payments. as well as transfers in the form of tariff concessions. The data source is the OECD statistical database.
4 **Private spending on environmental protection**. *Current expenditures on environmental protection* are monetary expenditures allocated by economic entities for activities aimed at preventing. reducing or combating environmental damage. The source of this data is the statistical offices of the EaP countries. *Expenditures for the rehabilitation of environmental fixed assets* represent a set of works and activities related to the restoration of the capacity or condition of buildings. structures. elements and their parts. including engineering structures and equipment. the result of which leads to an improvement in relation to the surrounding environment.
5 **Subsidies in organic farming.** *Subsidies in organic farming* are non-refundable and non-taxable financial support to support investments made in the development of organic farming.

Thus, the analysis captures the economic opportunities associated with green growth, assessing the effectiveness of policies in areas with a focus on technology and innovation; environmental goods and services; and investments and their financing, prices, taxes, and transfers.

Armenia

Green economy/environmental innovation

Armenia improved its ranking in the Global Innovation Index to 72nd place in 2023, up from 64th in 2019. In June 2022, the Gituzh Initiative was launched, comprising 200 founders and 18 associations, aimed at prioritizing the modernization of Armenia's science and technology industry. Despite facing geopolitical and economic challenges since independence, Armenia has emerged as a regional leader in innovation, particularly in the IT services sector. Over the past two decades, more than 1,000 start-ups have been established, offering a variety of IT services and independently developing new and innovative products. The IT sector's contribution to Armenia's GDP has increased from 1.2% in 2010 to 5.1% in 2020.

Public expenditure on environmental protection

In 2019, 54.8% of the total climate-related budgeting expenditures were financed from internal sources. Although during 2017–2019 (Table 3.29), the climate-related costs funded through internal sources decreased in absolute terms (decreasing from AMD 25.6 billion in 2017 to AMD 19.4 billion in 2019), the share of those expenditures in total climate-related spending increased from 42.8% in 2017 to 54.8% in 2019 (DFA, 2021, Energy Community (2017, IEA (2022)). Climate-related expenditures financed by external aid primarily targeted irrigation, energy, and road transportation, collectively covering approximately 87% of such expenditures. Additional areas receiving funding included waste collection, street lighting,

Table 3.29 Armenia: Current expenditure for nature protection and fixed assets 2014–2022.

	2014	*2015*	*2016*	*2017*	*2018*	*2019*	*2020*	*2021*	*2022*
Current expenditure for nature protection, million drams	10,959.5	8,473.1	8,775.5	9,818.7	12,121.7	9,507.5	9,978.3	11,819.7	12,600.4
Current expenditure for water resources protection and efficient use, million drams	4,148.3	4,213.6	4,499.7	4,858.6	5,314.8	4,094.1	4,196.7	4,933	3,914.6
Current expenditure for atmospheric air protection, million drams	369.4	537.1	597.7	959.5	925	1,985.6	810.2	923.5	1,209.5
Current expenditure for land protection against industrial waste and other hazardous substances, million drams	6,414.8	3,588.1	3,640.8	3,881.5	5,146.7	3,280.1	4,880.5	5,436.1	7,366.9
Current expenditure for land treatment (recultivation), million drams	27	134.3	37.3	119.1	735.2	147.7	90.9	527.1	109.5
Expenditure for current expenditure for nature protection per 1 organization, thousand drams	16,431	13,239.2	13,973.7	16,391.7	20,169.2	15,819.5	16,941	20,736.3	21,613.1
Expenditure for capital repair of fixed assets for nature protection, million drams	2,622.8	2,093.6	489.3	753.3	1027.3	872.1	1,837.5	1,079.4	1,197.5
Expenditure for capital repair of structures, facilities, attachments for hooking and clearance air	122	194.9	300.7	655.3	838.8	435.6	393	349.7	113.4
Expenditure for capital repair waste-water treatment, structures and facilities for water resources	2,298.9	1,881.7	172.9	82	178	425.9	1,361.4	700.6	770.9
Expenditure for capital repair of waste treatment, neutralizing and destruction, million drams	201.9	17	15.7	16	10.5	10.6	83.1	29.1	313.2

Source: https://statbank.armstat.am/pxweb/en/ArmStatBank/?rxid=9ba7b0d1-2ff8-40fa-a309-fae01ea885bb.

biodiversity, and environmental protection. Major international partner organizations providing financing for these expenditures included the World Bank (WB), the Asian Development Bank (ADB), the European Bank for Reconstruction and Development (EBRD), and France's Agence Française de Développement (AfD), which together accounted for about 78% of the total climate-related budget expenditures funded by external aid.

In 2019, climate-related spending was allocated as follows: mitigation-related expenditures accounted for approximately 35% of the total, while adaptation-related expenditures comprised about 51%. Over the period 2017–2019, there was an overall decrease in climate-related spending. Specifically, both mitigation and adaptation spending decreased during this time frame. Programme of the Government of the Republic of Armenia, 2021–2026. However, spending categorized as having mixed impacts—where activities contribute to both mitigation and adaptation objectives—increased slightly. This increase was primarily driven by higher expenditures related to forest protection initiatives (DFA, 2021).

Energy subsidies

The Public Services Regulatory Commission (PSRC) of Armenia, functioning as an independent regulatory body, oversees the pricing mechanisms for producers and consumers, as well as the transmission and distribution of natural gas and electricity. In Armenia, every electricity and natural gas consumer must have a meter installed to be connected to the grid. Consumer prices for natural gas are set higher than import prices, and there is a tiered pricing structure where larger consumers pay less per unit compared to smaller consumers. This approach aligns with Armenia's policy to phase out subsidies for natural gas consumption. Typically, the PSRC establishes natural gas tariffs based on monthly consumption thresholds, distinguishing rates for consumers using up to and above 10,000 m^3 per month (Figure 3.122).

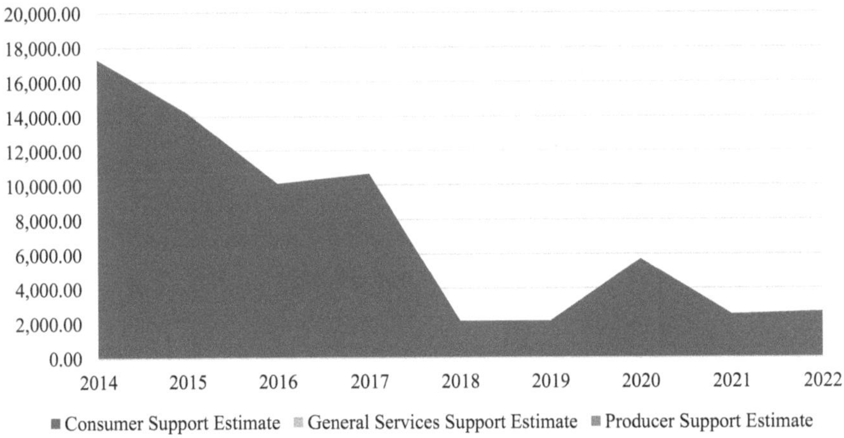

Figure 3.122 Armenia: Fossil fuel support by beneficiary (million AMD).

Source: OECD (2023).

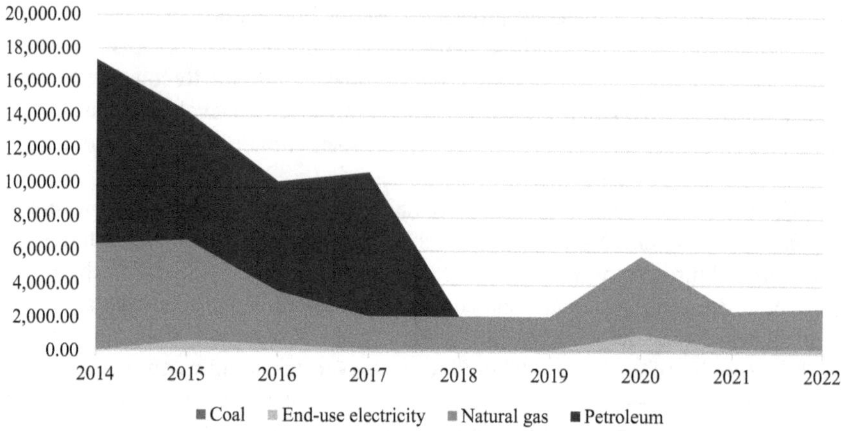

Figure 3.123 Armenia. Fossil fuel support by fuel type (million AMD).
Source: OECD (2023).

As for electricity prices for consumers, they are higher for groups of end users with lower voltage connections and lower for those with higher voltage connections. The highest price is paid by domestic consumers. This price structure reflects rising distribution costs at lower voltages (due to losses). There are no cross-subsidies from industrial consumers to households in Armenia (Figure 3.123).

In contrast, gas and diesel prices in Armenia are not regulated. However, the State Commission for the Protection of Economic Competition (SCPEC) monitors gasoline and diesel prices and keeps an eye on price cartels and super profits in any market segment (Figure 3.123).

The fiscal cost of fossil fuel support measures in Armenia amounted to AMD 2.63 billion in 2022, as indicated in Table 3.30. All of this support (100%) was directed to final beneficiaries rather than companies. The majority of support, totaling AMD 2.15 billion, or 81% of the total fiscal cost, came in the form of tax preferences. Direct transfers accounted for the remaining AMD 0.49 billion.

The fiscal cost of fossil fuel support measures has fallen by 75% since 2017. Since 2022, fiscal spending has increased by 7%, from AMD 2.02 billion to AMD 2.15 billion, and direct transfers have increased by 1%, from AMD 0.46 billion to

Table 3.30 Armenia: Fiscal cost of support measures for fossil fuels (in billions of national currency).

	2017	*2018*	*2019*	*2020*	*2021*	*2022*
Tax expenditures	10.306	1.779	1.838	1.874	2.018	2.146
Direct transfers	0.351	0.331	0.277	3.842	0.459	0.488
Total	10.657	2.110	2.115	5.716	2.477	**2.633**

Source: OECD (2023).

AMD 0.49 billion. All of the above growth rate percentages are expressed in nominal amounts in local currency (OECD, 2023).

Private spending on environmental protection

In Armenia, these economic instruments can be divided into two broad categories: natural resource royalties (and more recently, mineral royalties) and environmental fees. In May 2020, the Law "On targeted use of environmental tax paid by companies" was amended to expand the scope of companies required to pay environmental tax to the affected communities. The amendments stipulate that all companies eligible for production of metallic minerals will receive environmental tax deductions.

Subsidies in organic farming

The Organic Agriculture Support Initiative (OASI) project in Armenia, funded by the EU and co-implemented by the Austrian Development Agency (ADA), commenced in September 2015 with a total budget of EUR 3.3 million. This initiative aimed to promote organic farming by enhancing the legal and regulatory framework, providing robust marketing support, and facilitating successful market access for Armenian organic products both domestically and internationally. Key achievements of the project include establishing connections between Armenian farmers, processors, local buyers, and interested European and international companies. The initiative enabled Armenian organic producers to showcase their products at international organic fairs, enhancing visibility and market presence. Moreover, comprehensive support functions such as training and certification services were provided to strengthen the capacity of organic farming entities in Armenia. Financial and technical assistance was extended to individual farmers, farmer groups, cooperatives, and processors, resulting in a notable expansion of participants engaged in the organic products value chain (https://www.mineconomy.am).

On March 4, 2020, the "EU Green Agriculture Initiative in Armenia" (EU-GAIA), the largest EU-funded agricultural assistance project in Armenia, was officially launched in Yerevan. The project is funded by the European Union and co-financed and implemented by the Austrian Development Agency and partly by UNDP Armenia. The project partner on behalf of the Government of the Republic of Armenia is the RA Ministry of Economy. The objective of the project "EU Green Agriculture Initiative in Armenia" (EU-GAIA) is to support the development of sustainable, inclusive, innovative, and market-oriented agribusiness, particularly in the northern Marzes of Armenia: Lori, Tavush, and Shirak. The total budget of the project is 11.7 million euros. One of the main components of the project is the provision of direct technical assistance to producers and processors in the form of grants. The project will establish demonstration sites to show the use of modern infrastructure and green technologies. With the equipment and services provided by the project, selected agricultural producers and agribusiness enterprises will become more competitive in local and international markets (Lysenkov, 2021).

Azerbaijan

Green economy/environmental innovations

Although the Azerbaijani government is taking many measures to strengthen the innovative development of the economy, actively contributing to its growth and technical and technological development, the full development of the innovative technology sector is hindered by foreign producers, who occupy a leading position in the technology market (Yuzbashiyeva et al., 2022, Azerbaijan, 2021). This problem is closely related to the problem hindering the development of exports of innovative products and services from the country. The main condition for the transition is a change in the relative efficiency of lending and innovation. A lack of development of the innovation sector means a low demand for innovative products and services from the state and business (Table 3.31).

In Azerbaijan, common problems of innovative development are as follows (Yuzbashieva & Yuzbashiev, 2023):

- Lagging behind and growing a gap from developed countries. A small percentage of industrial enterprises (5–6%) are developing and implementing technical and technological innovations; innovative products do not reach 1%, the share of science-intensive products in the world trade volume does not exceed 0.3–0.5%.
- R&D spending is a small percentage of GDP.
- A low potential of applied science, which determines the sources of economic development. Science turned out to be unclaimed, its results are not used.
- In the adopted concepts, programs, strategies, and road map, there is no precise definition of "who is the subject" of innovative development, the role of the state apparatus in the implementation of innovative development directions, and existing personnel problems.
- At the heart of innovative development are not breakthrough, but inertial components.

Public expenditure on environmental protection

Spending on environmental protection in the 2014–2022 timeframe is on an upward trend, after declining in 2020 (Table 3.32).

Expenditures per thousand manat of GDP in the period 2019–2021 showed a downward trend, but an increase to 3.98% was recorded in 2022 (Table 3.33).

In the structure of capital investments aimed at the rational use of natural resources and environmental protection, it is worth highlighting the increase in value in the area of air protection. Expenditures in the field of land recultivation are still on the decline.

Energy subsidies

The electricity market in Azerbaijan is a closed market, operated mainly by the state-owned AzerEnerji JSC. AzerEnerji operates the country's thermal and hydroelectric power plants, with the exception of a few small hydropower plants that

Table 3.31 Azerbaijan: Expenditures to technological innovations in industry by types of innovations (thousand AZN).

Indicators	*2014*	*2015*	*2016*	*2017*	*2018*	*2019*	*2020*	*2021*	*2022*
All industry	**21,534.1**	**35,179.1**	**27,929.0**	**16,135.7**	**34,353.6**	**48,037.1**	**35,919.8**	**5,848.3**	**22,540.4**
Mining and quarrying	4,133.5	2671.5	179.6	31.7	1386.0	378.6	1001.1	529.8	19.3
Manufacturing	17,383.6	32,492.5	27,744.4	16,104.0	32,967.6	47,658.5	34,918.7	5,318.5	22,521.1
Manufacture of food products	1,156.7	-	-	81.5	-	208.7	8,667.0	98.1	195.1
Manufacture of beverages	2,089.0	12,792.0	1911.0	151.0	338.0	642.0	-	-	1,754.0
Manufacture of tobacco products	-	-	-	-	-	26,994.1	-	-	-
Manufacture of textiles	1,210.0	-	1,808.3	-	-	-	250.0	-	-
Manufacture of wearing apparel	-	-	-	-	-	-	-	-	-
Manufacture of wood and of products of wood and cork, except furniture	-	-	-	-	-	-	-	-	-
Printing and reproduction of recorded media	-	-	-	350.7	237.0	11.5	-	-	-
Manufacture of refined petroleum products	-	-	-	-	-	-	-	-	-
Chemical industry	178.8	199.5	180.7	664.7	215.4	-	-	-	16,010.1
Manufacture of rubber and plastic products	-	-	-	-	-	-	-	-	39.5
Manufacture of other non-metallic mineral products	-	-	11,928.2	-	3,081.6	-	512.2	340.3	338.6
Manufacture of basic metals	-	-	-	72.0	144.0	4,202.2	12,479.2	-	-
Manufacture of fabricated metal products, except machinery and equipment	-	-	-	1,415.0	1216.9	83.0	10.3	8.9	1.5
Manufacture of machinery and equipment	1,2667.0	15,871.2	8,227.7	12,525.1	17,215.6	15,500.0	9,500.0	4,700.0	124.5
Manufacture of furniture	-	399.9	922.3	676.3	534.9	-	3,500.0	126.0	3,025.1
Other manufacturing	-	-	-	-	-	-	-	43.2	-
Repair and installation of machinery and equipment	82.1	3,229.9	2,766.2	167.7	9,984.2	17.0	-	2.0	1,032.7
Electricity, gas and steam production, distribution and supply	**17.0**	**15.1**	**5.0**	-	-	-	-	-	-

Source: https://www.stat.gov.az.

Table 3.32 Azerbaijan: Expenses for protection of environment (thousand AZN).

	2014	*2015*	*2016*	*2017*	*2018*	*2019*	*2020*	*2021*	*2022*
Total	**283,414.6**	**136,208.3**	**155,817.2**	**189,044.1**	**319,256.1**	**387,680.4**	**239,764.5**	**141,342.7**	**231,193.6**
including:									
expenditures for carrying out of activities for the protection of environment	44,802.3	32,258.4	26,324.0	30,525.3	47,896.3	59,222.8	49,727.3	50,589.6	46,410.1
expenditures for capital repair of fixed assets on protection of environment	2,697.1	1,605.0	1,043.4	5,123.6	3,395.1	971.6	1,920.1	1,028.8	2,079.2
expenditures on maintenance of reserves, national parks, wild animals, fishes and their reproduction	6,151.9	5,949.8	6,777.6	6,895.9	6,807.5	6,837.4	6,206.0	6,785.9	7,682.0
expenditures for forestry	12,829.4	11,530.7	12,126.2	13,112.3	13,245.0	10,793.0	11,702.4	11,609	14,479.5
capital investments for rational use of natural resources and protection of environment	216,933.9	84,864.4	109,546.0	133,387.0	247,912.2	309,855.6	170,208.7	71,329.4	160,542.8
Expenditures per thsd. manat of GDP	9.51	2.50	5.34	6.47	10.77	7.06	4.56	2.54	3.98

Source: https://www.stat.gov.az.

Table 3.33 Azerbaijan: Current expenditures for carrying out of activities for environmental protection (thousand manat).

	2014	*2015*	*2016*	*2017*	*2018*	*2019*	*2020*	*2021*	*2022*
Total	**44,802.3**	**32,258.4**	**26,324.0**	**30,525.3**	**47,896.3**	**59,222.8**	**49,727.3**	**50,589.6**	**46,410.1**
including:									
protection of water resources and their rational use	20,940.5	17,276.2	15,274.8	16,016.7	20,518.8	31,984.1	28,998.1	20,318.6	25,374.9
air protection	4,297.6	2,518.6	2,419.4	3,708.1	5,694.7	5,710.2	5,793.3	6,096.5	6,403.8
protection from production and consumption pollutants	5,465.6	7,455.8	6,173.0	6,938.6	12,773.4	13,627.4	11,892.0	20,937.1	13,175.4
land recultivation	14,098.6	5,007.8	2,456.8	3,861.9	8,909.4	7,901.1	3,043.9	3,237.4	1,456

Source: https://www.stat.gov.az.

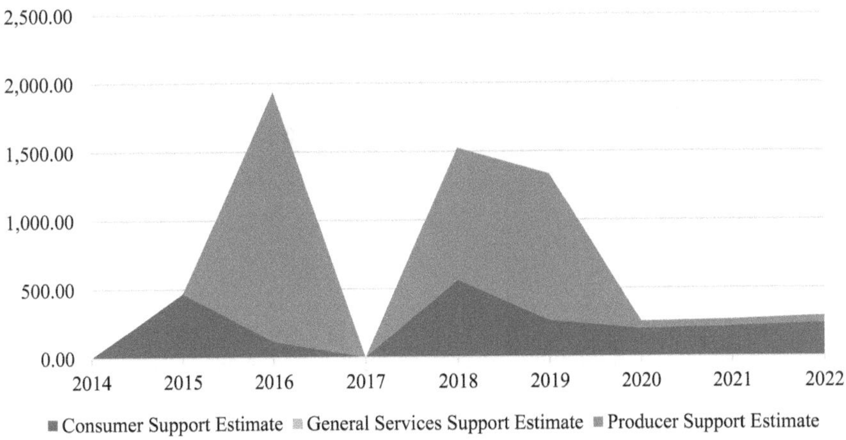

Figure 3.124 Azerbaijan. Fossil fuel support by beneficiary (million AZN).
Source: OECD (2023).

have been privatized. Until February 2015, AzerEnerji operated as an affiliated monopoly, managing the production, transmission, distribution, and sale of electricity. On February 10, 2015, Bakielektrikshabaka Open Joint Stock Company, a regional distribution company established to supply electricity to the capital Baku, was renamed AzerIshig OJSC and became a nationwide electricity distribution company. In 2020, methodologies for setting tariffs for the supply of electricity and heat were developed. In addition, a methodology for setting tariffs for natural gas has already been developed and submitted to the Council of Ministers for consideration. Total tax credits and support for fossil fuels in Azerbaijan are shown in Figures 3.124 and 3.125.

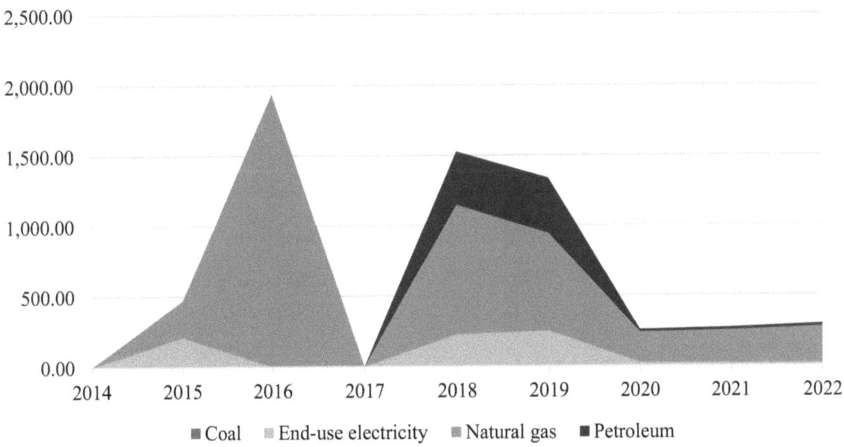

Figure 3.125 Azerbaijan. Fossil fuel support by fuel type (million AZN).
Source: OECD (2023).

Table 3.34 Azerbaijan: Fiscal cost of support measures for fossil fuels (million AZN).

	2017	*2018*	*2019*	*2020*	*2021*	*2022*
Tax expenditures	0.000	0.000	0.000	0.000	0.000	0.000
Direct transfers	0.107	1525.347	1335.580	257.212	270.549	295.959
Total	0.107	1525.347	1335.580	257.212	270.549	295.959

Source: OECD (2023).

The fiscal cost of fossil fuel support activities in Azerbaijan is estimated at AZN 295.96 million in 2022 (Table 3.34). Six percent was directed to final beneficiaries, compared to 94% to businesses. Support was provided mainly in the form of direct transfers (AZN 295.96 million) accounting for 100% of the total fiscal cost of support activities.

The fiscal cost of fossil fuel support measures has increased by 276,378% since 2017. Since 2021, direct transfers have increased by 10%, from AZN 270.55 million to AZN 295.96 million. All of the above growth rate percentages are expressed in nominal amounts in national currency.

Private spending on environmental protection

In the structure of lectures on capital repairs of environmental fixed assets (Tables 3.35 and 3.36), attention is drawn to the continuing upward trend during 2014–2017. The period 2018–2019 is a time of decline in spending, which began to gradually increase from 2020.

Table 3.35 Azerbaijan: Expenditures for capital repair of fixed assets on protection of environment (thousand AZN).

	2014	*2015*	*2016*	*2017*	*2018*	*2019*	*2020*	*2021*	*2022*
Total	**2,697.1**	**1,605.0**	**1,043.4**	**5,123.6**	**3,395.1**	**971.6**	**1,920.1**	**1,028.8**	**2,079.2**
including:									
treatment of sewage waters and rational use of water resources	1,944.0	1,115.4	624.5	4,281.2	1,315.4	548.2	1,802.7	458.4	828.1
treatment and disposal of air pollutant emissions	711.3	160.1	352.8	773.7	2,044.6	421.0	114.1	546.1	1,179.4
location and disposal of waste	41.8	329.5	66.1	68.7	35.1	2.4	3.3	24.3	71.7

Source: https://www.stat.gov.az.

Table 3.36 Azerbaijan: Capital investments directed to rational use of natural resources and protection of the environment (thousand AZN).

	2014	*2015*	*2016*	*2017*	*2018*	*2019*	*2020*	*2021*	*2022*
Total	**216,933.9**	**84,864.4**	**109,546.0**	**133,387.0**	**247,912.2**	**309,855.6**	**170,208.7**	**71,329.4**	**160,452.8**
including:									
capital investments for protection of water resources and their rational use	199,309.3	84,474.4	108,996.0	117,387.0	233,348.1	294,922.5	170,208.7	71,329.4	160,542.8
capital investments for air protection	8,889.4	-	-	16,000.0	13,498.5	10,198.2	-	-	-
capital investments for land protection and their rational use	8,735.2	390.0	550.0	-	1,065.6	4,734.9	-	-	-

Source: https://www.stat.gov.az.

Subsidies in organic farming

Back in 2005, the Ganja Agribusiness Association (GABA) initiated the development of a legal framework for organic farming in Azerbaijan. In 2008, the Law of the Republic of Azerbaijan on Organic Agriculture was enacted, establishing "organically clean" as a synonym for organic or biological practices (Republic of Azerbaijan, 2008). Despite the existence of this legislation and its regulatory provisions, practical implementation gaps persist, particularly concerning the registration, supervision, inspection, and certification functions. Consequently, these roles are currently fulfilled by foreign certification bodies. In the agricultural sector, the 2022 national budget allocates USD 587 million in grants and subsidies, marking a 5.8% increase from 2021. Of this amount, approximately USD 270 million is earmarked for enhancing food security and supporting irrigation agriculture (Gengenbach, 2022).

Belarus

Green economy/environmental innovations

In recent years, the Belarusian economy has faced substantial development challenges, characterized by a reluctance to undertake challenging reforms. The state budget primarily subsidizes economically vital sectors, such as through initiatives like the Belarusian Innovation Fund offering vouchers up to USD 25,000 and grants up to USD 10,000. The Belarusian government assumes an active regulatory role in utilizing available production capacities, with critical economic decisions typically made by the president, who wields significant authority in pivotal economic matters. However, the prevailing political and social conditions have had adverse effects on innovative enterprises, which frequently encounter regulatory delays that fail to keep pace with their forward-thinking initiatives in the sphere of innovation (Gródek-Szostak et al., 2021; Konferencja UNCTAD-15, 2021).

The implementation of environmental policy in Belarus is carried out within the framework of the implementation of the objectives of the Government Action Program for the period up to 2025, the implementation of the activities of the Social and Economic Development Program for 2021–2025, the State Program "Environmental Protection and Sustainable Use of Natural Resources" for 2021–2025, and others (Prikhodko, 2024).

The National Action Plan for the Development of a Green Economy in Belarus for 2021–2025 encompasses 12 strategic directions and 68 specific activities, involving collaboration among 48 relevant government agencies. Key among these initiatives is the formulation of a Strategy for the Development of a Circular Economy in Belarus by 2035, aimed at fostering long-term sustainable growth with minimal greenhouse gas emissions by 2050. Additionally, the plan focuses on establishing mechanisms for green financing to stimulate investment and attract funds towards projects dedicated to advancing the green economy. These efforts underscore Belarus's commitment to addressing environmental challenges through comprehensive policy frameworks and strategic initiatives (Prikhodko, 2024).

Work has begun on the establishment of four ecotourism clusters: on the basis of the Ozyory, Naliboki, Osveisky, and Eco-Rosa nature reserves. Action plans for their development for 2023–2024 have been drawn up for each of them, as well as guidelines for ecotourism development: on conducting responsible business in ecotourism; on trust councils in protected areas; on creating ecotourism clusters and ecotourism products; and on a system of voluntary ecocertification of ecotourism products (Prikhodko, 2024).

Public expenditure on environmental protection

For the 2015–2022 period, attention is drawn to the continued decline in public spending on environmental measures (Table 3.37). Belarus has various binding laws and other regulations that set policies and measures with targets for reducing greenhouse gas emissions and energy intensity of the economy. The National Strategy for Sustainable Development 2021–2030 places due emphasis on low-carbon development. Belarus has adopted a Green Economy Strategy to 2030, focusing on green innovation, improving the quality of life, and increasing the competitiveness of the national economy. The government is also integrating sustainable development goals into national development planning, investing in legal frameworks and public campaigns for action in this area. In terms of sustainable energy, Belarus has begun electrifying its transportation infrastructure and investing in energy efficiency. It is also actively supporting decentralized solar energy systems, focusing on hospitals, schools, and other public buildings. The national designated authority in the area of climate change is the Ministry of Natural Resources and Environmental Protection.

Energy subsidies

However, data on the scale of such support programs has not been made public. Data gaps, inconsistencies, and unavailability mean that findings can only indicate trends in fossil fuel subsidies (Table 3.38).

Table 3.37 Belarus: Expenditure structure by type of pro-environmental activities (billion BYN in 2015; million BYN during 2016–2022).

	2015	*2016*	*2017*	*2018*	*2019*	*2020*	*2021*	*2022*
Protection of atmospheric air, protection of the ozone layer of the climate	2,222.6	303.0	276.7	173.9	223.2	219.5	295.0	1,183.5
Collection and treatment of wastewater	4,453.2	469.2	509.6	375.3	389.5	423.6	443.0	546.0
Waste management and prevention of its harmful effects on the environment	1,284.3	151.5	165.0	185.6	232.3	255.0	279.4	346.4
Protection and reclamation of land, surface and underground waters	428.5	37.0	30.4	32.1	17.2	53.9	45.4	12.7
Protection of biodiversity and protection of natural areas	136.9	12.3	17.5	16.7	17.9	22.4	28.0	29.6

Source: http://dataportal.belstat.gov.by...

Table 3.38 Belarus: Fossil fuel subsidies in Belarus (million BYN).

Program	*Mechanism of support*	*Indicator*	*Fuel*	*2014*	*2015*	*2016*	*2017*	*2018*	*2019*
Funding for construction (reconstruction) of energy infrastructure in residential areas	direct transfer	PSE	electricity, natural gas	1,151,319	-	134	137	101	106
State support for development of the peat industry	direct transfer	PSE	peat	64,477	62,067	6	36	44	35
Development of power grid and gas supply networks in rural areas	direct transfer	PSE	electricity, natural gas	n.a.	n.a.	-	39	28	37
VAT exemption for utility tariffs for households	tax expenditure	CSE	electricity, natural gas, fuel oil, peat	2,038,000	-	n.a.	n.a.	n.a.	n.a.

Source: OECD (2021).

* n.a.: not applicable, -: not available.

Belarus abolished the VAT exemption on electricity and natural gas for households in January 2016, ending a USD 200 million per year subsidy. All estimated fossil fuel subsidies in 2018 are for individual producers. CSE measures in Belarus include housing subsidies for low-income households and partial compensation for the costs of utility providers.

Private spending on environmental protection

In 2022, the National Statistical Committee of Belarus reported that private spending on environmental protection amounted to nearly 917 million Belarusian rubles, almost 8% less than in 2021 at comparable prices (Belbiznespress, 2022). The structure of current spending on environmental protection is as follows:

- 47% - wastewater management economy (BYN 428.8 million);
- 29% - waste management (BYN 268.6 million); and
- 20% - air protection (BYN 181.4 million).

The majority of current expenditures have traditionally gone to manufacturing companies (50.3%); organizations involved in water supply, as well as waste collection, treatment, and disposal, and pollution elimination (26.7%); and organizations involved in the supply of electricity, gas, steam, hot water, and conditioned air (14.5%). In 2022, organizations in the Gomel region (BYN 254.9 million, or 27.8% of the republic's total), the Vitebsk region (BYN 133.9 million, or 14.6%), and the Minsk region (BYN 129.3 million, or 14.1%) spent the largest amounts on environmental protection activities.

Subsidies in organic farming

The efforts of environmentally conscious farmers were initially acknowledged by the public association Ecohome in 2009, which encouraged those adopting permaculture and pioneering environmentally friendly farming practices. Subsequently, Agro-Eco-Culture was founded to continue supporting these farmers. As of 2019, Belarus counted 25 organic producers, encompassing both growers and processors of organic products, all of whom have achieved organic certification. Each year sees the emergence of 5–7 new organic farms across the country (ecoidea.me).

Georgia

Green economy/environmental innovations

When analyzing the structure of implemented innovations in the 2016–2020 period, it is important to pay attention to the criterion of novelty of the innovation to the market and novelty to the enterprise (World Economic Forum, 2019). Novelty

Table 3.39 Georgia: The distribution of implemented innovations by categories (%) 2016–2022.

	2016	*2017*	*2018*	*2019*	*2020*	*2021*	*2022*
New to market	51.8%	57.9%	55.1%	48.1%	52.6%	39.4%	41.7%
New to enterprise	48.2%	42.1%	44.9%	51.9%	47.4%	60.6%	58.3%

Source: https://www.geostat.ge.

to the market means that an enterprise introduced a new or significantly improved product onto their market before their competitors (it may have already been available in other markets). In turn, novelty for enterprises means that an enterprise introduced a new or significantly improved product that was already available from their competitors in their market (Table 3.39).

In the case of innovations new to the market, it is noteworthy that the rate fell in 2021, but the following year saw an increase in the rate exceeding 40%. The year 2021, however, was a time for companies to invest in the development of innovations in their organizations (Figure 3.126).

Evaluating the environmental benefits achieved at the company (Figure 3.127), attention is drawn to the level of the indicator "reduced soil, noise, water, or air pollution," which in 2020 took the value of 20.9%, in 2021 the level of 19.4%, and in 2022 it reached 22.4%. Natiotal Statisctics Office of Georgia (2023a, 2023b). The lowest values in the analyzed period took the indicator "replaced a share of fossil energy with renewable energy sources," which in 2020 was equal to 11.5%, in 2021 it reached 8.4%, and in 2022 it took the value of 9.9%.

When evaluating the environmental benefits gained during the consumption or use of a good or service by the end user during 2020–2022, it is important to note the highest values of "reduced air, water, soil, or noise pollution," which remained at 29% throughout the period. Each of the studied parameters recorded an increase in 2022 compared to the previous period.

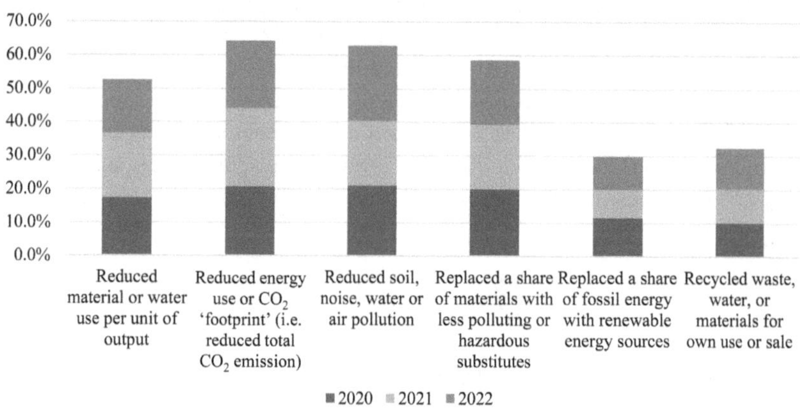

Figure 3.126 Georgia. Environmental benefits obtained within enterprise 2020–2022.

Source: https://www.geostat.ge.

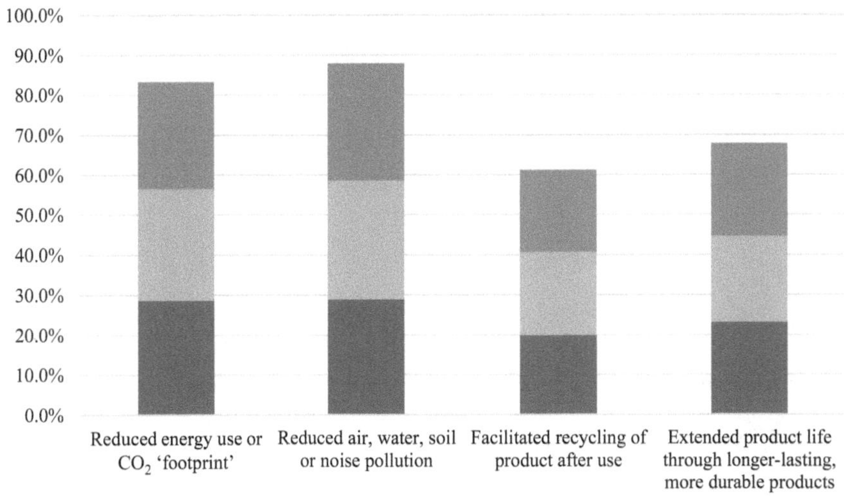

Figure 3.127 Georgia. Environmental benefits obtained during the consumption or use of a good or service by the end user 2020–2022.

Source: https://www.geostat.ge.

Public expenditure on environmental protection

The administrative framework overseeing environmental matters in Georgia comprises the lead ministry, presently the Ministry of Environmental Protection and Agriculture (MEPA), along with several independent agencies under its purview known as Legal Entities of Public Law (LEPL). These agencies include the Protected Areas Agency and the National Forestry Agency. The ministry is tasked with environmental protection and planning, pollution control and monitoring, and fulfilling international obligations (Martus, 2023).

Table 3.40 shows the changes in environmental spending as a percentage of total government spending from 2014 to 2022. As a result of the merger with the

Table 3.40 Georgia: General government spending on the environment.

Year	*Environmental protection expenditure (GEL million)*	*Environment as percentage of total general government expenditure*
2014	162.9	1.8
2015	133.2	1.4
2016	143.4	1.4
2017	144.6	1.3
2018	153.1	1.2
2019	269.7	1.9
2020	317.3	1.8
2021	403.1	2.1
2022	511.7	2.4

Source: https://www.geostat.ge.

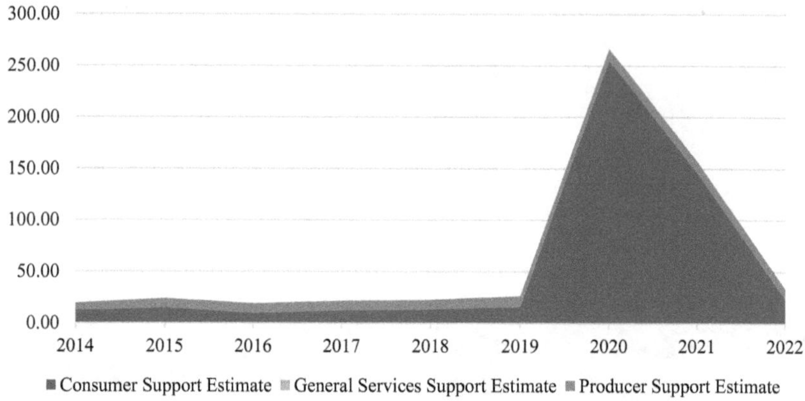

Figure 3.128 Georgia. Fossil fuel support by beneficiary (million GEL).
Source: OECD (2023).

Ministry of Agriculture, which as noted above is a larger and well-equipped ministry, there was an increase in spending from 1.2% of total spending in 2018 to 1.9% in 2019. During 2021–2022, spending exceeded 2% of total spending.

Energy subsidies

The Georgia Energy and Water Regulatory Commission (GNERC) sets tariffs for electricity and natural gas. A VAT rate of 18% applies to all energy products and is included in end-user tariffs. Total tax credits and support for fossil fuels in Georgia are shown in Figures 3.128 and 3.129.

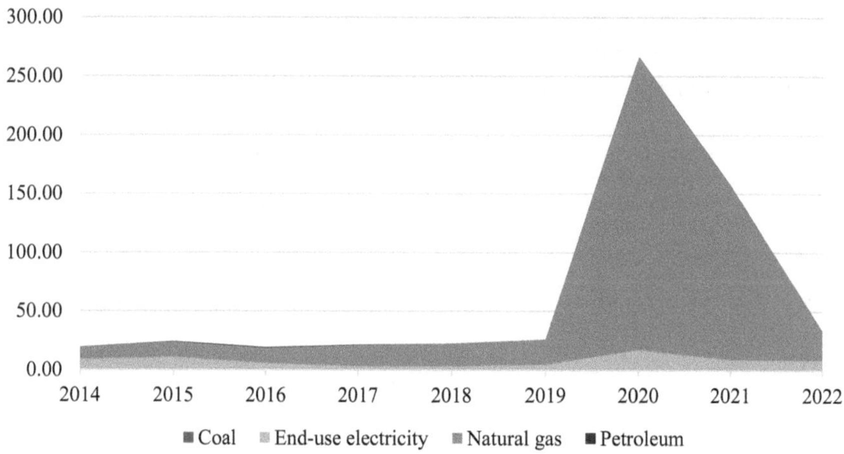

Figure 3.129 Georgia. Fossil fuel support by fuel type (million GEL).
Source: OECD (2023).

Table 3.41 Georgia: Fiscal cost of fossil fuel support measures (million GEL).

	2017	*2018*	*2019*	*2020*	*2021*	*2022*
Tax expenditures	9.488	9.545	10.411	11.323	11.367	10.366
Direct transfers	11.946	13.159	15.762	255.181	146.202	23.582
Total	21.435	22.704	26.173	266.504	157.570	**33.948**

Source: OECD (2023).

The fiscal cost of fossil fuel support activities in Georgia was estimated at GEL 33.95 million in 2022 (Table 3.41). As much as 69% was directed to final beneficiaries, compared to 31% directed to businesses. Support was provided mainly in the form of direct transfers (GEL 23.58 million), which accounted for 69% of the total fiscal cost of support activities. Fiscal expenditures amounted to GEL 10.37 million.

The fiscal cost of fossil fuel support measures has increased by 58% since 2017. From 2021, tax preferences fell by 9%, from GEL 11.37 million to GEL 10.37 million, and direct transfers fell by 48%, from GEL 146.20 million to GEL 23.58 million. All of the above growth rate percentages are expressed in nominal amounts in local currency.

Private spending on environmental protection

No data has been provided for this indicator.

Subsidies in organic farming

Georgia does not have an agricultural subsidy system (with the exception of the wine-growing sector), while this system is well implemented in neighboring countries that produce large quantities of wine (AGREEN, 2022).

Moldova

Green economy/environmental innovations

During the period 2021–2022, the proportion of innovative enterprises in the total number of enterprises decreased from 12.6% to 11.4%. The manufacturing industry constituted the largest segment of these innovative enterprises, comprising 46.2% of the total. Small- and medium-sized enterprises (SMEs) accounted for 89.8% of all innovative enterprises (Table 3.42).

Of the total number of innovative enterprises, 50.0% operated in industry (including 46.4% in manufacturing) and 50.0% in services (including 20.2% in wholesale trade, 11.4% in information and communications, and 8.8% in transportation and storage).

Environmental innovation can be assessed by the number of environment-related technologies in the total number of technologies. Thus, on average, about

Table 3.42 Moldova: Innovative companies by economic activity during 2021–2022.

Total	*Structure of innovative companies (%)*	
	2021–2022	*2019–2020*
	100.0	*100.0*
Industry – total	50.0	48.9
Mining industry	0.2	0.7
Manufacturing industry	46.2	44.6
Generation and supply of electricity and heat, gas, hot water, and air conditioning	1. 9	1.3
Water distribution; hygiene, waste management, decontamination activities	1.7	1.3
Services – total	50.0	51.1
Wholesale	20.2	22.3
Transport and storage	8.8	7.1
Information and communication	11.4	14.1
Financial and insurance operations	5.0	4.2
Professional, scientific, and technical activities	4.5	3.3

Source: www.statistica.gov.md.

one-fifth of new technologies used by local companies can be considered environmental or somehow related to the green economy. Most of these are related to environmental management and mitigation procedures in the energy or commodity production sector.

Public expenditure on environmental protection

For an extended period, Environmental Funds (specifically, the National Fund for Environmental Protection [NFEP] and previously, Local Environmental Funds) constituted the primary state instruments for environmental protection, funded through environmental fees. In 2017, this framework underwent revision, eliminating Local Environmental Funds and instituting an annual allocation to NFOŚ from the general state budget revenues. State expenditures in this realm are also channeled through the "Environmental Protection" budget program, aimed at aligning with pivotal elements from strategic planning documents, sector strategies, government action plans, and other policy frameworks. Over recent years, an average of MDL 240 million annually, or less than 0.1% of GDP, has been earmarked for the Environmental Program. This allocation reflects budgetary capacity yet underscores Moldova's challenge in fully matching environmental spending with revenues from environmental taxes. Furthermore, an analysis of approved versus realized expenditures reveals an average annual gap of nearly MDL 100 million (OECD, 2023).

According to the draft budget for 2024, supporting small- and medium-sized enterprises remains a priority, with over MDL 197 million allocated to finance various programs. Another focal area is the ongoing development of the transportation and infrastructure system, with funding totaling MDL 4,036.5 billion, including MDL 1,393.9 billion from external sources, and MDL 2,505.6 billion designated for the repair and maintenance of national and local roads. The 2024 state budget also earmarks MDL 1,600 billion to subsidize the agricultural sector, promote rural development, and integrate the domestic agro-industrial sector into the European economy. Additionally, allocations include MDL 322.1 million for energy efficiency initiatives, MDL 601.5 million for the National Fund for Regional and Local Development, and MDL 175 million to advance environmental sector policies.

Energy subsidies

Moldova's tax system consists of six general state taxes (value-added tax [VAT], excise tax, corporate income tax, personal income tax, customs tax, and road tax) and 14 local taxes (including property tax, land tax, and natural resources tax). Energy production and distribution in Moldova is not subject to any specific taxation other than taxes imposed on all types of commercial activities (Figures 3.130 and 3.131).

Consumption of gasoline and diesel fuel, as well as liquefied petroleum gas (LPG) is subject to excise taxes. Natural gas, compressed natural gas, electricity, and heat production are not subject to excise taxes. Moldova's Tax Code sets a reduced VAT rate (8%) on the supply of natural gas and LPG and 0% VAT on the supply of electricity and heat to households, while the standard VAT rate is 20%.

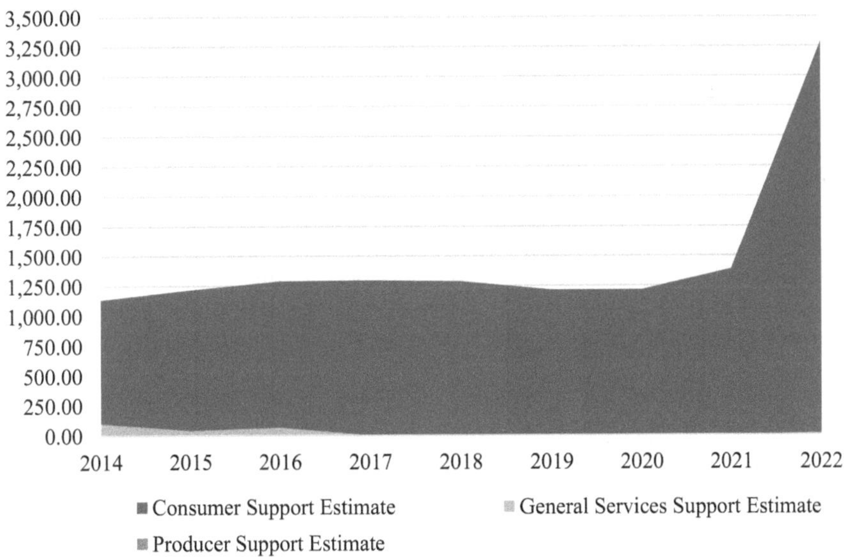

Figure 3.130 Moldova. Fossil fuel support by beneficiary (million MDL).

Source: OECD (2023).

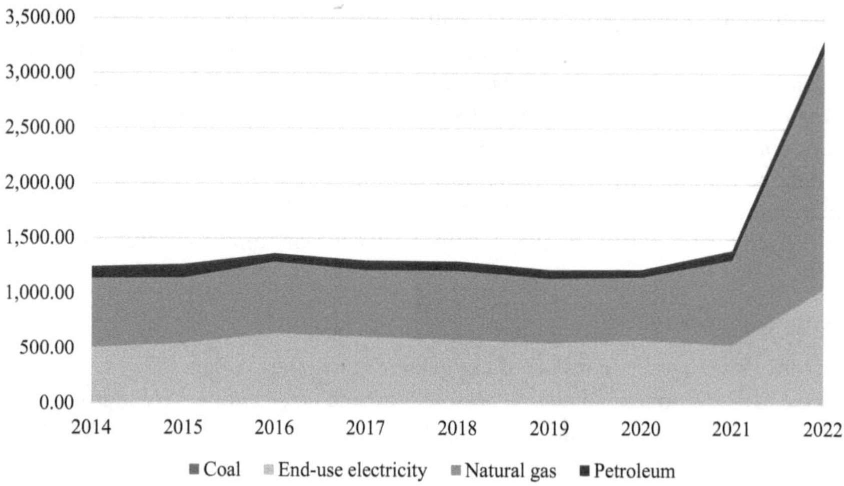

Figure 3.131 Moldova. Fossil fuel support by fuel type (million MDL).
Source: OECD (2023).

The key maintained subsidy programs in Moldova's energy sector are the following:

- reduced VAT rates for household consumption of heat and electricity, natural gas and LPG, and
- direct subsidies from the state budget to households to support energy consumption. Direct subsidies from the state budget to non-households for energy consumption were also provided in 2022.

Fiscal support for investments in energy infrastructure, particularly gas and electricity grids, was discontinued in 2018. Instead, government contributions have primarily been directed towards connecting Moldova to the European electricity grid.

The fiscal cost of fossil fuel support activities in Moldova amounted to MDL 3.30 billion in 2022 (Table 3.43). Ninety-nine percent (99%) of this support was directed to final beneficiaries, with none allocated to companies. Tax preferences constituted the majority of support, totaling MDL 2.23 billion, which accounted for

Table 3.43 Moldova: Fiscal cost of fossil fuel support measures (billion MDL).

	2017	*2018*	*2019*	*2020*	*2021*	*2022*
Tax expenditures	1.199	1.188	1.109	1.123	1.270	2.225
Direct transfers	0.096	0.100	0.105	0.093	0.120	1.078
Total	1.295	1.288	1.214	1.216	1.390	**3.303**

Source: OECD (2023).

67% of the total fiscal expenditure on aid activities. Direct transfers accounted for MDL 1.08 billion.

The fiscal cost of support measures for fossil fuels has increased by 155% since 2017. Since 2021–2022, tax expenditures have increased by 85%, from MDL 1.27 billion to MDL 2.23 billion and direct transfers increased by 1,031% from MDL 0.12 billion to MDL 1.08 billion. All growth rate percentages above are expressed in terms of nominal national currency amounts (OECD, 2023).

Private spending on environmental protection

In addition to public spending on environmental protection, the private sector makes a number of ongoing expenditures or investments. Some figures on private environmental spending refer to current and capital repairs expenditures on fixed assets. During 2019–2020, these expenditures remain roughly equal (about MDL 250 million) to public environmental spending (Tables 3.44 and 3.45). Most of this is for wastewater collection and treatment (66%) and waste management (23%),

Table 3.44 Moldova: Current expenditure on renovation of fixed assets of business entities by type of environmental activities, 2018–2022 (Thousand Lei (MDL).

	2018	*2019*	*2020*	*2021*	*2022*
	Current expenditures	*Current expenditures*	*Current expenditures*	*Current expenditures*	*Current expenditures*
Total	269,046.8	258,478.7	264,982.5	334,114.9	370,629.4
..for atmospheric air protection and prevention of climate change	7,496.8	3,573.5	5,553.0	8,753.2	13,844.4
..for collecting and treating wastewater	18,0161.5	179,276.3	182,530.3	189,528.0	204,167.6
..for waste management	64,765.6	61,266.7	66,258.6	124,585.9	117,284.6
..for soil protection and rehabilitation	3,829.0	4,742.3	3,553.8	3,205.8	1,686.0
..for protection and rehabilitation of groundwater and surface water	4,595.0	5,891.7	3,284.1	3,119.3	3,092.0
..for conservation of biodiversity and natural areas	615.4	70.7	173.5	125.0	89.8
..for other areas	7,583.5	3,657.5	3,629.2	4,797.7	30,465.0

Source: https://statbank.statistica.md.

Table 3.45 Moldova: Expenditures on renovation of fixed assets of business entities by type of environmental activities, 2018–2022 (Thousand Lei (MDL).

	2018	*2019*	*2020*	*2021*	*2022*
	Expenditures for the capital repair of fixed assets	*Expenditures for the capital repair of fixed assets*	*Expenditures for the capital repair of fixed assets*	*Expenditures for the capital repair of fixed assets*	*Expenditures for the capital repair of fixed assets*
Total	15,262.4	26,528.6	15,065.4	19,436.3	16,843.2
..for atmospheric air protection and prevention of climate change	493.1	15,269.7	5,284.0	2,303.0	1,837.2
..for collecting and treating wastewater	8,184.2	8,373.9	8,121.4	5,920.9	3,597.6
..for waste management	1,225.7	235.1	1,098.3	2,407.4	5,877.0
..for soil protection and rehabilitation	..	26.6	0.0	0.0	0.0
..for protection and rehabilitation of groundwater and surface water	2,691.0	1,681.2	508.1	8,370.1	266.7
..for conservation of biodiversity and natural areas	1,615.1	0.0	0.0	0.0	0.0
..for other areas	1,053.2	942.1	53.6	434.9	5,264.7

Source: https://statbank.statistica.md.

with the remainder for other areas (Tables 3.46 and 3.47). This allocation is mainly due to the increased regulation of economic activities in water consumption, as well as the rules of production waste management. Nevertheless, this amount of funding by the private sector is much lower than in European countries. On average (EUROSTAT, 2022) in the European Union, private spending on environmental protection is more than twice as high as public spending, reaching 1.9% of GDP in 2020. By comparison, Moldova managed to secure total environmental spending of only about 0.5% of GDP 2021–2022 (Tables 3.46 and 3.47).

In addition to government and private spending, external support programs play a crucial role in the broader assessment of environmental spending in Moldova. Moldova participates in the "EU4Environment" project alongside other Eastern

Table 3.46 Moldova: Ecological payments—within permissible limits—of operators calculated from evacuation of pollution by area, 2018–2022 (Thousand Lei (MDL).

	2018	*2019*	*2020*	*2021*	*2022*
	Within the permissible limits	*Within the permissible limits*	*Within the permissible limits*	*Within the permissible limits*	*Within the permissible limits*
Payments*total	9,148.4	6,058.6	9,716.1	7,737.4	9,493.8
..atmospheric air	1,388.8	1,254.2	1,955.3	2,328.1	3,294.6
..water bodies	6,473.6	3,820.4	4,019.3	4,104.8	3,248.6
..waste management	1,286.0	9,84.0	3,741.5	1,304.5	2,950.6

Source: https://statbank.statistica.md.

* Information is presented without the data on districts from the left side of the river Nistru and municipality Bender.

Partnership countries, benefiting from support aimed at ensuring the sustainable use of natural capital, improving environmental quality and population well-being, and stimulating economic growth.

Subsidies in organic farming

Moldova continues to support local agriculture through direct payments to operators, commonly known as agricultural subsidies. The main instrument for allocating these funds is the National Fund for the Development of Agriculture and the Rural Environment (Republic of Moldova, 2014). In 2020, the fund amounted to approximately 0.6% of GDP. Legislation includes a special program aimed at promoting and developing organic agriculture. Additionally, subsidies of up to

Table 3.47 Moldova: Ecological payments—for exceeding permissible limits—of operators calculated for evacuation of pollutants by area, 2018–2022 (Thousand Lei (MDL)).

	2018	*2019*	*2020*	*2021*	*2022*
	Exceeding permissible limits	*Exceeding permissible limits*	*Exceeding permissible limits*	*Exceeding permissible limits*	*Exceeding permissible limits*
Payments* total	5,953.3	3,414.7	3,525.8	6,544.5	10,374.4
..atmospheric air	1,648.4	1,294.3	183.4	211.5	5,733.9
..water bodies	4,177.9	2,043.2	3,171.3	6,168.6	4,454.8
..waste management	127.0	77.2	171.1	164.4	185.7

Source: https://statbank.statistica.md.

* Information is presented without the data on districts from the left side of the river Nistru and municipality Bender.

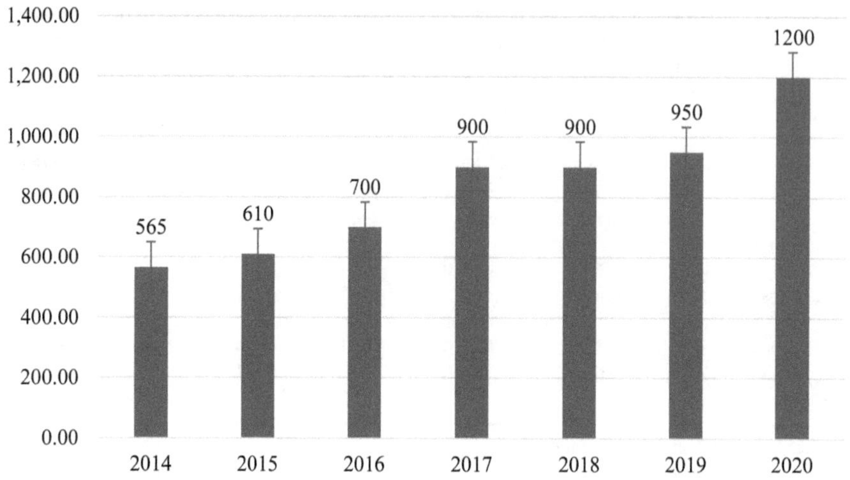

Figure 3.132 Moldova. Total subsidy found in organic agriculture (million MDL).
Source: EU4Environment (2022).

20% are provided to encourage the production of organic agri-foods. However, Figures 3.132 and 3.133 indicate that funding allocated to organic farmers remains extremely limited, averaging only MDL 2 million per year, which is less than 0.2% of the total subsidy fund (EU4Environment, 2022).

Even though the Fund is authorized to support organic farming, the share of subsidies allocated to the sector is rather small. This indicates the modest development of this sector and the challenges faced by farmers in meeting the general

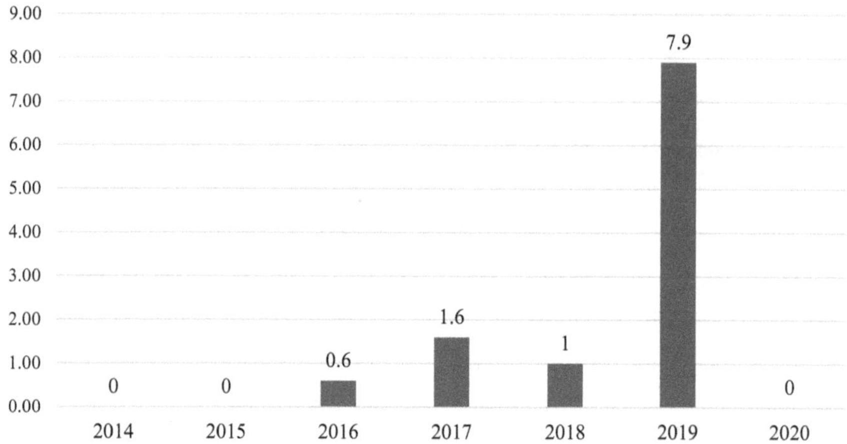

Figure 3.133 Moldova. Amount allocated for organic agriculture.
Source: EU4Environment (2022).

requirements of organic farming. In addition, the small number of operators and the small area of land farmed organically (only 1% of the total agricultural area) also indicate a lack of interest among most farmers in such activities (EU4Environment, 2022). There are a number of reasons related to both demand (i.e., little interest in the domestic market) and supply (i.e., increased certification requirements and the need for intensive investment).

Ukraine

Green economy/environmental innovation

Russia's large-scale aggression against Ukraine has shed light on long-standing barriers to achieving excellence in scientific research, disseminating knowledge to the public, and fostering competitive research, development, and innovation (Table 3.48) in Ukraine's industrial sector (OECD, 2021).

Corporate R&D spending typically accounts for 60% or more of total R&D spending in OECD countries, but in Ukraine, it only constitutes 20% of R&D spending, equivalent to 0.08% of GDP in 2020 (IEA, 2021). This contrasts with 0.88% in neighboring Poland, 1.21% in the Czech Republic, and an EU average of 1.53% (Guellec & van Pottelsberghe de la Potterie, 2004). Even this modest spending is largely self-funded by companies, with 85% coming from their own resources and less than 2% from the government budget (World Bank, 2022). Basic policy instruments such as innovation vouchers (Nature, 2022) and matching grants (Comin & Hobijn, 2010) have been implemented but have not significantly increased business R&D investment. Moreover, the low level of business R&D spending in Ukraine is likely attributed to challenging framework conditions. Insufficient funding for defense-related research has left the Science, Technology, and Innovation (STI) sector ill-prepared to support national defense efforts, prompting a shift in priorities under emergency conditions.

Table 3.48 Ukraine: Innovation costs of industrial enterprises 2014–2019.

Year, ***	*Share of innovation-active enterprises in the total number of industrial enterprises, %*	*Innovation costs, in million hryvnias*
2014	16.1	7,695.9
2015	17.3	13,813.7
2016	18.9	23,229.5
2017	16.2	9,117.5
2018	16.4	12,180.1
2019	15.8	14,220.9

Source: https://www.ukrstat.gov.ua.

* Data for 2014–2019 are given without including the temporarily occupied territory of the Autonomous Republic of Crimea, the city of Sevastopol, and parts of the temporarily occupied territories of the Donetsk and Luhansk regions.

** Data for 2015–2019 are given for legal entities engaged in industrial activities with average employment of 50 or more employees.

Public expenditure on environmental protection

Between 2014 and 2020, environmental expenditures from both state and local budgets nearly doubled, amounting to about UAH 9 billion (EUR 300 million). Despite this increase, they account for less than 1% of total annual spending. The classification of environmental protection and environmental resource management activities in Ukraine differs from those used in the European standard statistical classification system. Several budget programs considered to be environmental activities in Ukraine are not recognized as such by Eurostat or have unclear or missing environmental objectives.

As shown in Table 3.49, environmental spending in the consolidated budget increased from UAH 3.4 billion in 2014 to UAH 9.1 billion in 2020, accounting for 0.6–0.8% of total spending.

Administered by the Ministry of Defense, the budget program "Disposal of ammunition, liquid components of rocket fuel, weapons, military equipment and other military property, ensuring explosion and fire safety of arsenals, bases and depots of the Armed Forces of Ukraine" (code 2101210) aims to prevent man-made disasters in storage facilities for missiles, ammunition, and liquid components of rocket fuel (Ministry of Defence of Ukraine, 2020). In 2020, approximately UAH 2.5 billion was allocated under this program for the disposal of obsolete and surplus ammunition, liquid rocket fuel components, weapons, military equipment, and other military assets, as well as for the protection and defense of bases, depots, and arsenals (Ministry of Defence of Ukraine, 2020; State Treasury Service of Ukraine, 2021).

Table 3.49 Ukraine: Expenditures on environmental protection measures in the consolidated budget by functional budget classification (million UAH).

Program	*2014*	*2015*	*2016*	*2017*	*2018*	*2019*	*2020*	*2021p*
Protection and rational use of natural resources	1,534	1,820	2,371	1,981	1,751	1,866	1,532	2,216
Waste disposal	376	565	521	690	1,486	2,274	3,061	4,257
Elimination of other environmental pollution	969	1,910	2,343	2,794	1,943	2,193	1,923	2,496
Conservation of nature reserve fund	72	113	259	428	459	554	614	954
Fundamental and applied research and development in the field of environmental protection	66	81	85	104	130	197	168	121
Other activities in the field of environmental protection	456	1,040	677	1,352	2,472	2,646	1,767	2,520
Total	3,482	5,530	6,255	7,349	8,242	9,731	9,057	12,565
Share of environmental expenditures in the total consolidated budget expenditures, %	0.7	0.8	0.7	0.7	0.7	0.7	0.6	0.7

Source: Neuweg et al. (2023).
Note: p = provisional data.

Energy subsidies

From 2017 to 2021, energy pricing policy has undergone significant changes and revisions as part of a gradual transition towards fully liberalized market prices. Responsibility for setting energy prices is divided between the regulatory body (NEURC), the Council of Ministers, and local authorities. Total tax credits and support for fossil fuels in Ukraine are shown in Figures 3.134 and 3.135.

Government support for fossil fuels in Ukraine was estimated at UAH 44.56 billion in 2021 (Table 3.50). Eighty-three percent of the support was directed to end beneficiaries, compared to 17 percent of support to enterprises. Support was provided in the form of direct transfers (UAH 42.92 billion) accounting for 96% of the total support, the main component of which is compensation for electricity rate increases for certain categories of consumers. Tax expenditures amounted to UAH 1.64 billion.

Since 2016, government support for fossil fuels has fallen by 1%. In 2021, tax preferences fell by 22% (2021/2020), from UAH 3.57 billion to UAH 1.64 billion, and direct transfers fell by 65% from UAH 70.68 billion to UAH 42.92 billion (OECD, 2023).

Private spending on environmental protection

The "polluter pays" and "user pays" principles directly implement the "polluter pays" principle, with 80% of all revenues directed to Ukrainian environmental protection funds in the form of pollution payments. According to a study by Yevsuykov et al. (2021), in 2019, the state financed approximately 24.3% of the in-kind costs of the environmental protection system on average in Ukraine, while the remainder was covered by territorial environmental funds and local budgets.

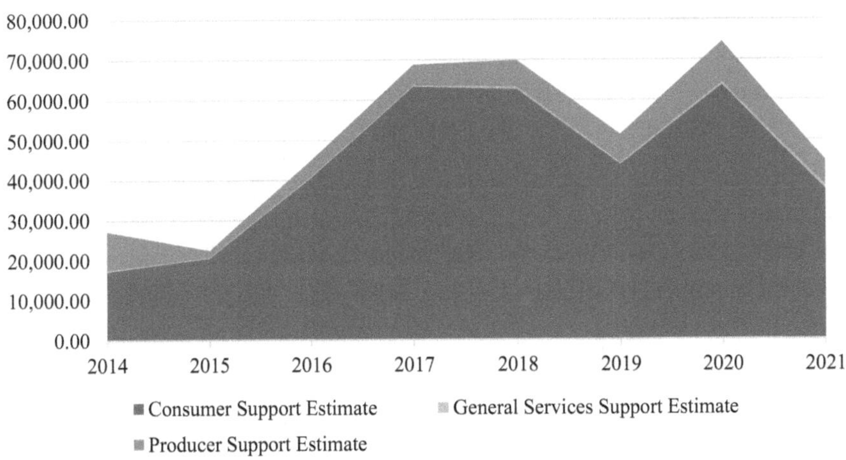

Figure 3.134 Ukraine. Fossil fuel support by beneficiary (million UAH).

Source: OECD (2023).

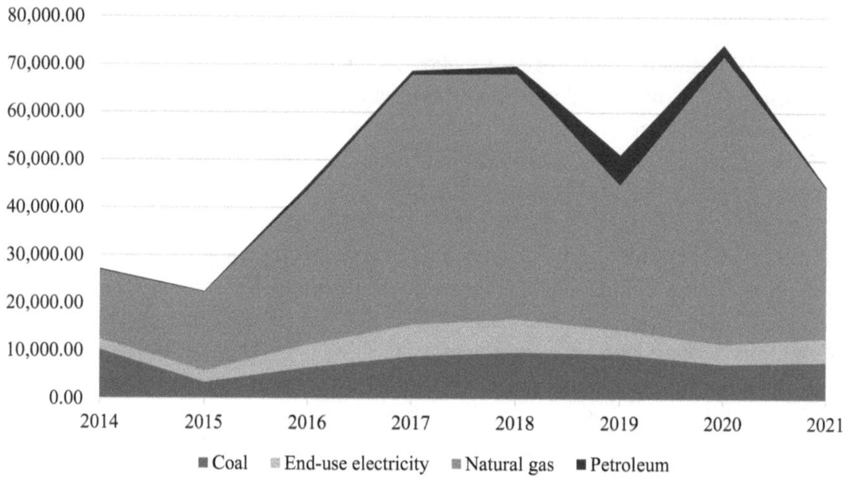

Figure 3.135 Ukraine. Fossil fuel support by fuel type (million UAH).
Source: OECD (2023).

Table 3.50 Ukraine: Government support to fossil fuels by mechanism (billion UAH).

	2016	*2017*	*2018*	*2019*	*2020*	*2021*
Tax expenditures	2.130	2.717	3.841	8.695	3.568	1.636
Direct transfers	42.699	65.919	65.883	42.494	70.680	42.924
Total	44.829	68.636	69.724	51.189	74.248	**44.561**

Source: OECD (2023).

Subsidies in organic farming

The Law on Organic Agriculture adopted by the Ukrainian Parliament in 2011 lacked detailed provisions on implementation and state control, functioning more as a statement of intent. Under the Association Agreement between Ukraine and the European Union, significant legislative revisions have been underway, resulting in a completely new version of the Law on Organic Agriculture developed with input from national regulatory bodies. Concurrently, subsidies for organic farming are being introduced as part of state agricultural subsidies, albeit implemented at the regional government level (oblast level) and not uniformly across all regions. These subsidies primarily cover inspection costs and provide assistance for the transition to organic farming (EcoConnect, 2020).

Summary

In conclusion, it is crucial to highlight that the economies of the Eastern Partnership countries bear equal responsibility for their geographic and economic activities, whether closer or wider in scope. Investments in new energy infrastructure within these countries must prioritize renewable energy sources, potentially including green hydrogen. The EaP countries possess significant potential for solar and wind energy, alongside existing hydropower resources. Embracing renewable energy not only enhances their energy independence from Russian oil and gas but also fosters integration into the European energy market.

Despite efforts by EaP countries to reform their economies, practical challenges remain in demonstrating environmentally friendly development. To address this, EaP countries need to accelerate the introduction of smart agricultural practices and decarbonization measures in industry. There is a need to increase knowledge of green technologies, enhance strategic capabilities, and gradually align the regulatory framework with EU standards and the requirements of the European Green Deal.

The current global trends towards green transformation in all spheres of the economy and public life have influenced the European Union, and in particular its policy towards its neighbors, including the EaP countries. The priorities of global Eurasian Economic Union (EEU) diplomacy impact the new directions of this policy towards the EaP. The Partnership countries are at different levels of integration with the political and legislative system of the EU. Georgia, Ukraine, and the Republic of Moldova have concluded some agreements relating to the EGD under the Association Agreement. Since none of these countries have a well-established program for national implementation of main challenges and benefits of the EGD, it is important to analyze the impact of this EU policy on EaP countries. In the context of the current global environmental and climate issues, as well as the dependence of the Partnership countries on the energy resources of the Russian Federation, the implementation of European green policy values in the countries of this region is timely and important.

Notes

1 Statistics for the Republic of Moldova do not include Transnistria.
2 The Red Book is the main document that summarizes the materials on the current state of rare and endangered species of plants and animals, on the basis of which scientific and practical measures are developed aimed at their protection, reproduction and rational use. The Red Book includes species of plants and animals that constantly or temporarily grow or live in natural conditions in a certain territory (mainly the territory of a single country) and are under threat of extinction. Species of animals and plants listed in the Red Book are subject to special protection throughout the entire individual territory covered by a specific edition of the Red Book.
3 Soil humus is the organic matter formed by the decomposition of plant residues. It is one of the main factors determining soil fertility.

References

Abrahamyan, R.M., Grigoryan, H.A., Astsatryan, H.V., et al. (2023). NO_2 data analytics and visualization service: improving air quality insights in Armenia and Belarus. *Programming and Computer Software*, 49(Suppl 1), S51–S60. https://doi.org/10.1134/S0361768823090025

Agency of Protected Areas (2024). National Park Info. https://apa.gov.ge/en/ accessed on 15.03.2024.

AGREEN (2022). Agreen cross-border alliance for climate-smart and green agriculture in the Black Sea Basin. Subsidy Contract No. BSB 1135.

Ahmadov, E. (2020). Water resources management to achieve sustainable development in Azerbaijan. *Sustainable Futures*, 2(1), 1–10.

Anuarul IPM (2021). Protecția mediului în Republica Moldova. Ministerul Mediului, Chisinau, 2022, p. 131. https://ipm.gov.md/ro/rapoarte-anuale accessed on 1.03.2024.

Armenian National Platform (2023). Equitable access to drinking water supply and sanitation in Armenia, Georgia and Moldova. https://eap-csf.am/equitable-access-to-drinking-water-supply-and-sanitation-in-armenia-georgia-and-moldova/ accessed on 10.04.2024.

Asian Development Bank (2014). Providing clean, safe water to Armenians. https://www.adb.org/results/providing-clean-safe-water-armenians accessed on 07.04.2024.

Atroshchanka, O.A. & Minkevich, S.I. (2004). Forestry inventory system in Belarus. https://www.fao.org/3/XII/0784-B1.htm accessed on 17.03.2024

Azerbaijan. (2021). President of the Republic of Azerbaijan Decree 2021. https://president.az/en/articles/view/50474

Azerbaijan FAA 119 (2020). Biodeversity analysis. USAID, pp. 8–9.

Azerbaijan Water (2024). People with no access to a safe drinking water source in Azerbaijan. https://www.worldometers.info/water/azerbaijan-water/#no-access-water accessed on 8.03.2024.

Baliuk, S.A., Kucher, A.V. & Maksymenko, N.V. (2021). Soil resources of Ukraine: state, problems and strategy of sustainable management. *Ukrainian Geographical Journal*, (2) 114, 03–11. https://doi.org/10.15407/ugz2021.02.003

Belbiznespress (2022). Belarus has calculated the costs of environmental protection. https://neg.by/novosti/otkrytj/prirodookhrannye-raskhody-predpriyatiy-v-2022-godu-sokratilis/ accessed on 24.03.2024.

BELTA (2024). Forests occupy almost 40% of the territory of Belarus. https://www.belta.by/economics/view/lesa-zanimajut-pochti-40-territorii-belarusi-384050-2020/ accessed on 17.03.2024.

Ber, J. (2023). Wojna z przyrodą. Wpływ rosyjskiej agresji na środowisko naturalne Ukrainy. Ośrodek Studiów Wschodnich, Warszawa. https://www.osw.waw.pl/pl/publikacje/komentarze-osw/2023-12-07/wojna-z-przyroda-wplyw-rosyjskiej-agresji-na-srodowisko accessed on 16.03.2024.

Biotica (January 29, 2021). Online google forms survey by authors, Chisinau.

Biroul Național de Statistică al Republicii Moldova (2023). Resursele naturale şi mediul în Republica Moldova, Chişinău, pp. 54–58.

Boyle, R. (2024). Greenhouse Gas Emissions in Azerbaijan. https://www.emission-index.com/countries/azerbaijan accessed on 10.04.2024.

CBITA (2011). Natural resources of Ukraine: characteristics of the main types. https://osvita.ua/vnz/reports/geograf/26416/ accessed on 14.03.2024.

Climate Watch Data (2024). www.climatewatchdata.org.

Comin, D. & Hobijn, B. (2010). Technology diffusion and postwar growth. *NBER Working Paper*, 16378. https://doi.org/10.3386/w16378

Convention on Biological Diversity (2020). Ukraine - country profile. https://www.cbd.int/countries/profile?country=ua accessed on 16.03.2024.

Convention on Biological Diversity (2024). Armenia - country profile. https://www.cbd.int/countries/profile?country=am accessed 16.03.2024.

Deraviaha, I. & Dubianok, S. (2020). кономические инструменты управления водными ресурсами и объектами и водохозяйственными системами в Республике Беларусь: тематические материалы проекта «Водная инициатива ЕС плюс для Восточного партнерства» [Economic instruments for the Management of Water Resources, Bodies of Water and Water Systems in the Republic of Belarus: Thematic Materials under the EU Water Initiative Plus for the Eastern Partnership]. Belarusian State Technological University, Minsk.

DFA (2021). Armenia: development finance assessment. https://www.undp.org/sites/g/files/zskgke326/files/2022-11/DFA%20Armenia_final.pdf

Dziarzhynskaya, N., Hindziuk, L. & Hindziuk, A. (2022). Air pollution monitoring and Its health impact in Belarus. [in.] *Hygiene and health in developing countries - recent advances*. Eds. S. Šostar Turk, U. Rozman. IntechOpen. https://doi.org/10.5772/intechopen.108198

EcoConnect (2020). Report on the status of organic agriculture and industry in Ukraine. http://www.ekoconnect.org/tl_files/eko/p/Projekte/MOE-Laenderberichte/Country-Report-Organic-UKRAINE-EkoConnect-2020.pdf

EcoConnect (2021). Country Report Organic. Armenia. Dresden, p. 8.

EcoConnect (2022). Country Report Organic. Azerbaijan. Dresden, p. 7.

EcoConnect (2022). Report on the Status of Organic Agriculture and Industry in Azerbaijan http://www.ekoconnect.org/tl_files/eko/p/Projekte/MOE-Laenderberichte/Country-Report-Organic-AZERBAIJAN-EkoConnect-2022.pdf accessed: 30.01.2024

Eco Future Project (2024). Belarus and water resources. https://efp.by/belarus_water.php accessed on 13.03.2024.

Energy Community (2017). Secretariat issues policy recommendations for Armenia. Energy Community News. https://energy-community.org/news/Energy-Community-News/2017/07/31.html accessed on 28.01.2024.

ENI SEIS II East (2019a). C4 – Household water use per capita in the Republic of Azerbaijan. https://eni-seis.eionet.europa.eu/east/indicators/c4-2013-household-water-use-per-capita-in-the-republic-of-azerbaijan accessed on 10.04.2024.

ENI SEIS II East (2019b). C4 – Household water use per capita in Georgia. https://eni-seis.eionet.europa.eu/east/indicators/c4-2013-household-water-use-per-capita-in-georgia#:~:text=In%202018%2C%20Georgian%20citizens%20used,per%20person%20on%20daily%20basis accessed on 11.04.2024.

ENI SEIS II East (2019c). C4 – Household water use per capita in the Republic of Moldova. https://eni-seis.eionet.europa.eu/east/indicators/c4-2013-household-water-use-per-capita-in-the-republic-of-moldova/ accessed on 11.04.2024.

EU4Environment (2021a). A partnership for green development in Azerbaijan. https://www.eu4environment.org/app/uploads/2020/09/Country-profile-Azerbaijan-2019-2020.pdf. accessed on 10.04.2024.

EU4Environment (2021b). Raport național bazat pe setul OCDE de indicatori ai creşterii verzi, Chişinau, p. 54.

EU4Environment (2022). Towards green transformation of the Republic of Moldova: state of play in 2021. Monitoring progress based on the OECD green growth indicators. https://www.eu4environment.org/app/uploads/2022/03/Report-Green-Growth-Indicators-Republic-Moldova-2021-ROM.pdf.

EU4Georgia (n.d.). Extended producer responsibility (EPR): business for the environment. https://eu4georgia.eu/wastemanagement/ accessed on 23.05.2024.

European Bank (2022). Moldova diagnostic 2022. https://www.ebrd.com/publications/country-diagnostics accessed on 11.04.2024.

European Environment Agency (2020). Water availability, surface water quality and water use in Eastern Partnership countries: an indicator-based assessment. https://www.eea.europa.eu/publications/regional-water-report accessed on 11.04.2024.

EUROSTAT (2022). https://ec.europa.eu/eurostat/statistics-explained/index.php?title=Government_expenditure_on_environmental_protection

EVN Report (2023). When untreated sewage is dumped into water resources. https://evnreport.com/law-society/when-untreated-sewage-is-dumped-into-water-resources/ accessed on 10.04.2024.

Excerpt N54 (2017). From the minutes of the RA Government session dated 28.12.2017, Concept of reforms and development of "Sevan" National Park.

FAO-FRA (2020). https://data.apps.fao.org/catalog/dataset/naturally-regenerating-forest-area-1990-2020-1000-ha accessed on 15.03.2024.

FiBi & IFOAM- Organics (2021) https://www.fibl.org/fileadmin/documents/shop/1150-organic-world-2021.pdf accessed: 30.01.2024

Fourth National Communication to the United Nations Framework Convention on Climate Change (2021). Republic of Azerbaijan, Baku, p. 19.

Gengenbach, H. (2022). Report on the status of organic agriculture and industry in Azerbaijan. https://orgprints.org/id/eprint/46065/1/Country-Report-Organic-AZERBAIJAN-EkoConnect-2022.pdf accessed on 08.03.2024.

German–Azerbeijan Chamber of Commerce (2023). Environment and water resource protection: measures to modernize water infrastructure in the South Caucasus, Baku, p. 23.

GGGI Technical Report (2023). Azerbaijan's transition to green and inclusive growth - a comparative assessment with the Central Asian Countries. https://greengrowthindex.gggi.org/wp-content/uploads/2023/12/Acosta-and-Hampel-2023-Azerbaijan-and-Central-Asia-green-growth.pdf accessed on 10.04.2024.

Ghazaryan, H. (2013). Soils in Armenia. [in.] *Soil resources of mediterranean and Caucasus countries*. Eds. Y. Yigini, P. Panagos, & L. Montanarella. Joint Research Centre, Luxemburg, p. 5.

Global Water Partnership (GWP) (n.d.). Water Resources Management in Armenia. National Report. https://www.gwp.org/globalassets/global/gwp-cacena_files/en/pdf/armenia.pdf accessed on 8.03.2024.

Global Water Partnership (GWP) (2024). Republic of Georgia - Country Report. Water resources of Georgia and their use. https://www.gwp.org/globalassets/global/gwp-cacena_files/en/pdf/georgia.pdf accessed on 14.03.2024.

Gródek-Szostak, Z., Kotulewicz-Wisińska, K., Lisiakiewicz, L., et al. (2021). *W poszukiwaniu bezpiecznej przystani. Perspektywy pracowników białoruskiego sektora IT w Polsce*. Centrum Polityk Publicznych, Uniwersytet Ekonomiczny w Krakowie.

Guellec, D. & van Pottelsberghe de la Potterie B. (2004). From R&D to productivity growth: Do the institutional settings and the source of funds of R&D matter? *Oxford Bulletin of Economics and Statistics*, 66(3), 353–378.

Heinz Gengenbach (2021). Raport Organic. Georgia, EcoConnect, Dresden, p. 8.

Hryhorczuk, D., Levy, B.S., Prodanchuk, M., et al. (2024). The environmental health impacts of Russia's war on Ukraine. *Journal of Occupational Medicine and Toxicology*, 19(1). https://doi.org/10.1186/s12995-023-00398-y

IEA (2021). Net zero by 2050: a roadmap for the global energy sector. https://doi.org/10.1787/c8328405-en

IEA (2022). Armenia 2022, IEA, Paris. https://www.iea.org/reports/armenia-2022 accessed on 14.02.2024.

IFAW (2023). War in Ukraine has devastating consequences for biodiversity. https://www.ifaw.org/international/press-releases/war-ukraine-biodiversity accessed on 16.03.2024.

IIR (2023). Informative Inventory Report (IIR) of the Republic of Armenia 2023. Submission under the UNECE Convention on Long-range Transboundary Air Pollution in Belarus more than 1,500 hectares of land are certified for growing organic products (2020). https://agronews.com/by/ru/news/agrosfera/2020-01-27/42192 accessed on 17.03.2024.

Index Mundi (2018). Ukraine - PM2.5 air pollution, mean annual exposure. https://www.indexmundi.com/facts/ukraine/indicator/EN.ATM.PM25.MC.M3 accessed on 15.04.2024.

IQAir (2024). Air quality in Yerevan. https://www.iqair.com accessed on 7.04.2024.

ISET (2021). Economic instruments for water management in Georgia. https://iset-pi.ge/storage/media/other/2021-10-06/8d25e1b0-2675-11ec-9ff4-81d57fbeb309.pdf accessed on 11.04.2024.

ISET Policy Brief Series (2023). Air quality in Georgia: need for urgent policy solutions. https://iset-pi.ge/storage/media/other/2023-02-03/b5df64d0-a3ac-11ed-a4d6-431f0ba6a3eb.pdf accessed on 11.04.2024.

Jorjadze, M.P. & Urushadze, T.T. (2015). Organic agriculture in Georgia. *Annals of Agricultural Science*, 13(4), 63.

Kerres, M. (2010). Adaptation to climate change in the Kura-Aras River Basin. Report for KfW Entwicklungsbank. http://www.kfw-entwicklungsbank.de/DE_Home/Sektoren/Wasser/Klimawandel/Kura-Aras.pdf accessed on 27.09.2022.

Konferencja UNCTAD-15 (2021). https://sputnik.by/20211006/makey-odnostoronnie-sanktsii-osobenno-nepriemlemy-v-period-pandemii-1057001984.html accessed on 23.02.2024.

Kostyushin, N. (2019). Sawdust and drip irrigation: organic agriculture is being developed in Belarus. https://soz.bio/opilki-i-kapelnyj-poliv-v-belarusi-razvivayut-organicheskoe-selskoe-hozyajstvo/ accessed on 17.03.2024.

Lysenkov, A. (2021). Report on the status of organic agriculture and industry in Armenia. https://orgprints.org/id/eprint/46040/1/Country-Report-Organic-ARMENIA-EkoConnect-2021.pdf

Maghedani, T. (2022). Air pollution regulation in Georgia: current needs and policies. https://ge.boell.org/en/2022/12/15/atmosperuli-haeris-dabindzurebis-kontroli-sakartveloshi-arsebuli-politika-da accessed on 11.04.2024.

Mammadova, S. (2015). Meteorological study of the air pollution in the cities of Azerbaijan. *International Journal of Engine Research*, 4(3), 93–98.

Mammadova, S. & Rostamnia, S. (2022). The ecogeographical impact of air pollution in the Azerbaijan cities: possible plant/synthetic-based nanomaterial solutions. *New Insights on Plant Mediated or Traditionally Prepared Nanomaterials for Biomedicine and Environmental Applications*, 1934554. https://doi.org/10.1155/2022/1934554

Martirosyana, S. & Khachatrian, T. (2020). Armenia's worsening air quality: particulate pollution in Yerevan tops Moscow. https://hetq.am/en/article/112482#:~:text=During%20the%20period%202000%2D2018,was%20in%202017%20%2D%20291%2C000%20tons accessed on 7.04.2024.

Martus, E. (2023). Building a green state? Environmental politics in Georgia. *Eurasian Geography and Economics*. https://doi.org/10.1080/15387216.2023.2169949

Matuszak, S. (2021). Spichlerz świata? Rozwój rolnictwa na Ukrainie, Ośrodek Studiów Wschodnich, Warszawa, p. 13.

Medvedev, I.V. (2021). Environmental protection: statistical collection. National Statistical Committee, Minsk, p. 202.

Ministerul Agriculturii şi Industriei Alimentare, https://www.madrm.gov.md/ro/content/agricultura-ecologic%C4%83 (2021) accessed on: 30.01.2024

Ministry of Defence of Ukraine (2020). Order of the Ministry of Defence No. 66 of 27 February 2020 on the Approval of the Passport of the Budget Programme, Ministry of Defence of Ukraine, Kyiv. https://www.mil.gov.ua/content/mou_orders/mou_2020/66_nm_2020.pdf. https://www.mineconomy.am/ accessed on 13.03.2024.

Ministry of Ecology and Natural Resources Republic of Azerbaijan (2021). Fourth National Communication to The United Nations Framework Convention on Climate Change. https://unfccc.int/sites/default/files/resource/FNC%20report.pdf

Ministry of Environmental Protection and Agriculture of Georgia (2015). Georgia's Fifth National Report to the Convention on Biological Diversity, Tbilisi, p. 11.

Ministry of Environmental Protection and Agriculture of Georgia (2019a). Georgia`s Greenhouse Gas Inventory 1990–2015 National Inventory Report. Under the United Nations Framework Convention on Climate Change, Tbilisi, p. 13.

Ministry of Environmental Protection and Agriculture of Georgia (2019b). Georgia`s Second Biennial Update Report Under the United Nations Framework Convention on Climate Change, Tbilisi, pp. 12–13.

Ministry of Environmental Protection and Agriculture of Georgia (2021). Fourth National Communication of Georgia under the United Nations Framework Convention on Climate Change, Tbilisi, p. 50.

Ministry of Environmental Protection and Agriculture of Georgia (2023a). First National Forest Inventory in Georgia, Tbilisi, pp. 27–29.

Ministry of Environmental Protection and Agriculture of Georgia (2023b). Georgia`s Long-term Low Emission Development Strategy, Tbilisi, p. 10.
Ministry of Natural Resources and Environment of the Republic of Belarus (2018). Seventh National Communication of the Republic of Belarus in Compliance with the Obligations under the UN Framework Convention on Climate Change, Minsk, p. 90.
Ministry for the Environment (2021). https://www.spyur.am/en/companies/water-committee/70058/
Minpriroda (2018). Стратегия управления водными ресурсами в условиях изменения климата на период до 2030 года (проект) [The Strategy of Water Resource Management in the Context of Climate Change Adaptation for the Period Until 2030: Draft]. Central Research Institute for Complex Use of Water Resources, Ministry of Natural Resources and Environmental Protection of the Republic of Belarus, Minsk.
Minpriroda (2024a). Biodiverity, p. 66. https://www.minpriroda.gov.by/uploads/files/000597_39187_part_5.pdf accessed on 17.03.2024.
Minpriroda (2024b). Biological and landscape diversity. https://minpriroda.gov.by/ru/biolog-landsh-raznoobr-ru/ accessed on 17.03.2024.
Minpriroda (2024c). Vodnyie resursy, p. 40. https://www.minpriroda.gov.by/uploads/files/000597_60789_part_4.pdf accessed on 13.03.2024.
MoE (2020). Fourth National Communication on Climate Change under The United Nations Framework Convention on Climate Change. https://unfccc.int/sites/default/files/resource/NC4_Armenia_.pdf accessed on 30.11.2023.
National Agency of Investments and Privatization (2020). Organic agriculture in the Republic of Belarus: current status and prospects, p. 15. https://investinbelarus.by/upload/medialibrary/b48/organicheskoe-selskoe-khozyaystvo-1_compressed-_4_.pdf accessed on 17.03.2024.
National Legal Internet Portal of the Republic of Belarus (2022). Decision No. 91 (2022) of the Council of Ministers of the Republic of Belarus, February 22. About the National Strategy for Water Resources Management in the Context of Climate Change for the Period until 2030. https://pravo.by/document/?guid=3871&p0=C22200091 accessed on 13.03.2024.
National Statistical Committee of the Republic of Belarus (2022). Air pollution and ozone depletion. https://www.belstat.gov.by/ofitsialnaya-statistika/makroekonomika-i-okruzhayushchaya-sreda/okruzhayuschaya-sreda/sovmestnaya-sistema-ekologicheskoi-informatsii2/a-zagryaznenie-atmosfernogo-vozduha-i-razrushenie-ozonovogo-sloya/ accessed on 10.04.2024.
National Statistics Office of Georgia (2022). Natural Resources of Georgia and Environmental Protection, Tbilisi, p. 16.
National Statistics Office of Georgia (2023a). Natural Resources of Georgia and Environmental Protection, Tbilisi, pp. 7, 39.
National Statistics Office of Georgia (2023b). Environment Statistics, Environmental Indicators, https://www.geostat.ge/en/modules/categories/73/environment-statistics
Nature (2022). Ukraine's scientists need help to rebuild their research system. *Nature*, 609(7). https://doi.org/10.1038/d41586-022-02760-2
NDC Registry (2023). Government of the Republic of Moldova, Updated Nationally Determined Contribution of the Republic of Moldova,, Document PDF from https://unfccc.int/NDCREG?page=1
Neuweg, I., Petkova, N., Michalak, K., et al. (2023). Review of environmental taxation and environmental expenditure in Ukraine. OECD Environment Working Papers, No. 231. OECD Publishing, Paris. https://doi.org/10.1787/921319bc-en
OECD (2021). OECD policy responses on the impacts of the war in Ukraine. https://www.oecd.org/ukraine-hub/policy-responses/building-back-a-better-innovation-ecosystem-in-ukraine-85a624f6/
OECD (2023). Inventory of support measures for fossil fuels: country notes. www.oecd.org/about/publishing/corrigenda.htm
Open Data Portal (2023). State cadastre of territories and objects of the nature reserve fund of Ukraine https://data.gov.ua/dataset/mepr_05 accessed on 16.03.2024.

Organic in Ukraine (2021). About organic. https://organic.com.ua/en/organic-in-ukraine/ accessed on 16.03.2024.

Ormax (January 31, 2021). Online Google Forms survey by authors, Chisinau.

Popovich, N., Migliozzi, B., Patanjali, K., et al. (2019). See how the world's most polluted. air compares with your city's. *New York Times*. https://www.nytimes.com/interactive/2019/12/02/climate/air-pollution-compare-ar-ul.html accessed on 7.04.2024.

Presidency of the Republic of Moldova (2021). The country's national afforestation program, discussed at the Presidency. https://www.presedinte.md/rom/comunicate-de-presa/programul-national-de-impadurire-a-tarii-discutat-la-presedintie accessed on 29.02.2024.

President of the Republic of Belarus (2024). Forestry industry https://president.gov.by/ru/belarus/economics/osnovnye-otrasli/selskoe-i-lesnoe-hozjajstvo, accessed on 16.03.2024.

Prikhodko, I. (2024). The first results of the green economy program implementation can be called successful. https://minpriroda.gov.by/printv/ru/news-ru/view/pervye-rezultaty-realizatsii-programmy-zelenoj-ekonomiki-mozhno-nazvat-uspeshnymi-ivan-prixodko-4940/ accessed on 24.05.2024.

Programme of the Government of the Republic of Armenia, 2021–2026., https://www.gov.am/en/gov-program/, 27.05.2024

Red List (2003). Biodiversity. http://promotegeorgia.com/en/data/unique-georgia/red-list-biodiversity accessed on 15.03.2024.

Reliefweb (2023). Ukraine: thousands of children lack safe drinking water as Kakhova Dam crisis unravels. https://reliefweb.int/report/ukraine/ukraine-thousands-children-lack-safe-drinking-water-kakhovka-dam-crisis-unravels accessed on 15.04.2024.

Republic of Armenia (April 22, 2021a). On Approval of the Nationally Determined Contribution 2021–2030 of the Republic of Armenia to Paris Agreement, Decision of The Government of The Republic of Armenia, N 610-L.

Republic of Armenia (2021b). Third Biennial Update Report. UNDP Armenia, Yerevan, p. 12.

Republic of Azerbaijan (2008). Law of Azerbaijan Republic on Organic Agriculture (No 650-IIIQ/13 June 2008).

Republic of Azerbaijan (2023). Updated document on nationally determined contributions (NDC), Baku, pp. 4–6.

Republic of Moldova (1998). Legea Nr. 1538/1998 privind fondul ariilor naturale protejate de stat, https://www.legis.md/cautare/getResults?doc_id=108578&lang=ro accessed on 13.03.2024.

Republic of Moldova (2014). HG Nr. 409/2014 cu privire la aprobarea Strategiei naționale de dezvoltare agricolă și rurală pentru anii 2014–2020. https://www.legis.md/cautare/getResults?doc_id=110039&lang=ro# accessed on 15.03.2024.

Republic of Moldova (2023). On the approval of the National Waste Management Programme for the years 2023–2027 and the Action Plan for its implementation for the period 2023–2027 (2023). Număr unic 651/MM/2023, https://cancelaria.gov.md/ro/content/cu-privire-la-aprobarea-programului-national-pentru-gestionarea-deseurilor-pentru-anii-2023 accessed on 1.02.2024.

SB News (2014). About 40 percent of Belarus is covered by forests. www.sb.by/articles/generous-in-its-gifts-for-friends.html accessed on 16.03.2024.

Shumilova, O., Tockner, K., Sukhodolov, A., et al. (2023). Impact of the Russia-Ukraine armed conflict on water resources and water infrastructure. *Nature Sustainability*, 6, 578–586.

State Forest Resources Agency of Ukraine (2024). General characteristic of Ukrainian forests. https://forest.gov.ua/en/areas-activity/forests-ukraine/general-characteristic-ukrainian-forests, accessed on 16.03.2024.

State Statistics Service of Ukraine (https://ukrstat.gov.ua/) (2021). Energy balance of Ukraine, https://stat.gov.ua/en/datasets/energy-balance-ukraine

Statistical Committee of Armenia (2022). https://statbank.armstat.am/pxweb/en/ArmStatBank/?rxid=9ba7b0d1-2ff8-40fa-a309-fae01ea885bb<

STAT (2019). Environmental protection. https://www.stat.gov.az/source/environment/?lang=en accessed on 10.04.2024.

State Treasury Service of Ukraine (2021). Reports on the Execution of the State Budget for the Period 2010–2021, State Treasury Service of Ukraine, Kyiv.

Statistical Committee Republic of Armenia (2023). https://armstat.am/en/ accessed on 28.02.2024.

Tăriță, A., Sandu, M. & Lozan, R. (2013). Apa este deminesiunea ecologică fundamentală a existenție. https://moldova-suverana.md/article/apa-este-dimensiunea-ecologic-fundamental-a-existenei_423 accessed on 29.03.2024.

The Solid Waste Management Company of Georgia (n.d.). About us. https://waste.gov.ge/ka/?page_id=20&lang=en accessed on May 23, 2024.

The State Statistical Committee of the Republic Azerbaijan (2023). Emissions of harmful substances into the atmospheric air. https://www.stat.gov.az/news/index.php?lang=en&id=5473 accessed on 7.04.2024.

Tomiltseva, A.I., Yatsyk, A.V., Mokin, V.B., et al. (2017). Ecological basics of water resources management: training. Institute of Ecological Management and Balanced Nature Management, Kyiv, p. 10.

Tsapko, A.V. (2018). Land resources of Belarus and their sustainable use. https://elar.urfu.ru/bitstream/10995/65039/1/978-5-8295-0567-7_2018-086.pdf accessed on 17.03.2024.

UNCG (2022). The 44% of the most valuable natural territories of Ukraine are covered by war. https://uncg.org.ua/44-pzf/ accessed on 16.03.2024.

UNDP (2022). Health impacts and social costs associated with air pollution in larger urban areas of Ukraine. https://www.undp.org/ukraine/publications/health-impacts-and-social-costs-associated-air-pollution-larger-urban-areas-ukraine accessed on 14.02.2024.

UNDP (2023). The low emissions development programme was approved, bringing Moldova one step closer towards a carbon-free economy. https://www.undp.org/moldova/press-releases/low-emissions-development-programme-was-approved-bringing-moldova-one-step-closer-towards-carbon-free-economy accessed on 15.03.2024.

UNECE (2004). Environmental performance reviews: Azerbaijan., https://www.un-ilibrary.org/content/books/9789210040693, 27.04.2024

UNECE (2019). Report on the national targets set under the Protocol on Water and Health in the Republic of Azerbaijan. https://unece.org/fileadmin/DAM/env/water/Protocol_on_W_H/Target_set_by_parties/Azerbaijan/Target_setting_report_AZ_final.pdf accessed on 10.04.2024.

UN Environment (2021). Third Biennial. Update Report of the Republic of Moldova, Chisinau, p.48.

UN Environment (2023).Third Biennial. Update Report of the Republic of Moldova, Chisinau, p. 48.

UNEP (2021). Nationally Determined Contribution of the Republic of Belarus to the reduction of greenhouse gas emissions until 2030. https://leap.unep.org/en/countries/by/national-legislation/nationally-determined-contribution-republic-belarus-reduction

UNEP/GRID-Arendal (2005). State of the environment Azerbaijan. http://www.grida.no

UNFCCC (1998). The first national communication on climate change. The United Nations Framework Convention on Climate Change, Kyiv, p. 3.

UNFCCC (2006a). National report on demonstrable progress in implementation of the Kyoto Protocol, Mińsk.

UNFCCC (2006b). Second report of Ukraine on climate change issues. The United Nations Framework Convention on Climate Change, Kyiv, p. 5.

UNFCCC (2016). Updated Nationally Determined Contribution of Ukraine to the Paris Agreement, Kyiv, p. 19.

UNFCCC (2023). The Doha Amendment. https://unfccc.int/process/the-kyoto-protocol/the-doha-amendment accessed on 1.01.2024.

UNICEF (2022). Schools ill-equipped to provide healthy and inclusive learning environments for all children. UNICEF, WHO. https://www.unicef.org/armenia/en/press-releases/

schools-ill-equipped-provide-healthy-and-inclusive-learning-environments-all accessed on 10.04.2024.
United Nations (2022). UN Report. SDG 6 snapshot in Belarus. https://sdg6data.org/en/country-or-area/Belarus accessed on 11.04.2024.
UNSDCF (2020). UN - Azerbaijan Sustainable Development Cooperation Framework 2021–2025. Common Country Analysis for UNSDCF and the 2030 Agenda. https://www.undp.org/sites/g/files/zskgke326/files/2022-08/UN%20Sustainable%20Development%20Cooperation%20Framework%202021-2025.pdf, 25.03.2024
Urushadze, T.F., Winfried E.H. Blum, J., et al. (2015). Soils of Georgia and problems of their use. *Annals of Agrarian Science*, 13(4), 8.
WAREG (2023). Assessing the damages and needs in Ukraine's water supply and sanitation sector: UN report highlights urgent reconstruction efforts. https://www.wareg.org/articles/assessing-the-damages-and-needs-in-ukraines-water-supply-and-sanitation-sector-un-report-highlights-urgent-reconstruction-efforts/ accessed on 15.04.2024.
Water Action Hub (2024). Georgia. Country overview. https://wateractionhub.org/geos/country/80/d/georgia/ accessed on 13.03.2024
Water Resources Management in Armenia (2024). National Report, https://www.gwp.org/globalassets/global/gwp-cacena_files/en/pdf/armenia.pdf, accessed: 8.03.2024
Willer, H. & Lernoud, J. (2016). Organic Agriculture Worldwide 2016: current statistics. Research Institute of Organic Agriculture (FiBL), Frick, Switzerland. https://www.expert-grup.org/ accessed on 11.04.2024.
Willer, H., Trávníček, J., Meier, C., et al. (2021). *World of organic agriculture statistics and emerging trends*. FiBL and IFOAM – Organics International, Frick and Bonn.
World Bank (2022). World Development Indicators. https://databank.worldbank.org/source/world-development-indicators
World Bank (2023a). Armenia forest landscape restoration note. International Bank for Reconstruction and Development. The World Bank, Washington, p. 14.
World Bank (2023b). Updated Ukraine recovery and reconstruction needs assessment. Available at: https://www.worldbank.org/en/news/press-release/2023/03/23/updated-ukraine-recovery-and-reconstruction-needs-assessment accessed on 14.04.2024
World Bank Blogs (2020). How a water supply and sanitation project helped Belarus exceed expectations. https://blogs.worldbank.org/en/water/how-water-supply-and-sanitation-project-helped-belarus-exceed-expectations accessed on 11.04.2024.
World Bank Open Data (2023). World Development Indicators, https://databank.worldbank.org/source/world-development-indicators
World Economic Forum (2019). The Global Competitiveness Report 2019, World Economic Forum, Geneva, http://www3.weforum.org/docs/WEF_TheGlobalCompetitivenessReport2019.pdf accessed on 28.012024.
World Health Organization (WHO) (2024). Ukraine [Country overview]. data.who.int, accessed on 15.04.2024.
World Resources Institute (2015). Aqueduct projected water stress country rankings. https://www.wri.org/data/aqueduct-projected-water-stress-country-rankings accessed on 10.04.2024.
WWF (2024). Forests of Armenia. https://www.wwf.am/en/our_work/forests/ accessed on 15.03.2024.
Yevsuykov, O.P., Shvydka, T.I., Streltsov, V.Y., et al. (2021). Financing environmental protection projects in Ukraine. *Ukrainian Journal of Ecology*, 11(1), 186–190.
Yolchiyeva, F., Hacjiyeva, S., Huseyinli, A.A., et al. (2020). Ecological problems of water resources in Azerbaijan and their impact on human health. *Central Asian Journal of Environmental Science and Technology Innovation*, 1(2), 71–76.
Yuzbashieva, G.Z. & Yuzbashiev, I.H. (2023). *Technical and technological modernization of Azerbaijan economy: solutions*. CIMS. https://fti.dp.ua/conf/2023/06057-1758/
Yuzbashiyeva G.Z., Yuzbahsiyev I.H., & Abasova S.H. (2022). Innovative Factors' Influencing to Azerbaijan National Economy Transformation. 07.07.2022. İARA conference – http://iaraconference.com/pdf/2nd-icctmr-souvenir.pdf

Part II

European Green Deal: essence, character, and mindset

4 Historical context

The premise of the concept of sustainable development was the global nature of ecological threats recognized by the international community and the need for a solidarity approach to environmental protection on a global scale. In 1969, the UN Secretary-General U'Thant announced a report entitled "Man and Environment," which drew attention to the need to solve environmental problems. However, the Rome Report prepared in 1972 indicated how great a threat the depletion of natural resources is to the future development of the world (Meadows et al., 1972). The economic pressure on the environment resulted in its significant degradation. At the same time, it limited the availability of resources necessary for economic development. In 1987, in the report "Our Common Future," the World Commission on Environment and Development, established by the United Nations and chaired by Gro Harlem Brundtland, indicated for the first time, sustainable development as the path to harmonious development without limiting the opportunities of next generations to meet their development needs in the future (Brundtland, 1987).

The detailed assumptions for sustainable development included in the report are as follows:

- level of exploitation of renewable natural resources, at which the rate of wear must not exceed the rate of their natural renewal;
- nonrenewable resources (e.g. minerals, fuels) must be used in such a way so that resources do not run out before their substitutes appear, and land must be reasonably reclamated;
- negative impacts on air, water, and other environmental elements must be minimized to maintain the overall integrity of the system;
- equal access to the environment and its resources must be guaranteed to all entities and citizens of the world;
- basic needs of societies must be secured;
- income and social security must be fairly distributed;
- there must be access to the environment and its resources and to recreation in a healthy environment.

DOI: 10.4324/9781003486732-7

The Brundtland Report (1987) was the subject of discussion at the United Nations Conference on Environment and Development (known as the "Earth Summit") in 1992 in Rio de Janeiro. At that time, action plans were adopted to implement the idea of sustainable development. It was to be achieved by reconciling the requirements of environmental protection and the development of the global economy.

During the Earth Summit, three documents on sustainable development were adopted:

1 A declaration specifying the rights and obligations of individual countries in implementing sustainable development.
2 Basic principles of sustainable development.
3 A set of more than 2,500 recommendations for actions for sustainable development on a global scale (the so-called Agenda 21 [United Nations, 1992]).

Among the 27 principles of sustainable development, the following were adopted from the point of view of the role of humans in environmental protection:

1 The human right to a healthy and productive life in harmony with nature, defining man as the subject of sustainable development.
2 Equal right to development for current and future generations.
3 The importance of environmental protection as an integral component of the sustainable development process.
4 The need to change consumption and production.
5 Public participation in the management of environmental resources.
6 Interconnectivity and indivisibility of development and environmental protection.

The declaration was supplemented with a set of 2,500 recommendations. They assume, among others, recognition of human mental development as the main goal of life, determination of the unsurpassable level of satisfaction of material needs, acceptance of the concept of sustainable development, stable and sustainable exploitation of natural resources, and creation of ecological market policies.

International cooperation on climate change was launched in 1992 as part of the UN Framework Convention and continues to this day. Agenda 21 identified humanity's problems in the 21st century and proposals to solve them. A new goal adopted in 1992 by most of the countries participating in UNCED, sustainable development, did not mean specific solutions. However, the goal of development was emphasized, which was a new model of prosperity that would protect the environment and meet the needs of humanity.

The ecological problems of sustainable development include (Spangenberg, 2002):

- global warming;
- destruction of ecosystems, species, and landscape diversity;
- depletion of nonrenewable resources;
- overexploitation of renewable resources;
- human health hazards (e.g., harmful substances, radiation, noise).

In turn, the following are indicated among the economic problems:

- lack of stability of national economies;
- insufficient satisfaction of basic needs;
- high degree of capital concentration, domination of economic power, and inflation;
- noneconomic imbalance, dependence on raw material supplies, and underdevelopment of many regions of the world;
- state debt, insufficient provision of public goods, and unfair distribution of income.

Among the sociocultural problems, the following were identified:

- Insufficient global development of democracy and the rule of law;
- gender inequality and wage disparities;
- lack of internal and external security (conflicts, violence, competition for influence);
- threats to human health and quality of life.

As a UN document, Agenda 21 adopted recommendations adapted to global, regional, national, and local development problems. These recommendations became the foundation for the development of EU and OECD programs.

In 1992, the United Nations Conference initiated international cooperation on the implementation of the idea of sustainable development, which is currently being continued. In the Rio Declaration, up to five principles recognized the fundamental role of partnership in creating and implementing the vision of development and building a civic society regionally. These include Principles 7, 10, 20, 21, and 22. Implementing the idea of sustainable development in environmental, spatial, economic, institutional, and political terms is impossible without cooperation with non-EU countries to contribute to peace, security, and self-sustaining development of the Earth (Treaty on European Union, 2004; Rogall, 2005).

The Johannesburg summit in 2002 was to review the implementation of Agenda 21 and other arrangements from ten years ago by the international community. The declaration and obligations of sustainable development adopted at the UN forum required the integration of activities in three key areas (Johannesburg Summit, 2002):

1 Economic growth and equitable distribution of benefits—achieving responsible, long-term growth that benefits all nations and communities requires an integrated approach to interconnected global economic systems.
2 Protection of natural resources and the environment—preserving the natural heritage and resources for future generations requires developing economically rational solutions that will limit the consumption of resources; this will stop environmental pollution and save natural ecosystems.

3 Social development—making every effort to ensure that the rich texture of cultural and social diversity is not violated and that all members of societies they had the instruments to shape their future, to address the global needs for work, food, education, energy, health care, water and sanitation.

Sustainable development assumes maintaining a balance between three dimensions: economic, social, and ecological (Pawłowski, 2009, Poveda, 2017). Taking into account the economic dimension of sustainable development means that the other two dimensions will not inhibit it. On the other hand, they can become stimulants through technological and technical progress forced by these dimensions. Thus, they will increase the level of society's education and participation in decision-making, create new jobs, increase activity and entrepreneurship, and improve the efficiency of the use of labor and natural resources. Sustainable development at the macroeconomic level should ensure the implementation of economic goals (social and material well-being), as well as ecological goals (environmental quality), and social goals (justice and security).

The recommendations of Agenda 21 on sustainable development are verified and updated during the regular sessions of the UN forum. In 2012, 20 years after the Earth Summit in Rio de Janeiro, another UN summit (Rio+20) was held to develop additional sustainable development goals. It was then that the declaration "The Future We Want" was adopted. It was divided into six parts and 280 articles renewing commitments to sustainable development in the 21st century (The Future We Want, 2012).

In 2015, the groundbreaking Sustainable Development Summit was held in New York. It formulated 17 goals and 169 detailed tasks in five separate areas: people, planet, prosperity, peace, and partnership. In turn, the United Nations Conference on Climate Change was held in 2015 in Paris and the next one in 2018 in Katowice. The latter concerned the development of rules for implementing the so-called "Paris Agreement" (Table 4.1).

The 2030 Agenda for Sustainable Development adopted in 2015 in New York during the UN Summit was a groundbreaking document. It defines the most important goals that determine the direction of the world's development by 2050 (United Nations, 2015). Subsequent conferences, which took place in Paris (2015) and Katowice (2018), served to develop global commitments to stop climate change in the long term. Problems related to sustainable development, including climate change, were the subject of the next UN conference held in New York in 2021. The agendas and goals adopted at the UN forum are recommendations for the implementation of sustainable development on a global, regional, and national scale.

During the 70th session of 2015, the General Assembly of the United Nations adopted the "2030 Agenda for Sustainable Development," identifying the following 17 sustainable development goals (United Nations, 2015):

Goal 1. End poverty in all its forms everywhere.
Goal 2. End hunger, achieve food security and improved nutrition, and promote sustainable agriculture.
Goal 3. Ensure healthy lives and promote well-being for all at all ages.

Table 4.1 The most important initiatives for sustainable development.

Initiative	*Document*	*Challenges*
Publication of the report of the Global Commission on Environment and Development, 1987.	Brundtland Report *Our Common Future*	The term *sustainable development* is understood as development in which the needs of the present generation can be met without compromising the opportunities to meet the needs of future generations.
United Nations Conference on Environment and Development in Rio de Janeiro, "Earth Summit," 1992.	Declaration on Environment and Development, UN Framework Convention on Climate Change, Agenda 21, Convention on the Conservation of Biological Diversity	Reaffirmation of the Declaration of the United Nations Conference on the Human Environment adopted in Stockholm in 1972. Adoption of 27 principles of sustainable development. Formulation of international cooperation assumptions regarding reducing greenhouse gas emissions, which were further specified in the Kyoto Protocol in 1997. A set of recommendations for implementing sustainable development programs.
United Nations Conference World Summit on Sustainable Development in Johannesburg, "Earth Summit," 2002.	Johannesburg Declaration on Sustainable Development	Commitments were made to work towards sustainable development by building a humanitarian, just, and responsive global society.
United Nations Conference on Sustainable Development in Rio de Janeiro, Rio+20, 2012.	"Agenda 21" 20 years later, "The Future We Want"	Renewing commitments to sustainable development and taking action to educate and promote the idea.
UN Sustainable Development Summit in New York, 2015.	2030 Agenda for Sustainable Development, "Transforming our world"	Sustainable development goals (17) were divided into 169 detailed tasks structured around the five pillars: people, planet, prosperity, peace, and Partnership.
United Nations Climate Change Conference, Paris, 2015.	UN Framework Convention on Climate Change, the "Paris Agreement"	The global agreement on climate change adopted under the so-called Conference of the Parties, COP 21, was a commitment to keep global warming to less than 2°C as a result of reducing carbon dioxide emissions.
United Nations Climate Change Conference (COP24), Katowice, 2018.	UN Framework Conference on Climate Change, the "Katowice Climate Package"	Establishing detailed rules for implementing the "Paris Agreement."

Source: Own study.

Goal 4. Ensure inclusive and equitable quality education and promote lifelong learning opportunities for all.
Goal 5. Achieve gender equality and empower all women and girls.
Goal 6. Ensure availability and sustainable management of water and sanitation for all.
Goal 7. Ensure access to affordable, reliable, sustainable and modern energy for all.
Goal 8. Promote sustained, inclusive and sustainable economic growth, full and productive employment and decent work for all.
Goal 9. Build resilient infrastructure, promote inclusive and sustainable industrialization, and foster innovation.
Goal 10. Reduce inequality within and among countries.
Goal 11. Make cities and human settlements inclusive, safe, resilient, and sustainable.
Goal 12. Ensure sustainable consumption and production patterns.
Goal 13. Take urgent action to combat climate change and its impacts by regulating emissions and promoting developments in renewable energy.
Goal 14. Conserve and sustainably use the oceans, seas and marine resources for sustainable development.
Goal 15. Protect, restore and promote sustainable use of terrestrial ecosystems, sustainably manage forests, combat desertification, and halt and reverse land degradation and halt biodiversity loss.
Goal 16. Promote peaceful and inclusive societies for sustainable development, provide access to justice for all and build effective, accountable and inclusive institutions at all levels.
Goal 17. Strengthen the means of implementation and revitalize the global partnership for sustainable development.

The assumption of sustainable development is to reduce the scope of poverty and social exclusion while ensuring similar development conditions for future generations. Sustainable development should enable economic development, maintaining appropriate proportions between development needs necessary to improve the standard of living and environmental protection. Several tasks were assigned to achieve each goal (Dalampira & Nastis, 2020).

At its core, the European Green Deal is an attempt to transform the European economy and European consumption patterns. However, this process involves a fundamental reconstruction of the European energy system and occupies a correspondingly high position on the EU policy agenda. However, the implementation of the European Green Deal will change relations between the EU and its neighbors and will redefine the priorities of the EU's global policy. Figure 4.1 presents the strategic implications of the European Green Deal for the further development of the EU.

For Europe to become climate neutral by 2050, the European Green Deal must have one main goal: changing the way energy is produced and consumed in the EU. Energy production and use in the economy account for more than 75% of EU greenhouse gas emissions (IEA, 2020). In 2022, wind and solar power generated a record 22% of the EU's electricity (EMBER, 2023), overtaking fossil gas (20%) and remaining above coal power (16%) for the first time. This situation will change completely by 2050, provided that the European Green Deal is successful. According to the forecasts adopted by the European Commission, in 2030, fossil fuels will

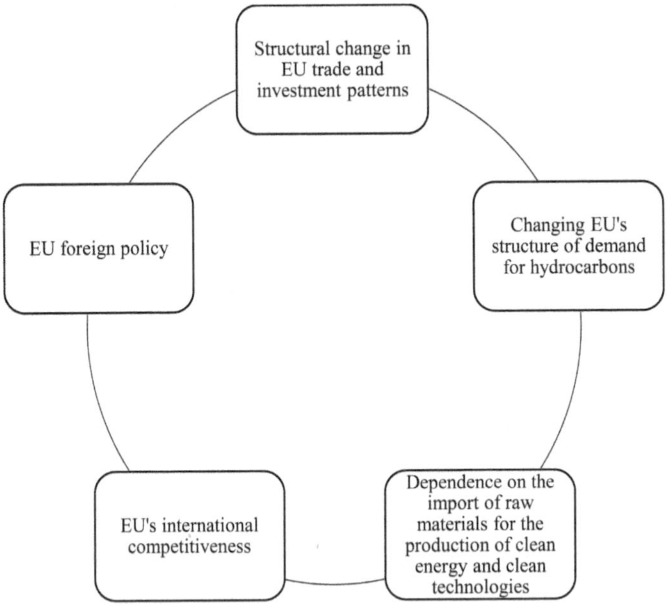

Figure 4.1 Strategic implications of the European Green Deal.

Source: Own study.

continue to provide approximately half of the EU's energy. However, please note that the intensity of fossil fuel pollution varies. By 2030, the use of coal, the most polluting element in the energy mix (Burke & Fishel, 2020) will have been significantly reduced. Crude oil, and especially natural gas, could be phased out at a later date. Most changes regarding oil and gas will occur between 2030 and 2050. It is expected that oil will be almost completely phased out during this period, while natural gas will provide only 10% of the EU's energy in 2050. This profound transformation of the EU's energy system will have various strategic geopolitical repercussions.

After Russia invaded Ukraine, it became immediately obvious that the European energy system must undergo a breakthrough change. Some expected that this new geopolitical landscape will halt the transition from fossil fuels to clean energy. Instead, the EU has made an ambitious energy transition its immediate priority, which is crucial as a response to the numerous emerging crises.

The strategic implications of global decarbonization naturally focus on the impact that reduced demand for oil and gas in large markets could have on producing countries. In the case of Europe, this applies in particular to its main gas suppliers in the Middle East, North Africa, the Caspian Sea region and Central Asia, which base their economies on revenues from the export of fossil fuels to the European Union. The projected decline in oil and gas imports into the EU will have an almost immediate effect of reducing investment in new fossil fuel infrastructure and even reducing efforts to maintain existing infrastructure. This will happen even though, as observed above, the EU is expected to keep imports of oil and natural gas more or less unchanged for at least the next decade (Leonard et al., 2021). Another potential long-term impact of the European Green Deal on the EU's neighbors must also be kept in mind: a possible increase in trade in green electricity and green hydrogen.

One of the main factors in implementing the European Green Deal is electrification (COM, 2020). To meet the growing demand for electricity from renewable sources over the next decades, Europe may rely on imports of solar and wind energy from neighboring regions. In particular, the Middle East and North Africa benefit from some of the best insolation in the world, from the Sahara to the Arabian Peninsula, as well as from world-class wind energy locations, from the Atlantic coast of Morocco to the Red Sea coast in Egypt (Leonard et al., 2021). The decline in global demand for oil resulting from the EU's transition to clean energy will also impact the global oil market, especially by a price decline. Its scale will, of course, also depend on the decarbonization trajectories of other countries. If the EU stands alone in significantly reducing its oil consumption, while other economies continue to rely on fossil fuels for their development, the demand in Asian, Latin American, and African markets could partially—and temporarily—offset Europe's withdrawal.

However, the European Green Deal can also create new threats to energy security. These could result in particular from the import of minerals and metals needed (rare earths) for the production of solar panels, wind turbines, lithium-ion batteries, fuel cells, and electric vehicles. Europe itself does not have significant mining and processing capacity for these key raw materials. In November 2023, the EU reached an interim agreement on the European Critical Raw Materials Act, because it was expected that the demand for rare earth elements will grow exponentially in the coming years. Critical raw materials are raw materials of great economic importance to the EU, with a high risk of supply disruption due to the concentration of sources and the lack of affordable and quality substitutes (COM, 2023).

The European Green Deal will have an impact on the EU's international competitiveness. If European companies assume the regulatory costs, which their foreign competitors do not bear, they will become less competitive both domestically and abroad. And if the EU tries to limit this loss and avoid carbon leakage by imposing tariffs on carbon-rich imports, it could be charged with disrupting international trade. This can lead to friction with the major trading partners, especially those with high carbon dioxide emissions, if they see the GHG border adjustment mechanism as an illegal trade barrier.

The European Green Deal is primarily about foreign policy because climate change is a global problem. All these foreign policy efforts will trigger a geopolitical response from the EU's international partners. Responses will include cooperation in implementing complementary climate policies, competitive efforts to redirect trade and investment flows, and downright hostile efforts to counter the effects of the Green Deal.

Climate changes, along with the public health crisis that was the COVID-19 pandemic, constitute one of the most dangerous threats of the 21st century (WHO, 2021). Global warming is, of course, an international problem. It requires coordinated action by all regions and countries in the world (Rahman et al., 2021). Therefore, individual regions and countries have taken various initiatives for sustainable development. They integrate environmental, economic, and social aspects to ensure the survival of current and future generations (Smol, 2022). Table 4.2 presents an overview of environmental initiatives similar to the European Green Deal in other parts of the world. This approach helps place European efforts in a global context.

Table 4.2 An overview of selected environmental initiatives in the context of the European Green Deal.

No.	*Country*	*Program name/ program document*	*Assumptions*
1.	USA	US Green New Deal (GND) Resolution *Recognizing the duty of the Federal Government to create a Green New Deal*	The GND emerged from the growing urgency of climate change. The resolution calls the phenomenon "a direct threat to the national security of the United States." The resolution is based on the statement that climate change poses a direct threat to the United States as it increases environmental, economic, and social instability. Therefore, the federal government has both the responsibility and the opportunity to make large public investments to accelerate the transition to a green, healthy economy through job training, creating jobs, infrastructure, health care, and housing (H. Res. 109, 2019). GND was the first to explicitly link unprecedented investment in social, economic and climate causes with a just transition for local communities and fairer climate outcomes for greenhouse gas emissions worldwide (Grantham Research Institute, 2019). The GND framework differs from other types of climate policy because they are based on large-scale investments to increase communities' resilience to climate disruptions and to reduce emissions. On the other hand, the goals of the GND proposal are not purely short-term, cost-effective changes to decarbonize the economy. They also include the long-term social and economic impacts on jobs, health, and social equality (Boyle et al., 2021). In general terms, GND can be described as an element of a just transition. that considers the employment impacts of the economic transition to renewable energy and the long-term harm to communities resulting from fossil fuel energy pollution (White, 2020). The goals of the Green New Deal include: • Emissions: To reduce net greenhouse gas emissions to zero within ten years. • Manufacturing: To stimulate "massive growth in clean manufacturing." • Energy consumption: To meet all US energy demand "through clean, renewable and emission-free energy sources." • Agriculture: To significantly reduce emissions and other pollutants from agriculture. • Infrastructure: To modernize infrastructure, including transport and housing, and to assure that all infrastructure bills considered by Congress take climate change into account. • Jobs: To guarantee work with a "family wage" for all. • Prosperity and social justice: To ensure quality health care, affordable housing, economic security, clean water, clean air, and healthy food for all in the United States while counteracting systemic social exclusion and injustice.

(Continued)

Table 4.2 (Continued)

No.	Country	Program name/ program document	Assumptions
			The US GND sets zero emissions as a goal to be achieved within a decade from the date of its initial implementation. GND emphasizes the implementation of climate/environmental goals along with specific social justice goals, not to mention the preservation of biodiversity and nature conservation. The US GND aims at sustainable development, emphasizing industry, climate, and community resilience. At the same time, it builds resilience to climate change-related disasters in building and strengthening infrastructure. Part of GND's appeal also centers on its job creation potential, with an emphasis on green growth (Lee et al., 2021). The US GND highlighted the creation of high-wage, sustainable jobs as a motivation and bargaining chip in many aspects of the GND proposal. First, it is intended to restore economic stability to the middle class. Second, it is a way to stimulate local production and reduce "exported" pollution. Third, it is believed to be a way to carry out an economic transformation and improve the conditions and structures of employee responsibility. When it comes to separating the use of natural resources from economic growth, the US Green New Deal does not specifically use the language of separation. However, this separation can possibly be derived from explicit propositions that concern the pressure on natural resources. The US GND targets industries such as agriculture and food. It highlights the importance of restructuring these industries to be more sustainable in ensuring soil health and working with farmers to "remove pollutants." When it comes to social inequality, the US GND is clearly visible in state policies aimed at addressing and remediating this area. One of the main goals of the proposal is to radically reduce social inequalities. The US GND is simple and ambitious in its purpose, which is to improve the standard of living. GND aims to ensure that "all people in the US have high-quality health care, affordable, safe and adequate housing, economic security, clean water, clean air, healthy and affordable food and access to nature (H. Res. 109, 2019)."

(Continued)

Table 4.2 (Continued)

No.	*Country*	*Program name/ program document*	*Assumptions*
2.	South Korea	The Korean Green New Deal (KGND)	South Korea's climate policy is characterized by a significant underreaction to the challenge of reducing greenhouse gas emissions and a failure to facilitate more sustainable consumption and production patterns (South Korean Government, 2020). At the same time, South Korea is very ambitious in its green industrial policy and international initiatives that support its "green growth" strategy (Kalinowski, 2021). The Korean New Deal, announced in Korean on July 14, 2020, was launched as a national development strategy to support post–COVID-19 recovery. It was also to lead international efforts to adapt to the structural changes needed to support a post-pandemic digital and green economy. As part of this policy proposal, the government included a financial package worth a total of KRW 277 trillion (USD 249 billion), including the third supplementary budget (Korean Ministry of Economy and Finance, 2020). The projected cost of the Green New Deal by 2025 is 160 trillion KRW (USD 144 billion). The government's goal is to transform South Korea into: • a smart country at the center of data-driven digital transformation, artificial intelligence networks, and infrastructure; • an ecological country and a responsible member of the global community that achieves balance between people, nature, and growth through the green transition towards net zero emissions; • a safe country that invests in human resources to create a strong employment and social safety net (Korean Ministry of Economy and Finance, 2020). The Korean New Deal consists of three main elements: the New Digital Deal, the Green New Deal, and a stronger safety network. The latter relates to jobs, social safety network systems, and building human resources (Korean Ministry of Economy and Finance, 2020). The Korean Green New Deal has three main priorities: • green infrastructure transformation to strengthen protection against climate and environmental risks against climate and environmental risks; • promoting low-emission and decentralized energy sources, with low-emission and decentralized energy sources that have been negatively affected by the transformation; • development of a green ecosystem of industrial innovations.

(Continued)

Table 4.2 (Continued)

No.	Country	Program name/ program document	Assumptions
			KGND does not set long-term goals, only short-term indicators (until 2025) with regard to the reduction of CO_2 emissions, new jobs and public spending. It focuses on implementing detailed projects that will contribute to achieving these goals. This highlights the stimulating nature of the strategy. The government expects to reduce greenhouse gas emissions by 12.3 $MtCO_2$ equivalent during 2021–2025 (total) through KGND, which is 20% of the total national reduction target (61.3 $MtCO_2$ equivalent) by 2025. Of this, 6.5 $MtCO_2$ equivalent is predicted in the energy sector and 2.3 $MtCO_2$ equivalent in the industrial sector. Furthermore, since KGND aims to transform the socioeconomic structure of the country in the wake of the COVID pandemic, an important performance indicator is job creation. The target is 659,000 jobs, which will be created by 2025 (Agora Energiewende, 2022). South Korea's Green New Deal has been hailed as a milestone for environmental policy planning in East Asia. It is run by the government of one of the richest and fossil fuel-dependent countries in the world, which has an ambitious vision of developing a sustainable economy. However, despite all the detailed lists of political projects, in which the costs have been fully assessed, the ambitions of the Korean Green New Deal lag behind similar US and EU plans in terms of climate goals (in particular the 2030 goals) and projected investment volumes in relation to GDP (Seung-Joon, 2021). This also relates to newly presented goals, which are merely a conversion of existing ones.
3.	Africa	The African Green Stimulus Program	The African Green Stimulus Program aims to strengthen action for environmental sustainability and prosperity in Africa, in line with the call contained in the Durban Declaration of the 17th Ordinary Session of the African Ministerial Conference on the Environment (AMCEN) held in South Africa in 2019 (African Ministerial Conference on the Environment, 2019). It also contributes to the implementation of the African Ministerial Declaration on Biodiversity adopted at the African Ministerial Summit on Biodiversity in November 2018 in Sharm El Sheikh. Arab Republic of Egypt and the Egyptian initiative to promote a Coherent Approach for Addressing Biodiversity Loss, Climate Change, and Land and Ecosystem Degradation endorsed by AMCEN in its Decision 17/1.

(Continued)

Table 4.2 (Continued)

No.	*Country*	*Program name/ program document*	*Assumptions*
			The principles of Partners for Inclusive Green Economies (PIGE) are underpinned by the premise that recovery should recognize the connections between human and environmental health, and go beyond responding to the pandemic in a conventional manner, and instead focus on building resilience to risks, including climate change, biodiversity collapse, and widening inequality. To achieve this stimulus and recovery efforts, they should address the underlying causes of these systemic risks through inclusive, practical, and targeted reforms and investments that balance socioeconomic and environmental priorities. It is considered important that Africa, as well as other developing countries, incorporate and adapt the relevant elements of these guiding principles into their recovery and reconstruction plans, depending on national circumstances. This African Green Stimulus Program aims to support the overall recovery program of the continent from COVID-19 and to contribute to the full implementation of the United Nations 2030 Agenda for Sustainable Development and the Sustainable Development Goals (SDGs). the AU's Agenda 2063. the United Nations Framework Convention on Climate Change (UNFCCC) and its Paris Agreement and Multilateral Environmental Agreements. It is envisaged that this African Green Stimulus Program will provide additional impetus to the realization of the African Regional Flagship Programs (RFPs). It is also recognized that the AGSP could contribute significantly to achieving and enhancing sustainable trade within the AfCFTA over the next decade. The Regional Flagship Programs (RFPs) were adopted at the 14th Session of AMCEN, held from 10–14 September, 2012, in Arusha, Tanzania, as a means for Africa to contribute to the effective implementation of the outcomes of the United Nations Conference on Sustainable Development (Rio +20), which took place in Rio de Janeiro, Brazil, in June 2012. The proposed Regional Flagship Programs as well as project design and finance, technical support requirements and modalities of implementation have been developed for the following five Regional Flagship Programs: 1 African Green Economy Partnership (AGEP); 2 Sustainable Land Management, Desertification, Biodiversity and Ecosystems-based Adaptation to Climate Change (LDBE); 3 Partnership for Sustainable Consumption and Production (SCP) in Africa (PSCPAfrica); 4 African Program on Sustainable Energy Development (APSED); 5 Africa Integrated Environmental Assessment for Sustainable Development (AIEASD).

(Continued)

Table 4.2 (Continued)

No.	*Country*	*Program name/ program document*	*Assumptions*
			Within the abovementioned context. the African Green Stimulus Program has the following objectives (African Union, 2013): • to respond urgently to support key sectors in Africa hardest hit by the Pandemic, such as ecotourism, waste management and the biodiversity economy; • to develop and support short- and medium-term interventions to enhance the implementation of key sectors identified in the African Green Stimulus Program; • to streamline focus, build synergies, and enhance coordination of existing climate change, biodiversity, desertification, land degradation, and green economy programs by consolidating and integrating these under identified key areas into one comprehensive Green Stimulus Program for Africa; • to enhance ambition and support to significantly scale up implementation of existing and new projects and programs in key areas through consolidated financial resource mobilization, technical support, and capacity building, as well as forging partnerships; • to support the development of longer-term transformative green economy programs that contribute to realizing the goals of Agenda 2063, the 2030 Agenda for Sustainable Development, and the Sustainable Development Goals, as well as addressing the imperatives of the Paris Agreement. This African Green Stimulus Program aims to support the continent's overall recovery program from COVID-19 and to contribute to the full implementation of the 2030 Agenda of the United Nations on Sustainable Development and Sustainable Development Goals, the Agenda 2063 of the United Arab Emirates, the UN Framework Convention on Climate Change (UNFCCC) and its Paris Agreement and Multilateral Environmental Agreements. This African Green Stimulus Program is expected to provide additional impetus for the realization of African Regional Flagship Programs (RFPs). It is also recognized that the AGSP could contribute significantly to achieving and enhancing sustainable trade within the AfCFTA over the next decade. Agenda 2063: The Future We Want is based on the African Union (AU) Vision for Africa, "to build an integrated prosperous and peaceful Africa. An Africa "led and governed by its own people and representing a dynamic force on the international stage" as an overarching guide to the future of the African continent. Agenda 2063 recognizes the importance of developing environmentally sustainable and climate-resilient economies and communities on the continent. When it comes to the continent's aspirations, in 2063, Africa will be globally recognized as a continent that respects its environment, is environmentally conscious, and has an established green economy and green energy. Africa's future prosperity will be based on inclusive growth and sustainable development (IRENA and AfDB, 2022).

(Continued)

Table 4.2 (Continued)

No.	*Country*	*Program name/ program document*	*Assumptions*
4.	China	Working Guidance for Carbon Dioxide Peaking and Carbon Neutrality in Full and Faithful Implementation of the New Development Philosophy ("Working Guidance") Action Plan for Reaching Carbon Dioxide Peak Before 2030 ("Action Plan")	In April 2019 China promoted the Belt and Road Initiative International Green Development Coalition as the first regional sustainable plan of China. In 2020, China launched its vision of peak carbon by 2030 and carbon neutrality by 2060 as two major projects aimed at improving air quality and environmental protection in the global context. China is a pioneer in the implementation of green financing to support green projects. Since March 2016, according to China's 13th Five-Year Plan for Economic and Social Development, the country has established a green financing system that includes green credit, green bonds, and green development funds (Sun et al., 2023). In February 2021, China's State Council published a roadmap for the transition towards green development and recycling by 2025. It also improved environmental protection in pursuit of the "beautiful China" goal by 2035 (China Briefing, 2022). In February 2022, the Chinese State Council announced guidelines to accelerate the establishment and improvement of a green and renewable economic system. In early November 2021, China released two key policy documents, further cementing its commitments to decarbonization. The two documents, the "Working Guidance for Carbon Dioxide Peaking and Carbon Neutrality in Full and Faithful Implementation of the New Development Philosophy" ("Working Guidance"), and the "Action Plan for Reaching Carbon Dioxide Peak Before 2030" ("Action Plan") also form the foundation for China's climate policy framework to achieve its carbon reduction targets. known as the "1+N" policy framework (China Briefing, 2022). Both references are "top-level design documents," to jointly set the direction for China's decarbonization efforts. However, the Action Plan goes far beyond its basic goals. It provides a comprehensive overview of the areas of the Chinese economy that will gradually be reduced or switched to sustainable energy and methods. These include heavy industry, agriculture, transport, and the circular economy. In February 2022, the State Council released the Guiding Opinions of the State Council on Accelerating the Establishment and Improvement of a Green, Low-carbon, and Recycling Economic System ("Guiding Opinion"). The document sets broader goals for China to transition to a green economy. The above series of documents will create a "1+N" policy system ("1" means one guideline, and "N" stands for action/implementation plan number). The system will have clear objectives, reasonable division of responsibility, strong measures, and orderly coordination to achieve carbon neutrality.

(Continued)

Table 4.2 (Continued)

No.	Country	Program name/ program document	Assumptions
			To achieve China's green and low-carbon transformation goals, decision makers have set the following specific tasks (China Briefing, 2022): • improving the production system (promoting green upgrading of industries, accelerating the green development of agriculture, improving the level of green development of the service industry; expending green and environmental protection industries, improving the level of recycling of industrial parks and industrial clusters; building a green supply chain); • improving the circulation system (creating a green supply chain, strengthening the recycling of renewable resources, establishing a green trade system, promoting the consumption of green products, advocating a green and low-carbon lifestyle); • improving the consumption system (promoting the consumption of green products and advocating a green and low-carbon lifestyle); • accelerating the green upgrading of infrastructure (promoting the green and low-carbon transformation of the energy system, promoting the construction and upgrading of urban environmental infrastructure, improving the green development of transportation infrastructure, as well as the urban and rural living environment); • building a market-oriented green technology innovation system (encouraging research and development of green and low carbon technologies, accelerating the transformation of scientific and technological achievements); • improving the system of laws, regulations, and policies (strengthening the support of laws and regulations, improving the price mechanism for green charges, increasing fiscal and tax support, vigorously developing green finance, improving green standards, green certification system and statistical monitoring system, cultivating green trading market mechanism). The Guideline suggests that China must first make breakthroughs in key areas, such as environmental protection, clean production, and clean energy before it fully implements the ecological modernization of its primary, secondary, and tertiary industry and infrastructure. The emphasis was also placed on the importance of innovation and the leading role of the market. This indicates that green technologies and private actors are expected to play an important role in China's green transformation.

(Continued)

Table 4.2 (Continued)

No.	*Country*	*Program name/ program document*	*Assumptions*
5.	India	Indian Green Deal (IGD)	The Green New Deal for India covers five sectors. which contribute to almost all greenhouse gas emissions in India (WEF, 2021): 1 Pillar 1 – Energy: The energy sector accounts for ~40% of India's GHG emissions, with coal being the dominant source of total fossil CO_2 emissions. Decarbonizing the energy sector is a fundamental priority for India's energy sector and will require a three-pronged approach: replace fossil fuels with renewables; reduce fossil CO_2 emissions from legacy infrastructure through enhanced efficiencies; and eliminate unavoidable carbon emissions through carbon sequestration. 2 Pillar 2 – Mobility: The mobility sector is highly dependent on oil and contributes to almost half of the India's oil demand. A green transformation of mobility will require a shift in the modal mix from road to rail, as well as a broad-based fuel diversification approach to encourage sustainable fuels (biofuels, CNG, LNG) in the immediate term, electrification in the medium term, and hydrogen-based heavy mobility in the long term. 3 Pillar 3 – Industry: Manufacturing is a key contributor to India's GHG emissions, with the iron and steel, cement, and chemicals and fertilizer sectors having the highest CO_2 footprint. A radical decarbonization of these sectors will need demand management measures such as circular economy acceleration; continued energy efficiency improvements; electrification of heat; carbon capture. utilization and storage; low-carbon fuels such as biomass and hydrogen; and innovative technologies with non-fossil feedstock. 4 Pillar 4 – Green Buildings. Infrastructure and Cities: India's top 25 cities contribute more than 15% of the country's estimated GHG emissions. India's transition to greener cities, buildings, and infrastructure will need a rethink of the country's approach to urban planning with a focus on transit-oriented urban development and an emphasis on low-carbon buildings and infrastructure construction. 5 Pillar 5 – Agriculture: The agricultural sector is the main contributor to nitrous oxide (N_2O) and methane emissions. To reduce agricultural emissions, India will need a national campaign to empower, educate, and enable more than 100 million farmers to adopt precision agriculture, sustainable animal husbandry, and green energy. These five pillars of India's green transformation depend on the continued development of three drivers of Indian growth: technological development, financial innovation, and strong political leadership.

(Continued)

Table 4.2 (Continued)

No.	*Country*	*Program name/ program document*	*Assumptions*
6.	Türkiye	Green Deal Action Plan of Türkiye	On July 16, 2021, the "Presidential Circular on the Action Plan" was first published in the Official Gazette. After the circular, the Ministry of Trade published the "Türkiye Green Deal Action Plan." In the action plan, it is understood that Türkiye will adapt to the changes envisaged in the European Green Deal. It aims to use resources effectively and efficiently for the transition to a sustainable and green economy. In this framework, the Action Plan includes a total of 32 targets and 81 actions under nine main headings. Actions and targets envisioned in the Action Plan: • Carbon border adjustments • Green and circular economy • Green finance • Clean, affordable, and secure energy supply • Sustainable agriculture • Sustainable smart mobility • Combating climate change • Diplomacy • Raising awareness regarding European Green Deal However, unlike the EU Green Deal adopted in 2019, the Türkish plan does not set any measurable goals or deadlines. Moreover, Türkiye's plan does not include a zero-pollution priority, which is the key to ensuring people's health. This is especially important. because in 2021, 42,000 people lost their lives due to the country's air pollution. The development and implementation of an ambitious Green Deal would also be an opportunity for Türkiye to take decisive steps to combat climate change (HEAL, 2023). In 2021, Türkiye outlined a series of measures as part of the Economic Reform Action Plan to grow the country's economy through investment-driven productivity, employment, and exports.

Source: Own study.

In summary, the implementation of the concept of the European Green Deal generates serious implications for both decision makers, academics, and active participants in the green transformation. The key challenges include the diversity of environmental, social, and economic conditions in which the changes proposed by decision makers and pro-environmental organizations should be implemented (Schumacher, 2020). Technological challenges should also be emphasized, because the presented Green Deal concepts recommend radical, not just gradual, sustainable technological changes (Tomaszewski, 2020). The participation of representatives from various sectors and industries is also an important element of the regional and national Green Deal strategies, as well as society itself, in shaping the policy. This is not easy, because it requires integrating equal environments and reconciling often-different and often-conflicting interests.

References

African Ministerial Conference on the Environment (AMCEN) (2019). Note by the Secretariat on Biodiversity Economy and Natural Capital Accounting in Africa. 17th Ordinary Session of AMCEN, Durban, South Africa. https://wedocs.unep.org/bitstream/handle/20.500.11822/34409/AGSP.pdf?sequence=3 accessed on 09.11.2023.

African Union (2013). Agenda 2063: the future we want. African Union Commission, Addis Ababa, Ethiopia.

Agora Energiewende (2022). The driving forces behind the green transition in Europe and South Korea – a comparison between the European Green Deal and the Korean Green New Deal https://static.agora-energiewende.de/fileadmin/Projekte/2022/2022-10_INT_Korea_Green_New_Deal/A-EW_280_Korean-Green-New-Deal_EN_WEB.pdf accessed on 08.11.2023.

Boyle, A.D., Leggat, G., Morikawa, L., Pappas, Y. & Stephens, J.C. (2021). Green new deal proposals: comparing emerging transformational climate policies at multiple scales. *Energy Research & Social Science*, 81, 102259. https://doi.org/10.1016/j.erss.2021.102259

Brundtland, G.H. (1987). *Our common future: report of the world commission on environment and development.* UN-Dokument A/42/427, Geneva. http://www.un-documents.net/ocf-ov.htm

Burke, A. & Fishel S. (2020). A coal elimination treaty 2030: fast tracking climate change mitigation, global health and security. *Earth System Governance*, 3, 100046. https://doi.org/10.1016/j.esg.2020.100046

China Briefing (2022). Investing in Green and Low-Carbon China. https://www.china-briefing.com/news/what-is-chinas-green-and-low-carbon-plan-and-why-is-it-relevant-to-foreign-investors/ accessed on 09.11.2023.

COM (2020). Stepping up Europe's 2030 climate ambition investing in a climate-neutral future for the benefit of our people. https://eur-lex.europa.eu/resource.html?uri=cellar:749e04bb-f8c5-11ea-991b-01aa75ed71a1.0001.02/DOC_1&format=PDF accessed on 20.02.2024.

COM (2023). 160 proposal for a regulation of the European Parliament and of the Council establishing a framework for ensuring a secure and sustainable supply of critical raw materials and amending regulations (EU) 168/2013, (EU) 2018/858, 2018/1724 and (EU) 2019/1020. https://eur-lex.europa.eu/legal-content/EN/TXT/?uri=CELEX:52023PC0160

Dalampira, E.S. & Nastis, S.A. (2020). Back to the future: simplifying sustainable development goals based on three pillars of sustainability. *International Journal of Sustainable Agricultural Management and Informatics*, 6(3), 226–240.

EMBER (2023). European electricity review 2023. https://ember-climate.org/insights/research/european-electricity-review-2023/ accessed on 20.02.2024.

Grantham Research Institute (2019). Policy brief: national laws and policies on climate change adaptation: a global review. https://www.lse.ac.uk/GranthamInstitute/wp-content/uploads/2019/12/National-laws-and-policies-on-climate-change-adaptation_A-global-review.pdf accessed on 08.11.2023.

H. Res. 109 (IH) - Recognizing the duty of the Federal Government to create a Green New Deal. 116th Congress (2019). https://www.govinfo.gov/app/details/BILLS-116hres109ih/summary accessed on 08.11.2023.

HEAL (2023). Health benefits of a Green Deal approach in Türkiye. https://www.env-health.org/health-benefits-of-a-green-deal-approach-in-turkey/#:~:text=Turkey's%20Green%20Deal%20Action%20Plan,any%20tangible%20targets%20or%20deadlines accessed on 10.11.2023.

IEA (2020). Energy policy review. https://iea.blob.core.windows.net/assets/ec7cc7e5-f638-431b-ab6e-86f62aa5752b/European_Union_2020_Energy_Policy_Review.pdf accessed on 20.02.2024.

IRENA and AfDB (2022). *Renewable energy market analysis: Africa and Its regions*. International Renewable Energy Agency and African Development Bank, Abu Dhabi and Abidjan. https://www.irena.org/-/media/Files/IRENA/Agency/Publication/2022/Jan/IRENA_Market_Africa_2022.pdf?rev=bb73e285a0974bc996a1f942635ca556

Johannesburg Summit (2002, August 26–September 4). *Report of the World Summit on Sustainable Development Johannesburg*. South Africa. https://documents.un.org/doc/undoc/gen/n02/636/93/pdf/n0263693.pdf?token=Thu9mycwH4XzLadcY4&fe=true accessed on 20.02.2024.

Kalinowski, T. (2021). The politics of climate change in a neo-developmental state: the case of South Korea. *International Political Science Review*, 42(1), 48–63. https://doi.org/10.1177/0192512120924741

Korean Ministry of Economy and Finance (2020). Korean new deal: national strategy for a great transformation. https://english.moef.go.kr/pc/selectTbPressCenterDtl.do?boardCd=N0001&seq=4948 accessed on 08.11.2023.

Lee, T., Kim, M. & Chifamb, N. (2021). Political framework of green new deal: a comparative analysis of the EU and US proposals. *The Korean Journal of International Studies*, 19(2), 221–246. https://doi.org/10.14731/kjis.2021.08.19.2.221

Leonard, M., Pisani-Ferry, J., Shapiro, J., Tagliapietra, S. &Wolff, G. (2021). The geopolitics of the European Green Deal. The European Council on Foreign Relations. https://ecfr.eu/wp-content/uploads/The-geopolitics-of-the-European-Green-Deal.pdf

Meadows, D.H, Meadows, D., Randers, J. & Behrens, W.W.III. (1972). *The limits to growth: a report for the Club of Rome's project on the predicament of mankind*. Universe Books, United States of America.

Pawłowski, A. (2009). The sustainable development revolution. *Problems of Sustainable Development*, 4(1), 65–76.

Poveda, C.A. (2017). The theory of dimensional balance of needs. *International Journal of Sustainable Development & World Ecology*, 24(2), 97–119.

Rahman, M.M., Bodrud-Doza, M., Shammi, M., Md Towfiqul Islam, A.R., & Moniruzzaman Khan, A.S. (2021). COVID-19 pandemic, dengue epidemic, and climate change vulnerability in Bangladesh: scenario assessment for strategic management and policy implications. *Environmental Research*, 192, 110303. doi: 10.1016/j.envres.2020.110303

Rogall, H. (2005). Climate protection as a Sphere of action towards a sustainable economy. Proceedings of the Rio 5—World Climate & Energy Event Proceedings. Rio de Janeiro, 9–18.

Schumacher, I. (2020). Perspectives on the economics of the environment in the shadow of coronavirus. *Environmental and Resource Economics*, 76, 447–517. https://doi.org/10.1007/s10640-020-00493-2

Seung-Joon, P. (2021). *Strengths and limitations of the Korean Green New Deal*. Heinrich-Böll-Stiftung. https://hk.boell.org/en/2021/04/08/strengths-and-limitations-korean-green-new-deal accessed on 08.11.2023.

Smol, M. (2022). Is the green deal a global strategy? Revision of the Green Deal definitions, strategies and importance in post-COVID recovery plans in various regions of the world. *Energy Policy*, 169, 113152. https://doi.org/10.1016/j.enpol.2022.113152

South Korean Government (2020). South Korean Government Launches Plan for a Green New Deal. https://www.iisd.org/sustainable-recovery/news/south-korean-government-launches-plan-for-a-green-new-deal/ accessed 10.11.2023.

Spangenberg, J.H. (2002). Environmental space and the prism of sustainability: frameworks for indicators measuring sustainable development. *Ecological Indicators*, 2(3), 295–309.

Sun, Y., Bao, Q., & Taghizadeh-Hesary, F. (2023). Green finance, renewable energy development, and climate change: evidence from regions of China. *Humanities and Social Sciences Communication*, 10, 107. https://doi.org/10.1057/s41599-023-01595-0

The Future We Want (June 20–22, 2012). *Outcome document of the United Nations Conference on Sustainable Development*. Rio de Janeiro, Brazil.

Tomaszewski, K. (2020). The Polish road to the new European Green Deal - challenges and threats to the national energy policy. *Polityka Energetyczna*, 23, 5–18. https://doi.org/10.33223/EPJ/123411

Treaty on European Union (2004). OJ 1992 C 191, p. 1: EUR-Lex - 11992M/TXT, Dziennik Ustaw [Journal of Laws] 2004, Supplement no. 2 to no 90, pos. 864, Vol. II, p. 492 and Vol. III, p. 493552.

United Nations (1992). Agenda 21: Programme of action for Sustainable Development.

United Nations (2015). Agenda for Sustainable Development 2030. https://sdgs.un.org/2030agenda

WEF (2021). *Mission 2070: A Green New Deal for a Net Zero India*. White Paper. https://www3.weforum.org/docs/WEF_Mission_2070_A_Green_New_Deal_for_a_Net_Zero_India_2021.pdf accessed on 09.11.2023.

White, D. (2020). Just transitions/design for transitions: preliminary notes on a design politics for a green new deal. *Capitalism nature socialism*, 31(2), 20–39.

WHO (2021). *COP26 special report on climate change and health*. The Health Argument for Climate Action. https://iris.who.int/bitstream/handle/10665/346168/9789240036727-eng.pdf?sequence=1

5 Objectives of the European Green Deal

In the European Union (EU), the concept of sustainable development has emerged as a central element of its strategy, permeating all aspects of EU policies. Consideration of the principles of sustainable development has been integral to many European Union programs, with sustainable development being among the three priorities of the EU strategy outlined in the publication "Europe 2020" on March 3, 2010. This approach contrasts with the assumptions of the Lisbon Strategy, in which sustainable development was criticized as a costly additional burden on the competitiveness of the European economy. The new strategy aimed to fulfill different objectives, focusing on smart and sustainable development as the long-term socioeconomic program of the EU (COM, 2010). The subsequent elevation in the importance of sustainable development was marked by the emergence of the concept of the green economy. It was envisioned as a catalyst for revitalizing development, a primary target for investment, and a means to generate new employment opportunities.

Consequently, the core of the European Union's development agenda between 2010 and 2020 aimed to mainstream the idea of the green economy across all EU policies and financial instruments. Declarative statements portrayed the green economy as more than just a set of commitments; it was seen as having the potential to serve as a pivotal tool in combating the effects of environmental degradation, a prerequisite for sustained economic growth, and a means of providing EU citizens with a safe living environment. The objectives of the EU Sustainable Development Strategy encompassed: (1) environmental protection, (2) social justice and cohesion, (3) economic prosperity, and (4) fulfillment of the EU's international commitments. EU policy on sustainable development was operationalized through action programs, with objectives defined within designated timeframes. The period 2013–2020 focused on actions to safeguard natural capital, promote health and well-being, and drive development and innovation within a resource-efficient, low-carbon economy (COM, 2013). Sustainable development was envisaged to stimulate the economic growth necessary for creating material wealth while considering social well-being, security, and continued progress.

Another new challenge for the European Union emerged with the adoption of the 2030 Agenda for Sustainable Development at the UN General Assembly in

DOI: 10.4324/9781003486732-8

2015. In response to the imperatives of the UN Agenda for Sustainable Development 2030 and the 2050 targets, the European Union developed the European Green Deal in 2019. This initiative is an integral component of the EU and member states' strategic framework (European Commission, 2019). It represents a novel approach to growth, aiming to reshape the EU into a just and prosperous society living in a modern, resource-efficient, and competitive economy. The goal is to achieve zero net greenhouse gas emissions by 2050 and to decouple economic growth from the consumption of natural resources.

The European Green Deal represents a response to contemporary challenges in environmental protection, the reduction of natural resource consumption and the promotion of sustainable practices in construction and mobility. In addition to striving for zero net greenhouse gas emissions, the initiative prioritizes safeguarding the health and well-being of citizens from the hazards and adverse impacts of environmental pollution. The European Green Deal encompasses the following areas:

- Reducing climate change impacts by 2050.
- Ensuring the provision of clean and affordable energy.
- Committing the industrial sector to a closed-loop economy.
- Achieving zero environmental pollution.
- Conducting construction and renovation activities in energy and resource-efficient ways.
- Protecting and restoring ecosystems and biodiversity.
- Establishing a healthy and environmentally sustainable food system.
- Promoting sustainable and intelligent mobility solutions.
- Supporting scientific research and innovation development.
- Enhancing education and training initiatives.
- Advancing automation and digitization processes.

The aforementioned domains of the Deal represent contemporary imperatives for individual EU countries, and ultimately for other nations aspiring to join the Community. The transition of the economy towards a sustainable future is intended to be facilitated through regulatory and fiscal measures (such as CO_2 fees on imported goods) as well as financial support within the EU. The tenets of the European Green Deal have been disseminated to all EU member states, both horizontally and across sectors. They constitute a comprehensive program of action that the European Union has embraced and integrated into all spheres of activity. At the European Commission level, a collaboration of experts from diverse backgrounds has resulted in the development of best practices at the local, regional, and national levels.

The aforementioned aspects of the European Green Deal delineate the contemporary trajectories pursued by individual countries in the realms of economy, environment, and society. Integral to realizing the objectives of the European Green Deal are the competences of individuals and the implementation of innovations. The transition of the economy towards sustainable development necessitates the optimization of processes for utilizing environmental resources in the production of sustainable goods, while also entailing a reduction in the consumption of natural resources. This transition involves the adoption of renewable energy sources, mitigation of air, soil, and water pollution, and ensuring safe working and living conditions for individuals (Gródek-Szostak & Adamczyk, 2021).

The EU's implementation of the 2030 Agenda for Sustainable Development is progressing in two phases. The initial phase focuses on the complete integration of the Sustainable Development Goals into the European policy framework and current priorities. Subsequently, the second phase entails the development of a long-term vision and the targeting of sectoral policies through 2050. Under the European Green Deal, the EU has set forth more ambitious objectives for 2030 and 2050, encompassing numerous specific actions and initiatives (see Table 5.1).

Table 5.1. outlines the ambitious goals of the European Green Deal along with a timetable for their implementation. However, these goals have not been achieved within the planned timeframe. This delay highlights the lack of unanimity among EU member states, as well as other challenges such as the COVID-19 pandemic and the war in Ukraine that arose during this period.

The European Green Deal is most commonly associated with addressing climate change, promoting renewable energy, and fostering a circular economy. The European Union aims to position Europe as a global leader in environmental and climate action. The primary strategic goal of the European Green Deal is to achieve climate neutrality by 2050, with an interim target of significantly reducing emissions by 2030 (Heyen et al., 2020). A key component of the Green Deal is the Just Transition Fund, designed to support regions most impacted by decarbonization. However, it currently lacks specific initiatives. In contrast, there are new proposals for emissions trading, which suggest that funds for climate protection and renewable energy investments should remain under EU control rather than being injected into national funds. Achieving the objectives outlined in the European Green Deal requires substantial investment. According to the European Commission's estimates, an additional 260 billion euros per year will be needed to meet the climate and energy targets set for 2030 (European Commission, 2019).

The European Green Deal is an integral part of EU and member state policies, encompassing key targets for environmental protection, reduction of natural resource consumption, and promoting sustainable consumption, construction, and mobility (European Commission, 2019). Transforming the EU economy for a sustainable future necessitates developing comprehensive strategies that enable a profound restructuring of economic processes. Implementing the European Green Deal requires overhauling clean energy supply strategies across various sectors, including industry, production and consumption, large-scale infrastructure, transportation, food and agriculture, construction, taxation, and social benefits. To achieve these goals, greater emphasis must be placed on protecting and restoring natural ecosystems, sustainable resource use, and improving human health. These areas require significant changes, which can yield the most substantial benefits for the economy, society, and the environment. The European Union also highlights the need for a digital transformation, advocating for the necessary tools and investments to facilitate the expected changes.

Table 5.1 European Green Deal – action plan and key initiatives.

Actions	*Timeline*
Ambitious climate goals	
Legislative proposal for a European "climate law" setting a goal of achieving climate neutrality in 2050.	March 2020
A comprehensive plan to responsibly increase the EU's 2030 climate target to at least 50% and closer to 55%.	Summer 2020
Legislative proposals to amend relevant legislative acts to achieve more ambitious climate goals. Adopted following the review of the ETS Directive; the Effort Sharing Regulation; the Land Use Regulation. land use change and forestry; the Energy Efficiency Directive; the Renewable Energy Directive; and CO2 emission standards for cars and vans.	June 2021
Legislative proposal to amend the energy taxation directive.	June 2021
Legislative proposal for border price adjustment mechanism with CO2 emissions.	2021
New EU climate change adaptation strategy.	2020/2021
Clean, affordable, and safe energy	
Evaluation of the final national energy and climate plans.	June 2020
Smart cross-sector integration strategy.	2020
The "renovation wave" initiative in the construction sector.	2020
Evaluation and review of the Trans-European Energy Network Regulation.	2020
Offshore wind energy strategy.	2020
Industrial strategy for a clean, circular economy	
EU industrial strategy.	March 2020
A roadmap for a circular economy, including a sustainable products initiative, with a focus on resource-intensive sectors, such as apparel, construction, electronics and plastics.	March 2020
Initiatives to stimulate pioneering markets for climate-neutral and closed-cycle products in energy-intensive industrial sectors.	since 2020
Legislative proposal to support carbon-free steel production by 2030.	2020
Battery legislation to support the strategic battery action plan and the circular economy.	October 2020
Proposals for legislative reforms in the field of waste.	since 2020
Sustainable and smart mobility	
Strategy for sustainable and smart mobility.	2020
Call for grant applications for the construction of public charging and refueling points for alternative fuel infrastructure.	since 2020
Evaluate legislative options to increase the production and supply of sustainable alternative fuels for various modes of transportation.	since 2020
Revised legislative proposal for a directive on combined transport.	2021
Review of the Alternative Fuels Infrastructure Directive and the Trans-European Transport Network Regulation.	2021
Initiatives to increase and better manage rail and inland waterway capacity.	since 2021
Legislative proposal for stricter air pollution emission standards for internal combustion engine vehicles.	2021

(Continued)

Table 5.1 (Continued)

Actions	*Timeline*
Greening the common agricultural policy/farm-to-fork strategy	
Analyze draft national strategic plans for ambitions related to the European Green Deal and farm-to-fork strategy.	2020–2021
Farm-to-fork strategy: Measures, including legislative, aimed at significantly reducing the use of chemical pesticides and their associated risks, and reducing the use of fertilizers and antibiotics.	spring 2020 2021
Conservation and protection of biodiversity	
EU biodiversity strategy to 2030.	March 2020
Measures to address the main drivers of biodiversity loss.	since 2021
New EU forestry strategy.	2020
Measures to support non-deforestation value chains.	since 2020
Strive for zero emissions for a non-toxic environment	
Chemicals strategy for sustainability.	summer 2020
Action plan for elimination of water, air and soil pollution.	2021
Review of measures to reduce pollution from large industrial installations	2021
Mainstreaming sustainability into all EU policies	
Legislative proposal on the fair transition mechanism, including the Fund for a Just Transition, and an investment plan for a sustainable Europe.	January 2020
Renewed strategy for sustainable financing.	autumn 2020
Review of the directive on non-financial reporting.	2020
Initiatives in the field of monitoring and modeling the green budgeting practices of member states and the EU.	since 2020
Review relevant state aid guidelines, including environmental and energy state aid guidelines.	2021
Align all new Commission initiatives with Green Deal goals and promote innovation.	since 2020
Identification by stakeholders and elimination of inconsistent legislation that limits the effectiveness of the European Green Deal.	since 2020
Integrating the Sustainable Development Goals into the European Semester.	since 2020
EU in the role of global leader	
The EU will continue to take a leadership role in international climate and biodiversity negotiations, thus consolidating the international policy framework.	since 2019
Strengthen EU green deal diplomacy together with member states.	since 2020
Bilateral efforts to encourage partners and ensure comparability of activities and policies.	since 2020
Green agenda for the Western Balkans.	since 2020
Cooperation—European Climate Pact	
Inauguration of the European Climate Pact.	March 2020
Legislative proposal for the 8th Environmental Action Program.	2020

Source: COM (2019).

The key challenges of the European Union's Sustainable Development Strategy under the European Green Deal include addressing climate change and promoting clean energy, improving transport systems, fostering sustainable consumption and production, conserving and managing natural resources, enhancing public health, promoting social inclusion, managing demography and migration, and tackling global poverty and sustainable development.

The European Green Deal is a comprehensive strategy encompassing various EU policy areas, including energy, construction, transport, industry, and agriculture. It outlines the EU's vision and development goals for the economy, environmental protection, and social progress through 2050 (Regulation EU, 2021). Implementing the European Green Deal requires a long-term strategy that considers the complex socioeconomic situations of the member states. The effects of this transformation will depend on the common arrangements and regulations established for individual economic sectors, driven by the EU's ambitious climate targets for 2030 and 2050.

The European Union's sustainable development strategy under the European Green Deal should include action in these areas:

1 Providing clean, affordable, and safe energy.
2 Transforming the industrial sector for a clean, circular economy.
3 Building and renovating in ways that conserve energy and resources.
4 Transitioning to sustainable and smart mobility. Creating an equitable, healthy, and environmentally friendly food system.
5 Protecting and restoring ecosystems and biodiversity.
6 Achieving zero emissions for a non-toxic environment.

Climate change is the most important and challenging strategic goal of the Green Deal. Therefore, the European Commission has prepared a plan to increase the EU's 2030 target for reducing greenhouse gas emissions to at least 50% and potentially to 55%, from 1990 levels (European Commission, 2019). As part of this strategy, the Commission has proposed a mechanism for adjusting the price of border tariffs to account for CO2 emissions in selected sectors, aiming to reduce the risk of emission transfer in imported goods.

As part of its latest Fit for 55 package, the European Commission has published a new document calling for a target of reducing CO_2 emissions by 90% by 2040. Additionally, the EC proposes tightening and accelerating climate policy, with contributions from taxes, a transition away from coal, a sharp reduction in oil and gas consumption, and substantial financial investments in renewable energy. The associated costs are estimated at EUR 1.5 trillion per year between 2031 and 2050 (COM, 2023).

The Council and the European Parliament have reached a preliminary agreement on the Net-Zero Industry Act. This new legislation aims to improve conditions for investment in green technologies by simplifying licensing procedures and supporting strategic projects. The goal is to meet 40% of the EU's demand for strategic carbon-neutral products and technologies, such as photovoltaic panels, wind turbines, batteries, and heat pumps. The act will accelerate the 2030 EU climate and energy goals and the achievement of climate neutrality. At the same time, it is expected to boost the competitiveness of European industry, create quality jobs, and support the EU's move toward energy independence.

Further decarbonization of the energy system is crucial to achieving the EU's 2030 and 2050 climate strategy goals. More than 75% of EU greenhouse gas emissions stem from the production and use of energy across various economic sectors. Attaining a climate-neutral Europe necessitates a circular economy, which involves transforming the industrial sector and all associated value chains. The roadmap for a circular economy will guide this transformation, initially focusing on resource-intensive sectors such as apparel, construction, electronics, and plastics. The construction, use, and renovation of buildings demand significant energy and mineral resources, leading to substantial financial outlays. By encouraging manufacturers and consumers to extend the life cycle of products, the new regulations will help reduce waste and promote more sustainable manufacturing models (European Council, 2024).

Following the announcement of the Fit for 55 package, the European Commission has introduced another set of legislative proposals to meet its climate goals. These proposals focus on decarbonizing the hydrogen and gas market, reducing methane emissions, developing low-carbon transportation, increasing the energy efficiency of buildings, and scaling up sustainable agriculture. Additionally, initiatives under the European Green Deal include farm-to-fork strategies and a new Circular Economy Action Plan, which aim to decarbonize the food sector and introduce circular economy principles, respectively. These proposed strategies will impact the production of food and goods not only within the Union but also in other countries. In alignment with the New Common Agricultural Policy, which took effect in the first quarter of 2023, and with the proposed regulations to implement the objectives of the new roadmap for a circular economy, companies from countries exporting food and goods to the Union will be required to adhere to stricter labeling and information regulations. However, these proposed regulations are still in the planning stage, since no stipulations regarding the meeting of standards for imported food products have been issued as of the first quarter of 2024. Protests by farmers in many EU member states, including Poland, which borders Ukraine, highlight concerns regarding the transfer of agricultural crops and food that not only do not meet EU standards, but also contain harmful substances banned in the EU.

The farm-to-fork strategy aims to contribute to achieving a circular economy by reducing the environmental impact of the food processing and retail sectors. This involves measures related to transportation, storage, packaging, and food waste. The strategy includes initiatives to address food labeling falsification through enhanced enforcement and increased investigative capacity at the EU level. Moreover, the initiative to explore innovative food and feed products must proceed with great care and diligence, aligning with the principle of "first, do no harm."

The achievement of climate goals is significantly influenced by transportation, which currently contributes to a quarter of the EU's greenhouse gas emissions, with this figure showing a continuous increase. Achieving climate neutrality requires a drastic reduction in emissions in the transport sector by 90% by 2050, which presents a significant challenge. The Council and the European Parliament have recently reached a preliminary political agreement on CO_2 emission standards for heavy vehicles. These new regulations aim to further reduce CO_2 emissions in the road transport sector and establish new targets for 2030, 2035, and 2040. They are crucial for advancing the EU's ambitious 2030 climate goals and achieving climate neutrality by 2050. However, it is worth noting that these standards do not apply to transport from non-EU countries. This not only undermines the competitiveness of EU carriers, but also leads to a substantial increase in emissions. For instance, the extensive transportation of food and agricultural products from Ukraine by trucks lacking environmental parameters exacerbates this issue. In contrast, ad hoc measures aimed at easing tensions, such as withdrawing from certain EU standards or providing subsidies to farmers from EU member states, offer only temporary relief to conflicts. A more sustainable approach, in line with the European Green Deal, would involve implementing consistent CO_2 standards for all heavy vehicles, including those entering EU territory (COM, 2024).

The biodiversity strategy will outline specific measures to attain the stated objectives. These measures may encompass quantitative targets for expanding the coverage of protected terrestrial and marine areas distinguished by abundant biodiversity, building upon the "Natura 2000" network. The Council and the European Parliament have reached a preliminary agreement on a directive concerning corporate sustainability due diligence. Large EU companies and non-EU companies operating within the EU will be required to undertake measures to identify any adverse impacts on business operations, as well as on the activities of their subsidiaries and business associates. Furthermore, large companies will need to ensure that their business practices align with the objective of the Paris Agreement to limit global warming to 1.5°C (European Council, 2023).

Among the critical goals outlined in Agenda 2030 and the European Green Deal are digitization and automation, which play an integral role in all sectors in achieving sustainable development objectives. Environmental protection necessitates initiatives to prevent new pollution and mitigate existing pollutants. To safeguard the citizens and ecosystems of Europe, the EU must improve the monitoring of air, water, soil, and consumer product pollution, along with implementing measures to prevent and remediate such pollution. Digital technologies play a pivotal role in advancing the sustainability objectives of the Green Deal across various sectors. Digitization can expedite and amplify the impact of policies on climate change and environmental protection through technologies like artificial intelligence, 5G, cloud computing, edge computing, and the Internet of Things (Reis et al., 2020). Furthermore, digitization paves the way for remote monitoring of water and air quality, as well as optimizing energy and resource utilization. Digital advancements are essential for realizing the European Green Deal, offering opportunities to enhance energy efficiency and circular economy practices.

According to the European Advancing Manufacturing Support Center, digitization will permeate various realms of activity:

- modern technologies in flexible manufacturing systems;
- sharing information throughout the manufacturing process;
- incorporating principles of circular economy to fully utilize raw materials and reduce emissions;
- fully implementing customers' expectations for environmentally friendly products;
- constructing workplaces conducive to leveraging individual differences among employees for organizational development;
- introducing integrated information systems capable of responding in real-time to changing environmental conditions (smart manufacturing, big data);
- organizations that respond to the needs of all participants in the value chain.

This new approach involves the evolution of the industry towards a production model that prioritizes not only technological innovation and economic growth but also responsible ecological and social practices. Simultaneously, it underscores the necessity for enhanced transparency and oversight concerning the environmental impact of electronic communications. It also advocates for the implementation of stringent regulations governing the deployment of new networks and the evaluation of systems for recycling unused equipment.

Additionally, it will emphasize strategies that improve supply chain resilience to potential threats and crises, as exemplified by the COVID-19 pandemic. The European Green Deal acknowledges the role of industry in achieving social objectives beyond job creation and production growth. It aims to ensure that production processes prioritize the well-being of workers and the protection of our planet, thus becoming a resilient provider of prosperity. Industrial sustainability is crucial because research and innovation help mitigate climate change and foster human-centered, crisis-resilient economic development (Breque et al., 2021). This sustainability is rooted in the European Commission's commitment to better integrate European social and environmental priorities with technological innovation, shifting the focus from individual technologies to a systems approach.

Digital transformation, impacting all areas of life and sectors of the economy, is critically important because, along with industrial transformation, it contributes to the realization of the 2030 and 2050 sustainable development goals. This transformation is intended to support social development, mitigate climate change and environmental degradation, and ultimately improve the quality of life for current and future generations. This includes promoting activities aimed at achieving specific technical and economic goals, such as increased production and productivity (Aagard, 2019). Equally important is the search for solutions to improve employee welfare, protect the environment, and increase the resilience of the supply chain to potential emergencies.

The European Green Deal, amid numerous regulations, reports, and current status and challenges of civilization, represents a strategic direction for economic development based on the principles of sustainable development. This initiative marks the beginning of changes that extend beyond the economic and political scope of the EU. The ambitious goals of the European Green Deal for protecting Europe's environment cannot be achieved by the EU alone, as the causes of climate change and biodiversity loss are global and transboundary issues. The EU can leverage its influence, expertise and financial resources to mobilize its neighbors and partners to join the effort to make Europe sustainable. A precursor to such efforts was the decision of March 18, 2020, which led to the European Commission and the European External Action Service issuing a joint communiqué entitled "The Eastern Partnership Policy after 2020. Post-2020 Eastern Partnership Policy Strengthening Resilience-Eastern Partnership which serves all." The overall vision outlined in the document reflects the EU's ongoing commitment to deepening political and economic relations with the Eastern Partnership (EaP) countries. The EaP has been aligned with the directions set for all of the European Union's external actions, with a strong emphasis on close cooperation and building resilience.

The special role of cooperation and resilience is clearly evident in the long-term goals defined for the Eastern Partnership program (Groza et al., 2018). According to these goals, partner countries are to undertake joint activities in pursuit of the five long-term objectives of the Eastern Partnership policy (JOIN, 2020):

- Resilient, sustainable, and integrated economies.
- Accountable institutions, rule of law, and security.
- Environmental resilience and climate resilience.
- Resilient digital transformation.
- Resilient, equitable, and inclusive societies.

The impact of the region's complex geopolitical situation on the shape and functioning of the Eastern Partnership was evident at the EaP Summit held in Brussels on December 15, 2021. The EU intends to continue leading international efforts in this area and forging alliances with like-minded partners. Recognizing the imperative to uphold EU security and competitiveness, closer cooperation is essential to achieve the goals of the European Green Deal. Central to Europe's environmental prospects in the near and distant future is the EU's strategy for sustainable development and environmental security, aiming to make Europe the first climate-neutral continent by 2050. Achieving this goal requires investments in innovation, research, and the transformation and modernization of EU industrial policy (Komunikat prasowy, 2023). The effectiveness of the green transformation for Europe hinges on proactive engagement by the EU's immediate neighbors under the Green Deal. To this end, the EU is planning a series of political and diplomatic initiatives aimed at fostering cooperation on environmental, energy, and climate issues with neighboring countries, including within the Eastern Partnership framework. Implementing the European Green Deal poses significant challenges for EU member states, and even more so for other European countries, whose participation is crucial for achieving the continent's climate neutrality.

The scale of the reforms announced and planned so far has sparked considerable controversy. On the one hand, some argue that the European Green Deal will be seen historically as akin to a new industrial revolution (Pawłowski, 2009). On the other hand, there are concerns that implementing such stringent standards could erode the competitiveness of the EU economy. This could potentially lead to economic downturns, social conflicts, and consequently undermine the security of EU member states, along with encountering resistance to the introduction of legislative changes.

The European Green Deal strategy marks the beginning of efforts to implement new sustainable and green development in Europe, but significant challenges are emerging:

- Will the European Green Deal concept succeed in going beyond economic policy and conflicting interests of member states?
- Will the European Green Deal concept succeed in going beyond the EU and be acceptable to the Eastern Partnership countries?

The European Union, despite the challenges anticipated during the implementation of the European Green Deal, aims to maintain its global leadership in climate action. Setting standards for the energy transition that consider the specific conditions of individual countries will be crucial. Requiring compliance with EU environmental regulations for access to the EU market will compel partners to adjust their environmental standards, which could pose difficulties. The EU should invite partners to collaborate to achieve the strategic goals of the European Green Deal by investing in renewable energy in these countries. This investment can help mitigate the economic impacts of the green transition. Moreover, it will enable EU companies to enter new markets and reap substantial economic benefits from renewable energy technology, thus enhancing EU foreign policy objectives. However, the cost-benefit analysis must also include financial assistance for least developed EU countries and EU Green Deal partners. In this way, the EU can foster a global coalition to combat climate change. International initiatives would establish the political framework for the European Green Deal and Europe's new green economy. The economic transition towards a green economy within individual EU member states should consider the social impact of these measures, particularly when neighboring countries do not adhere to similar regulations on climate change, environmental protection, or food products. Transfers of pollution and substandard products disregard borders and pose ongoing challenges.

The Eastern Partnership for the Green Deal presents an opportunity for Europe's green development. However, its success hinges on adapting implementation tasks and timelines to the specific conditions of individual EU member states, followed by similar cooperation with neighboring countries. Otherwise, stringent adherence to the objectives of the European Green Deal could adversely impact the competitiveness of the agriculture, economy, and transport sectors of the EU. This could result in imported food and other products not meeting EU environmental and safety standards gaining an advantage. Moreover, the challenges and costs associated with implementing European Green Deal requirements within EU member states will influence political and social sentiments, potentially fueling opposition to the Eastern Partnership within the EU and hampering its acceptance and adoption in other European countries. Consequently, achieving the ambitious goals of the European Green Deal, which is to transform the EU into a just and prosperous society with a modern, resource-efficient, and competitive economy with zero greenhouse gas emissions by 2050, alongside sustainable economic growth, could prove unattainable.

References

Aagard, A. (2019). *The concept and frameworks of digital business models*. [in.] *Digital business models: driving transformation and innovation*. Ed. A. Aagard. Palgrave Macmillan.

Breque, M., De Nul, L. & Petrides, A. (2021). Industry 5.0 - towards a sustainable, human - centric and resilient European industry. European Commission, 48.

COM (2010). Europe 2000. A strategy for smart, sustainable and inclusive growth, European Commission. Communication from the Commission to the European Council, Brussels.

COM (2013). Communication from the Commission to the European Parliament, the Council, the European Economic and Social Committee and the Committee of the Regions an EU Strategy on adaptation to climate change. https://eur-lex.europa.eu/legal-content/EN/TXT/?uri=CELEX:52013DC0216

COM (2019). Communication from the Commission to the European Parliament, the European Council, the Council, the European Economic and Social Committee and the Committee of the Regions the European Green Deal. https://eur-lex.europa.eu/legal-content/EN/TXT/?uri=COM%3A2019%3A640%3AFIN

COM (2023). 161 - Proposal for a regulation of the European Parliament and of the Council on establishing a framework of measures for strengthening Europe's net-zero technology products manufacturing ecosystem (Net Zero Industry Act). https://single-market-economy.ec.europa.eu/publications/net-zero-industry-act_en?prefLang=pl

COM (2024). Proposal for a regulation of the European Parliament and of the Council amending Regulation (EU) 2019/1242 as regards strengthening the CO2 emission performance standards for new heavy duty vehicles and integrating reporting obligations, and repealing Regulation (EU) 2018/956. https://www.consilium.europa.eu/media/70136/hdvs_provisional-agreement.pdf

European Council (2023). Corporate sustainability due diligence: Council and Parliament agree to protect environment and human rights. https://www.consilium.europa.eu/pl/press/press-releases/2023/12/14/corporate-sustainability-due-diligence-council-and-parliament-strike-deal-to-protect-environment-and-human-rights/

European Council (2024). Directive strengthening consumer rights in the ecological transformation process approved. https://www.consilium.europa.eu/pl/press/press-releases/2024/02/20/consumer-rights-final-approval-for-the-directive-to-empower-consumers-for-the-green-transition/

European Commission (2019). The European Green Deal. https://commission.europa.eu/strategy-and-policy/priorities-2019-2024/european-green-deal_en

Gródek-Szostak, Z. & Adamczyk, J. (November 23–24, 2021). *Assessment of Projects Financed from Structural Funds in the Sustainable Development Perspective*. Innovation Management and Sustainable Economic Development in the Era of Global Pandemic: Proceedings of the 38th International Business Information Management Association Conference (IBIMA), Eds. Seville, Spain & Khalid S. Soliman - King of Prussia, PA: International Business Information Management Association, pp. 159–165.

Groza, I., Jopp, M., Leancă, I. & Rusu, I. (2018). Challenges and perspectives for a sustainable transformation in the EU's Eastern neighbourhood. Institut für Europäische Politik: IEP Policy Paper, 1.

Heyen, D.A., Menzemer, L., Wolff, F., Beznea, A. & Williams, R. (2020). Just transition in the context of EU environmental policy and the European Green Deal. Issue Paper under Task, 3.

JOIN (2020). Joint communication: Eastern partnership policy beyond 2020: reinforcing resilience – an Eastern Partnership that delivers for all. https://www.eeas.europa.eu/sites/default/files/1_en_act_part1_v6.pdf

Komunikat prasowy (2023). Należyta staranność przedsiębiorstw w zakresie zrównoważonego rozwoju: zgoda Rady i Parlamentu w celu ochrony środowiska i praw człowieka (komunikat prasowy z 14 grudnia 2023). https://www.consilium.europa.eu/pl/press/press-releases/2023/12/14/corporate-sustainability-due-diligence-council-and-parliament-strike-deal-to-protect-environment-and-human-rights/

Pawłowski, A. (2009). The Sustainable Development Revolution. *Problems of sustainable development*, 4(1), 65–76.

Regulation EU (2021). 2021/1119 of the European Parliament and of the Council of 30 June 2021 establishing the framework for achieving climate neutrality and amending Regulations (EC) No 401/2009 and (EU) 2018/1999 ('European Climate Law'). https://eur-lex.europa.eu/legal-content/EN/TXT/?uri=CELEX:32021R1119

Reis, J., Amorim, M., Melão, N., Cohen, Y. & Rodrigues, M. (2020). Digitalization: a literature review and research agenda. Springer Nature Switzerland AG, pp. 443–456.

Index

FSC
www.fsc.org
MIX
Papier | Fördert
gute Waldnutzung
FSC® C083411

Kolibri 360 GmbH
Ferdinand-Jühlke-Straße 7
99095 Erfurt, Deutschland
produktsicherheit@kolibri360.de